# TCP/IP

**Fifth Edition**

## Tutorial and Technical Overview

EAMON MURPHY ■ STEVE HAYES ■ MATTHIAS ENDERS

Contributors to earlier editions: Gerard Bourbigot ■ Frank Vanderwiele ■
Bob Botts ■ Richard Ryniker ■ Bruce Wilder ■ Ricardo Haragutchi ■
Jim Curran ■ Paul D. Bosco ■ Frederic Debulois ■ Francis Li ■
Niels Christiansen ■ Philippe Beaupied ■ Lesia Antonowytsch Cox ■
Peter Frick ■ Carla Sadtler ■ Dave Shogren

D0564481

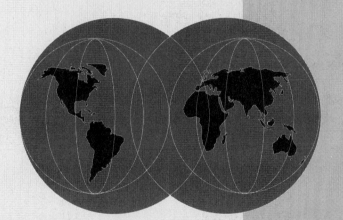

PRENTICE HALL PTR, UPPER SADDLE RIVER, NEW JERSEY 07458

## Fifth Edition

For information about redbooks:
http://www.redbooks.ibm.com/redbooks

Send comments to:
redbooks@vnet.ibm.com

Published by

Prentice Hall PTR
Prentice-Hall, Inc.
A Simon & Schuster Company
Upper Saddle River, NJ 07458

The publisher offers discounts on this book when ordered in bulk quantities. For more information, contact

> Corporate Sales Department,
> Prentice Hall PTR
> One Lake Street
> Upper Saddle River, NJ 07458
> Phone: 800-382-3419; FAX: 201-236-714
> E-mail (Internet): corpsales@prenhall.com

For book and bookstore information

http://www.prenhall.com

Printed in the United States of America

10  9  8  7  6  5  4  3  2  1

ISBN  0-13-460858-5

Prentice-Hall International (UK) Limited, *London*
Prentice-Hall of Australia Pty. Limited, *Sydney*
Prentice-Hall Canada Inc., *Toronto*
Prentice-Hall Hispanoamericana, S.A., *Mexico*
Prentice-Hall of India Private Limited, *New Delhi*
Prentice-Hall of Japan, Inc., *Tokyo*
Simon & Schuster Asia Pte. Ltd., *Singapore*
Editora Prentice-Hall do Brasil, Ltda., *Rio de Janeiro*

# Contents

# Figures

# Tables

# Preface

This document is for customers, networking specialists and consultants working on projects involving connectivity between IBM systems and equipment manufactured by other companies. It should be used to gain a basic understanding of the Transmission Control Protocol/Internet Protocol (TCP/IP) protocol suite and to gain an overview of the possible functionality of the IBM TCP/IP based products in heterogeneous networks.

The document is organized as follows:

- Chapter 1, "The Internet: Past, Present and Future"

  This chapter provides a brief history of the Internet and predicts how it is likely to develop in the future.

- Chapter 2, "Architecture and Protocols"

  This chapter gives the basics of the TCP/IP architecture and explains the protocols: IP, ICMP, ARP, RARP, UDP, TCP and DNS.

- Chapter 3, "Routing Protocols"

  This chapter describes the functionality of the TCP/IP routing protocols and explains the protocols: Hello, RIP, OSPF, EGP and BGP.

- Chapter 4, "Application Protocols"

  This chapter describes the functionality of the TCP/IP application protocols and their implementations in the IBM products.

- Chapter 5, "Connections"

  This chapter describes the connectivity supported by IBM products.

- Chapter 6, "Internet Access"

  This chapter provides an overview of Internet access methods and introduces a selection of Internet navigation tools.

# Special Notices

This publication is intended to help customers, FSC communications specialists and systems engineers understand the TCP/IP protocol suite and the characteristics of its implementation in the IBM TCP/IP products. The information in this publication is not intended as the specification of any programming interfaces that are provided by TCP/IP for VM, MVS, OS/400, AIX/RT, AIX PS/2, AIX/6000, AIX/370, OS/2 and DOS. See the PUBLICATIONS section of the IBM Programming Announcement for TCP/IP for

VM, MVS, OS/400, AIX/RT, AIX PS/2, AIX/6000, AIX/370, OS/2 and DOS for more information about what publications are considered to be product documentation.

References in this publication to IBM products, programs or services do not imply that IBM intends to make these available in all countries in which IBM operates. Any reference to an IBM product, program, or service is not intended to state or imply that only IBM's product, program, or service may be used. Any functionally equivalent program that does not infringe any of IBM's intellectual property rights may be used instead of the IBM product, program or service.

Information in this book was developed in conjunction with use of the equipment specified, and is limited in application to those specific hardware and software products and levels.

IBM may have patents or pending patent applications covering subject matter in this document. The furnishing of this document does not give you any license to these patents. You can send license inquiries, in writing, to the IBM Director of Commercial Relations, IBM Corporation, Purchase, NY 10577.

The information contained in this document has not been submitted to any formal IBM test and is distributed AS IS. The information about non-IBM (VENDOR) products in this manual has been supplied by the vendor and IBM assumes no responsibility for its accuracy or completeness. The use of this information or the implementation of any of these techniques is a customer responsibility and depends on the customer's ability to evaluate and integrate them into the customer's operational environment. While each item may have been reviewed by IBM for accuracy in a specific situation, there is no guarantee that the same or similar results will be obtained elsewhere. Customers attempting to adapt these techniques to their own environments do so at their own risk.

The following terms are trademarks of the International Business Machines Corporation in the United States and/or other countries:

| | |
|---|---|
| AIX | AIX/ESA |
| AIX/6000 | AIXwindows |
| AS/400 | CICS |
| CICS/ESA | CICS/MVS |
| DATABASE 2 | DB2 |
| Enterprise System/9000 | ES/9000 |
| ESA/390 | ESCON |
| graPHIGS | IBM |
| InfoExplorer | Micro Channel |
| OS/2 | OS/400 |
| Presentation Manager | PS/2 |
| RACF | RISC System/6000 |
| S/390 | System/370 |

System/390          VTAM
Xstation Manager

The following terms are trademarks of other companies:

AFS and Transarc are registered trademarks of the Transarc Corporation.
APOLLO is a registered trademark of the Hewlett-Packard Company.
AppleTalk is a trademark of Apple Computer Inc.
ARPANET was developed by the United States Department of Defense.
BSD is a trademark of the University of California, Berkeley.
C-bus is a trademark of Corollary, Inc.
Dasher 210 is a trademark of Data General Corporation.
DEC VT52, DEC VT100 and DEC VT220 are trademarks of the
Digital Equipment Corporation.
DECnet is a trademark of the Digital Equipment Corporation.
Digital Press is a trademark of the Digital Equipment Corporation.
Domain is a trademark of the Hewlett-Packard Company.
EtherLink is a trademark of the 3COM Corporation.
EtherLink/MC is a trademark of the 3COM Corporation.
3Com is a trademark of the 3COM Corporation.
HP and Hewlett Packard are trademarks of Hewlett Packard Corporation.
HYPERchannel is a trademark of the Network Systems Corporation.
IEEE is a trademark of the the Institute of Electrical and Electronics Engineers, Inc.
Interlink is a registered trademark of Interlink Computer Sciences, Incorporated.
IPX, Internet Packet Exchange and Novell are trademarks of Novell Inc.
Kerberos is a trademark of the Massachusetts Institute of Technology.
LSI/11 is a trademark of the Digital Equipment Corporation.
MCI is a trademark of MCI Communications Corporation.
Microsoft is a trademark of Microsoft Corporation.
NCS is a trademark of the Hewlett-Packard Company.
NDIS is a trademark of 3Com Corporation/Microsoft Corporation.
Network Computing System is a trademark of the Hewlett-Packard Company.
Network Computing Kernel is a trademark of the Hewlett-Packard Company.
Network File System and NFS are trademarks of SUN Microsystems, Inc.
NIC and NICps/2 are trademarks of Ungermann-Bass.
OSF/Motif is a registered trademark of Open Software Foundation, Inc.
OSF is a trademark of Open Software Foundation, Inc.
PC Direct is a trademark of Ziff Communications Company and is
used by IBM Corporation under license.
Portmapper is a trademark of SUN Microsystems, Inc.
PostScript is a trademark of Adobe Systems, Inc.
Project Athena is a trademark of the Massachusetts Institute of Technology.
SNS/SNA Gateway is a trademark of Interlink Computer Sciences, Incorporated.
SUN Microsystems is a trademark of SUN Microsystems, Inc.

Telenet is a trademark of GTE Telenet Communication Corporation.
Ungermann-Bass is a trademark of Ungermann-Bass Corporation.
UNIX is a registered trademark in the United States and other
countries licensed exclusively through X/Open Company Limited.
VT52, VT100, VT102, VT200, VT220 are trademarks of the Digital Equipment Corporation.
Western Digital is a trademark of the Western Digital Corporation.
Windows is a trademark of Microsoft Corporation.
Xerox and XNS are trademarks of the Xerox Corporation.
X/Open is a trademark of X/Open Company Limited.
X Window System and X Windows are trademarks of the Massachusetts
Institute of Technology.

Other trademarks are trademarks of their respective companies.

# Acknowledgments

The authors for this edition were:

**Eamon Murphy**          International Technical Support Organization, Raleigh
                          Center

**Matthias Enders**       IBM Germany

**Steve Hayes**           IBM UK

This publication is the result of a residency conducted at the International Technical
Support Organization, Raleigh Center.

Thanks to the following people for the invaluable advice and guidance provided in the
production of this document:

**Antonius Bekker**       EMEA Education, Raleigh

**Edward Britton**        TCP/IP Technology, Strategy and Cross Product, Raleigh

**Pete Haverlock**        NS Technical Support Center, Cary

**Alfred Christensen**    International Technical Support Organization, Raleigh
                          Center

**Barry Nusbaum**         International Technical Support Organization, Raleigh
                          Center

Contributors to earlier editions of this book were:

**Gerard Bourbigot**      IBM France

**Frank Vandewiele**      IBM Belgium

| | |
|---|---|
| **Bob Botts** | New Mexico Branch Office, Albuquerque |
| **Richard Ryniker** | IBM Research, Yorktown Heights |
| **Bruce Wilder** | TCP/IP Development, Raleigh |
| **Ricardo Haragutchi** | IBM Brazil |
| **Jim Curran** | TCP/IP Development, Raleigh |
| **Paul D. Bosco** | Network Systems Architecture and Hardware in Advanced Solutions Developed, Milford |
| **Frederic Debulois** | IBM France |
| **Francis Li** | IBM Canada |
| **Niels Christiansen** | International Technical Support Organization, Austin Center |

**Philippe Beaupied, Lesia Antonowytsch Cox, Peter Frick, Carla Sadtler, Dave Shogren** International Technical Support Organization, Raleigh Center

**TCP/IP Development, Raleigh**

**The staff of the International Technical Support Organization, Rochester Center**

**Telecommunications Education Center, Raleigh**

# Chapter 1. The Internet: Past, Present and Future

In this chapter we will describe how the Internet was formed, how it developed and how it is likely to develop in the future. We will also discuss IBM's involvement in and support for the Internet.

## 1.1 Introduction

Networks have become a fundamental, if not the most important, part of today's information systems. They form the backbone for information-sharing in enterprises, governmental and scientific groups. That information can take several forms. It can be notes and documents, data to be processed by another computer, files sent to colleagues, and even more exotic forms of data.

Most of these networks were installed in the late 60s and 70s, when network design was the "state of the art" topic of computer research and sophisticated implementers. It resulted in multiple networking models such as packet-switching technology, collision-detection local area networks, hierarchical enterprise networks, and many other excellent technologies.

From the early 70s on, another aspect of networking became important: protocol layering, which allows applications to communicate with each other. A complete range of architectural models were proposed and implemented by various research teams and computer manufacturers.

The result of all this great know-how is that today any group of users can find a physical network and an architectural model suitable for their specific needs. This ranges from cheap asynchronous lines with no other error recovery than a bit-per-bit parity function, through full-function wide area networks (public or private) with reliable protocols such as public packet-switching networks or private SNA networks, to high-speed but limited-distance local area networks.

The down side of this exploding information-sharing is the rather painful situation when one group of users wants to extend their information system to another group of users, who happen to have a different network technology and different network protocols. As a result, even if they could agree on a type of network technology to physically interconnect the two locations, their applications (such as mailing systems) still would not be able to communicate with each other because of the different protocols.

**1-1**

This situation was recognized rather early (beginning of the 70s) by a group of researchers in the US who came up with a new principle: *internetworking*. Other official organizations became involved in this area of interconnecting networks, such as ITU-T and ISO. All were trying to define a set of protocols, layered in a well-defined suite, so that applications would be able to talk to other applications, regardless of the underlying network technology and the operating systems where those applications run.

## 1.2 Internetworks

Those original designers, funded by the *Defense Advanced Research Projects Agency* (DARPA), of the *ARPANET protocol suite* introduced fundamental concepts such as *layering* and *virtualizing* in the world of networking, well before ISO even took an interest in networking.

The official organism of those researchers was the ARPANET Network Working Group, which had its last general meeting in October 1971. DARPA has continued its research for an internetworking protocol suite, from the early *NCP (Network Control Program)* host-to-host protocol to the TCP/IP protocol suite, which took its current form around 1978. At that time, DARPA was well known for its pioneering of packet-switching over radio networks and satellite channels. The first real implementations of the *Internet* were found around 1980 when DARPA started converting the machines of its research network (ARPANET) to use the new TCP/IP protocols. In 1983, the transition was completed and DARPA demanded that *all* computers willing to connect to its ARPANET use TCP/IP.

DARPA also contracted Bolt, Beranek, and Newman (BBN) to develop an implementation of the TCP/IP protocols for Berkeley UNIX on the VAX and funded the University of California at Berkeley to distribute that code free of charge with their UNIX operating system. The first release of the *Berkeley System Distribution* to include the TCP/IP protocol set was made available in 1983 (4.2BSD). From that point on, TCP/IP has been rapidly spreading among universities and research centers and has become the standard communications subsystem for all UNIX connectivity. The second release (4.3BSD) was distributed in 1986, with updates in 1988 (4.3BSD Tahoe) and 1990 (4.3BSD Reno). 4.4BSD was released in 1993. Due to funding constraints, 4.4BSD will be the last release of the BSD by the Computer Systems Research Group of the University of California at Berkeley.

As TCP/IP internetworking spread rapidly, new wide area networks were created in the US and connected to ARPANET. In turn, other networks in the rest of the world, not necessarily based on the TCP/IP protocols were added to the set of interconnected networks. The result is what is described as *The Internet*. Some examples of the different networks which have played key roles in this development are described in the next sections.

## 1.2.1 The Internet

What exactly is the Internet? First, the word *internet* (also *internetwork*) is simply a contraction of the phrase *interconnected network*. However when written with a capital "I" the Internet refers to a worldwide set of interconnected networks, so the Internet is an internet, but the reverse does not follow. The Internet is sometimes called the *connected Internet*.

The Internet consists of the following groups of networks (see the following sections for more information on some of these):

- Backbones: large networks which exist primarily to interconnect other networks. Currently the backbones are NSFNET in the US, EBONE in Europe and large commercial backbones.

- Regional networks connecting, for example, universities and colleges.

- Commercial networks providing access to the backbones to subscribers, and networks owned by commercial organizations for internal use which also have connections to the Internet.

- Local networks, such as campus-wide university networks.

In many cases, particularly for commercial, military and government networks, traffic between these networks and the rest of the Internet is restricted (see also 6.3, "Firewalls" on page 6-10). This leads to the question: how do I know if I am connected to the Internet? One workable approach is to ask the question: can I ping the host *ds.internic.net*? Ping, described in 2.5, "Ping" on page 2-63, is a program used for determining the reachability of hosts on internets, implemented on every TCP/IP platform. If the answer to this question is "no," then you are not connected. This definition does not necessarily mean that you are completely cut off from the Internet: many systems which would fail this test have, for example, electronic mail gateways to the Internet.

## 1.2.2 ARPANET

Sometimes referred to as the "grand-daddy of packet networks," the ARPANET was built by DARPA (which was called ARPA at that time) in the late 60s to accommodate research equipment on packet-switching technology and to allow resource sharing for the Department of Defense's contractors. The network interconnected research centers, some military bases and government locations. It soon became popular with researchers for collaboration through electronic mail and other services. It was developed into a research utility run by the Defense Communications Agency (DCA) by the end of 1975 and split in 1983 into MILNET for interconnection of military sites and ARPANET for interconnection of research sites. This formed the beginning of the "capital I" Internet.

In 1974, the ARPANET was based on 56 Kbps leased lines which interconnected *packet-switching nodes* (PSN) scattered across the continental US and western Europe. These were minicomputers running a protocol known as *1822* (after the number of a report describing it) and dedicated to the packet-switching task. Each PSN had at least two connections to other PSNs (to allow alternate routing in case of circuit failure) and up to 22 ports for user computer (*host*) connections. These 1822 systems offered reliable, flow-controlled delivery of a packet to a destination node. This is the reason why the original *NCP* protocol was a rather simple protocol. It was replaced by the TCP/IP protocols, which do not assume reliability of the underlying network hardware and can be used on other-than-1822 networks. This 1822 protocol did not become an industry standard, so DARPA decided later to replace the 1822 packet switching technology with the *CCITT X.25* standard.

Data traffic rapidly exceeded the capacity of the 56 Kbps lines that made up the network, which were no longer able to support the necessary throughput. Today the ARPANET has been replaced by new technologies in its role of backbone on the research side of the connected Internet (see NSFNET later in this chapter), whereas MILNET continues to form the backbone of the military side.

## 1.2.3 NSFNET

NSFNET, the National Science Foundation Network, is a three-level internetwork in the United States consisting of:

- The *backbone*: a network that connects separately administered and operated mid-level networks and NSF-funded supercomputer centers. The backbone also has transcontinental links to other networks such as EBONE, the European IP backbone network.
- *Mid-level networks*: of three kinds (regional, discipline-based and supercomputer consortium networks).
- *Campus networks*: whether academic or commercial, connected to the mid-level networks.

*First Backbone*

Originally established by the National Science Foundation (NSF) as a communications network for researchers and scientists to access the NSF supercomputers, the first NSFNET backbone used six DEC LSI/11 microcomputers as packet switches, interconnected by 56 Kbps leased lines. A primary interconnection between the NSFNET backbone and the ARPANET existed at Carnegie Mellon, which allowed routing of datagrams between users connected to each of those networks.

*Second Backbone*

The need for a new backbone appeared in 1987, when the first one became overloaded within a few months (estimated growth at that time was 100% per year). The NSF and MERIT, Inc., a computer network consortium of eight state-supported universities in Michigan, agreed to develop and manage a new, higher-speed backbone with larger transmission and switching capacities. To manage it they defined the *Information Services* (IS) which is comprised of an Information Center and a Technical Support Group. The Information Center is responsible for information dissemination, information resource management and electronic communication. The Technical Support Group provides support directly to the field. The purpose of this is to provide an integrated information system with easy-to-use-and-manage interfaces accessible from any point in the network supported by a full set of training services.

Merit and NSF conducted this project in partnership with IBM and MCI. IBM provided the software, packet-switching and network-management equipment, while MCI provided the long-distance transport facilities. Installed in 1988, the new network initially used 448 Kbps leased circuits to interconnect 13 *nodal switching systems* (NSS) supplied by IBM. Each NSS was composed of nine IBM RT systems (running an IBM version of 4.3BSD UNIX) loosely coupled via two IBM Token-Ring Networks (for redundancy). One Integrated Digital Network Exchange (IDNX) supplied by IBM was installed at each of the 13 locations, to provide:

- Dynamic alternate routing
- Dynamic bandwidth allocation

*Third Backbone*

In 1989, the NSFNET backbone circuits topology was reconfigured after traffic measurements and the speed of the leased lines increased to T1 (1.544 Mbps) using primarily fiber optics.

Due to the constantly increasing need for improved packet switching and transmission capacities, three NSSs were added to the backbone and the link speed was upgraded. The migration of the NSFNET backbone from T1 to T3 (45Mbps) was completed in late 1992. Advanced Network & Services, Inc. (a company formed by IBM, MCI, and Merit, Inc.) currently provides and manages the NSFNET.

The migration to gigabit levels has already started and will continue through the late 1990s. For an overview, please see 1.4, "Future" on page 1-20.

In April 1995 the US government intends to remove its funding of NFSNET. This is in part a reaction to the growing commercial use of NSFNET. For more on the commercial use of the Internet plus the US government plans refer to 1.2.12, "Commercial Use of the Internet" on page 1-9 and 1.2.13, "Information Super Highway" on page 1-10 respectively.

## 1.2.4 EBONE

EBONE, the Pan-European Multi-Protocol Backbone plays the same role in Europe for Internet traffic as the NSFNET backbone does in the United States. EBONE has kilobit and megabit links between five major centers.

## 1.2.5 CREN

Completed in October 1989, the merger of the two already well known networks CSNET (the Computer+Science Network) and BITNET (the *Because It's Time* Network) formed the Corporation for Research and Educational Networking. CREN draws on both of its historical CSNET and BITNET service families to provide a rich variety of network connection options:

| | |
|---|---|
| *PhoneNet* | Is the original CSNET network service and provides a store-and-forward electronic mail service using dial-up telephone lines (1200/2400 bps). It allows CSNET service members to exchange messages with other CREN members and with other major mail networks, including NSFNET, MILNET, etc. |
| *X.25Net* | Is a CSNET full-service Internet-connected network that uses TCP/IP protocols on top of X.25. It is the common method for international members to connect to CSNET, since they can use their local X.25 Public Data Network to reach Telenet in the US. It provides file transfer, remote login, and immediate electronic mail service between X.25Net hosts. |
| *Dial-up IP* | Is an implementation of SLIP (Serial Line IP) that allows sites using the switched telephone network (9600 bps) to send IP packets, by means of a central server, to the Internet. Users of this method thus have the same services as X.25Net sites. |
| *Leased Line IP* | Used by many CREN members to connect to CREN. A variety of link speeds are supported up to T1 rates. |
| *RSCS/NJE over BISYNC* | Traditionally runs over leased lines at 9600 bps and provides interactive messages, unsolicited file transfer and electronic mail. |
| *RSCS over IP* | Allows BITNET service hubs to relax the dedicated RSCS bisync line in preference to an Internet IP route, if one exists. |

## 1.2.6 Cypress

Cypress is a leased-line network that provides a low-cost, protocol-independent, packet switching system used primarily for interconnecting small sites to the TCP/IP Internet. Originally established as part of a joint research project with CSNET, it is now independent of CSNET.

There are no restrictions on its use, outside those imposed by other networks. Thus commercial traffic can pass between two industrial sites across Cypress. Industrial sites cannot pass commercial traffic onto the Internet due to restrictions imposed by government agencies that control the backbone networks (for example NSFNET).

## 1.2.7 DRI

The Terrestrial Wideband Network is a wide area network whose purpose is to provide a platform for research on high-speed networking protocols and applications (this role was formerly played by the ARPANET). This system includes both connection-oriented as well as connectionless service, broadcast and multicast service and real-time conferencing.

The Terrestrial Wideband Network was built and deployed by BBN Systems and Technologies Corporation during the first half of 1989 as part of the initial phase of the Defense Research Internet (DRI). Its main purpose was to carry cross-country Internet datagram traffic associated with DARPA-funded projects. It was composed of Internet gateways and Terrestrial Wideband Network packet switches (WPS) which communicated with each other using the Host Access Protocol (HAP) specified in RFC 1221. Wideband Monitoring Protocol (WB-MON) was used between the WPSs and the monitoring center. The backbone also supported a research environment for multimedia conferencing and voice/video conferencing using gateways that used a real-time connection-oriented protocol (ST-II - Stream Protocol - RFC 1190) over a connectionless network.

## 1.2.8 European Academic Research Network (EARN)

EARN, started in 1983, was the first and largest network serving academic and research institutions in Europe, the Middle East and Africa. EARN was initially started with help from IBM. It evolved to become a non-profit non-commercial traffic-based network serving academic and research institutions.

## 1.2.9 Réseaux Associés pour la Recherche Européenne (RARE)

RARE, founded in 1986, is the association of European networking organizations and their users. The association has 20 voting *Full National Members* (all of which are European countries), several *Associate National Members* (some European and Asian countries), *International Members* (for example EARN) and *Liason Members* (for example CREN).

It supports the principles of open systems as defined by the ISO as well as a number of mainly European groups, such as the *European Workshop for Open Systems* (EWOS) and the *European Telecommunications Standards Institute* (ETSI).

For more details, please refer to *Réseaux Associés pour la Recherche Européenne (RARE)*.

## 1.2.10  Réseaux IP Européens (RIPE)

Réseaux IP Européens (RIPE) coordinates TCP/IP networking for the research community in Europe.  It operates under the auspices of RARE.  RIPE has been functioning since 1989. By the early 1990s more than 60 organizations were participating in the work.  The objective of RIPE is to ensure the necessary administrative and technical coordination to allow the operation of a pan-European *IP* network.  Note that RIPE does *not* operate a network of its own. RIPE is the *IP* activity of RARE.

One of the activities of RIPE is to maintain a database of European IP networks, DNS domains and their contact persons.  The content of this database is considered to be public information.  The database can be accessed either via a *WHOIS* server on host *whois.ripe.net* (TCP port 43) or via anonymous FTP to *ftp.ripe.net*.

The RIPE NCC (Network Coordination Center) can be contacted via:

RIPE NCC
Kruislaan 409
NL-1098 SJ Amsterdam
The Netherlands
Phone: +31 20 592 5065
Fax: +31 20 592 5155
E-mail: ncc@ripe.net

## 1.2.11  Japanese Internet

Japan has many different networks. The following are some major ones.

- The Japanese BITNET was started in 1985.  It is funded by members and the Science University of Tokyo.  This network connects to CUNY (City University of New York) via a 56 Kbps link.

- N-1net is managed by the *National Center for Science and Information Systems* (NACSIS), a research institute funded by the Ministry of Education in Japan.  It started operation in 1980 using an X.25 packet-switching network.  N-1net has a 50 Kbps link to the NSF in Washington.

- Todai International Science Network (TISN) is used by physicists and chemists. TISN has a 128 Kbps link between Todai and Hawaii.

- *Widely Integrated Distributed Environment* (WIDE) is the Japanese Internet. It started as a research project in 1986. There are two links between WIDE and the rest of the Internet. One 192 Kbps link is from Keio University in Fujisawa to the University of Hawaii. A secondary 128 Kbps link from Todai to Hawaii serves as a backup.

For more details, please refer to [LaQuey] and [Malamud] listed in Appendix A, "Bibliography" on page A-1.

## 1.2.12 Commercial Use of the Internet

In recent years the Internet has grown in size and range at a greater rate than anyone could have predicted. In particular, more than half of the hosts now connected to the Internet are of a commercial nature. This is an area of potential and actual conflict with the initial aims of the Internet, which were to foster open communications between academic and research institutions. However, the continued growth in commercial use of the Internet is inevitable so it will be helpful to explain how this evolution is taking place.

One important initiative to consider is that of the *Acceptable Use Policy (AUP)*. The first of these policies was introduced in 1992 and applies to the use of NSFNET. A copy of this can be obtained at *nic.merit.edu/nsfnet/acceptable.use.policies*. At the heart of this AUP is a commitment "to support open research and education". Under "Unacceptable Uses" is a prohibition of "use for for-profit activities", unless covered by the General Principle or as a specifically acceptable use. However, in spite of this apparently restrictive stance the NSFNET has increasingly been used for a broad range of activities, including many of a commercial nature.

Apart from the NSFNET AUP, many of the internets that connect to NSFNET maintain their own AUPs. Some of these are relatively restrictive in their treatment of commercial activities while others are relatively liberal. The main thing to say is that AUPs will need to evolve as the inevitable growth in commercial use continues.

Let us now focus on the Internet service providers who have been most active in introducing commercial uses to the Internet. Two worth mentioning are PSINet and UUNET, which began in the late 80s to offer Internet access to both businesses and individuals. The California-based CERFnet provides services that are free of any AUP. An organization to interconnect PSINet, UUNET and CERFnet was formed soon after, called the Commercial Internet Exchange (CIX). To date CIX has more than 20 members connecting member internets in an AUP-free environment. At about the same time that CIX was conceived, a non-profit company, Advance Network and Services (ANS), was formed by IBM, MCI and Merit, Inc. to operate T1 backbone connections for

NSFNET. This group has been active in increasing the commercial presence on the Internet.

ANS also formed a commercially oriented subsidiary called ANS CO+RE to provide linkage between commercial customers and the research and education domains. ANS CO+RE provides AUP-free access to NSFNET as well as being linked to CIX.

## 1.2.13 Information Super Highway

One recent and important initiative has been the creation of the US Advisory Council on the National Information Infrastructure headed by Al Gore. In essence, this initiative makes the creation of a "network of networks" a national priority. This network would be similar to the existing Internet in some respects but with government and industry contributing those elements which it is best able to provide.

From a more international perspective The Group of Seven (G7) ministers met in Brussels in February 1995 to discuss the emerging Global Information Infrastructure (GII). The conference was attended by science, technology and economic ministers of Canada, the United Kingdom, France, Japan, Germany, Italy and the United States, and focused on technological, cultural and economic issues regarding the development of an international infrastructure.

A free electronic magazine called G7 Live was used to deliver daily wrap-ups, commentary and news about the conference to Internet users worldwide. Specific issues covered by G7 Live include intellectual property rights, infrastructure building, cultural and regulatory considerations and descriptions of the more than 100 technology exhibits that were present at the conference.

Both the NII and the GII described above are important initiatives which should ultimately lead to the "Information Super Highway" that is presently the subject of so much discussion in the media.

# 1.3 IBM and the Internet

In this section we will discuss the architectural and product support that IBM provides for the Internet.

## 1.3.1 The IBM Open Blueprint

In March 1992, IBM announced the Networking Blueprint which is, essentially, a framework for structuring network diversity and complexity with consistency and flexibility. Within this framework, you can create networking solutions best suited to your needs, irrespective of networking protocols and vendors.

The Open Blueprint is an expansion of the Networking Blueprint and incorporates the entire Networking Blueprint. The lower portion of the Open Blueprint is identical to the Networking Blueprint. The upper portion of the Open Blueprint is an expansion of the applications and application support layers of the Networking Blueprint to show more detail in the application environment. In this section only the networking portion of the Open Blueprint is discussed in greater detail.

What was the reason for the Networking Blueprint?

An organization's networking requirements are driven by the need for specific applications. Often the application requires a specific network protocol because all applications are written for a specific Application Programming Interface (API). Here are some examples:

- Most UNIX or AIX programs were written for TCP/IP transport using the Berkeley sockets API.

- Most SAA programs were written for SNA transport using CPI-C or other APPC interfaces.

All other popular transport protocols protocols such as OSI, DECnet, NetBIOS and IPX provide their own specific APIs.

As a result of this, you have to have multiple separate networks composed of different protocols, hardware components, bandwidth capabilities and network-specific management capabilities. Besides this you need skill in all these different segments.

The goals of the Networking Blueprint are:

- To allow you to buy and create applications without concern for the underlying networking components and services

- To enable the incorporation of multiple network protocols into a single network

- To permit an evolutionary exploitation of high bandwidth technologies and the emerging applications that use them

What the Networking Blueprint is not:

- The Blueprint is not a new architecture; it is a way to structure your systems.

- It is not proprietary, but on the contrary is based on international and industry standards.

- It does not imply totally new systems, but rather is bent on encompassing legacy systems, applications and devices as well as systems conforming to the new computing and communication models.

In order to reduce complexity, the Blueprint is separated into different components which are discussed below. See Figure 1-1 on page 1-12.

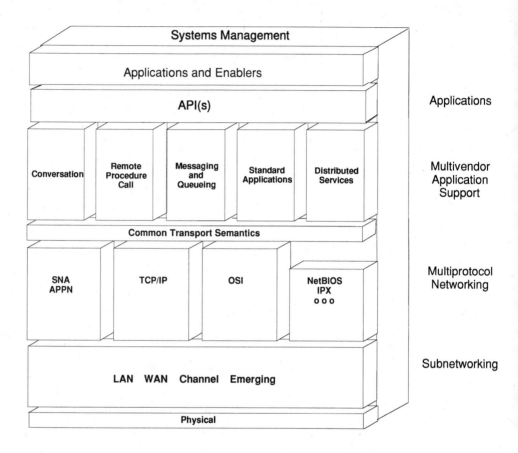

*Figure 1-1. IBM Networking Blueprint*

- Multivendor application support

  The multivendor application support addresses the problem of application portability and interoperability across the widest possible set of hardware and operating system platforms. It is essential that applications be developed independently of the systems they will run on. Therefore a number of APIs are recommended when new applications are to be written. These recommended APIs are:

  - CPI-C (transactional)

- RPC (client/server as per the OSF/DCE)

- MQI (Message Queuing Interface)

Most of these APIs are already available on the following platforms: MVS, VM, OS/2, OS/400 and AIX/6000 as shown in Table 1-1.

*Table 1-1. Availability of APIs for IBM Platforms*

| Platform | CPI-C | RPC | MQI |
|----------|-------|-----|-----|
| MVS | X | X | X |
| VM | X | X | |
| OS/2 | X | X | X |
| OS/400 | X | X | X |
| AIX/6000 | X | X | X |

The APIs are available on many platforms from other vendors as well.

It is IBM's strategy to offer application enabling systems that allow porting to IBM and non-IBM systems.

- Multiprotocol networking

The multiprotocol networking component addresses the problem of the multiplicity of networking protocols in most networks. A way of reducing the number of physical networks is a multiprotocol network processor such as the IBM 6611. It routes all the major protocols, including SNA APPN, and uses only standard mechanisms, such as OSPF, to communicate with other routers. In cases when standards do not exist, IBM contributes its technologies to the industry (for example, Data Link Switching (DLSw) was published as IETF RFC 1434).

The even more important step in this direction is the Multi-Protocol Transport Networking (MPTN) architecture. This technology makes it possible to minimize the number of protocols that must be supported in a network, and more significantly on the desktops and servers, by decoupling the application from the networking layer. MPTN was submitted to X/Open in December 1991. The IBM AnyNet product family fulfills this architecture. MPTN is part of the Common Transport Semantics (CTS) layer in the Blueprint. The CTS works as shown in Figure 1-2 on page 1-14.

CTS architecture offers:

- No interference when application and transport network protocol match

- MPTN function compensation and address mappings when applications and transport network do not match

– Functions delivered by industry standards such as RFC 1001/1002 for NetBIOS over TCP/IP

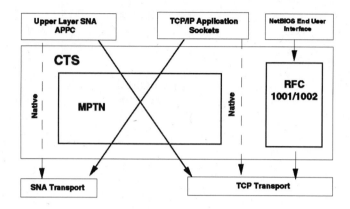

*Figure  1-2.  Common Transport Semantics*

Please see 1.3.2, "AnyNet" on page  1-15 for further information and a list of products already available.  For an architectural description see *MPTN Architecture Tutorial and Product Implementations.*

• Subnetworking

The subnetworking component addresses the rapid evolution of the telecommunication technologies. It identifies and recommends the use of ITU-T, IEEE and similar industry standards, to permit building LANs and WANs that are protocol transparent. The strategic protocols are 802.3, 802.5, X.25, frame relay (RFC 1490) and ATM. IBM's strategy fully acknowledges that tomorrow's networks will mostly be based on the ATM technology, which will allow the integration of audio, video and data and be an essential enabler for the full deployment of multimedia applications. An example of a product in this layer is the IBM 2220 Nways BroadBand Switch.

• Systems management

The system management component is the necessary glue that makes any network, large or small, operable. Network management applications will be written in such a way that they are portable across, and can interoperate with, a wide variety of IBM and non-IBM management platforms.

The application portability will be achieved with the deployment of the OSF/DME technology, including common APIs such as XMP. Multivendor interoperability will come from supporting the CMIP, SNMP and SNA/MS network management protocols.

For further information on the IBM Networking Blueprint or IBM Open Blueprint please refer to the IBM publications *G511-3096* and *G326-0395*.

## 1.3.2 AnyNet

The IBM AnyNet product family is the implementation of the Common Transport Semantics (CTS) in the IBM Networking Blueprint based on the emerging standard of Multiprotocol Transport Networking (MPTN). Please refer to Multiprotocol Networking described earlier in this chapter.

The idea behind AnyNet is to run matching applications which are designed to operate over one specific type of network over other networks. For example, you can run a host SNA printer application over a TCP/IP network. That means you don't have to install an SNA connection to this location beside the existing TCP/IP connection. The advantage of using AnyNet is the reduction of the number of different transport protocols. You can run all your applications over one kind of network if you like.

- Anynet/2 SNA over TCP/IP

  You have access from a TCP/IP workstation to any APPC database, terminal emulation or printer application running on the host, such as CICS, IMS, DB/2, or TSO. The "AnyNet partner" could be another AnyNet/2 station or AnyNet/MVS. See Figure 1-3 on page 1-16.

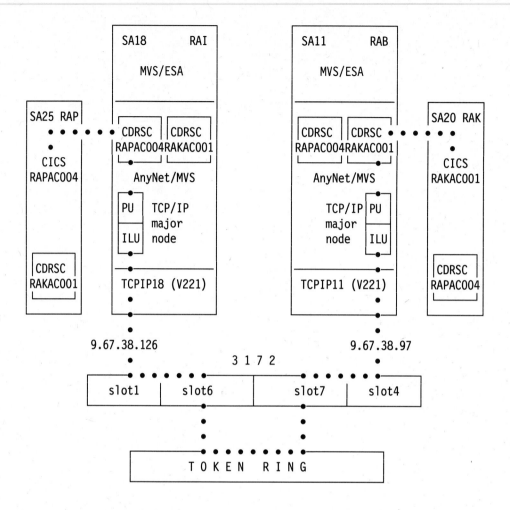

*Figure   1-3.   APPC over TCP/IP*

- AnyNet/2 Sockets over SNA

  With this you have access to Berkeley Software Distribution (BSD) Socket
  applications such as FTP, TELNET and NFS across an SNA network.

- AnyNet/2 Sockets over SNA Gateway

  This gateway enables all native TCP/IP workstations to connect to similar
  applications in an AnyNet/2 or AnyNet/MVS host across an existing SNA network.
  It is also possible to install multiple gateways in order to connect two TCP/IP
  networks across an existing SNA network.  See Figure  1-4 on page  1-17.

AnyNet/2 Sockets over SNA - Multiple Gateways

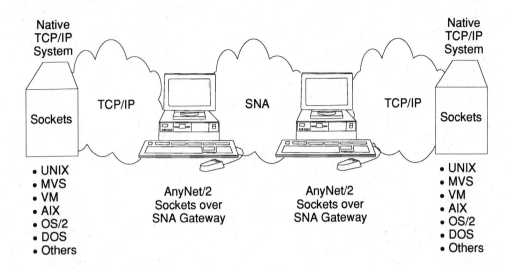

**Native TCP/IP System**

Sockets

• UNIX
• MVS
• VM
• AIX
• OS/2
• DOS
• Others

TCP/IP

AnyNet/2 Sockets over SNA Gateway

SNA

AnyNet/2 Sockets over SNA Gateway

TCP/IP

**Native TCP/IP System**

Sockets

• UNIX
• MVS
• VM
• AIX
• OS/2
• DOS
• Others

*Figure  1-4.  Multiple Gateways*

• AnyNet/2 NetBEUI over SNA

Enables you to run NetBIOS applications such as IBM LAN Server and Lotus Notes over an existing SNA network.

• AnyNet/MVS

This feature is available with VTAM 4.2 for MVS/ESA.

For details of Anynet implementations on selected platforms please see Table  1-2 on page  1-18.

| *Table 1-2.* *AnyNet Availability* | | | | | |
|---|---|---|---|---|---|
| **Functionality** | **OS/2** | **MVS** | **OS/400** | **AIX/6000** | **MS Windows** |
| APPC over TCP/IP | x | x | x | x | x |
| SNA over TCP/IP | x | x | | | |
| Sockets over SNA | x | x | x | x | |
| Sockets over SNA gateway | x | | | | |
| NetBEUI over SNA | x | | | | |
| IPX over SNA gateway | x | | | | |

## 1.3.3 IBM Global Network Services

The IBM Global Network is a business unit made up of Advantis in the USA, IBM Information Network organizations worldwide and wholly owned subsidiaries and joint ventures around the world providing a rich portfolio of value-added networking services.

IBM Global Network solutions are designed to ensure your success in the worldwide electronic marketplace, and feature:

- Network outsourcing

- Network services

- Networked applications

- Support services

You can connect to the IBM Global Network and extend your reach without having to manage the complexity of multi-vendor, multi-enterprise or multi-national network environments. Over 5,000 networking professionals in more than 60 countries design, install, manage and operate the network, saving you the cost of network hardware, software and personnel. For further information please refer to the Advantis web pages starting at *http://www.ibm.net/adv/*.

## 1.3.4 Internet Connection Services

The IBM Internet Connection Services, a global service, is accessible in each country and provides full Internet access. The following services are available:

- Access services

  - Direct Internet Access: extend current dial services options to include full TCP/IP node connectivity to the Internet.

- Secure access: enable the user to maintain the security of their corporate environment, while providing stand-alone access to Internet information resources.

- Global Access: extend the reach of Internet services through the IBM Global Network and its affiliates and joint ventures worldwide.

- Gateway Access: allow user participation in the Internet community through gateways located worldwide.

• Application services

- TCP/IP Protocol Support: TELNET, File Transfer Protocol (FTP), Simple Mail Transfer Protocol (SMTP), WHOIS, PING and other TCP/IP applications.

- Network News: user subscriptions and participation in news groups available on the Internet, including discussion groups designed specifically for IBM customers.

- Navigational Tools: Gopher and World Wide Web (WWW) browsers to assist the user in exploring the information available on the Internet.

- IBM Mail Exchange: Internet users can exchange mail with the users participating in IBM Mail Exchange with their electronic mail environment including support for multi-purpose Internet Mail Extensions (MIME) binary files. See 4.7, "Multipurpose Internet Mail Extensions (MIME)" on page 4-90.

- Information Exchange: extend your electronic trading partner circle to TCP/IP users.

• Support services

- Customer Support: assist IBM customers with their use of the Internet including access, navigation, setup and usage of other IBM Global Network services with Internet services.

- Server Support: provide an environment for customer information using Internet server technologies such as FTP, Gopher and WWW.

- Domain Name Services: perform the function of customer primary and secondary authoritative domain name servers.

## 1.3.4.1 Implementations

Included in the Bonus Pack of OS/2 Warp Version 3 is the Internet Access Kit which enables the user to connect to the Internet. Via a set of panels, you are requested to provide information needed for identification and registration. The billing is done via your credit card. The Internet Access Kit provides a complete set of Internet applications including WebExplorer, Gopher, Ultimail Lite, FTP etc.

Internet Connection for Windows provides a set of services and functions for the DOS/Windows environment that are similar to those described above for Warp. In particular, WebExplorer Mosaic provides WWW access capability. For more information about the World Wide Web refer to 6.2, "World Wide Web" on page 6-6.

The home page for the IBM Internet Connection is: *http://www.ibm.net/*.

# 1.4 Future

The long-term view described in the United States Federal High Performance Computing and Communications (HPCC) Program indicates that all the Internet networks will be absorbed into the National Research and Education Network (NREN).

The *High Performance Computing Act* of 1991 was signed into law in the United States in December 1991. This bill allocated to the NREN approximately US $100 million per year for the next five years.

The NREN network is being developed to provide distributed computing capability to research and educational institutions and to further advanced research on very high-speed networks and applications.

NREN has already scheduled the integration, coordinated by the NSF, of the DoD's Defense Research Internet (DRI), NSFNet, NASA (National Aeronautics and Space Administration) Science Internet (NSI) and Department of Energy (DOE) Energy Science Network (ESnet).

The NREN program specifies a three-phase project coordinated by the DARPA to increase data transmission speeds to 3 Gbps (gigabits per second) over the next 10 to 15 years. The program also includes the exploration of pricing mechanisms for network services and applications and the initiation of a *structured transition to commercial service*.

In August 1992, under the NREN program, the DOE awarded a five-year, US $50 million contract for high-speed public switched Asynchronous Transfer Mode (ATM) services to Sprint Corporation. Under this contract, Sprint Corporation will provide the DOE and NASA with ATM service at 45 Mbps (T3) speed. Livermore, California was an initial test site, with more sites added in 1993. Soon after, 15 DOE sites and 11 NASA sites were added to the production network.

At this time, the evolution of the NREN program towards high-speed networking is well advanced. It would be useful at this stage to describe the infrastructure of this developing high-speed network.

The *Network Access Point (NAP)* is a critical interchange in the new Internet architecture. A number of organizations have been selected by the National Science Foundation to operate the NAPs. Among these organizations are:

- Sprint Corporation - New York/New Jersey

- Ameritech - Chicago

- PacBell - San Francisco/Bay Area

- MFSdatanet - Washington DC

The *Network Service Provider (NSP)* is a provider of Internet services that qualifies to receive regional connectivity funding from NSF. This means that the NSP must connect to the three primary NAPs in California, Chicago and New York (see above). Among these organizations are:

- ANS (now owned by America Online)

- MCInet

- SprintLink

In addition, there are a number of *Internet Service Providers (ISPs)* who do not qualify for the NSF regional connectivity funding. Among these organizations are:

- AlterNet

- Net99

- PSI

A *Routing Arbitor (RA)* is an NSF funded organization that provides routing information at each NAP. A Routing Arbiter Database is maintained at *http://rrdb.merit.edu/grroverview.html on the World Wide Web.*

The NAPs are currently providing high-speed services based upon ATM, frame relay and FDDI to the NSPs and ISPs. For more information on ATM, Frame Relay and other high-speed networking technologies refer to the next section.

More information on selected NAPs is available via the World Wide Web at *http://rrdb.merit.edu/napsp3.html* and at *http://rrdb.merit.edu/pacbell.html.*

## 1.4.1 Future - High-Speed Networking

The future of NREN is influenced at least partially by advances in high-speed networking technology. We summarize here several emerging technologies and standards:

- **Frame relay** is a network interface protocol standard for interfacing to a packet network (the approved CCITT I.233, Q.922, Q.933 and I.370 standards and the approved ANSI T1.606, T1.618, T1.617 and T1.606 standards). It supports variable sized frames, and hence is not recommended for carrying isochronous traffic such as voice or video. (Note: voice must be transmitted with no more than a 100 ms delay for acceptable quality.) A network can be easily implemented on existing packet switching equipment using frame relay to gain throughput improvements. Currently, the frame relay access speed is defined up to T-1 (1.544 Mbps).

- **Distributed Queue Dual Bus (DQDB)** is a protocol designed to handle both isochronous (constant rate, voice) traffic and data traffic over a very high-speed optical link. The defined media and speed include:

    - *Fiber connection* at 35 Mbps and 155 Mbps
    - *SONET (Synchronous Optical Network) connection* starting at 51,840 Mbps.

  This protocol was accepted as the standard (IEEE 802.6) for Metropolitan Area Networks (MANs). It is the basis for a number of MANs. For example, the Switched Multi-megabit Data Service (SMDS) is a MAN service that was introduced in the U.S. in late 1992. Initially, SMDS operated (using copper connections) at T-1 (1.544 Mbps) but subsequently at T-3 (45 Mbps).

- **Asynchronous Transfer Mode (ATM)**, is a switching technology based on 53-byte fixed-length cell calls. It has very high-speed capabilities (defined at both 155 Mbps and 622 Mbps) and is suitable for carrying voice, video and data. Public networks are not expected to fully support ATM until the latter half of the 1990s.

- **Broadband-ISDN** is a newer, and not yet standardized, technology offering even higher speed starting at OC-3 ("Optical Carrier level 3", 155.52 Mbps). It too is not expected to be available until 1995 at the earliest.

# 1.5 Request For Comments (RFC)

The Internet protocol suite is still evolving through the mechanism of *Request For Comments* (RFC). New protocols (mostly application protocols) are being designed and implemented by researchers, and are brought to the attention of the Internet community in the form of an RFC.[1] The RFC mechanism is overseen by the Internet Architecture Board (IAB). The largest source of RFCs is the Internet Engineering Task Force (IETF) which is a subsidiary of the IAB. However, anyone may submit a memo proposed as an RFC to the RFC Editor. There are a set of rules which RFC authors must follow in order for an RFC to be accepted. These rules are themselves described in an RFC (RFC 1543) which also indicates how to submit a proposal for an RFC.

---

[1]  Some of these protocols, particularly those dated April 1, can be described as impractical at best. For instance, RFC 1149 (dated 1990 April 1) describes the transmission of IP datagrams by carrier pigeon and RFC 1437 (dated 1993 April 1) describes the transmission of people by electronic mail.

Once an RFC has been published, all revisions and replacements are published as new RFCs. A new RFC which revises or replaces an existing RFC is said to "update" or to "obsolete" that RFC. The existing RFC is said to be "updated by" or "obsoleted by" the new one. For example RFC 1521 which describes the MIME protocol is a "second edition," being a revision of RFC 1341 and RFC 1590 is an amendment to RFC 1521. RFC 1521 is therefore labelled like this: "Obsoletes RFC 1341; Updated by RFC 1590." Consequently, there is never any confusion over whether two people are referring to different versions of an RFC, since there are never different versions.

Some RFCs are described as *information documents* while others describe Internet protocols. The Internet Architecture Board (IAB) maintains a list of the RFCs that describe the protocol suite. Each of these is assigned a *state* and a *status*.

An Internet protocol can have one of the following states:

**Standard**

> The IAB has established this as an official protocol for the Internet. These are separated in two groups:
>
> 1. IP protocol and above, protocols that apply to the whole Internet.
> 2. Network-specific protocols, generally specifications of how to do IP on particular types of networks.

**Draft standard**

> The IAB is actively considering this protocol as a possible standard protocol. Substantial and widespread testing and comments are desired. Comments and test results should be submitted to the IAB. There is a possibility that changes will be made in a draft protocol before it becomes a standard.

**Proposed standard**

> These are protocol proposals that may be considered by the IAB for standardization in the future. Implementations and testing by several groups are desirable. Revision of the protocol is likely.

**Experimental**

> A system should not implement an experimental protocol unless it is participating in the experiment and has coordinated its use of the protocol with the developer of the protocol.

**Informational**

> Protocols developed by other standard organizations, or vendors, or that are for other reasons outside the purview of the IAB may be published as RFCs for the convenience of the Internet community as informational protocols. Such protocols may in some cases also be recommended for use on the Internet by the IAB.

**Historic**
> These are protocols that are unlikely to ever become standards in the Internet either because they have been superseded by later developments or due to lack of interest.

Definitions of protocol status:

**Required**   A system must implement the required protocols.

**Recommended** A system should implement the recommended protocol.

**Elective**   A system may or may not implement an elective protocol. The general notion is that if you are going to do something like this, you must do exactly this.

**Limited use** These protocols are for use in limited circumstances. This may be because of their experimental state, specialized nature, limited functionality, or historic state.

**Not recommended** These protocols are not recommended for general use. This may be because of their limited functionality, specialized nature, or experimental or historic state.

## 1.5.1 Internet Standards

Proposed standard, draft standard and standard protocols are described as being on the *Internet Standards Track*. The standards track is controlled by the *Internet Engineering Steering Group (IESG)* of the IETF. When a protocol reaches the standard state it is assigned a standard number (STD). The purpose of STD numbers is to clearly indicate which RFCs describe Internet standards. STD numbers reference multiple RFCs when the specification of a standard is spread across multiple documents. Unlike RFCs, where the number refers to a specific document, STD numbers do not change when a standard is updated. STD numbers do not, however, have version numbers since all updates are made via RFCs and the RFC numbers are unique. Thus to unambiguously specify which version of a standard one is referring to, the standard number and all of the RFCs which it includes should be stated. For instance, the Domain Name System (DNS) is STD 13 and is described in RFCs 1034 and 1035. To reference the standard, a form like "STD-13/RFC-1034/RFC-1035" should be used. For a description of the Standards Process, see *RFC 1602 – The Internet Standards Process - Revision 2*.

For some standards track RFCs the status category does not always contain enough information to be useful. It is therefore supplemented, notably for routing protocols by an *applicability statement* which is given either in STD 1 or in a separate RFC.

References to the RFCs and to STD numbers will be made throughout this book, since they form the basis of all TCP/IP protocol implementations.

Four Internet standards are of particular importance:

*STD 1 — Internet Official Protocol Standards*
> This standard gives the state and status of each Internet protocol or standard, and defines the meanings attributed to each different state or status. It is issued by the IAB approximately quarterly. At the time of writing this standard is in RFC 1780 (March 1995).

*STD 2 — Assigned Internet Numbers*
> This standard lists currently assigned numbers and other protocol parameters in the Internet protocol suite. It is issued by the Internet Assigned Numbers Authority (IANA). The current edition at the time of writing is RFC 1700 (October 1994).

*STD 3 — Host Requirements*
> This standard defines the requirements for Internet host software (often by reference to the relevant RFCs). The standard comes in two parts: *RFC 1122 — Requirements for Internet hosts – communications layer* and *RFC 1123 — Requirements for Internet hosts – application and support*.

*STD 4 — Gateway Requirements*
> This standard defines the requirements for Internet gateway (router) software. It is RFC 1009.

## 1.5.2 For Your Information (FYI)

A number of RFCs which are intended to be of wide interest to Internet users are classified as *For Your Information (FYI)* documents. They frequently contain introductory or other helpful information. Like STD numbers, an FYI number is not changed when a revised RFC is issued. Unlike STDs, FYIs correspond to a single RFC document. For example, *FYI 4 – FYI on Questions and Answers - Answers to Commonly asked "New Internet User" Questions* is currently in its fourth edition. The RFC numbers are 1177, 1206, 1325 and 1594.

## 1.5.3 Obtaining RFCs

All RFCs are available publicly, both in printed and electronic form from the Internet Network Information Center or InterNIC (*internic.net*). Prior to 1993, the NIC function was performed by the DDN NIC (*nic.ddn.mil*). See RFC 1400 for more information about the transition.

- RFCs can be obtained in printed form from:

> Network Solutions, Inc.
> Attn: InterNIC Registration Service
> 505 Huntmar Park Drive
> Herndon, VA 22070

Help Desk Telephone Number:
703-742-4777

FAX Number 703-742-4811

- To get the electronic form, users may use anonymous FTP to *ds.internic.net* (198.49.45.10) and retrieve files from the directory *rfc*, or Gopher to *internic.net* (198.41.0.5).

- For information on other methods of accessing RFCs by E-mail or FTP, send an E-mail message to "rfc-info@ISI.EDU" with the message body "help: ways_to_get_rfcs." For example:

```
To: rfc-info@ISI.EDU
Subject: getting rfcs

help: ways_to_get_rfcs
```

- If you have World Wide Web access, there are many sites that maintain RFC archives. One that you might try is the MAGIC Document Archive at *http://www.msci.magic.net/docs/rfc/rfc_by_num.html*.

- RFCs can also be obtained through the IBM VNET network using the following command:

```
EXEC TOOLS SENDTO ALMVMA ARCNET RFC GET RFCnnnn TXT *
```

Where *nnnn* refers to the number of the RFC.

To obtain the list of all the RFCs (and to know if they are available in TXT format or in PostScript format), use the command:

```
EXEC TOOLS SENDTO ALMVMA ARCNET RFC GET RFCINDEX TXT *
```

There is also an STDINDEX TXT file and an FYIINDEX TXT file which list those RFCs which have an STD or FYI number.

## 1.5.4  Major Internet Protocols

To give an idea of the importance of the major protocols, we list some of them together with their current state and status and STD number where applicable in Table  1-3 on page  1-27.  The complete list can be found in *RFC 1780 - Internet Official Protocol Standards*.

**Table 1-3.** *The Current state and status and STD numbers of Important Internet protocols*

| Protocol | Name | State | Status | STD |
|---|---|---|---|---|
| IP | Internet Protocol | Std. | Req. | 5 |
| ICMP | Internet Control Message Protocol | Std. | Req. | 5 |
| UDP | User Datagram Protocol | Std. | Rec. | 6 |
| TCP | Transmission Control Protocol | Std. | Rec. | 7 |
| TELNET | TELNET Protocol | Std. | Rec. | 8 |
| FTP | File Transfer Protocol | Std. | Rec. | 9 |
| SMTP | Simple Mail Transfer Protocol | Std. | Rec. | 10 |
| MAIL | Format of Electronic Mail Messages | Std. | Rec. | 11 |
| DOMAIN | Domain Name System | Std. | Rec. | 13 |
| DNS-MX | Mail Routing and the Domain System | Std. | Rec. | 14 |
| MIME | Multipurpose Internet Mail Extensions | Draft | Ele. | |
| SNMP | Simple Network Management Protocol | Std. | Rec. | 15 |
| SMI | Structure of Management Information | Std. | Rec. | 16 |
| MIB-I | Management Information Base | Hist. | Not | |
| MIB-II | Management Information Base-II | Std. | Rec. | 17 |
| NETBIOS | NetBIOS Services Protocol | Std. | Ele. | 19 |
| TFTP | Trivial File Transfer Protocol | Std. | Ele. | 33 |
| RIP | Routing Information Protocol | Std. | Ele. | 34 |
| ARP | Address Resolution Protocol | Std. | Ele. | 37 |
| RARP | Reverse Address Resolution Protocol | Std. | Ele. | 38 |
| GGP | Gateway to Gateway Protocol | Hist. | Not | |
| BGP3 | Border Gateway Protocol 3 | Draft | Ele. | |
| OSPF2 | Open Shortest Path First Protocol V2 | Draft | Ele. | |
| IS-IS | OSI IS-IS for TCP/IP Dual Environments | Prop. | Ele. | |
| BOOTP | Bootstrap Protocol | Draft | Rec. | |
| GOPHER | The Internet Gopher Protocol | Info. | | |
| SUN-NFS | Network File System Protocol | Info. | | |
| SUN-RFC | Remote Procedure Call Protocol Version 2 | Info. | | |

**Legend:**
**State:** Std. = Standard; Draft = Draft Standard; Prop. = Proposed Standard; Info. = Informational; Hist. = Historic
**Status:** Req. = Required; Rec. = Recommended; Ele. = Elective; Not = Not Recommended

At the time of writing there is no RFC associated with the HyperText Transfer Protocol used in World Wide Web implementations. However, the document *HyperText Transfer Protocol (HTTP)* written by Tim Berners-Lee may be obtained at *ftp://info.cern.ch/pub/www/doc/http-spec.text*.

In addition, the following RFCs describe the Uniform Resource Locator (URL) and associated concepts:

- *RFC 1630 — Universal Resource Identifiers in WWW*
- *RFC 1737 — Functional Requirements for Uniform Resource Names*
- *RFC 1738 — Uniform Resource Locators (URL)*

# Chapter 2.  Architecture and Protocols

In this chapter we start by introducing TCP/IP and describing its basic properties such as internetworking, protocol layering and routing.  We then discuss each of the specific protocols in more detail.

## 2.1  Architectural Model

The TCP/IP protocol suite is named for two of its most important protocols: Transmission Control Protocol (TCP) and Internet Protocol (IP).  Another name for it is the Internet Protocol Suite, and this is the phrase used in official Internet standards documents.  We shall use the more common term TCP/IP to refer to the entire protocol suite in this book.

### 2.1.1  Internetworking

The first design goal of TCP/IP was to build an interconnection of networks that provided universal communication services: an *internetwork*, or *internet*.  Each physical network has its own technology-dependent communication interface, in the form of a programming interface that provides basic communication functions (primitives).  Communication services are provided by software that runs between the physical network and the user applications and that provides a common interface for these applications, independent of the underlying physical network.  The architecture of the physical networks is hidden from the user.

The second aim is to *interconnect* different physical networks to form what appears to the the user to be one large network.  Such a set of interconnected networks is called an *internetwork* or an *internet*.

To be able to interconnect two networks, we need a computer that is attached to both networks and that can forward packets from one network to the other; such a machine is called a *router*.  The term *IP router* is also used because the routing function is part of the IP layer of the TCP/IP protocol suite (see 2.1.2.1, "Layered Protocols" on page  2-3).

Figure  2-1 on page  2-2 shows two examples of internets.

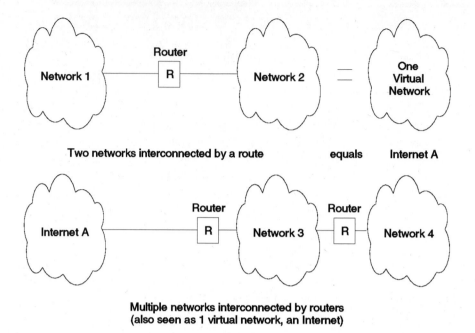

Two networks interconnected by a route        equals        Internet A

Multiple networks interconnected by routers
(also seen as 1 virtual network, an Internet)

*Figure  2-1. Internet Examples.* Two interconnected sets of networks, each seen as one logical network.

The basic properties of a router are:

- From the network standpoint, a router is a normal host.

- From the user standpoint, routers are invisible. The user sees only one large internetwork.

To be able to identify a host on the internetwork, each host is assigned an address, the *IP address*. When a host has multiple network adapters, each adapter has a separate IP address. The IP address consists of two parts:

```
IP address = <network number><host number>
```

The *network number* part of the IP address is assigned by a central authority and is unique throughout the Internet. The authority for assigning the *host number* part of the IP address resides with the organization which controls the network identified by the network number. The addressing scheme is described in detail in 2.2, "Addressing" on page 2-7.

## 2.1.2 Internet Architecture

The TCP/IP protocol suite has evolved over a time period of some 25 years. We will describe the most important aspects of the protocol suite in this and the following chapters.

### 2.1.2.1 Layered Protocols

TCP/IP, like most networking software, is modelled in layers. This layered representation leads to the term *protocol stack* which is synonymous with protocol suite. It can be used for situating (but *not* for comparing functionally) the TCP/IP protocol suite against others, such as SNA and Open System Interconnection (OSI). Functional comparisons cannot easily be extracted from this, as there are basic differences in the layered models used by the different protocol suites.

The Internet protocols are modeled in four layers:

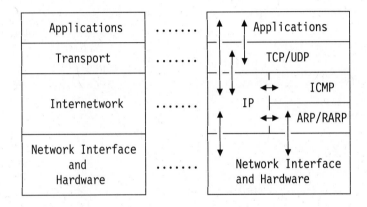

*Figure 2-2. Architectural Model.* Each layer represents a "package" of functions.

**Application**
> is a user process cooperating with another process on the same or a different host. Examples are TELNET (a protocol for remote terminal connections), FTP (File Transfer Protocol) and SMTP (Simple Mail Transfer Protocol). These are discussed in detail in Chapter 4, "Application Protocols" on page 4-1.

**Transport**
> provides the end-to-end data transfer. Example protocols are TCP (*connection-oriented*) and UDP (*connectionless*). Both are discussed in detail in 2.12, "Transmission Control Protocol (TCP)" on page 2-92 and 2.11, "User Datagram Protocol (UDP)" on page 2-88

### Internetwork

also called the *internet layer* or the *network layer*, the internetwork provides the "virtual network" image of internet (that is, this layer shields the higher levels from the typical network architecture below it). Internet Protocol (IP) is the most important protocol in this layer. It is a *connectionless* protocol which doesn't assume reliability from the lower layers. IP does *not* provide reliability, flow control or error recovery. These functions must be provided at a higher level, either at the Transport layer by using TCP as the transport protocol, or at the Application layer if UDP is used as the transport protocol. IP is discussed in detail in 2.3, "Internet Protocol (IP)" on page 2-36. A message unit in an IP network is called an *IP datagram*. This is the basic unit of information transmitted across TCP/IP networks. It is described in 2.3.1, "IP Datagram" on page 2-36 but we shall refer to it in this section to show how the different TCP/IP layers relate to an internet.

### Network Interface

also called the *link layer* or the *data-link layer*, the network interface layer is the interface to the actual network hardware. This interface may or may not provide reliable delivery, and may be packet or stream oriented. In fact, TCP/IP does not specify any protocol here, but can use almost any network interface available, which illustrates the flexibility of the IP layer. Examples are IEEE 802.2, X.25 (which is reliable in itself), ATM, FDDI, Packet Radio Networks (such as the AlohaNet) and even SNA. The possible physical networks and interfaces the IBM TCP/IP products can connect to are discussed in Chapter 5, "Connections" on page 5-1.

The actual interactions between the layers are shown by the arrows in Figure 2-2 on page 2-3. A more detailed "layering model" is shown in Figure 2-3.

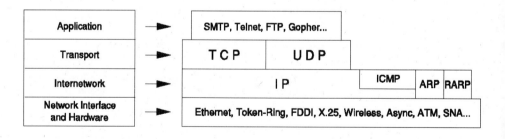

*Figure 2-3.* *Detailed Architectural Model*

## 2.1.2.2 Bridges, Routers and Gateways

Forming an internetwork by interconnecting multiple networks is done by *routers*. It is important to distinguish between a router, a bridge and a gateway.

*Bridge*  Interconnects LAN segments at the Network Interface layer level and forwards frames between them. A bridge performs the function of a MAC relay, and is independent of any higher layer protocol (including the Logical Link protocol). It provides MAC layer protocol conversion, if required. Examples of bridges are:

- A PS/2 running the IBM Token-Ring Network Bridge program
- The IBM 8229 LAN bridge

A bridge can be said to be *transparent* to IP. That is, when a host sends an IP datagram to another host on a network connected by a bridge, it sends the datagram directly to the host and the datagram "crosses" the bridge without the sending host being aware of it.

*Router*  Interconnects networks at the internetwork layer level and routes packets between them. The router must understand the addressing structure associated with the networking protocols it supports and take decisions on whether, or how, to forward packets. Routers are able to select the best transmission paths and optimal packet sizes. The basic routing function is implemented in the IP layer of the TCP/IP protocol stack. Therefore any host or workstation running TCP/IP may be used as a router. However, dedicated routers such as the IBM 6611 Network Processor provide much more sophisticated routing than the minimum function implemented by IP. Because IP provides this basic routing function, the term "IP router," is often used. Other, older, terms for router are "IP gateway," "Internet gateway" and "gateway." The term *gateway* is now normally used for connections at a higher level than the router level.

A router can be said to be *visible* to IP. That is, when a host sends an IP datagram to another host on a network connected by a router, it sends the datagram to the router and not directly to the target host.

*Gateway*  Interconnects networks at higher levels than bridges or routers. A gateway usually supports address mapping from one network to another, and may also provide transformation of the data between the environments to support end-to-end application connectivity. Gateways typically limit the interconnectivity of two networks to a subset of the application protocols supported on either one. For example, a VM host running TCP/IP may be used as an SMTP/RSCS mail gateway.

**Note:** The term "gateway," when used in this sense, is *not* synonymous with "IP gateway."

A gateway can be said to be *opaque* to IP. That is, a host cannot send an IP datagram through a gateway: it can only send it *to* a gateway. The higher-level protocol information carried by the datagrams is then passed on by the gateway using whatever networking architecture is used on the other side of the gateway.

Closely related to routers and gateways is the concept of a *firewall* or *firewall gateway* which is used to restrict access from the Internet to a network or a group of networks controlled by an organization for security reasons. See 6.3, "Firewalls" on page 6-10 for more information on firewalls.

### 2.1.2.3 IP Routing

Incoming datagrams will be checked to see if the local host is the IP destination host:

*yes*    The datagram is passed to the higher-level protocols.

*no*    The datagram is for a different host. The action depends on the value of the *ipforwarding* flag.

        *true*    The datagram is treated as an outgoing datagram and is routed to the *next hop* according to the algorithm described below.

        *false*    The datagram is discarded.

In the internet protocol, outgoing IP datagrams pass through the *IP routing* algorithm which determines where to send the datagram according to the destination IP address.

- If the host has an entry in its *IP routing table* (see 3.1, "Basic IP Routing" on page 3-1) which matches the destination IP address, the datagram is sent to the address in the entry.

- If the network number of the destination IP address is the same as the network number for one of the host's network adapters (that is, the destination and the host are on the same network) the datagram is sent to the physical address of the host matching the destination IP address.

- Otherwise, the datagram is sent to a *default router*.

This base algorithm, needed on all IP implementations, is sufficient to perform the base routing function.

As noted above, a TCP/IP host has basic router functionality included in the IP protocol. Such a router is adequate for simple routing, but not for complex networks. The protocols needed in complex cases are described in Chapter 3, "Routing Protocols" on page 3-1.

The IP routing mechanism combined with the "layered" view of the TCP/IP protocol stack, is represented in Figure 2-4 on page 2-7. This shows an IP datagram, going from one IP address (network number X, host number A) to another (network number Y, host number B), through two physical networks. Note that at the intermediate router, only the lower part of the TCP/IP protocol stack (the internetwork and the network interface layers) are involved.

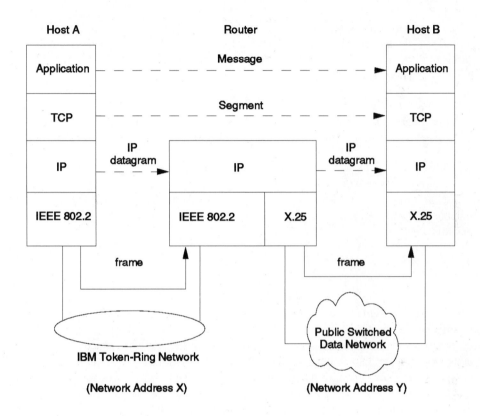

***Figure 2-4.*** *Internet Router.* The router function is performed by the IP protocol.

# 2.2 Addressing

Internet addresses can be symbolic or numeric. The symbolic form is easier to read, for example: myname@ibm.com. The numeric form is a 32-bit unsigned binary value which is usually expressed in a dotted decimal format. For example, 9.167.5.8 is a valid Internet address. The numeric form is used by the IP software. The mapping between the two is done by the *Domain Name System* discussed in 4.5, "Domain Name System

(DNS)" on page 4-39. We shall first look at the numeric form, which is called the IP address.

## 2.2.1 The IP Address

The standards for IP addresses are described in *RFC 1166 – Internet Numbers.*

To be able to identify a host on the internet, each host is assigned an address, the *IP address*, or *Internet Address*. When the host is attached to more than one network, it is called *multi-homed* and it has one IP address for each network interface. The IP address consists of a pair of numbers:

IP address = <network number><host number>

The *network number* part of the IP address is centrally administered by the Internet Network Information Center (the InterNIC) and is unique throughout the Internet.[1]

IP addresses are 32-bit numbers usually represented in a *dotted decimal* form (as the decimal representation of four 8-bit values concatenated with dots). For example *128.2.7.9* is an IP address with 128.2 being the network number and 7.9 being the host number. The rules used to divide an IP address into its network and host parts are explained below.

The binary format of the IP address 128.2.7.9 is:

        10000000 00000010 00000111 00001001

IP addresses are used by the IP protocol (see 2.3, "Internet Protocol (IP)" on page 2-36) to uniquely identify a host on the internet. IP datagrams (the basic data packets exchanged between hosts) are transmitted by some physical network attached to the host and each IP datagram contains a *source IP address* and a *destination IP address*. To send a datagram to a certain IP destination, the target IP address must be translated or mapped to a physical address. This may require transmissions on the network to find out the destination's physical network address (for example, on LANs the Address Resolution Protocol, discussed in 2.8, "Address Resolution Protocol (ARP)" on page 2-69, is used to translate IP addresses to physical MAC addresses).

The first bits of the IP address specify how the rest of the address should be separated into its network and host part.

---

[1] Prior to 1993, the NIC function was performed by the DDN NIC (nic.ddn.mil). See RFC 1400 for more information about this transition.

The terms *network address* and *netID* are sometimes used instead of network number, but the formal term, used in RFC 1166, is network number. Similarly, the terms *host address* and *hostID* are sometimes used instead of host number.

There are five classes of IP addresses. These are shown in Figure 2-5.

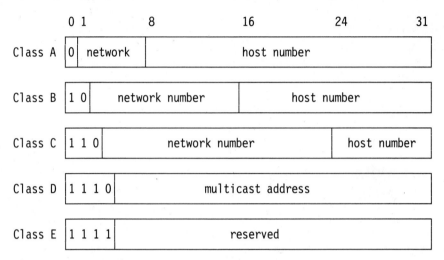

***Figure 2-5.*** *Assigned Classes of Internet Addresses*

**Note:** Two numbers out of each of the class A, class B and class C network numbers, and two host numbers out of every network are pre-assigned: the "all bits 0" number and the "all bits 1" number. These are discussed below in 2.2.3, "Special IP Addresses" on page 2-16.

- Class A addresses use 7 bits for the network number giving 126 possible networks (we shall see below that out of every group of network and host numbers, two have a special meaning). The remaining 24 bits are used for the host number, so each networks can have up to $2^{24}$-2 (16,777,214) hosts.
- Class B addresses use 14 bits for the network number, and 16 bits for the host number giving 16382 networks each with a maximum of 65534 hosts.
- Class C addresses use 21 bits for the network number and 8 for the host number giving 2,097,150 networks each with up to 254 hosts.
- Class D addresses are reserved for multicasting, which is used to address groups of hosts in a limited area. See 2.2.4.2, "Multicasting" on page 2-19 for more information on multicasting.
- Class E addresses are reserved for future use.

It is clear that a class A address will only be assigned to networks with a huge number of hosts, and that class C addresses are suitable for networks with a small number of hosts. However, this means that medium-sized networks (those with more than 254 hosts or where there is an expectation that there may be more than 254 hosts in the future) must use Class B addresses. The number of small- to medium-sized networks has been growing very rapidly in the last few years and it was feared that, if this growth had been allowed to continue unabated, all of the available Class B network addresses would have been used by the mid-1990s. This is termed the IP Address Exhaustion problem. The problem and how it is being addressed are discussed in 2.2.5, "The IP Address Exhaustion Problem" on page 2-21.

One point to note about the split of an IP address into two parts is that this split also splits the responsibility for selecting the IP address into two parts. The network number is assigned by the InterNIC, and the host number by the authority which controls the network. As we shall see in the next section, the host number can be further subdivided: this division is controlled by the authority which owns the network, and *not* by the InterNIC.

## 2.2.2 Subnets

Due to the explosive growth of the Internet, the use of assigned IP addresses became too inflexible to allow easy changes to local network configurations. These changes might occur when:

- A new physical network is installed at a location.
- Growth of the number of hosts requires splitting the local network into two or more separate networks.

To avoid having to request additional IP network addresses in these cases, the concept of *subnets* was introduced.

The host number part of the IP address is sub-divided again into a network number and a host number. This second network is termed a *subnetwork* or *subnet*. The main network now consists of a number of subnets and the IP address is interpreted as:

```
<network number><subnet number><host number>
```

The combination of the subnet number and the host number is often termed the "local address" or the "local part." "Subnetting" is implemented in a way that is transparent to remote networks. A host within a network which has subnets is aware of the subnetting but a host in a different network is not; it still regards the local part of the IP address as a host number.

The division of the local part of the IP address into subnet number and host number parts can be chosen freely by the local administrator; any bits in the local part can be used to form the subnet accomplished. The division is done using a *subnet mask* which is a 32 bit number. Zero bits in the subnet mask indicate bit positions ascribed to the host number, and ones indicate bit positions ascribed to the subnet number. The bit positions in the subnet mask belonging to the network number are set to ones but are not used. Subnet masks are usually written in dotted decimal form, like IP addresses.

The special treatment of "all bits zero" and "all bits one" applies to each of the three parts of a subnetted IP address just as it does to both parts of an IP address which has not been subnetted. See 2.2.3, "Special IP Addresses" on page 2-16. For example, a subnetted Class B network, which has a 16-bit local part, could use one of the following schemes:

- The first byte is the subnet number, the second the host number. This gives us 254 (256 minus 2 with the values 0 and 255 being reserved) possible subnets, each having up to 254 hosts. The subnet mask is 255.255.255.0.

- The first 12 bits 15 are used for the subnet number and the last four for the host number. This gives us 4094 possible subnets (4096 minus 2) but only 14 hosts per subnet (16 minus 2). The subnet mask is 255.255.255.240.

There are many other possibilities.

While the administrator is completely free to assign the subnet part of the local address in any legal fashion, the objective is to assign a *number* of bits to the subnet number and the remainder to the local address. Therefore, it is normal to use a contiguous block of bits at the beginning of the local address part for the subnet number because this makes the addresses more readable (this is particularly true when the subnet occupies 8 or 16 bits). With this approach, either of the subnet masks above are "good" masks, but masks like 255.255.252.252 and 255.255.255.15 are not.

## 2.2.2.1 Types of Subnetting

There are two types of subnetting: static and variable length. Variable length is the more flexible of the two. Which type of subnetting is available depends upon the routing protocol being used; native IP routing supports only static subnetting, as does the widely used RIP protocol. However, RIP Version 2 supports variable length subnetting as well. See 3.3.3, "Routing Information Protocol (RIP)" on page 3-17 for a description of RIP and RIP2. Chapter 3, "Routing Protocols" on page 3-1 discusses routing protocols in detail.

**Static Subnetting:**  Static subnetting means that all subnets in the subnetted network use the same subnet mask. This is simple to implement and easy to maintain, but it implies wasted address space for small networks. For example, a network of four hosts that uses a subnet mask of 255.255.255.0 wastes 250 IP addresses. It also makes the network more difficult to reorganize with a new subnet mask. Currently, almost every host and router supports static subnetting.

**Variable Length Subnetting:**  When variable length subnetting is used, the subnets that make up the network may use different subnet masks. A small subnet with only a few hosts needs a subnet mask that accommodates only these few hosts. A subnet with many hosts attached may need a different subnet mask to accommodate the large number of hosts. The possibility to assign subnet masks according to the needs of the individual subnets will help conserve network addresses. Also, a subnet can be split into two parts by adding another bit to the subnet mask. Other subnets in the network are unaffected by the change. Not every host and router supports variable length subnetting.

Only networks of the size needed will be allocated and routing problems will be solved by isolating networks with routers that support variable subnetting. A host that does not support this kind of subnetting would have to route to a router that supports variable subnetting.

**Mixing Static and Variable Length Subnetting:**  At first sight, it appears that the presence of a host which only supports static subnetting would prevent variable length subnetting from being used anywhere in the network. Fortunately this is not the case. Provided that the routers between subnets with different subnet masks are using variable length subnetting, the routing protocols employed are able to hide the difference between subnet masks from the hosts in a subnet. Hosts can continue to use basic IP routing and offload all of the complexities of the subnetting to dedicated routers.

## 2.2.2.2  A Static Subnetting Example

Assume that our IP network has been assigned the class B IP network number 129.112. We have to implement multiple physical networks throughout our network. and some of the routers we will be using do not support variable length subnetting. We must therefore choose a subnet mask for the whole network. We have a 16-bit local address for our whole network and must divide it into two parts appropriately. At the moment, we do not anticipate having more than 254 physical networks, nor more than 254 hosts per network, so a logical subnet mask to use is 255.255.255.0 (which also has the advantage of being an "easily readable" one). This decision should be made with care, since it will be difficult to change it later. If the number of networks or hosts grows beyond the planned numbers, we may have to implement variable length subnetting to make the best use of the 65,534 local addresses we have.

Figure  2-6 on page  2-13 shows an example of an implementation with three subnets.

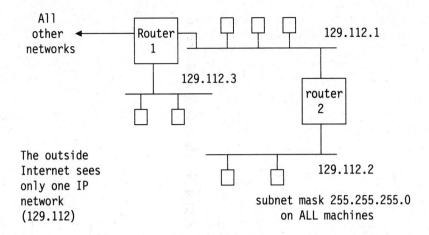

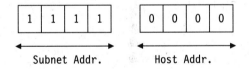

Figure   2-6.  A Subnet Configuration.   Three physical networks form one IP network.
The two routers are performing slightly different tasks.  Router 1 is acting as a router
between subnets 1 and 3 and as a router between the whole of our network and the rest of
the internet.  Router 2 acts only as a router between subnets 1 and 2.

Let us now consider a different subnet mask: 255.255.255.240.  The fourth octet is then
divided in two parts:

The following table contains the valid subnets using this subnet mask:

**Table   2-1  (Page   1  of   2).**  *Subnet Values for Subnet Mask 255.255.255.240*

| Hexadecimal value | Subnet number |
|-------------------|---------------|
| 0000 | 0 |
| 0001 | 16 |
| 0010 | 32 |
| 0011 | 48 |
| 0100 | 64 |
| 0101 | 80 |
| 0110 | 96 |
| 0111 | 112 |
| 1000 | 128 |
| 1001 | 144 |
| 1010 | 160 |
| 1011 | 176 |

***Table 2-1 (Page 2 of 2).*** *Subnet Values for Subnet Mask 255.255.255.240*

| Hexadecimal value | Subnet number |
| --- | --- |
| 1100 | 192 |
| 1101 | 208 |
| 1110 | 224 |
| 1111 | 240 |

For each of these subnet values, only 14 addresses (from 1 to 14) for hosts are available, because only the right part of the octet can be used and because addresses 0 and 15 (all bits set to one) have a special meaning as described in 2.2.3, "Special IP Addresses" on page 2-16.

Thus, subnet number 9.67.32.16 will contain hosts whose IP addresses are in the range of 9.67.32.17 to 9.67.32.30, and subnet number 9.67.32.32 will contain hosts whose IP addresses are in the range of 9.67.32.33 to 9.67.32.46, etc.

## 2.2.2.3 IP Routing with Subnets

To route an IP datagram on the network, the general IP routing algorithm has the following form:

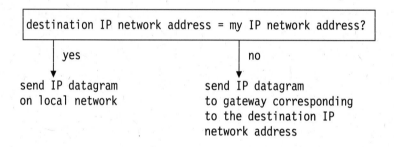

***Figure 2-7.*** *IP Routing without Subnets*

To be able to differentiate between subnets, the IP routing algorithm changes and has the following form:

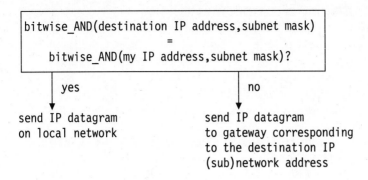

*Figure* 2-8. *IP Routing with Subnets*

Some implications of this algorithm are:

- It is a change to the general IP algorithm. Therefore, to be able to operate this way, the particular gateway must contain the new algorithm. Some implementations may still use the general algorithm, and will not function within a subnetted network, although they can still communicate with hosts in other networks which are subnetted.

- As IP routing is used in all of the hosts (and not just the routers), all of the hosts in the subnet must:
  1. Have an IP algorithm that supports subnetting.
  2. Have the same subnet mask (unless subnets are formed within the subnet).

- If the IP implementation on any of the hosts does not support subnetting, that host will be able to communicate with any host in its own subnet but not with any machine on another subnet within the same network. This is because the host sees only one IP network and its routing cannot differentiate between an IP datagram directed to a host on the local subnet and a datagram that should be sent via a router to a different subnet.

In case one or more hosts do not support subnetting, an alternative way to achieve the same goal exists in the form of *proxy-ARP*, which doesn't require any changes to the IP routing algorithm for single-homed hosts, but does require changes on routers between subnets in the network. This is explained in more detail in 2.8.5, "Proxy-ARP or Transparent Subnetting" on page 2-77.

All IBM TCP/IP implementations support subnetting but there is currently no support for proxy-ARP routers.

### 2.2.2.4 Obtaining a Subnet Mask

Usually, hosts will store the subnet mask to be used in a configuration file. However, sometimes this cannot be done, as for example in the case of a diskless workstation. The ICMP protocol includes two messages, address mask request and address mask reply, which allow hosts to obtain the correct subnet mask from a server. See 2.4.1.11, "Address Mask Request (17) and Address Mask Reply (18)" on page 2-61 for more information.

### 2.2.2.5 Addressing Routers and Multi-homed Hosts

Whenever a host has a physical connection to multiple networks or subnets, it is described as being *multi-homed*. All routers are multi-homed since their purpose is to join networks or subnets. A multi-homed host always has different IP addresses associated with each network adapter, since each adapter is in a different subnet or network.

There is one apparent exception to this rule: with some systems (for example VM and MVS) it is possible to specify the same IP address for multiple point-to-point links (such as channel-to-channel adapters) if the routing protocol used is limited to the basic IP routing algorithm. For example, a VM "hypervisor" system running TCP/IP connected to a token-ring LAN via a 3172 Interconnect Controller may run a number of "guest" VM and/or MVS systems. A very cost-effective solution for connecting these guests to the token-ring is to connect them to the hypervisor's TCP/IP with virtual channel-to-channel connections. The IP addresses can be chosen so that the channel-to-channel connected systems constitute their own subnet, in which case the hypervisor acts as a router. Because the routing protocols available on VM and MVS only support static subnetting, it may be difficult to find an additional subnet number if the address space is constrained. Therefore, the channel-to-channel connected systems may be given IP addresses in the same subnet as the token ring, in which case the hypervisor is taking the place of a bridge, and is *not* multi-homed. One disadvantage of this configuration is that other hosts on the LAN need static definitions to route datagrams for the hosts on the far side of the "bridge" via the hypervisor because the 3172 is not aware that it has this bridging responsibility. The "transparency" of bridges described in 2.1.2.2, "Bridges, Routers and Gateways" on page 2-5 is missing in this scenario.

## 2.2.3 Special IP Addresses

As noted above, any component of an IP address with a value "all bits 0" or all "all bits 1" has a special meaning

*all bits 0*         stands for "this": "this" host (IP address with <host number>=0) or "this" network (IP address with <network number>=0) and is only used when the real value is not known. This form is only used in source addresses when the host is trying to determine its IP addresses from a remote server. The host may know include its host number if known, but not its subnet or network number. See also 4.17, "BOOTstrap Protocol — BOOTP" on page 4-210.

*all bits 1*      stands for "all": "all" networks or "all" hosts. For example, 128.2.255.255 (a class B address with a host number of 255.255) means all hosts on network 128.2. These are used in broadcast messages, as described below.

There is another address of special importance: the "all bits 1" class A network number 127 is reserved for the *loopback address*. Anything sent to an address with 127 as the value of the high order byte, for example 127.0.0.1, must not be routed via a network but must be routed directly from the IP implementation's output driver to its input driver.[2]

## 2.2.4 Unicasting, Broadcasting and Multicasting

The majority of IP addresses refer to a single recipient: these are called *unicast* addresses. However, as noted above, there are two special types of IP address which are used for addressing multiple recipients: broadcast addresses and multicast addresses. These addresses are used for sending messages to multiple recipients. Any protocol which is *connectionless* may send broadcast or multicast messages as well as unicast messages. A protocol which is *connection-oriented* can only use unicast addresses because the connection exists between a specific pair of hosts. See 2.12, "Transmission Control Protocol (TCP)" on page 2-92 for more information on connection-oriented protocols.

### 2.2.4.1 Broadcasting

There are a number of addresses which are used for IP broadcasting: all use the convention that "all-bits 1" indicates "all." Broadcast addresses are never valid as source addresses, only as destination addresses. The different types of broadcast addresses are listed here:

*limited broadcast address*
          The address 255.255.255.255 (all bits 1 in all parts of the IP address) is used on networks which support broadcasting, such as token rings, and it refers to all hosts on the subnet. It does not require the host to know any IP configuration information at all. All hosts on the local network will recognize the address, but routers will never forward it.

          There is one exception to this rule, called *BOOTP forwarding*. The BOOTP protocol uses the limited broadcast address to allow a diskless workstation to

---

[2]  Older implementations, such as TCP/IP for MVS prior to Version 3 Release 1 and TCP/IP for VM prior to Version 2 Release 3 used 14.0.0.0 as the loopback address. Where an implementation supports both, such as the current MVS and VM versions, 127.0.0.1 is to be preferred to 14.0.0.0.

contact a boot server. BOOTP forwarding is a configuration option available on some routers, including the IBM 6611 and 2210 Network Processors to make an exception for UDP datagrams for ports 67 (used by the BOOTP protocol). Without this facility, a separate BOOTP server would be required on each subnet. However, this is not simple forwarding because the router also plays a part in the BOOTP protocol. See 4.17, "BOOTstrap Protocol — BOOTP" on page 4-210 for more information about BOOTP forwarding and 2.11, "User Datagram Protocol (UDP)" on page 2-88 for an explanation of UDP ports.

*network-directed broadcast address*

If the network number is a valid network number, the network is not subnetted and the host number is all ones (for example, 128.2.255.255), then the address refers to all hosts on the specified network. Routers should forward these broadcast messages unless configured otherwise. This is used in ARP requests (see 2.8, "Address Resolution Protocol (ARP)" on page 2-69) on unsubnetted networks.

*subnet-directed broadcast address*

If the network number is a valid network number, the subnet number is a valid subnet number and the host number is all ones, then the address refers to all hosts on the specified subnet. Since the sender's subnet and the target subnet may have different subnet mask, the sender must somehow find out the subnet mask in use at the target. The actual broadcast is performed by the router which receives the datagram into the subnet.

*all-subnets-directed broadcast address*

If the network number is a valid network number, the network is subnetted and the local part is all ones (for example, 128.2.255.255), then the address refers to all hosts on all subnets in the specified network. In principle routers may propagate broadcasts for all subnets but are not required to do so. In practice, they do not; there are few circumstances where such a broadcast would be desirable, and it can lead to problems, particularly if a host has been incorrectly configured with no subnet mask. Consider the wasted resource involved if a host 9.180.214.114 in the subnetted Class A network 9 thought that it was not subnetted and used 9.255.255.255 as a "local" broadcast address instead of 9.180.214.255 and all of the routers in the network respected the request to forward the request to all clients.

If routers do respect all-subnets-directed broadcast address they use an algorithm called *Reverse Path Forwarding* to prevent the broadcast messages from multiplying out of control. See RFC 922 for more details on this algorithm.

## 2.2.4.2 Multicasting

Broadcasting has a major disadvantage: its lack of selectivity. If an IP datagram is broadcast to a subnet, every host on the subnet will receive it, and have to process it to determine whether the target protocol is active. If it is not, the IP datagram is discarded. Multicasting avoids this overhead by using groups of IP addresses.

Each group is represented by a 28-bit number, which is included in a Class D address. Recall that a class D address has the format:

| 1 1 1 0 | multicast address |
|---------|--------------------|

So *multicast group addresses* are IP addresses in the range 224.0.0.0 to 239.255.255.255. For each multicast address there is a set of zero or more hosts which are listening to it. This set is called the *host group*. There is no requirement for any host to be a member of a group to send to that group. There are two kinds of host group:

*permanent*  The IP address is permanently assigned by IANA. The membership of a host group is not permanent: a host may leave or join the group at will. The list of IP addresses assigned permanent host groups is included in *STD 2 — Assigned Internet Numbers*. Important ones are:

224.0.0.0   Reserved base address
224.0.0.1   All systems on this subnet
224.0.0.2   All routers on this subnet

Some other examples used by the OSPF routing protocol (see 3.3.4, "Open Shortest Path First Protocol (OSPF) Version 2" on page 3-25) are:
224.0.0.5   All OSPF routers
224.0.0.6   OSPF Designated Routers

An application may also retrieve a permanent host group's IP address from the domain name system (see 2.2.8, "Domain Name System" on page 2-31) using the domain mcast.net, or determine the permanent group from an address by using a pointer query (see 2.2.8.6, "Mapping IP Addresses to Domain Names — Pointer Queries" on page 2-34) in the domain 224.in-addr.arpa. A permanent group exists even if it has no members.

*transient*  Any group which is not permanent is transient and is available for dynamic assignment as needed. Transient groups cease to exist when their membership drops to zero.

Multicasting on a single physical network which supports the use of multicasting is simple. To join a group, a process running on a host must somehow inform its network device drivers that it is wishes to be a member of the specified group. The device driver software itself must map the multicast address to a physical multicast address and enable the reception of packets for that address. The device driver must also ensure that the receiving process does not receive any spurious datagrams by checking the destination address in the IP header before passing it to the IP layer.

For example, Ethernet supports multi-casting if the high-order byte of the 48-byte address is X′01′ and IANA owns an Ethernet address block, which consists of the addresses between X′00005E000000′ and X′00005EFFFFFF′. The lower half of this range has been assigned by IANA for multicast addresses, so on an Ethernet LAN there is a range of physical addresses between X′01005E000000′ and X′01005E7FFFFF′ which is used for IP multicasting. This range has 23 usable bits, so the 28-bit multicast addresses are mapped to the Ethernet addresses by considering the low-order 23 bits, that is 32 multicast addresses are mapped to each Ethernet address. Because of this non-unique mapping, filtering by the device driver is required. There are two other reasons why filtering might still be needed:

- Some LAN adapters are limited to a finite number of concurrent multicast addresses and if this is exceeded they must receive all multicasts.

- Other LAN adapters tend to filter according to a hash table value rather than the whole address, which means that there is a chance that two multicast addresses with the same hash value might be in use at the same time and the filter might "leak."

Despite this requirement for software filtering of multicast packets, multicasting still causes much less overhead for hosts that are not interested. In particular, those hosts that are not in any host group are not listening to any multicast addresses and all multicast messages are filtered by the network interface hardware.

Multicasting is not limited to a single physical network. There are two aspects to multicasting across physical networks:

- A mechanism for deciding how widespread the multicast is (remember that unlike unicast addresses and broadcast addresses) multicast addresses cover the entire Internet.

- A mechanism for deciding whether a multicast datagram needs to be forwarded to a particular network.

The first problem is easily solved: the multicast datagram has a Time To Live (TTL) value like every other, which is decremented with each hop to a new network. When the Time to Live field is decremented to zero, the datagram can go no further. The mechanism for deciding whether a router should forward a multicast datagram is called *Internet Group Management Protocol (IGMP)* or *Internet Group Multicast Protocol*. This is described further in 2.7, "Internet Group Management Protocol (IGMP)" on page 2-66. IGMP and multicasting are defined in *RFC 1112 — Host extensions for IP multicasting*.

## 2.2.5 The IP Address Exhaustion Problem

The number of networks on the Internet has been approximately doubling annually for a number of years. However, the usage of the Class A, B and C networks differs greatly: nearly all of the new networks assigned in the late 1980s were Class B, and in 1990 it became apparent that if this trend continued, the last Class B network number would be assigned during 1994. On the other hand, Class C networks were hardly being used.

The reason for this trend was that most potential users found a Class B network to be large enough for their anticipated needs, since it accommodates up to 65534 hosts, whereas a class C network, with a maximum of 254 hosts, severely restricts the potential growth of even a small initial network. Furthermore, most of the class B networks being assigned were small ones. There are relatively few networks that would need as many as 65,534 host addresses, but very few for which 254 hosts would be an adequate limit. In summary, although the Class A, Class B and Class C divisions of the IP address are logical and easy to use (because they occur on byte boundaries), with hindsight they are not the most practical because Class C networks are too small to be useful for most organizations while Class B networks are too large to be densely populated by any but the largest organizations.

Table 2-2 shows the usage of network numbers between 1991 and 1994.

| Cls | Total | Year End 1990 | | | | Year End 1992 | | | | Year End 1994 | | | |
|---|---|---|---|---|---|---|---|---|---|---|---|---|---|
| | | Assigned | | Allocated | | Assigned | | Allocated | | Assigned | | Allocated | |
| | | Nbr | % | Nbr | % | Nbr | % | Nbr | % | Nbr | % | Nbr | % |
| A | 126 | 38 | 30 | 101 | 80 | 51 | 40 | 114 | 90 | 53 | 42 | 116 | 92 |
| B | 16382 | 3238 | 20 | 4079 | 25 | 6812 | 42 | 7919 | 48 | 8432 | 51 | 9976 | 61 |
| C | 2097150 | 7792 | 0.4 | 104404 | 5.0 | 23339 | 1.1 | 200742 | 10 | 52833 | 2.5 | 521489 | 25 |

*Table 2-2. IP network number usage between 1990 and 1994.* Source: netinfo/ip_network_allocations.95Jan from anonymous FTP site rs.internic.net

Some points about this table require explanation.

Assigned    The number of network numbers in use. The Class C figures are somewhat inaccurate, because the figures do not include many class C networks in Europe which were allocated to RIPE and subsequently assigned but which are still recorded as allocated.

Allocated    This includes all of the assigned networks and additionally, those networks which have either been reserved by IANA (for example the 63 class A networks are all reserved by IANA) or which have been allocated to regional registries by IANA and which will subsequently be assigned by those registries. For example, IANA allocated 64,783 Class C networks in August 1992, and 65,959 in July 1993.

**Note:** IANA actually reports a network as either assigned *or* allocated, but this table treats allocated as a superset of assigned so that the reader can subtract the Allocated percentage from 100 to easily determine how much "free" space is left.

Another way to look at these numbers is to examine the proportion of the address space which has been used: the figures in the table do not show for example that the Class A address space is as big as the rest combined, or that a single Class A network can theoretically have as many hosts as 66,000 Class C networks. Figure 2-9 shows the usage of the address space from this point of view. The full pie represents a 32-bit flat address space, that is $2^{32}$ or 4,294,967,296 addresses. The Class A, B and C address spaces are divided as follows:

*Assigned*   The portion of the address space which is found in networks which have been assigned. The true assigned figure is actually much lower than this, because each network itself is likely to have a considerable amount of free space, but since this space cannot be used outside the organization which runs the network, it is effectively used.

The assigned space is shown with "exploded" slices: the combined area of the exploded slices represents the proportion of the IP address space in use.

*Allocated*   The portion of the address space which is found in networks which have been allocated but not assigned plus the portion of the address space lost to reserved network numbers like the Class A networks 0 (this network) and 127 (loopback).

The allocated space is shown with shaded but not exploded slices.

*Unallocated* The remaining Class A, B and C space in each is "free"; it is shown with an unshaded slice.

The Class A, B and C slices are shown with progressively thinner borders. Class A starts at "3 o'clock" and moves counter-clockwise through Classes B, C and so on.

*Class D*   One sixteenth of the total space is absorbed by Class D multicast addresses. These are treated as being used and so the Class D slice is exploded.

*Class E*   The remaining sixteenth of the address space: that part corresponding to IP addresses with the four high-order bits set is reserved by IANA.

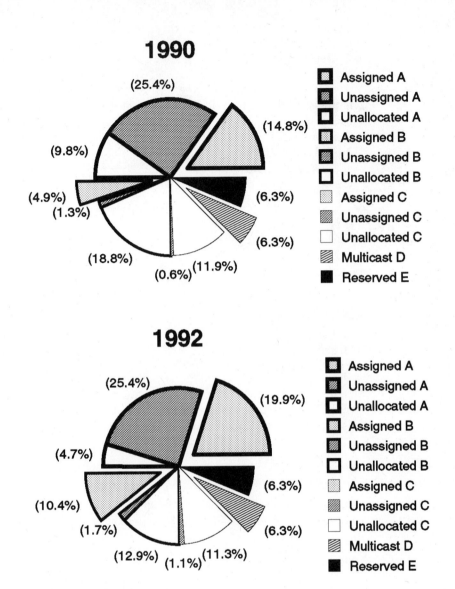

## 1990

(25.4%)
(14.8%)
(9.8%)
(4.9%)
(1.3%)
(6.3%)
(6.3%)
(18.8%)
(0.6%) (11.9%)

☒ Assigned A
▨ Unassigned A
☐ Unallocated A
▨ Assigned B
▨ Unassigned B
☐ Unallocated B
▨ Assigned C
▨ Unassigned C
☐ Unallocated C
▨ Multicast D
■ Reserved E

## 1992

(25.4%)
(19.9%)
(4.7%)
(6.3%)
(10.4%)
(1.7%)
(6.3%)
(12.9%) (1.1%) (11.3%)

☒ Assigned A
▨ Unassigned A
☐ Unallocated A
▨ Assigned B
▨ Unassigned B
☐ Unallocated B
▨ Assigned C
▨ Unassigned C
☐ Unallocated C
▨ Multicast D
■ Reserved E

*Figure 2-9 (Part 1 of 2). IP Address Space Usage*

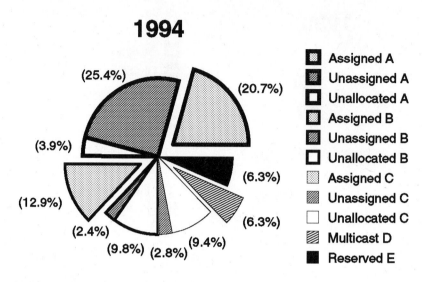

**1994**

Legend:
- Assigned A
- Unassigned A
- Unallocated A
- Assigned B
- Unassigned B
- Unallocated B
- Assigned C
- Unassigned C
- Unallocated C
- Multicast D
- Reserved E

(25.4%) (20.7%) (3.9%) (6.3%) (12.9%) (6.3%) (2.4%) (9.8%) (2.8%) (9.4%)

*Figure 2-9 (Part 2 of 2). IP Address Space Usage*

Examination of Table 2-2 on page 2-21 shows that since 1990, the number of assigned Class B networks has been increasing at a much lower rate than the total number of assigned networks and that the anticipated exhaustion of the Class B network numbers has not occurred. The reason for this is that the policies of the InterNIC on network number allocation were changed in late 1990 to preserve the existing address space, in particular to avert the exhaustion of the Class B address space. The new policies can be summarized as follows.

- The upper half of the Class A address space is reserved indefinitely to allow for the possibility of using it for transition to a new numbering scheme.

- Class B networks are only assigned to organizations which can clearly demonstrate a need for them. The same is, of course, true for Class A networks. The requirements for Class B networks are that the requesting organization

  - Has a subnetting plan which documents more than 32 subnets within its organizational network

  and

  - Has more than 4096 hosts

  Any requirements for a Class A network would be handled on an individual case basis.

- Organizations which do not fulfill the requirements for a Class B network are assigned a consecutively numbered block of Class C network numbers.

- The lower half of the Class C address space (network numbers 192.0.0 through 223.255.245) is divided into 8 blocks which are allocated to regional authorities as follows:

| | |
|---|---|
| *192.0.0 - 193.255.255* | Multi-regional |
| *194.0.0 - 195.255.255* | Europe |
| *196.0.0 - 197.255.255* | Others |
| *198.0.0 - 199.255.255* | North America |
| *200.0.0 - 201.255.255* | Central and South America |
| *202.0.0 - 203.255.255* | Pacific Rim |
| *204.0.0 - 205.255.255* | Others |
| *206.0.0 - 207.255.255* | Others |

The ranges defined as "Others" are to be where flexibility outside the constraints of regional boundaries is required. The range defined as "multi-regional" includes the Class C networks which had been assigned before this new scheme was adopted. The 192 networks were assigned by the InterNIC and the 193 networks had been previously allocated to RIPE in Europe.

The upper half of the Class C address space (208.0.0 to 223.255.255) remains unassigned and unallocated.

- Where an organization has a range of class C network numbers, the range provided is assigned is a *bit-wise contiguous* range of network numbers, and the number of networks in the range is a power of 2. That is, all IP addresses in the range have a common prefix, and every address with that prefix is within the range. For example, a European organization requiring 1500 IP addresses would be assigned 8 Class C network numbers (2048 IP addresses) from the number space reserved for European networks (194.0.0 through 195.255.255) and the first of these network numbers would be divisible by eight. A range of addresses satisfying these rules would be 194.32.136 through 194.32.143, in which case the range would consist of all of the IP addresses with the 21-bit prefix 194.32.136, or B' 110000100010000010001'.

The maximum number of network numbers assigned contiguously is 64, corresponding to a prefix of 18 bits. An organization requiring more than 4096 addresses but less than 16,384 addresses can request either a Class B or a range of Class C addresses. In general, the number of Class C networks assigned is the minimum required to provide the necessary number of IP addresses for the organization on the basis of a two-year outlook. However, in some cases, an organization may request multiple networks to be treated separately. For example, an organization with 600 hosts would normally be assigned four class C networks. However, if those hosts were distributed across 10 token-ring LANs with between 50 and 70 hosts per LAN, such an allocation would cause serious problems, since the organization would have to find 10 subnets within a 10-bit local address range. This would mean at least some of the LANs having a subnet mask of 255.255.255.192 which allows only 62 hosts per LAN. The intent of the rules is not to force the organization into complex subnetting of small networks, and the organization should request 10 different Class C numbers, one for each LAN.

The current rules are to be found in *RFC 1466 — Guidelines for Management of IP Address Space*. The reasons for the rules for the allocation of Class C network numbers will become apparent in the next section. The use of Class C network numbers in this way has averted the exhaustion of the Class B address space, but it is not a permanent term solution to the overall address space constraints that are fundamental to IP. The long-term solution is discussed in 2.16, "IP: The Next Generation (IPng)" on page 2-127.

## 2.2.6 Private Internets

Another approach to conservation of the IP address space is described in *RFC 1597 — Address Allocation for Private Internets*. Briefly, it relaxes the rule that IP addresses are globally unique by reserving part of the address space for networks which are used exclusively within a single organization and which do not require IP connectivity to the Internet. There are three ranges of addresses which have been reserved by IANA for this purpose:

*10*  A single Class A network

*172.16 through 172.31*  16 contiguous Class B networks

*192.168.0 through 192.168.255*  256 contiguous Class C networks

Any organization may use any addresses in these ranges without reference to any other organization. However, because these addresses are not globally unique, they cannot be referenced by hosts in another organization and they are not defined to any external routers. Routers in networks not using private addresses, particularly those operated by Internet service providers, are expected to quietly discard all routing information regarding these addresses. Routers in an organization using private addresses are expected to limit all references to private addresses to internal links; they should neither advertise routes to private addresses to external routers nor forward IP datagrams containing private addresses to via external routers. Hosts having only a private IP address do not have IP-layer connectivity to the Internet. This may be desirable and may even be a reason for using private addressing. All connectivity to external Internet hosts must be provided with application gateways.

## 2.2.7 Classless Inter-Domain Routing (CIDR)

There is a major problem with the use of a range of Class C addresses instead of a single Class B addresses: each network must be routed separately. Standard IP routing understands only the class A, B and C network classes. Within each of these types of network, subnetting can be used to provided better granularity of the address space within each network, but there is no way to specify that multiple class C networks are actually related. The result of this is termed the *routing table explosion* problem: a Class B network of 3000 hosts requires one routing table entry at each backbone router, but if the same network is addressed as a range of Class C networks, it requires 16 entries.

The solution to this problem is a scheme called *Classless Inter-Domain Routing (CIDR)*. CIDR is a *proposed standard protocol* with a status of *elective*.

CIDR does not route according to the class of the network number (hence the term classless) but solely according to the high order bits of the IP address which are termed the *IP prefix*. Each CIDR routing entry contains a 32 bit IP address and a 32 bit network mask, which together give the length and value of the IP prefix. This can be represented as <IP_address network_mask>. For example <194.0.0.0 254.0.0.0> represents the 7 bit IP prefix B′ 1100001′. CIDR handles the routing for a group of networks with a common prefix with a single routing entry. This is the reason why multiple Class C network numbers assigned to a single organization have a common prefix. This process of combining multiple networks into a single entry is termed *address aggregation* or *address summarization*. It is also called *supernetting* because routing is based upon network masks which are shorter than the *natural* network mask of the IP address, in contrast to *subnetting* where the network masks are longer than the natural mask.

Unlike subnet masks, which are normally contiguous but may have a discontiguous local part, supernet masks are *always* contiguous.

If IP addresses are represented with a tree showing the routing topology, with each leaf of the tree representing a group of networks which are considered as a single unit (called a *routing domain*) and the IP addressing scheme is chosen so that each fork in this tree corresponds to an increase in the length of the IP prefix, then CIDR allows address aggregation to be performed very efficiently. For example, if a router in North America routes all European traffic via a single link, then a single routing entry for <194.0.0.0 254.0.0.0> includes the group of Class C network addresses assigned to Europe as described above. This single entry takes the place of all the entries for all of the assigned network numbers in this range which is a possible maximum of $2^{17}$ or 131,072 numbers. At the European end of this link, there are routing entries with longer prefixes which map to the European network topology but this routing information is not needed at the American end of the link. CIDR uses a *longest match is best* approach, so if the router in the US needs to make an exception for one range of addresses, such as the 64 network range <195.1.64.0 255.555.192.0> it needs just one additional entry, since this entry overrides the more general (shorter) one for those networks it contains. It is apparent from this example that as the usage of the IP address space increases, particularly the Class C address space, the benefits of CIDR increase as well, provided that the assignment of addresses follows the network topology. The existing state of the IP address space does not follow such a scheme since it pre-dates the development of CIDR.

However, new Class C addresses are being assigned in such a way as to enable CIDR, and this should have the effect of alleviating the routing table explosion problem in the near term. In the longer term, a restructuring of the IP address space along topological lines may be necessary. This would involve the re-numbering of a large number of networks, implying an enormous amount of implementation effort, and so would be a gradual process.

It is an over-simplification to assume that routing topology can be represented as a simple tree; although most routing domains have a single attachment which provides access to the rest of the Internet, there are also many domains which have multiple attachments. Routing domains of these two types are called *single-homed* and *multi-homed*. Furthermore, the topology is not static. Not only are new organizations joining the Internet at an ever-increasing rate, but existing organizations may change places within the topology, for example if they change between service providers for commercial or other reasons. Although such cases complicate the practical implementation of CIDR-based routing and reduce the efficiency of address aggregation that can be achieved, they do not invalidate the approach.

The current Internet address allocation policies and the assumptions on which those policies were based is described in *RFC 1518 — An Architecture for IP Address Allocation with CIDR*. They can be summarized as follows:

- IP address assignment reflects the physical topology of the network and not the organizational topology; wherever organizational and administrative boundaries do not match the network topology, they should *not* be used for the assignment of IP addresses.

- In general, network topology will closely follow continental and national boundaries and therefore IP addresses should be assigned on this basis.

- There will be a relatively small set of networks which carry a large amount of traffic between routing domains and which will be interconnected in a non-hierarchical way and which will cross national boundaries. These are referred to as *transit routing domains (TRDs)*. Each TRD will have a unique IP prefix. TRDs will not be organized in a hierarchical way where there is no appropriate hierarchy. However, wherever a TRD is wholly within a continental boundary, its IP prefix should be an extension of the continental IP prefix.

- There will be many organizations which have attachments to other organizations which are for the private use of those two organizations and which do not carry traffic intended for other domains (transit traffic). Such private connections do not have a significant effect on the routing topology and can be ignored.

- The great majority of routing domains will be single-homed. That is, they will be attached to a single TRD. They should be assigned addresses which begin with that TRD's IP prefix. All of the addresses for all single-homed domains attached to a

TRD can therefore be aggregated into a single routing table entry for all domains outside that TRD.

**Note:** This implies that if an organization changes its Internet service provider, it should change all of its IP addresses. This is not the current practice, but the widespread implementation of CIDR is likely to make it much more common.

- There are a number of address assignment schemes which can be used for multi-homed domains. These include:

  - The use of a single IP prefix for the domain. External routers must have an entry for the organization which lies partly or wholly outside the normal hierarchy. Where a domain is multi-homed, but all of the attached TRDs themselves are topologically nearby, it would be appropriate for the domain's IP prefix to include those bits common to all of the attached TRDs. For example, if all of the TRD's were wholly within the United States, an IP prefix implying an exclusively North American domain would be appropriate.

  - The use of one IP prefix for each attached TRD, with hosts in the domain having IP addresses containing the IP prefix of the most appropriate TRD. The organization appears to be a set of routing domains.

  - Assigning an IP prefix from one of the attached TRDs. This TRD becomes a default TRD for the domain but other domains may explicitly route by one of the alternative TRDs.

  - The use of IP prefixes to refer to sets of multi-homed domains having the TRD attachments. For example there may be an IP prefix to refer to single-homed domains attached to network A, one to refer to single-homed domains attached to network B and one to refer to dual-homed domains attached to networks A and B.

- Each of these has various advantages, disadvantages and side effects. For example, the first approach tends to result in inbound traffic entering the target domain closer to the sending host than the second approach, and therefore in a larger proportion of the network costs being incurred by the receiving organization.

  Because multi-homed domains may vary greatly in character and none of the above schemes is suitable for all such domains, there is no single policy which is best and RFC 1518 does not specify any rules for choosing between them.

## 2.2.7.1 CIDR Implementation

The implementation of CIDR in the Internet is primarily based on *Border Gateway Protocol Version 4* (see 3.4.2.3, "Border Gateway Protocol Version 4 (BGP-4)" on page 3-64). In future CIDR will also be implemented by a variant of the ISO standard *Inter-Domain Routing Protocol (IDRP, ISO 10747)*, called IDRP for IP, which is closely related to BGP-4.

The implementation strategy, described in *RFC 1520 — Exchanging Routing Information Across Provider Boundaries in the CIDR Environment* involves a staged process through the routing hierarchy beginning with backbone routers. Network service providers are divided into four types:

*Type 1*     Those which cannot employ any default inter-domain routing.

*Type 2*     Those which use default inter-domain routing but which require explicit routes for a substantial proportion of the assigned IP network numbers.

*Type 3*     Those which use default inter-domain routing and supplement it with a small number of explicit routes.

*Type 4*     Those which perform all inter-domain routing using only default routes.

The CIDR implementation involves an implementation beginning with the Type 1 network providers, then the Type 2 and finally the Type 3 ones. CIDR has already been widely deployed in the backbone and over 9,000 class-based routes have been replaced by approximately 2,000 CIDR-based routes.

### 2.2.7.2 References

- *RFC 1467 — Status of CIDR Deployment in the Internet*
- *RFC 1517 — Applicability Statement for the Implementation of Classless Inter-Domain Routing (CIDR)*
- *RFC 1518 — An Architecture for IP Address Allocation with CIDR*
- *RFC 1519 — Classless Inter-Domain Routing (CIDR): an Address Assignment and Aggregation Strategy*
- *RFC 1520 — Exchanging Routing Information Across Provider Boundaries in the CIDR Environment*

## 2.2.8 Domain Name System

The Domain Name System protocol is a *standard protocol* (STD 13). Its status is *recommended*. It is described in:

- *RFC 1034 — Domain names – concepts and facilities*
- *RFC 1035 — Domain names – implementation and specification*

The early internet configurations required users to use only numeric IP addresses. Very quickly, this evolved to the use of symbolic host names. For example, instead of typing TELNET 128.12.7.14 one could type TELNET eduvm9, and eduvm9 is then translated in some way to the IP address 128.12.7.14. This introduces the problem of maintaining the mappings between IP addresses and high-level machine names in a coordinated and centralized way.

Initially, host names to address mappings were maintained by the Network Information Center (NIC) in a single file (HOSTS.TXT) which was fetched by all hosts using FTP. This is called a *flat namespace*.

Due to the explosive growth in the number of hosts, this mechanism became too cumbersome (consider the work involved in the addition of just one host to the Internet) and was replaced by a new concept: *Domain Name System*. Hosts may continue to use a local flat namespace (the HOSTS.LOCAL file) instead of or in addition to the Domain Name System, but outside small networks, the Domain Name System is practically essential. The Domain Name System allows a program running on a host to perform the mapping of a high-level symbolic name to an IP address for any other host without the need for every host to have a complete database of host names.

For the remainder of this section we will examine how the Domain Name System works from the user's point of view. See 4.5, "Domain Name System (DNS)" on page 4-39 for more details about the implementation of domain name resolvers and servers and the types of records stored in the Domain Name System.

### 2.2.8.1 The Hierarchical Namespace

Consider the internal structure of a large organization. As the chief executive cannot do everything, the organization will probably be partitioned into divisions, each of them having autonomy within certain limits. Specifically, the executive in charge of a division has authority to make direct decisions, without permission from his chief executive.

Domain names are formed in a similar way, and will often reflect the hierarchical delegation of authority used to assign them. For example, consider the name

```
lcs.mit.edu
```

Here, lcs.mit.edu is the lowest-level domain name, a subdomain of mit.edu, which again is a subdomain of edu (education) which is called a *top-level domain*. We can also represent this naming concept by a hierarchical tree (see Figure 2-10 on page 2-32).

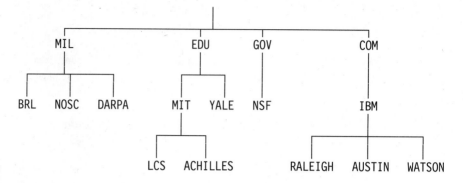

***Figure 2-10.*** *Hierarchical Namespace.* This figure shows the chain of authority in assigning domain names. This tree is only a tiny fraction of real namespace.

Figure 2-11 on page 2-33 shows some of the top-level domains. The single domain above the "top-level" domains has no name and is referred to as the *root domain*. The complete structure is explained in the following sections.

## 2.2.8.2 Fully Qualified Domain Names (FQDNs)

When using the Domain Name System, it is common to work with only a part of the domain hierarchy, for example the ral.ibm.com domain. The Domain Name System provides a simple method of minimizing the typing necessary in this circumstance. If a domain name ends in a dot (for example, wtscpok.itsc.pok.ibm.com.) it is assumed to be complete. This is termed a *Fully Qualified Domain Name (FQDN)* or an absolute domain name. If, however it does not end in a dot (for example, wtscpok.itsc) it is incomplete and the DNS resolver (see below) may complete this, for example by appending a suffix such as .pok.ibm.com to the domain name. The rules for doing this are implementation dependent and locally configurable.

## 2.2.8.3 Generic Domains

The three-character top-level names are called the *generic* domains or the *organizational* domains.

| Domain Name | Meaning |
| --- | --- |
| *edu* | Educational institutions |
| *gov* | Government institutions |
| *com* | Commercial organizations |
| *mil* | Military groups |
| *net* | Networks |
| *int* | International organizations |
| *org* | Other organizations |

*Figure   2-11.  The Generic Top-level Domains*

Since the Internet began in the United States, the organization of the hierarchical namespace initially had only US organizations at the top of the hierarchy, and it is still largely true that the generic part of the namespace contains US organizations. However, only the .gov and .mil domains are restricted to the US.

## 2.2.8.4 Country Domains

There are also top-level domains named for the each of the ISO 3166 international 2-character country codes (from *ae* for the United Arab Emirates to *zw* for Zimbabwe). These are called the *country* domains or the *geographical* domains. Many countries have their own second-level domains underneath which parallel the generic top-level domains. For example, in the United Kingdom, the domains equivalent to the generic domains .com and .edu are .co.uk and .ac.uk ("ac" is an abbreviation for academic). There is a .us top-level domain, which is organized geographically by state (for example, .ny.us refers to the state of New York). See RFC 1480 for a detailed description of the .us domain.

## 2.2.8.5 Mapping Domain Names to IP Addresses

The mapping of names to addresses, a process called domain name resolution, is provided by independent, cooperating systems called *name servers*. A name server is a server program answering requests from a client called a *name resolver*.

Each name resolver is configured with a name server to use (and possibly a list of alternatives to contact if the primary is unavailable). Figure  2-12 on page  2-34 shows schematically how a program uses a name resolver to convert a host name to an IP address. A user provides a host name, and the user program uses a library routine, called a stub resolver, to communicate with a name server which resolves the host name to an IP address and returns it to the stub, which returns it to the main program. The name server may obtain the answer from its name cache, its own database or another name server.

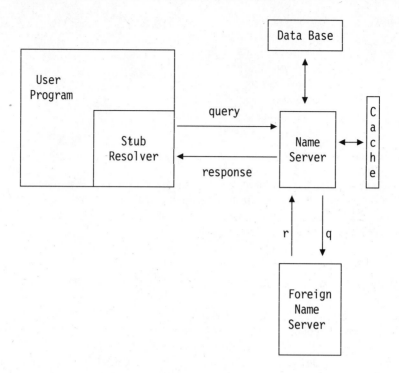

*Figure  2-12.  Domain Name Resolution*

## 2.2.8.6  Mapping IP Addresses to Domain Names — Pointer Queries

The Domain Name System provides for a mapping of symbolic names to IP addresses *and vice versa.*  While it is a simple matter in principle to search the database for an IP address given its symbolic name because of the hierarchical structure, the reverse process cannot follow the hierarchy.  Therefore, there is another namespace for the reverse mapping.  It is found in the domain in-addr.arpa ("arpa" because the Internet was originally the ARPA Internet).  Because IP addresses are normally written in dotted decimal format, there is one layer of domains for each hierarchy.  However, because domain names have the least-significant  parts of the name first but dotted decimal format has the most significant bytes first, the dotted decimal address is shown in reverse order.  For example, the domain in the domain name system corresponding to the IP address 129.34.139.30 is  30.139.34.129.in-addr.arpa.  Given an IP address, the Domain Name System can be used to find the matching host name.  A domain name query to find the host names associated with an IP address is called a "pointer query."

## 2.2.8.7 Other Uses for the Domain Name System

The Domain Name System is designed to be capable of storing a wide range of information. One of the most important of these is *mail exchange* information, which is used for electronic mail routing. This provides two facilities: transparent re-routing of mail to a different host than that specified and the implementation of mail gateways where electronic mail can be received by a mail gateway and re-directed using a different mail protocol from the intended recipient. This is explained in more detail in 4.6.2, "SMTP and the Domain Name System" on page 4-72.

## 2.2.8.8 References

For more details on the implementation of the Domain Name System and the format of the messages between Name Servers, see 4.5, "Domain Name System (DNS)" on page 4-39. The following RFCs define the Domain Name System standard and the information kept in the system.

- *RFC 1032 — Domain Administrator's Guide*
- *RFC 1033 — Domain Administrator Operations Guide*
- *RFC 1034 — Domain Names – Concepts and Facilities*
- *RFC 1035 — Domain Names – Implementation and Specification*
- *RFC 1101 — DNS Encoding of networks names and other types*
- *RFC 1183 — New DNS RR Definitions*
- *RFC 1706 — DNS NSAP Resource Records*

# 2.3 Internet Protocol (IP)

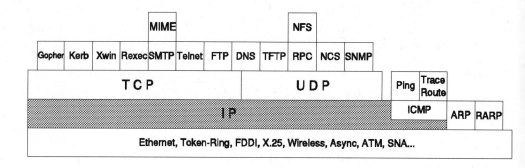

**Figure 2-13.** *Internet Protocol (IP)*

IP is a *standard protocol* with STD number 5 which also includes ICMP (see 2.4, "Internet Control Message Protocol (ICMP)" on page 2-52) and IGMP (see 2.7, "Internet Group Management Protocol (IGMP)" on page 2-66). Its status is *required*.

The current IP specification can be found in RFCs 791, 950, 919 and 922, with updates in RFC 1349.

IP is the protocol that hides the underlying physical network by creating a *virtual network* view. It is an unreliable, best-effort *connectionless* packet delivery protocol.

It adds no reliability, flow control or error recovery to the underlying network interface protocol. Packets (*datagrams*) sent by IP may be lost, out of order, or even duplicated, and IP will not handle these situations. It is up to higher layers to provide these facilities.

IP also assumes little from the underlying network mechanisms, only that the datagrams will "probably" (best-effort) be transported to the addressed host.

## 2.3.1 IP Datagram

The Internet datagram (IP datagram) is the base transfer packet in the Internet protocol suite. It has a header containing information for IP, and data that is relevant only to the higher level protocols.

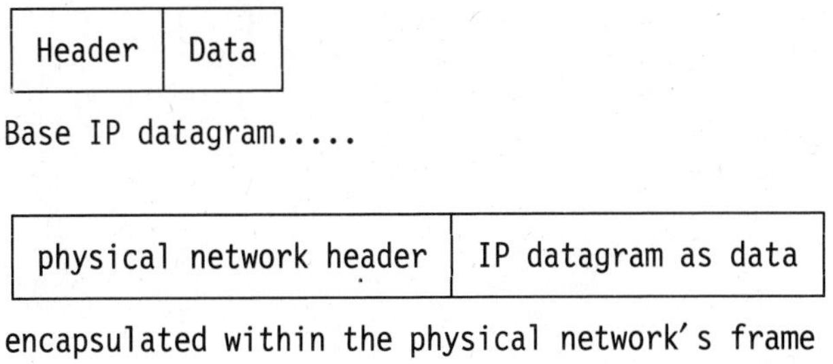

```
+--------+------+
| Header | Data |
+--------+------+
```

Base IP datagram.....

```
+-----------------------+-------------------+
| physical network header | IP datagram as data |
+-----------------------+-------------------+
```

encapsulated within the physical network's frame

*Figure   2-14. Base IP Datagram*

The IP datagram is encapsulated in the underlying network's frame, which usually has a maximum length or frame limitation, depending on the hardware used. For Ethernet, this will typically be 1500 bytes.  Instead of limiting the IP datagram length to some maximum size, IP can deal with *fragmentation* and *re-assembly* of its datagrams. In particular, the IP standard does not impose a maximum size, but states that all subnetworks should be able to handle datagrams of at least 576 bytes.

Fragments of a datagram all have a header, basically copied from the original datagram, and data following it. They are treated as normal IP datagrams while being transported to their destination.  Note, however, that if one of the fragments gets lost, the complete datagram is considered lost since IP does not provide any acknowledgment mechanism, so the remaining fragments will simply be discarded by the destination host.

## 2.3.1.1  IP Datagram Format

The IP datagram header is a minimum of 20 bytes long:

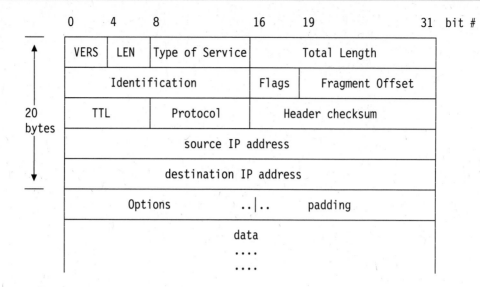

***Figure 2-15.*** *IP Datagram Format*

Where:

*VERS*

> The version of the IP protocol. The current version is 4. 5 is experimental and 6 is IPng (see 2.16, "IP: The Next Generation (IPng)" on page 2-127).

*LEN*

> The length of the IP header counted in 32-bit quantities. This does not include the data field.

*Type of Service*

> The type of service is an indication of the quality of service requested for this IP datagram.

```
0   1   2   3   4   5   6   7
┌───────────┬───────────┬───┐
│ Precedence│    TOS    │MBZ│
└───────────┴───────────┴───┘
```

Where:

*Precedence*    Is a measure of the nature and priority of this datagram:

> 000    Routine
> 001    Priority
> 010    Immediate

|     |                   |
| --- | ----------------- |
| 011 | Flash             |
| 100 | Flash override    |
| 101 | Critical          |
| 110 | Internetwork control |
| 111 | Network control   |

*TOS*  Specifies the *type of service* value:

|      |                       |
| ---- | --------------------- |
| 1000 | Minimize delay        |
| 0100 | Maximize throughput   |
| 0010 | Maximize reliability  |
| 0001 | Minimize monetary cost |
| 0000 | Normal service        |

*MBZ*  Reserved for future use ("must be zero" unless participating in an Internet protocol experiment which makes use of this bit)

A detailed description of the *type of service* can be found in the RFC 1349.

## Total Length

The total length of the datagram, header and data, specified in bytes.

## Identification

A unique number assigned by the sender to aid in reassembling a fragmented datagram. Fragments of a datagram will have the same identification number.

## Flags

Various control flags:

```
 0   1   2
+---+---+---+
|   | D | M |
| 0 | F | F |
+---+---+---+
```

Where:

*0*   Reserved, must be zero

*DF*  Don't Fragment: 0 means allow fragmentation, 1 means do not allow fragmentation.

*MF*  More Fragments: 0 means that this is the last fragment of this datagram, 1 means that this is not the last fragment.

*Fragment Offset*

Used with fragmented datagrams, to aid in reassembly of the full datagram. The value is the number of 64-bit pieces (header bytes are not counted) that are contained in earlier fragments. In the first (or only) fragment, this value is always zero.

*Time to Live*

Specifies the time (in seconds) this datagram is allowed to travel. Each router where this datagram passes is supposed to subtract from this field its processing time for this datagram. Actually a router is able to process a datagram in less than 1 second; thus it will subtract one from this field, and the TTL becomes a hop-count metric rather than a time metric. When the value reaches zero, it is assumed that this datagram has been traveling in a closed loop and it is discarded. The initial value should be set by the higher-level protocol which creates the datagram.

*Protocol Number*

Indicates the higher-level protocol to which IP should deliver the data in this datagram. Some important values are:

*0* Reserved
*1* Internet Control Message Protocol (ICMP)
*2* Internet Group Management Protocol (IGMP)
*3* Gateway-to-Gateway Protocol (GGP)
*4* IP (IP encapsulation)
*5* Stream
*6* Transmission Control (TCP)
*8* Exterior Gateway Protocol (EGP)
*9* Private Interior Routing Protocol
*17* User Datagram (UDP)
*89* Open Shortest Path First

The full list can be found in *STD 2 — Assigned Internet Numbers.*

*Header Checksum*

Is a checksum on the header only. It does not include the data. The checksum is calculated as the 16-bit one's complement of the one's complement sum of all 16-bit words in the header. For the purpose of this calculation, the checksum field is assumed to be zero. If the header checksum does not match the contents, the datagram is discarded because at least one bit in the header is corrupt, and the datagram may even have arrived at the wrong destination.

*Source IP Address*

The 32-bit IP address of the host sending this datagram.

*Destination IP Address*

The 32-bit IP address of the destination host for this datagram.

*Options*

Variable length. An IP implementation is not required to be capable of generating options in the datagrams it creates, but all IP implementations are required to be able to process datagrams containing options. The Options field is variable in length. There may be zero or more options. There are two option formats. The format for each is dependent on the value of the option number found in the first byte.

- A type byte alone.

- A type byte, a length byte and one or more option data bytes.

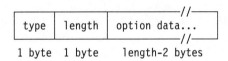

The type byte has the same structure in both cases:

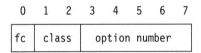

Where:

*fc*

Flag copy indicates whether (1) or not (0) the option field is to be copied when the datagram is fragmented.

*class*

The option class is a 2-bit unsigned integer:

*0* control
*1* reserved
*2* debugging and measurement
*3* reserved

*option number*

The option number is a 5-bit unsigned integer.

*0* End of option list. It has a class of 0, the fc bit is set to zero, and it has no length byte or data. That is, the option list is terminated by a X' 00' byte. It is only required if the IP header length (which is a multiple of 4 bytes) does not match the actual length of the options.

*1* No operation. It has a class of 0, the fc bit is not set and there is no length byte or data. That is, a X' 01' byte is a NOP. It may be used to align fields in the datagram.

*2* Security. It has a class of 0, the fc bit is set and there is a length byte with a value of 11 and 8 bytes of data). It is used for security information needed by US Department of Defense requirements.

*3* Loose Source Routing. It has a class of 0, the fc bit is set and there is a variable length data field. This option is discussed in more detail below.

*4* Internet Timestamp. It has a class of 2, the fc bit is not set and there is a variable length data field. The total length may be up to 40 bytes. This option is discussed in more detail below.

*7* Record Route. It has a class of 0, the fc bit is not set and there is a variable length data field. This option is discussed in more detail below.

*8* Stream ID. It has a class of 0, the fc bit is set and there is a length byte with a value of 4 and one data byte. It is used with the SATNET system.

*9* Strict Source Routing. It has a class of 0, the fc bit is set and there is a variable length data field. This option is discussed in more detail below.

*length*

counts the length (in bytes) of the option, including the type and length fields.

*option data*

contains data relevant to the option.

*padding*

If an option is used, the datagram is padded with all-zero bytes up to the next 32-bit boundary.

*data*

The data contained in the datagram is passed to a higher-level protocol, as specified in the *protocol* field.

## 2.3.1.2 Fragmentation

When an IP datagram travels from one host to another, it can cross different physical networks. Physical networks have a maximum frame size, called the *Maximum Transmission Unit (MTU)*, which limits the length of a datagram that can be placed in one physical frame. Therefore, a scheme has been put in place to fragment long IP datagrams into smaller ones, and to reassemble them at the destination host. IP requires that each link has an MTU of at least 68 bytes, so if any network provides a lower value than this, fragmentation and re-assembly must be implemented in the network interface layer in a way that is transparent to IP. 68 is the sum of the maximum IP header length of 60 bytes and the minimum possible length of data in a non-final fragment (8 bytes). IP implementations are not required to handle unfragmented datagrams larger than 576 bytes, but most implementations will handle larger values, typically slightly more than 8192 bytes or higher, and rarely less than 1500.

An unfragmented datagram has all-zero fragmentation information. That is, the more fragments flag bit is zero and the fragment offset is zero. When fragmentation is to be done, the following steps are performed:

- The DF flag bit is checked to see if fragmentation is allowed. If the bit is set, the datagram will be discarded and an error will be returned to the originator using ICMP.

- Based on the MTU value, the data field is split into two or more parts. All newly created data portions must have a length which is a multiple of 8 bytes, with the exception of the last data portion.

- All data portions are placed in IP datagrams. The header of these datagrams are copies of the original one, with some modifications:

  - The more fragments flag bit is set in all fragments except the last.

  - The fragment offset field in each is set to the location this data portion occupied in the original datagram, relative to the beginning of the original unfragmented datagram. The offset is measured in 8-byte units.

  - If options were included in the original datagram, the high order bit of the option type byte determines whether or not they will be copied to all fragment datagrams or just to the first one. For instance, source route options have to be copied in all fragments and therefore they have this bit set.

  - The header length field is of the new datagram is set.

  - The total length field of the new datagram is set.

  - The header checksum field is re-calculated.

- Each of these fragmented datagrams is now forwarded as a normal IP datagram. IP handles each fragment independently, that is, the fragments may traverse different routers to the intended destination, and they may be subject to further fragmentation if they pass through networks that have smaller MTUs.

At the destination host, the data has to be reassembled into one datagram. The identification field of the datagram was set by the sending host to a unique number (for the source host, within the limits imposed by the use of a 16-bit number). As fragmentation doesn't alter this field, incoming fragments at the receiving side can be identified, if this ID field is used together with the Source and Destination IP addresses in the datagram. The Protocol field is also be checked for this identification.

In order to reassemble the fragments, the receiving host allocates a buffer in storage as soon as the first fragment arrives. A timer routine is then started. When the timer timeouts and not all of the fragments have been received, the datagram is discarded. The initial value of this timer is called the IP datagram time-to-live (TTL) value. It is implementation dependent, and some implementations allow it to be configured; for example AIX Version 3.2 provides an *ipfragttl* option with a default value of 60 seconds.

When subsequent fragments of the datagram arrive, before the timer expires, the data is simply copied into the buffer storage, at the location indicated by the fragment offset field. As soon as all fragments have arrived, the complete original unfragmented datagram is restored, and processing continues, just as for unfragmented datagrams.

Note: IP does not provide the reassembly timer. It will treat each and every datagram, fragmented or not, the same way, that is, as individual messages. It is up to the higher layer to implement a timeout and to look after any missing fragments. The higher layer could be TCP for a connection-oriented transport network or the application for connectionless transport networks based upon UDP and IP.

The netstat command may be used on some TCP/IP hosts to list details of fragmentation that is occurring. An example of this is the `netstat -i` command in TCP/IP for OS/2.

## 2.3.1.3  IP Datagram Routing Options

The IP datagram Options field allows two methods for the originator of an IP datagram to explicitly provide routing information and one for an IP datagram to determine the route that it travels.

**Loose Source Routing:**   The Loose Source Routing option, also called the Loose Source and Record Route (LSRR) option, provides a means for the source of an IP datagram to supply explicit routing information to be used by the routers in forwarding the datagram to the destination, and to record the route followed.

```
┌──────────┬────────┬─────────┬──────────────┐─//─┐
│ 10000011 │ length │ pointer │  route data  │    │
└──────────┴────────┴─────────┴──────────────┘─//─┘
```

**Figure   2-16.**  *Loose Source Routing Option*

*1000011*    (decimal 131) is the value of the option type byte for loose source routing.

*length*    contains the length of this option field, including the type and length fields.

*pointer*    points to the option data at the next IP address to be processed. It is counted relative to the beginning of the option, so its minimum value is four. If the pointer is greater than the length of the option, the end of the source route is reached and further routing is to be based on the destination IP address (as for datagrams without this option).

*route data*    is a series of 32-bit IP addresses.

Whenever a datagram arrives at its destination and the source route is not empty (pointer < length) the receiving host will:

- Take the next IP address in the route data field (the one indicated by the pointer field) and put it in the Destination IP address field of the datagram.

- Put the local IP address in the source list at the location pointed to by the pointer field. The IP address for this is the local IP address corresponding to the network on which the datagram will be forwarded (routers are attached to multiple physical networks and thus have multiple IP addresses).

- Increment pointer by 4.

- Transmit the datagram to the new destination IP address.

This procedure ensures that the return route is recorded in the route data (in reverse order) so that the final recipient uses this data to construct a loose source route in the reverse direction. This is a *loose* source route because the forwarding router is allowed to use any route and any number of intermediate routers to reach the next address in the route.

**Note:**  The originating host puts the IP address of the first intermediate router in the destination address field and the IP addresses of the remaining routers in the path, including the target destination are placed in the source route option. The recorded route in the datagram when it arrives at the target contains the IP addresses of each of the routers that forwarded the datagram. Each router has moved one place in the source route, and normally a different IP address will be used, since the routers record the IP address of the outbound interface but the source route originally contained the IP address of the inbound interface.

**Strict Source Routing:**  The Strict Source Routing option, also called the Strict Source and Record Route (SSRR) option, uses the same principle as loose source routing except that the intermediate router *must* send the datagram to the next IP address in the source route via a directly connected network and not via an intermediate router.  If it cannot do so it reports an error with an ICMP Destination Unreachable message.

*Figure*   *2-17. Strict Source Routing Option*

*1001001*     (decimal 137) is the value of the option type byte for strict source routing

*length*       has the same meaning as for loose source routing

*pointer*      has the same meaning as for loose source routing

*route data*   is a series of 32-bit IP addresses

**Record Route:**  This option provides a means to record the route of an IP datagram.  It functions similarly to the source routing discussed above, but this time the source host has provided an empty routing data field, which will be filled in as the datagram traverses routers.  Note that sufficient space for this routing information must be provided by the source host: if the data field is filled before the datagram reaches its destination, the datagram is forwarded with no further recording of the route.

```
┌─────────┬────────┬─────────┬───────────────────//───┐
│00000111 │ length │ pointer │ route data          //  │
└─────────┴────────┴─────────┴───────────────────//───┘
```

*Figure*   *2-18. Record Route Option*

*0000111*     (decimal 7) is the value of the option type byte for record route

*length*       has the same meaning as for loose source routing

*pointer*      has the same meaning as for loose source routing

*route data*   is a multiple of four bytes in length chosen by the originator of the datagram

## 2.3.1.4  Internet Timestamp

A timestamp is an option forcing some (or all) of the routers on the route to the destination to put a timestamp in the option data.  The timestamps are measured in seconds and can be used for debugging purposes.  They cannot be used for performance measurement for two reasons:

- They are insufficiently precise because most IP datagrams will be forwarded in less than one second.

- They are insufficiently accurate because IP routers are not required to have synchronized clocks.

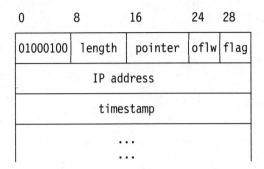

***Figure*** **2-19.** *Internet Timestamp Option*

Where

*01000100*

(Decimal 68) is the value of the option type for the internet time stamp option.

*length*

Contains the total length of this option, including the type and length-fields.

*pointer*

Points to the next timestamp to be processed (first free timestamp).

*oflw (overflow)*

Is a 4 bit unsigned integer of the number of IP modules that cannot register timestamps due to a lack of space in the data field.

*flag*

Is a 4-bit value which indicates how timestamps are to be registered. Values are:

*0* Timestamps only, stored in consecutive 32-bit words.
*1* Each timestamp is preceded by the IP address of the registering module.
*2* The IP address fields are pre-specified, and an IP module only registers when it finds its own address in the list.

*timestamp*

A 32-bit timestamp recorded in milliseconds since midnight UT (GMT).

The originating host must compose this option with a large enough data area to hold all the timestamps. If the timestamp area becomes full, no further timestamps are added.

## 2.3.2 IP Routing

An important function of the IP layer is *IP routing*. It provides the basic mechanism for routers to interconnect different physical networks. This means that an internet host can function as a normal host and a router simultaneously.

A basic router of this type is referred to as a *router with partial routing information*, because the router only has information about four kinds of destination:

- Hosts which are directly attached to one of the physical networks to which the router is attached

- Hosts or networks for which the router has been given explicit definitions

- Hosts or networks for which the router has received an ICMP redirect message

- A default destination for everything else

The last two items allow a basic router to begin with a very limited amount of information and to increase its information because a more sophisticated router will issue an ICMP redirect message if it receives a datagram and it knows of a better router on the same network for the sender to use. This process is repeated each time a basic router of this type is restarted.

Additional protocols are needed to implement a full-function router that can exchange information with other routers in remote network. Such routers are essential except in small networks, and the protocols they use are discussed in Chapter 3, "Routing Protocols" on page 3-1.

### 2.3.2.1 Direct and Indirect Destinations

If the destination host is attached to a network to which the source host is also attached, an IP datagram can be sent directly, simply by encapsulating the IP datagram in the physical network frame. This is called *direct routing*.

*Indirect routing* occurs when the destination host is not on a network directly attached to the source host. The only way to reach the destination is via one or more routers. The address of the first of these routers (the *first hop*) is called an *indirect route*. The first hop address is the only information needed by the source host: the router which receives a datagram has responsibility for the second hop and so on.

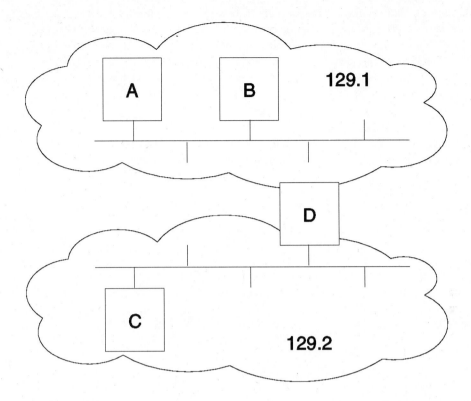

***Figure*** *2-20. Direct and Indirect IP Routes.* Host A has a *direct* route to hosts B and D, and an *indirect* route to host C. Host D is a router between the 129.1 and 129.2 networks.

A host can tell whether a route is direct or indirect by examining the network number and subnet number parts of the IP address.

1. If they match one of the IP addresses of the source host, the route is a direct one.

   The host needs to be able to address the target correctly using a lower-level protocol than ARP. This can either be done automatically using a network-specific protocol, such as ARP (see 2.8, "Address Resolution Protocol (ARP)" on page 2-69), which is used on broadcast LANs, or by statically configuring the host, for example when an MVS host has a TCP/IP connection over an SNA link.

2. For "indirect" routes, the only knowledge required is the IP address of a router leading to the destination network.

IP implementations may also support explicit host routes, that is, a route to a specific IP address. This is common for dial-up connections using Serial Line Internet Protocol (SLIP) which does not provide a mechanism for two hosts to inform each other of their IP addresses. Such routes may even have the same network number as the host, for example on subnets composed of point-to-point links. In general, however, routing information is done by network number and subnet number only.

## 2.3.2.2 IP Routing Table

Each host keeps the set of mappings between destination IP addresses and the IP addresses of the next hop routers for those destinations in a table called the *IP routing table*.

Three types of mappings can be found in this table:

1.  Direct routes, for locally attached networks

2.  Indirect routes, for networks reachable via one or more routers

3.  A default route, which contains the IP address of a router to be used for all IP addresses which are not covered by the direct and indirect routes.

See the network in Figure 2-21 for an example configuration.

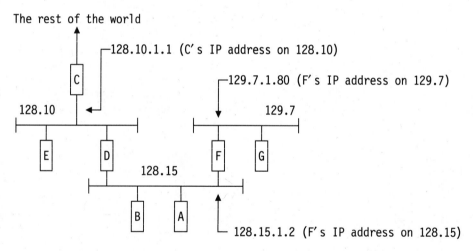

*Figure* *2-21. Example IP Routing Table*

The routing table of host D will contain the following entries

| Destination | route via |
|---|---|
| *128.10* | direct attachment |
| *128.15* | direct attachment |
| *129.7* | 128.15.1.2 |
| *default* | 128.10.1.1 |

## 2.3.2.3 IP Routing Algorithm

From the foregoing discussion, one can easily derive the steps that IP must take in order to determine the route for an outgoing datagram. This is called the *IP routing algorithm* and it is shown schematically in Figure 2-22.

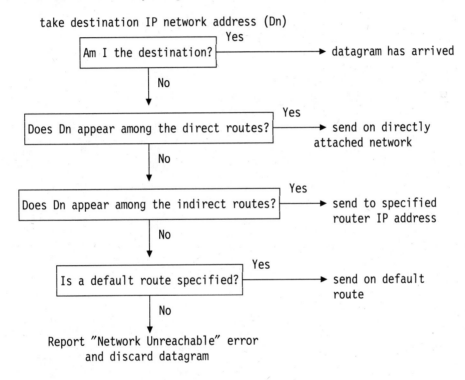

*Figure* 2-22. *IP Routing Algorithm*

Note that this is an iterative process. It is applied by every host handling a datagram, except for the host to which the datagram is finally delivered.

# 2.4 Internet Control Message Protocol (ICMP)

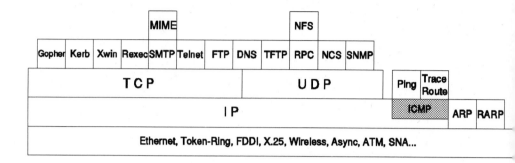

**Figure  2-23.** *Internet Control Message Protocol (ICMP)*

ICMP is a *standard protocol* with STD number 5 which also includes IP (see 2.3, "Internet Protocol (IP)" on page 2-36) and IGMP (see 2.7, "Internet Group Management Protocol (IGMP)" on page 2-66). Its status is *required.* It is described in RFC 792 with updates in RFC 950. It is part of STD 5 which also includes IP (see 2.3, "Internet Protocol (IP)" on page 2-36).

Path MTU Discovery is a *draft standard protocol* with a status of *elective.* It is described in RFC 1191.

ICMP Router Discovery is a *proposed standard protocol* with a status of *elective.* It is described in RFC 1256.

When a router or a destination host must inform the source host about errors in datagram processing, it uses the Internet Control Message Protocol (ICMP). ICMP can be characterized as follows:

- ICMP uses IP as if ICMP were a higher-level protocol (that is, ICMP messages are encapsulated in IP datagrams). However, ICMP is an integral part of IP and must be implemented by every IP module.

- ICMP is used to report some errors, *not* to make IP reliable. Datagrams may still be undelivered without any report on their loss. Reliability must be implemented by the higher-level protocols that use IP.

- ICMP can report errors on any IP datagram with the exception of ICMP messages, to avoid infinite repetitions.

- For fragmented IP datagrams, ICMP messages are only sent about errors on fragment zero. That is, ICMP messages never refer to an IP datagram with a non-zero fragment offset field.

- ICMP messages are never sent in response to datagrams with a destination IP address that is a broadcast or a multicast address.

- ICMP messages are never sent in response to a datagram which does not have a source IP address which represents a unique host. That is, the source address cannot be zero, a loopback address, a broadcast address or a multicast address.

- ICMP messages are never sent in response to ICMP error messages. They may be sent in response to ICMP query messages (ICMP types 0, 8, 9, 10 and 13 through 18).

- RFC 792 states that ICMP messages "may" be generated to report IP datagram processing errors, *not* "must." In practice, routers will almost always generate ICMP messages for errors, but for destination hosts, the number of ICMP messages generated is implementation dependent.

## 2.4.1 ICMP Messages

ICMP messages are described in RFC 792 and RFC 950, belong to STD 5 and are mandatory.

ICMP messages are sent in IP datagrams. The IP header will always have a Protocol number of 1, indicating ICMP and a type of service of zero (routine). The IP data field will contain the actual ICMP message in the format shown in Figure 2-24.

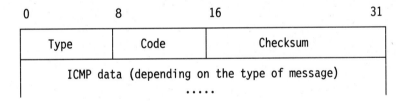

*Figure* *2-24. ICMP Message Format*

Where:

*Type*        Specifies the type of the message:

    **0**  Echo reply
    **3**  Destination unreachable
    **4**  Source quench
    **5**  Redirect
    **8**  Echo

**9** Router advertisement

**10** Router solicitation

**11** Time exceeded

**12** Parameter problem

**13** Timestamp request

**14** Timestamp reply

**15** Information request (obsolete)

**16** Information reply (obsolete)

**17** Address mask request

**18** Address mask reply

*Code*        Contains the error code for the datagram reported on by this ICMP message. The interpretation is dependent upon the message type.

*Checksum*    Contains the 16-bit one's complement of the one's complement sum of the ICMP message starting with the ICMP Type field. For computing this checksum, the checksum field is assumed to be zero. This algorithm is the same as that used by IP for the IP header. Compare this with the algorithm used by UDP and TCP (see 2.11, "User Datagram Protocol (UDP)" on page 2-88 and 2.12, "Transmission Control Protocol (TCP)" on page 2-92) which also include a *pseudo-IP* header in the checksum.

*Data*        Contains information for this ICMP message. Typically it will contain a part of the original IP message for which this ICMP message was generated. The length of the data can be determined from the length of the IP datagram that contains the message less the IP header length.

Each of the messages is explained below.

## 2.4.1.1 Echo Reply (0)
See 2.4.1.5, Echo (8) and Echo Reply (0).

## 2.4.1.2 Destination Unreachable (3)

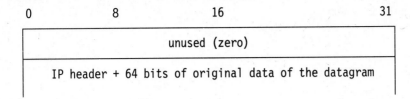

*Figure* **2-25.** *ICMP Destination Unreachable*

If this message is received from an intermediate router, it means that the router regards the destination IP address as unreachable.

If this message is received from the destination host, it means that the protocol specified in the protocol number field of the original datagram is not active, or that protocol is not active on this host or if the specified port is inactive (see 2.11, "User Datagram Protocol (UDP)" on page 2-88 for an introduction to the port concept).

The ICMP header code field will have one of the following values:

**0**  network unreachable
**1**  host unreachable
**2**  protocol unreachable
**3**  port unreachable
**4**  fragmentation needed but the *Do Not Fragment* bit was set
**5**  source route failed
**6**  destination network unknown
**7**  destination host unknown
**8**  source host isolated (obsolete)
**9**  destination network administratively prohibited
**10** destination host administratively prohibited
**11** network unreachable for this type of service
**12** host unreachable for this type of service
**13** communication administratively prohibited by filtering
**14** host precedence violation
**15** precedence cutoff in effect

If a router implements the Path MTU Discovery protocol, the format of the Destination unreachable message is changed for code 4 to include the MTU of the link which could not accept the datagram.

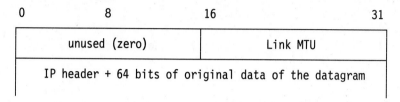

*Figure 2-26. ICMP Fragmentation Required with Link MTU*

## 2.4.1.3 Source Quench (4)

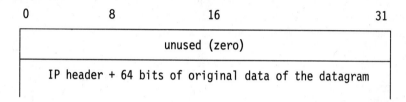

*Figure 2-27. ICMP Source Quench*

If this message is received from an intermediate router, it means that the router does not have the buffer space needed to queue the datagrams for output to the next network.

If this message is received from the destination host, it means that the incoming datagrams are arriving too quickly to be processed.

The ICMP header code field is always zero.

## 2.4.1.4 Redirect (5)

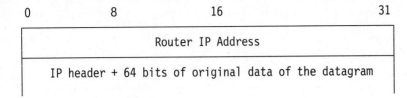

*Figure* *2-28. ICMP Redirect*

If this message is received from an intermediate router, it means that the host should send future datagrams for the network to the router whose IP address is given in the ICMP message. This preferred router will always be on the same subnet as the host which sent the datagram and the router which returned the IP datagram. The router will forward the datagram to its next hop destination. If the router IP address matches the source IP address in the original datagram header it indicates a routing loop. This ICMP will not be sent if the IP datagram contains a source route.

The ICMP header code field will have one of the following values:

**0** Network redirect
**1** Host redirect
**2** Network redirect for this type of service
**3** Host redirect for this type of service

## 2.4.1.5 Echo (8) and Echo Reply (0)

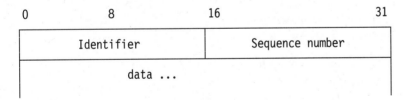

*Figure* *2-29. ICMP Echo and Echo Reply*

Echo is used to detect if another host is active on the network. The sender initializes the identifier and sequence number (which is used if multiple echo requests are sent), adds some data to the data field and sends the ICMP echo to the destination host. The ICMP header code field is zero. The recipient changes the type to Echo Reply and returns the datagram to the sender. This mechanism is used by the Ping command to determine if a destination host is reachable (see 2.5, "Ping" on page 2-63).

## 2.4.1.6 Router Advertisement (9) and Router Solicitation (10)

ICMP messages 9 and 10 are optional. They are described in RFC 1256 which is elective.

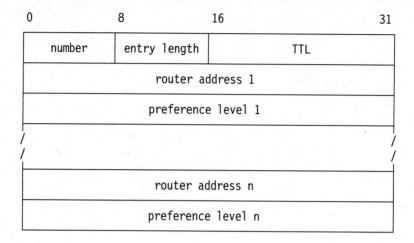

**Figure   2-30.** *ICMP Router Advertisement*

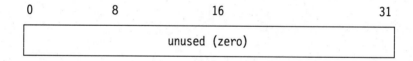

**Figure   2-31.** *ICMP Router Solicitation*

*number*

> The number of entries in the message.

*entry length*

> The length of an entry in 32-bit units. This is 2 (32 bits for the IP address and 32 bits for the preference value).

*TTL*

> The number of seconds that an entry will can be considered valid.

*router address*

> One of the sender's IP addresses.

*preference level*

> A signed 32-bit level indicating the preference to be assigned to this address when selecting a default router for a subnet. Each router on a subnet is

responsible for advertising its own preference level. Larger values imply higher preference, smaller values imply lower. The default is zero, which is in the middle of the possible range. A value of X' 80000000' $-2^{31}$ indicates that the router should never be used as a default router.

The ICMP header code field is zero for both of these messages.

These two messages are used if a host or a router supports the Router Discovery Protocol. The use of multicasting is recommended, but broadcasting may be used if multicasting is not supported on an interface. Routers periodically advertise their IP addresses on those subnets where they are configured to do so. Advertisements are made on the all-systems multicast address (224.0.0.1) or the limited broadcast address (255.255.255.255). The default behavior is to send advertisements every 10 minutes with a TTL value of 1800 (30 minutes). Routers also reply to solicitation messages they receive. They may reply directly to the soliciting host, or they may wait a short random interval and reply with a multicast. Hosts may send solicitation messages when they start until they receive a response. Solicitation messages are sent to the all-routers multicast address (224.0.0.2) or the limited broadcast address (255.255.255.255). Typically, three solicitation messages are sent at 3-second intervals. Alternatively a host may wait for periodic advertisements. Each time a host receives an advertisement, it updates its default router if the new advertisement has one with a higher preference value and sets the TTL timer for the entry to match the value in the advertisement. When the host receives a new advertisement for its current default router, it resets the TTL value to that in the new advertisement. This also provides a mechanism for routers to declare themselves unavailable: they send an advertisement with a TTL value of zero.

## 2.4.1.7  Time Exceeded (11)

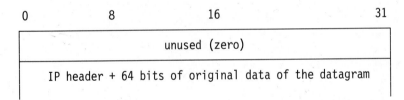

*Figure   2-32. ICMP Time Exceeded*

If this message is received from an intermediate router, it means that the time-to-live field of an IP datagram has expired.

If this message is received from the destination host, it means that the IP fragment reassembly time-to-live timer has expired while the host is waiting for a fragment of the datagram. The ICMP header code field may have the one of the following values:

**0** transit TTL exceeded
**1** reassembly TTL exceeded

## 2.4.1.8 Parameter Problem (12)

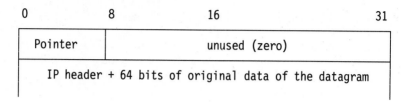

*Figure    2-33. ICMP Parameter Problem*

Indicates that a problem was encountered during processing of the IP header parameters. The pointer field points to the byte in the original IP datagram where the problem was encountered.  The ICMP header code field may have the one of the following values:

**0** unspecified error
**1** required option missing

## 2.4.1.9 Timestamp Request (13) and Timestamp Reply (14)

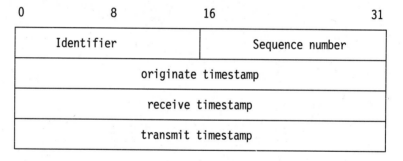

*Figure    2-34. ICMP Timestamp Request and Timestamp Reply*

These two messages are for performance measurements and for debugging.  They are not used for clock synchronization: the Network Time Protocol is used for that (see 4.22, "Time and Daytime Protocols" on page  4-221).

The sender initializes the identifier and sequence number (which is used if multiple timestamp requests are sent), sets the originate timestamp and sends it to the recipient. The receiving host fills in the receive and transmit timestamps, changes the type to Timestamp reply and returns it to the recipient.  The receiver has two timestamps in case there is a perceptible time difference between the receipt and transmit times, but in practice, most implementations will perform the two (receipt and reply) in one operation and will set the two timestamps to the same value. Timestamps are the number of milliseconds elapsed since midnight UT (GMT).

## 2.4.1.10 Information Request (15) and Information Reply (16)

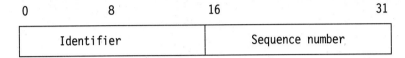

*Figure*   *2-35.  ICMP Information Request and Information Reply*

An Information Request is issued by a host to obtain an IP address for an attached network. The sender fills in the request with the destination IP address in the IP header set to zero (meaning this network) and waits for a reply from a server authorized to assign IP addresses to other hosts. The ICMP header code field is zero. The reply will contain IP network addresses in both the source and destination fields of the IP header. This mechanism is now obsolete. See also 2.9, "Reverse Address Resolution Protocol (RARP)" on page 2-79.

## 2.4.1.11 Address Mask Request (17) and Address Mask Reply (18)

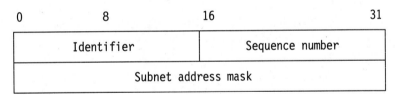

*Figure*   *2-36.  ICMP Address Mask Request and Reply*

An Address Mask Request is used by a host to determine the subnet mask in use on an attached network. Most hosts will be configured with their subnet mask(s), but some, such as diskless workstations, must obtain this information from a server. A host uses RARP (see 2.9, "Reverse Address Resolution Protocol (RARP)" on page 2-79) to obtain its IP address. To obtain a subnet mask, the host broadcasts an Address Mask Request. Any host on the network which has been configured to send Address Mask Replies will fill in the subnet mask, convert the packet to an Address Mask Reply and return it to the sender. The ICMP header code field is zero.

## 2.4.2 ICMP Applications

There are two simple and widely used applications which are based on ICMP: Ping and Traceroute. Ping uses the ICMP Echo and Echo Reply messages to determine whether a host is reachable. Traceroute sends IP datagrams with low TTL values so that they expire en route to a destination. It uses the resulting ICMP Time Exceeded messages to determine where in the internet the datagrams expired and pieces together a view of the route to a host. These applications are explained in 2.5, "Ping" on page 2-63 and 2.6, "Traceroute" on page 2-65.

## 2.4.3 ICMP for IP Version 6

The ICMP implementation above is specific to IP Version 4 (IPv4). IP Version 6 (IPv6, see 2.16.3, "IP Version 6 (IPv6)" on page 2-130) will require a new version of ICMP. The definitions of both new versions of ICMP and IP are not yet complete. Important features already known are:

- ICMP for IP Version 6 will use a new protocol number to distinguish it from ICMP Version 4.

- The ICMP header format will remain the same.

- Field lengths in messages will change to accommodate longer IPv6 messages.

- The Type and code values will be changed. Certain little used values will be removed.

- The size of ICMP messages will be increased to exploit the increased size of packets which IPv6 guarantees will be transmitted without fragmentation.

- The Fragmentation Required variant of the ICMP Destination unreachable message will be replaced by a Packet Too Big ICMP message which will include the outgoing link Maximum Transmission Unit (MTU) where the problem is identified.

- IGMP (see 2.7, "Internet Group Management Protocol (IGMP)" on page 2-66) will be merged with ICMP.

# 2.5 Ping

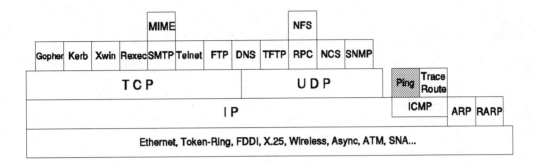

***Figure***   *2-37.  Packet InterNet Groper (PING)*

Ping is the simplest of all TCP/IP applications.  It sends one or more IP datagrams to a specified destination host requesting a reply and measures the round trip time.  The word *ping*, which is used as a noun and a verb, is taken from the sonar operation to locate an underwater object.  It is also an abbreviation for *Packet InterNet Groper*.

Traditionally, if you could ping a host other applications like Telnet or FTP could reach that host.  With the advent of security measures on the Internet, particularly firewalls (see 6.3, "Firewalls" on page 6-10), which control access to networks by application protocol and/or port number, this is no longer strictly true.  Nonetheless, the first test of reachability for a host is still to attempt to ping it.

The syntax that is used in different implementations of ping varies from platform to platform.  The syntax here is for the OS/2 implementation:

```
ping [-switches] host [size [packets]]
```

Where:

| | |
|---|---|
| *switches* | Switches to enable various ping options |
| *host* | The destination: either a symbolic name or an IP address |
| *size* | The size of the data portion of the packet |
| *packets* | The number of packets to send |

Ping uses the ICMP Echo and Echo Reply messages, as described in 2.4.1.5, "Echo (8) and Echo Reply (0)" on page 2-57.  Since ICMP is required in every TCP/IP implementation, hosts do not require a separate server to respond to pings.

Ping is useful for verifying a TCP/IP installation. Consider the following four forms of the command; each requires the operation of an additional part of the TCP/IP installation.

| | |
|---|---|
| *ping loopback* | Verifies the operation of the base TCP/IP software. |
| *ping my-IP-address* | Verifies whether the physical network device can be addressed. |
| *ping a-remote-IP-address* | Verifies whether the network can be accessed. |
| *ping a-remote-host-name* | Verifies the operation of the name server (or the flat namespace resolver, depending on the installation). |

Ping is implemented in all IBM TCP/IP products. TCP/IP for OS/2 (including the OS/2 Warp LAN Client version) also has a Presentation Manager program called PM Ping that uses ping to monitor a user-defined list of hosts stored in the file \TCPIP\ETC\PINGHOST.LST. This program can be iconized: when all hosts are responding, the icon is green, but if one or more hosts do not respond, the icon turns red.

# 2.6 Traceroute

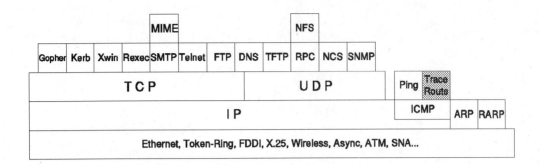

*Figure   2-38.* *Traceroute*

The Traceroute program can be useful when used for debugging purposes. Traceroute enables us to determine the route that IP datagrams follow from host to host.

Traceroute is based upon ICMP. It sends an IP datagram with a TTL of 1 to the destination host. The first router to see the datagram will decrement the TTL to 0 and return an ICMP Time Exceeded message as well as discarding the datagram. In this way, the first router in the path is identified. This process can be repeated with successively larger TTL values in order to identify the series of routers in the path to the destination host. Traceroute actually sends UDP datagrams to the destination host which reference a port number that is outside the normally used range. This enables Traceroute to determine when the destination host has been reached, that is, when an ICMP Port Unreachable message is received.

Traceroute is implemented in AIX/6000. It is also implemented in TCP/IP for OS/2.

# 2.7 Internet Group Management Protocol (IGMP)

IGMP is a *standard protocol* with STD number 5 which also includes IP (see 2.3, "Internet Protocol (IP)" on page 2-36) and ICMP (see 2.4, "Internet Control Message Protocol (ICMP)" on page 2-52). Its status is *recommended* and it is described in RFC 1112.

**Note:** IP and ICMP are *required*.

IGMP is best regarded as an extension to ICMP and occupies the same place in the IP protocol stack.[3]

See 2.2.4.2, "Multicasting" on page 2-19 for an introduction to multicasting.

## 2.7.1 IGMP Messages

ICMP messages are sent in IP datagrams. The IP header will always have a Protocol number of 2, indicating IGMP and a Type of Service of zero (routine). The IP data field will contain the 8-byte IGMP message in the format shown in Figure 2-39.

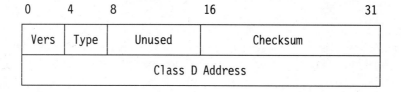

*Figure 2-39. ICMP Message Format*

Where:

*Vers*

> 4-bit IP version. Always 1.

*Type*

> Specifies a query or a report.
>
> *1* Specifies a query sent by a multicast router.
> *2* Specifies a report sent by a host.

---

[3] In IPv6 (see 2.16.3, "IP Version 6 (IPv6)" on page 2-130) IGMP is integrated into ICMP, since all IPv6 hosts will be required to support multicasting. In IPv4, multicasting support is optional so, unlike IP and ICMP, IGMP is not required.

*Checksum*
>A 16-bit checksum calculated as for ICMP.

*Class D Address*
>This is zero for a request, and is a valid multicast group address for a report.

## 2.7.2 IGMP Operation

Systems participating in IGMP fall into two types: hosts and multicast routers.

As described in 2.2.4.2, "Multicasting" on page 2-19, in order to receive multicast datagrams, a host must join a host group. When a host is multi-homed, it may join any group on one or more of its interfaces (attached subnets). The multicast messages that the host receives from the same group on two different subnets may be different. For example 244.0.0.1 is the group for "all hosts on this subnet," so the messages received on one subnet will always be different for this group from those on another. Multiple processes on a single host may be listening for messages for a multicast group on a subnet. If this is the case, the host joins the group once only, and keeps track internally of which processes are interested in that group.

To join a group, the host sends a report on an interface. The report is addressed to the multicast group of interest. Multicast routers on the same subnet receive the report and set a flag to indicate that at least one host on that subnet is a member of that group. No host has to join the all hosts group (224.0.0.1); membership is automatic. Multicast routers have to listen to all multicast addresses (that is, all groups) in order to detect such reports. The alternatives would be to use broadcasts for reports or to configure hosts with unicast addresses for multicast routers.

Multicast routers regularly, but infrequently (RFC 1112 mentions one-minute intervals), send out a query to the all hosts multicast address. Each host which still wishes to be a member of one or more groups replies once for each group of interest (but never the all hosts group, since membership is automatic). Each reply is sent after a random delay to ensure that IGMP does not cause bursts of traffic on the subnet. Since routers do not care how many hosts are members of a group and since all hosts which are members of that group can hear each other replying, any host which hears another claim membership of a group will cancel any reply that it is due to send in order to avoid wasting resources. If no hosts claim membership of a group within a specified interval, the multicast router decides that no host is a member of the group. When a host or a multicast router receives a multicast datagram, its action is dependent upon the TTL value and the destination IP address.

*0*     A datagram sent with a TTL value of zero is restricted to the source host.

*1*    A datagram with a TTL value of one reaches all hosts on the subnet which are members of the group. Multicast routers decrement the value to zero, but unlike unicast datagrams, they do not report this with an ICMP Time Exceeded message. Expiration of a multicast datagram is a normal occurrence.

*2+*   All hosts which are members of the group and all multicast routers receive the datagram. The action of the routers depends on the multicast group address.

> *224.0.0.0 - 224.0.0.255*
>
> This range is intended for single-hop multicasting applications only. Multicast routers will not forward datagrams with destination IP addresses in this range.
>
> It may seem at first as though a host need not bother reporting its membership of a group in this range since multicast routers will not forward datagrams from other subnets. However, the report also informs other hosts on the subnet that the reporting host is a member if the group. The only group which is never reported is 224.0.0.1 because all hosts know that the group consists of all hosts on that subnet.

> *other*
>
> Datagrams with other values for the destination address are forwarded as normal by the multicast router: it decrements the TTL value by at least one second as usual.
>
> This allows a host to locate the nearest server which is listening on a multicast address using what is called an *expanding ring search*. The host sends out a datagram with a TTL value of 1 (same subnet) and waits for a reply. If none is received, it tries a TTL value of 2, then 3, and so on. Eventually it will find the closest server.[4]

---

[4]  In general, the distance will be measured in hops, but strictly speaking the TTL value is, as always, "the time in seconds, with each hop being a minimum of one second."

# 2.8 Address Resolution Protocol (ARP)

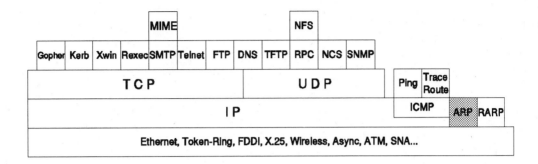

*Figure   2-40. Address Resolution Protocol (ARP)*

The ARP protocol is a *network-specific standard protocol*. Its status is *elective*.

The address resolution protocol is responsible for converting the higher-level protocol addresses (IP addresses) to physical network addresses. First, let's consider some general topics on Ethernet.

## 2.8.1 Ethernet versus IEEE 802.3

Two frame formats can be used on the Ethernet coaxial cable:

1. The standard issued in 1978 by Xerox Corporation, Intel Corporation and Digital Equipment Corporation, usually called *Ethernet* (or *DIX* Ethernet).

2. The international IEEE 802.3 standard, a more recently defined standard.

The difference between the two standards is in the use of one of the header fields, which contains a protocol-type number for Ethernet and the length of the data in the frame for IEEE 802.3.

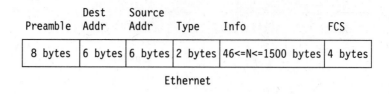

Ethernet

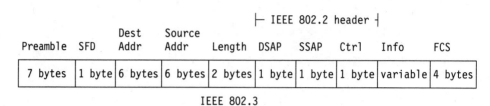

IEEE 802.3

*Figure*  *2-41.*  *Frame Formats for Ethernet and IEEE 802.3*

- The type field in Ethernet is used to distinguish between different protocols running on the coaxial cable, and allows their coexistence on the same physical cable.

- The maximum length of an Ethernet frame is 1526 bytes. This means a data field length of up to 1500 bytes.  The length of the 802.3 data field is also limited to 1500 bytes for 10 Mbps networks, but is different for other transmission speeds.

- In the 802.3 MAC frame, the length of the data field is indicated in the 802.3 header. The type of protocol it carries is then indicated in the 802.2 header (higher protocol level)/, see Figure  2-41

- In practice however, both frame formats can coexist on the same physical coax. This is done by using protocol type numbers (type field) greater than 1500 in the Ethernet frame.  However, different device drivers are needed to handle each of these formats.

Thus, for all practical purposes, the Ethernet physical layer and the IEEE 802.3 physical layer are compatible. However, the Ethernet data link layer and the IEEE 802.3/802.2 data link layer are incompatible.

**The 802.2 Logical Link Control (LLC) layer** above IEEE 802.3 uses a concept known as *Link Service Access Point* (LSAP) which uses a 3-byte header:

1 byte 1 byte 1 byte

| DSAP | SSAP | Ctrl |
|------|------|------|

*Figure*  *2-42.*  *IEEE 802.2 LSAP Header*

where DSAP and SSAP stand for Destination and Source Service Access Point respectively. Numbers for these fields are assigned by an IEEE committee.

Due to a growing number of applications using IEEE 802 as lower protocol layers, an extension was made to the IEEE 802.2 protocol in the form of the Sub-Network Access Protocol (SNAP). It is an extension to the LSAP header above, and its use is indicated by the value 170 in both the SSAP and DSAP fields of the LSAP frame above.

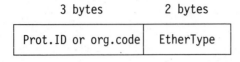

*Figure* **2-43.** *IEEE 802.2 SNAP Header*

**In the evolution of TCP/IP,** three standards were established, which describe the encapsulation of IP and ARP frames on these networks:

1. 1984: *RFC 894 — Standard for the Transmission of IP Datagrams over Ethernet Networks* specifies only the use of Ethernet type of networks. The values assigned to the type field are:

   *2048 (hex 0800)*     for IP datagrams
   *2054 (hex 0806)*     for ARP datagrams

2. 1985: *RFC 948 — Two Methods for the Transmission of IP Datagrams over IEEE 802.3 Networks* specifies two possibilities:

   a. The Ethernet compatible method: the frames are sent on a real IEEE 802.3 network in the same fashion as on an Ethernet network, that is, using the IEEE 802.3 data-length field as the Ethernet type field, thereby violating the IEEE 802.3 rules, but compatible with an Ethernet network.
   b. IEEE 802.2/802.3 LLC type 1 format: using 802.2 LSAP header with IP using the value 6 for the SSAP and DSAP fields.

   The RFC indicates clearly that the IEEE 802.2/802.3 method is the preferred method, that is, that all future IP implementations on IEEE 802.3 networks are supposed to use the second method.

3. 1987: *RFC 1010 - Assigned Numbers* (now obsoleted by RFC 1700 dated 1994) notes that as a result of IEEE 802.2 evolution and the need for more internet protocol numbers, a new approach was developed based on practical experiences exchanged during the August 1986 TCP Vendors Workshop. It states in an almost completely overlooked part of this RFC that from now on all IEEE 802.3, 802.4 and 802.5 implementations should use the Sub-Network Access Protocol (SNAP) form of the IEEE 802.2 LLC: DSAP and SSAP fields set to 170 (indicating the use of SNAP) and then SNAP assigned as follows:

- 0 (zero) as organization code.
- EtherType field:
  *2048 (hex 0800)*     for IP datagrams
  *2054 (hex 0806)*     for ARP datagrams
  *32821 (hex 8035)*    for RARP datagrams
  These are the same values as used in the Ethernet type field.

4. 1988: *RFC 1042 — Standard for the Transmission of IP Datagrams over IEEE 802 Networks.*

   As this new approach (very important for implementations) passed almost unnoticed in a little note of an unrelated RFC, it became quite confusing, and finally, in February 1988, it was repeated in an RFC on its own: *RFC 1042*, which obsoletes *RFC 948*.

The relevant IBM TCP/IP products implement RFC 894 for DIX Ethernet and RFC1010 (now RFC 1700) for IEEE 802.3 networks.

However, in practical situations, there are still TCP/IP implementations that use the older LSAP method (RFC 948 or 1042). *Such implementations will not communicate with the more recent implementations (such as IBM's).*

Note also that the last method covers not only the IEEE 802.3 networks, but also the IEEE 802.4 and 802.5 networks such as the IBM Token-Ring LAN.

## 2.8.2 ARP Overview

On a single physical network, individual hosts are known on the network by their physical hardware address. Higher-level protocols address destination hosts in the form of a symbolic address (IP address in this case). When such a protocol wants to send a datagram to destination IP address w.x.y.z, the device driver does not understand this address.

Therefore, a module (ARP) is provided that will translate the IP address to the physical address of the destination host. It uses a lookup table (sometimes referred to as the *ARP cache*) to perform this translation.

When the address is not found in the ARP cache, a broadcast is sent out on the network, with a special format called the *ARP request*. If one of the machines on the network recognizes its own IP address in the request, it will send an *ARP reply* back to the requesting host. The reply will contain the physical hardware address of the host and source route information (if the packet has crossed bridges on its path). Both this address and the source route information are stored in the ARP cache of the requesting host. All subsequent datagrams to this destination IP address can now be translated to a physical address, which is used by the device driver to send out the datagram on the network.

ARP was designed to be used on networks that support hardware broadcast. This means, for example, that ARP will not work on an X.25 network.

## 2.8.3 ARP Detailed Concept

ARP is used on IEEE 802 networks as well as on the older DIX Ethernet networks to map IP addresses to physical hardware addresses. To do this, it is closely related to the device driver for that network. In fact, the ARP specifications in RFC 826 only describe its functionality, not its implementation. The implementation depends to a large extent on the device driver for a network type and they are usually coded together in the *adapter microcode*.

### 2.8.3.1 ARP Packet Generation

If an application wishes to send data to a certain IP destination address, the IP routing mechanism first determines the IP address of the "next hop" of the packet (it can be the destination host itself, or a router) and the hardware device on which it should be sent. If it is an IEEE 802.3/4/5 network, the ARP module must be consulted to map the <protocol type, target protocol address> to a physical address.

The ARP module tries to find the address in this ARP cache. If it finds the matching pair, it gives the corresponding 48-bit physical address back to the caller (the device driver) which then transmits the packet. If it doesn't find the pair in its table, it *discards the packet* (assumption is that a higher-level protocol will retransmit) and generates a network *broadcast* of an ARP request.

```
                  +----------------------------+------------+
                  |   physical layer header    |  x bytes   |
                  +----------------------------+------------+
        A         |  hardware address space    |  2 bytes   |
        R         +----------------------------+------------+
        P         |  protocol address space    |  2 bytes   |
                  +-------------+--------------+------------+
        P         | hardware address|protocol address|      |
        a         | byte length (n) | byte length (m) | 2 bytes |
        c         +----------------------------+------------+
        k         |      operation code        |  2 bytes   |
        e         +----------------------------+------------+
        t         | hardware address of sender |  n bytes   |
                  +----------------------------+------------+
                  | protocol address of sender |  m bytes   |
                  +----------------------------+------------+
                  | hardware address of target |  n bytes   |
                  +----------------------------+------------+
                  | protocol address of target |  m bytes   |
                  +----------------------------+------------+
```

*Figure* **2-44.** *ARP Request/Reply Packet*

Where:

| | |
|---|---|
| *Hardware address space* | Specifies the type of hardware; examples are Ethernet or Packet Radio Net. |
| *Protocol address space* | Specifies the type of protocol, same as EtherType field in the IEEE 802 header (IP or ARP). |
| *Hardware address length* | Specifies the length (in bytes) of the hardware addresses in this packet. For IEEE 802.3 and IEEE 802.5 this will be 6. |
| *Protocol address length* | Specifies the length (in bytes) of the protocol addresses in this packet. For IP this will be 4. |
| *Operation code* | Specifies whether this is an ARP request (1) or reply (2). |
| *Source/target hardware address* | Contains the physical network hardware addresses. For IEEE 802.3 these are 48-bit addresses. |
| *Source/target protocol address* | Contains the protocol addresses. For TCP/IP these are the 32-bit IP addresses. |

For the ARP request packet, the target hardware address is the only undefined field in the packet.

## 2.8.3.2 ARP Packet Reception

When a host receives an ARP packet (either a broadcast request or a point-to-point reply), the receiving device driver passes the packet to the ARP module which treats it as shown in Figure 2-45 on page 2-76.

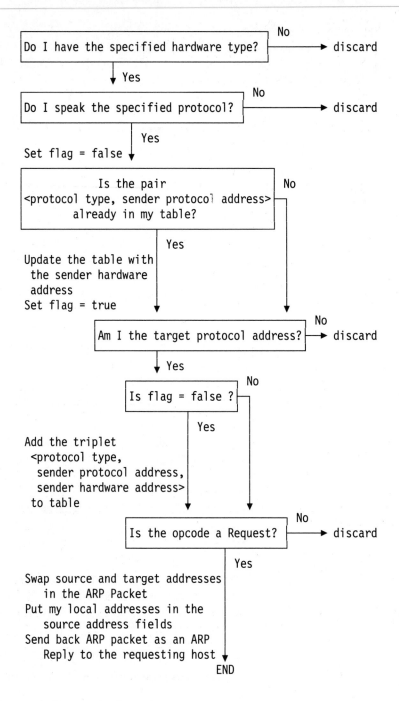

*Figure   2-45.  ARP Packet Reception*

The requesting host will receive this ARP reply, and will follow the same algorithm to treat it. As a result of this, the triplet <protocol type, protocol address, hardware address> for the desired host will be added to its lookup table (ARP cache). The next time a higher-level protocol wants to send a packet to that host, the ARP module will find the target hardware address and the packet will be sent to that host.

Note that because the original ARP request was a broadcast on the network, all hosts on that network will have updated the sender's hardware address in their table (only if it was already in the table).

## 2.8.4  ARP and Subnets

The ARP protocol remains unchanged in the presence of subnets. Remember that each IP datagram first goes through the IP routing algorithm. This algorithm selects the hardware device driver which should send out the packet. Only then, the ARP module associated with that device driver is consulted.

## 2.8.5  Proxy-ARP or Transparent Subnetting

Proxy-ARP is described in *RFC 1027 — Using ARP to Implement Transparent Subnet Gateways*, which is in fact a subset of the method proposed in *RFC 925 — Multi-LAN Address Resolution*. It is another method to construct local subnets, without the need for a modification to the IP routing algorithm, but with modifications to the routers, which interconnect the subnets.

### 2.8.5.1  Proxy-ARP Concept

Consider one IP network, which is divided into subnets, interconnected by routers. We use the "old" IP routing algorithm, which means that no host knows about the existence of multiple physical networks. Consider hosts A and B which are on different physical networks within the same IP network, and a router R between the two subnetworks:

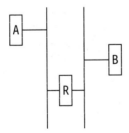

*Figure*   *2-46.  Hosts Interconnected by a Router*

When host A wants to send an IP datagram to host B, it first has to determine the physical network address of host B through the use of the ARP protocol.

As host A cannot differentiate between the physical networks, his IP routing algorithm thinks that host B is on the local physical network and sends out a broadcast ARP request. Host B doesn't receive this broadcast, but router R does. Router R understands subnets, that is, it runs the "subnet" version of the IP routing algorithm and it will be able to see that the destination of the ARP request (from the target protocol address field) is on another physical network. If router R's routing tables specify that the next hop to that other network is through a different physical device, it will reply to the ARP *as if it were host B*, saying that the network address of host B is that of the router R itself.

Host A receives this ARP reply, puts it in his cache and will send future IP packets for host B to the router R. The router will forward such packets to the correct subnet.

The result is transparent subnetting:

- Normal hosts (such as A and B) don't know about subnetting, so they use the "old" IP routing algorithm.
- The routers between subnets have to:
    1. Use the "subnet" IP algorithm.
    2. Use a modified ARP module, which can reply on behalf of other hosts.

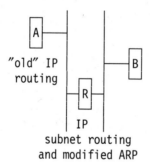

*Figure   2-47.  Proxy-ARP Router*

The IBM TCP/IP products do *not* implement proxy-ARP routing.

# 2.9 Reverse Address Resolution Protocol (RARP)

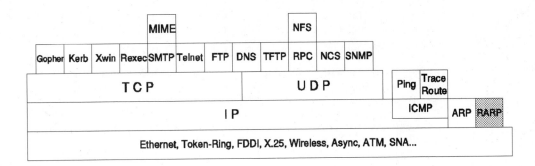

**Figure** *2-48. Reverse Address Resolution Protocol (RARP)*

## 2.9.1 RARP Overview

The RARP protocol is a *network-specific standard protocol*. Its status is *elective*.

Some network hosts, such as diskless workstations, do not know their own IP address when they are booted. To determine their own IP address, they use a mechanism similar to ARP (Address Resolution Protocol), but now the hardware address of the host is the known parameter, and the IP address the queried parameter. It differs more fundamentally from ARP in the fact that a "RARP server" must exist on the network which maintains a database of mappings from hardware address to protocol address.

## 2.9.2 RARP Concept

The reverse address resolution is performed the same way as the ARP address resolution. The same packet format (see Figure 2-44 on page 2-74) is used as for ARP.

An exception is the "operation code" field which now takes the following values:

3   for the RARP request
4   for the RARP reply

And of course, the "physical" header of the frame will now indicate RARP as the higher-level protocol (8035 hex) instead of ARP (0806 hex) or IP (0800 hex) in the *EtherType* field. Some differences arise from the concept of RARP itself:

- ARP only assumes that every host knows the mapping between its own hardware address and protocol address. RARP requires one or more server hosts on the network to maintain a database of mappings between hardware addresses and protocol addresses so that they will be able to reply to requests from client hosts.

- Due to the size this database can take, part of the server function is usually implemented outside the adapter's microcode, with optionally a small cache in the microcode. The microcode part is then only responsible for reception and transmission of the RARP frames, the RARP mapping itself being taken care of by server software running as a normal process in the host machine.

- The nature of this database also requires some software to create and update the database manually.

- In case there are multiple RARP servers on the network, the RARP requester only uses the first RARP reply received on its broadcast RARP request, and discards the others.

# 2.10 Ports and Sockets

In this section we will introduce the concepts of *port* and *socket*.

## 2.10.1 Ports

Each *process* that wants to communicate with another process identifies itself to the TCP/IP protocol suite by one or more *ports*. A port is a 16-bit number, used by the host-to-host protocol to identify to which higher-level protocol or application program (process) it must deliver incoming messages.

As some higher-level programs are themselves protocols, standardized in the TCP/IP protocol suite, such as TELNET and FTP, they use the same port number in all TCP/IP implementations. Those "assigned" port numbers are called *well-known ports* and the standard applications *well-known services*.

The "well-known" ports are controlled and assigned by the Internet Assigned Numbers Authority (IANA) and on most systems can only be used by system processes or by programs executed by privileged users. The assigned "well-known" ports occupy port numbers in the range 0 to 1023. The ports with numbers in the range 1024-65535 are not controlled by the IANA and on most systems can be used by ordinary user-developed programs.

Confusion due to two different applications trying to use the same port numbers on one host is avoided by writing those applications to request an available port from TCP/IP. Because this port number is dynamically assigned, it may differ from one invocation of an application to the next.

UDP, TCP and ISO TP-4 all use the same "port principle". (Please see Figure 2-52 on page 2-89 and Figure 2-56 on page 2-93.) To the extent possible, the same port numbers are used for the same services on top of UDP, TCP and ISO TP-4.

## 2.10.2 Sockets

Let us first consider the following terminologies:

- A *socket* is a special type of *file handle* which is used by a process to request network services from the operating system.

- A *socket address* is the triple:

    {*protocol, local-address, local-process*}

  In the TCP/IP suite, for example:

    {*tcp, 193.44.234.3, 12345*}

- A *conversation* is the communication link between two processes.

- An *association* is the 5-tuple that completely specifies the two processes that comprise a connection:

  {*protocol, local-address, local-process, foreign-address, foreign-process*}

  In the TCP/IP suite, for example:

  {*tcp, 193.44.234.3, 1500, 193.44.234.5, 21*}

  could be a valid association.

- A *half-association* is either:

  {*protocol, local-address, local-process*}

  or

  {*protocol, foreign-address, foreign-process*}

  which specify each half of a connection.

- The half-association is also called a *socket* or a *transport address*. That is, a socket is an end point for communication that can be named and addressed in a network.

The socket interface is one of several *application programming interfaces (APIs)* to the communication protocols. Designed to be a generic communication programming interface, it was first introduced by the 4.2BSD UNIX system. Although it has not been standardized, it has become a *de facto* industry standard.

4.2BSD allowed two different communication domains: Internet and UNIX. 4.3BSD has added the Xerox Network System (XNS) protocols and 4.4BSD will add an extended interface to support the ISO OSI protocols.

## 2.10.3 Basic Socket Calls

The following lists some basic socket interface calls. In the next section we shall see an example scenario of using these socket interface calls.

- Initialize a socket

  FORMAT: int *sockfd* = **socket**(int *family*, int *type*, int *protocol*)

  where:

  - *family* stands for *addressing family*. It can take on values such as AF_UNIX, AF_INET, AF_NS and AF_IUCV. Its purpose is to specify the method of addressing used by the socket.
  - *type* stands for the type of socket interface to be used. It can take on values such as SOCK_STREAM, SOCK_DGRAM, SOCK_RAW, and SOCK_SEQPACKET.
  - *protocol* can be UDP, TCP, IP or ICMP.
  - *sockfd* is an integer (similar to a file descriptor) returned by the **socket** call.

- Bind (Register) a socket to a port address

  FORMAT: int **bind**(int *sockfd*, struct sockaddr *\*localaddr*, int *addrlen*)

  where:

  - *sockfd* is the same integer returned by the **socket** call.
  - *localaddr* is the local address returned by the **bind** call.

  Note that after the **bind** call, we now have values for the first three parameters inside our 5-tuple association:

  > {*protocol, local-address, local-process, foreign-address, foreign-process*}

- Indicate readiness to receive connections

  FORMAT: int **listen**(int *sockfd*, int *queue-size*)

  where:

  - *sockfd* is the same integer returned by the **socket** call.
  - *queue-size* indicates the number of connection requests which can be queued by the system while the local process has not yet issued the **accept** call.

- Accept a connection

  FORMAT: int **accept**(int *sockfd*, struct sockaddr *\*foreign-address*, int *addrlen*)

  where:

  - *sockfd* is the same integer returned by the **socket** call.
  - *foreign-address* is the address of the foreign (client) process returned by the **accept** call.

  Note that this **accept** call is issued by a server process rather than a client process. If there is a connection request waiting on the queue for this socket connection, **accept** takes the first request on the queue and creates another socket with the same properties as *sockfd*; otherwise, **accept** will block the caller process until a connection request arrives.

- Request connection to the server

  FORMAT: int **connect**(int *sockfd*, struct sockaddr *\*foreign-address*, int *addrlen*)

  where:

  - *sockfd* is the same integer returned by the **socket** call.
  - *foreign-address* is the address of the foreign (server) process returned by the **connect** call.

  Note that this call is issued by a client process rather than a server process.

- Send and/or receive data

The **read**(), **readv**(*sockfd*, char *\*buffer*, int *addrlen*), **recv**(), **readfrom**(), **send**(*sockfd, msg, len, flags*), **write**() calls can be used to receive and send data in an established socket association (or connection).

Note that these calls are similar to the standard **read** and **write** file I/O system calls.

- Close a socket

  FORMAT: int **close**(int *sockfd*)

  where:

  – *sockfd* is the same integer returned by the **socket** call.

For more details, please refer to [Stevens] and the product implementation manuals listed in Appendix A, "Bibliography" on page A-1.

## 2.10.4 An Example Scenario

As an example, consider the socket system calls for a connection-oriented protocol.

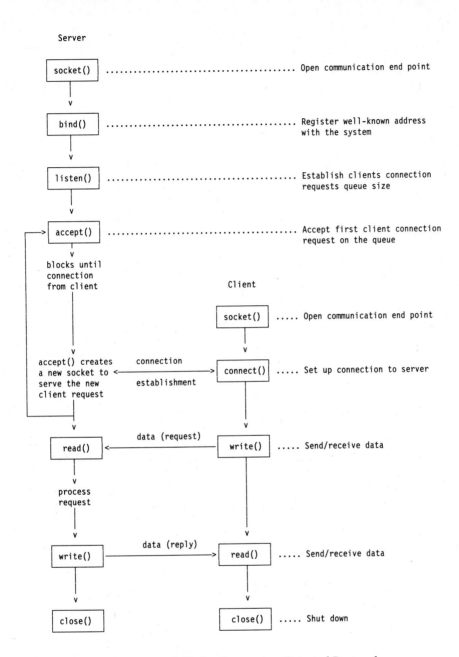

*Figure   2-49.  Socket System Calls for Connection-Oriented Protocol*

Consider the previous socket system calls in terms of specifying the elements of the association:

| | Protocol | Local Address , | Local Process | Foreign Address , | Foreign Process |
|---|---|---|---|---|---|
| connection-oriented server | socket() | bind() | | listen() accept() | |
| connection-oriented client | socket() | connect() | | | |
| connectionless server | socket() | bind() | | recvfrom() | |
| connectionless client | socket() | bind() | | sendto() | |

*Figure   2-50.  Socket System Calls and Association*

The socket interface is differentiated by the different services that are provided. Stream, datagram, and raw sockets each define a different service available to applications.

- **Stream socket interface** (SOCK_STREAM): It defines a reliable connection-oriented service (over TCP for example).  Data is sent without errors or duplication and is received in the same order as it is sent.  Flow control is built-in to avoid data overruns. No boundaries are imposed on the exchanged data, which is considered to be a stream of bytes. An example of an application that uses stream sockets is the File Transfer Program (FTP).

- **Datagram socket interface** (SOCK_DGRAM): It defines a connectionless service (over UDP for example). Datagrams are sent as independent packets.  The service provides no guarantees; data can be lost or duplicated, and datagrams can arrive out of order. No disassembly and reassembly of packets is performed.  An example of an application that uses datagram sockets is the Network File System (NFS).

- **Raw socket interface** (SOCK_RAW): It allows direct access to lower-layer protocols such as IP and ICMP.  This interface is often used for testing new protocol implementations.  An example of an application that uses raw sockets is the Ping command.

## 2.10.5  Implementations
In this section we discuss how sockets are implemented in the IBM TCP/IP products.

### 2.10.5.1  VM and MVS
The socket implementation in TCP/IP for VM and MVS supports two addressing families: *AF_INET*, and *AF_IUCV*. The AF_INET domain defines addressing in the Internet domain. The AF_IUCV domain defines addressing in the IUCV domain. In the IUCV domain, address spaces or virtual machines can use the socket interface to

communicate with other virtual machines or address spaces within the same operating system. Only stream sockets are supported in the AF_IUCV domain.

In an MVS OpenEdition environment AF_UNIX sockets are also supported.

### 2.10.5.2  OS/2 and DOS

TCP/IP for OS/2 and TCP/IP for DOS both support the *AF_INET* addressing family. They both support the Stream and Datagram socket interfaces.

### 2.10.5.3  AIX

All AIX implementations support the *AF_INET* and *AF_UNIX* addressing families.

They all support the 4.3BSD sockets and the datagram and stream socket interfaces.

# 2.11 User Datagram Protocol (UDP)

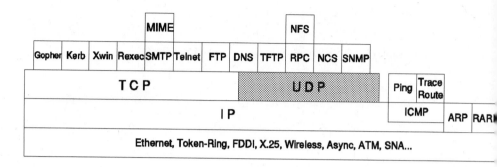

*Figure   2-51.  User Datagram Protocol (UDP)*

UDP is a *standard protocol* with STD number 6.  UDP is described by *RFC 768 — User Datagram Protocol*.  Its status is *recommended*, but in practice every TCP/IP implementation which is not used exclusively for routing will include UDP.

UDP is basically an application interface to IP.  It adds no reliability, flow-control or error recovery to IP.  It simply serves as a "multiplexer/demultiplexer" for sending and receiving datagrams, using *ports* to direct the datagrams as shown in Figure  2-52 on page  2-89.  For a more detailed discussion of ports refer to 2.10, "Ports and Sockets" on page  2-81.

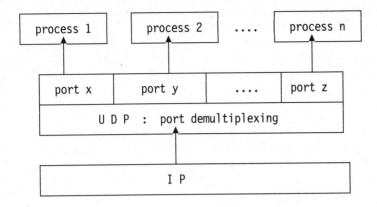

*Figure 2-52. UDP, A Demultiplexer Based on Ports*

UDP provides a mechanism for one application to send a datagram to another. The UDP layer can be regarded as being extremely thin and consequently has low overheads, but it requires the application to take responsibility for error recovery and so on.

## 2.11.1 Ports

The port concept was discussed earlier in 2.10, "Ports and Sockets" on page 2-81.

Applications sending datagrams to a host need to identify a target which is more specific than the IP address, since datagrams are normally directed to certain processes and not to the system as a whole. UDP provides this by using *ports*.

A port is a 16-bit number which identifies which process on a host is associated with a datagram. There are two types of port:

*well-known* Well-known ports belong to standard servers, for example TELNET uses port 23. Well-known port numbers range between 1 and 1023 (prior to 1992, the range between 256 and 1023 was used for UNIX-specific servers). Well-known port numbers are typically odd, because early systems using the port concept required an odd/even pair of ports for duplex operations. Most servers require only a single port. An exception is the BOOTP server which uses two: 67 and 68 (see 4.17, "BOOTstrap Protocol — BOOTP" on page 4-210).

The reason for well-known ports is to allow clients to be able to find servers without configuration information. The well-known port numbers are defined in *STD 2 — Assigned Internet Numbers*.

*ephemeral*   Clients do not need well-known port numbers because they initiate communication with servers and the port number they are using is contained in the UDP datagrams sent to the server. Each client process is allocated a port number as long as it needs it by the host it is running on. Ephemeral port numbers have values greater than 1023, normally in the range 1024 to 5000. A client can use any number allocated to it, as long as the combination of <transport protocol, IP address, port number> is unique.

**Note:**  TCP also uses port numbers with the same values. These ports are quite independent. Normally, a server will use either TCP or UDP, but there are exceptions. For example, Domain Name Servers (see 4.5, "Domain Name System (DNS)" on page 4-39) use both UDP port 53 and TCP port 53.

## 2.11.2  UDP Datagram Format

Each UDP datagram is sent within a single IP datagram. Although, the IP datagram may be fragmented during transmission, the receiving IP implementation will re-assemble it before presenting it to the UDP layer. All IP implementations are required to accept datagrams of 576 bytes, which, allowing for maximum-size IP header of 60 bytes means that a UDP datagram of 516 bytes is acceptable to all implementations. Many implementations will accept larger datagrams, but this is not guaranteed. The UDP datagram has a 16-byte header which is described in Figure 2-53.

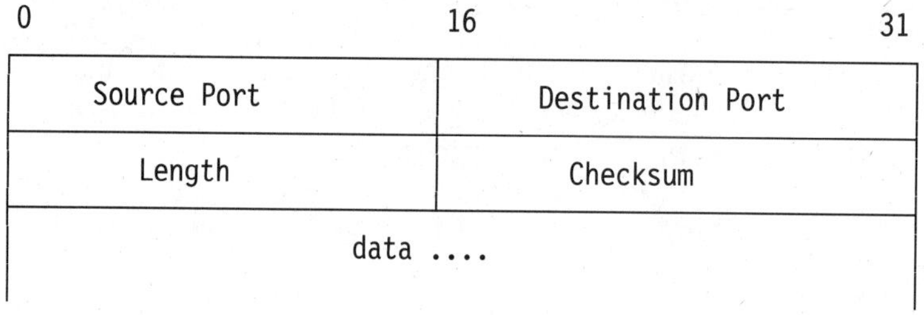

```
0                          16                        31
┌──────────────────────────┬──────────────────────────┐
│      Source Port         │    Destination Port       │
├──────────────────────────┼──────────────────────────┤
│        Length            │      Checksum             │
├──────────────────────────┴──────────────────────────┤
│                  data ....                           │
│                                                      │
└──────────────────────────────────────────────────────┘
```

*Figure*   *2-53. UDP Datagram Format*

Where:

*Source Port*        Indicates the port of the sending process. It is the port to which replies should be addressed.

*Destination Port*  Specifies the port of the destination process on the destination host.

*Length*             Is the length (in bytes) of this user datagram including the header.

*Checksum*           Is an optional 16-bit one's complement of the one's complement sum of a pseudo-IP header, the UDP header and the UDP data. The pseudo-IP header contains the source and destination IP addresses, the protocol and the UDP length:

```
0        8        16                          31
┌─────────────────────────────────────────────────┐
│              Source IP address                    │
├─────────────────────────────────────────────────┤
│            Destination IP address                 │
├──────────┬──────────┬─────────────────────────────┤
│   zero   │ protocol │        UDP length           │
└──────────┴──────────┴─────────────────────────────┘
```

*Figure  2-54.  Pseudo-IP Header*

The pseudo-IP header effectively extends the checksum to include the original (unfragmented) IP datagram.

## 2.11.3  UDP Application Programming Interface

The application interface offered by UDP is described in RFC 768.  It provides for:

- The creation of new receive ports.

- Receive operation that returns the data bytes and an indication of source port and source IP address.

- Send operation that has as parameters the data, source and destination ports and addresses.

The way this should be implemented is left to the discretion of each vendor.

Be aware that UDP and IP do not provide guaranteed delivery, flow-control or error recovery, so these must be provided by the application.

Standard applications using UDP include:

- Trivial File Transfer Protocol (TFTP)
- Domain Name System (DNS) name server
- Remote Procedure Call (RPC), used by the Network File System (NFS)
- Network Computing System (NCS)
- Simple Network Management Protocol (SNMP)

# 2.12 Transmission Control Protocol (TCP)

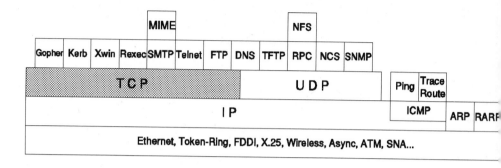

*Figure  2-55. Transmission Control Protocol (TCP)*

TCP is a *standard protocol* with STD number 7.  TCP is described by *RFC 793 — Transmission Control Protocol.*  Its status is *recommended*, but in practice every TCP/IP implementation which is not used exclusively for routing will include TCP.

TCP provides considerably more facilities for applications than UDP, notably error recovery, flow control and reliability.  TCP is a *connection-oriented* protocol unlike UDP which is *connectionless*.  Most of the user application protocols, such as TELNET and FTP, use TCP.

## 2.12.1 Sockets

The socket concept was discussed earlier in 2.10, "Ports and Sockets" on page  2-81.

Two processes communicate via *TCP sockets*.  The socket model provides a process with a full-duplex byte stream connection to another process.  The application need not concern itself with the management of this stream; these facilities are provided by TCP.

TCP uses the same port principle as UDP (see 2.11.1, "Ports" on page  2-89) to provide multiplexing.  Like UDP, TCP uses well-known and ephemeral ports.  Each side of a TCP connection has a *socket* which can be identified by the triple <TCP, IP address, port number>.  This is also called a *half-association*.  If two processes are communicating over TCP, they have a *logical connection* that is uniquely identifiable by the two sockets involved, that is by the combination <TCP, local IP address, local port, remote IP address, remote port>.  See Figure  2-56.  Server processes are able to manage multiple conversations through a single port.

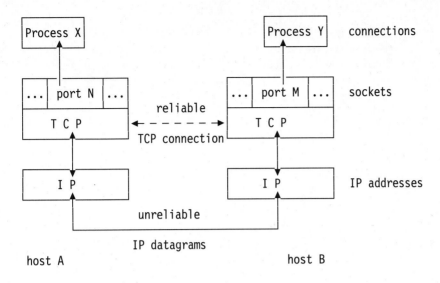

**Figure 2-56.** *TCP Connection.* Processes X and Y communicate over a TCP connection carried by IP datagrams.

## 2.12.2 TCP Concept

As noted above, the primary purpose of TCP is *to provide reliable logical circuit or connection service between pairs of processes.* It does *not* assume reliability from the lower-level protocols (such as IP) so TCP must guarantee this itself.

TCP can be characterized by the following facilities it provides for the applications using it:

*Stream Data Transfer*
> From the application's viewpoint, TCP transfers *a contiguous stream of bytes* through the internet. The application does not have to bother with chopping the data into basic blocks or datagrams. TCP does this by grouping the bytes in *TCP segments*, which are passed to IP for transmission to the destination. Also, TCP itself decides how to segment the data and it may forward the data at its own convenience.

> Sometimes, an application needs to be sure that all the data passed to TCP has actually been transmitted to the destination. For that reason, a *push* function is defined. It will push all remaining TCP segments still in storage to the destination host. The normal *close connection* function also pushes the data to the destination.

*Reliability*

TCP assigns a sequence number to each byte transmitted, and expects a positive acknowledgment (ACK) from the receiving TCP. If the ACK is not received within a timeout interval, the data is retransmitted. As the data is transmitted in blocks (TCP segments) only the sequence number of the first data byte in the segment is sent to the destination host.

The receiving TCP uses the sequence numbers to rearrange the segments when they arrive out of order, and to eliminate duplicate segments.

*Flow Control*

The receiving TCP, when sending an ACK back to the sender, also indicates to the sender the number of bytes it can receive beyond the last received TCP segment, without causing overrun and overflow in its internal buffers. This is sent in the ACK in the form of the highest sequence number it can receive without problems. This mechanism is also referred to as a *window*-mechanism and we will discuss it in more detail later in this chapter.

*Multiplexing*

Is achieved through the use of ports, just as with UDP.

*Logical Connections*

The reliability and flow control mechanisms described above require that TCP initializes and maintains certain status information for each "data stream." The combination of this status, including sockets, sequence numbers and window sizes, is called a logical connection. Each connection is uniquely identified by the pair of sockets used by the sending and receiving processes.

*Full Duplex*

TCP provides for concurrent data streams in both directions.

## 2.12.2.1 The Window Principle

A simple transport protocol might use the following principle: send a packet and then wait for an acknowledgment from the receiver before sending the next packet. If the ACK is not received within a certain amount of time, retransmit the packet.

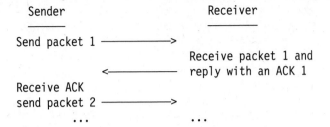

```
   Sender                    Receiver
   _____                    _____

Send packet 1 ──────────>
                                  Receive packet 1 and
                          <─────────── reply with an ACK 1
Receive ACK
send packet 2 ──────────>
      ...                     ...
```

*Figure* **2-57.** *The Window Principle*

While this mechanism ensures reliability, it only uses a part of the available *network bandwidth*.

Consider now a protocol where the sender groups its packets to be transmitted as Figure 2-58:

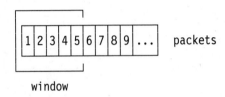

```
  ┌─┐
  │1│2│3│4│5│6│7│8│9│...│  packets
  └─┘
 window
```

*Figure* **2-58.** *Message Packets*

And uses the following rules:

- The sender may send all packets within the window without receiving an ACK, but must start a timeout timer for each of them.
- The receiver must acknowledge each packet received, indicating the sequence number of the last well-received packet.
- The sender slides the window on each ACK received.

In our example, the sender may transmit packets 1 to 5 without waiting for any acknowledgment:

```
            Sender                    Network
            ──────                    ───────
        Send packet 1        ──────>
        Send packet 2        ──────>
        Send packet 3        ──────>
        Send packet 4        ──────>
 ACK for packet 1 received <─────────── ACK 1
        Send packet 5        ──────>
```

*Figure   2-59.*  *Window Principle*

At the moment the sender receives the ACK 1 (acknowledgment for packet 1), it may
slide its window to exclude packet 1:

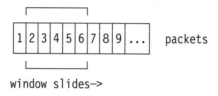

*Figure   2-60.*  *Message Packets*

At this point, the sender may also transmit packet 6.

Imagine some special cases:

- Packet 2 gets lost: the sender will not receive an ACK 2, so its window will remain in
  the position 1 (as last picture above).  In fact, as the receiver did not receive packet 2,
  it will acknowledge packets 3, 4 and 5 with an ACK 1, since packet 1 was the last
  one received "in sequence." At the sender's side, eventually a timeout will occur for
  packet 2 and it will be retransmitted. Note that reception of this packet by the
  receiver will generate an ACK 5, since it has now successfully received all packets 1
  to 5, and the sender's window will slide four positions upon receiving this ACK 5.

- Packet 2 did arrive, but the acknowledgment gets lost: the sender does not receive
  ACK 2, but will receive ACK 3. ACK 3 is an acknowledgment for *all* packets up to 3
  (including packet 2) and the sender may now slide his window to packet 4.

**Conclusion:** This window mechanism ensures:

- Reliable transmission.
- Better use of the network bandwidth (better throughput).

- Flow-control, as the receiver may delay replying to a packet with an acknowledgment, knowing its free buffers available and the window-size of the communication.

## 2.12.2.2 The Window Principle Applied to TCP

The above window principle is used in TCP, but with a few differences:

- As TCP provides a byte-stream connection, sequence numbers are assigned to each byte in the stream. TCP divides this contiguous byte stream into TCP segments to transmit them. The window principle is used at the byte level; that is, the segments sent and ACKs received will carry byte-sequence numbers and the window size is expressed as a number of bytes, rather than a number of packets.

- The window size is determined by the receiver, when the connection is established, and is *variable* during the data transfer. Each ACK message will include the window-size that the receiver is ready to deal with at that particular time.

The sender's data stream can now be seen as:

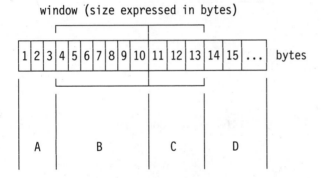

***Figure 2-61.*** *Window Principle Applied to TCP*

Where:

| | |
|---|---|
| *A* | Bytes that are transmitted and have been acknowledged. |
| *B* | Bytes that are sent but not yet acknowledged. |
| *C* | Bytes that may be sent without waiting for any acknowledgment. |
| *D* | Bytes that may not yet be sent. |

Remember that TCP will block bytes into segments, and a TCP segment only carries the sequence number of the first byte in the segment.

## 2.12.2.3 TCP Segment Format

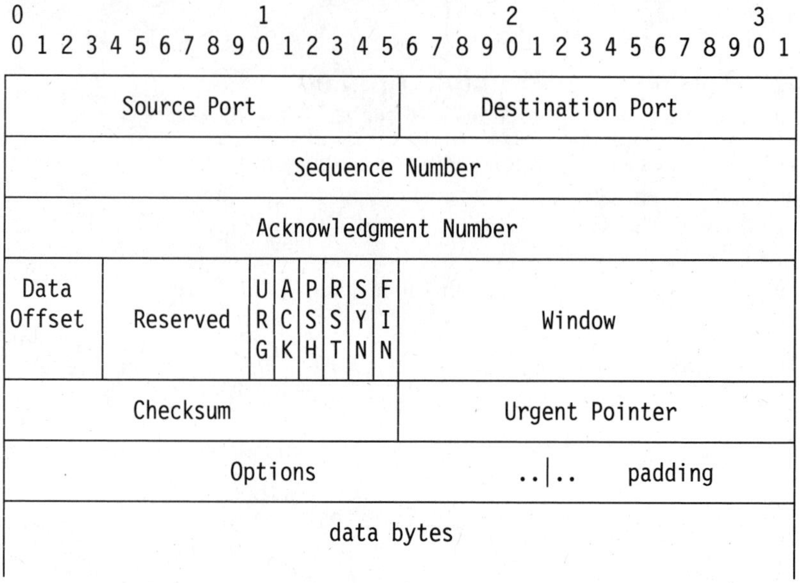

```
0                   1                   2                   3
0 1 2 3 4 5 6 7 8 9 0 1 2 3 4 5 6 7 8 9 0 1 2 3 4 5 6 7 8 9 0 1
```

| Source Port | | | | | | | Destination Port | |
|---|---|---|---|---|---|---|---|---|
| Sequence Number | | | | | | | | |
| Acknowledgment Number | | | | | | | | |
| Data Offset | Reserved | URG | ACK | PSH | RST | SYN | FIN | Window |
| Checksum | | | | | | | Urgent Pointer | |
| Options | | | | | | | .. \| ..    padding | |
| data bytes | | | | | | | | |

*Figure   2-62.  TCP Segment Format*

Where:

**Source Port**
The 16-bit source port number, used by the receiver to reply.

**Destination Port**
The 16-bit destination port number.

**Sequence Number**
The sequence number of the first data byte in this segment.  If the SYN control bit is set, the sequence number is the initial sequence number (n) and the first data byte is n+1.

**Acknowledgment Number**
If the ACK control bit is set, this field contains the value of the next sequence number that the receiver is expecting to receive.

**Data Offset**
The number of 32-bit words in the TCP header. It indicates where the data begins.

**Reserved**
Six bits reserved for future use; must be zero.

**URG**
Indicates that the urgent pointer field is significant in this segment.

| | |
|---|---|
| **ACK** | Indicates that the acknowledgment field is significant in this segment. |
| **PSH** | Push function. |
| **RST** | Resets the connection. |
| **SYN** | Synchronizes the sequence numbers. |
| **FIN** | No more data from sender. |
| **Window** | Used in ACK segments. It specifies the number of data bytes beginning with the one indicated in the acknowledgment number field which the receiver (= the sender of this segment) is willing to accept. |
| **Checksum** | The 16-bit one's complement of the one's complement sum of all 16-bit words in a pseudo-header, the TCP header and the TCP data. While computing the checksum, the checksum field itself is considered zero. |
| | The pseudo-header is the same as that used by UDP for calculating the checksum. It is a pseudo-IP-header, only used for the checksum calculation, with the format shown in Figure 2-63: |

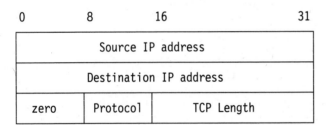

0          8          16                          31

*Figure* **2-63.** *Pseudo-IP Header*

| | |
|---|---|
| **Urgent Pointer** | Points to the first data octet following the urgent data. Only significant when the URG control bit is set. |
| **Options** | Just as in the case of IP datagram options, options can be either: |

- A single byte containing the option number, or
- A variable length option in the following format:

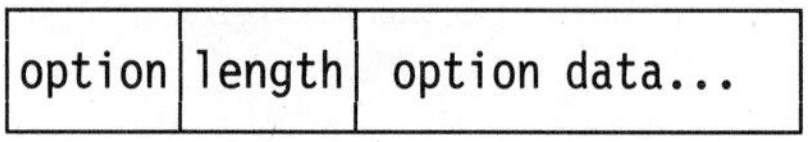

```
|option|length| option data...    |
```

*Figure* *2-64*. *IP Datagram Option.*  Variable length option.

There are currently only three options defined:

```
Kind  Length  Meaning
----  ------  -------
 0      -     End of option list.
 1      -     No-Operation.
 2      4     Maximum Segment Size.
```

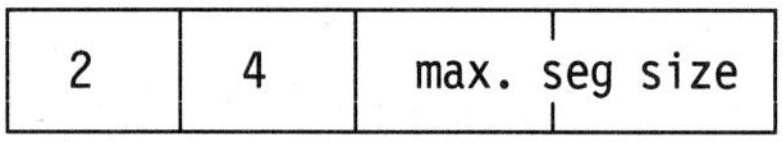

```
|   2   |   4   | max. seg size  |
```

*Figure* *2-65*. *Maximum Segment Size Option*

This option is only used during the establishment of the connection (SYN control bit set) and is sent from the side that is to receive data to indicate the maximum segment length it can handle. If this option is not used, any segment size is allowed.

**Padding**

All zero bytes used to fill up the TCP header to a total length that is a multiple of 32 bits.

## 2.12.2.4 Acknowledgments and Retransmissions

TCP sends data in variable length segments. Sequence numbers are based on a byte count. *Acknowledgments specify the sequence number of the next byte that the receiver expects to receive.*

Now suppose that a segment gets lost or corrupted. In this case, the receiver will acknowledge all further well-received segments with an acknowledgment referring to the first byte of the missing packet. The sender will stop transmitting when it has sent all the bytes in the window. Eventually, a timeout will occur and the missing segment will be retransmitted.

Suppose a window size of 1500 bytes, and segments of 500 bytes.

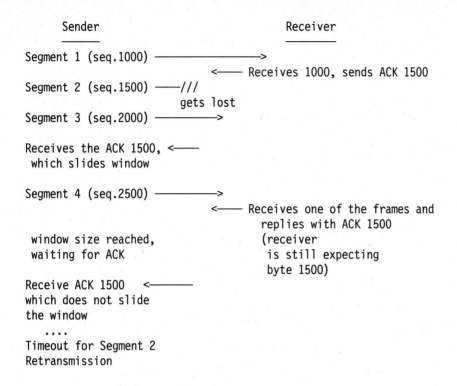

```
        Sender                          Receiver
        _____                          _____

Segment 1 (seq.1000)  ─────────────────>
                                <────── Receives 1000, sends ACK 1500
Segment 2 (seq.1500)  ─────///
                          gets lost
Segment 3 (seq.2000)  ─────────>

Receives the ACK 1500, <────
  which slides window


Segment 4 (seq.2500)  ─────────>
                                <────── Receives one of the frames and
                                        replies with ACK 1500
    window size reached,                (receiver
    waiting for ACK                      is still expecting
                                         byte 1500)

Receive ACK 1500  <─────────
which does not slide
the window
    ....
Timeout for Segment 2
Retransmission
```

***Figure*** *2-66. Acknowledgment and Retransmission Process*

A problem now arises, since the sender does know that segment 2 is lost or corrupted, but doesn't know anything about segments 3 and 4. The sender should at least retransmit segment 2, but it could also retransmit segments 3 and 4 (since they are within the current window). It is possible that:

1. Segment 3 has been received, and for segment 4 we don't know: it could be received, but ACK didn't reach us yet, or it could be lost also.
2. Segment 3 was lost, and we received the ACK 1500 upon the reception of segment 4.

Each TCP implementation is free to react to a timeout as the implementers wish. It could retransmit only segment 2, but in case 2 above, we will be waiting again until segment 3 times out. In this case, we lose all of the throughput advantages of the window mechanism. Or TCP might immediately resend all of the segments in the current window.

Whatever the choice, maximal throughput is lost. This is because the ACK does not contain a second acknowledgment sequence number indicating the actual frame received.

**Variable timeout intervals:**  Each TCP should implement an algorithm to adapt the timeout values to be used for the round trip time of the segments.  To do this, TCP records the time at which a segment was sent, and the time at which the ACK is received. A weighted average is calculated over several of these round trip times, to be used as a timeout value for the next segment(s) to be sent.

This is an important feature, since delays may be variable on an internet, depending on multiple factors, such as the load of an intermediate low-speed network or the saturation of an intermediate IP gateway.

## 2.12.2.5  Establishing a TCP Connection

Before any data can be transferred, a connection has to be established between the two processes. One of the processes (usually the server) issues a *passive OPEN* call, the other an *active OPEN* call.  The passive OPEN call remains dormant until another process tries to connect to it by an active OPEN.

On the network, three TCP segments are exchanged:

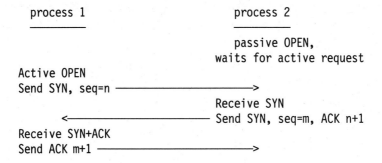

```
      process 1                        process 2
     ─────────                        ─────────
                                   passive OPEN,
                                   waits for active request

   Active OPEN
   Send SYN, seq=n  ──────────────────>
                                   Receive SYN
            <─────────────────────  Send SYN, seq=m, ACK n+1
   Receive SYN+ACK
   Send ACK m+1  ────────────────────────>


   The connection is now established and the two data streams
   (one in each direction) have been initialized (sequence numbers)
```

*Figure  2-67.  TCP Connection Establishment*

This whole process is known as *three-way handshake*.

Note that the exchanged TCP segments include the initial sequence numbers from both sides, to be used on subsequent data transfers.

*Closing* the connection is done implicitly by sending a TCP segment with the FIN bit (no more data) set.  As the connection is full-duplex (that is, we have two independent data streams, one in each direction), the FIN segment only closes the data transfer in one direction. The other process will now send the remaining data it still has to transmit and also ends with a TCP segment where the FIN bit is set. The connection is deleted (status information on both sides) once the data stream is closed in both directions.

### 2.12.2.6 TCP Segments Carried by IP Datagrams

TCP segments are transported in IP datagrams with the following parameter settings:

```
Type of Service = 00000000
    that is: Precedence = routine
             Delay      = normal
             Throughput = normal

Time to Live = 00111100 (1 minute)
```

# 2.12.3 TCP Application Programming Interface

The TCP application programming interface is not fully defined. Only some base functions it should provide are described in *RFC 793 - Transmission Control Protocol*. As is the case with most RFCs in the TCP/IP protocol suite, a great degree of freedom is left to the implementers, thereby allowing for optimal (operating system-dependent) implementations, resulting in better efficiency (greater throughput).

The following function calls are described in the RFC:

**Open**       To establish a connection, takes several parameters:
- Active/passive
- Foreign socket
- Local port number
- Timeout value (optional)
- And lots of other options

Returns a *local connection name*, which is used to reference this particular connection in all other functions.

**Send**       Causes data in a referenced user buffer to be sent over the connection. Can optionally set the URGENT flag or the PUSH flag.

**Receive**    Copies incoming TCP data to a user buffer.

**Close**      Closes the connection; causes a push of all remaining data and a TCP segment with FIN flag set.

**Status**     Is an implementation-dependent call that could return information such as:
- Local and foreign socket
- Send and receive window sizes
- Connection state
- Local connection name

**Abort**      Causes all pending Send and Receive operations to be aborted, and a RESET to be sent to the foreign TCP.

Full details can be found in *RFC 793 - Transmission Control Protocol* and the product implementation API in the *Programmer's Guides* listed in Appendix A, "Bibliography" on page A-1.

# 2.13 Asynchronous Transfer Mode (ATM)

ATM-based networks are of increasing interest for both local and wide area applications. There are already some products available to build your physical ATM network. The ATM architecture is new and therefore different from the standard LAN architectures. For this reason, changes are required so that traditional LAN products will work in the ATM environment. In the case of TCP/IP the main change required is in the network interface to provide support for ATM.

There are several approaches already available, two of which are important to the transport of TCP/IP traffic. They are described in 2.13.2, "Classical IP over ATM" on page 2-107 and 2.13.3, "ATM LAN Emulation" on page 2-112. They are also compared in 2.13.4, "Classical IP over ATM versus LAN Emulation" on page 2-116.

## 2.13.1 Address Resolution (ATMARP and InATMARP)

The address resolution in an ATM logical IP subnet is done by the ATM Address Resolution Protocol (ATMARP) based on RFC 826 and the Inverse ATM Address Resolution Protocol (InATMARP) based on RFC 1293. ATMARP is the same protocol as the ARP protocol with extensions needed to support ARP in a unicast server ATM environment. InATMARP is the same protocol as the original InARP protocol but applied to ATM networks. Use of these protocols differs depending on whether PVCs or SVCs are used.

Both ATMARP and InATMARP are defined in RFC 1577, which is a proposed standard with a state of elective.

The encapsulation of ATMARP and InATMARP requests/replies is described in 2.13.2, "Classical IP over ATM" on page 2-107.

### 2.13.1.1 InATMARP

The ARP protocol is used to resolve a host's hardware address for a known IP address. The InATMARP protocol is used to resolve a host's IP address for a known hardware address. In a switched environment you first establish a VC (Virtual Connection) of either PVC (Permanent Virtual Connection) or SVC (Switched Virtual Connection) in order to communicate with another station. Therefore you know the exact hardware address of the partner by administration but the IP address is unknown. InATMARP provides dynamic address resolution. InARP uses the same frame format as the standard ARP but defines two new operation codes:

- InARP request=8

- InARP reply=9

Please see 2.8.3.1, "ARP Packet Generation" on page 2-73 for more details.

Basic InATMARP operates essentially the same as ARP with the exception that InATMARP does not broadcast requests. This is because the hardware address of the destination station is already known. A requesting station simply formats a request by inserting its source hardware and IP address and the known target hardware address. It then zero fills the target protocol address field and sends it directly to the target station. For every InATMARP request, the receiving station formats a reply using the source address from the request as the target address of the reply. Both sides update their ARP tables. The *hardware type* value for ATM is 19 decimal and the *EtherType* field is set to 0x806, which indicates ARP according to RFC 1700.

## 2.13.1.2 Address Resolution in a PVC Environment

In a PVC environment each station uses the InATMARP protocol to determine the IP addresses of all other connected stations. The resolution is done for those PVCs which are configured for LLC/SNAP encapsulation. It is the responsibility of each IP station supporting PVCs to revalidate ARP table entries as part of the aging process.

## 2.13.1.3 Address Resolution in an SVC Environment

SVCs require support for ATMARP in the non-broadcast environment of ATM. To meet this need, a single ATMARP server must be located within the Logical IP Subnetwork (LIS) (see 2.13.2.1, "The Logical IP Subnetwork (LIS)" on page 2-109). This server has authoritative responsibility for resolving the ATMARP requests of all IP members within the LIS. For an explanation of ATM terms please refer to 2.13.2, "Classical IP over ATM" on page 2-107.

The server itself does not actively establish connections. It depends on the clients in the LIS to initiate the ATMARP registration procedure. An individual client connects to the ATMARP server using a point-to-point VC. The server, upon the completion of an ATM call/connection of a new VC specifying LLC/SNAP encapsulation, will transmit an InATMARP request to determine the IP address of the client. The InATMARP reply from the client contains the information necessary for the ATMARP server to build its ATMARP table cache. This table consists of:

- IP address
- ATM address
- Timestamp
- Associated VC

This information is used to generate replies to the ATMARP requests it receives.

**Note:** The ATMARP server mechanism requires that each client be administratively configured with the ATM address of the ATMARP server.

### ARP table add/update algorithm:

- If the ATMARP server receives a new IP address in an InATMARP reply the IP address is added to the ATMARP table.

- If the InATMARP IP address duplicates a table entry IP address and the InATMARP ATM address does not match the table entry ATM address and there is an open VC associated with that table entry, the InATMARP information is discarded and no modifications to the table are made.

- When the server receives an ATMARP request over a VC, where the source IP and ATM address match the association already in the ATMARP table and the ATM address matches that associated with the VC, the server updates the timeout on the source ATMARP table entry. For example, if the client is sending ATMARP requests to the server over the same VC that it used to register its ATMARP entry, the server notes that the client is still "alive" and updates the timeout on the client's ATMARP table entry.

- When the server receives an ARP_REQUEST over a VC, it examines the source information. If there is no IP address associated with the VC over which the ATMARP request was received and if the source IP address is not associated with any other connection, then the server adds this station to its ATMARP table. This is not the normal way because, as mentioned above, it is the responsibility of the client to register at the ATMARP server.

**ATMARP table aging:** ATMARP table entries are valid:

- In clients for a maximum time of 15 minutes
- In servers for a minimum time of 20 minutes

Prior to aging an ATMARP table entry, the ATMARP server generates an InARP_REQUEST on any open VC associated with that entry and decides what to do according to the following rules:

- If an InARP_REPLY is received, that table entry is updated and not deleted.
- If there is no open VC associated with the table entry, the entry is deleted.

Therefore, if the client does not maintain an open VC to the server, the client must refresh its ATMARP information with the server at least once every 20 minutes. This is done by opening a VC to the server and exchanging the initial InATMARP packets.

The client handles the table updates according to the following:

- When an ATMARP table entry ages, the ATMARP client invalidates this table entry.

- If there is no open VC associated with the invalidated entry, that entry is deleted.

- In the case of an invalidated entry and an open VC, the ATMARP client revalidates the entry prior to transmitting any non-address resolution traffic on that VC. There are two possibilities:

  - In the case of a PVC, the client validates the entry by transmitting an InARP_REQUEST and updating the entry on receipt of an InARP_REPLY.

  - In the case of an SVC, the client validates the entry by transmitting an ARP_REQUEST to the ATMARP server and updating the entry on receipt of an ARP_REPLY.

- If a VC with an associated invalidated ATMARP table entry is closed, that table entry is removed.

As mentioned above, every ATM IP client which uses SVCs must know its ATMARP server's ATM address for the particular LIS. This address must be named at every client during customization. There is at present no "well-known" ATMARP server address defined.

## 2.13.2  Classical IP over ATM

The definitions for implementations of classical IP over ATM (Asynchronous Transfer Mode) are described in RFC 1577 which is a proposed standard with a status of elective according to RFC 1720 (STD 1). This RFC considers only the application of ATM as a direct replacement for the "wires", local LAN segments connecting IP end-stations ("members") and routers operating in the "classical" LAN-based paradigm. Issues raised by MAC level bridging and LAN emulation are not covered.

For ATM Forum's method of providing ATM migration please see 2.13.3, "ATM LAN Emulation" on page  2-112.

Initial deployment of ATM provides a LAN segment replacement for:

- Ethernets, token-rings or FDDI networks

- Local-area backbones between existing (non-ATM) LANs

- Dedicated circuits of Frame Relay PVCs between IP routers

This RFC also describes extensions to the ARP protocol (RFC 826) in order to work over ATM. This is discussed separately in 2.13.1, "Address Resolution (ATMARP and InATMARP)" on page  2-104.

First some ATM basics:

*Cells*        All information (voice, image, video, data , etc.) is transported through the
               network in very short (48 data bytes plus a 5-byte header) blocks called
               "cells".

*Routing*      Information flow is along paths (called "virtual channels") set up as a series
               of pointers through the network.  The cell header contains an identifier that
               links the cell to the correct path that it will take towards its destination.

               Cells on a particular virtual channel always follow the same path through the
               network and are delivered to the destination in the same order in which they
               were received.

*Hardware-Based Switching*

               ATM is designed so that simple hardware-based logic elements may be
               employed at each node to perform the switching.  On a link of 1 Gbps a new
               cell arrives and a cell is transmitted every .43 microseconds.  There is not a
               lot of time to decide what to do with an arriving packet.

*Virtual Connection VC*

               ATM provides a Virtual Connection switched environment.  VC setup may
               be done on either a Permanent Virtual Connection (PVC) or a dynamic
               Switched Virtual Connection (SVC) basis. SVC call management is
               performed via implementations of the Q.93B protocol.

*End-User-Interface*

               The only way for a higher layer protocol to communicate across an ATM
               network is over the ATM AAL (ATM Adaptation Layer).  The function of
               this layer is to perform the mapping of PDUs (Protocol Data Units) into the
               information field of the ATM cell and vice versa.  There are four different
               AAL types defined, AAL1, AAL2, AAL3/4 and AAL5.  These AALs offer
               different services for higher layer protocols.  Here are the characteristics of
               AAL5 which is used for TCP/IP:

               • Message mode and streaming mode
               • Assured delivery
               • Non-assured delivery (used by TCP/IP)
               • Blocking and segmentation of data
               • Multipoint operation

               AAL5 provides the same functions as a LAN at the MAC (Medium Access
               Control) layer.  The AAL type is known by the VC endpoints via the cell
               setup mechanism and is not carried in the ATM cell header.  For PVCs the
               AAL type is administratively configured at the endpoints when the
               Connection (circuit) is set up.  For SVCs, the AAL type is communicated
               along the VC path via Q.93B as part of call setup establishment and the
               endpoints use the signaled information for configuration.  ATM switches
               generally do not care about the AAL type of VCs.  The AAL5 format

specifies a packet format with a maximum size of 64KB - 1 byte of user data. The "primitives" which the higher layer protocol has to use in order to interface with the AAL layer (at the AAL service access point - SAP) are rigorously defined. When a high-layer protocol sends data, that data is processed first by the adaptation layer, then by the ATM layer and then the physical layer takes over to send the data to the ATM network. The cells are transported by the network and then received on the other side first by the physical layer, then processed by the ATM layer and then by the receiving AAL. When all this is complete, the information (data) is passed to the receiving higher layer protocol. The total function performed by the ATM network has been the non-assured transport (it might have lost some) of information from one side to the other. Looked at from a traditional data processing viewpoint all the ATM network has done is to replace a physical link connection with another kind of physical connection - all the "higher layer" network functions must still be performed (for example IEEE 802.2).

*Addressing* An ATM Forum endpoint address is either encoded as a 20-byte OSI NSAP-based address (used for private network addressing, three formats possible) or is an E.164 Public UNI address (telephone number style address used for public ATM networks).[5]

*Broadcast, Multicast*

There are currently no broadcast functions similar to LANs provided. But there is a multicast function available. The ATM term for multicast is "point-to-multipoint connection".

## 2.13.2.1 The Logical IP Subnetwork (LIS)

The term LIS was introduced to map the logical IP structure to the ATM network. In the LIS scenario, each separate administrative entity configures its hosts and routers within a closed logical IP subnetwork (same IP network/subnet number and address mask). Each LIS operates and communicates independently of other LISs on the same ATM network. Hosts that are connected to an ATM network communicate directly to other hosts within the same LIS. This implies that all members of a LIS are able to communicate via ATM with all other members in the same LIS (VC topology is fully meshed). Communication to hosts outside of the local LIS is provided via an IP router. This router is an ATM endpoint attached to the ATM network that is configured as a member of one or more LISs. This configuration may result in a number of separate LISs operating over the same ATM network. Hosts of differing IP subnets must communicate via an

---

5   The ATM Forum is a worldwide organization, aimed at promoting ATM within the industry and the end-user community. The membership includes more than 500 companies representing all sectors of the communications and computer industries as well as a number of government agencies, research organizations and users.

intermediate IP router even though it may be possible to open a direct VC between the two IP members over the ATM network.

## 2.13.2.2 Multiprotocol Encapsulation

If you want to use more than one type of network protocol (IP, IPX, etc.) concurrently over a physical network, you need a method of multiplexing the different protocols. This can be done in the case of ATM either by VC-based multiplexing or LLC encapsulation. If you choose VC-based multiplexing you have to have a VC for each different protocol between the two hosts. The LLC encapsulation provides the multiplexing function at the LLC layer and therefore needs only one VC. TCP/IP uses, according to RFC 1577 and 1483, the second method because this kind of multiplexing was already defined in RFC 1042 for all other LAN types such as Ethernet, token-ring and FDDI. With this definition IP uses ATM simply as a LAN replacement. All the other benefits ATM has to offer, such as transportation of isochronous traffic etc., are not used. There is an IETF working group with the mission of improving the IP implementation and to interface with the ATM Forum in order to represent the interests of the Internet community for future standards.

To be exact, the TCP/IP PDU is encapsulated in an IEEE 802.2 LLC header followed by an IEEE 802.1a SNAP header (SubNetwork Attachment Point) and carried within the payload field of an AAL5 CPCS-PDU (Common Part Convergence Sublayer). The AAL5 CPCS-PDU format is shown in Figure 2-68.

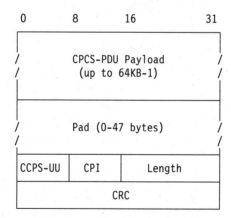

*Figure 2-68. AAL5 CPCS-PDU Format*

*CPCS-PDU Payload*
        The CPCS-PDU payload is shown in Figure 2-69.

*Pad*
        The Pad field pads out the CDCS-PDU to fit exactly into the the ATM cells.

*CPCS-UU*

The CPCS-UU (User-to-User identification) field is used to transparently transfer CPCS user-to-user information. This field has no function for the encapsulation and can be set to any value.

*CPI*

The CPI (Common Part Indicator) field aligns the CPCS-PDU trailer with 64 bits.

*Length*

The Length field indicates the length, in bytes, of the Payload field. The maximum value is 65535 which is 64KB - 1.

*CRC*

The CRC field protects the entire CPCS-PDU except the CRC field itself.

The payload format for routed IP PDUs is shown in Figure 2-69.

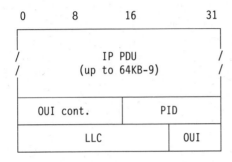

*Figure 2-69. CPCS-PDU Payload Format for IP PDUs*

*IP PDU*

Normal IP datagram starting with the IP header.

*LLC*

3-byte LLC header with the format DSAP-SSAP-Ctrl. For IP data it is set to 0xAA-AA-03 to indicate the presence of a SNAP header. The Ctrl field always has the value 0x03 specifying Unnumbered Information Command PDU.

*OUI*

The 3-byte OUI (Organizationally Unique Identifier) identifies an organization which administers the meaning of the following 2-byte Protocol Identifier (PID). To specify an EtherType in PID the OUI has to be set to 0x00-00-00.

*PID*

> The Protocol Identifier (PID) field specifies the protocol type of the following PDU. For IP datagrams the assigned EtherType or PID is 0x08-00.

The default MTU size for IP members in an ATM network is discussed in RFC 1626 and defined to be 9180 bytes. The LLC/SNAP header is 8 bytes; therefore, the default ATM AAL5 PDU size is 9188 bytes. The possible values can be between zero and 65535. You are allowed to change the MTU size but then all members of a LIS must be changed as well in order to have the same value. RFC 1755 recommends that all implementations should support MTU sizes up to and including 64KB.

The address resolution in an ATM network is defined as an extension of the ARP protocol and is described in 2.13.1, "Address Resolution (ATMARP and InATMARP)" on page 2-104.

There is no mapping from IP broadcast or multicast addresses to ATM "broadcast" or multicast addresses available. But there are no restrictions for transmitting or receiving IP datagrams specifying any of the four standard IP broadcast address forms as described in RFC 1122. Members, upon receiving an IP broadcast or IP subnet broadcast for their LIS, must process the packet as if addressed to that station.

### 2.13.2.3 Implementations

The following implementations of classical IP over ATM according to RFC 1577 are available at the time of writing:

- IBM AIX/6000
- IBM 8260, Switch/Control Point Module, for SNMP over ATM
- IBM Turboways 8282 ATM Workgroup Concentrator, for SNMP over ATM

## 2.13.3  ATM LAN Emulation

Another approach to provide a migration path to a native ATM network is ATM LAN emulation. ATM LAN emulation is still under construction by ATM Forum working groups. For the IETF approach please see 2.13.2, "Classical IP over ATM" on page 2-107. There is no ATM Forum implementation agreement available covering virtual LANs over ATM but there are some basic agreements on the different proposals made to the ATM Forum. The descriptions below are based on the IBM proposals.

The concept of ATM LAN emulation is to construct a system such that the workstation application software "thinks" it is a member of a real shared-medium LAN, such as a token-ring for example. This method maximizes the reuse of existing LAN software and significantly reduces the cost of migration to ATM. In PC LAN environments for example the LAN emulation layer could be implemented under the NDIS/ODI-type interface.  With such an implementation all the higher layer protocols, such as IP, IPX, NetBIOS and SNA for example, could be run over ATM networks without any change.

Refer to Figure 2-70 for the implementation of token-ring and Ethernet.

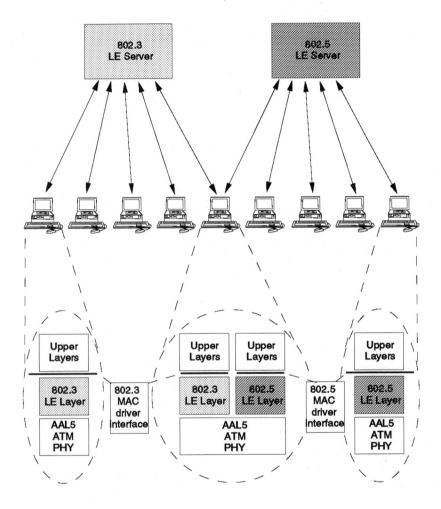

*Figure   2-70.  Ethernet and Token-ring LAN Emulation*

## 2.13.3.1  LAN Emulation Layer (Workstation Software)

Each workstation that performs the LE function needs to have software to provide the LE service.  This software is called the LAN emulation layer (LE layer).  It provides the interface to existing protocol support (such as IP, IPX, IEEE 802.2 LLC, NetBIOS, etc.)

and emulates the functions of a real shared-medium LAN. This means that no changes are needed to existing LAN application software to use ATM services. The LE layer interfaces to the ATM network through a hardware ATM adapter.

The primary function of the LE layer is to transfer encapsulated LAN frames (arriving from higher layers) to their destination either directly (over a "direct VC") or through the LE server. This is done by using AAL5 services provided by ATM.

Each LE layer has one or more LAN addresses as well as an ATM address.

A separate instance (logical copy or LE client) of the LE layer is needed in each workstation for each different LAN or type of LAN to be supported. For example, if both token-ring and Ethernet LAN types are to be emulated, then you need two LE layers. In fact they will probably just be different threads within the same copy of the same code but they are logically separate LE layers. Separate LE layers would also be used if one workstation needed to be part of two different emulated token-ring LANs. Each separate LE layer needs a different MAC address but can share the same physical ATM connection (adapter).

## 2.13.3.2 LAN Emulation Server

The basic function of the LE server is to provide directory, multicast and address resolution services to the LE layers in the workstations. It also provides a connectionless data transfer service to the LE layers in the workstations if needed.

Each emulated LAN must have an LE server. It would be possible to have multiple LE servers sharing the same hardware and code (via multithreading) but the LE servers are logically separate entities. As for the LE layers, an emulated token-ring LAN cannot have members that are emulating an Ethernet LAN. Thus an instance of an LE server is dedicated to a single type of LAN emulation. The LE server may be physically internal to the ATM network or provided in an external device, but logically it is always an external function which simply uses the services provided by ATM to do its job.

## 2.13.3.3 Default VCs

A default VC is a connection between an LE layer in a workstation and the LE server. These connections may be permanent or switched.

All LE control messages are carried between the LE layer and the LE server on the default VC. Encapsulated data frames may also be sent on the default VC.

The presence of the LE server and the default VCs is necessary for the LE function to be performed.

### 2.13.3.4 Direct VCs

Direct VCs are connections between LE layers in the end systems. They are always switched and set up on demand. If the ATM network does not support switched connections then you cannot have direct VCs and all the data must be sent through the LE server on default VCs. If there is no direct VC available for any reason then data transfer must take place through the LE server (there is no other way).

Direct VCs are set up on request by an LE layer (the server cannot set them up as there is no third party call setup function in ATM). The ATM address of a destination LE layer is provided to a requesting LE layer by the LE server. Direct VCs stay in place until one of the partner LE layers decides to end the connection (because there is no more data).

### 2.13.3.5 Initialization

During initialization the LE layer (workstation) establishes the default VC with the LE server. It also discovers its own ATM address - this is needed if it is to later set up direct VCs.

### 2.13.3.6 Registration

In this phase the LE layer (workstation) registers its MAC addresses with the LE server. Other things like filtering requirements (optional) may be provided.

### 2.13.3.7 Management and Resolution

This is the method used by ATM end stations to set up direct VCs with other end stations (LE layers). This function includes mechanisms for learning the ATM address of a target station, mapping the MAC address to an ATM address, storing the mapping in a table and managing the table.

For the server this function provides the means for supporting the use of direct VCs by end stations. This includes a mechanism for mapping the MAC address of an end system to its ATM address, storing the information and providing it to a requesting end station.

This structure maintains full LAN function and can support most higher layer LAN protocols. Reliance on the server for data transfer is minimized by using switched VCs for the transport of most bulk data.

### 2.13.3.8 Implementations

LAN emulation is provided by the following IBM products:

- IBM 8260, Switch/Control Point Module, for SNMP over ATM.

- IBM 8281 LAN Bridge to connect Ethernet or token-ring LANs to native attached ATM stations running LAN Emulation.

- IBM Turboways 25/100 ATM Adapter for ISA/MCA PCs. Token-ring LAN Emulation software for DOS/Windows is provided with the adapter. ATM LAN Emulation Server runs on a Novell NetWare server 3.12 or higher and requires a dedicated Turboways 100 ATM adapter.

- IBM 8282 Workgroup Concentrator to build an ATM network.

LAN Emulation software for OS/2, Ethernet and ATM Forum LAN Emulation Specification support is expected to follow during 1995.

## 2.13.4  Classical IP over ATM versus LAN Emulation

These two approaches to providing an easier way to migrate to ATM were made with different goals in mind.

Classical IP over ATM defines an encapsulation and address resolution method. The definitions are made for IP only and not for use with other protocols. So if you have applications requiring other protocol stacks (such as IPX or SNA for example) then IP over ATM will not provide a complete solution. On the other hand if you only have TCP or UDP-based applications then this might be the better solution, since this specialized adaptation of the IP protocol to the ATM architecture is likely to produce less overhead than a more global solution and therefore be more efficient. Another advantage of this implementation is the use of some ATM-specific functions, such as large MTU sizes, etc.

The major goal of the ATM Forum's approach is to run layer 3 and higher protocols unchanged over the ATM network. This means that existing protocols, such as TCP/IP, IPX, NetBIOS and SNA for example, and their applications can use the benefits of the fast ATM network without any changes. The mapping for all protocols is already defined. The LAN emulation layer provides all the services of a classic LAN; thus, the upper layer does not know of the existence of ATM. This is both an advantage and a disadvantage because the knowledge of the underlying network could be used to provide a more effective implementation.

In the near future both approaches will be used depending on the particular requirements. Over time, when the mapping of applications to ATM is fully defined and implemented, the scheme of a dedicated ATM implementation may be used.

## 2.14  TCP/IP and OSI

Figure 2-71 on page 2-117 shows an attempt to position the different TCP/IP and OSI architectural layers, but be aware of the basic differences discussed below.

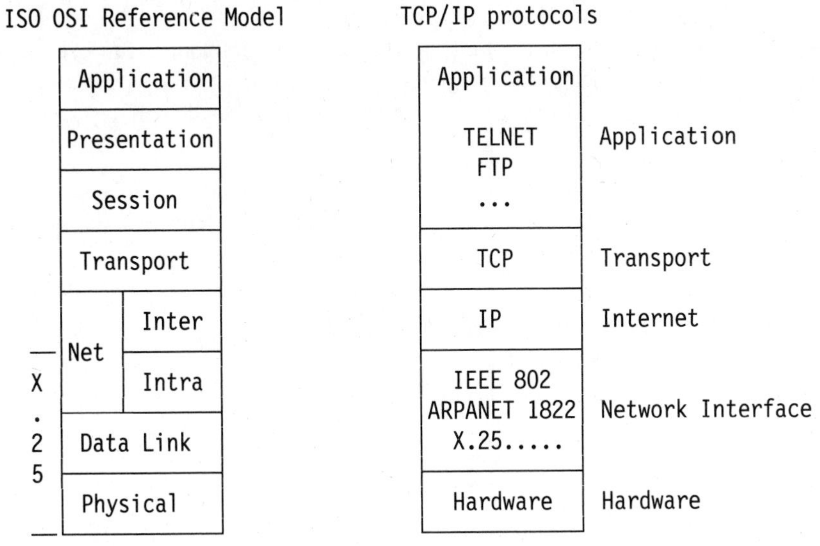

ISO OSI Reference Model          TCP/IP protocols

| ISO OSI Reference Model | | | TCP/IP protocols | |
|---|---|---|---|---|
| Application | | | Application | |
| Presentation | | | TELNET FTP ... | Application |
| Session | | | | |
| Transport | | | TCP | Transport |
| Net | Inter | | IP | Internet |
| X.25 | Intra | | IEEE 802 ARPANET 1822 X.25..... | Network Interface |
| | Data Link | | | |
| | Physical | | Hardware | Hardware |

*Figure*   *2-71. TCP/IP and OSI.*   Functional positioning of the layers.

## 2.14.1 Differences

One can only functionally position the internet model to the ISO OSI model because basic differences exist such as:

- In the internet protocol suite, a layer represents a reasonable packaging of function.

  The ISO view, on the other hand, treats layers as rather narrow functional groups, attempting to force modularity by requiring additional layers for additional functions.

  In the TCP/IP protocols, a given protocol can be used by other protocols within the same layer, whereas in the OSI model two separate layers would be defined in such circumstances. Examples of such "horizontal dependencies" are FTP, which uses the same common representation as TELNET on the "application layer," and ICMP, which uses IP for sending its datagrams on the "internetwork" layer.

  In practice, what we are discussing here is the difference between a de jure standard, OSI, and a de facto standard, TCP/IP. The focus in the TCP/IP world is on agreeing on a protocol standard which can be made to work in diverse heterogeneous networks. The focus in the OSI world has always been more on the standard than the implementation of the standard.

- Efficiency and feasibility. The OSI norms tend to be prescriptive (for instance the "layer N" must go through "all layers below it"), whereas the TCP/IP protocols are descriptive, and leave a maximum of freedom for the implementers. One of the advantages of the TCP/IP approach is that each particular implementation can use operating system-dependent features, generally resulting in a greater efficiency (fewer CPU cycles, more throughput for similar functions), while still ensuring "interoperability" with other implementations.

Another way to see this is that most of the internet protocols have first been developed (coded and tested), before being "described" in an RFC (usually by the implementer) which clearly shows the feasibility of the protocols.

## 2.14.2 The Internet World and OSI

The Department of Defense (DoD), funder of the original ARPANET research, made a statement on OSI in January '88, based on the Government OSI Profile (GOSIP) of April 22, 1987.

The following is an excerpt from the statement, which is published in *RFC 1039 - A DoD Statement on OSI*:

> "... It is intended to adopt the OSI protocols as a full **co-standard** with the DoD protocols when GOSIP is formally approved as a Federal Information Processing Standard. Two years thereafter, the OSI protocols would become the sole mandatory interoperable protocol suite; however, a capability for interoperation with DoD protocols would be provided for the expected life of systems supporting the DoD protocols. ..."

A lot of study has already been done by the internet world on possible transitions and coexistence of the protocols. The following list is a series of RFCs already issued for that purpose:

- *RFC 983 - ISO Transport Services on Top of the TCP.*
- *RFC 1006 - ISO Transport Services on Top of the TCP - Version 3.*
- *RFC 1039 - A DoD Statement on Open Systems Interconnection Protocols.*
- *RFC 1069 - Guidelines for the Use of Internet IP Addresses in the ISO Connectionless-Mode Network Protocol.*
- *RFC 1085 - ISO Presentation Services on Top of the TCP/IP-based Internets.*
- *RFC 1086 - ISO-TP0 Bridge between TCP and X.25.*
- *RFC 1090 - SMTP on X.25.*
- *RFC 1161 - SNMP over OSI.*
- *RFC 1195 - Use of OSI IS-IS for Routing in TCP/IP and Dual Environments.*
- *RFC 1238 - CLNS MIB for Use with Connectionless Network Protocol (ISO 8473) and End System to Intermediate System (ISO 9542).*

- *RFC 1240 - OSI Connectionless Transport Services on top of UDP: Version 1.*

- *RFC 1308 - Executive Introduction to Directory Services using the X.500 Protocol.*

- *RFC 1309 - Technical Overview of Directory Services using the X.500 Protocol.*

- *RFC 1327 - Mapping between X.400 (1988)/ISO 10021 and RFC 822.*

- *RFC 1328 - X.400 1988 to 1984 Downgrading.*

- *RFC 1330 - ESCC X.500/X.400 Task Force. Recommendations for the Phase I Deployment of OSI Directory Services (X.500) and OSI Message Handling Services (X.400) within the ESnet Community.*

- *RFC 1430 - A Strategic Plan for Deploying an Internet X.500 Directory Service.*

- *RFC 1487 - X.500 Lightweight Directory Access Protocol.*

- *RFC 1488 - The X.500 String Representation of Standard Attribute Syntaxes.*

- *RFC 1491 - A Survey of Advanced Usages of X.500.*

- *RFC 1562 - Naming Guidelines for the AARNet X.500 Directory Service.*

- *RFC 1567 - X.500 Directory Monitoring MIB.*

- *RFC 1608 - Representing IP Information in the X.500 Directory.*

- *RFC 1609 - Charting Networks in the X.500 Directory.*

- *RFC 1617 - Naming and Structuring Guidelines for X.500 Directory Pilots.*

- *RFC 1629 - Guidelines for OSI NSAP Allocation in the Internet.*

- *RFC 1632 - A Revised Catalog of Available X.500 Implementations.*

- *RFC 1684 - Introduction to White Pages Services based on X.500.*

- *RFC 1706 - DNS NSAP Resource Records.*

- *RFC 1729 - Using the Z39.50 Information Retrieval Protocol in the Internet Environment.*

- *RFC 1781 - Using the OSI Directory to Achieve User Friendly Naming.*

## 2.14.3  TCP/IP and OSI Coexistence Considerations

If your goal is TCP/IP-OSI coexistence, with an eye toward eventually going to pure OSI, you basically have five choices, which fall into two general categories: protocol-based and services-based.

Protocol-based approaches include dual stacks, application-layer gateways and transport-layer gateways. Services-based approaches include transport-service bridges and network tunnels.

### 2.14.3.1  Dual Stacks - The Simple Approach

The simplest way to integrate TCP/IP and OSI is to put both protocol stacks in every machine on the network.

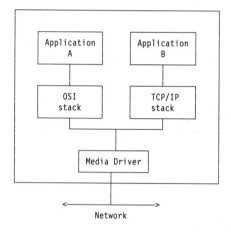

*Figure*   *2-72.  Dual Stacks*

Although this is a relatively straightforward approach, it involves a fundamental drawback: two networks will be running over the same set of wires, but the two sets of protocol cannot interoperate. Users are forced to choose between them. This disadvantage of having two separate networks can be an advantage. Those users who want to use TCP/IP can use TCP/IP, those who want to use OSI can use OSI. Another advantage is that an existing TCP/IP network will not be disturbed. But, dual stacks are memory-intensive, and they have to be put on every machine on the TCP/IP-OSI networks.

### 2.14.3.2  Application-Layer Gateways - The DoD Approach

This approach eliminates a major drawback of dual stacks (lack of application internetworking). The application-layer gateways convert protocol data units (PDU) from one stack's application protocol to the other's. With application-layer gateways it is possible to communicate from any TCP/IP system to any OSI system. It is not necessary to choose between protocols, because either application protocol will work on either stack.

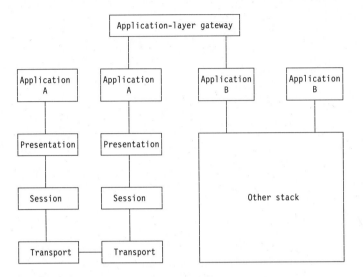

**Figure  2-73.** *Application-Layer Gateway Node*

Another advantage of application-layer gateways is that you do not have to add anything to, or otherwise modify, the end systems. This is because the application-layer gateway (which includes both protocol stacks) sits between the systems and handles all of the protocol conversion. But you will often lose functionality in the conversion from one application protocol to another because of imperfect mapping between the two protocols, mainly when going from OSI to TCP/IP applications. This is because OSI applications have richer functionalities. Another disadvantage of application-layer gateways is that they produce bottlenecks that will cause performance degradation if your gateway is not powerful enough.

## 2.14.3.3 Transport-Layer Gateways - The Wrong Approach

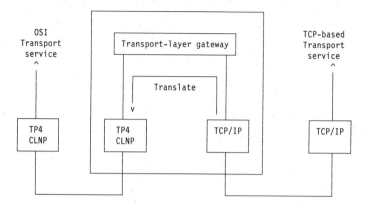

*Figure   2-74.* *Transport-Layer Gateway Node*

CLNP stands for *ConnectionLess Network Protocol* (see figure above).

If you have an environment with the TCP transport protocol on one side and the OSI TP4 transport protocol on the other, you need a software mechanism that dynamically translates TCP packets into TP4 packets.  This approach is considered to be wrong because no applications support TCP on one end and TP4 on the other, and because the addresses change on either part of the gateway, which involves loss of directories services.

The three approaches examined so far focus on protocol conversion.  However, it is possible to virtually ignore the protocol itself and to concentrate on emulating services. This is where transport-service bridges and network tunnels come into play.

## 2.14.3.4 Transport-Service Bridges - The ISODE Approach

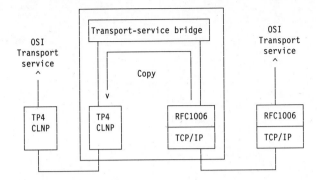

*Figure* **2-75.** *Transport-Service Bridge Node*

ISODE stands for *International Standards Organization Development Environment*. It is a publicly available collection of library routines and programs that implement OSI upper-layer services.

In a TCP-to-TP4 example, a transport-service bridge would make the TCP service look like a TP4 service. You accomplish this by emulating the TP4 service. With transport-service bridges you can run OSI applications over TCP/IP networks. One advantage of this approach is that you can use just one application protocol-OSI. Only the underlying layers need change between the two environments. A transport-service bridge is essentially a router that copies PDUs, as opposed to translating them. RFC 1006 defines the way to produce OSI transport services on top of TCP. The main disadvantage of this approach is that you do not have end-to-end (source to destination) checksum. In the example of TCP-to-TP4 environment, you have a TCP checksum on the source side of the transport-service bridge and a TP4 checksum on the destination side. Like gateways, transport-service bridges introduce a single point of failure. You can use transport-service bridges not only for TCP/IP-to-OSI implementations but also for OSI-to-OSI integration jobs. For example, OSI includes different transport protocols, such as TP0 for wide area networks and TP4 for local area networks. Transport-service bridges are viable candidates for linking those different OSI transports.

## 2.14.3.5 Network Tunnels - The Difficult Approach

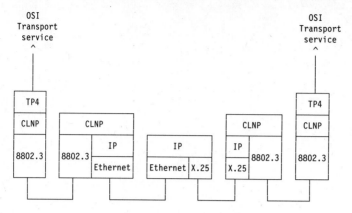

*Figure   2-76. Network Tunnels*

This approach eliminates the single point of failure and gives you end-to-end checksums. Network tunnels are one level down from the transport-service bridge approach. Instead of transport-service emulation, they use packet-level service emulation. Network tunnels operate at the network layer instead of at the transport layer.  They encapsulate OSI CLNP packets in IP packets and run them over IP networks. Network tunnels are essentially CLNP routers.

Network tunnels provide end-to-end checksums, a high degree of transparency, but they require OSI CLNP-based networks and are difficult to implement.

# 2.15  Data Link Switching: Switch-to-Switch Protocol

Data Link Switching (DLSw) was issued by IBM in March 1993 and is documented in RFC number 1795.  Its state is informational.

## 2.15.1  Introduction

Data Link Switching is a forwarding mechanism for the IBM SNA and IBM NetBIOS protocols. It does not provide full routing, but instead provides switching at the data link layer and encapsulation in TCP/IP for transport over the Internet. This Switch-to-Switch Protocol (SSP) is used between IBM 6611 Network Processors and/or IBM 2210 Nways Multiprotocol Routers. Routers of other vendors can participate if they comply to the above RFC or without DLSw capability as intermediate routers because the DLSw connection exists only between the two end routers.

## 2.15.2  Functional Description

DLSw was developed to provide support for SNA and NetBIOS in multiprotocol routers. Since SNA and NetBIOS are basically connection-oriented protocols, the data link control procedure that they use on the LAN is IEEE 802.2 Logical Link Control (LLC) Type 2.  DLSw also accommodates SNA protocols over WAN links via the SDLC protocol.

IEEE 802.2 LLC Type 2 was designed with the assumption that the network transit delay would be small and predictable (for example a local LAN).  Therefore LLC uses a fixed timer for detecting lost frames. When bridging is used over wide area lines (especially at lower speeds), the network delay is larger and can vary greatly based upon congestion. When the delay exceeds the timeout value LLC attempts to retransmit.  If the frame is not actually lost, only delayed, it is possible for the LLC Type 2 procedures to become confused, and as a result, the link is eventually taken down.

Given the use of LLC Type 2 services, DLSw addresses the following bridging problems:

- DLC timeouts
- DLC acknowledgments over the WAN
- Flow and congestion control
- Broadcast control of search packets
- Source-route bridging hop count limits

NetBIOS also makes extensive use of datagram services that use LLC Type 1. In this case, DLSw addresses the last two problems in the above list.  The principal difference between DLSw and bridging is that DLS terminates the data link control whereas bridging does not.  Figure  2-77 on page  2-126 illustrates this difference based upon two end systems operating with LLC Type 2 services.

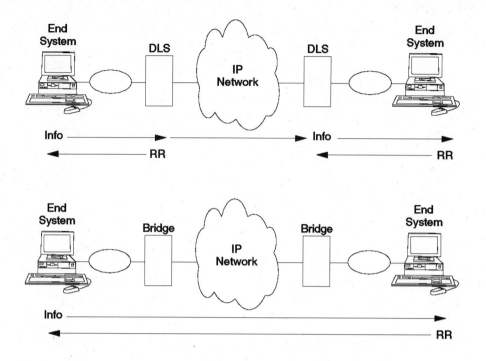

***Figure   2-77.*** *DLSw Compared to Bridging*

In traditional bridging, the data link control is end-to-end. DLSw terminates the LLC Type 2 connection at the switch.  This means that the LLC Type 2 connections do not cross the wide area network. The DLS multiplexes LLC connections onto a TCP connection to another DLS. Therefore, the LLC connections at each end are totally independent of each other. It is the responsibility of the data link switch to deliver frames that it has received from an LLC connection to the other end. TCP is used between the data link switches to guarantee delivery of frames.

As a result of this design, LLC timeouts are limited to the local LAN (for example they do not traverse the wide area). Also, the LLC Type 2 acknowledgments (RRs) do not traverse the WAN, thereby reducing traffic across the wide area links. For SDLC links, polling and poll response occurs locally, not over the WAN. Broadcast of search frames is controlled by the data link switches once the location of a target system is discovered. Finally, the switches can now apply back pressure to the end systems to provide flow and congestion control.

DLSw uses LAN addressing to set up connections between SNA systems. SDLC attached devices are defined with MAC addresses to enable them to communicate with LAN-attached devices. For NetBIOS systems, DLSw uses the NetBIOS name to forward datagrams and to set up connections for NetBIOS sessions. For circuit establishment, SNA systems send TEST (or in some cases, XID) frames to the null (x'00') SAP. NetBIOS systems have an address resolution procedure, based upon the Name Query and Name Recognized frames, that is used to establish an end-to-end circuit.

Since DLSw may be implemented in multiprotocol routers, there may be situations where both bridging and switching are enabled. SNA frames can be identified by their link SAP. Typical SAP values for SNA are x'04', x'08', and x'0C'. NetBIOS always uses a link SAP value of x'F0'.

For further details please refer to *RFC 1795*.

# 2.16  IP: The Next Generation (IPng)

The Internet has grown extremely rapidly in recent years, and by December 1994 it comprised over 32,000 networks connecting over 3.8 million computers in more than 90 countries. Since a 32-bit address field provides for over 4 billion possible addresses, it would seem that the IP addressing scheme is more than adequate to the task of addressing all of the hosts on the internet since there appears to be room for a thousand-fold increase before the IP addressing scheme is completely filled. Unfortunately, this is not the case, for a number of reasons, including the following:

- The IP address is divided into a network number and a local part which is administered separately. Although the address space within a network may be very sparsely filled, as far as the effective IP address space is concerned, if a network number is used then all addresses within that network are used.

- The address space for networks is structured into Class A, B and C networks of differing sizes, and the space within each needs to be considered separately.

- The IP addressing model requires that unique network numbers be assigned to all IP networks whether or not they are actually connected to the Internet.

- Growth of TCP/IP usage into new areas could result in a rapid explosion of the number of required IP addresses. For example, widespread use of TCP/IP for interconnecting electronic point-of-sale terminals or for cable television receivers would enormously increase the number of IP hosts.

- The current model of IP addressing with a single IP address for each (non-routing) host might change in the future (see *RFC 1681 − On Many Addresses per Host* for a discussion of some potential drivers for such a change).

These factors mean that the address space is much more constrained than our simple analysis would indicate. This problem is called *IP Address Exhaustion*. Methods of relieving this problem are already being employed (see the discussion beginning with 2.2.5, "The IP Address Exhaustion Problem" on page 2-21) but eventually, the present IP address space will be exhausted. The Internet Engineering Task Force (IETF) has a working group on *Address Lifetime Expectations (ALE)* with the express purpose of providing estimates of when exhaustion of the IP will become an intractable problem, and current estimates (as reported in the ALE working group minutes for December 1994) are that the IP address space will be exhausted at some point between 2005 and 2011. Before this happens, a replacement for the current version of IP will be required. Since there is also the possibility that a change in the usage trends of IP addresses could bring this forward, a replacement may need to be deployed by the turn of the century. This replacement is referred to as *IP: The Next Generation (IPng)*. When discussing IPng, the current version of IP (version 4) is referred to as *IPv4*. The responsibility for the decision on the final form of IPng lies with the *IPng Directorate*. There are a number of other IPng-related working groups: *IPng Requirements (IPNGREQ)*, *Transition and Co-existence including Testing (TACIT)* and one group for each of the proposed candidates for IPng. These groups are all temporary and are expected to disband or to be merged with other working groups in other areas when the IPng definition process has completed.

## 2.16.1 The Requirements for IPng

In July 1994, at an IETF meeting in Toronto, the IPng Area Directors of the IETF presented *RFC 1752 — The Recommendation for the IP Next Generation Protocol*. The recommendation was approved by the IETF in November 1994 and made a *proposed standard*.

These events were the culmination of much work and discussion which involved many interested parties. In this section we will look at crucial stages in getting to this point in the development of the IPng standard.

The IPng directorate published *RFC 1550 — IP: The Next Generation (IPng) White Paper Solicitation* requesting requirements for IPng. The important IPng requirements are summarized here:

- A dramatically larger address space: at least $10^9$ networks, preferably $10^{12}$; and at least $10^{12}$ hosts, preferably $10^{15}$. This would allow dramatic increases in IP address usage and at the same time leave the address space sparsely populated allowing IPng addresses to have more structure than is possible with IPv4.

- IPng should allow encapsulation of its own or other protocols' packets.

- IPng should add classes of service to distinguish types of data being transmitted, such as isochronous traffic like real-time audio and video.

- IPng must provide multicast addressing in a form which is more fully integrated with the rest of the protocol suite than the present implementation.

- IPng must provide authentication and encryption.

- IPng should preserve the virtues of IPv4: robustness, independence from the physical network characteristics, high performance, flexible topology, extensibility, datagram service, globally unique addressing, a built-in control protocol and freely available standards.

- The implementation of IPng must involve a simple transition plan.

- IPng must coexist with IPv4.

## 2.16.2  IPng Candidates

There were three main proposals for IPng which are described briefly below:

### 2.16.2.1  Common Architecture for the Internet (CATNIP)

CATNIP is a development of an older protocol (TP/IX) that integrates IPv4, Novell IPX and OSI Connectionless Networking Protocol (CLNP) and provides a common infrastructure. It is closest in design to CLNP and emphasizes ease of interoperability with existing implementations of all three. The CATNIP packet contains all of the information required by any of the three protocols in a compressed format using a packet header of 16 bytes or more. CATNIP uses a variable length address. Existing IPv4 addresses are mapped to 7-byte addresses of which the last 4 bytes are the IPv4 address. Existing IPv4 hosts would be limited to interoperating with CATNIP hosts with addresses in this form.

CATNIP is described in *RFC 1707 — CATNIP: Common Architecture for the Internet.*

### 2.16.2.2  TCP and UDP with Bigger Addresses (TUBA)

TUBA is also based on CLNP; simply put, CLNP replaces IPv4 in the TCP/IP protocol stack. It emphasises multiprotocol internets. Transition between IPv4 and IPng is done using a dual stack approach. The protocol stack has two independent internetwork layers and when attempting to communicate with another host, a dual stack host queries the Domain Name System for both the IP address and the *Network Service Access Point (NSAP)* that is the CLNP equivalent. If the Domain Name System returns both the IP address and the NSAP, the hosts communicate with CLNP as the internetwork protocol.

TUBA is described in *RFC 1347 — TCP and UDP with Bigger Addresses (TUBA), A Simple Proposal for Internet Addressing and Routing.* See also *RFC 1526 — Assignment of System Identifiers for TUBA/CLNP Hosts* and *RFC 1561 — Use of ISO CLNP in TUBA Environments.*

### 2.16.2.3 Simple Internet Protocol Plus (SIPP)

SIPP is a combination of the work of three earlier IETF working groups developing an IPng.

**IP Address Encapsulation (IPAE)**

> IPAE involved extensions to IPv4 to carry longer addresses, and how the transition between the two would be achieved.

**Simple Internet Protocol (SIP)**

> SIP was an IPv4 replacement with a simplified IP header and 64-bit addressing. SIP merged with IPAE taking the SIP header and the IPAE transition mechanisms.

**"P" Internet Protocol (Pip)**

> Pip was a brand new internet protocol designed with a wide range of advanced features and using variable length addressing. Pip merged with SIP when it was realized that the best features of Pip could be used with the SIP 64-bit addressing scheme and the IPAE transition mechanisms.

SIPP is an evolutionary development of IPv4. It emphasizes efficiency of operation over a wide range of network types and ease of interoperability. In addition to 64-bit addressing it includes a concept of extended addresses by using a routing option: the effective address length can be any multiple of 64 bits.

SIPP is described in *RFC 1710 — Simple Internet Protocol Plus White Paper.*

## 2.16.3  IP Version 6 (IPv6)

The IPng Directorate concluded that all three of these proposals (CATNIP, TUBA and SIPP) were insufficient to meet the accepted list of requirements, but that SIPP, as defined in RFC 1710, came closest. After some changes to the original proposal, for instance the use of 128-bit addresses instead of 64-bit ones, the IPng Directorate decided that SIPP was a suitable base for IPng and that features from the other proposals would be added to it to fulfill the remaining IPng requirements. The proposed solution is called *IP Version 6 (IPv6).*

The reader should be aware that the definition of IPv6 is still in progress, and the information presented here is based on Internet-Draft documents.[6]

---

6  Internet-Drafts may be obtained using anonymous FTP from directory Internet-Drafts from a number of sites, including ds.internic.net. The status of draft documents can be found in the file 1id-abstracts.txt in the same directory.

**Terminology:**   IPv6 uses the term *packet* rather than *datagram*, but the meaning is the
same, although the formats are different.

IPv6 introduces a new term, *node*, for a system running IPv6, that is, a host or a
router.  An IPv6 host is a node which does not forward IPv6 packets which are
not explicitly addressed to it.  A router is, as in IPv4, a node which does forward
IP packets not addressed to it.

The basic features of IPv6 as defined at the time of writing are described in the following
sections.

## 2.16.3.1  The IPv6 Header format

IPv6 increases the length of the IP header from 20 bytes to 40 bytes.  The IPv6 header
contains two 16-byte addresses (source and destination) preceded by 8 bytes of control
information as shown in Figure  2-78.  The IPv4 header (see Figure  2-15 on page  2-38)
has two 4-byte addresses preceded by 12 bytes of control information and possibly
followed by option data.  The reduction of the control information and the elimination of
options in the header are intended to optimize the processing of the majority of IP
datagrams (packets).  The infrequently used fields which have been removed from the
header are moved to optional extension headers.

```
      0         8        16        24     31
    ┌──────┬──────────────────────────────────┐
    │ Vers │          Flow Label              │
    ├──────┴─────────────────┬──────────┬──────┤
    │    Payload Length      │Next Header│Hop Limit│
    ├────────────────────────┴──────────┴──────┤
    │                                           │
    │           Source Address                  │
    │             (16 bytes)                    │
    │                                           │
    ├───────────────────────────────────────────┤
    │                                           │
    │                                           │
    │         Destination Address               │
    │             (16 bytes)                    │
    │                                           │
    └───────────────────────────────────────────┘
```

*Figure*    *2-78. IPv6 Header*

*Vers*

         4-bit Internet Protocol version number: 6.

*Flow Label*

         28-bit field. See 2.16.3.5, Flow Labels below.

*Payload Length*

         The length of the packet in bytes (excluding this header) encoded as a 16-bit unsigned integer. If length is greater than 64KB this field is 0 and an option header gives the true length.

*Next Header*

         Indicates the type of header immediately following this header. This is the same as the protocol number used in IPv4 (see the list in 2.3, "Internet Protocol (IP)" on page 2-36). The next header field is also used to indicate the presence of extension headers, which provide the mechanism for appending optional information to the IPv6 packet. The following values are important in addition to those mentioned for IPv4.

         *41*   IPv6 Header
         *43*   IPv6 Routing Header
         *44*   IPv6 Fragment Header
         *51*   IPv6 Authentication Header
         *?*    IPv6 End-to-End Options Header
         *?*    IPv6 ICMP Packet

         The values, except for the last two (which were undecided at the time of writing) are given in *STD 2 — Assigned Internet Numbers*, although the current edition of STD 2 at the time of writing (RFC 1700) mentions either

SIP or SIPP as the protocol. As noted above, IPv6 is a development of these two protocols.

The different types of extension header are discussed briefly below.

*Hop Limit*

This is the IPv4 TTL field but now it is measured in hops and not seconds. It was changed for two reasons:

- IP normally forwards datagrams at faster than one hop per second and the TTL field is always decremented on each hop, so in practice it is measured in hops and not seconds.

- Many IP implementations do not expire outstanding datagrams on the basis of elapsed time.

*Source Address*

A 128-bit address. IPv6 addresses are discussed in 2.16.3.4, "IPv6 Addresses" on page 2-139.

*Destination Address*

A 128-bit address. IPv6 addresses are discussed in 2.16.3.4, "IPv6 Addresses" on page 2-139.

A comparison between the IPv4 and IPv6 header formats will show that a number of IPv4 header fields have no direct equivalents in the IPv6 header.

*Type of Service*

Type of service issues in IPv6 will be handled using the *flow* concept, described in 2.16.3.5, "Flow Labels" on page 2-139.

*Identification, Fragmentation Flags and Fragment Offset*

Fragmented packets have an extension header rather than fragmentation information in the IPv6 header. This reduces the size of the basic IPv6 header. Since higher-level protocols, particularly TCP, tend to avoid fragmentation of datagrams, this reduces the IPv6 header overhead for the normal case. As noted below, IPv6 does not fragment packets en route to their destinations, only at the source.

*Header Checksum*

Because transport protocols implement checksums, and because IPv6 includes an optional authentication header which can also be used to ensure integrity, IPv6 does *not* provide checksum monitoring of IP packets.

Both TCP and UDP include a pseudo-IP header in the checksums they use, so in these cases, the IP header in IPv4 is being checked twice.

TCP and UDP, and any other protocols using the same checksum mechanisms running over IPv6 will continue to use a pseudo-IP header although, obviously, the format of the pseudo-IPv6 header will be different from the pseudo-IPv4 header. ICMP and IGMP and any other protocols which do not use a pseudo-IP header over IPv4 will use a pseudo-IPv6 header in their checksums.

*Options*

All optional values associated with IPv6 packets are contained in extension headers ensuring that the basic IP header is always the same size.

### 2.16.3.2  Packet Sizes

All IPv6 nodes are expected to dynamically determine the maximum transmission unit (MTU) supported by all links along a path (as described in *RFC 1191 — Path MTU Discovery*) and source nodes will only send packets which do not exceed the Path MTU. IPv6 routers will therefore not have to fragment packets in the middle of multihop routes and allow much more efficient use of paths which traverse diverse physical transmission media. It is currently proposed that IPv6 require that every link supports an MTU of 576 bytes, but this value, like all other parts of the IPv6 specification at the time of writing, is subject to change.

### 2.16.3.3  Extension Headers

Extension headers are placed between the IPv6 packet header and the data intended for the higher level protocol. They are counted as part of the payload length. Each header has an 8-bit *Next Header field* like that in the IPv6 header which identifies the type of the following header. All extensions defined at the time of writing have the Next Header field as the first byte of the header. The length of each header, which is always a multiple of 8 bytes, is encoded later in the header in a format specific to that header type. There are a limited number of IPv6 extension headers, any or all of which may be present once (and once only) in the IPv6 packet. IPv6 nodes which originate packets are required to place extension headers in a specific order although IPv6 nodes which receive packets are not required to verify that this is the case. The different types of extension header, as defined at the time of writing, are discussed briefly below. When the Next Header field contains a value other than one for an extension headers, this indicates the end of the IPv6 headers and the start of the higher-level protocol data.

IPv6 allows for encapsulation of IPv6 within IPv6 ("tunneling"). This is done with a Next Header value of 41 (IPv6). The encapsulated IPv6 packet may have its own extension headers. Because the size of a packet is calculated by the originating node to match the Path MTU, IPv6 routers should not add extension headers to a packet but instead should encapsulate the received packet within an IPv6 packet of their own making (which may be fragmented if necessary).

With the exception of the Hop-by-Hop header (which must immediately follow the IP header if present), extension headers are not processed by any route on the packet's path except the final one. Note that, as in IPv4, when a source route is included, the packet's destination IP address is actually the next node in the source route, and not the true destination, so this statement remains true but the word path means the path to the next destination listed in the source route.

IPv6 uses a common format called the *Type-Length-Value (TLV)* format for variable length fields which are found in the Hop-by-Hop and End-to-End option headers. The option has a 2-byte header followed by the option data.

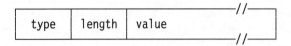

*Figure* **2-79.** *IPv6 Type-Length-Value Option Format*

*Type*        The type of the option. The option types all have a common format:

```
 0   1   2   3   4   5   6   7
┌───────┬───┬───────────────────┐
│  xx   │ y │      zzzzz         │
└───────┴───┴───────────────────┘
```

   *xx*    A 2-bit number indicating how an IPv6 node which does not recognize the option should treat it.

   *0* skip the option and continue

   *1* discard the packet quietly

   *2* discard the packet and inform the sender with an ICMP Unrecognized Type message

   *3* discard the packet and inform the sender with an ICMP Unrecognized Type message unless the destination address is a multicast address

   *y*    This bit has a specific meaning only for the Hop-by-Hop header. If set, it indicates that the value of the option may change en route and therefore it should be excluded from any integrity calculations performed on the packet. Since only hop-by-hop headers are examined by intermediate routers, only hop-by-hop options can be validly changed en route.

   *zzzzz*    The remaining bits define the option.

*Length*    The length of the option value field in bytes.

*Value*    The value of the option. This is dependent on the type.

To optimize the performance of IPv6 implementations, individual options are aligned so that multi-byte values are positioned on their natural boundaries. In many cases, this will result in the option headers being longer than otherwise necessary, but should allow nodes to process datagrams more quickly. To allow this alignment, all IPv6 implementations must recognize two padding options:

*Pad1*  A X′00′ byte used for padding a single byte. Longer padding sequences should be done with the PadN option.

*PadN*  An option in the TLV format described above. Its value is X′01′. The length byte gives the number of bytes of padding after the minimum two that are required.

The different extension headers are described (in the order in which they must be placed in the IPv6 packet) in the following sections.

**Hop-by-Hop Header:**  A Hop-by-Hop header contains options which must be examined by every node the packet traverses as well as the destination node. It must immediately follow the IPv6 header if present and is identified by the special value 0 in the Next Header field of the IPv6 header. This value is not a Protocol number but a special case to identify this unique type of extension header and the value 0 remains reserved in STD 2.

Initially, no Hop-by-Hop options (other than the pad options) are defined.

**Routing Header:**  The routing header is identified by the value 43 in the preceding Next Header field. It has its next header field as the first byte and a single byte routing type as the second. The only type defined initially is Loose Source Routing, which operates in the same way as IPv4.

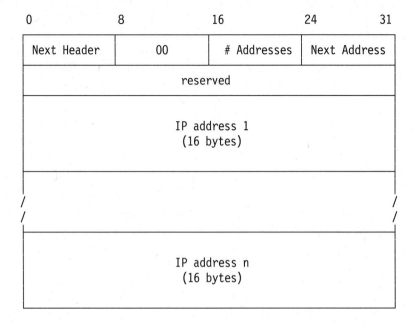

**Figure 2-80.** *IPv6 Loose Source Routing Header*

*Next Header* The type of next header after this one.

*00* Indicates loose source routing.

*#Addresses* Indicates the number of entries as an 8-bit unsigned integer. Compare this with IPv4 which uses a length byte to calculate the number of entries in the option field.

*Next Address* Index of the next address as an 8-bit unsigned integer to be processed (initialized to 0 by the originator) integer. Compare this with IPv4, which uses a pointer offset from the start of the source routing option.

*reserved* Initialized to zero for transmission and ignored on reception. This ensures that the header is a multiple of 16 bytes long. It does not ensure that addresses fall on 16-byte boundaries. IPv6 does not take account of alignment of fields longer than 8 bytes.

*Address n* A series of 16-byte IPv6 addresses which comprise the source route.

**Fragment Header:** The fragment header is identified by the value 44 in the preceding Next Header field.

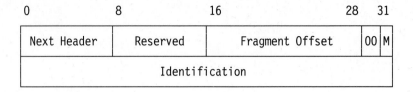

*Figure*  *2-81. IPv6 Fragment Header*

*Next Header* The type of next header after this one.

*reserved*     Initialized to zero for transmission and ignored on reception.

*Fragment Offset* A 13-bit unsigned integer giving the offset of the following payload
       relative to the beginning of the original unfragmented payload in 8-byte
       units. The field is a 13-bit count of 8-byte units instead of a 16-bit byte
       count because the payload is always fragmented on 8-byte boundaries, so
       the low order three bits of the byte offset are always zero.

*00*            Initialized to zero for transmission and ignored on reception.

*M*             More flag. If set it indicates that this is not the last fragment.

*Identification* Used to identify packets which are fragments of the same datagram. This
       is very similar to the IPv4 Identifier field, but it is twice as wide.

**Authentication Header:**   The authentication header is identified by the value 51 in
the preceding Next Header field.

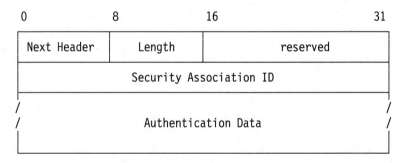

*Figure*  *2-82. IPv6 Fragment Header*

*Next Header*
       The type of next header after this one.

*Length*
       The length of the authentication data in 8-byte units.

*reserved*

Initialized to zero for transmission and ignored on reception.

*Security Association ID*

Used to identify the recipient (with the destination IP address).

*Authentication Data*

Dependent on the authentication algorithm in use. All IPv6 nodes will support a minimum authentication algorithm.

**End-to-End Header:** This has the same format as the Hop-by-Hop header, but it is only examined by the target node. Since it follows the routing header this is true regardless of any routing options which may be in effect. Again, only the padding options are initially specified. The value for the preceding Next Header field has not yet been defined.

## 2.16.3.4  IPv6 Addresses

IPv6 provides for an address of 128 bits in length. Unlike IPv4 which has a strictly codified form based on the address class indicated by the high-order bits of the address, IPv6 addresses are not structured in this way. Instead, they are designed to be used with Classless InterDomain Routing (CIDR) (see 2.2.7, "Classless Inter-Domain Routing (CIDR)" on page 2-26). The IPv6 address space is sufficiently large that it can encompass a wide range of existing and proposed address spaces. In keeping with the CIDR approach, the leading part of the IPv6 address, for example the first byte, would indicate the type of address. Such types would include a mapping of the current IPv4 address space to IPv6, OSI NSAPs, Novell IPX addresses and so on. Furthermore, the IPv6 routing header allows IP to encapsulate arbitrary addressing information in each packet. This could be used to extend the IPv6 scheme to address hypothetical systems which cannot be mapped to the IP address space. Given the length of the IPv6 address field, it is unlikely that this will be necessary in the near future.

## 2.16.3.5  Flow Labels

IPv6 introduces the concept of a *flow* which is a series of related packets from a source to a destination which requires a particular type of handling by the intervening routers, for example "real-time" service. The nature of that handling can either be conveyed by options attached to the datagrams (that is, by using the IPv6 Hop-by-Hop options header) or by a separate protocol.

Each IPv6 packet contains a flow label which is a 28-bit field:

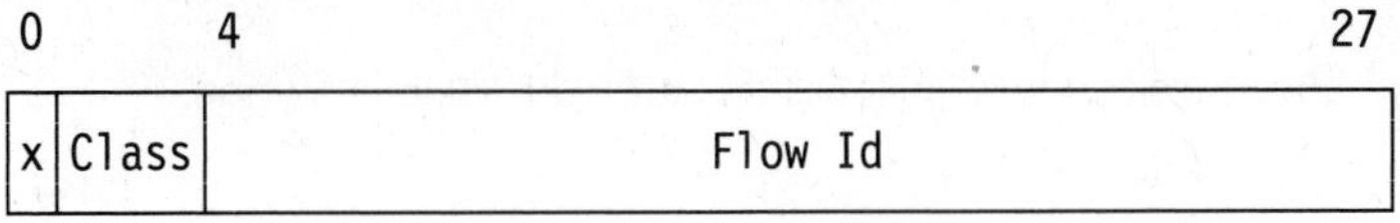

```
 0        4                                                      27
 ┌─┬─────┬──────────────────────────────────────────────────────┐
 │x│Class│                     Flow Id                          │
 └─┴─────┴──────────────────────────────────────────────────────┘
```

*Figure*   *2-83. IPv6 Flow Label*

*x*        A flag bit indicating whether the traffic is flow-controlled. If set, the traffic is not flow-controlled (there is no feedback from the recipients) otherwise there is flow control (for example the packets contain TCP segments).

*Class*    A 3-bit number identifying the traffic type. Although the protocol used to control the flow may redefine the values, the following recommended values are defined for flow-controlled traffic:

           *0* uncharacterized traffic

           *1* "filler" traffic

           *2* unattended data transfer, such as E-mail

           *3* reserved

           *4* attended bulk transfer, such as FTP

           *5* reserved

           *6* interactive traffic, such as TELNET

           *7* internet control traffic, such as routing protocols

           For non-flow controlled traffic, the class value is used as a priority when there is a problem. The lower the class value, the less concerned the sender is that the packet reaches its destination. For example, with a suitable protocol for high fidelity real-time video transport, loss of some packets may have a negligible effect on the viewer's perception compared with a backlog of packets or the arrival of packets in the wrong order.

*Flow ID*  A unique pseudo-random 24-bit number assigned to a flow by the source node. The value of zero is used for traffic which is not assigned to a flow. The randomness is needed to allow routers to employ a sequence of bits from the flow ID as a hash key.

## 2.16.3.6 Simple Internet Transition (SIT)

The techniques to be employed to convert the Internet from IPv4 to IPv6 are collectively termed *Simple Internet Transition (SIT)*. The emphasis in SIT is the ease of the process from the network user or operator's point of view. Compatibility features ensure investment protection for current IPv4 users, interoperability features ensure that the transition is gradual and does not impact the Internet's functionality. The transition employs the following techniques:

- Dual-stack IP implementations for hosts and routers which must interoperate between IPv4 and IPv6.

- Imbedding of IPv4 addresses in IPv6 addresses, IPv6 hosts will be assigned addresses which are interoperable with IPv4, and IPv4 host addresses will be mapped to IPv6.

- An IPv6-over-IPv4 tunneling mechanism.

The final technique is intended for use when the implementation of IPv6 is well advanced. It allows the implementation of IPv6-only nodes. Such nodes must exist within fully IPv6-capable networks.

- IPv4/IPv6 header translation by routers between IPv4 and IPv6 networks.

The techniques are also adaptable to other protocols, notably CLNP and IPX which have similar internetwork layer semantics and which have addressing schemes which can be mapped easily to a part of the IPv6 address space.

The transition model envisages different organizations migrating independently and in two phases. The first phase is a transition to a dual IPv6/IPv4 infrastructure. The second, which is *not* mandatory, is to an IPv6-only infrastructure. The second stage for any given site is only complete when that site no longer requires interoperability with IPv4. When this is complete, the restrictions imposed by the transition are removed.

The first stage is the easy one of the two, since all nodes are IPv4 capable. The second stage which involves IPv6-only areas in a network, requires more effort, particularly in the planning and deployment of routers which will perform the necessary header translation for IPv6-only nodes to interoperate with IPv4-only nodes.

**Deployment of IPv6/IPv4 nodes:** This involves the replacement of IPv4-only software with IPv6/IPv4 capable software. This should happen as part of normal product release cycles, and existing IPv4 nodes would continue to run in "IPv4-compatibility" mode.

Conceptually, the dual stack model envisages a doubling-up of the protocols in the internetwork layer only. However, related changes are obviously needed in all transport-layer protocols to operate using either stack, and possibly in applications if they are to exploit IPv6 capabilities, such as longer addresses.

## IPv4/IPv6 Addressing

**Notation:** IPv6 addresses are represented as a sequence of 4 hexadecimal digits (that is, 16-bit groups) separated by colons. For brevity, the sequence 0000 is contracted to 0. IPv6 addresses which are to be mapped to IPv4 are best represented as a 96-bit IPv6 prefix in a colon delimited form followed by a 32-bit IPv4 address in dotted decimal, for example 0:0:0:0:0:ffff:9.180.214.114

Three types of IPv6 address are defined:

*IPv4-compatible IPv6 address*
> An address indicating an IPv6-capable node which has an address that can be mapped directly and uniquely to the IPv4 address space. It has the IP prefix 0:0:0:0:0:ffff. For example, 0:0:0:0:0:ffff:9.180.214.114

*IPv4-mapped IPv6 address*
> An IPv6 address indicating an IPv4-only node. It has the IP prefix 0:0:0:0:0:0. For example, 0:0:0:0:0:0:9.180.214.114

It is important to realize that IPv4-compatible and IPv4-mapped addresses use the same IPv4 address space. The prefix only indicates whether or note the node is IPv6-capable.

*IPv6-only address*
> An IPv6 address indicating an IPv6-capable node where the low-order 32 bits do not necessarily contain an IPv4 address. The high-order 96 bits are something other than 0:0:0:0:0:ffff or 0:0:0:0:0:0.

A new type of record is defined for the Domain Name System (DNS). The AAAA record indicates an IPv6 address. The records found in the DNS for a node depend on which protocols it is running.

- IPv4-only nodes have only A records containing IPv4 addresses in the DNS. This simplifies DNS administration and means that the default behavior is the compatible one: IPv6 nodes interpret the contents of the pre-IPv6 DNS as containing only IPv4 nodes. An IPv6-node can obtain the IPv6 address of any IPv4-only node in the DNS by prefixing it with the 96-bit prefix 0:0:0:0:0:0.

- IPv6-capable nodes which can interoperate with IPv4-only nodes have AAAA records containing IPv4-compatible IPv6 addresses and A records containing the equivalent IPv4 addresses.

- IPv6-capable nodes which cannot interoperate with IPv4-only nodes have only AAAA records containing IPv6-only addresses.

Because IPv6/IPv4 nodes make decisions about which protocols to use based on the type of IPv6-address that a destination has, the incorporation of AAAA records in the DNS is a prerequisite to using the DNS with IPv6. This does not imply that name servers must use an IPv6-capable protocol stack, just that they support an additional record type.

**Interoperability Summary:** Whether two nodes can interoperate depends upon their capabilities and their addresses:

- An IPv6-capable node with an IPv4-compatible address can interoperate directly with all other nodes.

- An IPv6-only node with an IPv4-compatible address can interoperate with all other nodes. However, it requires a router to translate IPv6 headers to IPv4 headers and vice versa in order to interoperate with IPv4 nodes.

- An IPv6-capable node with an IPv6-only address cannot interoperate with IPv4 nodes.

- An IPv4-only node can directly interoperate with IPv6/IPv4 nodes which have IPv4-compatible addresses.

- An IPv4-only node can interoperate with IPv6-only nodes which have IPv4-compatible addresses. However, it requires a router to translate IPv4 headers to IPv6 headers and vice versa.

- An IPv4-only node cannot interoperate with IPv6-capable nodes which have IPv6-only addresses.

**Topological Model:** It is possible to divide the entire routing topology of the Internet into areas in such a way that every area falls into at least one of these two types:

*IPv4-complete*
> Every subnet in the area has at least one IPv4-router attached.

*IPv6-complete*
> Every subnet in the area has at least one IPv6-router attached.

It is possible for areas to be both IPv4- and IPv6-complete, but the model is simpler if such areas are treated as one or the other. We use the following rules for the deployment of non dual-stack nodes:

- IPv4-only nodes may not be deployed in IPv6-complete areas.

- IPv6-only nodes may not be deployed in IPv6-complete areas.

- All routers connecting IPv4-complete areas to IPv6-complete areas must translate IPv4 headers destined for the IPv6-complete area into IPv6 headers, and vice versa.

**Note:** An IPv4-complete area does not mean that no IPv6 routing can be used in the area, just that IPv4 routing is used throughout the entire area. The converse is true of IPv6-complete areas.

As noted above, the deployment of header-translating routers is part of the second phase of the transition. Therefore, IPv6-complete areas are unlikely to appear in most organizations immediately. The drivers for the introduction of IPv6-complete areas are likely to be requirements for new facilities which require IPv6, or exhaustion of the IPv4 address space. Which of these is seen as more important will vary between organizations. For example, commercial organizations with large, long-established internal IPv4 networks are unlikely to be driven by the problem of IP address exhaustion unless they also have a problem with address space within their own networks. They will, however, be likely to invest in IPv6 deployment if new business-critical applications require facilities which are only available on IPv6 or if they require connectivity to other organizations who are using IPv6-only addresses.

**IPv6-over-IPv4 Tunneling:**   IPv6 packets are tunnelled over IPv4 very simply; the IPv6 packet is encapsulated in an IPv4 datagram (which may be fragmented).

There are two kinds of tunneling of IPv6 packets over IPv4 networks: automatic and configured.

***Automatic Tunneling:***   As the name implies, automatic tunneling is done whenever it is needed. The decision is made by an IPv6/IPv4 host which has a packet to send across an IPv4-complete area, and it follows the following rules:

- If the destination is an IPv4-mapped address, send the packet using IPv4 because the recipient is not IPv6-capable.

Otherwise:

- If the destination is on the same subnet, send it using IPv6 because the recipient is IPv6-capable.

- If the destination is not on the same subnet but there is at least one default router on the subnet which is IPv6-capable, or there is a route configured to an IPv6 router for that destination, then send it to that router using IPv6.

Otherwise:

- If the address is an IPv4-compatible address, send the packet using automatic IPv6-over-IPv4 tunnelling.

Otherwise:

- The destination is a node with an IPv6-only address which is connected via an IPv4-complete area which is not also IPv6-complete and the destination is therefore unreachable.

**Note:**   The IP address must be IPv4-compatible for tunneling to be used. IPv6-only addresses cannot be tunneled to because they cannot be addressed using IPv4. Packets from IPv6/IPv4 nodes to IPv4-mapped addresses are not tunnelled to because they refer to IPv4-only nodes.

The rules listed above emphasize the use of an IPv6 router in preference to a tunnel for three reasons:

- There is less overhead because there is no encapsulating IPv4 header.

- IPv6-only features are available.

- The IPv6 routing topology will be used when it is deployed in preference to the pre-existing IPv4 topology.

A node does not need to know whether it is attached to an IPv6-complete or an IPv4-complete area: it will always use an IPv6-router if one is configured on its subnet and will use tunneling if one is not (in which case it can infer that it is attached to an IPv4-complete area).

Automatic Tunneling may be either host-to-host, or it may be router-to-host. A source host will send an IPv6 packet to an IPv6 router if possible, but that router may not be able to do the same, and will have to perform automatic tunneling itself. Because of the preference for the use of IPv6 routers rather than tunneling, the tunnel will always be as "short" as possible. However, the tunnel will always extend all of the way to the destination host: because IPv6 uses the same hop-by-hop routing paradigm, a host cannot determine if the packet will eventually emerge into an IPv6-complete area before it reaches the destination host. In order to use a tunnel which does not extend all of the way to the recipient, configured tunneling must be used. There is one exception to this rule: as described in "Header Translation" on page 2-146, all tunnels terminate at routers which perform header translation.

The mechanism used for automatic tunneling is very simple.

- The encapsulating IPv4 datagram uses the low-order 32 bits of the IPv6 source and destination addresses to create the equivalent IPv4 addresses and sets the protocol number to 41 (IPv6).

- The receiving node's network interface layer identifies the incoming packets (or packets if the IPv4 datagram was fragmented) as belonging to IPv4 and passes them upwards to the IPv4 part of the dual IPv6/IPv4 internetwork layer.

- The IPv4 layer then receives the datagram in the normal way, re-assembling fragments if necessary, notes the protocol number of 41, then removes the IPv4 header and passes the original IPv6 packet "sideways" to the IPv6 part of the internetwork layer.

- The IPv6 code then processes the original packet as normal. Since the destination IPv6 address in the packet is the IPv6 address of the node (an IPv4-compatible address matching the IPv4 address used in the encapsulating IPv4 datagram) the packet is at its final destination. IPv6 then processes any extension headers as normal and then passes the packet's remaining payload to the next protocol listed in the last IPv6 header.

With one exception, described in "Header Translation" on page 2-146, intermediate IPv6/IPv4 routers never examine or process the contents of an encapsulated IPv6 packet. The IPv4 datagram is treated in exactly the same way as other IPv4 datagrams forwarded by an IPv6/IPv4 router.

***Configured Tunneling:*** Configured tunneling is used for host-router or router-router tunneling of IPv6-over-IPv4. The sending host or the forwarding router is configured so that the route as well as having a next hop also has a "tunnel end" address (which is always an IPv4-compatible address because it must be an IPv6/IPv4 host which is reachable from an IP-complete area). The process of encapsulation is the same as for automatic tunnelling except that the IPv4 destination address is not derived from the low-order 32 bits of the IPv6 destination address, but from the low-order 32 bits of the tunnel end. When the router at the end of the tunnel receives the IPv4 datagram, it processes it in exactly the same way as a node at the end of an automatic tunnel. When the original IPv6 packet is passed to the IPv6 layer in the router, it recognizes that it is not the destination, and the router forwards the packet on to the final destination as it would for any other IPv6 packet.

It is, of course, possible that after emerging from the tunnel, the IPv6 packet is tunnelled again by another router.

**Header Translation:** Header translation is required for IPv6-only nodes to interoperate with IPv4-only nodes. Because there is no requirement for any node to be IPv6-only, header translation is regarded as an optional part of SIT. Header translation is performed by IPv6/IPv4 routers on the boundaries between IPv6-complete areas and IPv4-complete areas. Traffic crossing such a boundary can be categorized in two ways. First, traffic is either:

*IPv4*
> Traffic from an IPv4-complete area entering an IPv6-complete area

or

*IPv6*
> Traffic from an IPv6-complete area entering an IPv4-complete area

Secondly, each of these types may be described as either:

*Terminating*
> Addressed to a node within the area

or

*Transit*
> Addressed to a node outside the area

Routers translating between IPv4 and IPv6 must, in addition to correctly mapping between the the fields in the two headers, select the correct form of IP addresses to use:

- IPv4 addresses are obtained by taking the low-order 32 bits of the IP address. If either the source or the destination IPv6 address is IPv6 only, the header cannot be translated.

- IPv6 source addresses are created by adding the 96-bit prefix 0:0:0:0:0:0 to the IPv4 address to generate an IPv4-mapped IPv6 address.

- IPv6 destination addresses are created by adding the 96-bit prefix 0:0:0:0:0:ffff to the IPv4 address to generate an IPv4-compatible IPv6 address for terminating traffic or the 96-bit prefix 0:0:0:0:0:0 generate an IPv4-mapped IPv6 address for transit traffic. Therefore, Header translators must know the extent of their attached IP-complete area.[7]

There is one special case: tunnelled IPv6 traffic, that is, IPv6 packets encapsulated in IPv4 datagrams. If header translators treated tunnelled IPv6 traffic in the same way as other IPv4 traffic, the result would be an IPv6 packet encapsulated in another IPv6 packet. Therefore, header translators inspect the protocol number of an IPv4 datagram, and if it is 41 (IPv6) they "decapsulate" the packet rather than translate the IPv4 header. In effect, header translators always terminate tunnels.

Because of this effect, it is not possible, in general, for an IPv6/IPv4 node to send a packet to an IPv6-capable node with an IPv6-only address by using a configured tunnel to an IPv6/IPv4 router in the same IPv6-complete area as the target destination. If this were done, the tunnel could intersect a transit IPv6-complete area and the packet would be decapsulated, terminating the tunnel. The raw IPv6 packet could not then cross an IPv4-complete area because of its IPv6-only destination address.

In order for an IPv6/IPv4 node to send a packet to an IPv6-only address via an IPv4-capable router in the same IPv6-complete area as the target destination, the packet must contain a IPv6 source route consisting of the IPv4-capable router and the IPv6-only destination. This packet has an IPv4-compatible destination address until it reaches the target IPv6-complete area, so it can be safely tunneled through IPv4 regardless of the topology.

**Symmetry of the SIT model:**   Although the topological model used by SIT is symmetrical, as is its classification of nodes as IPv4-only, IPv6-only and IPv6/IPv4, other aspects of the scheme are not symmetrical:

---

[7] Topologically, header translators, or other IPv6-capable routers, connected to multiple IPv6-complete areas have the effect of combining these areas into a single IPv6-complete area. The same applies to IPv4-complete areas as well.

- Although all IPv4 addresses have an IPv6 equivalent (IPv4-mapped or IPv4-compatible), the reverse is not true. There are IPv6-only addresses and hosts with these addresses cannot interoperate with IPv4.

- IPv6/IPv4 hosts will use IPv6 in preference to IPv4 if possible.

- SIT does not define a mechanism for IPv4-over-IPv6 tunnelling.

## 2.17 Summary

The following chart shows the layered model of the TCP/IP protocol suite and also indicates the application programming interfaces (API) available to the user.

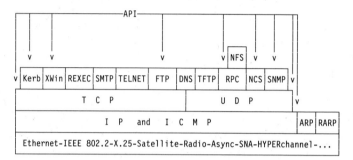

**Figure   2-84.** *TCP/IP Layered Model*

**Note:**  Remote Procedure Call uses both TCP and UDP. It has been placed upon UDP here since NFS only uses RPC over UDP.

**Note:**  ARP and RARP are only used on local area networks.


The IP/TCP/UDP socket API has been mentioned in 2.10, "Ports and Sockets" on page  2-81.  The other APIs will be explained in the next chapter:

- Kerberos (see 4.13, "Kerberos Authentication and Authorization System" on page  4-155)
- X Window (see 4.9, "X Window System" on page  4-118)
- FTP (see 4.4, "File Transfer Protocol (FTP)" on page  4-25)
- RPC (see 4.10, "Remote Procedure Call (RPC)" on page  4-129)
- NCS (see 4.11, "Network Computing System (NCS)" on page  4-136)
- SNMP DPI (see 4.14, "Network Management" on page  4-166)
- CICS Socket Interface (see 4.23.3, "CICS Socket Interface" on page  4-224).

# Chapter 3. Routing Protocols

One of the basic functions of IP is its ability to form connections between different physical networks. This is due to the flexibility of IP to use almost any physical network below it, and to the IP routing algorithm. A system which does this is termed a *router*, although the older term *IP gateway* is also used.

**Note:** In other sections of the book, we show the position of each protocol in the layered model of the TCP/IP protocol stack. The routing function is part of the internetwork layer, but the primary function of a routing protocol is to *exchange* routing information with other routers, and in this respect the protocols behave more like application protocols. The routing protocols described here use all three approaches to data transport: using UDP (for example RIP, described in 3.3.3, "Routing Information Protocol (RIP)" on page 3-17), TCP (see BGP in 3.4.2, "Border Gateway Protocol (BGP)" on page 3-52) and providing its own transport layer on top of IP (see OSPF in 3.3.4, "Open Shortest Path First Protocol (OSPF) Version 2" on page 3-25). Therefore, we shall not attempt to represent the position of these protocols in the protocol stack with a diagram as we do with the other protocols.

## 3.1 Basic IP Routing

The fundamental function for routers is present in *all* IP implementations:

> An *incoming* IP datagram that specifies a "destination IP address" other than the local host's IP address(es), is treated as a normal *outgoing* IP datagram.

This outgoing IP datagram is subject to the IP routing algorithm of the local host, which selects the *next hop* for the datagram (the next host to send it to). This new destination can be located on any of the physical networks to which the intermediate host is attached. If it is a physical network other than the one on which the host originally received the datagram, then the net result is that the intermediate host has *forwarded* the IP datagram from one physical network to another.

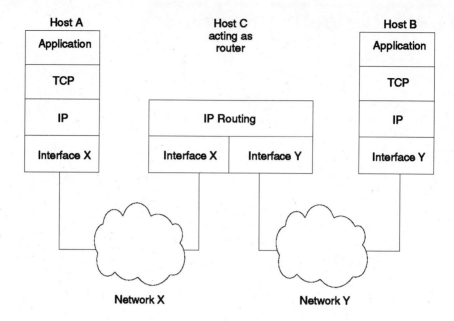

***Figure   3-1.*** *Router Operation of IP.*   Can be performed by *all* IP implementations.

The normal IP routing table contains information about the locally attached networks and the IP addresses of other routers located on these networks, plus the networks they attach to. It can be extended with information on IP networks that are farther away, and can also contain a default route, but it still remains a table with limited information; that is, it represents only a part of the whole internet. That is why this kind of router is called a *router with partial routing information.*

Some considerations apply to these routers with partial information:

- They do not know about all internet networks.
- They allow local sites autonomy in establishing and modifying routes.
- A routing entry error in one of the routers may introduce inconsistencies, thereby making part of the network unreachable.

Some error reporting should be implemented by routers with partial information via the Internet Control Message Protocol (ICMP) described in 2.4, "Internet Control Message Protocol (ICMP)" on page 2-52. They should be able to report the following errors back to the source host:

- Unknown IP destination network by an ICMP *Destination Unreachable* message.
- Redirection of traffic to more suitable routers by sending ICMP *Redirect* messages.

- Congestion problems (too many incoming datagrams for the available buffer space) by an ICMP *Source Quench* message.
- The "Time-to-Live" field of an IP datagram has reached zero. This is reported with an ICMP *Time Exceeded* message.
- Also, the following base ICMP operations and messages should be supported:
  - Parameter problem
  - Address mask
  - Time stamp
  - Information request/reply
  - Echo request/reply

A more intelligent router is required if:

- The router has to know routes to *all* possible IP networks, as was the case for the ARPANET *core* gateways.
- The router has to have dynamic routing tables, which are kept up-to-date with minimal or no manual intervention.
- The router has to be able to advertise local changes to other routers.

These more advanced forms of routers use additional protocols to communicate with each other. A number of protocols of this kind exist, and descriptions of the important ones will be given in the following sections. The reasons for this multiplicity of different protocols are basically fourfold:

- Using Internet terminology, there is a concept of a group of networks, called an *Autonomous System (AS)*, which is administered as a unit. The AS concept arose because the TCP/IP protocols were developed with the ARPANET already in place.

  Routing within an AS and routing outside an AS are treated as different issues and are addressed by different protocols.

- Over two decades several routing protocols were tested in the Internet. Some of them performed well, others had to be abandoned.

- The emergence of Autonomous Systems of different sizes called for different routing solutions. For small to medium sized ASs a group of routing protocols based upon Distance Vector (RIP, for example) became very popular. However, such protocols do not perform well for large interconnected networks. Link State protocols like OSPF are much better suited for such networks.

- To exchange routing information between ASs border gateway protocols were developed.

Before discussing the various routing protocols, we will review the routing architectures used in the early Internet, since this will help in understanding the role played by the differing routing protocols. This overview will also show the difference between *Interior* and *Exterior* routing. We will then discuss the various protocols used for the two types of routing.

## 3.1.1 Routing Daemons

The routing protocols are often implemented using one of two daemons:[1]

routed     Pronounced "route D." This is a basic routing daemon for interior routing supplied with the majority of TCP/IP implementations. It uses the RIP protocol (see 3.3.3, "Routing Information Protocol (RIP)" on page 3-17).

gated     Pronounced "gate D." This is a more sophisticated daemon on UNIX-based systems for interior and exterior routing. It can employ a number of additional protocols such as OSPF (see 3.3.4, "Open Shortest Path First Protocol (OSPF) Version 2" on page 3-25) and BGP (see 3.4.2, "Border Gateway Protocol (BGP)" on page 3-52).

              See 3.4.3, "IP Routing Protocols in IBM TCP/IP Products" on page 3-69 for details of routing daemon implementations in IBM products.

## 3.2 Historical Perspective

Initially, the ARPANET (see 1.2.2, "ARPANET" on page 1-3) played a central role in the development of the Internet, particularly in the area of routing. Although it was replaced in its role as the backbone of the Internet by the NSFNET in the late 1980s, the experience gained from its routing architecture had a direct effect on the later development of the current set of routing protocols.

## 3.2.1 The ARPANET Routing Architecture

At its heart was the concept of an *Autonomous System (AS)*: a collection of networks controlled by a single authority. Each AS is registered with the NIC (now the InterNIC) and has a 16-bit identification number called the *autonomous system number* or *AS number*. These are listed in *RFC 1166 — Internet Numbers*. The ARPANET core system was itself considered an autonomous system.

---

[1] Daemon, pronounced "demon," is a UNIX term for a background server process. Usually, daemons have names ending with a "d." An analogous concept for MVS is a server running in a separate address space from TCP/IP, for VM it is a separate service virtual machine, for OS/2 it is a separate OS/2 session, and so on. Although TCP/IP servers are often implemented differently on different platforms, the *routed* daemon is implemented like this on each of these platforms.

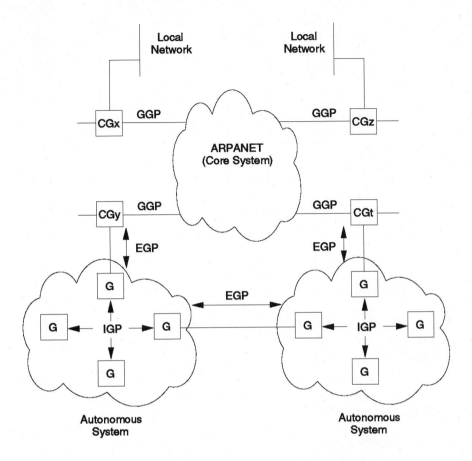

*Figure 3-2. The ARPANET Backbone.* The terms in the diagram are explained in the text which follows.

In keeping with the nomenclature used at the time, we shall refer to the routers between Autonomous Systems as *gateways*. All routing between gateways can be categorized as *intra-AS* (also termed *Interior*) if the gateways belong to the same AS or *inter-AS* (also termed *Exterior*) if they belong to different ones.

Intra-AS routing uses an *Interior Gateway Protocol (IGP)* and inter-AS routing uses an *Exterior Gateway Protocol (EGP)*. The ARPANET architecture did not specify which protocol should be used as an IGP, but it did specify a protocol to be used as an EGP. Confusingly, this protocol was also named *Exterior Gateway Protocol*.

**Note:** To avoid confusion, we shall use the term "EGP" to refer specifically to the EGP protocol, and "an EGP" to refer to a protocol belonging to the EGP group of protocols.

## 3.2.1.1 Core and Non-Core Gateways

In the ARPANET system, the *core gateways* which made up the backbone were maintained by a central authority, the Internet Network Operations Center. They provided reliable and authoritative routes for *all* possible Internet networks, and connected the ARPANET to the other Internet networks.

The core gateways (shown as CGx, CGy and so on in Figure 3-2 on page 3-5) had to know about all possible destinations in order to optimize the ARPANET traffic. A datagram travelling from one local network to another via the core system passed through exactly two core gateways. The ARPANET routing architecture specified that the core gateways communicated with the *Gateway-to-Gateway Protocol (GGP)*.

*Non-core gateways* (shown as G in Figure 3-2 on page 3-5) were maintained by the organizations responsible for the individual Autonomous Systems and forwarded information about networks in their areas to the core gateways using EGP.

## 3.2.1.2 Core Gateways

In addition to the simple ICMP error-reporting messages, an ARPANET core gateway also implemented:

- Gateway-to-Gateway Protocol (GGP) to exchange connectivity information between core gateways (see 3.2.1.4, "Gateway-to-Gateway Protocol (GGP)" on page 3-7).
- Exterior Gateway Protocol (EGP) to collect connectivity information from non-core gateways (see 3.4.1, "Exterior Gateway Protocol (EGP)" on page 3-49).
- Cross-Network Debugging Protocol (XNET), used to load the gateway and to create and examine the gateway's data.
- Host Monitoring Protocol (HMP) used to collect measurements and statistics information from the gateways (RFC 869).

## 3.2.1.3 Non-Core Gateways

Local internetworks created by individual groups can span multiple physical networks, tied together through gateways (non-core gateways). Such a group of networks is called an *autonomous system* (AS). Among its responsibilities, an AS must:

- Collect reachability information for all of its connected networks.
- Advertise reachability information to the core system using a standard protocol.
- Have a single administrative and technical point of contact.

An autonomous system must collect routing and reachability information about its own internal networks. Selected machines must forward that information to other autonomous systems and to the core gateways. As noted above, EGP must be used for this inter-AS communication. For inter-AS communication any suitable IGP may be used, the two most common being:

- The Hello protocol described in 3.3.2, "The Hello Protocol" on page 3-14
- Routing Information Protocol (RIP) described in 3.3.3.1, "Routing Information Protocol Version 1 (RIP, RIP-1)" on page 3-17

## 3.2.1.4 Gateway-to-Gateway Protocol (GGP)

GGP is an *historic protocol*. Its status is *not recommended*. It is described in detail in *RFC 823 — The DARPA Internet Gateway*.

As mentioned previously (see 3.2.1.1, "Core and Non-Core Gateways" on page 3-6), the original ARPANET core gateways used the *Gateway-to-Gateway Protocol*, to exchange routing information. In addition to this role, it had to route datagrams that were passing through the core system. Any datagram in transit through the core system should pass through two core gateways. The basic principles of GGP follow:

When a core gateway comes up, it is assigned core *neighbors*. A gateway only needs to propagate information about the networks it can reach to its neighbors. The neighbors will update their routing information with the received information and will send the changes to their assigned neighbors.

The information consists of sets (N,C) where:

$N$  is a network that is reachable by this gateway
$C$  is the cost of reaching that network. The cost is expressed in gateway hops (number of gateways to pass). A cost of zero corresponds to a network that is directly attached to the core gateway. Maximum cost corresponds to unreachable networks.

GGP messages are carried in IP datagrams, and typically contain a list of (N,C) pairs. They are sent by a gateway to its neighbors whenever one of the following occurs:

- A new network becomes reachable from the gateway.
- A network becomes unreachable.
- Routing data is changed due to reception of GGP messages from neighbor gateways.

Upon receipt of a GGP message from gateway G, the neighbor gateway A will compare an incoming (N,C) pair to the (N,C) pair in its local tables. If the cost to reach network N would be smaller by using the gateway G (originator of the GGP message) than when using the routing information in the local table, the routing path for network N is updated to point to gateway G, and as this is a route change, the gateway A will generate a GGP message to inform its neighbors of the change. Eventually, the information on network N will reach all the core gateways.

## 3.2.2 NSFNET Routing Architecture

As described in 1.2.3, "NSFNET" on page 1-4, the NSFNET backbone has been implemented in three phases and its routing architecture and protocols have evolved accordingly. This evolution and possible future alternatives are described in detail in:

- *RFC 1074 — The NSFNET Backbone SPF Based Interior Gateway Protocol.*
- *RFC 1092 — EGP and Policy Based Routing in the New NSFNET Backbone.*
- *RFC 1093 — The NSFNET Routing Architecture.*
- *RFC 1104 — Models of Policy Based Routing.*
- *RFC 1133 — Routing between the NSFNET and the DDN.*
- *RFC 1222 — Advancing the NSFNET Routing Architecture.*

The **first backbone** used the Hello protocol (see 3.3.2, "The Hello Protocol" on page 3-14) for interior routing. The client networks were mostly using RIP (see 3.3.3.1, "Routing Information Protocol Version 1 (RIP, RIP-1)" on page 3-17) as an IGP and they were connected to the backbone using a *gated* interface which acted as an interface between the Hello and RIP protocols.

The **second backbone** used a subset of the ANSI OSI Intermediate System to Intermediate System (IS-IS) routing protocol (see 3.3.4.3, "OSI Intermediate System to Intermediate System (IS-IS)" on page 3-47) as an IGP. It used EGP (see 3.4.1, "Exterior Gateway Protocol (EGP)" on page 3-49) to exchange reachability information between the backbone and the attached mid-level and peer networks. The routing is controlled by a distributed *routing policy database* that controls the acceptance and distribution of routing information. This database is managed by the Network Operations Center and is available through Information Services.

In the **third backbone**, EGP was progressively replaced by a true inter-AS routing protocol called the *Border Gateway Protocol (BGP)*, described in 3.4.2, "Border Gateway Protocol (BGP)" on page 3-52. One important aspect of BGP is its treatment of the Internet as an arbitrarily connected set of autonomous systems with no single core system. This removes the requirement for a single network such as NSFNET to play a central role and allows the backbone to be composed of many peer networks.

# 3.3 Interior Routing Protocols

*Interior routing protocols* or *interior gateway protocols (IGPs)* are used to exchange routing information between routers within a single autonomous system. They are also used by routers which run *exterior routing protocols* to collect network-reachability information for the autonomous system.

**Note:** The term interior routing protocol has no abbreviation in common use, so we shall use the abbreviation IGP as is usual in TCP/IP literature.

The most widely used IGPs are:

- The Hello protocol (see 3.3.2, "The Hello Protocol" on page 3-14).
- Routing Information Protocol (see 3.3.3, "Routing Information Protocol (RIP)" on page 3-17).
- The Open Shortest Path First protocol (see 3.3.4, "Open Shortest Path First Protocol (OSPF) Version 2" on page 3-25).

Before discussing these three protocols in detail, we shall look at two important groups of routing algorithm used in IGPs.

# 3.3.1 Routing Algorithms

In this section, we discuss the Vector-Distance and Link-State, Shortest Path First routing algorithms.

## 3.3.1.1 Vector-Distance

The term *Vector-Distance* refers to a class of algorithms that gateways use to update routing information. Each router begins with a set of routes for those networks or subnets to which it is directly attached, and possibly some additional routes to other networks or hosts if the network topology is such that the routing protocol will be unable to produce the desired routing correctly. This list is kept in a *routing table*, where each entry identifies a destination network or host and gives the "distance" to that network. The distance is called a *metric* and is typically measured in "hops."

Periodically, each router sends a copy of its routing table to any other router it can reach directly. When a report arrives at router B from router A, B examines the set of destinations it receives and the distance to each. B will update its routing table if:

- A knows a shorter way to reach a destination.

- A lists a destination that B does not have in its table.

- A's distance to a destination, already routed through A from B, has changed.

This kind of algorithm is easy to implement, but it has a number of disadvantages:

- When routes change rapidly, that is, a new connection appears or an old one fails, the routing topology may not stabilize to match the changed network topology because information propagates slowly from one router to another and while it is propagating, some routers will have incorrect routing information.

  Another disadvantage is that each router has to send a copy of its entire routing table to every neighbor at regular intervals. Of course, one can use longer intervals to reduce the network load but that introduces problems related to how well the network responds to changes in topology.

Vector-distance algorithms using hop counts as a metric do not take account of the link speed or reliability. Such an algorithm will use a path with hop count 2 that crosses two slow-speed lines, instead of using a path with hop count 3 that crosses three token-rings and may be substantially faster.

The most difficult task in a vector-distance algorithm is to prevent instability. Different solutions are available:

- **Counting to infinity**

  Let us choose a value of 16 to represent infinity. Suppose a network becomes inaccessible; all the immediately neighboring routers time out and set the metric to that network to 16. We can consider that all the neighboring routers have a piece of hardware that connects them to the vanished network, with a cost of 16. Since that is the only connection to the vanished network, all the other routers in the system will converge to new routes that go through one of those routers with a direct but unavailable connection. Once convergence has happened, all the routers will have metrics of 16 for the vanished network. Since 16 indicates infinity, all routers then regard the network as unreachable.

  The question with vector distance algorithms is not *will* convergence occur but *how long* will it take? Let us consider the configuration shown in Figure 3-3.

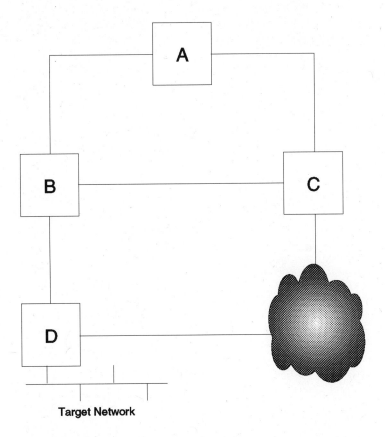

Target Network

*Figure* **3-3.** *The Counting to Infinity Problem.* All links have a metric of 1 except for the indirect route from C to D which has a metric of 10.

Let us consider only the routes from each gateway to the target network.

| Gateway | First Hop | Metric |
|---------|-----------|--------|
| D | = | 1 |
| B | D | 2 |
| C | B | 3 |
| A | B | 3 |

Now, consider that the link from B to D fails. The routes should now adjust to use the link from C to D. The routing changes start when B notices that the route to D is no longer usable. For RIP this occurs when B does not receive a routing update on its link to D for 180 seconds.

The following picture shows the metric to the target network, as it appears in the routing table of each gateway.

| Time | | | | | | | ..... | | | | |
|------|-----------|----------|----|---|----|---|-------|----|----|----|----|
| GW | First Hop | Metric | FH | M | FH | M | ..... | FH | M | FH | M |
| D | = | 1 | = | 1 | = | 1 | ..... | = | 1 | = | 1 |
| B | Unreach. | Unreach. | C | 4 | C | 5 | ..... | C | 11 | C | 12 |
| C | B | 3 | A | 4 | A | 5 | ..... | A | 11 | D | 11 |
| A | B | 3 | C | 4 | C | 5 | ..... | C | 11 | C | 12 |
| | Iteration #1 | | #2 | | #3 | | | #9 | | #10 | |

= : directly connected
Unreach: unreachable
FH : First hop
M : Metric

*Figure 3-4. The Counting to Infinity Problem*

The problem is that B can get rid of its route to D (using a timeout mechanism), but vestiges of that route persist in the system for a long time (time between iterations is 30 seconds using RIP). Initially, A and C still think they can reach D via B, so they keep sending updates listing metrics of 3. B will receive these updates and, in the next iteration, will claim that it can get to D via either A or C. Of course, it can't because the routes claimed by A and C (D reachable via B with a metric of 3) are now gone, but they have no way of knowing that yet. Even when they discover that their routes via B have gone away, they each think there is a route available via the other. Eventually the system will converge, when the direct link from C to D has a lower cost than the one received (by C) from B and A. The worst case is when a network becomes completely inaccessible from some part of the system: in that case, the metrics may increase slowly in a pattern like the one above until they finally reach "infinity." For this reason, the problem is called *counting to infinity*. Thus the choice of infinity is a trade off between network size and speed of convergence in case counting to infinity happens. This explains why we chose as low a value as 16 to represent infinity. 16 is the value used by RIP.

- The other solutions will be discussed within the RIP protocol (see 3.3.3, "Routing Information Protocol (RIP)" on page 3-17).

## 3.3.1.2 Link-State, Shortest Path First

The growth in networking over the past few years has pushed the currently available *Interior Gateway Protocols*, which use vector-distance algorithms, past their limits. The primary alternative to vector-distance schemes is a class of protocols known as *Link State, Shortest Path First*.

The important features of these routing protocols are:

- A set of physical networks is divided into a number of areas.
- All routers within an area have an identical database.
- Each router's database describes the complete topology (which routers are connected to which networks) of the routing domain. The topology of an area is represented with a database called a *Link State Database* describing all of the links that each of the routers in the area has.
- Each router uses its database to derive the set of optimum paths to all destinations from which it builds its routing table. The algorithm used to determine the optimum paths is called a *Shortest Path First (SPF)* algorithm.

In general, a link state protocol works as follows. Each router periodically sends out a description of its connections (the state of its links) to its neighbors (routers are neighbors if they are connected to the same network). This description, called a *Link State Advertisement (LSA)*, includes the configured cost of the connection. The LSA is flooded throughout the router's domain. Each router in the domain maintains an identical synchronized copy of a database composed of this link state information. This database describes both the topology of the router's domain and routes to networks outside of the domain such as routes to networks in other autonomous systems. Each router runs an algorithm on its topological database resulting in a shortest-path tree. This shortest-path tree contains the shortest path to every router and network the gateway can reach. From the shortest-path tree, the cost to the destination and the next hop to forward a datagram to is used to build the router's routing table.

Link-state protocols, in comparison with vector-distance protocols, send out updates when there is news, and may send out regular updates as a way of ensuring neighbor routers that a connection is still active. More importantly, the information exchanged is the state of a router's links, not the contents of the routing table. This means that link-state algorithms use fewer network resources than their vector-distance counterparts, particularly when the routing is complex or the autonomous system is large. They are, however, compute-intensive. In return, users get faster response to network events, faster route convergence, and access to more advanced network services.

## 3.3.2  The Hello Protocol

This was used in the "Fuzzball" software for LSI/11 minicomputers, which were widely used in Internet experimentation. The Hello protocol is described in *RFC 891 — DCN Local-Network Protocols*. It is not an Internet standard.

**Note:**  OSPF (see 3.3.4, "Open Shortest Path First Protocol (OSPF) Version 2" on page 3-25) includes a quite separate protocol for negotiation between routers which is also called the Hello protocol.

The communication in the Hello protocol is via Hello messages which are carried via IP datagrams. Hello uses protocol number 63 (reserved for "any local network").

The Hello protocol is significant partly because of its wide deployment during the early expansion of the Internet and partly because it provides an example of a vector-distance algorithm that does not use hop counts like RIP (see 3.3.3.1, "Routing Information Protocol Version 1 (RIP, RIP-1)" on page 3-17) but, instead, network delays as a metric for the distance.

A *Distributed Computer Network (DCN)* physical host is a PDP11-compatible processor which supports a number of cooperating sequential processses, each of which is given a unique 8-bit identifier called its port ID. Every DCN host contains one or more internet processes, each of which supports a virtual host given a unique 8-bit identifier called its host ID. There is a one-to-one correspondence between internet addresses and host IDs. Each DCN physical host is identified by a host ID for the purpose of detecting loops in routing updates, which establish the minimum-delay paths between the virtual hosts.

Each physical host contains two tables:

*Host Table*    This contains estimates of round-trip delay and logical-clock offset (that is, the difference between the logical clock of this host and the logical clock of the sender's host). It is indexed by the host number. The host table is maintained dynamically using updates generated by periodic (from 1 to 30 seconds) Hello messages.

*Net Table*    This contains an entry for every neighbor network that may be connected to the local network and certain other networks that are not neighbors. Each entry contains the network number, as well as the host number of the router (located on the local network) to that network. The Net table is fixed at configuration time for all hosts except those that support the GGP or EGP routing protocols. In these cases the Net table is updated as part of the routing operation.

In addition, entries in either table can be changed by operator commands.

The delay and offset estimates are updated by Hello messages exchanged on the links connecting physical neighbors.

Here is the format of a Hello message:

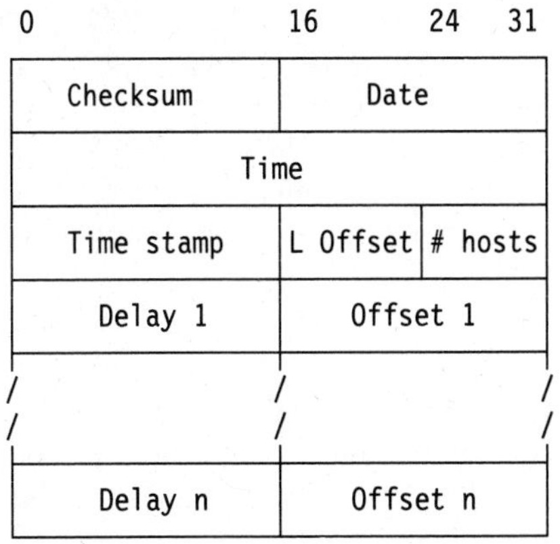

```
     0                  16       24   31
     +------------------+----------------+
     |    Checksum      |     Date       |
     +------------------+----------------+
     |              Time                 |
     +------------------+-------+--------+
     |   Time stamp     |L Offset|# hosts|
     +------------------+-------+--------+
     |    Delay 1       |    Offset 1    |
     +------------------+----------------+
     /                  /                /
     /                  /                /
     +------------------+----------------+
     |    Delay n       |    Offset n    |
     +------------------+----------------+
```

***Figure*** *3-5. Hello Message Format*

Where:

*Checksum*    contains a checksum covering the fields indicated

*Date*    is the local host's date

*Time*    is the local host's time

*Timestamp*    used in round-trip calculation (see below)

| | |
|---|---|
| *L Offset* | contains the offset of the block of entries of internet addresses used on the local network |
| *#hosts* | contains the number of entries from the host table that follows |
| *Delay n* | delay to reach host n |
| *Offset n* | offset from host n (difference between clocks) |

Let us consider the two main steps of the Hello protocol.

## 3.3.2.1 Round-Trip Delay Calculation

Periodically each host sends a Hello message to its neighbor on each of the communication links common to both of them. For each of these links the sender keeps a set of state variables, including a copy of the source-address field of the last Hello message received. When constructing a Hello message the sender sets the destination-address field to this state variable and the source-address field to its own address. It then fills in the date and time fields from its clock and the time stamp from another state variable. It finally copies the delay and offset values from its host table into the message.

Round-trip delay calculations are performed on the host receiving the Hello message. Each link has an internal state variable assigned, which is updated as each Hello message is received; this variable takes the value of the time field, minus the current time-of-day. When the next Hello message is transmitted, the value assigned to the time stamp field is computed as the low-order 16-bits of this variable minus the current time-of-day. The round trip delay is computed as the low-order 16-bits of the current time-of-day minus the value of the timestamp field.

## 3.3.2.2 Host Updates

When a Hello message arrives which results in a valid round trip-delay calculation, a host update process is performed. This consists of adding the round trip delay to each of the "Delay n" entries in the Hello message in turn and comparing each of these calculated delays to the delay field of the corresponding host table. Each entry is then updated according to the following rules:

- If the link connects to another host on the same network and the port ID of the link output process matches the port ID field of the entry, then update the entry.

- If the link connects to another host on the same network and the port ID of the link output process does not match the port ID field of the entry *and* the calculated delay is less than the host delay field of the host table by at least a specified switching threshold (currently 100 milliseconds), then update the entry. For example, if host A sends host B a Hello message, and if B's current delay to reach a given destination, D, is greater than the delay from A to D plus the delay from B to A, B changes its route and sends traffic to D via A.

The purpose of the switching threshold is to avoid (together with minimum delay specification) unnecessary switching between links and transient loops which can occur due to normal variations in propagation delays.

Please refer to RFC 891 for more details.

## 3.3.3 Routing Information Protocol (RIP)

There are two versions of RIP. Version 1 (RIP-1) is a widely deployed protocol with a number of known limitations. Version 2 (RIP-2) is an enhanced version designed to alleviate the limitations of RIP while being highly compatible with it. The term RIP is used to refer to Version 1, while RIP-2 refers to Version 2. Whenever the reader encounters the term RIP in TCP/IP literature, it is safe to assume that it is referring to Version 1 unless explicitly stated otherwise. We shall use this nomenclature in this section except when the two versions are being compared, when we shall use the term RIP-1 to avoid possible confusion.

### 3.3.3.1 Routing Information Protocol Version 1 (RIP, RIP-1)

RIP is a *standard protocol* (STD 34). Its status is *elective*. It is described in RFC 1058, although many RIP implementations pre-date this RFC by a number of years. RIP is generally implemented with a daemon named *routed*. RIP is also supported by *gated* daemons.

RIP was based on the Xerox PUP and XNS routing protocols. It is widely used, as the code is incorporated in the routing code of Berkeley BSD UNIX which provides the basis for many UNIX implementations.

RIP is a straightforward implementation of vector-distance routing for local networks. RIP communication uses UDP as a transport protocol, with port number 520 as the destination port (see 2.11, "User Datagram Protocol (UDP)" on page 2-88 for a description of UDP and ports). RIP operates in one of two modes: *active* (normally used by routers) and *passive* (normally used by hosts). The difference between the two is explained below. RIP messages are sent in UDP datagrams and each contains up to 25 pairs of numbers as shown in Figure 3-6 on page 3-18.

```
0          8          16                    31
┌─────────┬─────────┬──────────────────────────┐
│ Command │ Version │            0             │
├─────────┴─────────┼──────────────────────────┤
│  Address family   │            0             │
├───────────────────┴──────────────────────────┤
│              IP address 1                     │
├───────────────────────────────────────────────┤
│                   0                           │
├───────────────────────────────────────────────┤
│                   0                           │
├───────────────────────────────────────────────┤
│       hop count metric for address 1          │
├──/────────────────────────────────────/──────┤
│ /                                       /     │
├───────────────────┬──────────────────────────┤
│  Address family   │            0             │
├───────────────────┴──────────────────────────┤
│              IP address 25                    │
├───────────────────────────────────────────────┤
│                   0                           │
├───────────────────────────────────────────────┤
│                   0                           │
├───────────────────────────────────────────────┤
│       hop count metric for address 25         │
└───────────────────────────────────────────────┘
```

*Figure* *3-6. RIP Message.* Between 1 and 25 routes may be listed in a RIP message. With 25 routes the message is 504 bytes long (25×20+4) which is the maximum size message that can be transmitted in a 512-byte UDP datagram.

| | |
|---|---|
| *Command* | is 1 for a RIP request or 2 for a RIP reply. |
| *Version* | is 1. |
| *Address Family* | is 2 for IP addresses. |
| *IP address* | is the IP address for this routing entry: either a host or a subnet (in which case the host number is zero). |
| *Hop count metric* | is the number of hops to the destination. The hop count for a directly connected interface is 1, and each intermediate router increments it by 1 to a maximum of 15, with 16 indicating that no route exists to the destination. |

Both active and passive RIP participants listen to all broadcast messages and update their routing table according to the vector-distance algorithm described earlier.

## Basic Operation

- When RIP is started it sends a message to each of its neighbors (on well-known UDP port 520) asking for a copy of the neighbor's routing table. This message is a query (command set to 1) with an address family of 0 and a metric of 16. The neighboring routers return a copy of their routing tables.

- When RIP is in active mode it sends all or part of its routing table to all of its neighbor routers (by broadcasting and/or by sending it on any point-to-point links to its neighbors). This is done every 30 seconds. The routing table is sent as a reply (command is 2, even though it is unsolicited).

- When RIP discovers a metric has changed, it broadcasts the change to other routers.

- When RIP receives a reply, the message is validated and the local routing table is updated if necessary.

  To improve performance and reliability, RIP specifies that once a router (or host) learns a route from another router, it must keep that route until it learns of a better one (with a strictly lower cost). This prevents routes from oscillating between two or more equal cost paths.

- When RIP receives a request, other than one for the entire table, it is returned as the response with the metric for each entry set to the value from the local routing table. If no route exists in the local table, the metric is set to 16.

- RIP routes learned from other routers time out unless they are re-advertised within 180 seconds (6 broadcast cycles). When a route times out, its metric is set to infinity, the invalidation of the route is broadcast to the router's neighbors, and 60 seconds later, the route is deleted from the local routing table.

**Limitations:**   RIP is not designed to solve every possible routing problem. RFC 1720 (STD 1) describes these technical limitations of RIP as "serious" and the IETF is evaluating candidates for a new standard "open" protocol to replace RIP. Possible candidates include OSPF (see 3.3.4, "Open Shortest Path First Protocol (OSPF) Version 2" on page  3-25) and OSI IS-IS (see 3.3.4.3, "OSI Intermediate System to Intermediate System (IS-IS)" on page  3-47). However, RIP is widely deployed and therefore is unlikely to be completely replaced for some time. RIP has the following specific limitations:

- The maximum cost allowed in RIP is 16 which means that the network is unreachable. Thus RIP is inadequate for large networks (that is, those in which legitimate hop counts approach 16).

- RIP does not support variable length subnet masks *(variable subnetting)*. There is no facility in a RIP message to specify a subnet mask associated with the IP address.

- RIP has no facilities to ensure that routing table updates come from authorized routers. It is an unsecure protocol.

- RIP only uses fixed metrics to compare alternative routes. It is not appropriate for situations where routes need to be chosen based on real-time parameters such as measured delay, reliability, or load.

- The protocol depends upon *counting to infinity* to resolve certain unusual situations. As described earlier (3.3.1.1, "Vector-Distance" on page 3-9), the resolution of a loop would require either much time (if the frequency of updates was limited) or much bandwidth (if updates were sent whenever changes were detected). As the size of the routing domain grows, the instability of the vector-distance algorithm in the face of changing topology becomes apparent. RIP specifies mechanisms to minimize the problems with counting to infinity (these are described below) which allows RIP to be used for larger routing domains, but eventually RIP will be unable to cope. There is no fixed upper limit, but the practical maximum depends upon the frequency of changes to the topology, the details of the network topology itself, and what is deemed as an acceptable maximum time for the routing topology to stabilize.

Solving the *counting to infinity* problem is done by using the *split horizon*, *poisoned reverse* and *triggered updates* techniques.

**Split horizon with poisoned reverse:**   Let's consider our example network (shown in Figure 3-7) again.

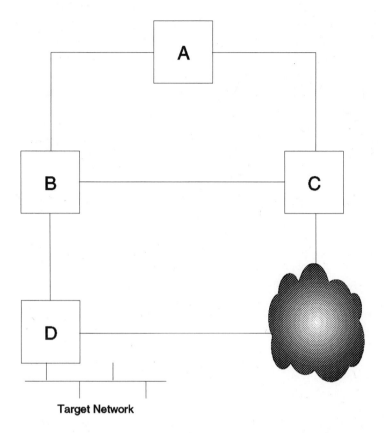

*Figure 3-7. The Counting to Infinity Problem.* All links have a metric of 1 except for the indirect route from C to D which has a metric of 10.

As described in 3.3.1.1, "Vector-Distance" on page 3-9 the problem was caused by the fact that A and C are engaged in a pattern of mutual deception. Each claims to be able to reach D via the other. This can be prevented by being more careful about where information is sent. In particular, it is never useful to claim reachability for a destination network to the neighbor from which the route was learned (reverse routes). The *split horizon with poisoned reverse* scheme includes routes in updates sent to the router from which they were learned, but sets their metrics to infinity. If two routers have routes pointing at each other, advertising reverse routes with a metric of 16 will break the loop immediately. If the reverse routes are simply not advertised (this scheme is called *simple split horizon*), the erroneous routes will have to be eliminated by waiting for a timeout. Poisoned reverse does have a disadvantage: it increases the size of the routing messages.

**Triggered updates:** Split horizon with poisoned reverse will prevent any routing loop that involves only two gateways. However, it is still possible to end up with patterns in which three routers are engaged in mutual deception. For example, A may believe it has a route through B, B through C, and C through A. This cannot be solved using split horizon. This loop will only be resolved when the metric reaches infinity and the network or host involved is then declared unreachable. Triggered updates are an attempt to speed up this convergence. Whenever a router changes the metric for a route, it is required to send update messages almost immediately, even if it is not yet time for one of the regular update messages (RIP specifies a small time delay, between 1 and 5 seconds, in order to avoid having triggered updates generate excessive network traffic).

## 3.3.3.2 Routing Information Protocol Version 2 (RIP-2)

RIP-2 is a *draft standard protocol*. Its status is *elective*. It is described in RFC 1723.

RIP-2 extends RIP-1. It is less powerful than other recent IGPs such as OSPF (see 3.3.4, "Open Shortest Path First Protocol (OSPF) Version 2" on page 3-25) and IS-IS (see 3.3.4.3, "OSI Intermediate System to Intermediate System (IS-IS)" on page 3-47), but it has the advantages of easy implementation and lower overheads. The intention of RIP-2 is to provide a straightforward replacement for RIP which can be used on small to medium-sized networks, can be employed in the presence of variable subnetting (see 2.2.2, "Subnets" on page 2-10) or supernetting (see 2.2.7, "Classless Inter-Domain Routing (CIDR)" on page 2-26) and importantly, can interoperate with RIP-1.

RIP-2 takes advantage of the fact that half of the bytes in a RIP-1 message are reserved (must be zero) and that the original RIP-1 specification was well designed with enhancements in mind, particularly in the use of the version field. One notable area where this is not the case is in the interpretation of the metric field. RIP-1 specifies it as being a value between 0 and 16 stored in a four-*byte* field. For compatibility, RIP-2 preserves this definition, meaning that it agrees with RIP-1 that 16 is to be interpreted as infinity, and wastes most of this field.

**Note:** Neither RIP-1 nor RIP-2 are properly suited for use as an IGP in an AS where a value of 16 is too low to be regarded as infinity, because high values of infinity exacerbate the counting to infinity problem. The more sophisticated Link-State protocol used in OSPF and IS-IS provides a much better routing solution when the AS is large enough to have a legitimate hop count close to 16.

Provided that a RIP-1 implementation obeys the specification in RFC 1058, RIP-2 can interoperate with RIP-1. The RIP message format is extended as shown in Figure 3-8 on page 3-23.

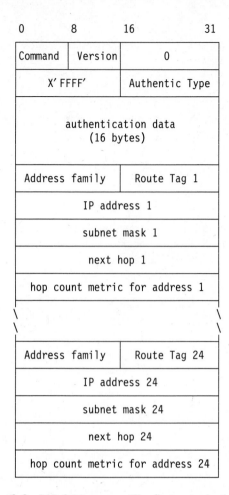

*Figure* *3-8. RIP-2 Message.* The first entry in the message may be an authentication entry, as shown here, or it may be a route as in a RIP-1 message. If the first entry is an authentication entry, only 24 routes may be included in a message; otherwise the maximum is 25 as in RIP-1.

The fields in a RIP-2 message are the same as for a RIP-1 message except as follows:

*Version*

> Is 2. This tells RIP-1 routers to ignore the fields designated as "must be zero" (if the value is 1, RIP-1 routers are required to discard messages with non-zero values in these fields since the messages originate with a router claiming to be RIP-1-compliant but sending non-RIP-1 messages).

*Address Family*

May be X′ FFFF′ in the first entry only, indicating that this entry is an authentication entry.

*Authentication Type*

Defines how the remaining 16 bytes are to be used. The only defined types are 0 indicating no authentication and 2 indicating that the field contains password data.

*Authentication Data*

The password is 16 bytes, plain text ASCII, left adjusted and padded with ASCII NULLs (X′ 00′ ).

*Route Tag*

Is a field intended for communicating information about the origin of the route information. It is intended for interoperation between RIP and other routing protocols. RIP-2 implementations must preserve this tag, but RIP-2 does not further specify how it is to be used.

*Subnet Mask*

The subnet mask associated with the subnet referred to by this entry.

*Next Hop*

A recommendation about the next hop that the router should use to send datagrams to the subnet or host given in this entry.

To ensure safe interoperation with RIP, RFC 1723 specifies the following restrictions for RIP-2 routers sending over a network interface where a RIP-1 router may hear and operate on the RIP messages.

1. Information internal to one network must never be advertised into another network.

2. Information about a more specific subnet may not be advertised where RIP-1 routers would consider it a host route.

3. *Supernet* routes (routes with a subnet mask shorter than the natural or "unsubnetted" network mask) must not be advertised where they could be misinterpreted by RIP-1 routers.

RIP-2 also supports the use of multicasting rather than simple broadcasting. This can reduce the load on hosts which are not listening for RIP-2 messages. This option is configurable for each interface to ensure optimum use of RIP-2 facilities when a router connects mixed RIP-1/RIP-2 subnets to RIP-2-only subnets. Similarly, the use of authentication in mixed environments can be configured to suit local requirements.

RIP-2 is implemented in recent versions of the *gated* daemon, often termed *gated Version 3*. Since the draft standard is new at the time of writing, many implementations will comply with the earlier version described in RFC 1388.  Such implementations will interoperate with those adhering to RFC 1723.

For more information on RIP-2, see:

- *RFC 1721 — RIP Version 2 Protocol Analysis*

- *RFC 1722 — RIP Version 2 Protocol Applicability Statement*

- *RFC 1723 — RIP Version 2 − Carrying Additional Information*

- *RFC 1724 — RIP Version 2 MIB Extension*

## 3.3.4  Open Shortest Path First Protocol (OSPF) Version 2

**Note:**   The term OSPF is invariably used to refer to OSPF Version 2 (OSPF-2).  OSPF Version 1, which is described in RFC 1131, is obsolete.

OSPF is a *draft standard protocol*.  Its status is *elective*, but RFC 1370 contains an *applicability statement* for OSPF which says that any router implementing a protocol other than simple IP-based routing must implement OSPF (this does not preclude a router implementing other protocols as well, of course).  OSPF is described in RFC 1583, which obsoletes RFC 1247.  OSPF implementations based on RFC 1583 are backward-compatible with implementations based on RFC 1247 and will interoperate with them.  Readers interested in the development of OSPF Version 2 from Version 1 should refer to Appendix F of RFC 1247 and Appendix E of RFC 1583.

OSPF is an interior routing protocol, but it is designed to operate with a suitable exterior protocol, such as BGP.  See 3.4.2.2, "BGP OSPF Interaction" on page  3-64.

OSPF is a complex standard when compared to RIP: RFC 1583 runs to 216 pages, whereas RIP, specified in RFC 1058 has 33 pages and RIP-2 (RFC 1723) adds only another 9.  Much of the complexity of OSPF is directed towards a single purpose: ensuring that the topological databases are the same for all of the routers within an area.  Because the database is the basis for all routing choices, if routers were to have independent databases, they could make mutually conflicting decisions.

OSPF communicates using IP (it is protocol number 89).  It is a *Link-State, Shortest Path First* protocol as described in 3.3.1.2, "Link-State, Shortest Path First" on page  3-13.  OSPF supports different kinds of networks such as  point-to-point networks, broadcast networks, such as Ethernet and token-ring, and non-broadcast networks, such as X.25.

The OSPF specification makes use of *state machines* to define the behavior of routers complying with the protocol.  Aspects of a router's operation which are important to OSPF, such as its network interfaces and its neighboring routers, are described as being in one of a finite number of *states* (for example, a neighbor may be in the down state).

There is a separate state machine for each separate component (for example, two network interfaces have separate state machines) and the state of one is independent of the state of another. The possible states are sufficient to describe all possible conditions relevant to the protocol, so a state machine is always in one, and only one, of its possible states. State changes occur only as a result of *events*. There is a finite set of events for each type of state machine which is sufficient to describe all possible occurrences relevant to the protocol. The behavior of the state machine in response to an event is defined for all possible combinations of state and event. For example, if the state machine for a network interface experiences an InterfaceDown event, the state machine changes to the down state unconditionally. The InterfaceDown event is generated by the OSPF implementation whenever it receives an indication from a lower-level protocol that the interface is not functioning. See RFC 1583 for a complete description of each of the state machines, their possible states and events and the changes associated with them.

Here are some definitions which are necessary to understand the sequence of operations described later in this section:

*Area*

A set of networks within a single autonomous system that have been grouped together. The topology of an area is hidden from the rest of the autonomous system, and each area has a separate topological database (see below). Routing within the autonomous system takes place on two levels, depending on whether the source and destination of a packet reside in the same area (*intra-area routing*) or different areas (*inter-area routing*).

Intra-area routing is determined only by the area's own topology. That is, the packet is routed solely on information obtained within the area; no routing information obtained outside the area can be used.

Inter-area routing is always done via the *backbone*.

The division of an autonomous system into areas enables a significant reduction in the volume of routing traffic required to manage the routing database for a large autonomous system.

*Backbone*

The backbone consists of those networks not contained in any area, their attached routers, and those routers that belong to multiple areas. The backbone *must* be logically contiguous. If it is not physically contiguous, the separate components must be connected using *virtual links* (see below). The backbone is responsible for the distribution of routing information between areas. The backbone itself has all the properties of an area; its topology is separate from that of the areas.

*Area Border Router*

A router connected to multiple areas. An area border router has a copy of the topological database for each area that it is connected to. An area border router is always part of the backbone. Area border routers are responsible for the propagation of inter-area routing information into the areas to which they are connected.

*Internal Router*

A router which is not an area border router.

*AS Border Router (ASBR)*

A router which exchanges routing information with routers belonging to other autonomous systems. All routers in the AS know the path to all AS boundary routers. An ASBR may be an area border router *or* an internal router. It need not be part of the backbone.

**Note:** The nomenclature for this type of router is somewhat varied. RFC 1583, which describes OSPF uses the term *AS Boundary Router*. RFC 1267 and 1268 which describe BGP use the terms *Border Router* and *Border Gateway*. RFC 1340 which describes the interaction between OSPF and BGP uses the term *AS Border Router*. We shall use the last term consistently when describing both OSPF and BGP.

*Virtual Link*

A virtual link is part of the backbone. Its endpoints are two area border routers which share a common non-backbone area. The link is treated like a point-to-point link with metrics cost equal to the intra-area metrics between the endpoints of the links. The routing through the virtual link is done using normal intra-area routing.

*Transit Area*

An area through which a virtual route is physically connected.

*Stub Area*

An area configured to use default routing for inter-AS routing. A stub area can be configured where there is only a single exit from the area, or where any exit may be used without preference for routing to destinations outside the autonomous system. By default inter-AS routes are copied to all areas, so the use of stub areas can reduce the storage requirements of routers within those areas for autonomous systems where a lot of inter-AS routes are defined.

*Multiaccess Network*

A physical network that supports the attachment of multiple routers. Each pair of routers on such a network is assumed to be able to communicate directly.

*Hello Protocol*

The part of the OSPF protocol used to establish and maintain neighbor relationships. This is *not* the Hello protocol described in 3.3.2, "The Hello Protocol" on page 3-14.

*Neighboring routers*

Two routers that have interfaces to a common network. On multiaccess networks, neighbors are dynamically discovered by the Hello protocol.

Each neighbor is described by a state machine which describes the conversation between this router and its neighbor. A brief outline of the meaning of the states follows. See the section immediately following for a definition of the terms *adjacency* and *designated router*.

*Down*

Initial state of a neighbor conversation. It indicates that there has been no recent information received from the neighbor.

*Attempt*

A neighbor on a non-broadcast network appears down and an attempt should be made to contact it by sending regular Hello packets.

*Init*

A Hello packet has recently been received from the neighbor. However, bidirectional communication has not yet been established with the neighbor (that is, the router itself did not appear in the neighbor's Hello packet).

*2-way*

In this state, communication between the two routers is bidirectional. Adjacencies can be established, and neighbors in this state or higher are eligible to be elected as (backup) designated routers.

*ExStart*

The two neighbors are about to create an adjacency.

*Exchange*

The two neighbors are telling each other what they have in their topological databases.

*Loading*

The two neighbors are synchronizing their topological databases.

*Full*

The two neighbors are now fully adjacent; their databases are synchronized.

Various events cause a change of state. For example, if a router receives a Hello packet from a neighbor that is down, the neighbor's state changes to init, and an inactivity timer is started. If the timer fires (that is, no further OSPF packets are received before it expires) the neighbor will return to the down state. Refer to RFC 1583 for a complete description of the states and information on the events which cause state changes.

*Adjacency*

A relationship formed between selected neighboring routers for the purpose of exchanging routing information. *Not* every pair of neighboring routers become adjacent. In particular, not every pair of routers will stay synchronized. If all neighbors were to be synchronized, the number of synchronized pairs on a multiaccess network such as a LAN would be $n(n-1)/2$ where $n$ is the number of routers on the LAN. In large networks, the synchronization traffic would swamp the network, rendering it unusable. The concept of adjacencies is used to limit the number of synchronized pairs to $2n-1$, ensuring that the amount of synchronization traffic is manageable.

*Link State Advertisement*

Refers to the local state of a router or network. This includes the state of the router's interfaces and adjacencies. Each link state advertisement is flooded throughout the routing domain. The collected link state advertisements of all routers and networks form the area's topological database.

*Flooding*

The process of ensuring that each link state advertisement is passed between adjacent routers to reach every router in the area. The flooding procedure is reliable.

*Designated Router*

Each multiaccess network that has at least two attached routers, has a Designated Router. The Designated Router generates a link state advertisement for the multiaccess network. It is elected by the Hello protocol. It becomes adjacent to all other routers on the network. Since the topological databases of all routers are synchronized through adjacencies, the Designated Router plays a central part in the synchronization process.

*Backup Designated Router*

In order to make the transition to a new Designated Router smoother, there is a Backup Designated Router for each multiaccess network. The Backup Designated Router is also adjacent to all routers on the network, and becomes Designated Router when the previous Designated Router fails. Because adjacencies already exist between the Backup Designated Router and all other routers attached to the network, new adjacencies do not have to be formed when the Backup Designated Router takes over from the Designated Router, shortening the time required for the takeover considerably. The Backup designated router is elected using the Hello protocol.

*Interface*

The connection between a router and one of its attached networks. Each interface has state information associated with it which is obtained from the underlying lower-level protocols and the OSPF protocol itself. A brief description of each state is given here. Please refer to RFC 1583 for more details, and for information on the events that will cause an interface to change its state.

*Down*

The interface is unavailable. This is the initial state of an interface.

*Loopback*

The interface is looped back to the router. It cannot be used for regular data traffic.

*Waiting*

The router is trying to determine the identity of the Designated Router or its backup.

*Point-to-Point*

The interface is to a point-to-point network or is a virtual link. The router forms an adjacency with the router at the other end.

**Note:** The interfaces do not need IP addresses. Since the remainder of the internet has no practical need to see the routers' interfaces to the point-to-point link, just the interfaces to other networks, any IP addresses for the link would be needed only for communication between the two routers. To conserve the IP address space, the routers can dispense with IP addresses on the link. This has the effect of making the two routers appear to be one to IP but this has no ill effects. Such a link is called an *unnumbered* link.

*DR Other*

The interface is on a multiaccess network but this router is neither the Designated Router nor its backup. The router forms adjacencies with the Designated Router and its backup.

*Backup*

The router is the Backup Designated Router. It will be promoted to Designated Router if the present Designated Router fails. The router forms adjacencies with every other router on the network.

*DR*

The router itself is the Designated Router. The router forms adjacencies with every other router on the network. The router must also originate a network links advertisement for the network node.

*Type of Service (TOS) metrics*

> In each type of link state advertisement, different metrics can be advertised for each IP Type of Service. A metric for TOS 0 (used for OSPF routing protocol packets) must always be specified. Metrics for other TOS values can be specified; if they are not, these metrics are assumed equal to the metric specified for TOS 0.

*Link State Database*

> Also called the *directed graph* or the *topological database*. It is created from the link state advertisements generated by the routers in the area.

> **Note:** RFC 1583 uses the term Link State Database in preference to topological database. The former term has the advantage that it describes the contents of the database, the latter is more descriptive of the purpose of the database – to describe the topology of the area. We have previously used the term topological database for this reason, but for the remainder of this section where we discuss the operation of OSPF in more detail, we will refer to it as the Link State Database.

*Shortest-Path Tree*

> Each router runs the Shortest Path First (SPF) algorithm on the Link State Database to obtain its shortest-path tree. The tree gives the route to any destination network or host as far as the area boundary. It is used to build the routing table.

> **Note:** Because each router occupies a different place in the area's topology, application of the SPF algorithm gives a different tree for each router, even though the database is identical.

> Area border routers run multiple copies of the algorithm but build a single routing table.

*Routing table*

> The routing table contains entries for each destination: network, subnet or host. For each destination, there is information for one or more types of service (TOS). For each combination of destination and type of service, there are entries for one or more optimum paths to be used.

*Area ID*

> A 32-bit number identifying a particular area. The backbone has an Area ID of zero.

*Router ID*

> A 32-bit number identifying a particular router. Each router within the AS has a single router ID. One possible implementation is to use the lowest numbered IP address belonging to a router as its router ID.

*Router Priority*

An 8-bit unsigned integer, configurable on a per-interface basis indicating this router's priority in the selection of the (backup) Designated Router. A Router Priority of zero indicates that this router is ineligible to be the Designated Router.

## 3.3.4.1 Overview of OSPF Operation

The basic sequence of operations performed by OSPF routers is:

1. Discovering OSPF neighbors

2. Electing the Designated Router

3. Forming adjacencies

4. Synchronizing databases

5. Calculating the routing table

6. Advertising Link States

Routers will go through these steps when they first come up, and will repeat these steps in response to events which occur in the network. Each router must perform each of these steps for each network it is connected to, except for the calculation of the routing table. Each router generates and maintains a single routing table for all networks.

Each of these steps is described in the following sections.

**Discovering OSPF Neighbors:** When OSPF routers start, they initiate and sustain relationships with their neighbors using the Hello protocol. The Hello protocol also ensures that communication between neighbors is bidirectional. Hello packets are sent periodically out to all router interfaces. Bidirectional communication is indicated when the router sees itself in the neighbor's Hello packet. On a broadcast network, Hello packets are sent using multicast; neighbors are then discovered dynamically. On non-broadcast networks each router that may potentially become a Designated Router has a list of all routers attached to the network and will send Hello packets to all other potential Designated Routers when its interface to the non-broadcast network first becomes operational.

The OSPF header is described in Figure 3-9.

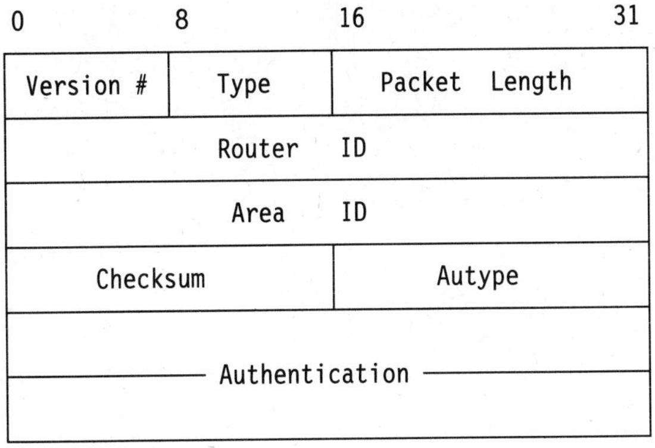

```
0          8         16                    31
┌──────────┬─────────┬──────────────────────┐
│Version # │  Type   │  Packet   Length      │
├──────────┴─────────┴──────────────────────┤
│          Router   ID                       │
├────────────────────────────────────────────┤
│            Area   ID                       │
├────────────────────┬───────────────────────┤
│     Checksum       │      Autype            │
├────────────────────┴───────────────────────┤
│                                            │
│          ──── Authentication ────           │
│                                            │
└────────────────────────────────────────────┘
```

*Figure* **3-9.** *OSPF Packet Header*

*Version #*
> The OSPF version number (2).

*Type*
> Hello (1), database description (2), Link-State Request (3), Link-State Update (4), or Link-State Acknowledgment (5).

*Packet length*
> Length of the protocol packet in bytes including the OSPF header.

*Router ID*
> The ID of the router originating the packet.

*Area ID*
> The area that the packet is being sent into.

*Checksum*
> The standard IP checksum of the entire contents of the packet, excluding the 64-bit authentication field.

*AuType*
> Identifies the authentication scheme to be used for the packet. The authentication type is configurable on a per-area basis. Additional authentication data is configurable on a per-interface basis. The authentication types currently defined are 0 (No authentication) and 1 (plain text 64-bit password).

*Authentication*
> A 64-bit field for use by the authentication scheme.

The format of the OSPF Hello packet is given in Figure 3-10.

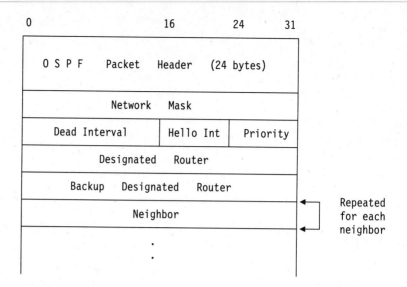

*Figure   3-10.  OSPF Hello Packet*

*Network Mask*
>The network mask associated with this interface.  This is the subnet mask if subnetting is implemented, or the equivalent mask for a non-subnetted network (for example, 255.255.255.0 for a non-subnetted Class C  network).

*Dead Interval*
>The number of seconds that must elapse before returning a silent neighbor to the down state.

*Hello Int (Hello Interval)*
>The number of seconds between this router's Hello packets.

*Priority*
>This router's Router Priority (for this interface).

*Designated Router*
>The IP address of the Designated Router for this network, according to the sending router.  This is set to 0 if no Designated Router is known.

*Backup Designated Router*
>The IP address of the Backup Designated Router for this network, according to the sending router.  This is set to 0 if no Backup Designated Router is known.

*Neighbor*

The Router IDs of each router from whom valid Hello packets have been received recently from the network. Recently means within the last Dead Interval.

**Determining the Designated Router:** This is done using the Hello protocol. A brief description of the process is given here. See RFC 1583 for a full description. The router examines the list of its neighbors, discards any with which it does not have bidirectional communication or which have a Router Priority of zero, and records the Designated Router, Backup Designated Router and Router Priority declared by each one. The router adds itself to the list, using the Router Priority configured for the interface and zero (unknown) for the Designated Router and Backup Designated Router values, if the calculating router has just come up.

The following rules are used to determine the Backup Designated Router:

- If one or more routers declare themselves to be the Backup Designated Router and not to be the Designated Router, then the one with the higher Router Priority wins.

- In the event of a tie, the router with the highest Router ID wins.

- If no router has declared itself to be the Backup Designated Router, then the Router with the highest Router Priority is elected unless it has declared itself to be the Designated Router.

- Again, in the event of a tie, the router with the highest Router ID wins.

Because the calculating router is in the list, it may determine that it is to become the Backup Designated Router. A similar process is followed for the Designated Router:

- If one or more routers declare themselves to be the Designated Router, then the one with the higher Router Priority wins.

- In the event of a tie, the router with the highest Router ID wins.

- If no router has declared itself to be the Backup then the Backup Designated Router becomes the Designated Router.

The actual process is considerably more complex than this, because the Hello messages transmitted include changes to the fields recorded on other routers, and these changes cause events in those routers which in turn will trigger state changes or other actions. The intent behind the mechanism is twofold:

- That when a router comes up, it should not usurp the position of (Backup) Designated Router from the current holder even if it has a higher Router priority.

- That the promotion of a Backup Designated Router to Designated Router should be orderly and require the Backup to accept its responsibilities.

The algorithm does not always result in the router with the highest priority being the Designated Router, nor in the one with the second highest priority being the Backup.

The Designated Router has the following responsibilities:

- The Designated Router generates the network links advertisement on behalf of the network. This advertisement is *flooded* throughout the area and describes this network to all routers in all networks in this area.

- The Designated Router becomes adjacent to other routers on the network. These adjacencies are central to the flooding procedure used to ensure that link state advertisements reach all routers in the area and therefore that the topological database used by all routers remains the same.

The Backup Designated Router has the following responsibility

- The Designated Router becomes adjacent to all other routers on the network. This ensures that it can take over from the Designated Router rapidly.

**Forming adjacencies:** After a neighbor has been discovered, bidirectional communication ensured, and (on a multiaccess network) a Designated Router elected, a decision is made regarding whether or not an adjacency should be formed with the neighbor:

- On multiaccess networks, all routers become adjacent to both the Designated Router and the Backup Designated Router.

- On point-to-point links (or virtual links), the router always forms an adjacency with the router at the other end.

If the decision is made to not form an adjacency, the state of the neighbor communication remains in the 2-way state.

Adjacencies are established using *Database Description* packets. These contain a summary of the sender's link state database. Multiple packets may be used to describe the database: for this purpose a poll-response procedure is used. The router with the higher router ID will become the master, the other will become the slave. Database Description packets sent by the master (*polls*) are acknowledged by Database Description packets sent by the slave (*responses*). The packets contain sequence numbers to ensure a match between polls and responses. This is called the *Database Exchange Process*.

The format of the OSPF Database Description packet is shown in Figure 3-11.

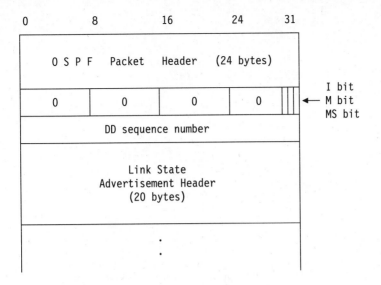

*Figure* *3-11.* *OSPF Database Description Packet*

*0*  Reserved, must be 0.

*I bit*  Init bit. Set to 1 when the packet is the first in the sequence of database description.

*M bit*  More bit. Indicates that more data descriptions are to follow.

*MS bit*  Master/slave bit. Set to 1 when the router is the master, 0 when it is the slave.

*DD sequence number* Used to sequence the collection of database description packets.

The rest of the packet contains a list of some or all of the contents of the topological database. Each item in the database is a link state advertisement. The database description packets contain the headers from these advertisements. The headers are sufficient to uniquely identify each advertisement. This information is used in the subsequent database synchronization. The format of a Link State Header is shown in Figure 3-12.

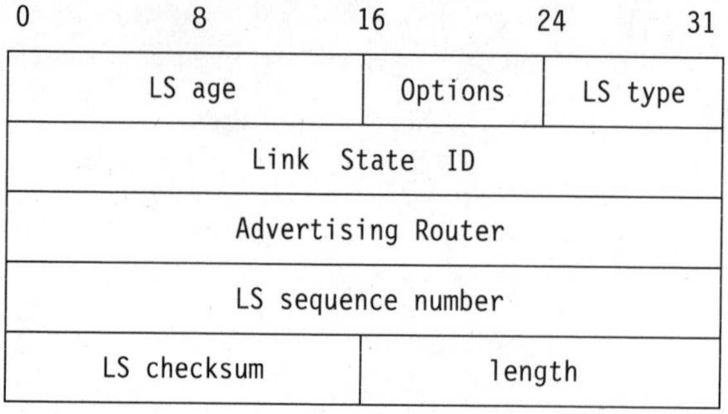

```
0          8          16         24         31
+--------------------+----------+-----------+
|       LS age       | Options  |  LS type  |
+--------------------+----------+-----------+
|            Link  State  ID                |
+-------------------------------------------+
|            Advertising Router             |
+-------------------------------------------+
|            LS sequence number             |
+--------------------+----------------------+
|    LS checksum     |        length        |
+--------------------+----------------------+
```

*Figure  3-12. OSPF Link State Advertisement Header*

The fields in the link state advertisement header are:

*LS age*

A 16-bit number indicating the time in seconds since the origin of the advertisement. It is increased as the link state advertisement resides in a router's database and with each hop it travels as part of the flooding procedure. When it reaches a maximum value, it ceases to be used for determining routing tables and is discarded unless it is still needed for database synchronization. The age is also to determine which of two otherwise identical copies of an advertisement a router should use.

*Options*

Two bits which describe optional OSPF capabilities. The E-bit indicates an external routing capability: it is set unless the advertisement is for a router, network links or summary link in a stub area. The E-bit is used for information only and does not affect the routing table. The T-bit indicates that the advertisement describes paths for types of service in addition to TOS 0.

*LS type*

The types of the link state advertisement are:

1 Router links. These describe the states of a router's interfaces.
2 Network links. These describe the routers attached to a network.
3 Summary links. These describe inter-area, intra-AS routes. They are created by area border routers and allow routes to networks within the AS but outside the area to be described concisely.
4 Summary links. These describe routes to the boundary of the AS (that is, to AS boundary routers). They are created by area border routers. They are very similar to type 3.

5 AS external links. These describe routes to networks outside the AS. They are created by AS boundary routers. A default route for the AS can be described this way.

*Link State ID*

A unique ID for the advertisement which is dependent on the Link State Type. For types 1 and 4 it is the Router ID, for types 3 and 5 it is an IP network number, and for type 2 it is the IP address of the Designated Router.

*Advertising Router*

The Router ID of the router that originated the link state advertisement. For type 1 advertisements, this field is identical to the Link State ID. For type 2, it is the Router ID of the network's Designated Router. For types 3 and 4, it is the Router ID of an area border router. For type 5, it is the Router ID of an AS boundary router.

*LS sequence number*

Used to allow detection of old or duplicate link state advertisements.

*LS checksum*

Checksum of the complete link state advertisement excluding the LS age field.

**Synchronization of databases:** After the Database Exchange Process is over, each router has a list of those link advertisements for which the neighbor has more up-to-date instances. These are then requested in *Link State Request* packets. The response to a Link State Request packet is a Link State Update packet which contains some or all of the link state advertisements requested. At most one Link State Request can be outstanding: if no response is received, the requester must retry the request.

Link state advertisements come in five formats. The format of a Router Links Advertisement (Type 1) is shown in Figure 3-13.

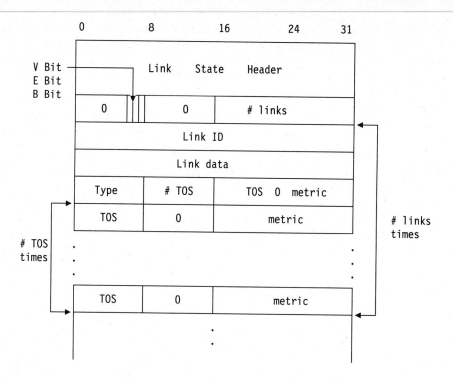

*Figure 3-13. OSPF Router Links Advertisement.* This advertisement is itself encapsulated in an OSPF packet.

*V Bit*

When set, this router is the endpoint of a virtual link which is using this area as a transit area.

*E Bit*

When set, the router is an AS boundary router.

*B Bit*

When set, the router is an area border router.

*# links*

The number of links described by this advertisement.

*Link ID*

Identifies the object that this link connects to. The value depends upon the type field (see below).

*1* Neighboring router's Router ID
*2* IP Address of the Designated Router

*3* This value depends on what the inter area route is to:

> For a stub network it is the IP network/subnet number
> For a host it is X′ FFFFFFFF′
> For the AS-external default route it is X′ 00000000′

*4* Neighboring router's Router ID

*Link Data*

This value also depends upon the type field (see RFC 1583 for details).

*Type*

What this link connects to.

*1* Point-to-point connection to another router
*2* Connection to a transit network
*3* Connection to a stub network or to a host
*4* Virtual link

*# metric*

The number of different TOS metrics given for this link in addition to the metric for TOS 0.

*TOS 0 metric*

The cost of using this outbound link for TOS 0. All OSPF routing protocol packets are sent with the IP TOS field set to 0.

*TOS*

IP type of service that this metric refers to. RFC 1349 defines the possible TOS values in an IP header (see also 2.3, "Internet Protocol (IP)" on page 2-36) using a 4-bit sequence. OSPF encodes these by treating the sequence as a number and doubling it (there is a reserved bit of 0 immediately following the TOS value field in the IP datagram, so OSPF allows for its future inclusion in the TOS value). There are five defined values:

| OSPF | RFC 1349 | Type of Service |
|------|----------|-----------------|
| 0 | 0000 | Normal service |
| 2 | 0001 | Minimize monetary cost |
| 4 | 0010 | Maximize reliability |
| 8 | 0100 | Maximize throughput |
| 16 | 1000 | Minimize delay |

***Table  3-1.*** *Type of Service Values*

*metric*

The cost of using this outbound router link for traffic of the specified Type of Service.

As an example, suppose the point-to-point link between routers RT1 (IP address: 192.1.2.3) and RT6 (IP address: 6.5.4.3) is a satellite link. To encourage the use of this line for high bandwidth traffic, the AS administrator may set an artificially low metric for that TOS. Router RT1 would then originate the following router links advertisement (assuming RT1 is an area border router and is not an AS boundary router):

```
; RT1's router links advertisement

LS age = 0                       ; always true on origination
LS type = 1                      ; indicates router links
Link State ID = 192.1.2.3        ; RT1's Router ID
Advertising Router = 192.1.2.3   ; RT1
bit E = 0                        ; not an AS boundary router
bit B = 1                        ; area border router
#links = 1
        Link ID = 6.5.4.3        ; neighbor router's Router ID
        Link Data = 0.0.0.0      ; interface to unnumbered SL
        Type = 1                 ; connects to router
        # other metrics = 1
        TOS 0 metric = 8
            TOS = 2              ; high bandwidth
            metric = 1           ; traffic preferred
```

The format of a Network Links Advertisement (Type 2) is shown in Figure 3-14.

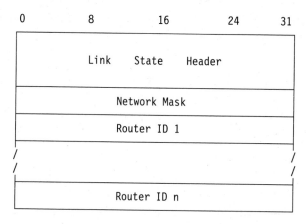

***Figure*** *3-14. OSPF Network Links Advertisement.* This advertisement is itself encapsulated in an OSPF packet.

*Network Mask*

> The IP address mask for the network. For example a Class A network would have the mask 255.0.0.0.

*Router ID 1-n*

> The IP addresses of all routers on the network which are adjacent to the Designated Router (including the sending router). The number of routers in the list is deduced from the length field in the header.

The format of a Summary Links Advertisement (Type 3 or 4) is shown in Figure 3-15.

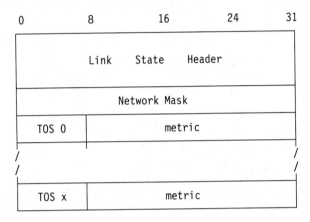

***Figure 3-15. OSPF Summary Links Advertisement.*** This advertisement is itself encapsulated in an OSPF packet.

*Network Mask*

> For a Type 3 link state advertisement, this is the IP address mask for the network. For a Type 4 link state advertisement, this is not meaningful and must be zero.

*TOS 0*

> zero

*metric*

> The cost of this route for this type of service in the same units used for TOS metrics in Type 1 advertisements.

*TOS x*

> Zero or more entries for additional types of service. The number of entries can be determined from the length field in the header.

The format of an External Links Advertisement is shown in Figure 3-16.

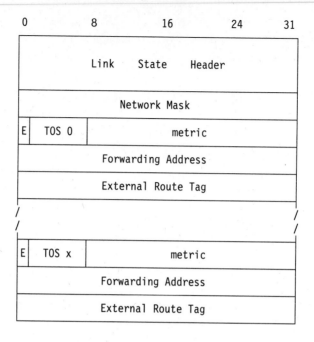

```
  0         8          16         24      31
  +-------------------------------------------+
  |                                           |
  |         Link    State    Header           |
  |                                           |
  +-------------------------------------------+
  |              Network Mask                 |
  +-+-------+---------------------------------+
  |E| TOS 0 |             metric              |
  +-+-------+---------------------------------+
  |           Forwarding Address              |
  +-------------------------------------------+
  |           External Route Tag              |
  /                                           /
  /                                           /
  +-+-------+---------------------------------+
  |E| TOS x |             metric              |
  +-+-------+---------------------------------+
  |           Forwarding Address              |
  +-------------------------------------------+
  |           External Route Tag              |
  +-------------------------------------------+
```

**Figure   3-16.** *OSPF External Links Advertisement.*   This advertisement is itself
encapsulated in an OSPF packet.

*Network Mask*

> The IP address mask for the network.

*Bit E*

> The type of external metric.  If set, the type is 2, otherwise it is 1.
>
> *1* The metric is directly comparable to OSPF Link State metrics
>
> *2* The metric is considered larger than all OSPF Link State metrics

*TOS 0*

> zero

*metric*

> The cost of this route.  Interpretation depends on the E-bit.

*Forwarding Address*

> The IP address that data traffic for this type of service intended for the
> advertised destination is to be forwarded to.  The value zero indicates that
> traffic should be forwarded to the AS boundary router that originated the
> advertisement.

*External Route Tag*

A 32-bit value attached to the external route by an AS boundary router. OSPF does not define or use this value, but see 3.4.2.2, "BGP OSPF Interaction" on page 3-64 for its use when BGP is being used as an external routing protocol.

*TOS x*

Zero or more entries for additional types of service. The number of entries can be determined from the length field in the header.

When all Link State Request packets have been answered, the databases are synchronized and the routers are described as fully adjacent. This adjacency is now added to the two routers' link state advertisements.

**Calculating the routing table:** Using its attached areas' link state databases as input, a router runs the SPF algorithm to build its routing table. The routing table is always built from scratch: updates are never made to an existing routing table. An old routing table is not discarded until changes between the two tables have been identified. Briefly, the calculation consists of the steps listed below. See RFC 1583 for more details about how the algorithm is implemented.

1. The intra-area routes are calculated building the shortest path tree for each attached area using the router itself as the root of the tree. The router also calculates whether the area can act as a transit area for virtual links.

2. The inter-area routes are calculated through examination of summary link advertisements. For area border routers (which are part of the backbone) only link advertisements corresponding to the backbone are used (that is, an area border router will always route inter-area traffic through the backbone).

3. If the router is connected to one or more transit areas, the router replaces any routes it has calculated by routes through transit areas if these are superior.

4. AS external routes are calculated through examination of AS external link advertisements. The locations of the AS boundary routers are already known because these are determined like any other intra-area or inter-area routes.

When the algorithm produces multiple equal cost routes, OSPF can distribute the load across them evenly. The maximum supported number of equal cost routes is implementation dependent.

**Advertising Link States:** A router periodically advertises its link state, so the absence of a recent advertisement indicates to a router's neighbors that the router is down. All routers which have established bidirectional communication with a neighbor run an inactivity timer to detect such an occurrence. If the timer is not reset, it will eventually pop, and the associated event places the state machine corresponding to that neighbor in the down state. This means that communication must be re-established from the beginning, including re-synchronization of databases. A router also re-issues its advertisements when its state changes.

A router can issue several link state advertisements into each area. These are propagated throughout the area by the flooding procedure. Each router issues a Router Links Advertisement. If the router is also the Designated Router for one or more of the networks in the area, then it will originate Network Links Advertisements for those networks. Area border routers issue one Summary Link Advertisement for each known inter-area destination. AS boundary routers originate one AS External Link Advertisement for each known external destination. Destinations are advertised one at a time so that the change in any single route can be flooded without reflooding the entire collection of routes. During the flooding procedure, many link state advertisements can be carried by a single Link State Update packet.

## 3.3.4.2 Summary of Features for OSPF

OSPF is a complex routing protocol, as will be clear from the preceding sections. The benefits of this complexity (over RIP) are as follows:

- Because of the synchronized Link State databases, OSPF routers will converge much faster than RIP routers after topology changes. This effect becomes more pronounced as autonomous systems get larger.

- It includes *Type of Service (TOS)* routing that is designed to compute separate routes for each type of service. For any destination, multiple routes can exist, each route supporting one or more different Types of Service.

- It uses weighted metrics for different speed links. For example, a T1 1.544 Mbps link might be assigned a metric of 1 and a 9600 bps SLIP link might be assigned a metric of 10.

- It provides load balancing since an OSPF gateway can use more than one equal minimum cost path to a destination.

- A subnet mask is associated with each route, allowing variable-length subnetting (see 2.2.2, "Subnets" on page 2-10) and supernetting (see 2.2.7, "Classless Inter-Domain Routing (CIDR)" on page 2-26).

- All exchanges between routers may be authenticated by the use of passwords.

- OSPF supports host-specific routes, network-specific routes as well as subnet routes.

- OSPF allows contiguous networks and hosts to be grouped together into *areas* within an AS, simplifying the topology and reducing the amount of routing information which must be exchanged. Knowledge of an area's topology remains hidden from other areas.

- It minimizes broadcasts by allowing a more complex graph topology in which multiaccess networks have a *Designated Router* which is responsible for describing that network to the other networks in the area.

- It allows external routing information exchange, that is, routing information learned from another autonomous system.

- It allows routing within the AS to be configured according to a virtual topology rather than just the physical interconnections. Areas can be joined using virtual links which cross other areas without requiring complicated routing.

- It allows the use of point-to-point links without IP addresses which can save scarce resources in the IP address space.

**References:** A detailed description of OSPF can be found in the following RFCs:

- *RFC 1245 — OSPF Protocol Analysis*
- *RFC 1246 — Experience with the OSPF Protocol*
- *RFC 1253 — OSPF Version 2: Management Information Base*
- *RFC 1370 — Applicability Statement for OSPF*
- *RFC 1583 — OSPF Version 2*

## 3.3.4.3 OSI Intermediate System to Intermediate System (IS-IS)

Intermediate System to Intermediate System (IS-IS) is a similar protocol to OSPF: it also uses a Link State, Shortest Path First algorithm (see 3.3.1.2, "Link-State, Shortest Path First" on page 3-13 for more details). However, IS-IS is an OSI protocol used for routing *Connectionless Network Protocol (CLNP)* packets within a routing domain. CLNP is the OSI protocol most comparable to IP.

*Integrated IS-IS* extends IS-IS to encompass TCP/IP. Integrated IS-IS is described in RFC 1195. Its goal is to provide a *single* (and efficient) routing protocol for TCP/IP *and* for OSI. Its design makes use of the OSI IS-IS routing protocol, augmented with IP-specific information, and provides explicit support for IP subnetting, variable subnet masks, TOS-based (type of service) routing, and external routing. It provides a provision for authentication information. Integrated IS-IS is based on the same SPF routing algorithm as OSPF.

Integrated IS-IS does not employ mutual encapsulation of IP and CLNP packets: both types are forwarded "as-is," nor does it change the behavior of the router as expected by either protocol suite. Integrated IS-IS behaves like an IGP in a TCP/IP network and in an OSI network. The only change is the addition of additional IP-related information.

IS-IS uses the term *Intermediate System (IS)* to refer to an IS-IS router, but we shall use the term router, since this is freely used in the Integrated IS-IS standard.

IS-IS groups networks into domains in a fashion that is analogous to OSPF. A *routing domain* is analogous to an Autonomous system, and it is subdivided into *areas* just like OSPF. Here is an overview of some of the more important aspects of IS-IS routing. Where possible, comparisons are made with equivalent concepts used in OSPF but it is dangerous to draw too close a parallel, since there are fundamental differences between the two protocols.

- Routers are divided into Level 1 routers, which know nothing of the topology outside their areas, and Level 2 routers, which do know about the higher-level topology, but know nothing about the topology inside the areas unless they are also Level 1 routers.

- A Level 1 router may belong to more than one area, but unlike OSPF this is not for routing purposes but for ease of management of the domain, and would normally be short term. A Level 1 router recognizes another as a neighbor if they are both in the same area.

- A Level 2 router recognizes all other Level 2 routers as neighbors. A Level 2 router may also be a Level 1 router in one area, but not more.

- A Level 1 router in IS-IS cannot have a link to an external router (in OSPF an internal router can be an AS border router).

- There is a Level 2 backbone containing all Level 2 routers, but unlike in OSPF, it must be physically connected.

- The OSI addressing scheme explicitly identifies the target area for a packet, allowing simple selection of routing choices as follows:

  - Level 2 routers route towards the area without regard to its internal structure.

  - Level 1 routers route towards the destination if it is within their area, or to the nearest Level 2 router if it is not.

- Multiaccess networks use a Designated Router concept. To avoid the "$n(n-1)/2$" problem described under OSPF, IS-IS implements a *pseudonode* for the LAN. Each LAN-attached router is regarded as having a link to the pseudonode but no link to any of the other routers on the LAN. The Designated Router then acts on behalf of the pseudonode.

Integrated IS-IS permits considerable mixing of the two protocol suites, subject to certain restrictions on the topology. Three types of router are defined:

*IP-only*     A router which uses IS-IS as the routing protocol for IP and does not otherwise support OSI protocols (for example, such routers would not be able to forward OSI CLNP packets).

*OSI-only*     A router which uses IS-IS as the routing protocol for OSI but not IP.

*Dual*      A router which uses IS-IS as a single integrated routing protocol for both IP and OSI.

It is possible to have a mixed domain containing IS-IS routers, some of which are IP-only, some OSI-only and some are dual. Each area within a mixed domain is configured to be OSI, IP or dual. Areas which are to carry mixed traffic must have dual routers for all of the Level 1 routers. Similarly, the Level 2 routers in a mixed domain must all be dual routers if mixed traffic is to be routed between areas.

### 3.3.4.4 Co-existence of TCP/IP and OSI Routing Protocols without IS-IS

As its name suggests, Integrated IS-IS offers an integrated routing solution for multi-protocol networks. OSPF, like other TCP/IP routing protocols, uses an approach termed *Ships In the Night (SIN)* to handle coexistence issues. In the SIN approach, each multiprotocol router runs a separate process for each network layer (IP and OSI). A SIN router allows network managers to insert new SIN-based routing protocols, such as OSPF, one by one in the network, but the protocols exist independently of one another, and their frames pass each other like ships in the night.

Since the customer base of independent router vendors remains largely TCP/IP-focused, most of these vendors are choosing, for now, to stick with SIN even if it means their routers will not be able to work in OSI networks. A few of them have announced that they will support Integrated IS-IS in the future.

# 3.4 Exterior Routing Protocols

*Exterior Routing Protocols* or *Exterior Gateway Protocols (EGPs)* are used to exchange routing information between routers in different autonomous systems.

**Note:** The term Exterior Routing Protocol has no abbreviation in common use, so we shall use the abbreviation EGP as is usual in TCP/IP literature.

Two EGPs are in common use

- Exterior Gateway Protocol (see 3.4.1, "Exterior Gateway Protocol (EGP)").
- Border Gateway Protocol (see 3.4.2, "Border Gateway Protocol (BGP)" on page 3-52).

EGP is being replaced progressively by BGP. We shall discuss the two protocols in turn.

## 3.4.1 Exterior Gateway Protocol (EGP)

EGP is a *standard protocol*. Its status is *recommended*.

The Exterior Gateway Protocol is the protocol used for exchange of routing information between *exterior* gateways (not belonging to the same autonomous system).

EGP gateways may only forward reachability information for networks within their autonomous system. This routing information must be collected by this EGP gateway, usually via an *Interior Gateway Protocol* (IGP), used to exchange information between gateways within an autonomous system (see Figure 3-2 on page 3-5).

EGP is based on periodic polling using *Hello/I Hear You* message exchanges, to monitor neighbor reachability and poll requests to solicit update responses. EGP restricts exterior gateways by allowing them to advertise only those destination networks reachable entirely within that gateway's autonomous system. Thus, an exterior gateway using EGP passes along information to its EGP neighbors but does not advertise reachability information about its EGP neighbors (gateways are neighbors if they exchange routing information) outside the autonomous system. It has three main features:

- It supports a *neighbor acquisition protocol*. Two gateways may be regarded as neighbors if they are connected by an *internet* which is transparent to them. EGP does not specify the way in which one gateway initially decides that it wants to become a neighbor of another. To become a neighbor it must send an *Acquisition confirm* message as a response to an *Acquisition Request* message. This step is necessary to obtain routing information from another gateway.
- It supports a *neighbor reachability protocol*. It is used by a gateway to keep real-time information as to the reachability of its neighbors. The EGP protocol provides two message types for that purpose: a *Hello* message and an *I Hear You* message (response to Hello).
- It supports update messages (also called *network reachability (NR) messages*) that carry routing information. No gateway is required to send NR messages to any other gateway, except as a response to a *poll request*.

To perform these three basic functions, EGP defines 10 message types:

*Acquisition Request*
> Request a gateway to become a neighbor (or peer)

*Acquisition Confirm*
> Positive response to acquisition request

*Acquisition Refuse*
> Negative response to acquisition request

*Cease Request*
> Request termination of neighbor relationship

*Cease Confirm*
> Confirmation response to cease request

*Hello*
> Request neighbor to respond if alive

*I Hear You*
> Response to Hello message

*Poll Request*
> Request network routing table

*Routing Update*
> Network reachability information

*Error*
> Response to incorrect message

Let us consider the EGP routing update message shown in Figure 3-17.

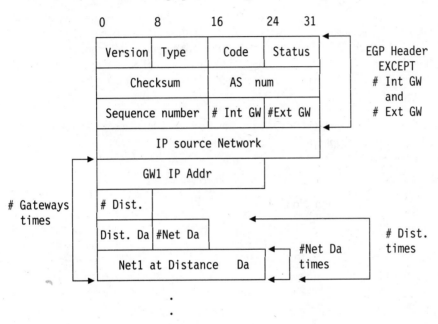

***Figure 3-17.*** *EGP Routing Update Message*

The different fields are as follows (the EGP header is not considered; refer to RFC 904 for more details):

*#Int GW*    Number of interior gateways (in the AS) appearing in this message.

*#Ext GW*    Number of exterior gateways (outside the AS) appearing in this message.

*IP Source Network*
> The IP network number about which all reachability is measured.

*GW1 IP addr*
> IP address (without network number) of the gateway from which the distances are measured.

*#Dist.*    Number of distances in the gateway block.

*Dist.Da*   Distance value.

*#Net Da*   Number of networks at a given distance (Da).

*Net1 at distance Da*
> IP network number reachable via GW1 and at distance Da from GW1.

As indicated above, the EGP routing information messages associate a *distance* qualifier to each route. But, EGP *does not interpret these distance values.* They merely serve as an indication of the reachability or unreachability of a network (a value of 255 means that the network is unreachable). The value cannot be used to compute the shorter of two routes unless those routes are both contained within a single autonomous system. For this reason, EGP cannot be used as a routing algorithm. As a result there will be only one path from the exterior gateway to any network.

EGP is gradually being replaced by the more functional Border Gateway Protocol (BGP). For a more detailed description of BGP refer to the next section.

## 3.4.2  Border Gateway Protocol (BGP)

**Note:** There are four different versions of BGP defined. Where BGP is specified without a version number, it normally refers to BGP Version 3 unless the document pre-dates the publication of the BGP-3 definition. BGP-3 is described in this section and BGP-4 in 3.4.2.3, "Border Gateway Protocol Version 4 (BGP-4)" on page 3-64. BGP-1 and BGP-2, described in RFC 1105 and RFC 1163, are obsolete. Changes from BGP-1 and BGP-2 to BGP-3 are documented in Appendix 2 and 3 of RFC 1267.

### 3.4.2.1  Border Gateway Protocol Version 3 (BGP-3)

BGP-3 is a *draft standard protocol.* Its status is *elective.* It is described in RFC 1267.

BGP-3 is an *inter-Autonomous System* (inter-AS) routing protocol based on experience gained from EGP (see 3.4.1, "Exterior Gateway Protocol (EGP)" on page 3-49). Unlike other routing protocols which communicate via packets or datagrams, BGP-3 is *connection oriented*; it uses TCP as a transport protocol. The well-known port number is 179. See 2.12, "Transmission Control Protocol (TCP)" on page 2-92 for information on TCP and port numbers.

Recall that the EGP was designed as a protocol to exchange *reachability* information between autonomous systems, rather than a true *routing* protocol. Because inter-AS routing information is not available, EGP cannot detect the presence of a loop caused by a set of EGP routers all believing that one of the others can reach another AS to which none of them is connected. A further problem with EGP has to do with the amount of information exchanged; as the number of IP networks known to the NSFNET increased, the size of the EGP Neighbor Reachability (NR) messages became quite large and the amount of time it took to process them became significant.

BGP-3 has replaced EGP in the NSFNET backbone for these reasons. However, BGP-3 as described in RFC 1268 does not require the NSFNET or any other backbone to play any central role. Compare this to the Core System role played by the ARPANET in the early days of the Internet. Instead, BGP-3 views the Internet as an arbitrary collection of autonomous systems, and it does not take account of the internal topology of an AS nor of the IGP (or possibly multiple IGPs) used within an AS.

Before giving an overview of BGP-3 operation, we shall define some terms used in BGP-3:

*BGP speaker*
> A system running BGP.

*BGP neighbors*
> A pair of BGP speakers exchanging inter-AS routing information. BGP neighbors may be of two types:
>
> > *Internal*    A pair of BGP speakers in the same autonomous system. Internal BGP neighbors must present a consistent image of the AS to their External BGP neighbors. This is explained in more detail below.
> >
> > *External*    A pair of BGP neighbors in different autonomous systems. External BGP neighbors must be connected by a BGP connection as defined below. This restriction means that in most cases where an AS has multiple BGP inter-AS connections, it will also require multiple BGP speakers.

*BGP session*
> A TCP session between BGP neighbors which are exchanging routing information using BGP. The neighbors monitor the state of the session by sending a *keepalive* message regularly (the recommended interval is 30 seconds).[2]

---

2  This keepalive message is implemented in the application layer, and is independent of the keepalive message available in many TCP implementations.

*AS Border Router (ASBR)*

A router which has a connection to multiple autonomous systems.

**Note:** The nomenclature for this type of router is somewhat varied. RFC 1583, which describes OSPF, uses the term *AS Boundary Router*. RFC 1267 and 1268, which describe BGP-3, use the terms *Border Router* and *Border Gateway*. RFC 1340, which describes the interaction between OSPF and BGP-3, uses the term *AS Border Router*. We shall use the last term consistently when describing both OSPF and BGP. BGP-3 defines two types of AS Border Router, depending on its topological relationship to the BGP speaker which refers to it.

*internal*    A next hop router in the same AS as the BGP speaker.

*external*    A next hop router in a different AS from the BGP speaker.

The IP address of a border router is specified as a next hop destination when BGP-3 advertises an AS path (see below) to one of its external neighbors. Next hop border routers must share a physical connection (see below) with both the sending and receiving BGP speakers. If a BGP speaker advertises an external border router as a next hop, that router must have been learned of from one of that BGP speaker's peers.

*AS connection*

BGP-3 defines two types of inter-AS connection.

*physical connection*

An AS shares a physical network with another AS, and this network is connected to at least one border router from each AS. Since these two routers share a network, they can forward packets to each other without requiring any inter-AS or intra-AS routing protocols (that is, they require neither an IGP nor an EGP to communicate).

*BGP connection*

A BGP connection means that there is a BGP session between a pair of BGP speakers, one in each AS, and this session is used to communicate the routes through the physically connected border routers that can be used for specific networks. BGP-3 requires that the BGP speakers must be on the same network as the physically connected border routers so that the BGP session is also independent of all inter-AS or intra-AS routing protocols. The BGP speakers do not need to be border routers, and vice versa. In fact, BGP speakers do not need to be routers: it is quite feasible for a host to provide the BGP function and to pass exterior routing information to one or more border routers with another protocol.

**Note:** The term BGP connection can be used to refer to a session between two BGP speakers in the same AS.

*Traffic type*

BGP-3 categorizes traffic in an AS as one of two types:

local    Local traffic is traffic which either originates in or terminates in that AS. That is, either the source or the destination IP address is in the AS.

transit    Transit traffic is all non-local traffic.

One of the goals of BGP is to minimize the amount of transit traffic.

*AS Type*    An AS is categorized as one of three types:

stub    A stub AS has a single inter-AS connection to one other AS. A stub AS only carries local traffic.

multihomed
         A multihomed AS has connections to more than one other AS but refuses to carry transit traffic.

transit    A transit AS has connections to more than one other AS and will carry transit traffic. The AS may impose policy restrictions on what transit traffic will be carried.

*AS number*    A 16-bit number uniquely identifying an AS. This is the same AS number used by GGP and EGP.

*AS path*    A list of all of the AS numbers traversed by a route when exchanging routing information. Rather than exchanging simple metric counts, BGP-3 communicates entire paths to its neighbors.

*Routing Policy*

A set of rules constraining routing to conform to the wishes of the authority which administers the AS. Routing policies are not defined in the BGP-3 protocol, but are selected by the AS authority and presented to BGP-3 in the form of implementation-specific configuration data. Routing policies may be selected by the AS authority in whatever way that authority sees fit. For example:

- A multihomed AS can refuse to act as a transit AS. It does this by not advertising routes to networks other than those directly connected to it.

- A multihomed AS can limit itself to being a transit AS for a restricted set of adjacent ASs. It does this by advertising its routing information to this set only.

- An AS can select which outbound AS should be used for carrying transit traffic.

An AS can also apply performance-related criteria when selecting outbound paths:

- An AS can optimize traffic to use short AS paths rather than long ones.

- An AS can select transit routes according to the service quality of the intermediate hops. This service quality information could be obtained using mechanisms external to BGP-3.

It can be seen from the definitions above that a stub AS or a multihomed AS has the same topological properties as an AS in the ARPANET architecture: that is it never acts as an intermediate AS in an inter-AS route. In the ARPANET architecture, EGP was sufficient for such an AS to exchange reachability information with its neighbors, and this remains true with BGP-3. Therefore, a stub AS or a multihomed AS may continue to use EGP (or any other suitable protocol) to operate with a transit AS. However, RFC 1268 recommends that BGP-3 is used instead of EGP for these types of AS because it provides an advantage in bandwidth and performance. Additionally, in a multihomed AS, BGP-3 is more likely to provide an optimum inter-AS route than EGP, since EGP only addresses reachability and not "distance."

**Path Selection:** Each BGP speaker must evaluate different paths to a destination from the border router(s) for an AS connection, select the best one that complies with the routing policies in force and then advertise that route to all of its BGP neighbors at that AS connection.

BGP-3 is a vector-distance protocol but, unlike traditional vector-distance protocols such as RIP where there is a single metric, BGP-3 determines a preference order by applying a function mapping each path to a preference value and selects the path with the highest value. The function applied is generated by the BGP-3 implementation according to configuration information.

Where there are multiple viable paths to a destination, BGP-3 maintains all of them but only advertises the one with the highest preference value. This approach allows a quick change to an alternate path should the primary path fail.

**Routing Policies:** RFC 1268 includes a recommended set of policies for all implementations:

- A BGP-3 implementation should be able to control which routes it announces. The granularity of this control should be at least at the network level for the announced routes and at the AS level for the recipients. For example, BGP-3 should allow a policy of announcing a route to a specific network to a specific adjacent AS.

- BGP-3 should allow a weighting policy for paths. Each AS can be assigned a weight and the preferred path to a destination is then the one with the lowest aggregate weight.

- BGP-3 should allow a policy of excluding an AS from all possible paths. This can be done with a variant of the previous policy; each AS to be excluded is given an "infinite" weight and the route selection process refuses to consider paths of infinite weight.

**AS Consistency:**  BGP-3 requires that a transit AS present the same view to every AS using its services. If the AS has multiple BGP speakers, they must agree on two aspects of topology: intra-AS and inter-AS. Since BGP-3 does not deal with intra-AS routing at all, a consistent view of intra-AS topology must be provided by the interior routing protocol(s) employed in the AS. Naturally, a protocol such as OSPF (see 3.3.4, "Open Shortest Path First Protocol (OSPF) Version 2" on page 3-25) or Integrated IS-IS (see 3.3.4.3, "OSI Intermediate System to Intermediate System (IS-IS)" on page 3-47) which implements synchronization of router databases lends itself well to this role. Consistency of the external topology *may* be provided by all BGP speakers in the AS having BGP sessions with each other, but BGP-3 does not require that this method be used, only that consistency be maintained.

**Routing Information Exchange:**  BGP-3 only advertises routes that it uses itself to its neighbors. That is, BGP-3 conforms to the normal Internet hop-by-hop paradigm, even though it has additional information in the form of AS paths and theoretically could be capable of informing a neighbor of a route it would not use itself.

When two BGP speakers form a BGP session, they begin by exchanging their entire routing tables. Routing information is exchanged via UPDATE messages (see below for the format of these messages). Since the routing information contains the complete AS path to each listed destination in the form of a list of AS numbers in addition to the usual reachability and next hop information used in traditional vector distance protocols, it can be used to suppress routing loops and to eliminate the *counting-to-infinity* problem found in RIP. After BGP neighbors have performed their initial exchange of their complete routing databases, they only exchange updates to that information.

**BGP-3 Message formats:**  All BGP-3 messages have a common basic format. They vary between 19 and 4096 bytes in length, are transmitted over TCP and are processed in their entirety (that is, a BGP speaker does not begin to process the message until it has received the whole message). Each message has a header shown in Figure 3-18.

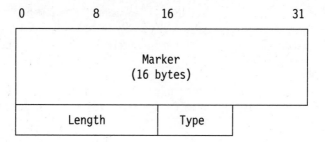

*Figure* *3-18. BGP-3 Header*

Marker    A value which can be predicted by the receiver, used for authentication and
          for identifying loss of synchronization. It is set to "all ones" when the
          Authentication Code is 0 (see below).

Length    Total length of the message including the header, in bytes. The message
          must not be padded since the length is used to calculate the length of the last
          field of the message in many cases.

type      An 8-bit unsigned value.

          *1* OPEN[3]
          *2* UPDATE
          *3* NOTIFICATION
          *4* KEEPALIVE

OPEN messages are used to initiate the BGP-3 session. The format of an OPEN message
is shown in Figure 3-19.

---

[3] RFC 1267 uses uppercase to name BGP messages, so we shall do the same in this section.

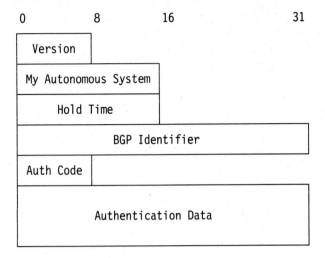

*Figure    3-19.  BGP-3 OPEN Message*

*Version*      3 for BGP-3 (1 byte)

*My Autonomous System*
            The AS number of the sender (2 bytes)

*Hold time*   The maximum length of time in seconds that may elapse between the receipt
            of successive KEEPALIVE and/or UPDATE and/or NOTIFICATION
            messages (2 bytes).

*BGP Identifier*
            A unique 32-bit number identifying the BGP speaker.  It is the IP address of
            any one of the speaker's interfaces.  The same number is used for all
            interfaces and all BGP neighbors.

*Authentication Code*
            Defines the interpretation of the Authentication Data (1 byte).  BGP-3
            defines no authentication codes other than zero (for no authentication).

*Authentication Data*
            Dependent on the Authentication Code.  The length is variable and is
            inferred from the message length.  For authentication code zero, the data is
            omitted (it has a length of zero).

UPDATE messages are used to transfer routing information.  The format of an UPDATE
message is shown in Figure  3-20.

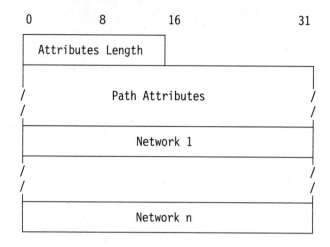

*Figure 3-20. BGP-3 UPDATE Message*

*Attributes Length*
> Length of the path attributes field in bytes (2 bytes).

*Path Attributes*
> Each path attribute is a triple: *<attribute type, attribute length, attribute value>* where:

> *attribute type*
>> is a 2-byte field, consisting of an attribute flag byte and a 1-byte *attribute type code*. The bits in the flag byte are:

>> X' 80'
>>> Optional attribute. If set, the attribute is *optional*, otherwise it is *well-known*. Well-known attributes are those that all BGP-3 implementations must handle. There are two types: *mandatory* attributes must be included in every UPDATE message, *discretionary* attributes may be omitted from UPDATE messages.

>>> Optional attributes are those that BGP-3 implementations are not required to recognize. If a receiving BGP speaker does not recognize the attribute, it should handle it according to the transitive bit. BGP speakers are allowed to make appropriate updates to attributes in messages which they receive from peers before relaying them to other BGP speakers.

X' 40'

> Transitive attribute. This bit must be set if the attribute is mandatory. For optional attributes, if this bit is set, the attribute is *transitive*, otherwise it is *non-transitive*. An unrecognized transitive optional attribute must be passed on to other BGP peers after setting the partial bit. An unrecognized non-transitive optional attribute must be quietly discarded. BGP speakers may add transitive optional attributes to the path attributes in an UPDATE message before relaying it to a peer.

X' 20'

> Partial attribute. This bit indicates that a transitive optional attribute was passed on by a BGP speaker that did not recognize it or was added by a BGP speaker other than the originator of the message. In all other cases it must be zero.

X' 10'

> Extended length. The attribute length field is two bytes if this bit is set and one byte if not.

The low order four bits must be zero and must be ignored by the recipient.

Refer to RFC 1267 for more details of how these bits are interpreted.

The attribute type codes defined are shown in Table 3-2.

*Table 3-2. BGP-3 UPDATE Path Attribute Type Values*

| Code | Name | Length | Attributes |
|------|------|--------|------------|
| 1 | ORIGIN | 1 | well-known, mandatory |
| 2 | AS_PATH | variable | well-known, mandatory |
| 3 | NEXT_HOP | 4 | well-known, mandatory |
| 4 | UNREACHABLE | 0 | well-known, discretionary |
| 5 | INTER-AS METRIC | 2 | optional, non-transitive |

ORIGIN

> The method by which this path was learned by the originating AS.

> *0* IGP – the networks listed are within the originating AS.

*1* EGP – the networks listed are outside the originating AS and the reachability information was learned from EGP.

*2* INCOMPLETE – the networks listed were learned by some other means.

AS_PATH
The 2-byte AS numbers of each AS in the path to the destination network(s). The number of hops in the path can be calculated by dividing the attribute length by 2.

NEXT_HOP
The IP address of the border router that is the next hop on the path to the listed network(s). This field is ignored for internal BGP connections.

UNREACHABLE
Previously advertised routes have now become unreachable.

INTER-AS METRIC
This value may be used to choose between multiple paths to one AS. If all other factors are equal, the path with the lower metric is to be preferred. This value may be sent to a BGP speaker in a neighboring AS, and if received over an external BGP connection, it may be propagated over internal BGP connections. A BGP speaker may not relay an INTER-AS METRIC in an UPDATE message which it receives from a peer to an external peer.

*attribute length*
One or two byte length (depending on the value of the extended length bit).

*attribute value*
Dependent upon the value of the attribute type code.

Each attribute can be specified only once. The end of the attributes is determined from the path attributes length field.

*Network 1* The 32-bit network number of the first network described by the preceding path attributes. Subnets and hosts are explicitly disallowed.

*Network n* The network number of the last network described by the preceding path attributes. The number of networks can be calculated by subtracting the lengths of the BGP-3 header and the path attributes information from the length of the message and dividing by 4.

NOTIFICATION messages are used to inform the neighbor of an error. The BGP connection is terminated after the message is sent. The format of a NOTIFICATION message is shown in Figure 3-21.

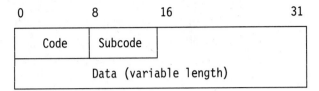

*Figure*  *3-21. BGP-3 NOTIFICATION Message*

*Code*  One byte indicating the type of error. The following codes are defined:

*1* Message Header Error
*2* OPEN Message Error
*3* UPDATE Message Error
*4* Hold Timer Expired
*5* Finite State Machine Error
*6* Cease

*Subcode*  A single byte providing more information about the nature of the error. The value 0 (unspecific) indicates that no more appropriate subcode exists. In addition the following subcodes are defined:

Message Header Error Subcodes
*1*  Connection Not Synchronized
*2*  Bad Message Length
*3*  Bad Message Type

OPEN Message Error Subcodes
*1*  Unsupported Version Number
*2*  Bad Peer AS
*3*  Bad BGP Identifier
*4*  Unsupported Authentication Code
*5*  Authentication Failure

UPDATE Message Error Subcodes
*1*  Malformed Attribute List
*2*  Unrecognized Well-known Attribute
*3*  Missing Well-known Attribute
*4*  Attribute Flags Error
*5*  Attribute Length Error
*6*  Invalid ORIGIN Attribute
*7*  AS Routing Loop

8    Invalid NEXT_HOP Attribute

9    Optional Attribute Error

10   Invalid Network Field

*Data*       Variable length information dependent upon the code and subcode which can be used to diagnose the cause of the error. The length can be calculated by subtracting 21 from the total message length.

KEEPALIVE messages are used to ensure that the connection is still working. The KEEPALIVE message consists of just the header.

**References:**   A detailed description of BGP-3 may be found in the following RFCs:

- *RFC 1265 — BGP Protocol Analysis*
- *RFC 1266 — Experience with the BGP protocol*
- *RFC 1267 — A Border Gateway Protocol 3 (BGP-3)*
- *RFC 1268 — Application of the Border Gateway Protocol in the Internet*

### 3.4.2.2 BGP OSPF Interaction

There is a *proposed standard protocol* with a status of *elective* defining how BGP-3 (an exterior routing protocol) should interact with OSPF (an interior routing protocol). Any host or router which dynamically exchanges information between BGP-3 and OSPF should adhere to this standard. It is described in *RFC 1654 — BGP OSPF Interaction*.

BGP OSPF interaction covers the conversion from OSPF fields in an External Links Advertisement to BGP path attributes, and vice versa, for three properties of a route definition.

*Table   3-3. BGP OSPF Attribute-Field Mapping*

| OSPF Field | BGP Attribute |
| --- | --- |
| Type and Metric | INTER-AS METRIC |
| External Tag | ORIGIN and AS PATH |
| Forwarding Address | NEXT HOP |

The standard defines how these mappings should be done and what restrictions there are on what may be done automatically. Please refer to the RFC for more information.

### 3.4.2.3 Border Gateway Protocol Version 4 (BGP-4)

BGP-4 is a *proposed standard protocol*. Its status is *elective*. It is described in RFC 1654. The main changes are to support *supernetting* or *Classless Inter-Domain Routing (CIDR)* which is described in 2.2.7, "Classless Inter-Domain Routing (CIDR)" on page 2-26. In particular BGP-4 supports IP prefixes and path aggregation. Because CIDR is radically different from the normal Internet routing architecture, BGP-4 is incompatible with BGP-3. However, BGP does define a mechanism for two BGP speakers to negotiate a version which they both understand. This is done using the OPEN message. Therefore, it is possible to implement "multi-lingual" BGP speakers which will allow inter-operation of BGP-3 and BGP-4.

The following items identify the major changes between BGP-3 and BGP-4.

- The BGP Version Number in the header field is 4.

- CIDR removes the concept of a network class from inter-domain routing, replacing it with the concept of an IP prefix.

- The list of networks in an UPDATE message is replaced by *network layer reachability information (NLRI)*.

- BGP-4 introduces the aggregation of multiple routes or AS paths into single entries or *aggregates*. The use of aggregates can dramatically reduce the amount of routing information required.

   A new attribute for an AS path (ATOMIC_AGGREGATE) can be used to insure that certain aggregates are not de-aggregated. Another new attribute (AGGREGATOR) can be added to aggregate routes in order to advertise which AS and which BGP speaker within that AS caused the aggregation.

- BGP-4 conceptually models the data held by a BGP speaker into three sets of *Routing Information Bases (RIB)*: one set (Adj-RIBs-In) for data obtained from BGP neighbors; one RIB (Loc-RIB) for local data obtained by the operation of the local routing policies on the Adj-RIBs-In; and one set (Adj-RIBs-Out) for data that is to be advertised in update messages.

- BGP-4 allows negotiation of Hold Times on a per-connection basis so that both ends of a connection are using the same value.

- BGP-4 changes the format of the UPDATE message to that shown in Figure 3-22.

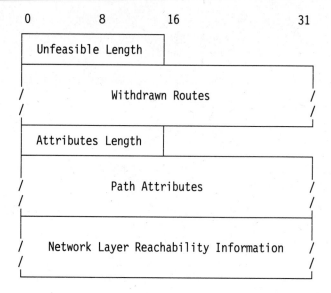

*Figure   3-22. BGP UPDATE Message*

*Unfeasible Length*

This is a contraction of *Unfeasible Routes Length* and is a 2-byte field giving the length of the Withdrawn Routes data. It may be zero, indicating no withdrawn routes.

*Withdrawn Routes*

A list of IP address prefixes that are being withdrawn from service. Each entry is of the form *<length, prefix>* where *length* is a single byte giving the length of the prefix in bits, and prefix is the IP address prefix padded to the next byte boundary. A length of zero matches all IP addresses.

*Attributes Length*

A 2-byte field giving the length of the path attributes field in bytes.

*Path Attributes*

These have the same values as for BGP-3 except as noted here:

*attribute type*

The following attribute type codes are defined:

| Code | Name | Length | Attributes |
|------|------|--------|------------|
| 1 | ORIGIN | 1 | well-known, mandatory |

| Code | Name | Length | Attributes |
|------|------|--------|------------|
| 2 | AS_PATH | variable | well-known, mandatory |
| 3 | NEXT_HOP | 4 | well-known, mandatory |
| 4 | MULTI_EXIT_DISC | 4 | optional, non-transitive |
| 5 | LOCAL-PREF | 4 | well known, discretionary |
| 4 | ATOMIC_AGGREGATE0 | | well known, discretionary |
| 5 | AGGREGATOR | 6 | optional, transitive |

ORIGIN

> The method by which this path was learned by the originating AS.
>
> *0* IGP — the networks listed are within the originating AS.
>
> *1* EGP — the networks listed are outside the originating AS and the reachability information was learned from EGP.
>
> *2* INCOMPLETE – the networks listed were learned by some other means.

AS_PATH

> A sequence of *AS Path segments*. Each of these is of the form *<path segment type, path segment length, path segment value>*
>
> *path segment type*
>> A 1-byte value indicating how the path segment is to be interpreted.
>>
>> *1* AS_SET: an unordered set of those ASs that a route in the UPDATE message has traversed
>>
>> *2* AS_SEQUENCE: an ordered set of ASs that a route in the UPDATE message has traversed
>
> *path segment length*
>> A 1-byte value containing the number of ASs in the path segment field.
>
> *path segment length*
>> A series of 2-byte AS numbers.

NEXT_HOP
> The IP address of the border router that is the next hop on the path to the listed destination(s).

MULTI_EXIT_DISC
> This value may be used to choose between multiple paths to one AS. It replaces the BGP-3 INTER-AS METRIC. If all other factors are equal, the path with the lower value is to be preferred. This value may be sent to a BGP speaker in a neighboring AS, and if received over an external BGP connection, it may be propagated over internal BGP connections. A BGP speaker may not relay a MULTI_EXIT_DISC value in an UPDATE message which it receives from a peer to an external peer.

LOCAL_PREF
> Used by a BGP speaker to inform other BGP speakers in its own AS of its degree of preference for an advertised route.

ATOMIC_AGGREGATE
> Used by a BGP speaker to inform other BGP speakers that the local system selected a less specific route without selecting a more specific route which is included in it.

AGGREGATOR
> The 2-byte AS number of the last AS number that formed the aggregate route followed by the IP address of the BGP speaker that formed the aggregate route.

*attribute length*
> One or two byte length (depending on the value of the extended length bit).

*attribute value*
> Dependent upon the value of the attribute type code.

> Each attribute can be specified only once. The end of the attributes is determined from the path attributes length field.

*Network Reachability Information*
> A series of IP prefixes described by the preceding path attributes. The end of the data can be determined by reference to the length of the message. Each entry is of the form *<length, prefix>* where *length* is a single byte giving the length of the prefix in bits, and prefix is the IP address prefix padded to the next byte boundary. A length of zero matches all IP addresses.

- The following error subcodes are added to the NOTIFICATION message definition:

**OPEN Message Error Subcodes**

*6* Unacceptable Hold Time

**UPDATE Message Error Subcodes**

*11* Malformed AS_PATH

- BGP-4 defines the following rules for creating AS_PATHs or modifying AS_PATHs learned from a BGP neighbor.

  The following two rules describe how to create a new AS_PATH:

  - When advertising it to a BGP speaker in the same AS, an AS-PATH of zero length is created.

  - When advertising it to a BGP speaker in a different AS, the AS_PATH includes only the sender's AS number.

  The following two rules describe how to handle AS_PATHs learned from a neighbor:

  - When advertising it to a BGP speaker in the same AS, the AS-PATH is left unchanged.

  - When advertising it to a BGP speaker in the same AS, the advertising BGP adds its own AS number to the beginning the AS-PATH. If the AS_PATH begins with a segment which is an AS_SEQUENCE, it adds its AS number to the beginning of that sequence, but if it begins with an AS-SET, the advertising BGP adds a new segment of the AS_SEQUENCE type to the beginning of the AS_PATH.

**References:** A detailed description of BGP-4 can be found in the following RFCs:

- *RFC 1654 — A Border Gateway Protocol 4 (BGP-4)*
- *RFC 1655 — Application of the Border Gateway Protocol in the Internet*
- *RFC 1656 — BGP-4 Protocol Document Roadmap and Implementation Experience*

# 3.4.3  IP Routing Protocols in IBM TCP/IP Products

The *routed* program which supports RIP is implemented on the following IBM TCP/IP platforms:

MVS
VM
AIX
OS/2
DOS

The routed program is not implemented on OS/400.

The *gated* program which supports RIP, Hello, EGP and BGP is implemented on AIX. On AIX 4.1, gated additionally supports OSPF Version 2 and RIP Version 2.

The IBM 6611 Network Processor implements RIP, RIP Version 2, Hello, OSPF, EGP and BGP.

The IBM 2210 Nways Network Processor implements RIP, OSPF and EGP.

# Chapter 4.  Application Protocols

The highest-level protocols are called *application protocols*. They communicate with applications on other internet hosts and are the user-visible interface to the TCP/IP protocol suite.

## 4.1.1  Characteristics of Applications

All of the higher-level protocols have some characteristics in common:

- They can be user-written applications or applications standardized and shipped with the TCP/IP product. Indeed, the TCP/IP protocol suite includes application protocols such as:

  - TELNET for interactive terminal access to remote internet hosts.

  - FTP (file transfer protocol) for high-speed disk-to-disk file transfers.

  - SMTP (simple mail transfer protocol) as an internet mailing system.

  These are the most widely implemented application protocols, but a lot of others exist. Each particular TCP/IP implementation will include a more or less restricted set of application protocols.

- They use either UDP or TCP as a transport mechanism. Remember that UDP is unreliable and offers no flow-control, so in this case the application has to provide its own error recovery and flow-control routines. It is often easier to build applications on top of TCP, a reliable, connection-oriented protocol. Most application protocols will use TCP, but there are applications built on UDP to provide better performance through reduced protocol overhead.

- Most of them use the client/server model of interaction.

## 4.1.2  Client/Server Model

TCP is a peer-to-peer, connection-oriented protocol.  There are no master/slave relations. The applications, however, use a client/server model for communications.

A *server* is an application that offers a service to internet users; a *client* is a requester of a service.  An application consists of both a server and a client part, which can run on the same or on different systems.

Users usually invoke the client part of the application, which builds a *request* for a particular service and sends it to the server part of the application using TCP/IP as a transport vehicle.

**4-1**

The server is a program that receives a request, performs the required service and sends back the results in a *reply*. A server can usually deal with multiple requests (multiple clients) at the same time.

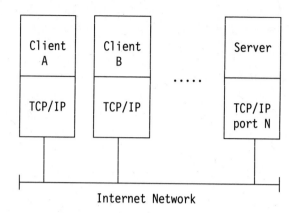

*Figure* **4-1.** *The Client/Server Model of Applications*

Some servers wait for requests at a *well-known port* so that their clients know to which IP socket they must direct their requests. The client uses an arbitrary port for its communication. Clients that wish to communicate with a server that does not use a well-known port must have another mechanism for learning to which port they must address their requests. This mechanism might employ a registration service such as Portmap, which uses a well-known port.

The next sections discuss the most widely used application protocols.

# 4.2 TELNET

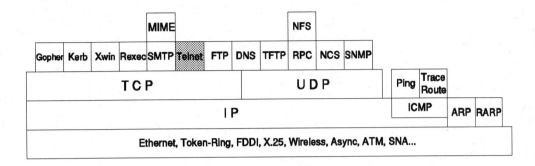

*Figure 4-2. TELNET.* Remote Login Protocol.

TELNET is a *standard protocol* with STD number 8. Its status is *recommended*. It is described in *RFC 854 — TELNET Protocol Specifications* and *RFC 855 — TELNET Option Specifications*.

The TELNET protocol provides a standardized interface, through which a program on one host (the TELNET client) may access the resources of another host (the TELNET server) as though the client were a local terminal connected to the server.

For example, a user on a workstation on a LAN may connect to a host attached to the LAN as though the workstation were a terminal attached directly to the host. Of course, TELNET may be used across WANs as well as LANs.

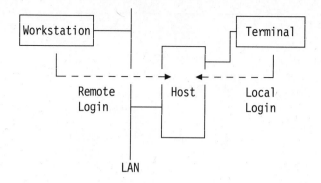

*Figure 4-3. Remote Login using TELNET.* TELNET allows the LAN-attached user to log in the same way as the local terminal user.

Most TELNET implementations do not provide you with graphics capabilities.

## 4.2.1 TELNET Operation

TELNET protocol is based on three ideas:

- The *Network Virtual Terminal (NVT)* concept. An NVT is an imaginary device having a basic structure common to a wide range of real terminals. Each host maps its own terminal characteristics to those of an NVT, and assumes that every other host will do the same.

- A symmetric view of terminals and processes

- Negotiation of terminal options. The principle of negotiated options is used by the TELNET protocol, because many hosts wish to provide additional services, beyond those available with the NVT. Various options may be negotiated. Server and client use a set of conventions to establish the operational characteristics of their TELNET connection via the "DO, DON'T, WILL, WON'T" mechanism discussed later in this chapter.

The two hosts begin by verifying their mutual understanding. Once this initial negotiation is complete, they are capable of working on the minimum level implemented by the NVT. After this minimum understanding is achieved, they can negotiate additional options to extend the capabilities of the NVT to reflect more accurately the capabilities of the real hardware in use. Because of the symmetric model used by TELNET, both the host and the client may propose additional options to be used.

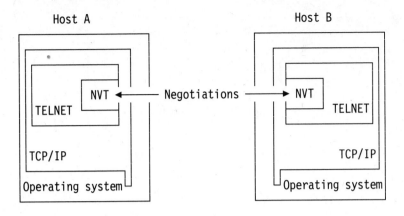

*Figure* *4-4. The Symmetric TELNET Model.* The negotiations start on the NVT basis.

## 4.2.1.1 Network Virtual Terminal

The NVT has a printer (or display) and a keyboard. The keyboard produces outgoing data, which is sent over the TELNET connection. The printer receives the incoming data. The basic characteristics of an NVT, unless they are modified by mutually agreed options are:

- The data representation is 7-bit ASCII transmitted in 8-bit bytes.
- The NVT is a half-duplex device operating in a line-buffered mode.
- The NVT provides a local echo function.

All of these may be negotiated by the two hosts. For example, a local echo is preferred because of the lower network load and superior performance but there is an option for using a remote echo, although no host is required to use it.

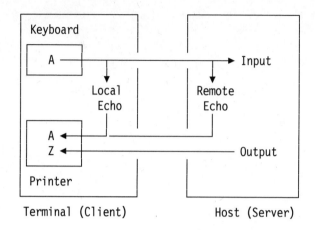

*Figure 4-5. Echo Option.* The remote echo function can be used instead of the local echo if both parties agree.

An NVT Printer has an unspecified carriage width and page length. It can handle printable ASCII characters (ASCII code 32 to 126) and understands some ASCII control characters such as:

| Command | ASCII | Action |
|---|---|---|
| NULL (NUL) | 0 | No Operation. |
| Line Feed (LF) | 10 | Moves the printer to the next print line, keeping the same horizontal position. |
| Carriage Return (CR) | 13 | Moves the printer to the left margin. |
| BELL (BEL) | 7 | Produces an audible or visible signal. |
| Back Space (BS) | 8 | Moves the print head one character position toward the left margin. |
| Horizontal Tab (HT) | 9 | Moves the printer to the next horizontal tab stop. |
| Vertical Tab (VT) | 11 | Moves the printer to the next vertical tab stop. |
| Form Feed (FF) | 12 | Moves the printer to the top of the next page, keeping the same horizontal position. |

## 4.2.1.2 TELNET Options

There is an extensive set of TELNET options, and the reader should consult *STD 1 — Official Internet Protocol Standards* for the standardization state and status for each of them. At the time of writing, the following options were defined:

| Table 4-1 (Page 1 of 2). TELNET Options | | | | |
|---|---|---|---|---|
| **Num** | **Name** | **State** | **RFC** | **STD** |
| 255 | Extended-Options-List | Standard | 861 | 32 |
| 0 | Binary Transmission | Standard | 856 | 27 |
| 1 | Echo | Standard | 857 | 28 |
| 3 | Suppress Go Ahead | Standard | 858 | 29 |
| 5 | Status | Standard | 859 | 30 |
| 6 | Timing Mark | Standard | 860 | 31 |
| 34 | Linemode | Draft | 1184 | |
| 2 | Reconnection | Proposed | | |
| 4 | Approx Message Size Negotiation | Proposed | | |
| 7 | Remote Controlled Trans and Echo | Proposed | 726 | |
| 8 | Output Line Width | Proposed | | |
| 9 | Output Page Size | Proposed | | |
| 10 | Output Carriage-Return Disposition | Proposed | 652 | |
| 11 | Output Horizontal Tabstops | Proposed | 653 | |
| 12 | Output Horizontal Tab Disposition | Proposed | 654 | |
| 13 | Output Formfeed Disposition | Proposed | 655 | |
| 14 | Output Vertical Tabstops | Proposed | 656 | |
| 15 | Output Vertical Tab Disposition | Proposed | 657 | |
| 16 | Output Linefeed Disposition | Proposed | 658 | |
| 17 | Extended ASCII | Proposed | 698 | |
| 18 | Logout | Proposed | 727 | |
| 19 | Byte Macro | Proposed | 735 | |
| 20 | Data Entry Terminal | Proposed | 1043 | |
| 21 | SUPDUP | Proposed | 736 | |
| 22 | SUPDUP Output | Proposed | 749 | |
| 23 | Send Location | Proposed | 779 | |
| 24 | Terminal Type | Proposed | 1091 | |
| 25 | End of Record | Proposed | 885 | |
| 26 | TACACS User Identification | Proposed | 927 | |
| 27 | Output Marking | Proposed | 933 | |

| Table 4-1 (Page 2 of 2). TELNET Options | | | | |
|---|---|---|---|---|
| Num | Name | State | RFC | STD |
| 28 | Terminal Location Number | Proposed | 946 | |
| 29 | TELNET 3270 Regime | Proposed | 1041 | |
| 30 | X.3 PAD | Proposed | 1053 | |
| 31 | Negotiate About Window Size | Proposed | 1073 | |
| 32 | Terminal Speed | Proposed | 1079 | |
| 33 | Remote Flow Control | Proposed | 1372 | |
| 35 | X Display Location | Proposed | 1096 | |
| 39 | TELNET Environment Option | Proposed | 1572 | |
| 37 | TELNET Authentication Option | Experimental | 1416 | |

All of the standard options have a status of *recommended* and the remainder have a status of *elective*. There is an *historic* version of the TELNET Environment Option which is *not recommended*; it is TELNET option 36 and was defined in RFC 1408.

**Full-Screen Capability:** Full-screen TELNET is possible provided the client and server have compatible full-screen capabilities. For example, VM and MVS provide a TN3270-capable server. To use this facility, a TELNET client must support TN3270.

## 4.2.1.3 TELNET Command Structure

The communication between client and server is handled with internal commands, which are not accessible by users. All internal TELNET commands consist of 2 or 3-byte sequences, depending on the command type.

The Interpret As Command (IAC) character is followed by a command code. If this command deals with option negotiation, the command will have a third byte to show the code for the referenced option.

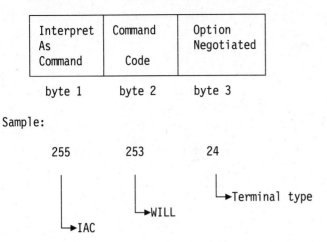

Sample:

Figure   *4-6. Internal TELNET Command Structure.*   This command proposes
negotiation about terminal type.

| Command name | Code | Comments |
|---|---|---|
| SE | 240 | End of sub-negotiation parameters. |
| NOP | 241 | No operation. |
| Data Mark | 242 | The data stream portion of a synch.  This should always be accompanied by a TCP urgent notification. |
| Break | 243 | NVT character BRK. |
| Go ahead | 249 | The GA signal. |
| SB | 250 | Indicates that what follows is sub-negotiation of the option indicated by the immediately following code. |
| WILL | 251 | Shows the desire to use, or confirmation that you are now using, the option indicated by the code immediately following. |
| WON'T | 252 | Shows the refusal to use, or to continue to use, the option indicated by the code immediately following. |
| DO | 253 | Requests that the other party uses, or confirms that you are expecting the other party to use, the option indicated by the code immediately following. |
| DON'T | 254 | Demands that the other party stop using, or confirms that you are no longer expecting the other party to use, the option indicated by the code immediately following. |
| IAC | 255 | Interpret As Command.  Indicates that what follows is a TELNET command, not data. |

## 4.2.1.4  Option Negotiation

Using internal commands, TELNET in each host is able to negotiate options.  The
starting base of negotiation is the NVT capability: each host to be connected must agree
to this minimum.  Every option can be negotiated by the use of the four command codes
WILL, WON'T, DO, DON'T described above.

In addition, some options have sub-options: if both parties agree to the option, they use the SB and SE commands to manage the sub-negotiation. Here is a simplified example of how option negotiation works.

| Send | Reply | Meaning |
|------|-------|---------|
| DO transmit binary | WILL transmit binary | |
| DO window size | WILL window size | Can we negotiate window size? |
| SB Window Size 0 80 0 24 SE | | Specify window size |
| DO terminal type | WILL terminal type | Can we negotiate terminal type? |
| SB terminal type SE | | Send me your terminal characteristics. |
| | SB terminal type IBM-3278-2 SE | My terminal is a 3278-2 |
| DO echo | WON'T echo | |

The terminal types are defined in *STD 2 — Assigned Numbers*.

### 4.2.1.5 TELNET Basic Commands

The primary goal of the TELNET protocol is the provision of a standard interface for hosts over a network. To allow the connection to start, the TELNET protocol defines a standard representation for some functions:

| | |
|---|---|
| *IP* | Interrupt Process |
| *AO* | Abort Output |
| *AYT* | Are You There |
| *EC* | Erase Character |
| *EL* | Erase Line |
| *SYNCH* | Synchronize |

## 4.2.2 Implementations

### 4.2.2.1 VM

The TELNET client is a CMS program, that is, you must log on to a VM user ID running CMS to use it. The TELNET server runs in the TCP/IP virtual machine and uses the *CCS System service to create logical terminals for incoming TELNET clients. VTAM (GCS) is not required to use the TELNET protocol on a VM system.

**Full-Screen Emulation:**  When you use the *TELNET* command to connect to a host, you have to choose the mode of operation.  Line mode or transparent mode are the two possibilities.  In line mode you will be connected as a start-stop TTY terminal.  In transparent mode, the TELNET command supports IBM 3270-type display stations.  Examples of stations are:

IBM 3278 Display Station Models 2, 3, 4, and 5

IBM 3279 Display Station Models 2, and 3.

The mode of operation depends on the ability of both hosts to agree on a terminal type.

**Translate Tables:**  The translation tables used to convert EBCDIC data to ASCII do not always include desired characters.  This becomes evident when you use the National Language Support Option (NLS) with your operating system. TCP/IP for VM provides standard tables.  If needed, you can create and customize your own translate tables, without having to recompile the source.  The TELNET CLIENT function only works in 7-bit mode.  For more details, please refer to *IBM TCP/IP Version 2 Release 3 for VM: Planning and Customization.*

### Command Format

```
TELNET ( foreignhost ( portnumber ))(( linemode ) translate filename ))
```

*Linemode*   makes line mode instead of full-screen mode of connection.

*Translate*   defines the translation table to be used.

While in a TELNET session, you may invoke subcommands such as:

*AO*       stop display output

*AYT*      query connection

*HELP*    help

*IP*         interrupt process

*PA1*      send PA1 keystroke

*QUIT*    quit session

*SYNCH* clear data path

For more details, please refer to *IBM TCP/IP Version 2 Release 3 for VM: User's Guide.*

## 4.2.2.2  MVS

TELNET provides:

1. Client and server 3270 full screen (transparent mode).

2. Client and server line mode.

3. Server for 3270 DBCS transfer mode which supports all full-screen access from a VT100 or VT282 remote TELNET client.

4. Client VT100 and VT220 full-screen support with either Communication Subsystem For Interconnection (CSFI) from IBM or similar products from third-party vendors.

TELNET functionality:

- Session establishment

  When a 3270 connection is established, the MVS TELNET server allows you to choose which VTAM application a client will be automatically connected to (usually this *default application* is a network solicitor). If you want the incoming users to be able to choose between different VTAM applications (that is, you do not specify a default application), the TELNET server will ask for the application name. It is possible to restrict the use of an application to some users (or none) and to have logical units (LU) reserved for some specific users.

- Unformatted system services (USS) message 10 support

  USS message 10 support provides the ability to emulate the VTAM USS message 10 support. You may define one or more USS message 10 screens. The actual USS message 10 screen to be used for a TELNET session can be selected via the LU mapping functions.

- IP address to LU name mapping

  The IP-address-to-LU-name mapping function provides for the selection of both an LU type 2 name and an application screen (or USS message 10 screen) for incoming TELNET sessions. The selection is made by the following:

  - IP address
  - Group of IP addresses
  - Subnet
  - Used link to the MVS host

- Support for 3270 DBCS transform

  3270 DBCS transform mode provides 3270 full-screen emulation where the 3270 protocol processing is performed entirely by IBM TCP/IP for MVS. The remote TELNET client may be emulating either a VT100 or VT282 type terminal.

- SMF reporting

  The TELNET server also provides *user accounting* and *control information* using the MVS *SMF* (System Management Facility) records. For example, client identity, IP address, timestamp of LOGON and LOGOFF and VTAM LU can be recorded.

  A standard record type (SMF record type 118) has been registered.

- Modify console command

  The console operator may now query the status of active or inactive LUs in use by the TELNET server.

- User set limits

  The user set option permits the user to control the number of TCP connections or UDP ports that may be open at one time.

- Binary option for line mode

  With this option the line mode client is able to bypass the ASCII to EBCDIC translation.

VTAM and TSO (refer to *IBM TCP/IP Version 3 Release 1 for MVS: Customization and Administration Guide* for more details about the requirements) are required to use TELNET (both client and server).

The capabilities of the TELNET function under MVS are the same as under VM.

A programmable workstation may use either a TN3270 client or an rlogin client to reach OpenEdition MVS services.

## 4.2.2.3 OS/400

The OS/400 TELNET provides both client and server functions. The OS/400 TELNET supports negotiations of the data transmission in one of the following four operating modes: VT100 full-screen mode, ASCII line mode, 5250 full-screen mode (see RFC 1205 for details) or 3270 full-screen mode.

- VT100 mode considerations:

  Although the AS/400 TELNET server supports VT100 clients, this is not the preferred mode to use. A TN3270 or TN5250 client is preferred. The VT100 terminal is a character mode device, while the OS/400 is a block mode system. In general, this results in larger amount of overhead associated with the transmission of each VT100 keystroke. In contrast, the 5250 or 3270 block devices buffer all keystrokes at the client system until an Attention Identifier (AID) key is pressed.

  The OS/400 VT100 server requires the VT100 client to have the autowrap option turned on. The Change Keyboard Map (CHGKBDMAP) and the Set Keyboard Map (SETKBMAP) commands are available for keyboard remapping.

- ASCII line mode considerations:

  ASCII line mode is the standard TELNET network virtual terminal (NVT) support and is assumed when 5250 full-screen mode or 3270 full-screen mode cannot be negotiated. The client ASCII line mode provides one input line and several scrollable output lines. Since the OS/400 operates in full-screen mode and has screens with multiple input fields, this ASCII line mode TELNET server implementation has several considerations. For example, a sign-on screen for the AS/400 system is not automatically displayed when ASCII line mode is negotiated. Please refer to *AS/400 TCP/IP Guide* for details.

- 5250 full-screen considerations:

5250 full-screen support can only be satisfactorily negotiated with a TELNET application running on a system that supports 5250 TELNET. The client support is similar to the OS/400 display station pass-through between two OS/400 systems. A TELNET user at the client OS/400 will receive an OS/400 5250 sign-on display from the server system and will be able to run applications on the remote system as if the display were locally attached to the server.

The OS/400 server TELNET requires virtual controllers and devices (which are automatically created by the system) to direct output on the client system. OS/400 server TELNET must be allowed to automatically configure virtual controllers and 5250 or 3270 devices.

- 3270 full-screen considerations:

3270 full-screen support is negotiated with any TELNET application that supports 3270 TELNET. The TELNET user at the local OS/400 receives a 3270 logon screen (for example, a VM logo screen) and is able to run applications on the 3270 host as if his display were locally attached. The 3270 TELNET server support allows the IBM S/370 family systems and non-AS/400 systems client TELNET users to sign on and run OS/400 5250 full-screen applications as if they were locally attached to the AS/400. Automatic configuration of controllers and devices is allowed. The OS/400 3270 full-screen mode TELNET server supports 3270 extended attributes, 3270-to-5250 keyboard re-mapping and workstation type negotiations.

### 4.2.2.4 AIX/6000

AIX for RISC System/6000 supports both the TELNET client and server functions.

The following options are supported:

Binary Transmission (used in TELNET 3270 sessions)
Suppress Go-Ahead (the RISC System/6000 system suppresses go-ahead)
Timing Mark (recognized, but has a negative response)
Extended Options List (recognized, but has a negative response)
Echo (a user-changeable command)
Term Type (allows the server to determine the terminal type used by the client)
SAK (Secure Attention Key)
NAWS (Negotiate About Window Size)

The telnetd server (also know as a daemon) is a subserver controlled by the inetd subsystem (also known as the super daemon).

The telnet command is identical to the tn and the TN3270 commands. It operates in two different modes:

- Command Mode

  When the telnet command is issued without arguments, it enters the command mode. The user may enter telnet subcommands.

- Input Mode

  When the telnet command is issued with arguments, it performs an open subcommand with those arguments and then enters input mode. The type of input mode is either character-at-a-time or line-by-line, depending on what the remote system supports.

The terminal-type negotiation will take place between the *telnet* command and the remote system when none of the following is used:

1. The -e command line flag

2. The emulate environment variable

3. The TN3270 command

The 3270, DEC VT100 and NONE (no emulation) terminal types are supported. In the case of 3270 emulation mode, keyboard remapping is supported.

The rlogin command and the rlogind server (daemon) can also be used if both the local and the target hosts are AIX (or UNIX) systems. The rlogin and rlogind programs are considered as not-trusted because the remote host does not require password authentication when one or both of the following conditions is satisfied:

1. The local host is included in the remote /etc/hosts.equiv file, the local user is not the root user, and the -l User flag is not specified.

2. The local host and user name is included in the $HOME/.rhosts file in the remote user account.

For security reasons, any $HOME/.rhosts file must be owned by either the remote user or root and should allow write access only by the owner.

Since rlogin and rlogind are considered as not-trusted, they can be disabled by running the securetcpip command. The securetcpip command is used to enable additional TCP/IP security environment by disabling commands that are not trusted. The telnet command and the ftpd daemon are considered as trusted command and daemon, respectively. For more details, please refer to *AIX Version 3.2 for RISC System/6000 Communication Concepts and Procedures*.

## 4.2.2.5 AIX/ESA

AIX/ESA supports both client and server TELNET functions.

The TELNET server supports the following options: binary, echo/no echo, suppress go ahead, timing mark and terminal type.

The client function is implemented by the telnet and TN3270 commands. It operates in two modes: *command mode* and *input mode*. The type of input mode used is either *character-at-a-time* or *line-by-line*.

If an HFT terminal is being used (the terminal supports the High-Function Terminal driver such as the PS/2 console), TELNET can emulate either a DEC VT100 terminal or an IBM 3270 terminal. The 3270 terminal types supported are: 3277-1, 3278-1, 3278-2, 3278-3, 3278-4 and 3278-5. If TELNET 3270 mode command is being used with a color display, then 3279 terminal type is supported.

In addition, the rlogin command can also be used to log into an AIX/ESA or AIX/ESA-compatible system, if your local system is listed in the /etc/hosts.equiv file on the remote system, or your system and your user name are listed in the .rhosts file in your home directory on the remote system.

**Note:** Any login operation is subject to the AIX/ESA security features in effect. For more details, please refer to *AIX/ESA Security Features User's Guide*.

## 4.2.2.6 OS/2

TCP/IP for OS/2 supports the following ASCII-based TELNET clients: TelnetPM, Telnet, Ansiterm, Telneto. The terminal types supported by these clients are VT220, VT100, ANSI, HFT and NVT. Supported 3270 terminal emulator TELNET clients are: PMANT, 3270 TELNET (PM) and TN3270. In addition, TN5250, which provides a PM-based 5250 emulation client, is supported.

- *VT220* - Uses emulation type VT220 to log on to a foreign host.

- *VT100* - Uses emulation type VT100 to log on to a foreign host.

  This implements a superset of VT100, since it supports all 12 function keys instead of just four.

- *ANSI* - Uses command Ansiterm to log on to a foreign host using ANSI mode, which is the native screen driver for an OS/2 command shell.

- *Telneto* - Uses command Telneto to log on to a foreign host using VT100 terminal emulation in true line mode.

  This is equivalent to VT200 in protocol support, and implements linemode capabilities as defined in RFC 1184.

- *PMANT* - Uses command PMANT to log on to a foreign host as a 3270 terminal.

PMANT is an OS/2 Presentation Manager application which allows for keyboard remapping, VIO font selections, terminal screen size definitions (24x80, 32x80, 43x80, 27x132), extended colors support, extended highlighting support and OS/2 clipboard support.

- *3270 TELNET* - 3270 TELNET is a new client which is integrated in the OS/2 WorkPlace Shell. Apart from the improved GUI features, it provides similar functions to those of PMANT.

- *TN3270* - Use command TN3270 to log on to a foreign host as a 3270 terminal.

  TN3270 is a text application running under either an OS/2 window or full-screen session. It is similar to PMANT but does not include the Presentation Manager interface. TN3270 is recommended in lieu of PMANT when using TCP/IP for OS/2 over slower serial lines, such as SLIP. It supports keyboard remapping, alternative screen sizes and extended colors. Selectable fonts and copy to clipboard are also supported in an OS/2 window session. It only supports 80-column screens.

For any terminal type, a TELNET server must be running on the foreign host that supports that specific terminal type.

TCP/IP V2.0 for OS/2 can be a TELNET server, supporting VT220, VT100, ANSITERM or TN clients. Note that TELNET users that log into an OS/2 TELNET server have the capability of running any applications with the exception of OS/2 Presentation Manager (PM) applications.

## 4.2.2.7 DOS

TCP/IP for DOS provides three TELNET client implementations:

- DOS TELNET: To be used from the DOS command line.

- DOS TN3270: To be used from the DOS command line.

- Windows TELNET: To be used through the Windows interface.

TCP/IP for DOS does not provide a TELNET Server implementation.

The SETTERM command allows the configuration of a DOS TELNET client. This program is menu driven and allows the following settings:

- Key assignment: Specifies how keys are interpreted for the currently defined session. For example, PF8 can be assigned to the Down function.
- Character translations: Specifies how a particular character is translated. The decimal value (in the range of 0 to 255) for the byte to be translated must be entered. After this value is supplied, the system prompts for the replacement value (in the range of 0 to 255).
- Video attributes: Specifies foreground, background, and highlighting attributes.

- Terminal choices: Specifies the order of preference for terminals (five emulators are available) to use during a TELNET session.
- Session hot-key definitions: TELNET can open up to eight different sessions. You can assign a hot-key to each session. The session hot key is used to quickly switch among active sessions.

The modifications are stored in an ASCII file which can be referenced when the TELNET command is issued. It is possible      to have different configuration files for different settings.

TELNET offers four terminal emulators:

- VT220
- VT100
- IBM-3278-2
- ANSITERM

Windows TELNET offers six terminal emulators:

- VT220
- VT100
- IBM-3278-2 through 3278-5
- ANSI
- TTY
- 5250

The terminal preference is generally handled through the SETTERM command but it can be specified with the TELNET command. All the TELNET sessions must be opened from a full-screen window.

TELNET provides a menu-driven interface that makes it easy to supply the information needed to begin a TELNET session.

When you TELNET to a remote host from a DOS workstation, at the same time you can initiate the TFTP server. Then from the remote host, you will be able to execute a TFTP session between that host and the PC running DOS. When a file transfer request is detected, the TFTP Request menu is displayed. You can now decide the appropriate action to take (accept this transfer, deny this transfer, accept all future transfers, deny all future transfers). TELNET also allows you to temporarily go back to a DOS shell.

## 4.2.2.8  TELNET Server Client Cross Table

| | TELNET function | |
|---|---|---|
| | Server | Client |
| VM | Yes | Yes |
| MVS | Yes | Yes |
| AIX/6000 | Yes | Yes |
| AIX/ESA | Yes | Yes |
| DOS | No | Yes |
| OS/2 | Yes | Yes |
| OS/400 | Yes | Yes |

*Figure   4-7.  TELNET Server and Client*

## 4.2.2.9  3270 Full-Screen Cross Table

| | Client | Server | Extended data stream |
|---|---|---|---|
| VM | Yes | Yes | Yes |
| MVS | Yes | Yes | Yes |
| AIX/6000 | Yes | No | No |
| AIX/ESA | Yes | No | No |
| DOS | Yes | No | No |
| OS/2 | Yes | No | Yes |
| OS/400 | Yes | Yes | Yes(server) |

*Figure   4-8.  3270 Full-Screen Server and Client*

## TELNET Scenario

- User connected to host A needs to run a job on host B.

- Host A runs TCP/IP for IBM PC.

- Host B runs TCP/IP for VM.

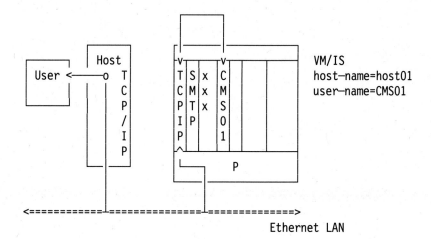

```
1) Login to        |    TELNET     host01
   remote host     |    LOGIN      cms01
                 v      PASSWORD   cmspw
```

2) Use the workstation as a local VM connected terminal.
   Using the standard VM procedures, you may for example:
       Dial, Note, Send file perform another remote login
   or run jobs under VM.

```
3) End of operation   |
                    v     QUIT
```

*Figure  4-9.  TELNET Scenario*

# 4.3  Trivial File Transfer Protocol (TFTP)

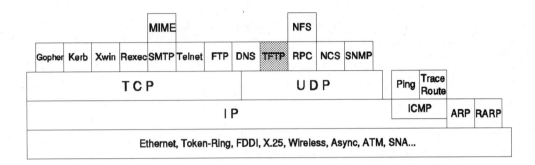

*Figure*  *4-10.*  *Trivial File Transfer Protocol (TFTP)*

The TFTP protocol is a *standard protocol* with STD number 33.  Its status is *elective* and it is described in *RFC 1350 — The TFTP Protocol (Revision 2).*

TCP/IP file transfer is a disk-to-disk data transfer, as opposed to, for example, the VM SENDFILE command, a function that is considered in the TCP/IP world as a mailing function, where you send out the data to someone's mailbox (reader in the case of VM).

TFTP is an extremely simple protocol to transfer files.  It is implemented on the internet UDP layer (User Datagram Protocol) and lacks most of the features of FTP (see 4.4, "File Transfer Protocol (FTP)" on page  4-25).  The only thing it can do is read/write a file from/to a server.

**Note:**   It has no provisions for user authentication: it is an unsecure protocol.

## 4.3.1  Usage

The command:

```
TFTP <hostname>
```

takes you to the interactive prompt where you can enter subcommands:

```
Connect <host>
```
          specify destination host ID

```
Mode <ascii/binary>
```
          specify the type of transfer mode

```
Get <remote filename> [<local filename>]
```
        retrieve a file

```
Put <remote filename> [<local filename>]
```
        store a file

```
Verbose
```
        toggle verbose mode, which displays additional information during file
        transfer, on or off

```
Quit
```
        exit TFTP

For a full list of these commands, see the user's guide of your particular TFTP
implementation.

## 4.3.2 Protocol Description

Any transfer begins with a request to read or write a file. If the server grants the request,
the connection is opened and the file is sent in blocks of 512 bytes (fixed length). Blocks
of the file are numbered consecutively, starting at 1. Each data packet must be
acknowledged by an acknowledgment packet before the next one can be sent.
Termination of the transfer is assumed on a data packet of less than 512 bytes.

Almost all errors will cause termination of the connection (lack of reliability). If a packet
gets lost in the network, a timeout will occur, after which a retransmission of the last
packet (data or acknowledgment) will take place.

There was a serious bug, known as the Sorcerer's Apprentice Syndrome, in RFC 783. It
may cause excessive retransmission by both sides in some network delay scenarios. It
was documented in RFC 1123 and was corrected in RFC 1350. For details, please refer
to the RFCs.

### 4.3.2.1 TFTP Packets

Only five types of packets exist:

| Opcode | Operation |
|--------|-----------|
| 1 | Read Request (RRQ) |
| 2 | Write Request (WRQ) |
| 3 | Data (DATA) |
| 4 | Acknowledgment (ACK) |
| 5 | Error (ERROR) |

The TFTP header contains the *opcode* associated with the packet.

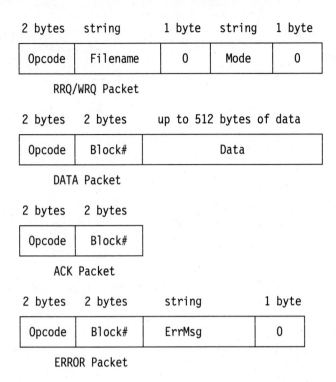

```
  2 bytes    string       1 byte   string   1 byte
 ┌────────┬───────────┬─────────┬─────────┬─────────┐
 │ Opcode │ Filename  │    0    │  Mode   │    0    │
 └────────┴───────────┴─────────┴─────────┴─────────┘
          RRQ/WRQ Packet

  2 bytes    2 bytes       up to 512 bytes of data
 ┌────────┬───────────┬─────────────────────────────┐
 │ Opcode │  Block#   │             Data            │
 └────────┴───────────┴─────────────────────────────┘
           DATA Packet

  2 bytes    2 bytes
 ┌────────┬───────────┐
 │ Opcode │  Block#   │
 └────────┴───────────┘
         ACK Packet

  2 bytes    2 bytes      string          1 byte
 ┌────────┬───────────┬─────────────┬──────────────┐
 │ Opcode │  Block#   │   ErrMsg    │      0       │
 └────────┴───────────┴─────────────┴──────────────┘
          ERROR Packet
```

*Figure   4-11.  TFTP Packets*

## 4.3.2.2  Data Modes

Three modes of transfer are currently defined in RFC 1350:

*NetASCII*   US-ASCII as defined in *USA Standard Code for Information Interchange* with modifications specified in *RFC 854 — Telnet Protocol Specification* and extended to use the high order bit.  That is, it is an 8-bit character set, unlike US-ASCII which is 7-bit.

*Octet*   Raw 8-bit bytes, also called binary.

*Mail*   This mode was originally defined in RFC 783 and was declared obsolete by RFC 1350.  It allowed for sending mail to a user rather than transferring to a file.

The mode used is indicated in the Request for Read/Write packet (RRQ/WRQ).

## 4.3.3 Implementations

TFTP is implemented in the IBM TCP/IP products for VM (client only), AIX/6000, AIX/ESA, OS/2 and DOS.

### 4.3.3.1 AIX/ESA

Both the TFTP client and server functions are available.

**Note:** The TFTP functions are usually disabled due to security requirements. This is especially the case in AIX/ESA. For more details, please refer to *AIX/ESA Security Features User's Guide*.

### 4.3.3.2 AIX/6000

The tftpd server (daemon) is a subserver controlled by the inetd subsystem (also known as the super daemon).

The tftp and utftp client commands are available, but they are not recommended for use in a secure environment. The securetcpip command can be used to disable tftpd, tftp and utftp.

### 4.3.3.3 OS/2

Because of the above-mentioned lack of authorization, there are two different ways to start the TFTP daemon (TFTPD) in an OS/2 machine (TEMP is used as an example: it could be another name):

- Via the TFTPD C:TEMP command: This restricts the directory where files can be written to the TEMP directory on drive C:.
- Via the TFTPD C:TEMP command: This restricts the names of the file that are written. For example, if a client host writes a file named CONFIG.SYS, the file will be known as TEMPCONF.SYS on your OS/2 system.

### 4.3.3.4 DOS

TCP/IP for DOS provides a TFTP client. This is started from the DOS prompt using the tftp command.

# 4.4 File Transfer Protocol (FTP)

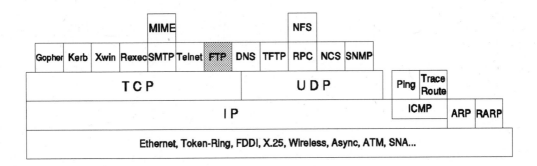

*Figure* *4-12.* *File Transfer Protocol (FTP)*

FTP is a *standard protocol* with STD Number 9. Its status is *recommended.* It is described in *RFC 959 — File Transfer Protocol (FTP).*

Copying files from one machine to another is one of the most frequently used operations. The data transfer between client and server can be in either direction. The client may send a file to the server machine. It may also request a file from this server.

To access remote files, the user must identify himself to the server. At this point the server is responsible for authenticating the client before it allows the file transfer.

From an FTP user's point of view, the link is connection-oriented. In other words, it is necessary to have both hosts up and running TCP/IP to establish a file transfer.

## 4.4.1 Overview of FTP

FTP uses TCP as a transport protocol to provide reliable end-to-end connections. Two connections are used: the first is for login and follows the TELNET protocol and the second is for managing the data transfer. As it is necessary to log into the remote host, the user must have a user name and a password to access files and directories. The user who initiates the connection assumes the client function, while the server function is provided by the remote host.

On both sides of the link the FTP application is built with a protocol interpreter (PI), a data transfer process (DTP), and a user interface (see Figure 4-13 on page 4-26).

The user interface communicates with the protocol interpreter, which is in charge of the control connection. This protocol interpreter has to communicate the necessary information to its own file system.

On the opposite side of the link, the protocol interpreter, besides its function of responding to the TELNET protocol, has to initiate the data connection. During the file transfer, the data management is performed by DTPs. After a user's request is completed, the server's PI has to close the control connection.

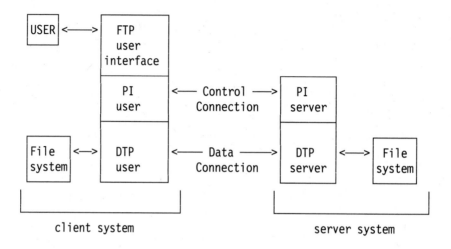

```
PI : protocol interpreter
DTP: data transfer process
```

*Figure    4-13.  FTP Principle*

## 4.4.2  FTP Operations

When using FTP, the user will perform some or all of the following operations:

- Connect to a remote host
- Select a directory
- List files available for transfer
- Define the transfer mode
- Copy files to or from the remote host
- Disconnect from the remote host

### 4.4.2.1  Connect to the Remote Host

To execute a file transfer, the user begins by logging into the remote host.  This is the primary method of handling the security.  The user must have a user ID and password for the remote host, unless using Anonymous FTP which is described in 4.4.5.1, "Anonymous FTP" on page  4-31.

There are three commands which are used:

*Open*   Selects the remote host and initiates the login session

*User*   Identifies the remote user ID

*Pass*   Authenticates the user

*Site*   Sends information to the foreign host that is used to provide services specific to that host

### 4.4.2.2  Select a Directory

When the control link is established, the user may use the cd (change directory) subcommand to select a remote directory to work with.  Obviously, user can only access directories for which the remote user ID has the appropriate authorization.  The user may select a local directory with the lcd (local change directory) command.  The syntax of theses commands depends upon the operating system in use.

### 4.4.2.3  List Files Available for Transfer

This is done using the dir or ls subcommands.

### 4.4.2.4  Specifying the Transfer Mode

Transferring data between dissimilar systems often requires transformations of the data as part of the transfer process.  The user has to decide on two aspects of the data handling:

- The way the bits will be moved from one place to another.
- The different representations of data upon the system's architecture.

This is controlled using two subcommands:

*Mode*   Specifies whether the file is to be treated as having a record structure in a byte stream format.

    *Block*   Logical record boundaries of the file are preserved.

    *Stream*   The file is treated as a byte stream.  This is the default, and provides more efficient transfer but may not produce the desired results when working with a record-based file system.

*Type*   Specifies the character sets used for the data.

| | |
|---|---|
| *ASCII* | Indicates that both hosts are ASCII-based, or that if one is ASCII-based and the other is EBCDIC-based, that ASCII-EBCDIC translation should be performed. |
| *EBCDIC* | Indicates that both hosts use an EBCDIC data representation. |
| *Image* | Indicates that data is to be treated as contiguous bits packed in 8-bit bytes. |

Because these subcommands do not cover all possible differences between systems, the SITE subcommand is available to issue implementation-dependent commands.

### 4.4.2.5 Copy Files

| | |
|---|---|
| *Get* | Copies a file from the remote host to the local host. |
| *Put* | Copies a file from the local host to the remote host. |

### 4.4.2.6 End the Transfer Session

| | |
|---|---|
| *Quit* | Disconnects from the remote host and terminates FTP. Some implementations use the BYE subcommand. |
| *Close* | Disconnects from the remote host but leaves the FTP client running. An open command may be issued to work with a new host. |

## 4.4.3 Reply Codes

In order to manage these operations, the client and server conduct a dialog using the TELNET convention. The client issues commands, and the server responds with *reply codes*. The responses also include comments for the benefit of the user, but the client program uses only the codes.

Reply codes are three digits long, with the first digit being the most significant.

*Table 4-2. FTP Reply Codes.* The second and third digits provide more details about the response.

| Reply code | Description |
|---|---|
| 1xx | Positive preliminary reply. |
| 2xx | Positive completion reply. |
| 3xx | Positive intermediate reply. |
| 4xx | Transient negative completion reply. |
| 5xx | Permanent negative completion reply. |

**Example:** For each user command, shown like `this`, the FTP server responds with a message beginning with a 3-digit reply code, shown like `this`:

**FTP foreignhost**
220 service ready
**USERNAME cms01**
331 user name okay
**PASSWORD xyxyx**
230 user logged in
**TYPE Image**
200 command okay

## 4.4.4 FTP Scenario

A LAN user has to transfer a file from his workstation to a system running VM. The file has to be transferred from his disk to the minidisk 191 owned by the CMS's user cms01. There is no Resource Access Control Facility (RACF) installed. The symbolic name corresponding to an Internet address is host01.itsc.raleigh.ibm.com.

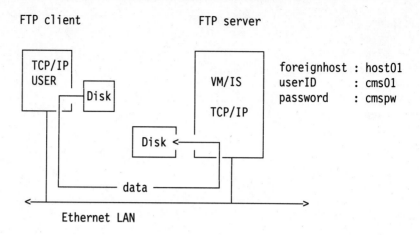

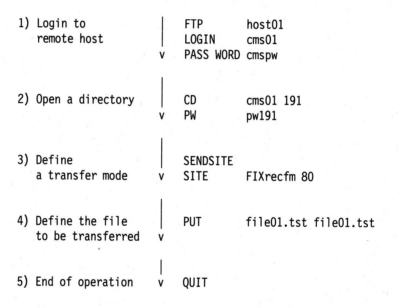

**Figure 4-14.** *FTP Scenario*

## 4.4.5  A Sample FTP Session

```
[C:SAMPLES]ftp host01.itsc.raleigh.ibm.com
Connected to host01.itsc.raleigh.ibm.com.
220 host01 FTP server (Version 4.1 Sat Nov 23 12:52:09 CST 1991) ready.
Name (rs60002): cms01
331 Password required for cms01.
Password: xxxxxx
230 User cms01 logged in.
ftp> put file01.tst file01.tst
200 PORT command successful.
150 Opening data connection for file01.tst (1252 bytes).
226 Transfer complete.
local: file01.tst remote: file01.tst
1285 bytes received in 0.062 seconds (20 Kbytes/s)
ftp> close
221 Goodbye.
ftp> quit
```

*Figure   4-15. A Sample FTP Session.*   Transfer a file to a remote host

### 4.4.5.1  Anonymous FTP

Many TCP/IP sites implement what is known as *anonymous FTP*, which means that these sites allow public access to some file directories.  The remote user only needs to use the login name *anonymous* and password *guest* or some other common password conventions, for example the user's Internet E-mail ID.  The password convention used on a system is explained to the user during the login process.

## 4.4.6  Implementations

### 4.4.6.1  VM

TCP/IP for VM is implemented with server and client functions of FTP.  This implementation provides you with most of the capabilities useful for file transfer.  Please refer to *IBM TCP/IP Version 2 Release 3 for VM: User's Guide* for a list of the subcommands that may be used.

The file transfer process can be automated using the EXEC interface which allows you to read the FTP subcommands from a file (using the FILEDEF command) or from the program stack.  By default, the results of your FTP dialog are printed on your terminal. A file may be defined as the output device for the FTP dialog using the FILEDEF command, in which case the dialog output is placed in the file rather than typed on the console.  Please refer to the *IBM TCP/IP Version 2 Release 3 for VM: User's Guide* for more information about the EXEC interface.

While in an FTP session you can issue CMS commands on your local (client) VM system.

The Resource Access Control Facility (RACF) allows FTP servers to act as *surrogates* for other user IDs.  This means that the FTP server can access those disks available to that user ID (the one entered during the logon procedure).  Please refer to *IBM TCP/IP Version 2 Release 3 for VM: Planning and Customization* for more information about RACF considerations.

## 4.4.6.2  MVS

TCP/IP for MVS is implemented with both server and client functions of FTP.  This implementation provides you with most of the capabilities useful for file transfer.  Please refer to *IBM TCP/IP Version 3 Release 1 for MVS: User's Guide* for a list of the subcommands that may be used.

There are two FTP servers available in MVS:

- The old Pascal-based FTP server (module FTPSERVE)

- The new C-based FTP server (module EZAFTSRV), which is recommended

The C FTP Server provides an FTP server specifically designed for MVS TCP/IP.  In addition to providing all the functions found in the Pascal-based FTP server (except RDW), C FTP Server uses native MVS file interfaces; has a structured design; takes advantage of MP support, reducing the need for multiple servers; improves the RAS characteristics for FTP server; adds struct-r support; provides delete/catalog options if file transfer fails.  The C FTP Server is available in an MVS/ESA environment only.

The C FTP Server will be the basis for future enhancements of the FTP server.  No enhancements are planned for the Pascal server in further releases.

**SQL Query to DB2:**  MVS FTP also supports the DATABASE 2 (DB2) SQL query function.  Only the *SELECT* DML operation is supported. That is, other DML (INSERT, UPDATE or DELETE) and DDL operations are not supported.  The SQL query may be submitted to a DB2 subsystem at either the local or the remote site, as illustrated below:

1. *put* (submit) a local file containing an *SQL query* to any DB2 subsystem at the *remote* MVS FTP server and *get* (retrieve) the SQL query results in a file from the remote MVS FTP server

2. *put* a local file containing an SQL query to any DB2 subsystem at the *local* MVS FTP client; upon completion of the query operation, the local MVS FTP client will transfer the SQL query output file to the remote FTP server

The *site* and *locsite* FTP subcommands are used to switch the *filetype* to *sql* and to identify the name of the DB2 subsystem. Please refer to *IBM TCP/IP Version 3 Release 1 for MVS: User's Guide* for the syntax of these FTP subcommands.

An FTP installation may also have the flexibility of defining the following user security exits: Check IP and PORT Addresses, Check USER and PASSWORD, Check the Command, and Check use of JES.

The FTP server also provides *user accounting* and *control information* using the MVS *SMF* (System Management Facility) records. For example, client identity, IP addresses, used commands and failed logon attempts can be recorded.

IBM TCP/IP for MVS uses SMF record type 118 for all SMF records.

The file transfer process can be automated using the EXEC interface that allows you to read the FTP subcommands from a disk (*ALLOC DA(FTPIN) DD(INPUT) SHR REU*) or from a program stack (*QUEUE* command). As the default, the results of your FTP dialog are printed on your terminal. If a disk file is defined as the output device (*ALLOC DA(FTPOUT) DD(OUTPUT) SHR REU* ), the dialog results go into the file. Please refer to the *IBM TCP/IP Version 3 Release 1 for MVS: User's Guide* for more information about the EXEC interface. You can also run FTP as a batch job, but you must supply the JCL and submit it as a job with TSO job submission facility.

While in an FTP session you can issue TSO commands on your local (client) MVS system.

**Job Submission via JES:** The MVS FTP server allows you to interface with MVS Job Entry System (JES). First an FTP session must be established between the client and the FTP MVS server (The SET FILETYPE=JES command activates the JES interface).

The FTP server provides four functions in its JES interface:

1. Submit a job. The JCL is created on the client and sent to the MVS server using FTP.
2. Display the status of all the user's jobs.
3. Receive the spool output of the job (JCL messages and SYSOUT). Automatic return of JES output to the FTP client is possible.
4. Delete a job.

Please refer to *IBM TCP/IP Version 3 Release 1 for MVS: Customization and Administration Guide* for more information about the JES interface.

## Special SITE parameters for transferring files between two MVS systems

- Data Compression as defined in RFC 959

   Data is transmitted in a compressed format.

- Checkpoint and Restart as defined in RFC 959

Both the block and the compressed transfer mode supports checkpoint/restart. When checkpointing is used, the sending side inserts checkpoint markers into the data being transmitted. Now assume that your connection breaks down in the middle of the transfer of a large file. All you have to do now is to start the FTP client again, reconnect to the server, reestablish your mode and type settings, and issue the restart command.

### 4.4.6.3 OS/400

Both the FTP client and server functions are supported in OS/400.

FTP supports the following functions:

- Creating libraries, files, and members using the OS/400 FTP server subcommands.

  Since the FTP protocol limits remote FTP server subcommand names to 4 characters or less, the OS/400 FTP server supports abbreviated AS/400 CL commands. For example, CRTL is the abbreviated subcommand for CRTLIB

- Using ASCII and EBCDIC mapping tables for AS/400 servers and FTP clients to map incoming and outgoing data.

- Running FTP unattended in batch mode by using either a REXX EXEC or a CL program.

- Submitting and accepting remote CL commands.

- Transferring binary files without changes.

- Sending document files in EBCDIC format or translating them to ASCII (the default format).

- Converting double-byte character set (DBCS) data from AS/400 EBCDIC code pages to and from internet ASCII code pages.

- Sending or receiving physical files, source files, logical files, save files, hierarchical file system files (HFS), including Client Access/400 files and document library object (DLO) files.

- Sending or receiving files greater than 16 million bytes.

The FTP client can be started with the FTP or the STRCPFTP command. OS/400 files must be specified in the following format (otherwise, the default may not be the name you expect or want):

```
{Libraryname/}Filename.membername
```

## 4.4.6.4 AIX/6000

AIX/6000 provides a full implementation of FTP. It supports the standard set of subcommands with the addition of NLIST, RSTATUS, RHELP, SIZE and SYSTEM. Both the client and server functions are supported, via the ftp and the ftpd programs, respectively.

The ftpd server (also known as a daemon) is a subserver controlled by the inetd subsystem (also known as the super daemon).

The $HOME/.netrc file can be used to specify automatic login information for the user ID and password to use at the foreign host. Since this file is not encrypted, the automatic login feature is not available when your AIX system has been configured with the securetcpip command.

The rcp command and the rshd server (daemon) can be used to transfer files between AIX systems. They provide two additional features: copying file attributes and copying recursively subdirectory files. Since rcp and rshd do not provide a secure environment for transferring files, they are disabled by running the securetcpip command.

The securetcpip command is used to enable additional security environments by disabling commands that are not trusted. For more information about the securetcpip command, please refer to *AIX Version 3.2 for RISC System/6000 Communication Concepts and Procedures*.

## 4.4.6.5 AIX/ESA

Both the FTP client and server functions are provided in AIX/ESA. In addition, the rcp command may also be used, if your local system is listed in the /etc/hosts.equiv file on the remote system; or, your system and your user name are listed in the .rhosts file in your home directory on the remote system.

**Note:** Any copy operation is subject to the AIX/ESA security features in effect. For more details, please refer to *AIX/ESA Security Features User's Guide*.

## 4.4.6.6 OS/2

TCP/IP for OS/2 implements both the client and server functions of FTP.

Two files are used by the FTP to enable or automate various functions. These files are:

- TRUSERS - Used by the FTP server to define access authorization to users on the foreign host. You can assign user IDs, passwords, and authority (read or write) on a directory basis.

  Here is an example of a TRUSERS file:

```
user: bill buffalo
rd:   d:\
wr:   d:\tmp

user: jane calamity
wr∧: c:\etc
```

Where:

- bill is the user ID
- buffalo is his password
- rd:   d: allows Bill to read any file whose access path begins with d:.
- wr:   d:tmp allows Bill to write into any file whose access path begins with d:tmp.

- jane is the user ID
- calamity is her password
- wr∧:   c:etc gives Jane access to read or write to any file except those whose access path begin with c:etc.

- NETRC - Used by FTP clients as a source for user ID and password values and macros (the init macro is the one that executes when the session is established).

Here is an example of NETRC file:

```
machine fsc5 login debulois password xxxxxx macdef init
pwd

macdef go
lcd c:\work
binary
hash
put miam.miam crunch.crunch

machine reso login debulois password yyyyyy macdef init
pwd
```

When the command FTP fsc5 is issued the following sequence takes place:

1. The NETRC file is read from the line machine fsc5
2. The password and user ID are transmitted to the server
3. The init macro is executed (that is, the pwd FTP subcommand is executed) and control is returned to the keyboard
4. The go macro can be executed under the FTP command prompt.

The FTP -n fsc5 command allows you to log on to the host named fsc5 without reading the NETRC file.

These two files can be hidden by the File Manager and their location can be customized.

A Presentation Manager FTP client application is also provided (FTPPM).

The FTP server can be initiated by the INETD super server or by the ftpd command.

The High Performance File System (HPFS) is supported.

TCP/IP for OS/2 also includes an API that allows applications to have a client interface for file transfer. Applications written to this interface can communicate with multiple FTP servers at the same time (256 connections maximum). The interface also allows third-party proxy transfers between pairs of FTP servers. In addition to the FTP specific API calls, a ping() call is included to allow the application to determine whether the remote host is alive before attempting FTP transfers. The programs may be compiled and linked using the IBM C-Set/2 32-bit compiler or alternatively, the Microsoft C Compiler Version 6.0A.

The REXX FTP Application Program Interface (API) package, which is provided in the TCP/IP V2.0 for OS/2 Base Kit, provides access to the OS/2 TCP/IP FTP APIs. The REXX FTP API function names are similar to the FTP subcommands.

## 4.4.6.7 DOS
TCP/IP for DOS implements both the client and server functions of FTP. In particular, a DOS-based FTP server and client are provided as well as a Windows-based FTP client.

The FTP server function is implemented as a dedicated, foreground process and can support multiple concurrent FTP client sessions. It supports DOS wild card characters for multiple file transfers. Its security function is similar to that of the OS/2 implementation of a trusted users file named TRUSERS.

Once in the FTP command shell (ftp>) you can (basic FTP subcommands not included):

- Enter DOS command with the ! subcommand
- Reserve space on the host to accommodate the file to be transferred with the allocate subcommand
- Transfer a single file from a host and append it to a file on your PC with the getappend subcommand
- Read the FTP subcommands from a file on your PC with the take subcommand
- Inform the FTP server that your byte-size is eight bits with the tenex subcommand

A file transfer from TCP/IP for DOS can be automated using a command file with the ftp -f command_file command.

TCP/IP for DOS also includes an API which allows applications to have a client interface for file transfer. Applications written to this interface can communicate with multiple

FTP servers at the same time (256 connections maximum). The interface also allows third-party proxy transfers between pairs of FTP servers. In addition to the FTP specific API calls, a ping() call is included to allow the application to determine whether the remote host is alive before attempting FTP transfers.

# 4.5  Domain Name System (DNS)

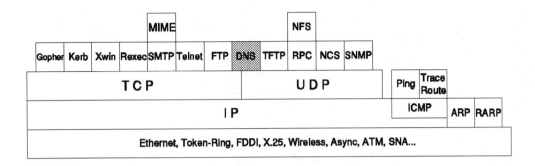

*Figure   4-16.  The Domain Name System*

The Domain Name System is a *standard protocol* with STD number 13.  Its status is *recommended*.  It is described in RFC 1034 and RFC 1035.  This section explains the implementation of the Domain Name System, and the implementation of name servers. See 2.2.8, "Domain Name System" on page 2-31 for an overview of the Domain Name System and its relationship to the IP addressing scheme.

## 4.5.1  The Distributed Name Space

The Domain Name System uses the concept of a *distributed name space*.  Symbolic names are grouped into *zones of authority*, or more commonly *zones*.  In each of these zones, one or more hosts has the task of maintaining a database of symbolic names and IP addresses and providing a server function for clients who wish to translate between symbolic names and IP addresses.  These local *name servers* are then (through the internet on which they are connected) logically interconnected into a hierarchical tree of *domains*.  Each zone contains a part or a *subtree* of the hierarchical tree and the names within the zone are administered independently of names in other zones.  Authority over zones in vested in the name servers.  Normally, the name servers which have authority for a zone will have domain names belonging to that zone, but this is not required. Where a domain contains a subtree which falls in a different zone, the name server(s) with authority over the superior domain are said to *delegate authority* to the name server(s) with authority over the subdomain.  Name servers may also delegate authority to themselves; in this case, the domain name space is still divided into zones moving down the domain name tree, but authority for two zones is held by the same server.  The division of the domain name space into zones is accomplished using resource records stored in the Domain Name System:

*Start of Authority (SOA) Records*
> Defines the start of a zone

*Name Server (NS) Records*
> Marks the end of a zone started by an SOA record and points to a name server having authority for the next zone

In this context, the start of a domain is closer to the root of the tree than the end. At the root, there can be no higher name servers to delegate authority: authority for the zone encompassing the root of the name space is vested in a set of *root name servers*.[1]

The results of this scheme are:

- Rather than having a central server for the database, the work that is involved in maintaining this database is off-loaded to hosts throughout the name space.
- Authority for creating and changing symbolic host names and responsibility for maintaining a database for them is delegated to the organization owning the zone (within the name space) containing those host names.
- From the user's standpoint, there is a single database that deals with these address resolutions. The user may be aware that the database is distributed, but generally need not be concerned about this.

**Note:** Although domains within the namespace will frequently map in a logical fashion to networks and subnets within the IP addressing scheme, this is not a requirement of the Domain Name System. Consider a router between two subnets: it has two IP addresses, one for each network adapter, but it would not normally have two symbolic names.

## 4.5.2 Domain Resolution

Domain resolution is a client/server process. The client function (called the *resolver* or *name resolver*) is transparent to the user and is called by an application to resolve symbolic high-level names into real IP-addresses or vice versa. The name server (also called a *domain name server*) is a server application providing the translation between high-level machine names and the IP addresses. The basic process is shown in Figure 4-17 on page 4-41 and Figure 4-18 on page 4-42. The former shows a program called a *full resolver*, which is a program distinct from the user program, which forwards all queries to a name server for processing. Responses are cached by the name server for future use, and often by the name server. The latter shows a *stub resolver*, which is a routine linked with the user program, which forwards the queries to a name server for processing. Responses are cached by the name server but not usually by the resolver

---

[1]  At the time of writing there were nine root servers. The current list is available by anonymous FTP from ftp.rs.internic.net in the file netinfo/root-servers.txt

although this is implementation dependent. On UNIX, the stub resolver is implemented by two library routines: gethostbyname() and gethostbyaddr() for converting host names to IP addresses and vice versa. Other platforms have the same or equivalent routines. Stub resolvers are much more common than full resolvers.

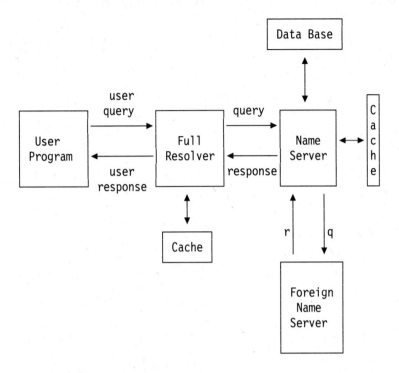

*Figure* **4-17.** *Using a Full Resolver for Domain Name Resolution*

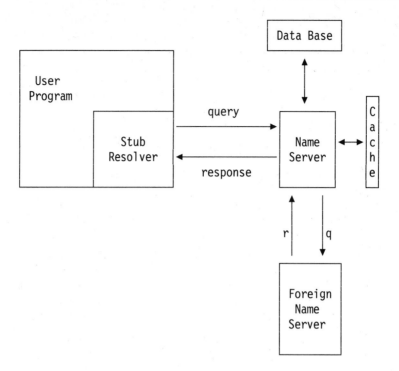

*Figure* *4-18.* *Using a Stub Resolver for Domain Name Resolution*

## 4.5.2.1 Domain Name Resolver Operation

Domain name queries can be one of two types: *recursive* or *iterative* (also termed *non-recursive*). A flag bit in the domain name query specifies whether the client desires a recursive query and a flag bit in the response specifies whether the server supports recursive queries. The difference between a recursive and an iterative query arises when the server receives a request for which it cannot supply a complete answer by itself. A recursive query requests that the server should issue a query itself to determine the requested information and return the complete answer to the client. An iterative query means that the name server should return what information it has available and also a list of additional servers for the client to contact to complete the query.

Domain name responses can be one of two types: *authoritative* and *non-authoritative*. A flag bit in the response indicates which type a response is. When a name server receives a query for a domain in a zone over which it has authority, it returns all of the requested information in a response with the authoritative answer flag set. When it receives a query for a domain over which it does not have authority, its actions depend upon the setting of the recursion desired flag in the query.

If the recursion desired flag is set and the server supports recursive queries, it will direct its query to another name server. This will either be a name server with authority for the domain given in the query, or it will be one of the root name servers. If the second server does not return an authoritative answer (for example if it has delegated authority to another server) the process is repeated.

When a server (or a full resolver program) receives a response, it will cache it to improve the performance of repeat queries. The cache entry is stored for a maximum length of time specified by the originator in a 32-bit *time-to-live (TTL)* field contained in the response. 172,800 seconds (two days) is a typical TTL value.

If the recursion desired flag is not set or the server does not support recursive queries, it will return whatever information it has in its cache and also a list of additional name servers to be contacted for authoritative information.

## 4.5.2.2 Domain Name Server Operation

Each name server has *authority* for zero or more zones. There are three types of name server:

*primary*    A primary name server loads a zone's information from disk, and has authority over the zone.

*secondary*  A secondary name server has authority for a zone, but obtains its zone information from a primary server using a process called *zone transfer*. To remain synchronized, the secondary name servers query the primary on a regular basis (typically every three hours) and re-execute the zone transfer if the primary has been updated.

A name server can operate as a primary or a secondary name server for multiple domains, or a primary for some domains and as a secondary for others. A primary or secondary name server performs all of the functions of a caching only name server.

*caching-only* A name server that does not have authority for any zone is called a caching-only name server. A caching-only name server obtains all of its data from primary or secondary name servers as required. It requires at least one NS record to point to a name server from which it can initially obtain information.

When a domain is registered with the root and a separate zone of authority established, the following rules apply:

- The domain must be registered with the root administrator.

- There must be an identified administrator for the domain.

- There must be at least two name servers with authority for the zone which are accessible from outside and inside the domain to ensure no single point of failure).

It is also recommended that name servers which delegate authority also apply these rules, since the delegating name servers are responsible for the behavior of name servers under their authority.

## 4.5.3 Domain System Resource Records

The Domain Name System's distributed database is composed of *resource records (RRs)*. They provide a mapping between domain names and *network objects*. The most common network objects are the addresses of Internet hosts, but the Domain Name System is designed to accommodate a wide range of different objects. The general format of a resource record is:

```
name ttl class type rdata
```

where:

*name*   Is the domain name to be defined. The domain name system is very general in its rules for the composition of domain names. However, it recommends a syntax for domain names which will minimize the likelihood of applications which use a DNS resolver (that is, nearly all TCP/IP applications) from misinterpreting a domain name. A domain name adhering to this recommended syntax will consist of a series of labels consisting of alphanumeric characters or hyphens, each label having a length of between 1 and 63 characters, starting with an alphabetic character. Each pair of labels is separated by a dot (period) in human readable form, but not in the form used within DNS messages. Domain names are not case-sensitive.

*ttl*   Is the *time-to-live (TTL)* time in seconds that this resource record will be valid in a name server cache. This is stored in the DNS as an unsigned 32-bit value. 86400 (one day) is a typical value for records pointing to IP addresses.

*class*   Identifies the protocol family. Commonly used values are:

   *IN*   The Internet system
   *CH*   The Chaos system

*type*   Identifies the type of the resource in this resource record.

   The different types are described in detail in RFCs 1034, 1035 and 1706. Each type has a name and a value. Commonly used types include:

   | Type | Value | Meaning |
   | --- | --- | --- |
   | A | 1 | A host address. |
   | CNAME | 5 | Canonical name of an alias; specifies an alias name for a host. |

| Type | Value | Meaning |
|------|-------|---------|
| HINFO | 13 | The CPU and OS used by the host; this is only a comment field. |
| MX | 15 | A mail exchange for the domain; specifies a domain name for a mailbox. This is used by SMTP (see 4.6.2, "SMTP and the Domain Name System" on page 4-72 for more information). |
| NS | 2 | The authoritative name server for a domain. |
| PTR | 12 | A pointer to another part of the domain name space. |
| SOA | 6 | The start of a zone of authority in the domain name space. |
| WKS | 11 | Well-known services; specifies that certain services (for instance SMTP) are expected to be always active on this host. |

*Rdata*    The value depends on the type, for example:

| | |
|---|---|
| *A* | A 32-bit IP address (if the class is IN) |
| *CNAME* | A domain name |
| *MX* | A 16-bit preference value (low values being preferred) followed by a domain name. |
| *NS* | A host name |
| *PTR* | A domain name |

## 4.5.4  Domain Name System Messages

All messages in the Domain Name System protocol use a single format. This format is shown in Figure 4-19 on page 4-46. This frame is sent by the resolver to the name server. Only the header and the question section are used to form the query. Replies and/or forwarding of the query use the same frame, but with more sections filled in (the answer/authority/additional sections).

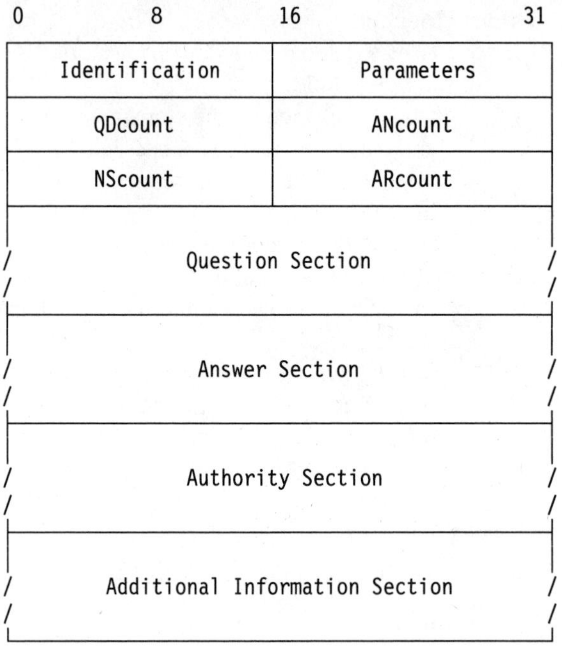

```
      0         8        16                    31
      ┌─────────────────────┬──────────────────────┐
      │    Identification   │      Parameters      │
      ├─────────────────────┼──────────────────────┤
      │       QDcount       │       ANcount        │
      ├─────────────────────┼──────────────────────┤
      │       NScount       │       ARcount        │
      ├─────────────────────┴──────────────────────┤
      /                                             /
      /            Question Section                 /
      ├─────────────────────────────────────────────┤
      /                                             /
      /             Answer Section                  /
      ├─────────────────────────────────────────────┤
      /                                             /
      /            Authority Section                /
      ├─────────────────────────────────────────────┤
      /                                             /
      /        Additional Information Section       /
      └─────────────────────────────────────────────┘
```

*Figure   4-19.  DNS Message Format*

## 4.5.4.1 Header Format

The header section is always present and has a fixed length of 12 bytes. The other sections are of variable length.

*ID*  A 16-bit identifier assigned by the program. This identifier is copied in the corresponding reply from the name server and can be used for differentiation of responses when multiple queries are outstanding at the same time.

*Parameters*

A 16-bit value in the following format:

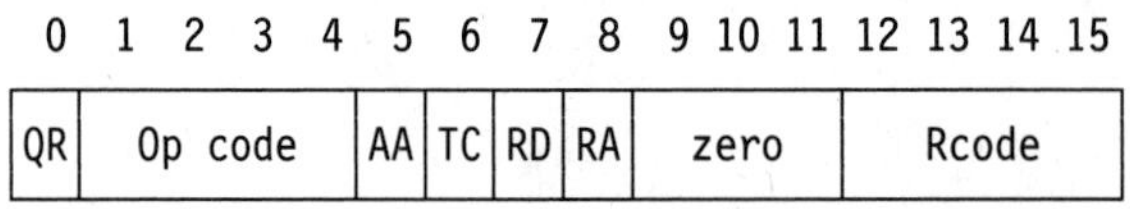

```
 0  1  2  3  4  5  6  7  8  9 10 11 12 13 14 15
┌──┬───────────┬──┬──┬──┬──┬──────────┬────────────┐
│QR│  Op code  │AA│TC│RD│RA│   zero   │   Rcode    │
└──┴───────────┴──┴──┴──┴──┴──────────┴────────────┘
```

*QR*  Flag identifying a query (0) or a response(1)

*Op code*
> 4-bit field specifying the kind of query:

> *0* standard query (QUERY)
> *1* inverse query (IQUERY)
> *2* server status request (STATUS)
> Other values are reserved for future use

*AA* Authoritative answer flag. If set in a response, this flag specifies that the responding name server is an authority for the domain name sent in the query.

*TC* Truncation flag. Set if message was longer than permitted on the physical channel.

*RD* Recursion desired flag. This bit signals to the name server that recursive resolution is asked for. The bit is copied to the response.

*RA* Recursion available flag. Indicates whether the name server supports recursive resolution.

*zero*
> 3 bits reserved for future use. Must be zero.

*Rcode*
> 4-bit response code. Possible values are:

> *0* No error.
> *1* Format error. The server was unable to interpret the message.
> *2* Server failure. The message was not processed because of a problem with the server.
> *3* Name error. The domain name in the query does not exist. This is only valid if the AA bit is set in the response.
> *4* Not implemented. The requested type of query is not implemented by name server
> *5* Refused. The server refuses to respond for policy reasons.
> Other values are reserved for future use.

*QDcount* An unsigned 16-bit integer specifying the number of entries in the question section.

*ANcount* An unsigned 16-bit integer specifying the number of RRs in the answer section.

*NScount* An unsigned 16-bit integer specifying the number of name server RRs in the authority section.

*ARcount* An unsigned 16-bit integer specifying the number of RRs in the additional records section.

## 4.5.4.2 Question Section

The next section contains the queries for the name server. It contains QDcount (usually 1) entries, each in the format shown in Figure 4-20.

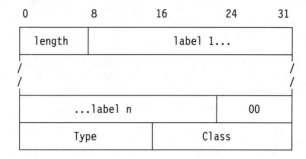

**Figure 4-20.** *DNS Question Format.* All of the fields are byte-aligned. The alignment of the Type field on a 4-byte boundary is for example purposes and is not required by the format.

*length*   A single byte giving the length of the next label.

*label*    One element of the domain name (for example "ibm" from ral.ibm.com) characters. The domain name referred to by the question is stored as a series of these variable length labels, each preceded by a 1-byte length.

*00*       X' 00' indicates the end of the domain name and represents the null label of the root domain.

*Type*     2 bytes specifying the type of query. It may have any value from the Type field in a resource record.

*Class*    2 bytes specifying the class of the query. For Internet queries, this will be "IN".

For example, the domain name raleigh.ibm.com would be encoded with the following fields:

```
X'07'
"raleigh"
X'03'
"ibm"
X'03'
"com"
X'00'
```

Thus the entry in the question section for raleigh.ibm.com would require 21 bytes: 17 to store the domain name and 2 each for the Qtype and Qclass fields.

## 4.5.4.3 Answer, Authority and Additional Resource Sections

These three sections contain a variable number of resource records. The number is specified in the corresponding field of the header. The resource records are in the format shown in Figure 4-21.

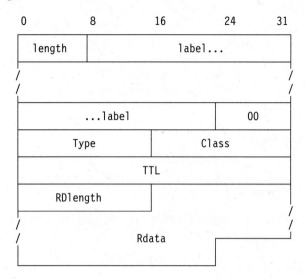

***Figure 4-21.*** *DNS Answer Record Entry Format.* All of the fields are byte-aligned. The alignment of the Type field on a 4-byte boundary is for example purposes and is not required by the format.

Where the fields before the TTL field have the same meanings as for a question entry and:

*TTL*        A 32-bit time-to-live value in seconds for the record. This defines how long it may be regarded as valid.

*RDlength*    A 16-bit length for the Rdata field.

*Rdata*      A variable length string whose interpretation depends on the Type field.

## 4.5.4.4 Message Compression

In order to reduce the message size, a compression scheme is used to eliminate the repetition of domain names in the various RRs. Any duplicate domain name or list of labels is replaced with a pointer to the previous occurrence. The pointer has the form of a 2-byte field:

- The first 2 bits distinguish the pointer from a normal label, which is restricted to a 63-byte length plus the length byte ahead of it (which has a value of <64).
- The offset field specifies an offset from the start of the message. A zero offset specifies the first byte of the ID field in the header.
- If compression is used in an Rdata field of an answer, authority or additional section of the message, the preceding RDlength field contains the real length after compression is done.

## 4.5.5  A Simple Scenario

Consider a stand-alone network (no outside connections), consisting of two physical networks: one has an internet network address 129.112, the other has a network address 194.33.7, interconnected by an IP gateway (VM2).

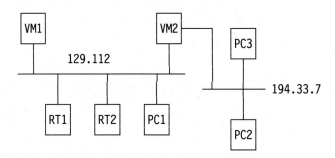

*Figure*  *4-22.*  *A Simple Configuration.*   Two networks connected through an IP gateway.

Let us assign the name server function to VM1.  Remember that the domain hierarchical tree forms a logical tree, completely independent of the physical configuration. In this simple scenario, there is only one level in the domain tree. Let's give this configuration the domain name test.example.

The zone data for the name server will then be as shown in Figure  4-23.

```
;note: an SOA record has no TTL field
;
$origin test.example.                                        ;note 1
;
@           IN SOA VM1.test.example. ADM.VM1.test.example.
                (870611            ;serial number for data
                 1800             ;secondary refreshes every 30 mn
                 300              ;secondary reties every 5 mn
                 604800           ;data expire after 1 week
                 86400)           ;minimum TTL for data is 1 week
;
@       99999 IN NS  VM1.test.example.                       ;note 2
;
VM1     99999 IN A   129.112.1.1                             ;note 3
        99999 IN WKS 129.112.1.1 TCP (SMTP                   ;note 4
                                      FTP
                                      TELNET
                                      NAMESRV)
;
RT1     99999 IN A    129.112.1.2
              IN HINFO IBM RT/PC-AIX                         ;note 5
RT2     99999 IN A    129.112.1.3
              IN HINFO IBM RT/PC-AIX
PC1     99999 IN A    129.112.1.11
PC2     99999 IN A    194.33.7.2
PC3     99999 IN A    194.33.7.3
;
;VM2 is an IP gateway and has 2 different IP addresses
;
VM2     99999 IN A    129.112.1.4
        99999 IN A    194.33.7.1
        99999 IN WKS  129.112.1.4 TCP (SMTP FTP)
              IN HINFO IBM-3090-VM/CMS
;
4.1.112.129.in-addr.arpa.  IN  PTR  VM2                      ;note 6
;
;Some mailboxes
;
central 10    IN MX  VM2.test.example.                       ;note 7 and 8
;
;a second definition for the same mailbox, in case VM2 is down
;
central 20    IN MX  VM1.test.example.
waste   10    IN MX  VM2.test.example.
```

*Figure   4-23.  Zone Data for the Name Server*

**Notes:**

*1* The `$origin` statement sets the @ variable to the zone name (test.example.). Domain names which do not end with a period are suffixed with the zone name. Fully qualified domain names (those ending with a period) are unaffected by the zone name.

*2* Defines the name server for this zone.

*3* Defines the Internet address of the name server for this zone.

*4* Specifies well-known services for this host. These are expected to be always available.

*5* Gives information about the host.

*6* Used for inverse mapping queries (see 2.2.8.6, "Mapping IP Addresses to Domain Names — Pointer Queries" on page 2-34).

*7* Will allow mail to be addressed to user@central.test.example.

*8* See 4.6.2, "SMTP and the Domain Name System" on page 4-72 for the use of these definitions.

## 4.5.6 Extended Scenario

Consider the case where a connection is made to a third network (129.113) which has an existing name server with authority for that zone.

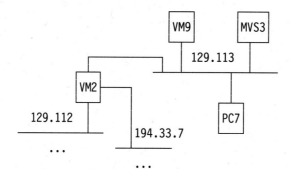

*Figure 4-24. Extended Configuration.* A third network is connected to the existing configuration.

Let us suppose that the domain name of the other network is tt.ibm.com and that its name server is located in VM9.

All we have to do is add the address of this name server to our own name server database, and to reference the other network by its own name server. The following two lines are all that is needed to do that:

```
tt.ibm.com.        99999  IN NS    VM9.tt.ibm.com.
VM9.tt.ibm.com.    99999  IN A     129.113.1.9
```

This simply indicates that VM9 is the authority for the new network, and that all queries for that network will be directed to that name server.

## 4.5.7 Transport

Domain Name System Messages are transmitted either as datagrams (UDP) or via stream connection (TCP).

**UDP usage:**  Server port 53 (decimal).

Messages carried by UDP are restricted to 512 bytes. Longer messages are truncated and the TC bit is set in the header.  Since UDP frames can be lost, a retransmission strategy is required.

**TCP usage:**  Server port 53 (decimal).

In this case, the message is preceded by a 2-byte field indicating the total message frame length.

*STD 3 — Host Requirements* requires that:

- A Domain Name System resolver or server that is sending a non-zone-transfer query *must* send a UDP query first.  If the answer section of the response is truncated and if the requester supports TCP, it should try the query again using TCP.  UDP is preferred over TCP for queries because UDP queries have much lower overhead, and the use of UDP is essential for a heavily loaded server.  Truncation of messages is rarely a problem given the current contents of the Domain Name System database, since typically 15 response records can be accommodated in the datagram, but this may change as new record types are added to the Domain Name System.
- TCP must be used for zone transfer activities because the 512-byte limit for a UDP datagram will always be inadequate for a zone transfer.
- Name servers must support both types of transport.

## 4.5.8 References

The following RFCs define the Domain Name System standard and the information kept in the system:

- *RFC 1032 — Domain Administrator's Guide*
- *RFC 1033 — Domain Administrator Operations Guide*
- *RFC 1034 — Domain Names – Concepts and Facilities*
- *RFC 1035 — Domain Names – Implementation and Specification*
- *RFC 1101 — DNS Encoding of Networks Names and Other Types*
- *RFC 1183 — New DNS RR Definitions*

• *RFC 1706 — DNS NSAP Resource Records*

## 4.5.9 DNS Applications

Three common utilities for querying name servers are provided with many DNS implementations:

*host*  Obtains an IP address associated with a host name or a host name associated with an IP address.

*nslookup* Allows you to locate information about network nodes, examine the contents of a name server database and establish the accessibility of name servers.

*dig*  Allows you to exercise name servers, gather large volumes of domain name information and execute simple domain name queries. DIG stands for Domain Internet Groper.

## 4.5.10 Implementations

All of the IBM TCP/IP platforms use stub resolvers in each client application. All except OS/400 and DOS include a name server implementation, which we will discuss in detail in the following sections.

### 4.5.10.1 VM

TCP/IP for VM allows for the use of a local site tables or the use of the Domain Name System.

The use of local site tables or the use of the Domain Name System is specified in the TCPIP DATA file using the NSINTERADDR statement. If this statement is omitted, then TCP/IP will use a local site table. If this statement exists, TCP/IP will use the Domain Name System. If the parameter on the NSINTERADDR statement is the *loopback* address (127.0.0.1)[2] then the local name server will be used. Otherwise one (or more) more remote name servers specified on the NSINTERADDR statements will be used. This provides a total of five possible configurations.

**Using a local site table:** To use a local site table, omit the NSINTERADDR statement from the TCPIP DATA file. Name resolvers need access to a *site table* to resolve symbolic names. The source for this is the HOSTS LOCAL file which must be converted into a machine-readable form by running the MAKESITE utility. MAKESITE generates two files, HOSTS ADDRINFO and HOSTS SITEINFO, which comprise the site table. The site table is used if no name server is available, that is, if no name server is specified or if the specified name server(s) are unavailable. The only exception is SMTP, which never uses the site tables if it is configured to use a name server.

---

2 VM also supports 14.0.0.0 as a loopback address for compatibility with older releases.

**Using a remote name server:** The resolver program obtains the IP addresses of the remote name server(s) from the NSINTERADRR statement(s) in the TCPIP DATA file. If multiple NSINTERADDR statements are found, then connections to the remote name servers are attempted in the order they appear in this configuration file. The number of times that each connection is tried and the timeout interval for the server to respond to the UDP datagram containing the query are specified on the RESOLVERUDPRETRIES and RESOLVERTIMEOUT statements.

**Caching-only name server:** The name server software is run in a service virtual machine, normally called NAMESRV. Resolver programs use the loopback address specified on the NSINTERADDR statement in the TCPIP DATA file. The server does not have any data available locally, other than a set of resource records specifying the IP addresses name servers to query for particular domains (and possibly an initial set of other resource records). However, the server caches data locally so that subsequent queries for the same domain name can be quickly answered, and it also provides for recursion if recursive resolution is asked by the client resolver. The only data required are the IP addresses of the remote server(s).

The name server configuration file name is specified in the PROFILE EXEC on the NAMESRV 191 minidisk as an argument to the NSMAIN command which starts the name server. The default is NSMAIN DATA. In this configuration file, the entry:

```
CACHINGONLY fn ft fm
```

specifies the file name of the data file to be used. The information is written in standard resource record format, for example:

```
PARIS.IBM.COM                   IN NS    VMA.PARIS.IBM.COM
LAHULPE.IBM.COM                 IN NS    MIDVMB.LAHULPE.IBM.COM
  ..                            IN NS    SRI-NIC.ARPA
SRI-NIC.ARPA                    IN A     10.0.0.51
                                IN A     26.0.0.73
VMA.PARIS.IBM.COM               IN A     9.37.17.2
MIDVMB.LAHULPE.IBM.COM          IN A     9.36.1.4
```

This simply means that all queries for domain PARIS.IBM.COM will be forwarded to VMA.PARIS.IBM.COM, all queries for LAHULPE.IBM.COM to MIDVMB.LAHULPE.IBM.COM, and all others to the root server SRI-NIC.ARPA.

**Full-function name server:** The name server software is run in the NAMESRV service virtual machine and resolver programs use the loopback address. The name server can operate as a primary and/or a secondary name server. The domain data is stored in an SQL/DS table.

*Mail eXchanger (MX)* records are supported. They are only used by SMTP ( see 4.6.2, "SMTP and the Domain Name System" on page 4-72 for more details about the use of MX records).

The NSMAIN DATA contains PRIMARY and/or SECONDARY statements instead of a CACHINGONLY statement. An example is shown in Figure 4-25.

```
;*********************************************************
; This file is read by the name server upon initialization.
; The default name of this file is NSMAIN DATA *.
; A different file may be read by suppling a parameter when
; the name server is started... NSMAIN MY FILE B for example.
;
; This file contains the startup parameter values which define
; the name server as authoritative for stn.mlv.fr and
; tst.mlv.fr.   The data for stn.mlv.fr is defined locally,
; whereas the data for  tst.mlv.fr is defined remotely and zone
; transferred to the local name server.
;
; If you are not using SQL, remove all PRIMARY and SECONDARY
; statements and use the CACHINGONLY statement to define a
; database of remote name servers.
;*********************************************************
;
; The PRIMARY and SECONDARY statements are used if you are using an
; SQL database.
;
PRIMARY stn.mlv.fr STN  ; Use authoritative tables STN0 & STN1
SECONDARY tst.mlv.fr TST 152.9.271.2
;                       ; Use authoritative tables TST0 & TST1
;                       ; Transfer domain data for tst.mlv.fr into tables
;                       ; TST0 and TST1 from 152.9.271.2
;
; The CACHINGONLY statement is used to define a caching only name server
; that obtains all records from remote name servers.
;
; CACHINGONLY  NSMAIN CACHE A     ; Sample CACHINGONLY data file
;
;
NEGATIVECACHING                  ; The NS will store negative query answers
STANDARDQUERYCACHE       100     ; The number of Standard queries to cache
INTERMEDIARYQUERYCACHE   50      ; The number of Intermediary queries to cache
INVERSEQUERYCACHE        5       ; The number of Inverse queries to cache
DATABASEQUERYCACHE       5       ; The number of Data Base queries to cache
;
;
LRUTIME                  300     ; Time an entry must be in the cache before it
                                 ; can be replaced by the LRU algorithm
HOSTNAMECASE        LOWER        ; Host names in the SQL tables are in lower case
DOMAINNAMEPORT           53      ; Listen on port N, default is 53
; UDPONLY                        ; Use UDP only when contacting a remove NS
UDPRETRYINTERVAL         5       ; After N seconds, try next remote NS
; NORECURSION                    ; Prevents NS from performing recursion
MSGNOH                           ; Specifies the NS use CP MSGNOH, not CP MSG
SMSGUSERFILE     VALIDUSR EXEC A ; SMSG userid authorization file
TRACE               QUEUE        ; Display query origination and query name
```

*Figure*  *4-25. Sample NSMAIN DATA File for VM*

**User Applications:**  VM provides the NSLOOKUP and DIG programs to query name servers.  For more information on these programs, please refer to *IBM TCP/IP Version 2 Release 3 for VM: User's Guide*.

## 4.5.10.2 MVS

**Note:**  Consult *IBM TCP/IP Version 3 Release 1 for MVS: Customization and Administration Guide* for information on the search order used for TCP/IP data sets.

TCP/IP for MVS supports both local site tables and the Domain Name System.

The use of local site tables or the use of the Domain Name System is specified in the TCPIP.DATA data set using the NSINTERADDR statement.  If this statement is omitted, TCP/IP will use a local site table.  If this statement exists TCP/IP will use the Domain Name System.  If the parameter on the NSINTERADDR statement is the *loopback* address (127.0.0.1)[3] then the local name server will be used, otherwise one (or more) more remote name servers specified on the NSINTERADDR statements will be used. This provides a total of five possible configurations.

**Using a local site table:**  To use a local site table, omit the NSINTERADDR statement from the TCPIP.DATA data set.  Name resolvers need access to a *site table* to resolve symbolic names.  The source for this is the HOSTS.LOCAL data set, which must be converted into a machine-readable form by running the MAKESITE utility. MAKESITE generates two data sets, HOSTS.ADDRINFO and HOSTS.SITEINFO, which comprise the site table.  The site table is used if no name server is available, that is, if no name server is specified or if the specified name server(s) are unavailable.  The only exception is SMTP, which never uses the site tables if it is configured to use a name server.

**Using a Remote Name Server:**  The resolver program obtains the IP addresses of the remote name server(s) from the NSINTERADRR statement(s) in the TCPIP.DATA data set.  If multiple NSINTERADDR statements are found then connections to the remote name servers are attempted in the order they appear in this configuration file.  The number of times that each connection is tried and the timeout interval for the server to respond to the UDP datagram containing the query are specified on the RESOLVERUDPRETRIES and RESOLVERTIMEOUT statements.

**Caching-only name server:**  The name server software is run in a separate address space.  Resolver programs use the loopback address specified on the NSINTERADDR statement in the TCPIP DATA file.  The server does not have any data available locally, other than a set of resource records specifying the IP addresses name servers to query for

---

[3]  MVS also supports 14.0.0.0 as a loopback address for compatibility with older releases.

particular domains (and possibly an initial set of other resource records). However, the server caches data locally so that subsequent queries for the same domain name can be quickly answered, and it also provides for recursion if recursive resolution is asked by the client resolver. The only data required are the IP addresses of the remote server(s).

The NSMAIN.DATA configuration data set contains the entry:

```
CACHINGONLY data_set_name
```

which gives the name of the data set containing these IP addresses. The information is written in standard resource record format, for example:

```
PARIS.IBM.COM              IN NS    MVSA.PARIS.IBM.COM
LAHULPE.IBM.COM            IN NS    MIDVMB.LAHULPE.IBM.COM
  ..                       IN NS    SRI-NIC.ARPA
SRI-NIC.ARPA               IN A     10.0.0.51
                           IN A     26.0.0.73
MVSA.PARIS.IBM.COM         IN A     9.37.17.2
MIDVMB.LAHULPE.IBM.COM     IN A     9.36.1.4
```

This simply means that all queries for domain paris.ibm.com will be forwarded to mvsa.paris.ibm.com, all queries for lahulpe.ibm.com to midvmb.lahulpe.ibm.com, and all others to the root server sri-nic.arpa.

**Full-function name server:**  The name server software is run in a separate address space and resolver programs use the loopback address. The name server can operate as a primary and/or a secondary name server. The domain data is stored in a DB2 SQL table.

The name server software is run in the NAMESRV service virtual machine and resolver programs use the loopback address. The name server can operate as a primary and/or a secondary name server. The domain data is stored in an SQL/DS database.

*Mail eXchanger (MX)* records are supported. They are only used by SMTP (see 4.6.2, "SMTP and the Domain Name System" on page 4-72 for more details about the use of MX records).

The NSMAIN DATA contains PRIMARY and/or SECONDARY statements instead of a CACHINGONLY statement. An example is shown in Figure 4-26.

```
;
DB2SYSNAME SYS1          ; Define Local DB2 subsystem
PRIMARY watson.ibm.com WATSON  ; Use authoritative tables WATSON0, WATSON1
SECONDARY ibm.com IBM 129.34.128.245
;                           ; Transfer domain data for ibm.com into tables
;                           ; IBM0 and IBM1 from 129.34.128.245
;
NEGATIVECACHING                        ; The NS will store negative query answers
STANDARDQUERYCACHE       100           ; The number of Standard queries to cache
INTERMEDIARYQUERYCACHE   50            ; The number of Intermediary queries to cache
INVERSEQUERYCACHE        5             ; The number of Inverse queries to cache
;
;
LRUTIME                  300           ; Time an entry must be in the cache before it
                                       ; can be replaced by the LRU algorithm
HOSTNAMECASE             UPPER         ; Host names in the DB2 tables are in upper case
DOMAINNAMEPORT           53            ; Listen on port N, default is 53
UDPONLY                              ; Use UDP only when contacting a remove NS
UDPRETRYINTERVAL         5             ; After N seconds, try next remote NS
; NORECURSION                          ; Prevents NS from performing recursion
TRACE                    QUEUE         ; Display query origination and query name
```

**Figure** *4-26. Sample NSMAIN DATA File for MVS*

A sample DB2 configuration is shown schematically in Figure 4-27.

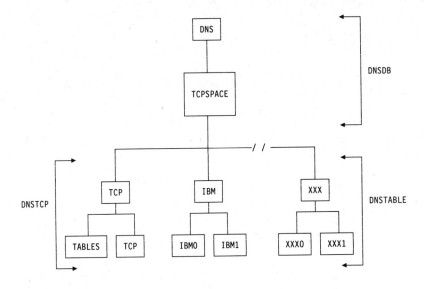

```
DNS = Storage Group
TCPSPACE = Data base
TCP, IBM, XXX = Tablespace
TABLES, TCP, IBM0, IBM1, XXX0, XXX1 = SQL Tables
```

*Figure* *4-27. DB2 Storage Group, Tablespace, and Table Definition*

**User Applications:**  MVS provides the NSLOOKUP and DIG programs to query name servers.  For more information on these programs, please refer to *IBM TCP/IP Version 3 Release 1 for MVS: User's Guide.*

For more information on their installation, please refer to the *IBM TCP/IP Version 3 Release 1 for MVS: Customization and Administration Guide.*

## 4.5.10.3 OS/400

TCP/IP on OS/400 systems does not support the name server function but can use a remote name server (that is, the user applications include a stub resolver).  A flat name space is supported and the local host table is configured using the OS/400 TCP/IP configuration panels.

## 4.5.10.4 AIX

Domain name services are fully implemented in AIX/6000.  AIX/ESA provides similar services.  We shall concentrate on the AIX/6000 implementation here.  The following types of name server are supported:

1. Primary name server
2. Secondary name server

3. Caching-only server
4. Forwarder or client server (not on AIX/ESA)
5. Remote server

The AIX resolver routines, gethostbyaddr() and gethostbyname(), attempt to resolve names using the following procedure:

- If the file /etc/resolv.conf does not exist, then the resolver routines assume that the local network is a flat network. They then use the /etc/hosts file to map the name to an address.

- Otherwise, they assume the local network is a domain network and attempt to use the following sources in the order listed:

  1. The domain name server
  2. The local /etc/hosts file

The *named* daemon provides the name server function. It is controlled by the AIX SRC (system resource control). It can be started automatically with each system restart by either using the *smit stnamed* fastpath command or by editing the rc.tcpip file to uncomment the line:

```
#start /etc/named "$src_running"
```

The named daemon can also be started by issuing the *startsrc -s named* command.

An AIX host can be configured to use a name server by using the following steps:

- Create the /etc/resolv.conf file to include the domain name and up to 16 name server entries. For example:

```
domain itsc.raleigh.ibm.com
nameserver 9.67.38.101
nameserver 9.67.38.96
```

- Create the /etc/named.boot file to specify the name and the type of the local named daemon.

- Create the /etc/named.* files to define further data for the daemon. The format of the files follows the standard Resource Record format.

The daemon also supports resource records for mail of types MB (mailbox domain name), MR (mail rename domain name), MG (mail group member), MINFO (mailbox or mail list information) and MX (mail exchange).

**User Applications:**  AIX/6000 includes the host and nslookup programs. AIX/6000 also provides the dig program to query name servers.

## 4.5.10.5 OS/2

TCP/IP for OS/2 provides a similar implementation to that in AIX. The following types of name server are supported:

1. Primary name server
2. Secondary name server
3. Caching-only server
4. Remote server
5. Flat name space

In order to use any of the first three, the *named* server which is included in the Domain Name Server kit is required.

The OS/2 resolver routines, gethostbyaddr() and gethostbyname() attempt to resolve names using the following procedure:

- If the file \TCPIP\ETC\RESOLV does not exist, then the resolver routines assume that the local network is a flat network. They then use TCPIP\ETC\HOSTS file to map the name to an address.

- Otherwise, they assume the local network is a domain network and attempt to use the following sources in the order listed:

    1. The domain name server.

    2. The local \TCPIP\ETC\HOSTS file.

The *named* daemon provides the name server function. It is configured using the \TCPIP\ETC\NAMEDB\NAMED.BT file.

**User Applications:** The HOST and NSLOOKUP programs are included in TCP/IP for OS/2.

Please refer to *IBM TCP/IP Version 2.0 for OS/2: User's Guide* for more details about the HOST and NSLOOKUP commands.

## 4.5.10.6 DOS

TCP/IP for DOS system does not support the name server function but can use a remote name server (that is, the user applications include a stub resolver). A flat name space is supported and the local host table is found in the \TCPDOS\ETC\HOSTS file.

**User Applications:** The HOST program is included with TCP/IP for DOS.

Please refer to *IBM TCP/IP Version 2.1.1 for DOS: User's Guide* for more details about the HOST command.

# 4.6  Simple Mail Transfer Protocol (SMTP)

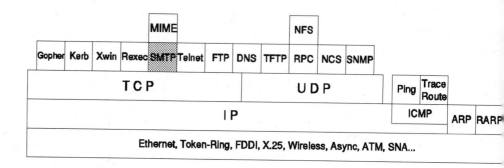

***Figure   4-28.*** *Simple Mail Transfer Protocol (SMTP)*

Electronic mail (E-mail) is probably the most widely used TCP/IP application. The basic Internet mail protocols provide mail (note) and message exchange between TCP/IP hosts; facilities have been added for the transmission of data which cannot be represented as 7-bit ASCII text.

There are three *standard protocols* which apply to mail of this kind.  Each is *recommended.*  The term SMTP is frequently used to refer to the combined set of protocols,  since they are so closely inter-related, but strictly speaking SMTP is just one of the three.  Normally, it is evident from the context which of the three protocols is being referred to.  Whenever some doubt might exist, we shall refer to the STD or RFC numbers to avoid ambiguity.  The three standards are:

- A standard for exchange of mail between two computers (STD 10/RFC 821), which specifies the protocol used to send mail between TCP/IP hosts.  This standard is SMTP itself.

- A standard (STD 11) on the format of the mail messages, contained in two RFCs. RFC 822 describes the syntax of mail header fields and defines a set of header fields and their interpretation.  RFC 1049 describes how a set of document types other than plain text ASCII can be used in the mail body (the documents themselves are 7-bit ASCII containing imbedded formatting information:  Postscript, Scribe, SGML, TEX, TROFF and DVI are all listed in the standard).

  The official protocol name for this standard is MAIL.

- A standard for the routing of mail using the Domain Name System, described in RFC 974. The official protocol name for this standard is DNS-MX.

The STD 10/RFC 821 dictates that data sent via SMTP is 7-bit ASCII data, with the high-order bit cleared to zero. This is adequate in most instances for the transmission of English text messages, but is inadequate for non-English text or non-textual data. There are two approaches to overcoming these limitations:

- Multipurpose Internet Mail Extensions (MIME), defined in RFC 1521 and RFC 1522, which specifies a mechanism for encoding text and binary data as 7-bit ASCII within the mail envelope defined by RFC 822. MIME is described in 4.7, "Multipurpose Internet Mail Extensions (MIME)" on page 4-90.

- SMTP Service Extensions, which define a mechanism to extend the capabilities of SMTP beyond the limitations imposed by RFC 821. There are three current RFCs which describe SMTP Service Extensions:

  - A standard for a receiver-SMTP to inform a sender-SMTP which service extensions it supports (RFC 1651).

    RFC 1651 modifies RFC 821 to allow a client SMTP agent to request that the server respond with a list of the service extensions that it supports at the start of an SMTP session. If the server SMTP does not support RFC 1651 it will respond with an error and the client may either terminate the session or attempt to start a session according to the rules of RFC 821. If the server does support RFC 1651, it may also respond with a list of the service extensions that it supports. A registry of services is maintained by IANA: the initial list defined in RFC 1651 contains those commands listed in *RFC 1123 — Requirements for Internet Hosts — Application and Support* as optional for SMTP servers.

Other service extensions are defined via RFCs in the usual manner. The next two RFCs define specific extensions:

  - A protocol for 8-bit text transmission (RFC 1652) which allows an SMTP server to indicate that it can accept data consisting of 8-bit bytes. A server which reports that this extension is available to a client must leave the high order bit of bytes received in an SMTP message unchanged if requested to do so by the client.

    The MIME and SMTP Service Extension approaches are complementary rather than competing standards. In particular, RFC 1652 is titled *SMTP Service Extension for 8bit-MIMEtransport*, since the MIME standard allows messages to be declared as consisting of 8-bit data rather than 7-bit data. Such messages cannot be transmitted by SMTP agents which strictly conform to RFC 821, but can be transmitted when both the client and the server conform to RFCs 1651 and 1652. Whenever a client SMTP attempts to send 8-bit data to a server which does not support this extension, the client SMTP must either encode the message contents into a 7-bit representation compliant with the MIME standard or return a permanent error to the user.

This service extension does not permit the sending of arbitrary binary data because RFC 821 defines the maximum length of a line which an SMTP server is required to accept as 1000 characters. Non-text data could easily have sequences of more than 1000 characters without a <CRLF> sequence.

**Note:** The service extension specifically limits the use of non-ASCII characters (those with values above decimal 127) to message bodies — they are *not* permitted in RFC 822 message headers.

- A protocol for message size declaration (RFC 1653) which allows a server to inform a client of the maximum size message it can accept. Without this extension, a client can only be informed that a message has exceeded the maximum size acceptable to the server (either a fixed upper limit or a temporary limit imposed by a lack of available storage space at the server) after transmitting the entire message. When this happens, the server discards the failing message. If both client and server support the Message Size Declaration extension, the client may declare an estimated size of the message to be transferred and the server will return an error if the message is too large.

Each of these SMTP Service Extensions is a *draft standard protocol* and each has a status of *elective*.

## 4.6.1 How SMTP Works

SMTP (that is, STD 11/RFC 821) is based on *end-to-end delivery*; an SMTP client will contact the destination host's SMTP server directly to deliver the mail. It will keep the mail item being transmitted until it has been successfully copied to the recipient's SMTP. This is different from the store-and-forward principle that is common in many mailing systems, where the mail item may pass through a number of intermediate hosts in the same network on its way to the destination and where successful transmission from the sender only indicates that the mail item has reached the first intermediate hop.

In various implementations, there is a possibility to exchange mail between the TCP/IP SMTP mailing system and the locally used mailing systems. These applications are called *mail gateways* or *mail bridges*. Sending mail through a mail gateway may alter the end-to-end delivery specification, since SMTP will only guarantee delivery to the mail-gateway host, not to the real destination host, which is located beyond the TCP/IP network. When a mail gateway is used, the SMTP end-to-end transmission is host-to-gateway, gateway-to-host or gateway-to-gateway; the behavior beyond the gateway is not defined by SMTP. CSNET provides an interesting example of mail gateway service. Started as a low-cost facility to interconnect scientific and corporate research centers, CSNET operates a mail gateway service that allows subscribers to send and receive mail across the Internet using only a dial-up modem. The mail gateway polls the subscribers at regular times, delivers mail that was addressed to them and picks up the outgoing mail. Although this is not a direct end-to-end delivery, it has proven to be a very useful system.

Each message has:

- A header, or envelope, the structure of which is strictly defined by RFC 822.

  The mail header is terminated by a null line (that is, a line with nothing preceding the <CRLF> sequence). However, some implementations (for example VM, which does not support zero-length records in files) may interpret this differently and accept a blank line as a terminator.

- Contents

  Everything after the null (or blank) line is the message body which is a sequence of lines containing ASCII characters (that is, characters with a value less than 128 decimal).

RFC 821 defines a client/server protocol. As usual, the client SMTP is the one which initiates the session (that is, the sending SMTP) and the server is the one which responds (the receiving SMTP) to the session request. However, since the client SMTP frequently acts as a server for a user mailing program, it is often simpler to refer to the client as the sender-SMTP and to the server as the receiver-SMTP.

## 4.6.1.1 Mail Header Format

The user normally doesn't have to worry about the message header, since it is taken care of by SMTP itself. A short reference is included below for completeness.

RFC 822 contains a complete lexical analysis of the mail header. The syntax is written in a form known as the augmented Backus-Naur Form (BNF). RFC 822 contains a description of augmented BNF, and many RFCs which are related to RFC 822 use this format. RFC 822 describes how to parse a mail header to a *canonical representation*, unfolding continuation lines, deleting insignificant spaces, removing comments and so on. The syntax is powerful, but relatively difficult to parse. A basic description is given here, which should be adequate for the reader to interpret the meaning of simple mail headers that he or she encounters. However, this description is too great a simplification to understand the details workings of RFC 822 mailers; for a full description, refer to RFC 822.

Briefly, the header is a list of lines, of the form:

`field-name: field-value`

Fields begin in column 1: lines beginning with white space characters (SPACE or TAB) are continuation lines which are unfolded to create a single line for each field in the canonical representation. Strings enclosed in ASCII quotation marks indicate single tokens within which special characters such as the colon are not significant. Many important field values (such as those for the "To" and "From" fields) are "mailboxes." The most common forms for these are:

octopus@garden.under.the.sea
The Octopus <octopus@garden.under.the.sea>
"The Octopus" <octopus@garden.under.the.sea>

The string "The Octopus" is intended for human recipients and is the name of the mailbox owner. The string "octopus@garden.under.the.sea" is the machine-readable address of the mailbox (the angle brackets are used to delimit the address but are not part of it). One can see that this form of addressing is closely related to the Domain Name System concept. In fact, the client SMTP uses the Domain Name System to determine the IP address of the destination mailbox.

Some frequently used fields are:

| keyword | value |
|---|---|
| *to* | Primary recipients of the message. |
| *cc* | Secondary ("carbon-copy") recipients of the message. |
| *from* | Identity of sender. |
| *reply-to* | The mailbox to which responses are to be sent. This field is added by the originator. |
| *return-path* | Address and route back to the originator. This field is added by the final transport system that delivers the mail. |
| *Subject* | Summary of the message. This is usually provided by the user. |

## 4.6.1.2 Mail Exchange

The SMTP design is based on the model of communication shown in Figure 4-29. As a result of a user mail request, the sender-SMTP establishes a two-way connection with a receiver-SMTP. The receiver-SMTP can be either the ultimate destination or an intermediate (mail gateway). The sender-SMTP will generate commands which are replied to by the receiver-SMTP.

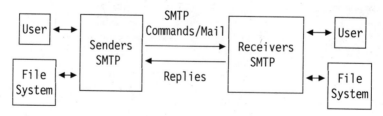

*Figure 4-29. Model for SMTP*

**SMTP mail transaction flow:** Although mail commands and replies are rigidly defined, the exchange can easily be followed in Figure 4-30 on page 4-70. All exchanged commands/replies/data are text lines, delimited by a <CRLF>. All replies have a numeric code at the beginning of the line.

1. The sender SMTP establishes a TCP connection with the destination SMTP and then waits for the server to send a *220 Service ready* message or a *421 Service not available* message when the destination is temporarily unable to proceed.

2. HELO (HELO is an abbreviation for hello) is sent, to which the receiver will identify himself by sending back its domain name. The sender-SMTP can use this to verify if it contacted the right destination SMTP.

   If the sender-SMTP supports SMTP Service Extensions as defined in RFC 1651, it may substitute an EHLO command in place of the HELO command. A receiver-SMTP which does not support service extensions will respond with a *500 Syntax error, command unrecognized* message. The sender-SMTP should then retry with HELO, or if it cannot transmit the message without one or more service extensions, it should send a QUIT message.

   If a receiver-SMTP supports service extensions, it responds with a multi-line *250 OK* message which includes a list of service extensions which it supports.

3. The sender now initiates the start of a mail transaction by sending a MAIL command to the receiver. This command contains the reverse-path which can be used to report errors. Note that a path can be more than just the *user mailbox@host domain name* pair. In addition, it can contain a list of routing hosts. Examples of this are when we pass a mail bridge, or when we provide explicit routing information in the destination address. If accepted, the receiver replies with a *250 OK*.

4. The second step of the actual mail exchange consists of providing the server SMTP with the destinations for the message (there can be more than one recipient). This is done by sending one or more RCPT TO:*<forward-path>* commands. Each of them will receive a reply *250 OK* if the destination is known to the server, or a *550 No such user here* if it isn't.

5. When all RCPT commands are sent, the sender issues a *DATA* command to notify the receiver that the message contents are following. The server replies with *354 Start mail input, end with <CRLF>.<CRLF>*. Note the ending sequence that the sender should use to terminate the message data.

6. The client now sends the data line by line, ending with the 5-character sequence <CRLF>.<CRLF> line upon which the receiver acknowledges with a *250 OK* or an appropriate error message if anything went wrong.

7. We now have several possible actions:

- The sender has no more messages to send; he will end the connection with a QUIT command, which will be answered with a *221 Service closing transmission channel* reply.
- The sender has no more messages to send, but is ready to receive messages (if any) from the other side. He will issue the TURN command. The two SMTPs now switch their role of sender/receiver and the sender (previously the receiver) can now send messages by starting with step 3 above.
- The sender has another message to send, and simply goes back to step 3 to send a new MAIL command.

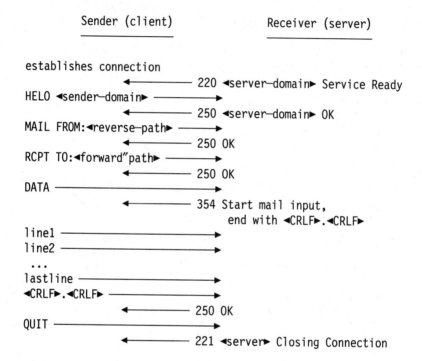

```
          Sender (client)              Receiver (server)
          _____             _____


establishes connection
                        ◄─────────── 220 ◄server─domain► Service Ready
HELO ◄sender─domain► ──────────►
                        ◄─────────── 250 ◄server─domain► OK
MAIL FROM:◄reverse─path► ──────►
                        ◄─────────── 250 OK
RCPT TO:◄forward"path► ────────►
                        ◄─────────── 250 OK
DATA ──────────────────────────►
                        ◄─────────── 354 Start mail input,
                                         end with ◄CRLF►.◄CRLF►
line1 ─────────────────────────►
line2 ─────────────────────────►
 ...
lastline ──────────────────────►
◄CRLF►.◄CRLF► ──────────────────►
                        ◄─────────── 250 OK
QUIT ──────────────────────────►
                        ◄─────────── 221 ◄server► Closing Connection
```

*Figure   4-30. Normal SMTP Data Flow.*   One mail message is delivered to one destination mailbox.

**The SMTP destination address (a mailbox address),** in its general form
*local-part@domain-name*, can take several forms:

*user@host*            For a direct destination on the same TCP/IP network.

*user%remote-host@gateway-host*
           For a user on a non-SMTP destination remote-host, via the mail
           gateway gateway-host.

*@host-a,@host-b:user@host-c*
           For a *relayed* message. This contains explicit routing
           information. The message will first be delivered to host-a, who
           will resend (relay) the message to host-b. Host-b will then
           forward the message to the real destination host-c. Note that the
           message is stored on each of the intermediate hosts, so we don't
           have an end-to-end delivery in this case.

In the above description, only the most important commands were mentioned. All of
them are commands that must be recognized in each SMTP implementation. Other
commands exist, but most of those are only optional; that is, the RFC standard does not
require them to be implemented everywhere. However, they implement very interesting
functions such as relaying, forwarding, mailing lists, etc.

For a full list of command verbs, see the official *RFC 821 — Simple Mail Transfer
Protocol* and *RFC 1123 — Requirements for Internet Hosts — Application and Support*.
For details of SMTP service extensions, see *RFC 1651 — SMTP Service Extensions, RFC
1652 — SMTP Service Extension for 8bit-MIMEtransport* and *RFC 1653 — SMTP
Service Extension for Message Size Declaration.*

**Example:** In the following scenario, user abc at host vm1.stockholm.ibm.com sends a
note to users xyz, opq and rst at host delta.aus.edu. The lines preceded by R: are lines
sent by the receiver, the S: lines are sent by the sender.

```
R: 220 delta.aus.edu Simple Mail Transfer Service Ready
S: HELO stockholm.ibm.com
R: 250 delta.aus.edu

S: MAIL FROM:<abc@stockholm.ibm.com>
R: 250 OK

S: RCPT TO:<xyz@delta.aus.edu>
R: 250 OK
S: RCPT TO:<opq@delta.aus.edu>
R: 550 No such user here
S: RCPT TO:<rst@delta.aus.edu>
R: 250 OK
```

```
S: DATA
R: 354 Start mail input, end with <CRLF>.<CRLF>
S: Date: 23 Jan 89  18:05:23
S: From: Alex B. Carver <abc@stockholm.ibm.com>
S: Subject: Important meeting
S: To:  <xyz@delta.aus.edu>
S: To:  <opq@delta.aus.edu>
S: cc:  <rst@delta.aus.edu>
S:
S: Blah blah blah
S: etc.....
S: .
R: 250 OK

S: QUIT
R: 221 delta.aus.edu Service closing transmission channel
```

Note that the message header is part of the data being transmitted.

## 4.6.2  SMTP and the Domain Name System

If the network is using the domain concept, an SMTP cannot simply deliver mail sent to TEST.IBM.COM by opening a TCP connection to TEST.IBM.COM. It must first query the name server to find out to which host (again a domain name) it should deliver the message.

For message delivery, the name server stores resource records (RRs) known as MX RRs. They map a domain name to two values:

- A preference value. As multiple MX resource records may exist for the same domain name, a preference (priority) is assigned to them. The lowest preference value corresponds to the most preferred record. This is useful whenever the most preferred host is unreachable; the sending SMTP then tries to contact the next (less preferred) host.
- A host name.

It is also possible that the name server responds with an empty list of MX RRs. This means that the domain name is in the name server's authority, but has no MX assigned to it. In this case, the sending SMTP may try to establish the connection with the host name itself.

An important recommendation is given in RFC 974. It recommends that after obtaining the MX records, the sending SMTP should query for WKS (*Well-Known Services*) records for this host, and should check that the referenced host has SMTP as a WKS-entry.

**Note:** This is only an option of the protocol but is already widely implemented.

Here is an example of MX Resource Records:

```
fsc5.stn.mlv.fr.        IN    MX 0   fsc5.stn.mlv.fr.
                        IN    MX 2   psfred.stn.mlv.fr.
                        IN    MX 4   mvs.stn.mlv.fr.
                        IN    WKS    152.9.250.150 TCP (SMTP)
```

In the above example, mail for fsc5.stn.mlv.fr should by preference, be delivered to the host itself, but in case the host is unreachable, the mail might also be delivered to psfred.stn.mlv.fr or to mvs.stn.mlv.fr (if psfred.stn.mlv.fr is unreachable, too).

## 4.6.3 Post Office Protocol Mail Servers

Since an SMTP mail receiver is a server program, and SMTP is an end-to-end application rather than a store-and-forward one, it is necessary for the server to be available when a client (sender) wishes to transmit mail. If the SMTP server resides on an end-user workstation or PC, that workstation must be running the server when the client wishes to send. Some clients, such as the SMTP service virtual machine on VM (which are themselves servers for a user mail program) can periodically retry the server for a finite period of time, others such as the MAIL program on DOS cannot. In either case, if the server is unavailable it will sooner or later be regarded as unreachable by the SMTP client and the sending process will fail. This is not generally a problem for multi-user systems because the systems are normally unavailable only for relatively short periods of time. For single-user systems, however, this is not the case, and a method for ensuring that the user has an accessible mailbox on a different server is required. There are a number of other reasons why it may be desirable to off-load mail server functions from a user workstation, including a lack of resources on small workstations, the lack of, or expense of, continuous TCP/IP connectivity and so on.

The simplest approach, of course, is for the user to use a multi-user host system for mail functions, but this is frequently not desirable – perhaps the user does not use a host system for any other purpose, or the user wants access to workstation files when composing mail messages without uploading them. Alternatively, the end-user may run a client program which communicates with a server program on a host. This server program acts as both a sender and a receiver SMTP. An example of this is *Ultimedia Mail/2*: an OS/2 Presentation Manager client/server multimedia capable mail program which is described in more detail in 4.7.6, "Implementations" on page 4-108. In either of these cases, the end users mailbox resides on the server, and mail to other users is sent by the server system.

An intermediate approach is to off-load the SMTP server function from the end-user workstation, but not the SMTP client function. That is, the user sends mail directly from the workstation, but has a mailbox which resides on a server system. The user must then connect to the mail server system to collect mail from the mailbox.

The Post Office Protocol (POP) describes how a program running on an end-user workstation may receive mail stored on a mail server system. "maildrop" to refer to a mailbox managed by a POP server. Post Office Protocol Version 3 is a *draft standard protocol* and its status is *elective*. The older Post Office Protocol Version 2 is an *historic protocol* with a status of *not recommended*.

## 4.6.3.1 Addressing Mailboxes on Server Systems

When a user employs a server system for all mail functions, the mailbox address seen by other SMTP users refers exclusively to the mail server system. For example if two OS/2 systems are named:

> hayes.itso.ral.ibm.com

and

> itso180.itso.ral.ibm.com

with the first one being used as an UltiMail client and the second as an UltiMail server, the mailbox address might be:

> hayes@itso180.itso.ral.ibm.com

This mailbox address would appear in the "From:" header field of all outgoing mail and in the SMTP commands to remote servers issued by the UltiMail server system.

When the user uses a POP server, however, the mailbox address on outbound mail items contains the workstation's hostname (for example steve@hayes.itso.ral.ibm.com). In this case, the sender should include a "Reply-To:" field in the mail header to indicate that replies should *not* be sent to the originating mailbox. For example, the mail header might look like this:

```
Date: Fri, 10 Feb 95 15:38:23
From: steve@hayes.itso.ral.ibm.com
To: "Steve Hayes" <tsgsh@gford1.warwick.uk.ibm.com>
Reply-To: hayes@itso180.itso.ral.ibm.com
Subject: Test Reply-To: header field
```

The receiving mail agent is expected to send replies to the "Reply-To:" address and not the "From:" address.

**Using the Domain Name System to Direct Mail:** An alternative approach to using the "Reply-To:" header field is to use the Domain Name System to direct mail to the correct mailbox. The administrator for the Domain Name Server with authority for the domain containing the user's workstation and the name server can add MX resource records to the Domain Name System to direct mail appropriately, as described in 4.6.2,

"SMTP and the Domain Name System" on page 4-72. For example, the following MX records indicate to client SMTPs that, if the SMTP server on hayes.itso.ral.ibm.com is not available, there is a mail server on itso.180.ral.ibm.com (9.24.104.180) which should be used instead.

```
itso180.itso.ral.ibm.com.   IN     WKS  9.24.104.180 TCP (SMTP)

hayes.itso.ral.ibm.com.     IN     MX 0 hayes.itso.ral.ibm.com.
                            IN     MX 1 itso180.itso.ral.ibm.com.
```

## 4.6.4 References

A detailed description of the SMTP, MAIL and DNS-MX standards can be found in the following RFCs:

- *RFC 821 — Simple Mail Transfer Protocol*
- *RFC 822 — Standard for the format of ARPA Internet text messages*
- *RFC 974 — Mail Routing and the Domain System*
- *RFC 1049 — A Content Type Header Field for Internet messages*

A detailed description of the Post Office Protocol can be found in the following RFCs:

- *RFC 937 — Post Office Protocol – Version 2*
- *RFC 1725 — Post Office Protocol – Version 3*

## 4.6.5 Implementations

This section discusses the various SMTP implementations on different systems, with particular emphasis on how SMTP is integrated with the system's native mail facilities.

### 4.6.5.1 VM

There are two possible approaches to using SMTP on VM: the use may send mail directly via the SMTP server, or via the RSCS Data Interchange Manager.

**Direct User Interface to SMTP:**  The SMTP mailing capabilities are directly accessible from the normal mailing functions.

NOTE        A new NOTE EXEC is shipped with VM TCP/IP. It allows a user to address both SMTP and RSCS destinations in the usual CMS *user ID at hostname* format or in the SMTP *user ID@hostname* address format. SMTP format addresses given on the note command are converted to CMS format in the note header (although the case of the addresses is preserved). Nicknames are supported through the user ID NAMES file. The NOTE EXEC adds a *Subject:* line to the note header to provide minimum compliance with the RFC 822 standard. As with the standard NOTE EXEC, notes are sent using SENDFILE with the NOTE option.

**SENDFILE** A new SENDFILE EXEC is shipped with TCP/IP for VM. Like the NOTE EXEC, it is used both for RSCS and SMTP destinations. When a file is sent to an SMTP destination, it is delivered as a mail message. Furthermore, since SMTP is a 7-bit ASCII protocol as noted above, files other than English text files are liable to corruption by the conversion to 7-bit ASCII.

When sending files via SMTP, SENDFILE EXEC adds a minimum set of RFC 822 header records to the file, wraps the note in an RFC 821 format "Batch SMTP" envelope then sends it to SMTP for transmission. Files to non SMTP-users are sent exactly as with the supplied CMS SENDFILE EXEC.

When sending notes via SMTP, SENDFILE EXEC converts the CMS format note header records to the equivalent RFC 822 header records, wraps the note in an RFC 821 format "Batch SMTP" envelope then sends it to SMTP for transmission. For example, a CMS NOTE header of the form:

```
Date: 8 February 1995, 15:49:33 EST
From: Steve Hayes                                     HAYES     at WTSCP
To:   TSGSH at gford1.warwick.uk.ibm.com
Subject: Testing TCP/IP NOTE EXEC
```

is converted to the following for SMTP recipients:

```
Date: Wed, 8 Feb 95 15:50:28 EST
From: "Steve Hayes" <HAYES@WTSCPOK.ITSC.POK.IBM.COM>
To:   TSGSH@gford1.warwick.uk.ibm.com
Subject: Testing TCP/IP NOTE EXEC
```

Notes to non SMTP-users are sent exactly as with the supplied CMS SENDFILE EXEC.

**OfficeVision/VM** PROFS and OfficeVision/VM: provide a limited SMTP interface as follows:

- A copy of the note has to be addressed to the SMTP virtual machine (*Send To* field or .cc or .ad commands).
- The TCP/IP recipient has to be specified using the *.ddn* command. The specification follows the normal *hostname(user ID)* PROFS format. Multiple recipients may be entered this way, as well as a mix of TCP/IP and RSCS recipients. For example:

```
Send To : SMTP
...
.ddn vm90(peter) paris2(gerard).
```

Incoming mail from a TCP/IP sender will arrive from the SMTP user ID, so the REPLY function cannot be used since this would send the reply to SMTP itself. A new note must be used instead.

The RSCS Data Interchange Manager can be used to provide a more natural SMTP interface for OV/VM or PROFS users.

For notes and files sent from CMS or from OV/VM, there is an SMSG interface. The user sends an SMSG to the SMTP service machine with a single word command. The commands supported are:

**QUeues**    to determine mail queue lengths

**STats**    for information on operating statistics

**HElp**    for a list of valid commands

The following commands are valid for authorized users only:

**CLosecon**    Close the virtual console

**REboot**    Re-IPL CMS

**SHutdown** Log off the virtual machine

**TRace**    ´ Enable resolver tracing

**NOTrace**    Disable resolver tracing

**DEbug**    Enable session debugging

**NODebug**    Disable session debugging

**RSCS Data Interchange Manager:** The RSCS Data Interchange Manager (DIM) allows CMS users and OfficeVision/VM (PROFS) users to send mail via SMTP using standard CMS or OV/VM facilities without the need to specify mailbox addresses in the SMTP *user@host.domain* format. RSCS DIM maintains a nickname table which maps 1 to 8-character nicknames to SMTP mailbox addresses, and manages a dummy RSCS link which provides the access to and from SMTP via the RSCS DIM service virtual machine. Users send mail to an SMTP network using CMS or OfficeVision (PROFS) notes, giving the nickname for the SMTP mailbox and the RSCS node associated with RSCS DIM. The RSCS service machine re-directs the note to the RSCS DIM service machine which changes the RSCS user IDs and nodenames in the header to SMTP mailbox addresses and then packages the resulting RFC 822-compliant note to SMTP. For example, if the following entry appears in the RSCS DIM nickname table:

```
steve    tsgsh@itso180.itso.ral.ibm.com
```

and the RSCS node associated with RSCS DIM is SMTPGATE, then a CMS user would send notes to STEVE at SMTPGATE. RSCS DIM would convert the CMS note header of the form:

```
Date: 8 February 1995, 15:15:46 EST
From: ENDERS at WTSCPOK
To:   STEVE at SMTPGATE

Subject: A test of RSCS Interchange
```

to one like this:

```
Date:  Wed, 8 Feb 95 15:15:46 -0500
From: <enders@wtscpok.itsc.pok.ibm.com>
To: <tsgsh@itso180.itso.ral.ibm.com>
Subject: A test of RSCS Interchange
```

before forwarding it via SMTP. In the reverse direction, RSCS DIM applies the opposite changes, and also adds a "Return-Path:" record. An RFC 822 header of the form:

```
Date: Wed, 8 Feb 95 15:20:34 -0500
From: Steve Hayes <tsgsh@itso180.itso.ral.ibm.com>
To:   Matthias Enders <enders@wtscpok.itsc.pok.ibm.com>
Subject: A test of RSCS Interchange
```

is converted to one like this:

```
Date: 8 February 95, 15:20:34 EST
From: Steve Hayes                     STEVE at SMTPGATE
To:   Matthias Enders                 ENDERS   at WTSCPOK

Subject: A test of RSCS Interchange
Return-Path: <tsgsh@itso180.itso.ral.ibm.com>
```

RSCS DIM privileged user may add, change and delete nicknames and restrict access to the RSCS DIM by user ID. By default, general users may also add nicknames (which are publicly visible) and change or delete nicknames which they added. Users may also create temporary nicknames by embedding lines of the form:

```
<nickname>:user@host.domain
```

immediately after the note header.

**Note:** RSCS DIM nicknames are independent of end-user nicknames. A user may refer to an RSCS DIM nickname via a CMS or PROFS nickname file exactly as though it were a conventional user ID at a remote node.

**SMTP Server:** The SMTP server is implemented as a disconnected VM service machine. Outgoing mail is sent to the SMTP service as a NETDATA format note or punch file via the SPOOL. The note contains the mail item surrounded by an "Batch

SMTP" envelope. This envelope contains the SMTP commands that the SMTP virtual machine (the SMTP client) is to issue to the remote SMTP server. The SMTP virtual machine receives the spool file, validates the SMTP commands in the envelope then begins an SMTP session with the server, executing the commands given in the envelope. It is possible to send multiple mail items in a single Batch SMTP file, but the SENDFILE and NOTE EXECs supplied with TCP/IP do not do this. A VM host with TCP/IP and SMTP running can act as a gateway between a TCP/IP network and an RSCS network. See 4.6.6, "SMTP Gateways" on page 4-86 for more details.

A local site is allowed to customize the SMTP mail headers with the REWRITE822HEADER statement. This is implemented in conformance with the guidelines set forth by RFC 822.

Mail Exchange (MX) records defined in RFC 974 are also supported when SMTP is used in conjunction with a name server. This allows the mail server to deliver mail to alternate hosts or hold for future delivery if the primary destination is not available.

## 4.6.5.2 MVS

The MVS TCP/IP SMTP functions are very similar to the VM TCP/IP ones.

**User Interface to SMTP:** This is provided through a TSO/E interface.

**SENDNOTE** SMTPNOTE REXX sample is provided with TCP/IP for MVS. It requires some customization at installation time, and uses TSO EDIT commands to allow the user to enter note text and then prefixes the note text with the BATCH SMTP headers. As with the NOTE EXEC on VM, mailbox addresses are converted to the correct form automatically.

**XMIT** Data sets may be sent using the TSO XMIT command. However, the necessary header records must be included in the data set, and the XMIT command must specify the SMTP address space, not the mailbox address.

**SMSG** The SMSG interface is the same as VM, except that it does not include the REBOOT and CLOSECON commands which are not appropriate on MVS.

**DISOSS** No links are provided with DISOSS.

**SMTP Server:** The SMTP server on MVS is closely analogous to that on VM. It resides in a separate started task and receives outgoing mail in NETDATA format via JES. The mail has the true mail item surrounded by a Batch SMTP envelope containing the commands that the SMTP server issues to send the mail to the remote user. When a name server is being used, SMTP supports Mail Exchange records. The REWRITE822HEADER configuration statement is also available.

SMTP can also be configured to act as a TCP-to-NJE Mail Gateway. See 4.6.6, "SMTP Gateways" on page 4-86 for more details.

### 4.6.5.3 OS/400

For consistency with other OS/400 mail functions, SMTP is coupled to the OS/400 delivery services (SNADS). SNADS is part of the OS/400 operating system and it contains extensions to support SMTP. This allows you to send mail to various types of users (not just SMTP users) but with one consistent user interface.

Configuring an OS/400 system to use SMTP can be an extensive process. The benefits of this extensive configuration are in the usability of the product: after configuration, the use of SMTP is not different from any of the OS/400 mail protocols. The user does not need to know whether the mail is being delivered by SNADS to another SNADS system, or via SMTP. SMTP may be configured to operate as an SMTP/SNADS Gateway. See 4.6.6, "SMTP Gateways" on page 4-86 for more details.

Because SNADS interfaces with SMTP, much of the configuration process is SNADS configuration. The steps to perform are the following:

1. Configure TCP/IP.
2. Configure the local domain name.
3. Add a routing entry to the QSNADS subsystem.
4. Create a SNADS distribution queue (normally QSMTPQ) pointing to the remote location TCPIPLOC so that SNADS can transfer mail to TCP/IP.
5. Update the system directory. Entries may be added for remote hosts by adding a group entry with *ANY as the user ID and a SNADS address which is used to refer to the remote host, or for remote users with a SNADS user ID and a SNADS address which are used together to refer to the remote user. Each entry uses the same system name, which is usually TCPIP.
6. Update the SNADS routing table to direct mail to the TCPIP system via the QSMTPQ distribution queue.
7. Update the SMTP alias table. Entries are needed in the SMTP Alias table in four different circumstances:

    a. When the local and remote users are both on AS/400s, the mail is being sent by SMTP and the remote user has a SNADS address that is different from the host system name.

    b. When the local or remote user has an abbreviated SNADS or SMTP name.

    c. If the SMTP user ID or host name contains more than eight characters and/or special characters.

    d. If the mail address includes specific routing information (that is, it is of the form @host-a,@host-b:user@host-c).

If none of these is true, an Alias is not required and the remote SMTP user can be identified with a SNADS user ID, address and host system name.

There are two alias tables: a system alias table and a personal alias table. The former offers better performance, requires less storage and allows generic entries (*ANY) for remote systems. The latter gives individual users the ability to add to or override the aliases in the system alias table.

8. Optionally, SMTP can be configured to use another system as a mail router. This is useful when the SMTP using a local host table rather than a remote name server and the local host table does not contain all SMTP hosts that the local users communicate with.

9. Enroll OfficeVision/400 users.

SMTP can be configured so that incoming mail from remote SMTP users causes SMTP to automatically generate SNADS directory entries and SMTP alias table entries for the sending user so that the local user can reply to the mail without having to manually register the SMTP user. The directory user IDs added are of the form QSMnnnnn (nnnnn is a numeric string in the range 01 to 99999) with a SNADS address of QSMRMTAD and system name TCPIP. An entry is added to the system alias table to associate this SNADS entry with the real SMTP mailbox address.

**User Interface to SMTP:**  OfficeVision/400 provides the user interface to SMTP. Additionally, mail can also be sent and received using CL commands.

The AS/400 user sees incoming mail as though it came from SNADS. If automatic registration of incoming users is enabled or if the sender has been previously registered, then the SNADS user ID and address will be valid and can be used for replying to the mail. If neither of these is true, the sender will be invalid and the user will have to add an entry to the alias table in order to reply to the mail. The registration must be explicit; SMTP looks for exact matches with the user ID and address in the alias tables, ignoring *ANY group entries when dealing with incoming mail.

The AS/400 can send mail to a user in the SMTP network by specifying the SNADS user ID and address, provided that a system directory entry for the SMTP exists. This may be an individual entry for the user ID and host (either manually or automatically registered), a group reference to the host (that is one with *ANY as the user ID) or even the "*ANY *ANY" entry.[4] If no entry is found an error is returned to the user. SMTP then searches the alias tables for the SNADS user ID and address or the SNADS address alone; if an entry is found it is used as the SMTP mailbox address of the recipient.

**Addressing AS/400 Users:**  A SNADS user is identified by a user ID, address and system name while an SMTP mailbox address has a user ID and a host name. The SMTP user ID of a SNADS user is created by concatenating the SNADS user ID and address,

---

4  Use of the *ANY *ANY entry to route mail for unknown recipients via SMTP is not recommended because it may cause the mail to loop indefinitely.

separated by a *delimiter character* (the default delimiter is "?"). The SMTP host name is the local AS/400 system name concatenated with the local domain name, separated by a period. Thus, the address looks like this:

`userid?address@systemid.domain1.domain2.domain3`

Local user IDs may also have an entry in the system alias table. If there is a match for the SNADS user ID and address in the table, the alias is used as the SMTP user ID and the address looks like this:

`alias@systemid.domain1.domain2.domain3`

When SMTP sends outbound mail, it uses the alias form if one exists or the userid?address form if not.

When SMTP receives incoming mail, it attempts to interpret the To: mailbox address as a SNADS address. The first token after the "@" and before the next period is the SMTP host name. This is verified against the local host table and if it is not found, the mail is rejected. If it is found, the mailbox address is interpreted like this:

*octopus@here.there.everywhere*

> If there is an entry for OCTOPUS in the system alias table, then the SNADS user ID and address are taken from the alias table entry. If there is no entry, then the SNADS user ID is OCTOPUS and the address is HERE.

*octopus?garden@here.there.everywhere*

> The SNADS user ID is OCTOPUS and the address is GARDEN.

*octopus%shade@here.there.everywhere*

> If this OS/400 system is operating as a mail router for the sending system then this system will attempt to route the mail to the system SHADE (an entry for SHADE must be in the local host table). If not, the string between the % and the @ is ignored.

*octopus?garden%shade@here.there.everywhere*

> If this OS/400 system is operating as a mail router for the sending system then this system will attempt to route the mail to the system SHADE (an entry for SHADE must be in the local host table). If not, the string between the % and the @ is ignored.

### 4.6.5.4 AIX

All AIX implementations of SMTP provide a similar user interface through:

- The *mesg* user command

- The *mail* user command
- The Message Handler (MH) subcommands
- The *sendmail* daemon

The sendmail configuration file is */etc/sendmail.cf*. In AIX/6000, the sendmail daemon is normally started at system boot time. This can be done by uncommenting the sendmail entry in the */etc/rc.tcpip* file. For an understanding of the use of these standard AIX functions, refer to the documentation available for the AIX system you are using.

Also the *Basic Network Utilities (uucp)* can use the TCP/IP interface program for sending and receiving files and commands between systems. The *uucpd* daemon shipped with BNU provides BNU facilities over an internet.

The Post Office Protocol (POP) Versions 2 and 3 are also supported by AIX.

## 4.6.5.5 OS/2

Both the SMTP client and server functions are implemented in TCP/IP for OS/2 by the SENDMAIL program. Incoming mail is stored by the SENDMAIL program in the subdirectory ETC\MAIL. Outgoing mail and temporary files are stored in the subdirectory ETC\MQUEUE. The user may send a file to a remote mail destination by executing the SENDMAIL program from an OS/2 command session. To receive mail, the SENDMAIL program must be running in the background as a server.

SENDMAIL also supports the MX records (See 4.6.2, "SMTP and the Domain Name System" on page 4-72).

Mail can be sent with a TYPE command, or with the SENDMAIL command itself, but the main mail administrator is the *LaMail* program. LaMail is an OS/2 application that provides a LAN-attached user with a Presentation Manager interface to SENDMAIL. It includes file editing, spell checking, synonym and user environment configuration functions. It displays mail delivered by SENDMAIL in an In-basket object, and allows the user to configure additional folders for storing sent and received mail items. All of these objects are displayed within the main LaMail window and are opened by double-clicking with the mouse as usual for Presentation Manager applications. LaMail allows the user to create "nicknames" for frequently used correspondents via a pull-down menu (the nicknames are stored in the *\TCPIP\LaMail/nickname.nam* file in a format which matches that of a VM NAMES file).

OS/2 users may also use *UltiMedia Mail/2 (UltiMail)* which is a MIME-compliant OS/2 Presentation Manager client/server multimedia mail program. See 4.7, "Multipurpose Internet Mail Extensions (MIME)" on page 4-90 for more information on MIME and UltiMail.

### 4.6.5.6 OS/2 Warp

The OS/2 Warp Internet Connection provides a SENDMAIL program but, instead of LaMail, it contains *UltiMail Lite* which is MIME-compliant and contains a POP3 client. Because the Internet Connection is intended for SLIP modem connections, a POP client is essential in order for most home and small office users to receive mail without being permanently connected to the Internet. UltiMail Lite is also provided as part of TCP/IP for OS/2 Version 3.0 which is supplied with OS/2 Warp Connection. Since this version of Warp is intended for use with permanent TCP/IP connections, mail may be sent directly to the OS/2 system, with SENDMAIL providing the SMTP server, or it may be sent to a POP3 server, and the POP3 client used to collect mail. See 4.7, "Multipurpose Internet Mail Extensions (MIME)" on page 4-90 for more information on MIME and UltiMail.

### 4.6.5.7 DOS

Mail support is provided through SMTP and Post Office Protocol (POP) functions.

- There are two SMTP client functions: a MAIL program for DOS users and a Microsoft Windows client.

- There is a Microsoft Windows SMTP server.

- There are two POP client functions: a POPGET program for DOS users and a Microsoft Windows client. The POPGET program supports POP Version 2 servers, and the Windows client supports POP Version 2 and POP Version 3 servers.

- There is source code for a POP server (pcpopd) which can be compiled and run on a UNIX or AIX host. pcpopd is a POP Version 2 server.

The IBM TCP/IP MAIL program (WMAIL) is a Windows program that provides a common interface to all of the mailing functions. Users can perform mail tasks such as send and receive mail, display, reply to and delete incoming mail, and create mail items with the user's preferred editor and other utility functions such as printing and nickname management. Files may be attached to mail items by selecting the Attach File from the File pull-down menu. This uses the UUENCODE utility supplied with TCP/IP for DOS.[5] Mail may be received with WMAIL using either SMTP or POP or both. The WMAIL program must be active for remote users to send mail directly to the DOS system, since the SMTP server is part of WMAIL. POP allows mail to be sent to a mailbox on a remote mail server when WMAIL is not running; the user receives mail by selecting the Retrieve Mail item from the Mail pull-down menu. When receiving mail, there is an

---

[5] UUencode and UUdecode are a pair of UNIX utilities for encoding 8-bit binary data in a form that is safe for use with the UUCP program. This approach is in common use, but is not an Internet standard. It is inferior to MIME in most respects, but will safely transmit encoded 8-bit binary data through 7-bit ASCII gateways. It is not reliable through all gateways that perform ASCII-EBCDIC translation.

Unattach File option on the File pull-down menu. This uses the UUDECODE utility (also supplied with TCP/IP for DOS).[5]

The MAIL program is a DOS-based SMTP client which will send a file from disk to an SMTP destination. The MAIL program prefixes the file with a set of RFC 822 headers, for example, the command:

```
mail tsgsh@gford1.warwick.uk.ibm.com c:\mail.dat
```

where the c:\mail.dat file contains:

```
Reply-To: hayes@rs60007.itso.ral.ibm.com
Subject: test dos mail function

testing, testing 1, 2, 3.
```

results in the following mail item being sent:

```
Date: 2/10/1995
From: pcuser@dos2.itso.ral.ibm.com
Subject: This mail comes from a PC Station.
To: tsgsh@gford1.warwick.uk.ibm.com

Reply-To: hayes@rs60007.itso.ral.ibm.com
Subject: test dos mail function

testing, testing 1, 2, 3.
```

Note that MAIL does not interpret the contents of the MAIL.DAT file as containing RFC 822 header records, so the Reply-To: line in the mail item is in the body of the mail (because it is after the <CRLF><CRLF> sequence and so will be ignored by RFC 822-compliant mail readers).

MAIL supports a "-u" option to "UUencode" files with binary data.

The POPGET program is a DOS-based POP client which will download files from the mail server to a *mail directory* specified in the \TCPIP\ETC\TCPDOS.INI file. Normally, this is the \TCPIP\ETC\MAIL directory. For example, if the user ID HAYES is registered with password STEVE at a POP server running on the AIX system rs60007.itso.ral.ibm.com, then the command:

```
popget steve -s rs60007.itso.ral.ibm.com -u hayes
```

will download each of the items in the mailbox to a file in the mail directory, where they can be viewed with an ASCII editor. If a mail item contains a "UUencoded" file, the UUDECODE program must be used to extract the original file from the file downloaded to the mail directory.

A complete description of the configuration and all the mail programs can be found in
*IBM TCP/IP Version 2.1.1 for DOS: User's Guide.*

## 4.6.6 SMTP Gateways

An SMTP gateway is a host that has two *links* connected to different networks. SMTP
gateways may be implemented to connect many different kinds of networks.

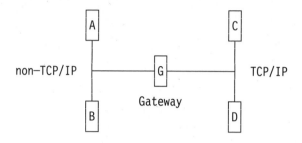

**Figure   4-31.**  *SMTP-RSCS/NJE Mail Gateway*

### 4.6.6.1 VM and MVS

VM and MVS are both secure gateway capable.

An SMTP-RSCS/NJE gateway is configured using the SMTP configuration file as shown
below.  To configure a host which is *not* to act as a gateway, the GATEWAY statement
should not be specified.

```
 . . . . . . . . .
;
GATEWAY                  ; accept mail from and deliver mail to RSCS host
RSCSDOMAIN RSCSNET       ; pseudo domain name of associated RSCS network
LOCALFORMAT NETDATA      ; local recipients receive mail in Netdata format
RSCSFORMAT NETDATA       ; RSCS recipients receive mail in Netdata format
REWRITE822HEADER NO      ; Only set to no if you do not want SMTP to
                         ; rewrite the 822 headers on all mail passing
                         ; from RSCS to TCP through gateway.
 . . . . . . . . . .
```

A user on a host on the TCP/IP network will have to write the destination in the following
way to send it to a VM or MVS host located on the RSCS/NJE network:

```
user%nodeid@gateway
```

The mail gateway needs to have some information in order to identify the nodes in the
RSCS/NJE network.

- On VM, the SMTPRSCS procedure must be run against the RSCS CONFIG file and the resulting file (SMTPRSCS HOSTINFO) must be located on a minidisk accessed by SMTP.

- On MVS, the SMTPNJE program is used to create the SMTP.NJE.HOSTINFO data set.

On VM systems in the RSCS/NJE network, in order to use the mail gateway, the TCP/IP NOTE and SENDFILE EXECs must be available together with a TCPIP DATA file specifying the local host name and domain name (see *IBM TCP/IP Version 2 Release 3 for VM: Planning and Customization* for more details). On MVS systems, a properly configured SMTPNOTE CLIST is needed (see *IBM TCP/IP Version 3 Release 1 for MVS: Customization and Administration Guide* for more details).

Specific users and/or nodes in the RSCS/NJE network may be prevented from using the gateway by coding a RESTRICT statement in the SMTP configuration. Alternatively, the gateway may be made a *secure gateway* where only explicitly authorized users in the RSCS/NJE network can use it by adding a SECURE statement to the SMTP configuration file. When operating in secure gateway mode, only those RSCS or NJE addresses in an SMTP security table are authorized to send and receive mail. In addition, SMTP source routing is disabled to prevent the gateway from relaying mail to unauthorized users. SMTP rejects mail from or to unauthorized RSCS or NJE users.

Here is an example of an SMTP security table:

```
*
* <userid>  <nodeid>  <nickname>  <primary_nick?>  <primary_mbox?>
*
  DEBULOI    MLVFSC0
  DEBULOIS   MLVFSC1    FRED0       Y                N
  DEBULOIS   MLVFSC5    FRED1       N                Y
  TCPMAINT   MLVFSC5    TCP0        N                N
  DEBULOIS   MLVFSC1    TCP1        Y                Y
```

According to the previous table (assuming that the host name of the gateway is SMTP-GW.IBM.COM), mail sent from the following RSCS/NJE addresses is rewritten to the following TCP network addresses:

```
DEBULOI at MLVFSC0     >>>>>>     DEBULOI%MLVFSC0@SMTP-GW.IBM.COM
DEBULOIS at MLVFSC1    >>>>>>     TCP1@SMTP-GW.IBM.COM
DEBULOIS at MLVFSC5    >>>>>>     FRED1@SMTP-GW.IBM.COM
TCPMAINT at MLVFSC5    >>>>>>     TCP0%MLVFSC5@SMTP-GW.IBM.COM
```

Mail sent from the following TCP addresses is forwarded to the following RSCS/NJE network addresses:

```
DEBULOI%MLVFSCO@SMTP-GW.IBM.COM  >>>>>>>   DEBULOI   at MLVFSCO
FRED1@SMTP-GW.IBM.COM            >>>>>>>   DEBULOIS  at MLVFSC5
TCP1@SMTP-GW.IBM.COM             >>>>>>>   DEBULOIS  at MLVFSC1
TCPO%MLVFSC5@SMTP-GW.IBM.COM     >>>>>>>   TCPMAINT  at MLVFSC5
```

Please refer to *IBM TCP/IP Version 2 Release 3 for VM: Planning and Customization* and *IBM TCP/IP Version 3 Release 1 for MVS: Customization and Administration Guide* for more details.

### 4.6.6.2 OS/400

An OS/400 TCP/IP system may be configured to act as a gateway. OS/400 users on remote AS/400s refer to SMTP users in the TCP/IP network by SNADS addresses. As before, the OS/400 gateway provides SMTP access to remote users in a form that is very well integrated with AS/400 Office mail, but requires configuration work to enable this seamless integration. Automatic registration of users sending mail via SMTP may be employed to reduce the administrative overhead of updating aliases. Each AS/400 system using the gateway needs an entry in its system directory for each host in the SMTP network. SMTP hosts have a matching SNADS address in the gateway's system directory in which case the sending system requires an entry in its directory to route mail for that SMTP host. Individual SMTP users may also have entries manually created at the gateway, which also need matching entries at the systems using the gateway. Finally, if automatic registration is being employed, there will be SMTP users with a SNADS address of QSMRMTAD. The systems using the gateway should route mail for *ANY QSMMRTAD to the gateway.

**Note:** Because remote SNADS users do not have access to the alias tables used by SMTP, aliases cannot be created on remote systems: all new SMTP users must be registered at the gateway, either manually by the gateway system's administrator or security officer or automatically by the SMTP user sending a mail item via the gateway.

## 4.6.7 SMTP and X.400

Since SMTP-based mail systems are widely used in the Internet, and many Internet users require communications with other users using other mail systems, there is a need to establish inter-mail system mapping (or translation) facilities. The most important group of mail systems requiring SMTP interoperability are the X.400-based systems.

In contrast to SMTP over TCP/IP networks, the CCITT 1988 X.400 Series of Recommendations specify a mail protocol over OSI networks. Commonly known as X.400 (88) Message Handling System, it has a much richer set of functions than those described in STD 10 and STD 11, in particular the contents of an X.400 (88) message may contain objects which are not representable as text data, for which there is no STD 11/RFC 822 equivalent. Furthermore, the elements of RFC 822 message headers and X.400 message envelopes are organized differently, and the addressing mechanisms for the two protocols are syntactically very different. An older version of X.400, commonly known as X.400 (1984) was specified in 1984. This too is richer than RFC 822.

The process of conversion of the elements of an RFC 822 message to an X.400 message is termed mapping. A detailed description of the protocol for the mapping between X.400 (1988) and RFC 822 can be found in *RFC 1327 — Mapping between X.400 (1988) / ISO 10021 and RFC 822*. A historic protocol for the mapping between X.400 (1984) and RFC 822 can be found in *RFC 987 — Mapping between X.400 and RFC 822*. The current protocols view the mapping process between X.400 (84) and RFC 822 as a two stage process, with X.400 (88) being the intermediate stage. This is a logical view only: implementations are not required to perform two mappings, only to produce results which are consistent with such a process. When converting from RFC 822 to X.400 (84), the mapping involves downgrading the logical X.400 (88) intermediate to X.400 (84) This protocol is defined in *RFC 1328 — X.400 1988 to 1984 downgrading*.

MIME (see 4.7, "Multipurpose Internet Mail Extensions (MIME)" on page 4-90) extends RFC 822 considerably, and as far as possible mappings between the parts of MIME message bodies and X.400 (88) are defined. These definitions are given in *RFC 1494 — Mapping between X.400 and RFC-822 Message Bodies*. Since RFCs 1327 and 1328 pre-date MIME, they have both been updated to define the behavior of gateways which are MIME-compliant. These updates are: *RFC 1495 — between X.400 and RFC-822 Message Bodies* and *RFC 1496 — Rules for Downgrading Messages from X.400/88 to X.400/84 When MIME Content-Types are Present in the Messages*.

**Note:** All of the RFCs mentioned here describe *proposed standard protocols* All of these protocols have a status of *elective* with the exception of RFC 987 which is replaced by RFC 1327 and is an *historic* protocol.

A useful document on this subject is *RFC 1506 — A Tutorial on Gatewaying between X.400 and Internet Mail*.

Many vendors have product implementations of mail systems supporting translation between SMTP and X.400 (1984).

The following is a list of current IBM products implementing interoperability between SMTP and X.400-based mail systems. For more details, please refer to the corresponding product references.

- MVS: X.400 DISOSS Connection, Open Network Distrution Services (ONDS) and OSI/Communications Subsystem (OSI/CS)

- AIX/6000: OpenMail for AIX and OSI Services/600 (which support X.400 (88) and OSI Messaging and Filing/6000 (OSIMFS/6000)for X.400 (84)

- OS/400: OSI Message Services/400 (OSIMS/400) and OSI Communications Subsystem/400 (OSICS/400)

# 4.7 Multipurpose Internet Mail Extensions (MIME)

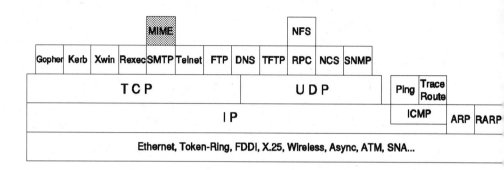

*Figure 4-32. Multipurpose Internet Mail Extensions (MIME)*

MIME is a *draft standard protocol*. Its status is *elective*.

Electronic mail (as described in 4.6, "Simple Mail Transfer Protocol (SMTP)" on page 4-64) is probably the most widely used TCP/IP application. However, SMTP (that is, an STD 10/RFC 821 compliant mailing system) is limited to 7-bit ASCII text with a maximum line length of 1000 characters which results in a number of limitations.

- SMTP cannot transmit executable files or other binary objects. There are a number of ad hoc methods of encapsulating binary items in SMTP mail items, for example:
    - Encoding the file as pure hexadecimal
    - The UNIX UUencode and UUdecode utilities which are used to encode binary data in the UUCP mailing system to overcome the same limitations of 7-bit transport
    - The Andrew Toolkit representation

    None of these can be described as a de facto standard. UUencode is perhaps the most pervasive due to the pioneering role of UNIX systems in the Internet.

- SMTP cannot transmit text data which includes national language characters since these are represented by codepoints with a value of 128 (decimal) or higher in all character sets based on ASCII.

- SMTP servers may reject mail messages over a certain size. Any given server may have permanent and/or transient limits on the maximum amount of mail data it can accept from a client at any given time.

- SMTP gateways which translate from ASCII to EBCDIC and vice versa do not use a consistent set of code page mappings, resulting in translation problems.

- SMTP gateways to X.400 networks cannot handle non-textual data included in X.400 mail messages. The standards for mapping X.400 messages to STD 11/RFC 822[6] which pre-dated MIME required that non-textual parts of an X.400 message body must either be converted to (not encoded in) an ASCII format, or discarded and the RFC 822 recipient informed that discarding has occurred.

  Obviously, this is undesirable since the element is presumably important to the recipient who may be able to view or otherwise use it even though it is not understood by the mailing system. Discarding the element obviously means it is not available to the user. Converting it to ASCII involves clearing the high-order byte, which for non-textual data almost certainly means corruption beyond repair. The problem is particularly acute in the case where both the sender and recipient are on X.400 networks but the mail item passes through an intermediate RFC 822 network (this is termed "tunnelling") since the X.400 users would naturally expect to send and receive X.400 mail messages without loss of information.

- Some SMTP implementations or other mail transport agents (MTAs) in the Internet do not adhere completely to the SMTP standards defined in RFC 821. Common problems include:

  - Removal of trailing white space characters (TABs and SPACEs)

  - Padding of all lines in a message to the same length

  - Wrapping of lines longer than 76 characters

  - Changing of new line sequences between different conventions (for instance <CR> characters may be converted to <CRLF> sequences)

  - Conversion of TAB characters to multiple SPACEs.

---

6  RFC 822 format messages are not restricted to SMTP (RFC 821) networks but may be transmitted over any network supporting 7-bit ASCII (for example, UUCP networks). STD 11/RFC 822 format messages can also be encoded in EBCDIC and transmitted over RSCS/NJE networks, although problems arise with the mapping of certain characters such as "[" and "]" which are syntactically important in RFC 822 header fields.

MIME is a standard which includes mechanisms to solve these problems in a manner which is highly compatible with existing RFC 822 standards. Because mail messages are frequently forwarded through mail gateways, it is not possible for an SMTP client to distinguish between a server which manages the destination mailbox and one which acts as a gateway to another network. Since mail which passes through a gateway may be tunnelled through further gateways, some or all of which may be using a different set of messaging protocols, it is not possible in the general case for a sending SMTP to determine the lowest common denominator capability common to all stages of the route to the destination mailbox. For this reason, MIME assumes the worst: 7-bit ASCII transport which may not strictly conform to or be compatible with RFC 821. It does not define any extensions to RFC 821, but limits itself to extensions within the framework of RFC 822. Thus, a MIME message is one which can be routed through any number of networks which are loosely compliant with RFC 821 or which are capable of transmitting RFC 821 messages.

MIME is a *draft standard protocol* with a status of *elective*. It is described in two parts:

- Protocols for including objects other than US ASCII text mail messages within the bodies of messages conforming to RFC 822. These are described in RFC 1521.

- A protocol for encoding non-US ASCII text in the header fields of mail messages conforming to RFC 822. This is described in RFC 1522.

Although RFC 1521 provides a mechanism suitable for describing non-textual data from X.400 messages in a form that is compatible with RFC 822, it does not say how X.400 message parts are to be mapped to MIME message parts. The conversion between X.400 and MIME is defined in RFCs 1494, 1495 and 1496 which update the protocols for the conversion between RFC 822 and X.400.

The MIME standard was designed with the following general order of priorities:

1. Compatibility with existing standards such as RFC 822.

   There are two areas where compatibility with previous standards is not complete.

   - RFC 1049 (which is part of STD 11) described a "Content-Type:" field used to indicate the type of (ASCII text) data in a message body. PostScript or SGML would allow a user mail agent to process it accordingly. MIME retains this field, but changes the values that are defined for it. Since the correct response for a mail agent on encountering an unknown value in this field is basically to ignore it, this does not raise any major compatibility concerns.

   - RFC 934 discussed encapsulation of messages in the context of message forwarding and defined encapsulation boundaries: lines indicating the beginning and end of an encapsulated message. MIME retains broad compatibility with RFC 934, but does not include the "quoting" mechanism used by RFC 934 for lines in encapsulated messages that could otherwise be misinterpreted as boundaries.[7]

The most important compatibility issue is that the "standard" form of a MIME message is readable with an RFC 821 compliant mail reader. This is, of course, the case: in particular the default "encoding" for MIME message bodies is no encoding at all, just like RFC 822.

2. Robustness across existing practice. As noted above, there are many widely-deployed MTAs in the Internet which do not comply with STD 10/RFC 821. The encoding mechanisms specified in RFC 1521 are designed to always circumvent the most common of these – folding of lines as short as 76 characters and corruption of trailing white space characters – by only transmitting short lines with no trailing white space characters, and to allow encoding of any data in a mail safe fashion.

**Note:** MIME does *not* require mail items to be encoded – the decision is left to the user and/or the mail program. For binary data, transmitted across (7-bit) SMTP, encoding is invariably required, but for data consisting mostly of text, this may not be the case.

The preferred encoding mechanism for "mostly text" data is such that, at a minimum, it is "mail-safe" with any compliant SMTP agent on an ASCII system and at maximum is mail-safe with all known gateways and MTAs. The reason why MIME does not require maximum encoding is that the encoding hampers readability when the mail is transmitted to non-MIME compliant systems.

3. Ease of extension. RFC 1521 categorizes elements of mail bodies into seven *content-types* which have *subtypes*. The content-type/subtype pairs in turn have parameters which further describe the object concerned. The RFC defines a mechanism for registering new values for these and other MIME fields with the Internet Assigned Numbers Authority (IANA). This process is itself updated by RFC 1590.

For the current list of all MIME values, consult *STD 2 — Assigned Internet Numbers*. The remainder of this chapter describes only the values and types given in RFC 1521.

---

[7] The reason for this departure is that MIME allows for deeply nested encapsulation, but encodes text in such a way as to reversibly spill text lines at or before column 76 to avoid the lines being spilled irreversibly by non-conforming SMTP agents. The RFC 934 quoting mechanism can result in lines being lengthened with each level of encapsulation, possibly past column 76.

One consequence of this approach is that, to quote RFC 1521, "some of the mechanisms [used in MIME] may seem somewhat strange or even baroque at first. In particular, compatibility was always favored over elegance."

Because RFC 822 defines the syntax of message headers (and deliberately allows for additions to the set of headers it describes) but not the composition of message bodies, the MIME standard is largely compatible with RFC 822, particularly the RFC 1521 part that defines the structure of message bodies and a set of header fields that are used to describe that structure.

MIME can be seen as a high-level protocol; since it works entirely within the boundaries of STD 10 and STD 11, it does not involve the transport layer (or lower layers) of the protocol stack at all.

## 4.7.1  How MIME works

A MIME-compliant message must contain a header field with the following verbatim text:

MIME-Version: 1.0

As is the case with RFC 822 headers, the case of MIME header field names is never significant but the case of field values may be, depending on the field name and the context. For the MIME fields described below, the values are case-insensitive unless stated otherwise.

The general syntax for MIME header fields is the same as that for RFC 822, so the following field:

MIME-Version: 1.0 (this is a comment)

is valid since parenthetical phrases are treated as comments and ignored.

Five header fields are defined for MIME.

*MIME-Version* As noted above, this must have the value "1.0"

*Content-Type* This describes how the object within the body is to be interpreted. The default value is "text/plain; charset=us-ascii" which indicates unformatted 7-bit ASCII text data (that is a message body by the RFC 822 definition).

*Content-Transfer-Encoding* This describes how the object within the body was encoded so that it could be included in the message in a mail-safe form.

*Content-Description* A plain text description of the object within the body which is useful when the object is not readable (for example audio data).

*Content-ID* A world-unique value specifying the content of this part of this message.

**Note:** RFC 1521 includes a definition of the term "body" as used above and also the terms "body part" "entity" and "message." Unfortunately the four definitions are circular because a general MIME message can recursively contain MIME messages to an arbitrary depth. The simplest example of a body is the body of message as defined by RFC 822.

The first two of these fields are described in more detail in the following sections.

## 4.7.2 The Content-Type Field

The body of the message is described with a *Content-Type* field of the form:

`Content-Type:` *type/subtype ;parameter=value ;parameter=value*

The allowable parameters are dependent on the type and subtype. Some type/subtype pairs have no parameters, some have optional ones, some have mandatory ones and some have both. The subtype parameter may *not* be omitted, but the whole field may be, in which case the default value is *text/plain*.

There are seven standard content-types:

*text*      A single subtype is defined:

     *plain*     Unformatted text. The character set of the text may be specified with the *charset* parameter. The following values are permitted.

         *us-ascii* The text consists of ASCII characters in the range 0 to 127 (decimal). This is the default (for compatibility with RFC 822).

         *iso-8859-x* where "x" is in the range 1 to 9 for the different parts of the ISO-8859 standard. The text consists of ISO characters in the range 0 to 255 (decimal). All of the ISO-8859 character sets are ASCII-based with national language characters and so on in the range 128 to 255. Note, if the text contains no characters with values above 127, the character set should be specified as "us-ascii" because it can be adequately represented in that character set.

     Further subtypes may be added to describe other readable text formats (such as word processor formats) which contain formatting information for an application to enhance the appearance of the text, provided that the correct software is not required to determine the meaning of the text.

*multipart*   The message body contains multiple objects of independent data types. In each case, the body is divided into parts by lines called encapsulation boundaries. The contents of the boundary are defined with a parameter in the content-type field, for example:

```
Content-Type: multipart/mixed; boundary="1995021309105517"
```

The boundary should not appear in any of the parts of the message. It is case-sensitive and consists of 1-70 characters from a set of 75 which are known to be very robust through mail gateways, and it may not end in a space. (The example uses a 16-digit decimal timestamp.) Each encapsulation boundary consists of the boundary value prefixed by a <CRLF> sequence and two hyphens (for compatibility with RFC 934). The final boundary which marks the end of the last part also has a suffix of two hyphens. Within each part there is a MIME header, which like ordinary mail headers is terminated by the sequence *<CRLF><CRLF>* but which may be blank. The header fields define the content of the encapsulated message.

Four subtypes are defined:

*mixed*         The different parts are independent but are to be transmitted together. They should be presented to the recipient in the order that they appear in the mail message.

*parallel*      This differs from the mixed subtype only in that no order is ascribed to the parts and the receiving mail program may, for example, display all of them in parallel.

*alternative*   The different parts are alternative versions of the same information. They are ordered in increasing faithfulness to the original, and the recipient's mail system should display the "best" version to the user.

*digest*        This is a variant on multipart/mixed where the default type/subtype is message/rfc822 (see below) instead of text/plain. It is used for the common case where multiple RFC 822 or MIME messages are transmitted together.

An example of a complex multipart message is shown in Figure 4-33 on page 4-97.

*message*   The body is an encapsulated message, or part of one. Three subtypes are defined:

*rfc822*        The body itself is an encapsulated message with the syntax of an RFC 822 message. However, unlike "top-level" RFC 822 messages it is not required to have the minimum set of "From:," "To:" and at least one destination header.

                **Note:** "rfc822" refers to the syntax of the encapsulated message envelopes and does not preclude MIME messages for example.

```
MIME-Version: 1.0
From: Steve Hayes <steve@hayessj.bedfont.uk.ibm.com>
To:   Matthias Enders <enders@itso180.itso.ral.ibm.com>
Subject: Multipart message
Content-type: multipart/mixed; boundary="1995021309105517"
```

This section is called the preamble.  It is after the header but before the
first boundary.  Mail readers which understand multipart messages must
ignore this.
```
--1995021309105517
```

The first part.  There is no header, so this is text/plain with
charset=us-ascii by default.  The immediately preceding <CRLF> is part of
the <CRLF><CRLF> sequence that ends the null header.  The one at the end is
part of the next boundary, so this part consists of five lines of text with
four <CRLF>s.
```
--1995021309105517
Content-type: text/plain; charset=us-ascii
Comments: this header explicitly states the defaults
```

One line of text this time, but it ends in a line break.

```
--1995021309105517
Content-Type: multipart/alternative; boundary=_
Comments:    An encapsulated multipart message!
```

Again, this preamble is ignored.  The multipart body contains a still image
and a video image encoded in Base64.  See4.7.3.5, "Base64 Encoding" on page 4-104
One feature is that the character "_" which is allowed in multipart
boundaries never occurs in Base64 encoding so we can use a very simple
boundary!
```
--_
Content-type: text/plain
```

---

*Figure   4-33  (Part  1  of  2).  A Complex Multipart Example*

    *partial*   This type is used to allow fragmentation of large mail items in a
                  similar way to IP fragmentation.  Because SMTP agents may
                  impose upper limits on maximum mail sizes, it may be
                  necessary to send large items as fragments.  The intent of the
                  message/partial mail items is that the fragmentation is
                  transparent to the recipient.  The receiving user agent should
                  re-assemble the fragments to create a new message with

This message contains images which cannot be displayed at your terminal.
This is a shame because they're very nice.

--
Content-type: image/jpeg
Content-transfer-encoding: base64
Comments: This photograph is to be shown if the user's system cannot display
        MPEG videos.  Only part of the data is shown in this book because
        the reader is unlikely to be wearing MIME-compliant spectacles.

Qk1OAAAAAAAAE4EAABAAAAAQAEAAPAAAAABAAgAAAAAAAAAAAAAAAAAAAAAAAABAAAAAQAAAAAA
AAAAAAAAAAAAAAAAAAAAAAB4VjQSAAAAAAAAgAAAkgAAAJKAAKoAAACqAIAAqpIAAMHBwQDJyckA
/9uqAKpJAAD/SQAAAGOAAFVtAACqbQAA/2OAAAAkAABVkgAAqiQAAP+SAAAAtgAAVbYAAKq2AAD/
<base64 data continues for another 1365 lines>
--
Content-type: video/mpeg
Content-transfer-encoding: base64

AAABswoAeBn//+CEAAABsgAAOgAAAG4AAAAAAAAQAAT/////wAAAGy//8AAAEBQ/Zl1IwwBGWCX
+pqMiJQDjAKywS/1NRrtXcTCLgzVQymqqHAfOsL1sMgMq4SWLCwOTYRdgyAyrhNYsLhhF3DLjAGg
BdwDXBv3yMV8/4tzrp3zsAWIGAJg1IBKTeFFI2IsgutIdfuSaAGCTsBVnWdz8afdMMAMgKgMEkPE
<base64 data continues for another 1839 lines>
-- --
That was the end of the nested multipart message.  This is the epilogue.
Like the preamble it is ignored.
--1995021309105517--
And that was the end of the main multipart message.  That's all folks!

*Figure   4-33  (Part 2 of 2). A Complex Multipart Example*

identical semantics to the original.  There are three parameters for the "Content-type:" field:

*id=* A unique identifier common to all parts of the message.

*number=* The sequence number of this part, with the first part being numbered 1.

*total=* The total number of parts.  This is optional on all but the last part.  The last part is identified by the fact that it has the same value for the number and total parameters.

The original message is always a message according to RFC 822 rules.  The first part is syntactically equivalent to a message/rfc822 message (that is the body itself contains message headers), and the subsequent parts are syntactically equivalent to text/plain messages. When re-building the message, the RFC 822 header fields are taken from the top-level message, not from the enclosed message, with the exception of those fields which cannot be copied from the inner message to the outer when fragmentation is performed (for example, the "Content-Type:" field).

**Note:** It is explicitly permitted to fragment a message/partial message further. This allows mail gateways to freely fragment messages in order to ensure that all parts are small enough to be transmitted. If this were not the case, the mail agent performing the fragmentation would have to know the smallest maximum size limit that the mail items would encounter en route to the destination.

*external-body* This type contains a pointer to an object which exists elsewhere. It has the syntax of the message/rfc822 type. The top-level message header defines how the external object is to be accessed, using the *access-type:* parameter of the "Content-Type:" field and a set of additional parameters which are specific to the access type. The intent is for the mail reader to be able to synchronously access the external object using the specified access type. The following access types are defined:

| | |
|---|---|
| **ftp** | File Transfer Protocol. The recipient will be expected to supply the necessary user ID and password – for security reasons, these are never transmitted with the message. |
| **tftp** | Trivial File Transfer Protocol. |
| **anon-ftp** | Anonymous FTP. |
| **local-file** | The data is contained in a file accessible directly via the recipient's local file system. |
| **afs** | The data is contained in a file accessible via the global Andrew File System. |
| **mail-server** | The data is accessible via a mail server. Unlike the others, this access is necessarily asynchronous. |

When the external object has been received, the desired message is obtained by appending the object to the message header encapsulated within the body of the message/external-body message. This encapsulated message header defines how the resulting message is to be interpreted (it is required to have a "Content-ID:" and will normally have a

"Content-Type:" field). The encapsulated message body is not used (the real message body is elsewhere, after all) and it is therefore termed the "phantom body." There is one exception to this: if the access-type is mail-server the phantom body contains the mail server commands necessary to extract the real message body. This is because mail server syntaxes vary widely and so it is much simpler to use the otherwise redundant phantom body than to codify a syntax for encoding arbitrary mail server commands as parameters on the "Content-Type:" field.

*image*    The body contains image data requiring a graphical display or some other device such as a printer to display it. Two subtypes are defined initially:

   *jpeg*    The image is in JPEG format, JFIF encoding.

   *gif*    GIF format.

*video*    The body contains moving image data (possibly with synchronized audio) requiring an intelligent terminal or multimedia workstation to display it. A single subtype is defined initially:

   *mpeg*    MPEG format.

*audio*    The body contains image data requiring a speaker and sound card (or similar hardware) to "display" it. A single subtype is defined initially:

   *basic*    A lowest common denominator format in the absence of any de facto standards for audio encoding. Specifically, it is single-channel 8-bit ISDN mu-law encoding at a sample rate of 8kHz.

*application*  This type is intended for types which do not fit into other categories, and particularly for data to be processed by an application program before being presented to the user, such as spreadsheet data. It is also intended for application programs which are intended to be processed as part of the mail reading process (for example, see the PostScript type below). This type of usage poses serious security risks unless an implementation ensures executable mail messages are run in a safe or "padded cell" environment.

Two subtypes are defined initially:

*PostScript*  Adobe Systems PostScript (Level 1 or Level 2).

   **Security Issues:** Although PostScript is often thought of as a format for printer data, it is a programming language and the use of a PostScript interpreter to process application/PostScript types poses serious security problems. Any mail reader which automatically interprets PostScript programs is equivalent, in principle, to one which automatically runs executable programs it receives. RFC 1521 outlines the issues involved.

*octet-stream* This subtype indicates general binary data consisting of 8-bit bytes. It is also the subtype that a mail reader should assume on encountering an unknown type or subtype. Any parameters are permitted, and RFC mentions two: a *type=* parameter to inform the recipient of the general type of the data and *padding=* to indicate a bit stream encoded in a byte stream (the padding value is the number of trailing zero bits added to pad the stream to a byte boundary).

Implementations are recommended to offer the user the option of using the data as input to a user program or of storing it in a file (there is no standard for the default name of such a file, although RFC 1521 does mention a "Content-Disposition:" field to be defined in a later RFC.

**Security Issues:** RFC strongly recommends against an implementation executing an application/octet-stream part automatically or using it as input to a program specified in the mail header. To do so would expose the receiving system to serious security risks and could impact the integrity of any networks that the system is connected to.

Obviously, there are many types of data which do not fit into any of the subtypes above. Co-operating mail programs may, in keeping with the rules of RFC 822, use types and/or subtypes beginning with "X-" as private values. No other values are permitted unless they have first been registered with the Internet Assigned Numbers Authority (IANA). See RFC 1590 for more details. The intention is that few, if any, additional types will be needed, but that many subtypes will be added to the set.

## 4.7.3 The Content-Transfer-Encoding Field

As already noted, SMTP agents and mail gateways can severely constrain the contents of mail messages which can be transmitted safely. The MIME types described above list a rich set of different types of object which can be included in mail messages and the majority of these do not fall within these constraints. Therefore, it is necessary to encode data of these types in a fashion which can be transmitted, and to decode them on receipt. RFC 1521 defines two forms of encoding which are mail safe. The reason for two forms rather than one is that it is not possible, given the small set of characters known to be mail safe, to devise a form which can both encode text data with minimal impact to the readability of the text and yet can encode binary data which consists of characters distributed randomly across all 256 byte values compactly enough to be practical.

These two encodings are used only for bodies and not for headers. Header encoding is described in 4.7.4, "Using Non-ASCII Characters in Message Headers" on page 4-106. The *Content-Transfer-Encoding:* field defines the encoding used. Although cumbersome, this field name emphasizes that the encoding is a feature of the transport process and not an intrinsic property of the object being mailed. Although there are only two encodings defined, this field can take on *five* values (as usual, the values are case insensitive). Three of the values actually specify that no encoding has been done; where they differ is that they imply different reasons why this is the case. This is a subtle but important point. MIME is not restricted to SMTP as a transport agent, despite the prevalence of (broadly) SMTP-compliant mail systems on the Internet. It therefore allows a mail agent to transmit data which is not mail-safe by the standards of SMTP (that is STD 10/RFC 821). If such a mail item reaches a gateway to a more restrictive system, the "encoding" mechanism specified allows the gateway to decide on an item-by-item basis whether the body must be encoded to be transmitted safely.

The five "encodings" are:

- 7bit (the default if the "Content-Transfer-Encoding:" header is omitted).
- 8bit
- Binary
- Quoted-Printable
- Base64

These are described in the sections that follow.

### 4.7.3.1 7bit Encoding

7bit "encoding" means that no encoding has been done and the body consists of lines of ASCII text with a length of not greater than 1000 characters. It is therefore known to be mail-safe with any mail system that *strictly* conforms with STD 10/RFC 821. This is the default, since these are the restrictions which apply to pre-MIME STD 11/RFC 822 messages.

**Note:** 7bit encoding does *not* guarantee that the contents are truly mail safe for two reasons. First, gateways to EBCDIC networks have a smaller set of mail-safe characters, and secondly because of the many non-conforming SMTP implementations. The Quoted-Printable encoding is designed to overcome these difficulties for text data.

### 4.7.3.2 8bit Encoding

8bit "encoding" implies that lines are short enough for SMTP transport, but that there may be non-ASCII characters (that is, octets with the high-order bit set). Where SMTP agents support the *SMTP Service Extension for 8bit-MIMEtransport*, described in RFC 1652, 8bit encoding is possible. Otherwise, SMTP implementations should set the high-order bit to zero, so 8bit encoding is not valid.

## 4.7.3.3 Binary Encoding

Binary "encoding" indicates that non-ASCII characters may be present and that the lines may be too long for SMTP transport (that is, there may be sequences of 999 or more characters without a CRLF sequence). There are currently no standards for the transport of unencoded binary data by mail based on the TCP/IP protocol stack, so the only case where it is valid to use binary encoding in a MIME message sent on the Internet or other TCP/IP based network is in the header of an external-body part (see the message/external-body type above). Binary encoding would be valid if MIME were used in conjunction with other mail transport mechanisms, or with a hypothetical SMTP Service Extension which did support long lines.

## 4.7.3.4 Quoted-Printable Encoding

This is the first of the two "real" encodings and it is intended to leave text files largely readable in their encoded form.

- It represents non-mail safe characters by the hexadecimal representation of their ASCII characters.

- It introduces reversible (soft) line breaks to keep all lines in the message to a length of 76 characters or less.

Quoted-Printable encoding uses the equals sign as a "quote character" to indicate both of these cases. It has five rules which are summarized as follows:

1. Any character except one which is part of a new line sequence (that is, a X′ 0D0A′ sequence on a text file) can be represented by "=XX" where XX are two uppercase hexadecimal digits. If none of the other rules apply, the character must be represented like this.

2. Any character in the range X′ 21′ to X′ 7E′ exceptX′ 3D′ ("=") may be represented as the ASCII character.

3. ASCII TAB (X′ 09′ ) and SPACE (X′ 20′ ) may be represented as the ASCII character except when it is the last character on the line.

4. A line break must be represented by a <CRLF> sequence (X′ 0D0A′ ). When encoding binary data, X′ 0D0A′ is not a line break and should be coded, according to rule 1, as "=0D=0A."

5. Encoded lines may not be longer than 76 characters (excluding the <CRLF>). If a line is longer than this, a soft line break must be inserted at or before column 75. A soft line break is the sequence "=<CRLF>" (X′ 3D0D0A′ ).

This scheme is a compromise between readability, efficiency and robustness. Since rules 1 and 2 use the phrase "may be encoded," implementations have a fair degree of latitude on how many characters are "quoted." If as few characters are quoted as possible within the scope of the rules, then the encoding will work with well-behaved ASCII SMTP agents. Adding the following set of ASCII characters:

! " # $ @ [   ] ^   { | } ~

to the list of those to be quoted is adequate for well-behaved EBCDIC gateways. For total robustness, it is better to quote *every* character except for the 73-character set known to be invariant across all gateways, that is the letters and digits (A-Z, a-z and 0-9) and the following 11 characters:

' ( ) + , - . / : = ?

**Note:** This invariant list does not even include the SPACE character! For practical purposes, when encoding text files, only a SPACE at the end of a line should be quoted. Otherwise readability is severely impacted.

## 4.7.3.5  Base64 Encoding

This encoding is intended for data which does not consist mainly of text characters. Quoted-printable replaces each non-text character with a 3-byte sequence which is grossly inefficient for binary data. Base64 encoding works by treating the input stream as a bit stream, regrouping the bits into shorter bytes, padding these short bytes to 8 bits and then translating these bytes to characters which are known to be mail-safe. As noted in the previous section, there are only 73 safe characters, so the maximum byte length usable is 6 bits which can be represented by 64 unique characters (hence the name Base64). Since the input and output are both byte streams, the encoding has to be done in groups of 24 bits (that is 3 input bytes and 4 output bytes). The process can be seen as follows:

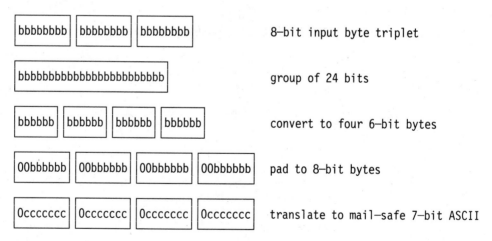

*Figure 4-34. Base64 Encoding.* How 3 input bytes are converted to 4 output bytes in the Base64 encoding scheme.

The translate table used is called the *Base64 Alphabet*.

| Base64 value | ASCII char. | Base64 value | ASCII char. | Base64 value | ASCII char. | Base64 value | ASCII char. |
|---|---|---|---|---|---|---|---|
| 0 | A | 16 | Q | 32 | g | 48 | w |
| 1 | B | 17 | R | 33 | h | 49 | x |
| 2 | C | 18 | S | 34 | i | 50 | y |
| 3 | D | 19 | T | 35 | j | 51 | z |
| 4 | E | 20 | U | 36 | k | 52 | 0 |
| 5 | F | 21 | V | 37 | l | 53 | 1 |
| 6 | G | 22 | W | 38 | m | 54 | 2 |
| 7 | H | 23 | X | 39 | n | 55 | 3 |
| 8 | I | 24 | Y | 40 | o | 56 | 4 |
| 9 | J | 25 | Z | 41 | p | 57 | 5 |
| 10 | K | 26 | a | 42 | q | 58 | 6 |
| 11 | L | 27 | b | 43 | r | 59 | 7 |
| 12 | M | 28 | c | 44 | s | 60 | 8 |
| 13 | N | 29 | d | 45 | t | 61 | 9 |
| 14 | O | 30 | e | 46 | u | 62 | + |
| 15 | P | 31 | f | 47 | v | 63 | / |

*Figure* *4-35. The Base64 Alphabet*

One additional character (the "=" character) is needed for padding. Because the input is a byte stream which is encoded in 24-bit groups it will be short by zero, 8 or 16 bits, as will the output. If the output is of the correct length, no padding is needed. If the output is 8 bits short, this corresponds to an output quartet of two complete "bytes," a "short byte" and a missing byte. The short byte is padded with two low-order zero bits. The missing byte is replaced with an "=" character. If the output is 16 bits short, this corresponds to an output quartet of one complete "byte," a "short byte" and two missing bytes. The short byte is padded with 6 low-order zero bits. The 2 missing bytes are replaced with an "=" character. If "zero characters" (that is "A"s) were used, the receiving agent would not be able to tell when decoding the input stream if trailing X′ 00′ characters in the last or last two positions of the output stream were data or padding. With pad characters, the number of "="s (0, 1 or 2) gives the length of the input stream modulo 3 (0, 2 or 1 respectively).

## 4.7.3.6 Conversion between Encodings

The Base64 encoding can be freely translated to and from the binary encoding without ambiguity since both treat the data as an octet-stream. This is also true for the conversion from Quoted-Printable to either of the other two (in the case of the Quoted-Printable to Binary conversion the process can be viewed as involving an intermediate binary encoding) by converting the quoted character sequences to their 8-bit form, deleting the soft line breaks and replacing hard linebreaks with <CRLF> sequences. This is not strictly true of the reverse process since Quoted-Printable is actually a record-based system: there is a semantic difference between a hard line break and an imbedded "=0D=0A" sequence (for example when decoding Quoted-Printable on a EBCDIC record-based system such as VM, hard line breaks map to record boundaries but =0D=0A sequences map to X′ 0D25′ sequences).

### 4.7.3.7 Multiple Encodings

MIME does *not* allow nested encodings. Any Content-Type that recursively includes other Content-Type fields (notable the multipart and message types) may not use a Content-Transfer-Encoding other than 7bit, 8bit or binary. All encodings must be done at the innermost level. The purpose of this restriction is to simplify the operation of user mail agents. If nested encodings are not permitted, the structure of the entire message is always visible to the mail agent without the need to decode the outer layer(s) of the message.

This simplification for user mail agents has a price: complexity for gateways. Because a user agent may specify an encoding of 8bit or binary, a gateway to a network where these encodings are not safe must encode the message before passing it to the second network. The obvious solution, to simply encode the message body and to change the "Content-Transfer-Encoding:" field, is not allowed for the multipart or message types since it would violate the restriction described above. The gateway must therefore correctly parse the message into its components and re-encode the innermost parts as necessary.

There is one further restriction: messages of type message/partial must *always* have 7bit encoding (8bit and binary are also disallowed). The reason for this is that if a gateway needs to re-encode a message, it requires the entire message to do so, but the parts of the message may not all be available together (parts may be transmitted serially because the gateway is incapable of storing the entire message at once or they may even be routed independently via different gateways). Therefore message/partial body parts must be mail safe across lowest common denominator networks; that is, they must be 7bit encoded.

## 4.7.4 Using Non-ASCII Characters in Message Headers

All of the mechanisms above refer exclusively to bodies and not to headers. The contents of message headers must be still be coded in US-ASCII. For header fields which include human-readable text, this is not adequate for languages other than English. A mechanism to include national language characters is defined by the second part of MIME (RFC 1522). This mechanism differs from the Quoted-Printable encoding, which would be used in a message body for the following reasons:

- The format of message headers is strictly codified by RFC 822, so the encoding used by MIME for header fields must work within a narrower set of constraints than that used for bodies.

- Message relaying programs frequently change message headers, for example re-ordering header fields, deleting some fields but not others, re-ordering mailboxes within lists or spilling fields at different positions than the original message.

- Some message handling programs do not correctly handle some of the more arcane features of RFC 822 (such as the use of the "" character to "quote" special characters like "<" and ">.").

The approach used by MIME is to reserve improbable sequences of legal ASCII characters which are not syntactically important in RFC 822 for use with this protocol. Words in headers fields which need national characters are replaced by *encoded words* which have the form:

`=?charset?encoding?word?=`

where:

charset    is the value allowed for the charset parameter used with text/plain MIME type, that is: "us-ascii" or "iso-8859-1" through "iso-8859-9."

encoding   "B" or "Q."   "B" is identical to the Base64 encoding used in message bodies.  "Q" is similar to the Quoted-Printable encoding but uses "_" to represent X′ 20′ (ASCII SPACE).[8] Q encoding requires the encoding of "_" characters and does not allow line breaks.  Any printable ASCII character other than "_," "=" and SPACE may be left unquoted within an encoded word unless it would be syntactically meaningful when the header field is parsed according to RFC 822.

*charset* and *encoding* are both case-insensitive.

word       is a string of ASCII text characters other than SPACE which conforms to the rules of the encoding given.

An encoded word must have no imbedded white space characters (SPACE or TAB), may be up to 75 characters long, and may not be on a line that is greater than 76 characters long (excluding the <CRLF>).  These rules ensure that gateways will not fold encoded words in the middle of the word.  Encoded words can generally be used in the "human-readable" parts of header fields. For example, if a mailbox is specified in the form:

`The Octopus <octopus@garden.under.the.sea>`

---

8   The underscore character is not strictly mail-safe, but it is used because the use of any other character to indicate a SPACE would seriously hamper readability.

an encoded word could be used in the "The Octopus" section but not in the address part between the "<" and the">"). RFC 1522 specifies precisely where encoded words may be used with reference to the syntax of RFC 822.

## 4.7.5 References

A detailed description of MIME can be found in the following RFCs:

- *RFC 1521 – MIME (Multipurpose Internet Mail Extensions) Part One: Mechanisms for Specifying and Describing the Format of Internet Message Bodies.*
- *RFC 1522 – MIME (Multipurpose Internet Mail Extensions) Part Two: Message Header Extensions for Non-ASCII Text*

## 4.7.6 Implementations

As can be seen from the above, MIME, while being flexible enough for many kinds of mail transport, places particular emphasis on body types that are used in multimedia applications (the image, audio and video types). MIME-compliant mailers are provided in the *UltiMail* family of products.

There are two different UltiMail products. The original version of the the product is *UltiMedia Mail/2*, providing MIME compliance, a client/server structure, and multimedia capabilities of OS/2 Version 2.1. This was originally announced as an optional kit of TCP/IP V2.0 for OS/2. It is now part of the IBM WorkGroup product. The newer version provides improvements in usability, robustness and function. It is called *UltiMail Lite* and is included with the OS/2 Warp products. It is intended for single user use while the former, mentioned above, is intended for group users.

Both of them have the same basic structure.

- The OS/2 SENDMAIL program provides the SMTP (that is, STD 10/RFC 821) server and client programs. It is responsible for receiving incoming mail, and for transmitting outgoing mail.

- The UltiMail server program provides the STD 11/RFC 822 and MIME implementations. It converts mail items between the MIME format necessary for mail transmission and the object-based structure understood by the mail client. The server is a *System Object Model (SOM)*[9] application. Each user has an in-basket object, folder objects containing mail that has been sent and received, and address book objects containing names and addresses of regular mail contacts. Within the in-basket and the folders are letter objects, and within the letter objects are the parts which comprise the mail item. The SOM implementation maps this to a directory

---

9  System Object Model is the technology used to implement the object-oriented Workplace Shell Environment in OS/2 Version 2 and OS/2 Warp Version 3.

structure. Each user has a directory structure managed by the server. Within this directory structure, sub-directories are used to hold mail items. Physically, each mail item itself is a directory, and within that directory are files containing the different parts contained in the mail item.

When an item is sent, UltiMail assembles the components of the mail item into a single MIME message and transmits it using SENDMAIL. The server also watches constantly for mail delivered by SENDMAIL. When an incoming mail item is detected, the server converts the mail item to a set of objects which can be understood by the UltiMail client, and if the destination user is connected to the server, it informs the client program that mail has arrived.

- The UltiMail Client

The end user works with mail via the client program. This provides an object-oriented interface which will be familiar to OS/2 WorkPlace Shell users. The in-basket, folders and address books are represented by icons in the main UltiMail window. Double-clicking on an icon open a view of the object it represents. When creating or receiving mail items, a formatted window is displayed with entry boxes for the header fields, icons representing the parts in the message, an icon bar for common functions like sending, replying, adding images and so on. An example session is shown in Figure 4-36 on page 4-110.

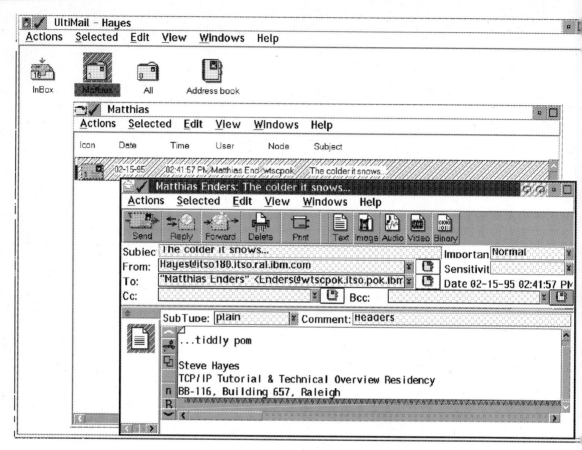

*Figure 4-36. A Sample UltiMail Session*

## 4.7.6.1 UltiMedia Mail/2

UltiMedia Mail/2, the original UltiMail product, supports multiple clients for each server and multiple servers for each clients. The server and client may be on the same system or on separate systems (a TCP socket connection is used in the second case). It supports SMTP but not POP, so the server must be running in order to receive mail. It supports MultiMedia mail using the MMPM/2 component of OS/2.

## 4.7.6.2 UltiMail Lite

UltiMail Lite is provided with OS/2 Warp Version 3, in the Internet Connection provided with the BonusPak. In UltiMail Lite, the server and the client components share the same process, and are always run together. In fact the client/server structure of the program is not apparent to the user. UltiMail Lite does not support including video and audio types in mail messages, but does support all of the other MIME types, and will recognize video and audio clips which are included in a mail message but will not display them. In addition it includes a POP3 client for retrieving mail from a POP3 server. When configured to use POP3, UltiMail Lite retrieves the mail from the POP3 server and queues it to itself as though it had arrived directly via SENDMAIL. When using the IBM Internet Access Kit, the POP server is accessed via a SLIP connection. Users of IBM's connections services have mailbox addresses of the form *user ID*@ibm.net and mail from other users is re-directed to the POP server using MX records in the Domain Name System as described in 4.6.3.1, "Addressing Mailboxes on Server Systems" on page 4-74.

### 4.7.6.3 IBM WorkGroup

The version of UltiMail included in IBM WorkGroup is the full-function client/server equivalent of UltiMail Lite. It includes separate client and server components and full multimedia support with MMPM/2.

# 4.8 Remote Execution Command Protocol (REXEC)

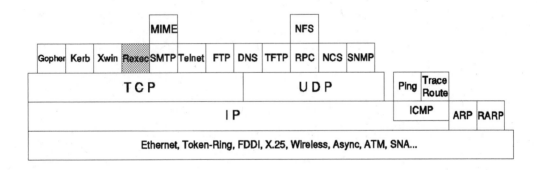

*Figure 4-37. Remote Execution Command Protocol (REXEC)*

REXECD (*Remote EXEcution Command Daemon*) is a server that allows execution of the REXEC or RSH (Remote Shell Protocol) command from a remote host over the TCP/IP network. The client function is performed by the REXEC process.

## 4.8.1 Principle of Operation

REXECD is a server (or daemon). It handles commands issued by foreign hosts, and transfers orders to slave virtual machines for job execution. The daemon performs automatic login, and user authentication when user ID and password are entered.

REXEC command is used to define user ID, password, host address, and the process to be started on the remote host. Both server and client are linked over the TCP/IP network.

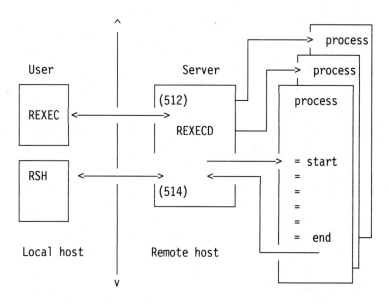

*Figure   4-38.  REXECD Principle*


## 4.8.2 Implementations

### 4.8.2.1 VM

The REXECD service machine supports both the remote execution protocol (REXEC) on port 512, and the remote shell protocol (RSH) on port 514.

Both client and server functions are implemented under VM.

The REXECD machine can transfer commands to a user machine, or slave machine. A slave machine is useful for the user who does not have his own virtual machine defined in the VM system where he wants to execute some process.

Slave machines are autologged when REXECD executes its *PROFILE EXEC*. The following is an example of the *REXECD* parameters. This is part of the *PROFILE EXEC*. This file can be shared between the REXECD virtual machine and the slave machine(s).

```
.....
'REXECD -d -r -s VMUSER14 PASSW1 -s SLAV2 PSW2'
```

Where:

- REXECD is the name of the module
- -d is the DEBUG option
- -r is the RACF option
- -s slave machines' parameters
- VMUSER14, SLAV2 are the slave virtual machines
- PASSW1, PSW2 are the passwords of the slave virtual machines.

When using the REXECD VM server from another host, you are prompted for a user ID and a password. You can either enter a valid user ID and its RACF password (if the RACF option is enabled) or the keyword guest and a null password to use one of the slave machines. To enable the RACF option (that is to use the RACF password to autolog a user ID) the following steps must be performed:

1. Start REXECD with the -r option
2. Copy the *VALIDATE EXEC* (from FTPSERVE.191) on REXECD.191
3. Copy the *VALIDATE MODULE* on REXECD.191 as *RPIVAL MODULE*.

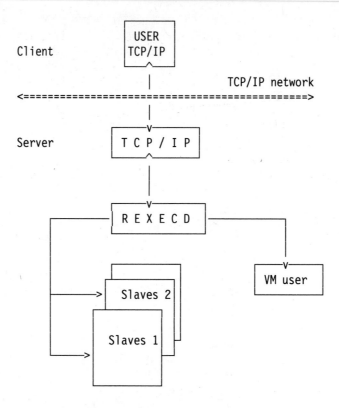

*Figure   4-39.   REXECD Scheme under VM*

When using the client function from VM (*REXEC* command) the *NETRC DATA* file may provide you with an alternative to specifying the user ID and password as REXEC parameters. This file should be stored using the A0 filemode.

Example of NETRC DATA A0 file:

```
machine fsc5 login guest password xxx
machine psfred login FRED password pass
```

The first entry identifies a slave machine (the password does not matter).

The following is a sample response that is displayed as a result of using the REXEC command and the *NETRC DATA* file:

```
rexec fsc5 q t
TIME IS 05:43:10 EUR FRIDAY 02/10/95
CONNECT= 00:01:58 VIRTCPU= 000:02.41 TOTCPU= 000:04.59
Ready; T=0.39/0.71 05:43:14
```

## 4.8.2.2 MVS

TCP/IP for MVS includes both server and client remote execution functions (REXEC).
The implementation is as follows:

- The REXEC - remote execution client

  The remote execution protocols allow your TSO users to execute commands on
  remote TCP/IP hosts and receive the results on their TSO terminal.

- The RSH - remote shell client

  See REXEC above.

- The REXECD - remote execution server

  The remote execution command daemon (REXECD) is the server that allows
  execution of a TSO batch command that has been received from a remote TCP/IP
  host. This server supports both the remote execution protocol (REXEC) and the
  remote shell protocol (RSH).

  **Note:** The RSH protocols are supported for the REXEC functions only. Remote
  login (RLOGIN) is not supported. If the MVS system runs OpenEdition, an
  RLOGIN server is supplied with OpenEdition MVS.

- The RSHD - remote shell server

  See REXECD above.

Another possibility to submit jobs to an MVS/JES subsystem is the job submission
facility from an MVS FTP server (see 4.4.6.2, "MVS" on page 4-32 for more
information).

## 4.8.2.3 AIX

All AIX systems are implemented with both REXEC client and server.

## 4.8.2.4 AIX/6000

The rexecd daemon is a subserver controlled by the inetd subsystem (also known as the
super daemon).

The $HOME/.netrc file can be used to specify automatic login information for the user ID and password to use at the foreign host. Since this file is not encrypted, the automatic login feature is not available when your AIX system has been configured with the securetcpip command.

The rsh command and the rshd server (daemon) can be used. Since rsh and rshd do not provide a secure environment for transferring files, they are disabled by running the securetcpip command.

The securetcpip command is used to enable additional TCP/IP security environment by disabling commands that are not trusted. For more information about the securetcpip command, please refer to *AIX Version 3.2 for RISC System/6000 Communication Concepts and Procedures*.

### 4.8.2.5 OS/2

TCP/IP for OS/2 provides client and server functions of REXEC. Before activating the REXEC server, the variables *USERID* and *PASSWORD* have to be defined. They are used to define which remote users can access your system. REXECD and REXEC are the commands used for server and client respectively. The REXEC command uses the /ETC/NETRC file to automate the login process.

OS/2 provides client and server (RSHD) functions of RSH. Before activating the RSH server, the RHOSTS file in the ETC directory must be created. It is used by the RSH server to verify the authorization of remote hosts. You must specify the full domain name (for example, *joe.watson.ibm.com*) of the remote hosts.

The following is an example REXEC session from OS/2 to AIX V3.

```
[C:\]rexec rs60002 -l paul -p mypasswd ls -ls
total 368
    4 drwxr-xr-x   2 li        staff        512 Sep 09 18:49 hippi
    4 drwxr-xr-x   3 li        staff        512 Sep 09 11:07 info
   84 -rw-r--r--   1 li        staff      83913 Sep 18 11:51 krypto.ps.Z
    4 drwxr-xr-x   4 li        staff        512 Sep 17 11:10 mit
    4 -rw-r--r--   1 li        staff       1818 Sep 17 11:14 x11r5doc.du
```

### 4.8.2.6 DOS

TCP/IP for DOS is implemented with the client REXEC and the RSH commands. REXEC requires an REXEC Daemon to be running on the foreign host. This REXEC command is used to provide the necessary parameters, user name, password, internet address, and command to be executed on the foreign host. RSH requires a RSH server to be running on the foreign host. Like REXEC, the RSH command executes a command on the remote host. However, RSH neither requires nor allows you to supply a password.

# 4.9 X Window System

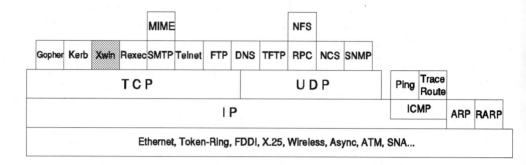

*Figure* *4-40.* *X Window System*

The X Window System (hereafter referred to as X) is one of the most widely used *Graphical User Interface (GUI)*, or bitmapped-window display systems. It is supported by all major workstation vendors, and is used by a large and growing number of users worldwide. The X Window System offers more than just a raw environment. It also offers a platform for uniquely incorporated commercial packages. In addition to writing application software, some industry groups have created proprietary software packages and standards for interfaces which leverage the display capabilities of the X Window System. These packages are then integrated into applications to improve the *look and feel* of them. The two most significant commercial packages in this area are the Open Software Foundation's *MOTIF* and UNIX International's *Open Look*. X was the brainchild of Robert Scheifler, Jim Gettys, and others at MIT, as part of *Project Athena*, a research project devoted to the examination of very large networks of personal computers and workstations. (For an overview of the Project Athena, please refer to *Project Athena: Supporting Distributed Computing at MIT*). As part of this study, a unifying window system environment extending over all systems was deemed necessary. X was envisioned as this window system, one that could be used among the varied heterogeneous computers and networks.

As Project Athena progressed, X evolved into a portable network-based window system. Much of the early work on X was derived from an extant Stanford window system called W. In fact the name X was simply a play on the previous name W. The MIT X Consortium, founded in 1988, is dedicated to the advancement of the X Window System and to the promotion of cooperation within the computer industry in standardizing the X Window System interfaces.

Current X releases contain two numbers: the *version number* indicating major protocol or standards revisions, and a *release number* indicating minor changes. At the time of writing, the latest version is X11 Release 6, also known as X11R6. The latest release of OSF/MOTIF is V1.2 (based on X11R5). Major revisions of X are incompatible, but there is backward compatibility with minor releases within major revision categories.

The aim of X was to allow the user to control all sessions from one screen, with applications either running in a window, or in separate virtual terminals but with an icon on the primary screen reminding him of the existence of that application (the same function as OS/2 Presentation Manager).

The X Window System provides the capability of managing both local and remote windows. Remote windows are established through TCP/IP, and local windows through the use of BSD *sockets*.

## 4.9.1 Functional Concept

Basically there are two parts communicating with each other:

1.  The application, which gets input from the user, executes code and sends output back to the user. Instead of reading and writing directly to a display, the application uses the Xlib programming interface to send and receive data to/from the user's terminal. The application part is also called the X client.

2.  The user's terminal, running a display-managing software which receives/sends data from/to the application and is called the X server.

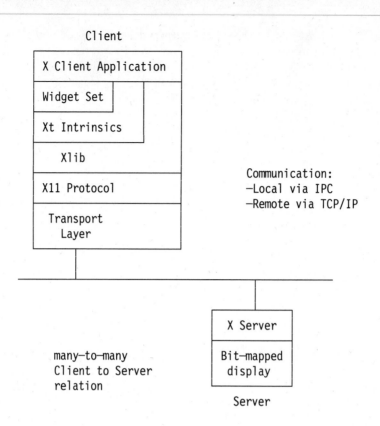

**Figure 4-41.** *Concept of X Window System.* Clients and servers communicating together.

Terminology:

- **X Server**: This is a dedicated program that provides display services on a graphic terminal, on behalf of a user, at the request of the user's X client program. It controls the screen and handles the keyboard and the mouse (or other input devices) for one or more X clients. Equally, it is responsible for output to the display, the mapping of colors, the loading of fonts and the keyboard mapping. Typically X server programs run on high performance graphics PCs and workstations, as well as "X terminals", which are designed to run only the X server program.

  The X11R5 X server has provided some speed improvements and new font interfaces. An *X Font Service Protocol* is available to allow the X servers to delegate the task of managing fonts to a font server.

- **X Client**: This is the actual *application* and is designed to employ a graphical user interface to display its output. Typically, many X clients compete for the service of one X server per display per user. Conflict for services are resolved by the X

Window Manager, a separate entity altogether. *Xterm* and *Xclock* are two examples of X clients.

X11R5 added some more clients, new demos and a completely new implementation of bitmap and xmag.

- **X Window Manager**: This is an X client program located on the workstation where the X server runs. While windows can be created without a window manager in place, a window manager permits windows to be resized, moved, and otherwise modified on demand.

- **X Protocol**: This runs within the network connection, and allows requests-responses between client and server. It uses a reliable byte stream connection (that is TCP) and describes the format of messages exchanged between client and server over this connection.

- **Xlib**: The rudimentary application programming interface is contained in the Xlib. It is a collection of C primitive subroutines embedded in all X clients, which gives the lowest level access to the X protocol. The procedures in Xlib translate client requests to X protocol requests, parse incoming messages (events, replies, and errors) from the X server, and provide several additional utilities, such as storage management and operating system independent operations. It is possible to write application programs entirely with Xlib. In fact, most existing X clients are or were developed in this fashion.

  X11R5 added two new major pieces of functionality to Xlib:

  – Device-independent color
  – Internationalization (i18n): this means that X client application programs can adapt to the requirements of different native languages, local customs, and character string encodings.

- **X Toolkits**: The complexity of the low-level Xlib interface and of the underlying X Protocol is handled by an increasing variety of available X *Toolkits*. The X Toolkits are software libraries that provide high-level facilities for implementing common user-interface *objects* such as buttons, menus, and scrollbars, as well as layout tools for organizing these objects on the display. The basis for a family of toolkits is provided with the standard X releases from MIT. The library, called the **X Intrinsics** or **Xt**, forms the building blocks for sets of user interface objects called *widgets*.

- **Widgets**: For toolkits based on the X Intrinsics, a common interface mechanism called a *widget* is used. A widget is essentially an X window plus some additional data and a set of procedures for operating on that data. Widgets are a client-side notion only. Neither the X server nor the X protocol understand widgets. A sample widget set, *Xaw*, more commonly referred to as the *Athena Widget Set*, is distributed by MIT with the X11 source.

Functionality:

- X client and X server can be on different hosts. Then they use the TCP/IP protocol to communicate over the network. They can also be on the same machine, using IPC (inter-process communication) to communicate (through sockets).

- There is only one X server per terminal. Multiple X client applications can communicate with this one X server. The duty of the X server is to display the application windows and to send the user input to the appropriate X client application.

- It is up to the X client to maintain the windows that it created. It is notified by *events* from the X server whenever something is changed on the display by other clients. However, they don't have to care about which part of their windows are visible or not when they are drawing or redrawing their windows.

- The X server keeps track of the visibility of the windows, by maintaining *stacks*. A stack contains all *"first generation" children* of a parent window. A child window can also be a parent window by having one or more child windows itself, which are again held in a *substack*. The *primary stack* is the stack which holds all the windows located directly below the root. See Figure 4-42 on page 4-123 for an illustration. Subwindows can only be fully visible when their parent is on the top of its respective stack and mapped to the display.

- X server itself has no management functions; it only performs window clipping according to its stacks. Every client is responsible for its own windows. There is a *Window Manager* which manipulates the top level windows of all the clients. The Window Manager is not part of the X server but is itself a client. As soon as the Window Manager changes something on the screen (for instance resizing a window), it makes the X server send out an exposure event to all the other clients.

- The client applications send *request messages* to the X server, which replies with a *reply message* or an *error message*. The X server can also send *event messages* to the applications. Event messages indicate changes to the windows (and their visibility), and user input (mouse and keyboard).

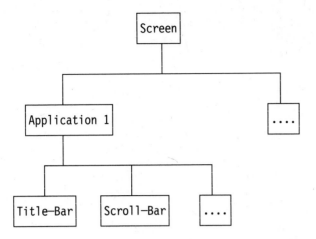

**Figure 4-42.** *X Window System Window Structure.* Each window is a child of another window, the whole display being the root.

Applying this client/server concept gives the following advantages:

- Applications don't have to know the hardware characteristics of the terminal.

- Applications don't have to be on the same computer as the terminal.

- Programs written to Xlib are portable.

- New terminal types can be added by providing an appropriate X server.

- The programmers do not have to deal with the communications. They just write graphic applications to Xlib, regardless of whether the users will be remote or local.

## 4.9.2 Protocol

An X Window System protocol can be implemented on top of any reliable byte stream transport mechanism. It uses a simple block protocol on top of the stream layer. Four kinds of messages are used:

- Request format. Requests flow from the client application to the X server.

| major | length | minor | data |
|-------|--------|-------|------|

Where:

> Major and minor are opcodes, each 1-byte long.
> Length is 2-bytes long.
> Data may be zero or more bytes, depending on the request.

- Reply format: 32-byte block.

- Error format: 32-byte block.

- Event format: 32-byte block.

Reply, error and event messages are sent by the X server to the X client applications.

Displays are always numbered from zero. For TCP connections, display number N is associated with port 5800+N (hex 5800) and port 5900+N. The X server treats connections on the 58xx ports as connections with hosts which use the "low-order byte first" format, and the 59xx ports as "high-order byte first".

There are more than a hundred different possible requests, each corresponding to an *Xlib* application call. As this document is not a programmer's guide, we will not deal with the *Xlib* functions. *RFC 1013 - X Window System Protocol, Version 11* contains the 1987 alpha update of the X11 protocol. For documentation on the current release X11R6, please contact either MIT or a commercial computer books publisher. For documentation on IBM X Windows implementations, please see the appropriate section in Appendix A, "Bibliography" on page A-1.

## 4.9.3 Implementations

### 4.9.3.1 VM
The TCP/IP for VM API is from the X Window System Version 11, Release 4 and includes the following components:

- X11LIB TXTLIB (Xlib, Xmu, Xext, and Xau routines).
- OLDXLIB TXTLIB (X Release 10 compatibilty routines).
- XTLIB TXTLIB (Xt Intrinsics).
- XAWLIB TXTLIB (Athena Widget set).
- Header files (H files) needed for compiling X clients.
- Standard MIT X clients.
- Sample X clients (Xlib sample program, Athena Widget set sample program, OSF/Motif-based widget sample program).

In addition, it also includes an API based on Version 1.1.2 of the OSF/Motif-based widget set which has the following components:

- XMLIB TXTLIB (OSF/Motif-based widget set)

- Header files needed for compiling clients using the OSF/Motif-based widget set.

GDDMXD is an interface to the Graphical Data Display Manager/VM (GDDM/VM or GDDM/VMXA). This interface permits graphics display output from the IBM GDDM/VM to be displayed on workstations that support the X Window System. The interface translates the data stream, created by GDDM, to the X protocol, and transmits it by TCP/IP to the X server. If GDDMXD is installed on your system, but is not active, GDDM transmits data as if the interface were not present. The X GDDM interface should be installed by the person responsible for installing GDDM, because the shared segment of GDDM needs to be reinstalled during X GDDM interface installation. Please refer to *IBM TCP/IP Version 2 Release 3 for VM: Planning and Customization* for more details about the installation of the X GDDM interface, and to *IBM TCP/IP Version 2 Release 3 for VM: Programmer's Reference* for more programming considerations.

No X server function is provided for VM users.

## 4.9.3.2 MVS

The TCP/IP for MVS API is from the X Window System Version 11, Release 4 and includes the following components:

- *tcpip*.SEZAX11L (Xlib, Xmu, Xext, and Xau routines).
- *tcpip*.SEZAOLDX (X Release 10 compatibilty routines).
- *tcpip*.SEZAXTLB (Xt Intrinsics).
- *tcpip*.SEZAXAWL (Athena Widget set).
- Header files (H files) needed for compiling X clients.
- Standard MIT X clients.
- Sample X clients (Xlib sample program, Athena Widget set sample program, OSF/Motif-based widget sample program).

In addition, it also includes an API based on Version 1.1.2 of the OSF/Motif-based widget set which has the following components:

- *tcpip*.SEZAXMLB (OSF/Motif-based widget set)

- Header files needed for compiling clients using the OSF/Motif-based widget set.

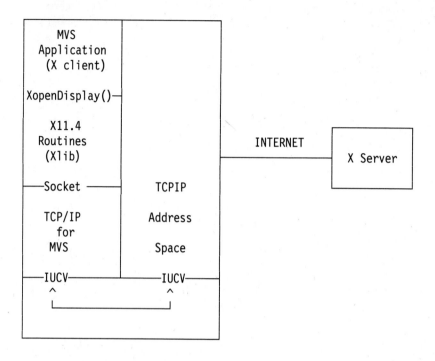

*Figure* *4-43.* *MVS X Window System Application to Server*

GDDMXD is an interface that allows graphics from the IBM Graphical Data Display Manager/MVS to be displayed on workstations that support the X Window System.

The interface translates the data stream, created by GDDM, to the X protocol, and transmits it by TCP/IP to the X server. GDDMXD was implemented such that existing GDDM applications can function as X Window clients without modifications or relink.

If the GDDMXD is installed on your system and not activated, or has been made inactive, GDDM transmits data as if the interface were not present. Please refer to *IBM TCP/IP Version 3 Release 1 for MVS: Customization and Administration Guide* for more details about the installation of the GDDMXD interface, and to *IBM TCP/IP Version 3 Release 1 for MVS: Programmer's Reference* for more programming considerations.

IBM TCP/IP for MVS supports the OpenEdition/MVS with the following set of object libraries with the X Windows routines compiled with the C/370 RENT compiler option (Reentrant):

- *tcpip.v3r1*.SEZAROE1

- *tcpip.v3r1*.SEZAROE2

- *tcpip.v3r1*.SEZAROE3

These libraries can be used as input for linking reentrant OpenEdition/MVS X Windows applications.

No X server function is provided for MVS users.

### 4.9.3.3 AIX/6000 V3.2.5

Both a client and server X Window System is implemented by *AIXwindows Environment/6000* Version 1.2.5.

AIXwindows Environment/6000 Version 1.2.5 provides a graphical interface to AIX/6000 V3.2.5. It is based on and compatible with the industry-accepted X Window System and the OSF/Motif 1.2.2 graphical user interface. It can also interact with other AIX and other equipment manufacturer systems implementing the X Window System and OSF/Motif interfaces. AIXwindows Environment/6000 provides a sophisticated graphical desktop (AIXwindows Desktop) that can be tailored for integrating and launching applications. AIXwindows Environment/6000 provides the facilities to execute and develop X applications, OSF/Motif applications or applications requiring Display PostScript support.

If you require 3D capability, the AIXwindows/3D feature provides the facilities for the development and execution of 3D applications using a variety of industry standard APIs. This includes hardware accelerated support for PEXlib, graPHIGS and GL 3.2 as well as a pure software implementation of OpenGL, PEXlib and graPHIGS, referred to as Softgraphics. Softgraphics allows all 3D functions to be performed by software where the graphics adapter is used simply as a frame buffer to display the image. This implementation makes it possible to run 3D applications on any 2D graphics adapter.

### 4.9.3.4 AIX/6000 Version 4.1.1

AIX Version 4.1.1 contains the AIXwindows 2D environment, and this function is loaded automatically at installation time upon detection of a supported graphics card. The AIXwindows 2D environment is based upon X11R5 and Motif 1.2.3.

A new graphical user interface based on the Common Desktop Environment (CDE) was added.

### 4.9.3.5 AIX/ESA

*AIXwindows Environment/ESA Version 1 Release 2* implements the X Window System Version X11R5 and OSF/Motif Version 1.1.4 with single byte, double byte, and multibyte data streams in which characters can be encoded up to 4 bytes each. The code set support in AIX/ESA Version 2 Release 2 includes the support of ISO 8859-1, ISO 8859-7 (Greek), ISO 8859-9 (Turkish), IBM PC Code Page 850, IBM PC Code Page 932 (Shift-JIS), and IBM Japanese EUC (Extended UNIX Code).

*AIXwindows Environment/ESA* provides the X Window System client functions.

### 4.9.3.6 OS/2

The X server function is available in the X Window Server Kit (PMX) of TCP/IP V2.0 for OS/2 (X11R5).

The X server function uses OS/2 PM as the X Window manager and supports all the keyboard, display, and pointer functions that are supported by OS/2 PM. Using PM as the X Window manager enables OS/2 PM windowed applications and X client applications to share the same screen. As a result, X client applications cannot act as the X Window manager for the OS/2 X server.

The X client function is available in the X Window Client Kit of TCP/IP V2.0 for OS/2 (X11R5).

Motif 1.2 function is available in the OSF/Motif Kit of TCP/IP V2.0 for OS/2. The X Window Client Kit mentioned above is a prerequisite for the OSF/Motif Kit.

# 4.10 Remote Procedure Call (RPC)

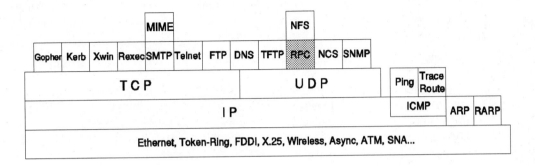

**Figure 4-44.** *Remote Procedure Call (RPC)*

Sun-RPC is a *proposed standard protocol*. Its status is *elective*.

Remote Procedure Call is a standard developed by SUN Microsystems and used by many vendors of UNIX systems. The current Sun-RPC specification can be found in *RFC 1057 - RPC: Remote Procedure Call Protocol Specification Version 2.*

The Remote Procedure Call protocol is an application programming interface (API) available for developing distributed applications. It allows programs to call subroutines that are executed at a remote system. The caller program (called a *client*) sends a *call message* to the *server process*, and waits for a *reply message*. The call message includes the procedure's parameters and the reply message contains the procedure's results.

Sun RPC consists of the following parts:

- *RPCGEN*: a compiler that takes the definition of a remote procedure interface, and generates the client stubs and the server stubs.
- *XDR (eXternal Data Representation)*: a standard way of encoding data in a portable fashion between different systems. It imposes a big-endian byte ordering and the minimum size of any field is 32 bits. This means that both the client and the server have to perform some translation.
- A run-time library.

## 4.10.1 RPC Concept

The RPC concept can be simplified as follows:

- The caller process sends a call message and waits for the reply.

- On the server side a process is dormant awaiting the arrival of call messages. When one arrives, the server process extracts the procedure parameters, computes the results and sends them back in a reply message.

See Figure 4-45 for a conceptual model of RPC.

This is only a possible model, as the SUN RPC protocol doesn't put restrictions on the concurrency model. In the model above, the caller's execution blocks until a reply message is received. Other models are possible; for instance, the caller may continue processing while waiting for a reply, or the server may dispatch a separate task for each incoming call so that it remains free to receive other messages.

The remote procedure calls differ from local procedure calls in the following ways:

- Use of global variables as the server has no access to the caller program's address space.
- Performance may be affected by the transmission times.
- User authentication may be necessary.
- Location of server must be known.

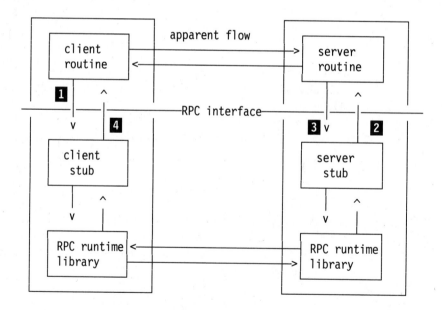

**Figure 4-45. RPC.** Remote Procedure Call Model

## 4.10.1.1 Transport

The RPC protocol can be implemented on any transport protocol. In the case of TCP/IP, it can use either TCP or UDP as the transport vehicle. The type of the *transport* is a parameter of the RPCGEN command. In case UDP is used, remember that this does not provide reliability, so it will be up to the caller program itself to ensure this (using timeouts and retransmissions, usually implemented in RPC library routines). Note that even with TCP, the caller program still needs a timeout routine to deal with exceptional situations such as a server crash.

The call and reply message data is formatted to the XDR standard.

## 4.10.1.2 RPC Call Message

The RPC call message consists of several fields:

- Program and procedure numbers

  Each call message contains three fields (unsigned integers):

  - Remote program number
  - Remote program version number
  - Remote procedure number

  that uniquely identify the procedure to be executed. The remote program number identifies a functional group of procedures, for instance a file system, which would include individual procedures like "read" and "write". These individual procedures are identified by a unique procedure number within the remote program. As the remote program evolves, a version number is assigned to the different releases.

  Each remote program is attached to an internet port. The number of this port can be freely chosen, except for the reserved "well-known-services" port numbers. It is evident that the caller will have to know the port number used by this remote program.

  Assigned program numbers:

  | | |
  |---|---|
  | 00000000 - 1FFFFFFF | defined by Sun |
  | 20000000 - 3FFFFFFF | defined by user |
  | 40000000 - 5FFFFFFF | transient (temporary numbers) |
  | 60000000 - FFFFFFFF | reserved |

- Authentication fields

  Two fields, *credentials* and *verifier*, are provided for the authentication of the caller to the service. It is up to the server to use this information for user authentication. Also, each implementation is free to choose the varieties of supported authentication protocols. Some authentication protocols are:

  - Null authentication.

- UNIX authentication. The callers of a remote procedure may identify themselves as they are identified on the UNIX system.
- DES authentication. In addition to user ID, a timestamp field is sent to the server. This timestamp is the current time, enciphered using a key known to the caller machine and server machine only (based on the *secret key* and *public key* concept of DES).

- Procedure parameters

  Data (parameters) passed to the remote procedure.

### 4.10.1.3 RPC Reply Message
Several replies exist, depending on the action taken:

- SUCCESS: procedure results are sent back to the client.
- RPC_MISMATCH: server is running another version of RPC than the caller.
- AUTH_ERROR: caller authentication failed.
- PROG_MISMATCH: if program is unavailable or if the version asked for does not exist or if the procedure is unavailable.

For a detailed description of the call and reply messages, see *RFC 1057 - RPC: Remote Procedure Call Protocol Specification Version 2*, which also contains the type definitions (typedef) for the messages in XDR language.

### 4.10.1.4 Portmap or Portmapper
As stated above, the caller has to know the exact port number used by a specific RPC program to be able to send a call message to it. Portmap is a server application that will map a program number and its version number to the internet port number used by the program. Because Portmap is assigned a reserved (*well-known service*) port number 111, all the caller has to do is ask the Portmap service on the remote host about the port used by the desired program. See Figure 4-46 on page 4-133.

Portmap only knows about RPC programs on the host it runs on (only RPC programs on the local host).

In order for Portmap to know about the RPC program, every RPC program should register itself with the local Portmap when it starts up. It should also cancel its registration when it closes down.

Normally, the calling application would contact Portmap on the destination host to obtain the correct port number for a particular remote program, and then send the call message to this particular port. A variation exists when the caller also sends the procedure data along to Portmap and then the remote Portmap directly invokes the procedure.

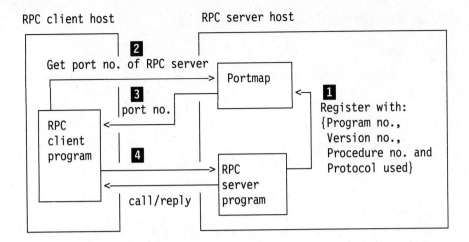

**RPC client host**　　　　　　**RPC server host**

*Figure 4-46. Portmap.* Informs the caller which port number a program on its host occupies.

## 4.10.1.5 RPCGEN

RPCGEN is a tool that generates C code to implement an RPC protocol. The input to RPCGEN is a file written in a language similar to C, known as the RPC language. Assuming that an input file named *proto.x* is used, RPCGEN produces the following output files:

- A header file called *proto.h* that contains common definitions of constants and macros
- Client stub source file, *protoc.c*
- Server stub source file, *protos.c*
- XDR routines source file, *protox.c*

## 4.10.2 Implementations

### 4.10.2.1 VM

VM provides an RPC application programming interface (API) for both the client and the server side.

For the client side, there are calls to:

- Invoke (send) a remote procedure call.
- Query the remote Portmap application about ports.

For the server side, there are calls to:

- Attach the program to a port number.
- Register the program and its port number with the local Portmap application.
- Cancel registration with Portmap.
- Send a reply back to the caller.

This programming interface is available for programs written in the C language. In addition to this, the XDR type definitions are shipped with the product, in the form of C header files.

The *rpcinfo* command can be used to display the list of currently active RPC server programs on a host.

### 4.10.2.2 MVS

MVS TCP/IP provides the same RPC support as VM TCP/IP.

### 4.10.2.3 OS/400

The RPC programming interface is included in the licensed program offering DCE Base Services/400 Version 3.

The RPC facility consists of an application development tool and a runtime library. When developing a DCE application, you simply define an RPC interface between the client application and the server application. DCE uses the DCE interface definition language (IDL) to define this interface. The language is similar to ANSI C definitions. The application development tool consists of an IDL compiler that compiles your interface definitions into portable C-language source code. This IDL-generated source code can be compiled with your application code using the ILE C compiler and linked to the DCE runtime library to form the distributed application.

To allow RPC to participate in an open distributed computing environment, the RPC interface must be uniquely identified. This is accomplished by giving the interface a universal unique identifier (UUID). A UUID is a hexadecimal number that contains information that makes it unique from all other UUIDs. The application development tool also includes a UUID generator that generates and automatically includes a UUID in the RPC interface description.

The runtime service implements the network protocols by which the client and server sides of an application communicate.

## 4.10.2.4 AIX/6000
Full client and server RPC functions are available in AIX/6000.

The following programming interfaces are available:

- RPCGEN protocol compiler.

- High layer interface - This interface is actually a method for using RPC routines, rather than a part of RPC proper. An example is *rnusers( )*.

- Middle layer interface - This interface is RPC proper. That is, the programmer only needs to make RPC calls, but need not consider details about sockets or other low-level implementation mechanisms. On this interface, RPC does not allow timeout specifications, choice of transport, or process control in case of errors. Nor does it support multiple types of call authentication. Example routines are *registerrpc( ),callrpc( )* and *svc_run( )*.

- Low layer interface - This interface allows the programmer greatest control but also requires more low-level coding efforts. This interface may be necessary if for example, the programmer needs to use TCP instead of UDP (used by the two higher layers). Example routines are *svctcp_create( ) and clnt_call( )*.

For details about the RPC programming interface for AIX, see the documentation available for each implementation and *AIX Distributed Environments*, GG24-3489.

## 4.10.2.5 AIX/ESA
Full RPC client and server functions are provided in the AIX/ESA environment.

## 4.10.2.6 OS/2
Full RPC client and server functions are provided in the OS/2 environment.

## 4.10.2.7 DOS
TCP/IP for DOS provides full RPC client functionality.

# 4.11  Network Computing System (NCS)

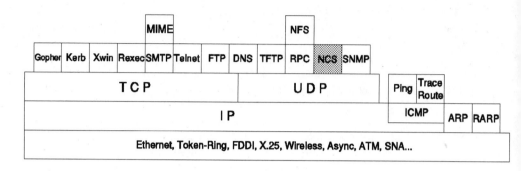

*Figure  4-47.*  *Network Computing System (NCS)*

The APOLLO Network Computing System (NCS) is an implementation of the Network
Computing Architecture developed to provide tools for designing, implementing and
supporting applications requiring distributed data and distributed computing. This is
achieved through implementation of NCS on top of the Remote Procedure Call interface,
which is different from Sun RPC.

The Network Computing Architecture is object-oriented. This allows programs to access
objects through interfaces no matter which machines they communicate with. These
types of programs have a simpler design and are less susceptible to hardware and
network changes.

An object is an entity managed by defined operations having a type specifying the class
or category. For example, a disk file is an object and it can be an ASCII type.

An interface is a set of operations that manipulate the objects.

The Network Computing Architecture uses an expanded concept called replicated
objects which are copies of an object that have the same identifier.  It can be weakly or
strongly consistent. Weakly consistent replicated objects can be accessed even if they are
not identical. Strongly consistent replicated objects can only be accessed when they are
identical. The use of one or the other depends on the performance, availability and
consistency required.

Distributed data and processing is achieved through the use of the following components:

1. The *Remote Procedure Call* (RPC) runtime library
2. The *Network Interface Definition Language* (NIDL) compiler
3. The *Location Broker*

The *Network Computing Kernel* consists of the Location Broker and the RPC runtime library, which provides runtime support for network computing. This kernel and the NIDL compiler support the development and implementation of distributed applications.

## 4.11.1.1 NCS RPC

The NCS RPC can use the Domain network communications protocols (DDS) and the DARPA Internet Protocols (UDP/IP). The selection is made by the destination address given so that a program can access a Domain and non-Domain entity.

The Berkeley socket concept is used in NCS RPC. It can listen to more than one socket identified by a socket address divided into address family (which defines the structure of the address), network address (host address) and port number (endpoint address).

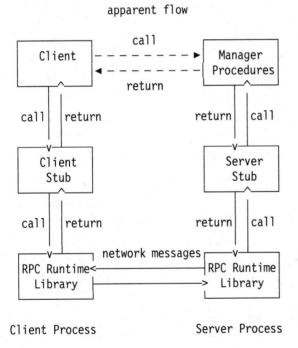

*Figure* **4-48.** *NCS (Components of the Network Computing System)*

The client procedure uses standard procedure calling conventions, but it is remotely executed by the server. The program that makes remote procedure calls to request operations is called an RPC client. It does not know how an interface is implemented and may not know the location of the server.

The process that receives the operation request packet from the RPC runtime library is the RPC server. It is responsible for sending the response with the results of the operation. A server can export an interface for more than one object.

The client process has three components: the client procedure that makes calls, the client stub and the RPC runtime library. The client stub is responsible for making use of the RPC runtime library to have the client procedure's calls executed.

The server process has three components: the manager procedures corresponding to the client application, the server stub corresponding to the client stub and the RPC runtime library. The server can be called a manager.

When the client requests an operation on a particular object through an RPC it must indicate the object on which the operation is to be performed and the server that exports the interface containing the operation. This information is passed by a handle, created and managed by several calls provided by NCS. The representation of the server in the handle is called binding. The client may or may not bind the handle by requesting an RPC with the following states:

- Unbound - no identification (RPC broadcasts to all hosts on the local network and accepts the first response)

- Bound-to-host - handle contains host identification without a specific server (an RPC is sent to the host and the Local Location Broker finds the right port)

- Bound-to-server - handle contains full identification (an RPC is sent to the specific server port).

The stubs are responsible for making the remote call as transparent as possible. They mediate between the client and the manager procedures, converting data for the use of RPC runtime routines.

The RPC runtime library transmits RPC packets containing routines, tables and data for supporting communication between the client and server stub. There are three types of calls:

- Client calls used to manipulate the handle and to send packets.
- Server calls used to create sockets, register interfaces and return object identification.
- Conversion calls used to determine the socket address for a specific host and return the host name and socket port number related to a socket address.

## 4.11.1.2 Network Interface Definition Language

The NIDL is a development language that completely defines the interface and each RPC's parameters. Two syntaxes can be used, one more comfortable for C programmers and the other for Pascal programmers.

The NIDL compiler translates the NIDL commands into executable stubs that will be linked with clients and servers. These stubs will be generated in C source code but are fully compatible with Pascal programs.

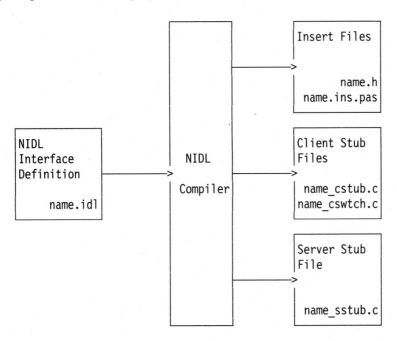

*Figure  4-49. NIDL Compiler.  Generated files.*

The NIDL Compiler generates two client stub files: name_cstub.c and name_cswtch.c. The second one is a switch file used to create replicated servers to provide access to a replicated object and ensure consistency. The client calls are sent to the client switch that contains the public procedures, leaving the client stub only with the private procedures.

The stub generated can have two major responsibilities:

- Copying and converting data - The simplest stubs have only this procedure of argument passing and data conversion. All stubs marshal and unmarshal values into and from the RPC packet. The client stub marshals the input parameters to send the packet to the server and unmarshals the output parameters from the reply packet. The server stub unmarshals the input parameters from the RPC packet sent from the client and sends them to the interface manager and marshals the output parameters to send them to the client. In addition each stub checks the data representation format indicated in the transmitted packet. Every system sends data in its native format and the stubs convert them to the receiver's representation. It's important to note that no stub sends data in a standard format so, if both systems use the same data representation, there is no need to convert data.

- Binding with a remote interface - NIDL manages the object and binding information in the following ways:

  - Explicit handle - the client explicitly passes the handle parameter in each operation which is passed to the server's manager routines

  - Implicit handle - the handle is a single global variable making the RPC look more like an ordinary procedure call but restricting it to a one-server system

  - Manual binding - the client makes all calls that create and manage the handle

  - Automatic binding - the client calls an auto-binding routine for each RPC and an auto-unbinding routine after the response, thus trading performance for convenience.

## 4.11.1.3 The Location Broker

The Location Broker is used by the client to request information about objects and interfaces. This information is registered in the Location Broker by the servers.

The Location Broker is composed of three components:

- Local Location Broker (LLB) - maintains information about objects and interfaces on the local host and provides it to remote or local application programs. It also provides the client with the LLB's forwarding facility, which eliminates the need for a client to know the specific port that a server uses.

- Global Location Broker (GLB) - maintains information about objects and interfaces throughout the network.

- Location Broker Client Agent - is a set of routines called by application programs to access LLB and GLB databases. The client may know the host on which the object is located and can directly interrogate the remote host's LLB; otherwise it would take the GLB route.

The GLB may have several replicas running to ensure the availability of the information. To ensure the consistency of the replicas' data all the manipulation is done by the Data Replication Manager (DRM), which propagates any change in the database. The DRM uses a replica list containing the location of every replica. Clients are allowed to do lockups and updates even in the propagation procedures, which gives weak consistency but high availability.

The Location Broker database has the following fields:

- Object UUID - object identifier
- Type UUID - type of the object identifier
- Interface UUID - interface of the object identifier
- Flags - indication of a global object
- Annotation - user defined
- Socket address length - socket address field length
- Socket address - location of the server

Here are some definitions:

- *UUID* stands for *Universal Unique IDentifier*, that is, a 128-bit value used for identification. No other object, type, or interface can use a UUID that is already assigned.
- *Object*: an entity that is manipulated by well-known operations. Disk files and printers are examples of objects. Objects are accessed through interfaces. Every object has a type.
- *Type*: a class of object. All objects of a specific type can be accessed through the same interface or interfaces.
- *Interface*: a set of operations. The Network Computing Architecture specifies a Network Interface Definition Language (NIDL) for defining interfaces.
- *NIDL*: a declarative language for the definitions of interfaces.
- *NIDL Compiler*: an NCS tool that converts an interface definition, written in NIDL, into several program modules, including source code for client and server stub.

# 4.11.2  Implementations

## 4.11.2.1  VM

The following list indicates the parts and versions of NCS that were ported to VM:

- NIDL Compiler 1.0
- Network Computing Kernel (NCK) 1.1

The IBM VM implementation of NCS differs from the Apollo Computer, Inc. implementation of NCS:

- The IBM VM implementation of NCS contains support for the Non-Replicated Global Location Broker Daemon (NRGLBD).
- It does not contain support for the Global Location Broker Daemon (GLBD).
- It does not contain support for the Data Replication Manager Administrative Tool (DRM_ADMIN).
- It does not support multitasking, forking, spanning a task, or Apollo's Concurrent Program Support (CPS).
- It only supports the Internet Protocol (IP).

- It fixed several EBCDIC-to-ASCII translation table errors as well as the IBM floating point and IEEE floating point translation errors which were present in the NCS V1.0.
- The NCS regular enum data type requires fullword (4 bytes) enumeration usage in the IBM C/370 Compiler.

The VM implementation of NCS consists of three virtual machines:

- NCS virtual machine, which has two minidisks:
  1. 191 minidisk: the files stored there should be accessible to anyone who wants to run NCS. This disk is a repository for the NCS executables, NCS IDL and header files, LIBNCK (RPC runtime library), sample programs.
  2. 195 minidisk: These files should be accessible only to qualified users who are acting as NCS database or network administrators. The NCS 195 disk contains the NCS executable LB_ADMIN. The LB_ADMIN function allows the user to add, delete, or update any record in the NCS Global Location Broker or Local Location Broker databases.
- NCSGLBD virtual machine, where the NCS Non-Replicated Global Location Broker daemon is run. It controls the Global Location Broker database, that is, it helps clients to locate servers on the network or internet. The NRGLBD should be running on this host only if neither GLBD or NRGLBD is running anywhere else in your network.
- NCSLLBD virtual machine, where the NCS Local Location Broker daemon (LLBD) is run. It manages the LLB database where information about local NCS-based servers are stored. The LLBD must be run on each host where NCS-based programs are run.

## 4.11.2.2 MVS

The same parts and versions of NCS were ported to MVS as in VM. Please refer to 4.11.2.1, "VM" on page 4-141.

The MVS implementation of NCS consists of two servers:

- NCSGLBD server, where the NCS Non-Replicated Global Location Broker daemon is run. It controls the Global Location Broker database. It also helps clients to locate servers on the network. The NRGLLD should be running on this host only if neither GLBD or NRGLBD is running anywhere else in your network.
- NCSLLBD server: where the NCS Local Location Broker daemon (LLBD) is run. It manages the LLB database where information about local NCS-based servers are stored. The LLBD must be run on each host where NCS-based programs are run.

  The runnidl, runcpp, uuid@gen and lb@admin commands are available. Please refer to *IBM TCP/IP Version 3 Release 1 for MVS: User's Guide* and *IBM TCP/IP Version 3 Release 1 for MVS: Programmer's Reference* for details.

### 4.11.2.3 OS/400

NCS is not implemented in TCP/IP on the OS/400 system.

### 4.11.2.4 AIX/ESA

*NCS for IBM AIX/ESA* is a port of Hewlett-Packard/Apollo's NCS Version 1.5.1 to the IBM AIX/ESA. For details, please refer to *Network Computing System for AIX/ESA Planning and Administration*.

### 4.11.2.5 AIX/6000

NCS with the Network Computing Kernel, runtime services and the NIDL compiler are supported in both AIX Versions.

The implementation includes the *Local Location Broker* (llbd daemon) and the *Non-replicated Global Location Broker* (nrglbd daemon). Both daemons are controlled by the SRC (System Resource Controller) and can be started by uncommenting the *#startsrc -s llbd* and *#startsrc -s nrglbd* lines in the **/etc/rc.ncs** file. For more details, please refer to *AIX Version 3.2 for RISC System/6000 Communication Concepts and Procedures* and *AIX Version 3.2 for RISC System/6000 General Programming Concepts*.

The *lb_admin*, *nidl* and *uuid_gen* commands are available. Please see the online InfoExplorer facility for details.

### 4.11.2.6 OS/2

NCS is not implemented in TCP/IP for OS/2.

### 4.11.2.7 DOS

NCS is not implemented in TCP/IP for DOS.

# 4.12 Network File System (NFS)

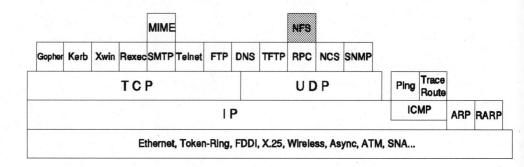

*Figure 4-50.* *Network File System (NFS)*

The SUN Microsystems Network File System (NFS) protocol enables machines to share file systems across a network. The NFS protocol is designed to be machine-, operating system-, and transport protocol-independent. This is achieved through implementation on top of Remote Procedure Call (see 4.10, "Remote Procedure Call (RPC)" on page 4-129). RPC establishes machine independence by using the External Data Representation convention.

SUN-NFS is a *proposed standard protocol.* Its status is *elective.* The current Sun-NFS specification can be found in *RFC 1094 - NFS: Network File System Protocol specification.* This RFC documents NFS Version 2. Although this RFC mentions an NFS Version 3, nobody has submitted a new RFC nor an Internet-Draft discussing a possible Version 3 specification.

## 4.12.1 Concept

NFS allows authorized users to access files located on remote systems as if they were local. Two protocols serve this purpose:

1. The *Mount* protocol to specify the remote host and file system to be accessed and where to locate them in the local file hierarchy.
2. The *NFS* protocol to do the actual file I/O to the remote file system.

Both Mount and NFS protocol are RPC applications (caller/server concept) and are *transported by UDP.*

## 4.12.1.1 Mount Protocol

The Mount protocol is an RPC-application shipped with NFS. It is program number 100005. The Mount protocol is transported by UDP. Mount is an RPC-server program and provides a total of six procedures:

| | |
|---|---|
| *NULL* | Does nothing, useful for server response testing. |
| *MOUNT* | Mount function, returns a file handle pointing to the directory. |
| *DUMP* | Returns the list of all mounted file systems. |
| *UMOUNT* | Removes a mount list entry. |
| *UNMTALL* | Removes all mount list entries for this client. |
| *EXPORT* | Returns information about the available file systems. |

The *MOUNT*-call returns a file handle to the directory. The file handle is a 32-byte field, which will be used subsequently by the client to access files. File handles are a fundamental part of NFS because each directory and file will be referenced through a handle. Some implementations will encrypt the handles for security reasons (for example, NFS on VM can optionally use the VM encryption programs to provide this).

The user interface to this RPC application is provided through the MOUNT command. The user issues a MOUNT command to locate the remote file system in his own file hierarchy.

For example, consider a VM NFS server. The concept of subdirectories (hierarchical file system) does not exist here; there are only minidisks (to be considered as one directory each). Now consider an AIX client (AIX does have a subdirectory file system). The client can access the user 191 VM minidisk as its local subdirectory /u/vm/first by issuing the MOUNT command:

```
MOUNT -o options
        host:user.191,ro,pass=password,record=type,names=action
        /u/vm/first
```

Where:

| | |
|---|---|
| *options* | System options such as message size. |
| *host* | The TCP/IP name of the remote host. |
| *user* | VM user ID. |
| *191* | Minidisk address. |
| *pass=* | Link password that will allow the NFS machine to access the minidisk. |
| *record=* | Specifies what translation processing is to be done on the CMS records: |
| | **binary** No processing performed. |
| | **text** Code conversion between EBCDIC (server) and ASCII (client). |
| | **nl** EBCDIC-to-ASCII translation, and new line characters are interpreted as CMS record boundaries. |
| *names=* | Specifies the handling of a file name: |

> ***fold*** file names supplied by the client are translated to uppercase.
> ***mixed*** file names are used as supplied by the client.
> If no name translation option is specified, case folding is performed and, in addition, client names that are not valid in CMS will be converted into valid CMS names.

The result is that the VM minidisk is now seen by the client machine as a local subdirectory:

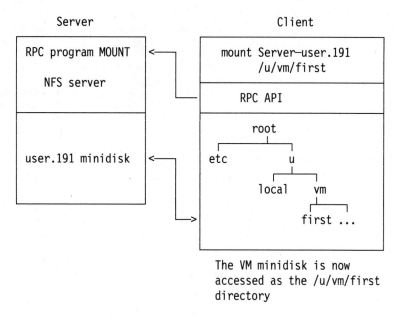

```
         Server                              Client
┌────────────────────────┐    ┌────────────────────────────────────┐
│ RPC program MOUNT    <──┼─┐  │    mount Server-user.191            │
│                        │ │  │         /u/vm/first                 │
│ NFS server             │ └──┼──────────────────────────────────── │
│                        │  ┌─┼───      RPC API                     │
├────────────────────────┤  │ │                                     │
│                        │  │ │              root                   │
│                        │  │ │               │                     │
│ user.191 minidisk    <─┼──┘ │     etc          u                  │
│                        │    │                  │                  │
│                        │    │              local    vm            │
│                        │  ┌─┼─>                      │            │
│                        │  │ │                    first ...         │
└────────────────────────┘    └────────────────────────────────────┘
```

The VM minidisk is now
accessed as the /u/vm/first
directory

***Figure 4-51. NFS Mount Command.*** The client *mounts* the VM minidisk user.191 as its local directory */u/vm/first*.

Obviously, the previous command:

```
MOUNT -o options host:user.191,ro,pass=password,record=type,names=action
/u/vm/first
```

has three parts:

1. -o options is the *client* part. It has to be understood by the NFS client only. This means, it depends on the client host and is documented in the client's documentation.
2. host:user.191,ro,....,names=action is the *server* part. The syntax depends on the server's file system (obviously, user.191 does not mean anything to an MVS NFS server). Refer to the documentation of the NFS server to know what parameters it will accept.

3. /u/vm/first is a *client* part and is called the *mount point*, that is, where the remote file system will be hooked on the local file system.

The *UMOUNT* command removes the remote file system from the local file hierarchy. Following the example above:

UMOUNT /u/vm/first

will remove the /u/vm/first directory.

## 4.12.1.2 NFS Protocol

NFS is the RPC application program providing file I/O functions to a remote host, once it has been requested through a MOUNT command. It has program number 100003 and sometimes uses IP port 2049. As this is not an officially assigned port and several versions of NFS (and mount) already exist, port numbers may change. It is advised to go to Portmap (port number 111) (see 4.10.1.4, "Portmap or Portmapper" on page 4-132) to obtain the port numbers for both Mount and NFS. The NFS protocol is transported by UDP.

The NFS program supports 18 procedures, providing for all basic I/O operations such as:

| | |
|---|---|
| *LOOKUP* | Searches for a file in the current directory and if found, returns a file handle pointing to it plus information on the file's attributes. |
| *READ and WRITE* | Basic read/write primitives to access the file. |
| *RENAME* | Renames a file. |
| *REMOVE* | Deletes a file. |
| *MKDIR and RMDIR* | Creation/deletion of subdirectories. |
| *GET and SET-ATTR* | Gets or sets file attributes. |

Other functions are also provided.

These correspond to most of the file I/O primitives used in the local operating system to access local files. In fact, once the remote directory is mounted, the local operating system just has to "re-route" the file I/O primitives to the remote host. This makes all file I/Os look alike, regardless of whether the file is located locally or remotely. The user can operate his normal commands and programs on both kinds of files; in other words, this *NFS protocol is completely transparent to the user.* See Figure 4-52 on page 4-148.

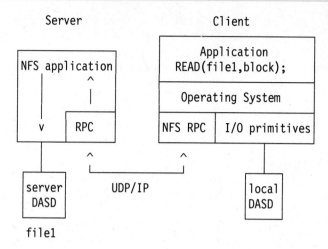

*Figure 4-52. NFS File I/O.* Intercepted at the operating system level, thereby making it transparent to the user.

### 4.12.1.3 NFS File System

NFS assumes a hierarchical file system (directories). Files are unstructured streams of uninterpreted bytes; that is, files are seen as a contiguous byte stream, without any record-level structure.

This is the kind of file system used by AIX and PC/DOS, so these environments will easily integrate an NFS-client extension in their own local file system. File systems used in VM and MVS lend themselves less readily to this kind of extension.

With NFS, all file operations are *synchronous*. This means that the file-operation call only returns when the server has completed all work for this operation. In case of a write request, the server will physically write the data to disk and if necessary, update any directory structure, before returning a response to the client. This ensures file integrity.

NFS also specifies that servers should be *stateless*. That is, a server does not need to maintain any extra information about any of its clients in order to function correctly. In case of a server failure, clients only have to retry a request until the server responds, without having to reiterate a mount operation.

## 4.12.2 Implementations

### 4.12.2.1 VM

TCP/IP for VM includes the NFS server function only. This means that other hosts running NFS will be able to access VM minidisks, but that the VM user is not able to access the remote hosts' file systems.

The VM NFS server uses UDP port number 2049. It also requires that the PORTMAP virtual machine be started.

The VM NFS server saves information about the file handles it distributes to clients in the file *VMNFS HISTORY*. This is done because the 32-byte file handle cannot hold all information needed to uniquely identify a CMS file. So, instead, each file handle is associated with a record of the history file. The *VMNFS HISTORY* will also record the CP LINK password the client sends when he wants to access a minidisk. Appropriate actions should be taken to ensure security of this file (on NFS 191 disk).

To prevent a client from manipulating the contents of an obtained file handle, provision is made for encryption of these file handles. The client must return this encrypted file handle for each file operation. The *NFSFHCIP ASSEMBLE* file is shipped with the product. It invokes a subroutine to encode or decode a file handle. As shipped, it will call the *Information Protection System Cryptographic Programs for VM/CMS*, program number 5796-PPK. This file should be modified to contain the cryptographic key needed for the encryption. By changing the assembly source, one may also call upon other cryptographic programs, or not use any encoding at all. The *VMNFS MODULE* will need to be rebuilt only if some form of encryption is used. See *IBM TCP/IP Version 2 Release 3 for VM: Planning and Customization* for more information on encryption and for other installation parameters.

Another security feature for the VM NFS implementation is the possibility to send the CP LINK password (sent by client to the server) separately from the MOUNT command, because all the information transmitted with the MOUNT command (passwords for example) are stored on the client. This is provided through the MOUNT -v or MOUNTPW commands.

If RACF is installed on your server, it can be used to secure the access to the minidisks. Please refer to *IBM TCP/IP Version 2 Release 3 for VM: Planning and Customization* for more details.

The VM NFS server uses, when possible, the multiple-block *BLOCKIO, a fast VM Control Program system service, to improve the write operations.

The SMSG command allows an authorized user to transmit commands to NFS while NFS is executing. For example, displaying a summary of its activity, detaching a mounted minidisk, writing internal trace table to disk, or refreshing a mounted minidisk.

The following shows a sample output from a query command.

```
SMSG VMNFS M QUERY
MSG FROM VMNFS   : M 200 ro  TCPMAINT.192
MSG FROM VMNFS   : M VM NFS server start time 02Apr91 13:12:21.
MSG FROM VMNFS   : M   2 RPC (0 duplicate XID),  4 SMSG, 4 *BLOCKIO
MSG FROM VMNFS   : M   0 null, 0 getattr, 0 setattr, 0 lookup, 0 read, 0 write
MSG FROM VMNFS   : M   0 create, 0 remove, 0 rename, 0 readdir, 1 statfs
MSG FROM VMNFS   : M   1 mount, 0 mountpw, 0 mountnull, 0 unmount, 0 unsupported
MSG FROM VMNFS   : M End of reply.
```

The SHOWEXP command is not supported. That is, you cannot display from a client the *export list* (the minidisks that can be mounted) of a VM NFS server.

An alternative NFS implementation for the VM/ESA environment is LAN File Services/ESA.

## 4.12.2.2 MVS

NFS in the MVS environment is delivered as part of Data Facility Systems Managed Storage/MVS (DFSMS/MVS). NFS in the MVS environment supports the server function only.

It provides access to data sets for users of workstations which support the NFS client function. NFS uses the MVS access methods to read, write, create or delete MVS data sets.

The NFS server reads or writes binary and text data. In a file that contains text, record boundaries are translated into line terminators. A file that contains binary data is stored in the MVS system and retrieved without text translation.

In order to get access to the NFS server, an NFS client will be required to submit a user ID and password. This security function is provided by PCNFSD. PCNFSD replaces the *mvslogin* and *mvslogout* commands which performed a similar function in earlier MVS NFS implementations.

Unlike VM, the SHOWEXP command is supported.

An alternative NFS implementation for the MVS/ESA environment is LAN File Services/ESA.

With LFS/ESA on MVS, an NFS client is able to access OpenEdition MVS Hierarchical File System (HFS) files on MVS.

## 4.12.2.3 OS/400

NFS for OS/400 is available by installing the TCP/IP File Server Support/400. This product allows other systems to access AS/400 system files (both Native Database and Shared Folder).

TCP/IP File Server Support/400 is a server only implementation of NFS.

TCP/IP File Server Support/400 supports NFS Protocol Version 2. TCP/IP File Server Support is designed to be compatible with clients running ONC/NFS Version 4.x.

NFS support (NFS/400) will be integrated into OS/400 in 1995. The new NFS support will provide both client and server capability and will be compatible with SUN Microsystems NFS.

## 4.12.2.4 AIX/6000

NFS on RISC System/6000 supports:

- Server and client functions
- Network Information Services (NIS)
- Network Lock Manager and Status Monitor
- Automounter support
- Diskless support (Sun diskless booting from RISC System/6000)
- User authentication provided via RPC's use of Data Encryption Standard (DES)
- XDR library routines
- Support for PC-NFS V4.0 (Sun System on PC)
- Support of Access Control Lists between AIX/6000 systems
- Remote mapped file support, which allows a RS/6000 NFS client to take advantage of the enhanced virtual memory management function of AIX/6000
- Kernel extension support, which allows users to install NFS without rebuilding the base AIX kernel
- System Management Interface Tool (SMIT) support designed to provide an easy-to-use menu/dialog user interface for NFS configuration and management
- System Resource Control (SRC) support designed to provide an easy-to-use and consistent way to start and stop the NFS daemons

Information about NFS on all AIX implementations has been collected in the publication: *AIX Distributed Environments*, GG24-3489.

## 4.12.2.5 AIX/ESA

*NFS for IBM AIX/ESA Version 2 Release 1* supports:

- Server and client functions
- Network information services (NIS)
- Network Lock Manager and Status Monitor
- XDR library routines

It is compliant with SUN NFS Version 2.

### 4.12.2.6 OS/2

TCP/IP for OS/2 includes the NFS client and server functions.

The client runs in the *NFSCTL* program. The following commands are shipped with the product:

- NFSC: to start the client NFSCTL.

- MOUNT: to mount a directory on an NFS server as a local drive. It takes advantage of PCNFSD if it is available on the UNIX server (this prevents you from having to remember your UIDs and GIDs on each of the UNIX machines to which you have access). If PCNFSD is not running, MOUNT will prompt you for a UID and GID (if you did not supply them on the command line). You can use different UIDs and GIDs for different servers.

- UMOUNT: to dismount previously mounted NFS drives.

- MVSLOGIN: to authenticate an NFS client's access to a data set on a specific MVS server.

- MVSLOGUT: to end the session with an MVS NFS server.

- QMOUNT: to query the characteristics of a drive.

- UNIX2OS2: to convert text files from the UNIX format (lines end in a *line-feed (LF)* character only) to OS/2 format (lines end in a *carriage-return line-feed (CRLF)* sequence).

- OS22UNIX: to convert from the OS/2 format to the UNIX format.

- NFSDIR: to quickly display a directory from an NFS mounted drive.

- SHOWEXP: to display a list of exported file systems for a specific host running an NFS server.

- LN: to create symbolic links on an NFS mounted drive.

The OS/2 NFS server is started by the NFSD command. It requires Portmap to be started via the PORTMAP command. It also requires the \ETC\EXPORTS file which is read only during NFSD startup. Please refer to *IBM TCP/IP Version 2.0 for OS/2: Installation and Administration* for more considerations about the \ETC\EXPORTS file.

PCNFSD support is provided in the OS/2 NFS Server.

## 4.12.2.7 DOS

TCP/IP for DOS includes the NFS client function only. Both native DOS and Microsoft Windows implementations are provided in a separately orderable kit.

The following commands are available:

- MOUNT: to mount a directory on an NFS server as a local drive. It takes advantage of PCNFSD if it is available on the UNIX server (this prevents you from having to remember your UIDs and GIDs on each of the UNIX machines on which you have access). If PCNFSD is not running, MOUNT will prompt you for a UID and GID (if you did not supply them on the command line).

- MVSLOGIN: to authenticate an NFS client's access to an MVS NFS server.

  **Note:** The MVS NFS server requires that uid and gid be set to -2. Before using the MOUNT or MVSLOGIN commands, either issue the following two commands or put them in the CONFIG.SYS file:

      set unix.uid=-2
      set unix.gid=-2

- MVSLOGUT: to end the session with an MVS NFS server.

- QMOUNT: to display a list of mounted drives.

- SHOMOUNT: to display the list of clients who currently have a directory mounted on an NFS server.

- SHOWEXP: to display the list of exported file systems available for mounting for a specific host running an NFS server (if supported by the server).

- UMOUNT: to dismount previously mounted drives.

- TODOS: to convert text files from the UNIX format (lines end in a *line-feed (LF)* character only) to DOS format (lines end in a *carriage-return line-feed (CR LF)* two-character sequence).

- TOUNIX: to convert from the DOS format to the UNIX format.

- NFSDOWN: to shut down and remove the DOSNFS TSR from memory.

- NFSPRINT: to allow spooling and printing files with NFS. Two servers participate in the print-spool services: the PCNFSD server, and the print server. These servers can run on the same machine, but this is not necessary.

- NFSSET: If the NFS server is a UNIX host, when a file is created in a mounted file system it has a *umask* assigned to it, which indicates the file permissions associated with it. By default, all files created on a mounted drive have a umask of 600, which means that the owner of these files has the ability to read and write to them, and no one else can access them. The NFSSET command allows you to change the umask (3-digit octal number that indicates how the user, the members of the user's group, and the other system users can access the file. The default is 600 (which means that the owner of the file has the ability to read and write to it, and no one else has access to them). The flash variable default is OFF (if set to ON the scroll light is flashed whenever a mounted file system is accessed).

- NFSPING: To check the status of an NFS server (different daemons can be *pinged* such as PCNFSD, the MOUNT daemon, and the NFS daemon).

- NFSSTAT: To display the status of NFS, including the umask and the current status of the flash variable.

Please refer to *IBM TCP/IP Version 2.1.1 for DOS: User's Guide* for more details about the NFS commands.

# 4.13 Kerberos Authentication and Authorization System

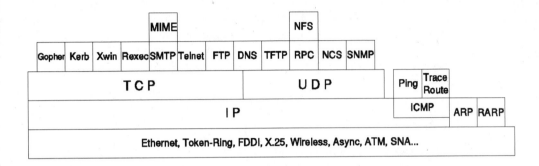

*Figure* *4-53. Kerberos Authentication and Authorization System*

According to *The Enlarged Devil's Dictionary (Ambrose Bierce)*, Kerberos is "the watchdog of Hades, whose duty it was to guard the entrance against whom or what does not clearly appear; Kerberos is known to have had three heads."

The Kerberos Authentication and Authorization System is an encryption-based security system that provides mutual authentication between the users and the servers in a network environment. The assumed goals for this system are:

- Authentication to prevent fraudulent requests/responses between users and servers that must be confidential and on groups of at least one user and one service.

- Authorization can be implemented independently from the authentication by each service that wants to provide its own authorization system. The authorization system can assume that the authentication of a user/client is reliable.

- Permits the implementation of an accounting system that is integrated, secure and reliable, with modular attachment and support for "chargebacks" or billing purposes.

The Kerberos system is mainly used for authentication purposes, but it also provides the flexibility to add authorization information.

The current versions of the Kerberos protocol are Versions 4 and 5. Version 4 is widely used and is the version most commonly implemented in commercial products. Version 5 is currently an Internet-Draft. It is based on Version 4 and incorporates a number of new features and improvements.

## 4.13.1 Assumptions

Kerberos assumes the following:

- The environment using this security system will include: public and private workstations that can be located in areas with minimal physical security; a campus network without link encryption that can be composed of dispersed local networks connected by backbones or gateways; centrally operated servers in locked rooms with moderate physical security and centrally operated servers with considerable physical security.

- Confidential data or high-risk operations such as a bank transaction may not be part of this environment without additional security, because once you have a workstation as a terminal you can emulate certain conditions and normal data will be flowing without any encryption protection.

- One of the cryptosystems used is the Data Encryption Standard (DES), which is available in the U.S. market but may not be exported without an official export license, so the Kerberos designers developed it to be modular and replaceable.

- Kerberos assumes a loosely synchronized clock in the whole system so the workstation has to have a synchronization tool like the Time server provided.

## 4.13.2 Naming

A *Principal Identifier* is the name that identifies a client or a service for the Kerberos system.

In Version 4, the identifier consists of three components:

- The *principal* name is unique for each client and service assigned by the Kerberos Manager.

- The *instance* name used for distinct authentication is an added label for clients and services which exist in several forms. For users, an instance can provide different identifiers for different privileges. For services, an instance usually specifies the host name of the machine that provides this service.

- The *realm* name used to allow independently administered Kerberos sites. The principal name and the instance are qualified by the realm to which they belong, and are unique only within that realm. The realm is commonly the domain name.

In Version 4, each of the three components has a limit of 39 characters long. Due to conventions, the period (.) is not an acceptable character.

In Version 5, the identifier consists of two parts only, the *realm* and the *remainder*, which is a sequence of however many components are needed to name the principal. Both the realm and each component of the remainder are defined as ASN.1 (Abstract Syntax Notation One, ISO standard 8824) *GeneralStrings*. This puts few restrictions on the characters available for principal identifiers.

## 4.13.3 Kerberos Authentication Process

In the Kerberos system, a client that wants to contact a server for its service, first has to ask for a *ticket* from a mutually trusted third party, the Kerberos Authentication Server (**KAS**). This ticket is obtained as a function where one of the components is a private key known only by the service and the Kerberos Authentication Server, so that the service can be confident that the information on the ticket originates from Kerberos. The client is known to the KAS as a principal name (**c**). The private key ($K_c$) is the authentication key known only to the user and the Kerberos Authentication Server (KAS).

In this chapter, the symbol {**X,Y**} indicates a message containing information (or data) X and Y. {**X,Y**}$K_z$ indicates that a message which contains the data X and Y, has been enciphered using the key $K_z$.

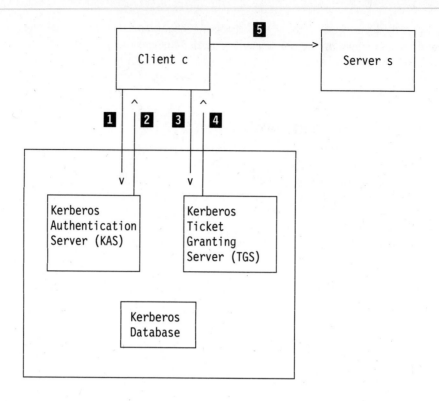

1 Client —> KAS: c, tgs, n
2 KAS —> Client: $\{K_{c,tgs}, n\}K_c$, $\{T_{c,tgs}\}K_{tgs}$
3 Client —> TGS: $\{A_c\}K_{c,tgs}$, $\{T_{c,tgs}\}K_{tgs}$, s, n
4 TGS —> Client: $\{K_{c,s}, n\}K_{c,tgs}$, $\{T_{c,s}\}K_s$
5 Client —> Server: $\{A_c n\}K_{c,s}$, $\{T_{c,s}\}K_s$

**In Kerberos Version 4:**

message 2 was: KAS —> Client: $\{K_{c,tgs}, n, \{T_{c,tgs}\}K_{tgs}\}K_c$
message 4 was: TGS —> Client: $\{K_{c,s}, n, \{T_{c,s}\}K_s\}K_{c,tgs}$

*Figure  4-54. Kerberos Authentication Scheme*

The authentication process consists of exchanging five messages (see Figure  4-54):

1 Client -> KAS

The client sends a message {c, tgs, n}, to the KAS, containing its identity (c), a nonce (a timestamp or other means to identify this request), and requests for a ticket for use with the ticket-granting server (TGS).

**2** KAS -> Client

The authentication server looks up the client name (c) and the service name (the ticket-granting server, tgs) in the Kerberos database, and obtains an encryption key for each ($K_c$ and $K_{tgs}$).

The KAS then forms a response to send back to the client. This response contains an initial ticket $T_{c,tgs}$, that grants the client access to the requested server (the ticket-granting server). $T_{c,tgs}$ contains $K_{c,tgs}$, c, tgs, nonce, lifetime and some other information. The KAS also generates a random encryption key $K_{c,tgs}$, called the session key. It then encrypts this ticket using the encryption key of the ticket-granting server ($K_{tgs}$). This produces what is called a *sealed ticket* $\{T_{c,tgs}\}K_{tgs}$. A message is then formed consisting of the sealed ticket and the TGS session key $K_{c,tgs}$.

**Note:** In Kerberos Version 4, the message is:

$$\{K_{c,tgs}, n, \{T_{c,tgs}\}K_{tgs}\}K_c$$

While in Kerberos Version 5, the message is of a simpler form:

$$\{K_{c,tgs}, n\}K_c, \{T_{c,tgs}\}K_{tgs}$$

This simplifies the (unnecessary) double encryption of the ticket.

**3** Client -> TGS

Upon receiving the message, the client decrypts it using its secret key $K_c$ which is only known to it and the KAS. It checks to see if the nonce (n) matches the specific request, and then caches the session key $K_{c,tgs}$ for future communications with the TGS.

The client then sends a message to the TGS. This message contains the initial ticket $\{T_{c,tgs}\}K_{tgs}$, the server name (s), a nonce, and a new authenticator $A_c$ containing a timestamp. $A_c$ is {c, nonce}. The message is:

$$\{A_c\}K_{c,tgs}, \{T_{c,tgs}\}K_{tgs}, s, n$$

**4** TGS -> Client

The ticket-granting server (TGS) receives the above message from the client (c), and first deciphers the sealed ticket using its TGS encryption key (this ticket was originally sealed by the Kerberos authentication server in step 2 using the same key). From the deciphered ticket, the TGS obtains the TGS-session-key. It uses this TGS-session-key to decipher the sealed authenticator (validity is checked by comparing the client name both in the ticket and in the authenticator, the TGS server name in the ticket, the network address that must be equal in the ticket, in the authenticator, and in the received message). Finally, it checks the current time in the authenticator to make certain the message is recent. *This requires that all the clients and servers maintain their clocks within some prescribed tolerance.* The TGS now looks up the server name from the message in the Kerberos database, and obtains the encryption key ($K_s$) for the specified service.

The TGS forms a new random session key $K_{c,s}$ for the benefit of the client (c) and the server (s), and then creates a new ticket $T_{c,s}$ containing:

$K_{c,s}$, n, nonce, lifetime,

It then assembles and sends a message to the client.

**Note:** In Kerberos Version 4, the message is:

$\{K_{c,s},n,\{T_{c,s}\}K_s\}K_{c,tgs}$

While in Kerberos Version 5, the message is of a simpler form:

$\{K_{c,s},n\}K_{c,tgs}, \{T_{c,s}\}K_s$

This simplifies the (unnecessary) double encryption of the ticket.

**5** Client -> Server

The client receives this message and deciphers it using the TGS-session-key that only it and the TGS share. From this message it obtains a new session key $K_{c,s}$ that it shares with the server(s) and a sealed ticket that it cannot decipher because it is enciphered using the server's secret key $K_s$.

The client builds an authenticator and seals it using the new session key $K_{c,s}$. At last, it sends a message containing the sealed ticket and the authenticator to the server (s) to request its service.

The server (s) receives this message and first deciphers the sealed ticket using its encryption key, which only it and KAS know. It then uses the new session key contained in the ticket to decipher the authenticator and does the same validation process that was described in step **4** .

Once the server has validated a client, an option exists for the client to validate the server. This prevents an intruder from impersonating the server. The client requires then that the server sends back a message containing the timestamp (from the client's authenticator, with one added to the timestamp value). This message is enciphered using the session key that was passed from the client to the server.

Let us summarize some of the central points in this scheme:

- In order for the workstation to use any end server, a ticket is required. All tickets, other than the first ticket (also called the *initial ticket*) are obtained from the TGS. The first ticket is special: it is a ticket for the TGS itself and is obtained from the Kerberos authentication server.

- Every ticket is associated with a session key that is assigned every time a ticket is allocated.

- Tickets are reusable. Every ticket has a lifetime, typically eight hours. After a ticket has expired, you have to identify yourself to Kerberos again, entering your login name and password.

- Unlike a ticket, which can be reused, a new authenticator is required every time the client initiates a new connection with a server. The authenticator carries a timestamp within it, and the authenticator expires a few minutes after it is issued (this is the reason why clocks must be synchronized between clients and servers).

- A server should maintain a history of previous client requests for which the timestamp in the authenticator is still valid. This way a server can reject duplicate requests that could arise from a stolen ticket and authenticator.

## 4.13.4  Kerberos Database Management

Kerberos needs a record for each user and service in its realm and each record keeps only the needed information as follows:

- Principal identifier (c,s)
- Private key for this principal ($K_c,K_s$)
- Date of expiration for this identity
- Date of the last modification in this record
- Identity of the principal who last modified this record (c,s)
- Maximum lifetime of tickets to be given to this principal (Lifetime)
- Attributes (unused)
- Implementation data (not visible externally)

The private key field is enciphered using a master key so that removing the database will not cause any problem as the master key is not in it.

The entity responsible for managing this database is the Kerberos Database Manager (KDBM). There is only one KDBM in a realm, but it is possible to have more than one Kerberos Key Distribution Server (KKDS), each one having a copy of the Kerberos database. This is done to improve availability and performance so that the user can choose one in a group of KKDSs to send its request to. The KKDS performs read-only operations, leaving the actualization to the KDBM, which copies the entire database a few times a day. This is done to simplify the operation using a Kerberos protected protocol. This protocol is basically a mutual authentication between KDBM and KKDS before a file transfer operation with checkpoints and checksum.

## 4.13.5  Kerberos Authorization Model

The Kerberos Authentication Model permits only the service to verify the identity of the requester but it gives no information on whether the requester can use the service or not. The Kerberos Authorization Model is based on the principle that each service knows the user so that each one can maintain its own authorization information. However, the Kerberos Authentication System could be extended by information and algorithms which could be used for authorization purposes. (This is made easier in Version 5. Please see the next section.) The Kerberos could then check if a user/client is allowed to use a certain service.

Obviously, both the client and the server applications must be able to handle the Kerberos authentication process. That is, both the client and the server must be *kerberized*.

## 4.13.6  Kerberos Version 5 Enhancements

Kerberos Version 5 has a number of enhancements over Version 4. Some of the important ones are:

- Use of encryption has been separated into distinct program modules which allows for supporting multiple encryption systems.

- Network addresses that appear in protocol messages are now tagged with a type and length field. This allows support of multiple network protocols.

- Message encoding is now described using the ASN.1 (Abstract Syntax Notation 1) syntax in accordance with ISO standards 8824 and 8825.

- The Kerberos Version 5 ticket has an expanded format to support new features (for example, the inter-realm cooperation).

- As mentioned in 4.13.2, "Naming" on page 4-156, the principal identifier naming has changed.

- Inter-realm support has been enhanced.

- Authorization and accounting information can now be encrypted and transmitted inside a ticket in the authorization data field. This facilitates the extension of the authentication scheme to include an authorization scheme as well.

- A binding is provided for the GSSAPI (Generic Security Service API) to the Kerberos Version 5 implementation.

For more detail on the difference between the two versions of Kerberos, please refer to [Kohl, Neuman and Ts'o]. For details on the GSSAPI, please refer to [Linn].

## 4.13.7 Implementations

### 4.13.7.1 VM

The Kerberos Version 4 is implemented in TCP/IP for VM using two virtual machines:

- *VMKERB*: This runs the Kerberos authentication server and the ticket-granting server. It must reside on the same host as the Kerberos database and it requires access to the C/370 runtime library. It uses UDP port 750 and TCP port 750.

- *ADM_SERV*: This runs the Kerberos database remote administration server. It must reside on the same host as the Kerberos database and it requires access to the C/370 runtime library. It uses UDP port 751 and TCP port 751.

The structure of the Kerberos database is shown in Figure 4-55.

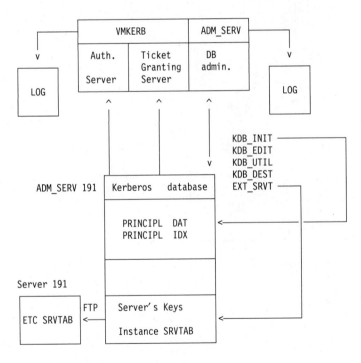

*Figure 4-55. Kerberos Database*

Where:

- *KDB_INIT*: is used to build and format the Kerberos database

- *KDB_UTIL*: is used to load or dump the Kerberos database
- *KDB_EDIT*: is used to register users to the Kerberos database
- *KDB_DEST*: is used to erase Kerberos database files
- *EXT_SRVT*: is used to generate key files for specified instance
- *PRINCIPL DAT* and *PRINCIPL IDX*: are files created using the KDB_INIT command.

The Kerberos database can be maintained remotely (please refer to *IBM TCP/IP Version 2 Release 3 for VM: User's Guide* for more information).

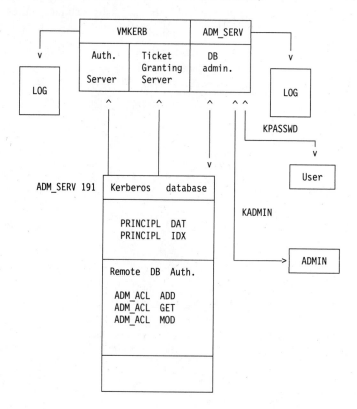

**Figure   4-56.** *Kerberos Database Remote Administration*

Where:

- *KADMIN*: is used to remotely add, retrieve, or modify a Kerberos user with instance as null.
- *ADM_ACL XXX*: are files used for authorization purposes.
- *KPASSWD*: this command is used by the user to change his password.

### 4.13.7.2 MVS

The MVS implementation is very similar to that of the VM. Please refer to 4.13.7.1, "VM" on page 4-163. The naming differences are: MVSKERB address space instead of VMKERB; ADM@SERV virtual machine instead of ADM_SERV virtual machine.

### 4.13.7.3 OS/2

TCP/IP for OS/2 does not implement Kerberos.

### 4.13.7.4 DOS

TCP/IP for DOS does not implement Kerberos.

# 4.14 Network Management

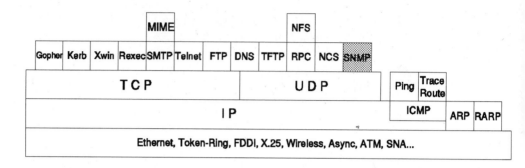

*Figure 4-57. Network Management*

With the growth in size and complexity of the TCP/IP-based internets the need for network management became very important. The current network management framework for TCP/IP-based internets consists of:

1. SMI (RFC 1155) - describes how managed objects contained in the MIB are defined. (It will be discussed in 4.14.2, "Structure and Identification of Management Information (SMI)" on page 4-168.)

2. MIB-II (RFC 1213) - describes the managed objects contained in the MIB. (It will be discussed in 4.14.3, "Management Information Base (MIB)" on page 4-169.)

3. SNMP (RFC 1098) - defines the protocol used to manage these objects. (It will be discussed in 4.14.4, "Simple Network Management Protocol (SNMP)" on page 4-174.)

The Internet Architecture Board issued an RFC detailing its recommendation, which adopted two different approaches:

- In the short term SNMP should be used.

  The IAB recommends that all IP and TCP implementations be network manageable. At the current time, this implies implementation of the Internet MIB-II (RFC 1213), and at least the recommended management protocol SNMP (RFC 1157).

  Note that the historic protocols SGMP (*Simple Gateway Monitoring Protocol*, RFC 1028) and MIB-I (RFC-1156) are not recommended for use.

- In the long term, use of the emerging OSI network management protocol (CMIP) would be investigated. This is known as *CMIP over TCP/IP* (CMOT). (It will be discussed in 4.14.5, "Common Management Information Protocol over TCP/IP (CMOT)" on page 4-177.)

Both the SNMP and CMOT use the same basic concepts in describing and defining management information called *Structure and Identification of Management Information* (SMI) described in RFC 1155 and *Management Information Base* (MIB) described in RFC 1156.

## 4.14.1 Standards

SNMP (*Simple Network Management Protocol*) is an Internet *standard protocol*. Its status is *recommended*. Its current specification can be found in *RFC 1157 - Simple Network Management Protocol (SNMP)*.

MIB-II is an Internet *standard protocol*. Its status is *recommended*. Its current specification can be found in *RFC 1213 - Management Information Base for Network Management of TCP/IP-based Internets: MIB-II*.

CMIP (*Common Management Information Protocol*) and CMIS (*Common Management Information Services*) are defined by the ISO/IEC 9595 and 9596 standards.

CMOT (*CMIS/CMIP Over TCP/IP*) is an Internet *proposed standard protocol*. Its status is *elective*. Its current specification can be found in *RFC 1189 - Common Management Information Services and Protocols for the Internet (CMOT) and (CMIP)*.

OIM-MIB-II is an Internet *proposed standard protocol*. Its status is *elective*. Its current specification can be found in *RFC 1214 - OSI Internet Management: Management Information Base*.

Other RFCs issued by IAB on this subject are:

- RFC 1052 - *IAB Recommendations for the Development of Internet Network Management Standards*.
- RFC 1085 - *ISO Presentation Services on Top of TCP/IP-based Internets*.
- RFC 1155 - *Structure and Identification of Management Information for TCP/IP-based Internets*.
- RFC 1156 - *Management Information Base for Network Management of TCP/IP-based Internets*.
- RFC 1215 - *Convention for Defining Traps for Use with the SNMP*.
- RFC 1227 - *SNMP MUX Protocol and MIB*.
- RFC 1228 - *SNMP-DPI: Simple Network Management Protocol Distributed Programming Interface*.
- RFC 1230 - *IEEE 802.4 Token Bus MIB*.

- RFC 1231 - *IEEE 802.5 Token-Ring MIB.*
- RFC 1239 - *Reassignment of Experimental MIBs to Standard MIBs.*
- RFC 1351 - *SNMP Administrative Model.*
- RFC 1352 - *SNMP Security Protocols.*

## 4.14.2 Structure and Identification of Management Information (SMI)

The SMI defines the rules for how managed objects are described and how management protocols may access these objects. The description of managed objects is made using a subset of the ASN.1 (Abstract Syntax Notation 1, ISO standard 8824), a data description language. The object type definition consists of five fields:

- Object: A textual name, termed the *object descriptor*, for the object type along with its corresponding *object identifier* defined below.

- Syntax: The abstract syntax for the object type. It can be a choice of SimpleSyntax (Integer, Octet String, Object Identifier, Null) or an ApplicationSyntax (NetworkAddress, Counter, Gauge, TimeTicks, Opaque) or other application-wide types (see RFC 1155 for more details).

- Definition: A textual description of the semantics of the object type.

- Access: One of read-only, read-write, write-only or not-accessible.

- Status: One of mandatory, optional, or obsolete.

As an example, we can have:

```
OBJECT
        sysDescr { system 1 }
Syntax  OCTET STRING
Definition This value should include the full name and version
        identification of the system's hardware type, software
        operating-system, and networking software. It is
        mandatory that this contain only printable ASCII
        characters.
Access  read-only.
Status  mandatory.
```

This example shows the definition of an object contained in the Management Information Base (MIB). Its name is sysDescr and it belongs to the system group (see 4.14.3, "Management Information Base (MIB)" on page 4-169).

A managed object not only has to be described but identified, too. This is done using the ASN.1 Object Identifier in the same way as a telephone number, reserving group of numbers to different locations. In the case of TCP/IP-based network management the number allocated was 1.3.6.1.2 and SMI uses it as the base for defining new objects.

The number 1.3.6.1.2 is obtained by joining groups of numbers with the following meaning:

- The first group defines the node administrator:
    - (1) for ISO
    - (2) for CCITT
    - (3) for the joint ISO-CCITT.
- The second group for the ISO node administrator defines (3) for use by other organizations.
- The third group defines (6) for the use of the U.S. Department of Defense (DoD).
- In the forth group the DoD has not indicated how it will manage its group so the Internet community assumed (1) for its own.
- The fifth group was approved by IAB to be:
    - (1) for the use of OSI directory in the Internet
    - (2) for objects identification for management purposes
    - (3) for objects identification for experimental purposes
    - (4) for objects identification for private use.

In the example the {system 1} beside the object name means that the object identifier is 1.3.6.1.2.1.1.1. It is the first object in the first group (system) in the Management Information Base (MIB).

## 4.14.3  Management Information Base (MIB)

### 4.14.3.1  Overview
The MIB defines the objects which may be managed for each layer in the TCP/IP protocol. There are two versions, MIB-I and MIB-II.  MIB-I was defined in RFC 1156, and is now classified as a *historic* protocol with a status of *not recommended*.

| Group | Objects for | # |
|---|---|---|
| system | basic system information | 7 |
| interfaces | network attachments | 23 |
| at | address translation | 3 |
| ip | internet protocol | 38 |
| icmp | internal control message protocol statistics | 26 |
| tcp | transmission control protocol | 19 |
| udp | user datagram protocol | 7 |
| egp | exterior gateway protocol | 18 |
| transmiss. | transmission. Media—specific | 0 |
| snmp | snmp applications entities | 30 |

#: Number of objects in the group

*Figure   4-58. Management Information Base II (MIB-II).   Group definition.*

Each managed node supports only those groups that are appropriate. For example, if there is no gateway, the EGP group need not be supported. But if a group is appropriate, all objects in that group must be supported.

The list of managed objects defined has been derived from those elements considered essential. This approach of taking only the essential objects is not restrictive, since the SMI provides extensibility mechanisms like definition of a new version of the MIB and definition of private or non-standard objects.

Below are some examples of objects in each group. The complete list is defined in RFC 1213.

- System Group

    - sysDescr - Full description of the system (version, HW, OS)
    - sysObjectID - Vendor's object identification
    - sysUpTime - Time since last re-initialization
    - sysContact - Name of contact person
    - sysServices - Services offered by device

- Interfaces Group

    - ifIndex - Interface number
    - ifDescr - Interface description
    - ifType - Interface type

- ifMtu - Size of the largest IP datagram
- ifAdminisStatus - Status of the interface
- ifLastChange - Time the interface entered in the current status
- ifINErrors - Number of inbound packets that contained errors
- ifOutDiscards - Number of outbound packets discarded

- Address Translation Group

  - atTable - Table of address translation
  - atEntry - Each entry containing one network address to physical address equivalence
  - atPhysAddress - The media-dependent physical address
  - atNetAddress - The network address corresponding to the media-dependent physical address

- IP Group

  - ipForwarding - Indication of whether this entity is an IP gateway
  - ipInHdrErrors - Number of input datagrams discarded due to errors in their IP headers
  - ipInAddrErrors - Number of input datagrams discarded due to errors in their IP address
  - ipInUnknownProtos - Number of input datagrams discarded due to unknown or unsupported protocol
  - ipReasmOKs - Number of IP datagrams successfully re-assembled
  - ipRouteMask - Subnet-mask for route

- ICMP Group

  - icmpInMsgs - Number of ICMP messages received
  - icmpInDestUnreachs - Number of ICMP destination-unreachable messages received
  - icmpInTimeExcds - Number of ICMP time-exceeded messages received
  - icmpInSrcQuenchs - Number of ICMP source-quench messages received
  - icmpOutErrors - Number of ICMP messages not sent due to problems within ICMP

- TCP Group

  - tcpRtoAlgorithm - Algorithm to determine the timeout for retransmitting unacknowledged octets
  - tcpMaxConn - Limit on the number of TCP connections the entity can support
  - tcpActiveOpens - Number of times TCP connections have made a direct transition to the SYN-SENT state from the CLOSED state
  - tcpInSegs - Number of segments received, including those received in error
  - tcpConnRemAddress - The remote IP address for this TCP connection
  - tcpInErrs - Number of segments discarded due to format error
  - tcpOutRsts - Number of resets generated

- UDP Group

  - udpInDatagrams - Number of UDP datagrams delivered to UDP users
  - udpNoPorts - Number of received UDP datagrams for which there was no application at the destination port
  - udpInErrors - Number of received UDP datagrams that could not be delivered for reasons other than the lack of an application at the destination port
  - udpOutDatagrams - Number of UDP datagrams sent from this entity

- EGP Group

  - egpInMsgs - Number of EGP messages received without error
  - egpInErrors - Number of EGP messages with errors
  - egpOutMsgs - Number of locally generated EGP messages
  - egpNeighAddr - The IP address of this entry's EGP neighbor
  - egpNeighState - The EGP state of the local system with respect to this entry's EGP neighbor

This is not the complete MIB definition but it is presented as an example of the objects defined in each group.

To illustrate this, the Interfaces Group contains two top-level objects: the number of interface attachments on the node (*ifNumber*) and a table containing information on those interfaces (*ifTable*). Each entry (*ifEntry*) in that table contains the objects for a particular interface. Among those, the interface type (*ifType*) is identified in the MIB tree using the ASN.1 notation by 1.3.6.1.2.1.2.2.1.3. and for a token-ring adapter the value of the corresponding variable would be 9, which means "iso88025-tokenRing" (see Figure 4-59 on page 4-173).

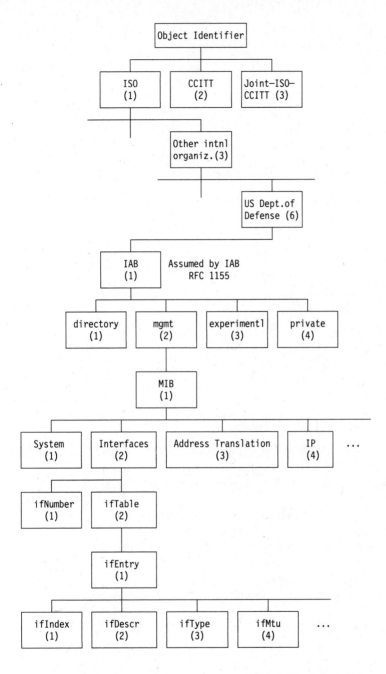

***Figure 4-59.*** ***Object Identifier.*** Allocation for TCP/IP-based Network.

### 4.14.3.2 IBM-Specific MIB Part

IBM has added the following objects in the MIB-II database:

```
* IBM SNMP agent DPI UDP port
DPI_port                1.3.6.1.4.1.2.2.1.1.    number        2

* IBM "ping" round-trip-time table
RTTaddr                 1.3.6.1.4.1.2.2.1.3.1.  internet      60
minRTT                  1.3.6.1.4.1.2.2.1.3.2.  number        60
maxRTT                  1.3.6.1.4.1.2.2.1.3.3.  number        60
aveRTT                  1.3.6.1.4.1.2.2.1.3.4.  number        60
RTTtries                1.3.6.1.4.1.2.2.1.3.5.  number        60
RTTresponses            1.3.6.1.4.1.2.2.1.3.6.  number        60
```

Where:

- *DPI_port* returns the port number between the agent and the subagent.

- *RTT* allows an SNMP manager to ping remote hosts. RTT stands for Round Trip Table.

  - RTTaddr: host address
  - minRTT: minimum round trip time
  - maxRTT: maximum round trip time
  - aveRTT: average round trip time
  - RTTtries: number of pings yet to be performed
  - RTTresponses: number of responses received

## 4.14.4 Simple Network Management Protocol (SNMP)

The SNMP added the improvement of many years of experience in SGMP and allowed it to work with the objects defined in the MIB with the representation defined in the SIM.

RFC 1157 defines the Network Management Station (NMS) as the one that executes network management applications (NMA) that monitor and control network elements (NE) such as hosts, gateways and terminal servers. These network elements use a management agent (MA) to perform the network management functions requested by the network management stations. The Simple Network Management Protocol (SNMP) is used to communicate management information between the network management stations and the agents in the network elements.

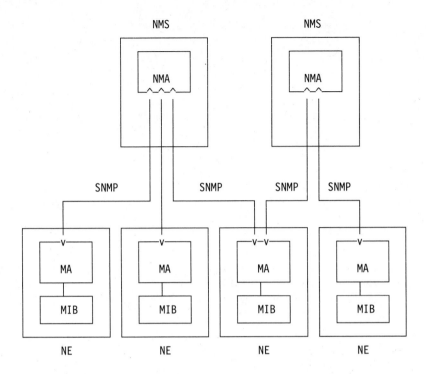

NMS — Network Management Station
NMA — Network Management Application
NE  — Network Element
MA  — Management Agent
MIB — Management Information Base

*Figure   4-60.  SNMP.*   Components of the Simple Network Management Protocol.

All the management agent functions are only alterations (set) or inspections (get) of variables limiting the number of essential management functions to two and avoiding more complex protocols. In the other direction, from NE to NMS, a limited number of unsolicited messages (traps) are used to inform about asynchronous events. In the same way, trying to preserve the simplicity, the interchange of information requires only an unreliable datagram service and every message is entirely and independently represented by a single transport datagram. This means also that the mechanisms of the SNMP are generally suitable for use with a wide variety of transport services. The RFC 1157 specifies the exchange of messages via the UDP protocol, but a wide variety of transport protocols can be used.

The entities residing at management stations and network elements that communicate with one another using the SNMP are termed SNMP application entities. The peer processes that implement it are the protocol entities. An SNMP agent with some arbitrary set of SNMP application entities is called an SNMP community, where each one is named by a string of octets that need to be unique only to the agent participating in the community.

A message in the SNMP protocol consists of a version identifier, an SNMP community name and a protocol data unit (PDU). It is mandatory that all implementations of the SNMP support the five PDUs:

- **GetRequest**: Retrieve the values of a specific object from the MIB
- **GetNextRequest**: Walk through portions of the MIB
- **SetRequest**: Alter the values of a specific object from the MIB
- **GetResponse**: Response from a GetRequest, a GetNextRequest and a SetRequest
- **Trap**: Capability of the network elements to generate events to network management stations such as agent initialization, agent restart and link failure. There are seven trap types defined in RFC 1157: coldStart, warmStart, linkDown, linkUp, authenticationFailure, egpNeighborLoss and enterpriseSpecific.

The formats of these messages are as follows:

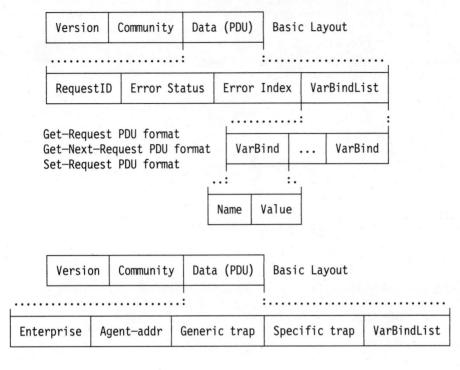

Figure 4-61. SNMP Message Format. Request, Set and Trap PDU format.

## 4.14.5 Common Management Information Protocol over TCP/IP (CMOT)

CMOT is the network management architecture that has been developed to move towards a closer relationship with the Open System Interconnection (OSI) network management standards named Common Management Information Protocol (CMIP). With these premises CMOT, as in the OSI model, can be divided into an organizational model, functional model and informational model.

In the organizational and informational models the same OSI concept is used in CMOT and in SNMP. The object identification is formed using the subtree related to the DoD with subdivisions in management, directory, experimental and private. All the management objects are defined in the Management Information Base (MIB) being represented by the Structure and Identification of Management Information (SMI), a subset of the ASN.1 (OSI Abstract Syntax Notation 1).

In the functional model CMOT adopted the OSI model that divides the management components into managers and agents. The agent collects information, performs commands and executes tests and the manager receives data, generates commands and sends instructions to the agents. This manager and agent are formed by a set of specific management information per communication layer named the Layer Management Entities (LME).

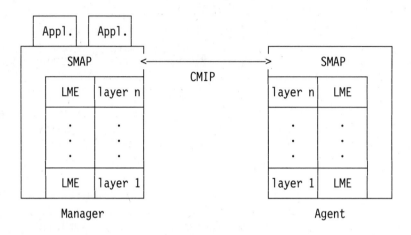

*Figure 4-62. CMOT.* Components of the CMIP over TCP/IP.

All the LME are coordinated by a System Management Application Process (SMAP) that can communicate between different systems over the Common Management Information Protocol (CMIP).

In the OSI approach the management can occur only over fully established connections between the managers and the agents. CMOT allows management information exchange over connectionless services (datagram). But to maintain the same service interface required by CMIP, called Common Management Information Services (CMIS), the CMOT architecture defined a new communication layer, the Lightweight Presentation Protocol (LPP). This layer has been defined to provide the presentation services required for the CMIP so that the entirely defined network management standards defined by OSI will fit in the TCP/IP CMOT architecture.

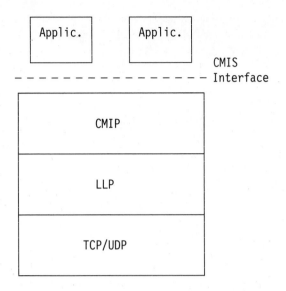

*Figure* *4-63.* *Lightweight Presentation Protocol (LPP)*

# 4.14.6 SNMP Distributed Programming Interface (SNMP DPI)

SNMP defines a protocol that permits operations on a collection of variables. This set of variables (MIB) and a core set of variables have previously been defined. However, the design of the MIB makes provision for extension of this core set. Unfortunately, conventional SNMP agent implementations provide no means for an end user to make new variables available. The SNMP DPI addresses this issue by providing a light-weight mechanism that permits end users to dynamically add, delete, or replace management variables in the local MIB without requiring recompilation of the SNMP agent. This is achieved by writing the so-called subagent that communicates with the agent via the SNMP DPI. It is described by G. Carpenter and B. Wijnen (T.J. Watson Research Center, IBM Corp.) in RFC 1228.

The SNMP DPI allows a process to register the existence of a MIB variable with the SNMP agent. When requests for the variable are received by the SNMP agent, it will pass the query on to the process acting as a subagent. This subagent then returns an appropriate answer to the SNMP agent. The SNMP agent eventually packages an SNMP response packet and sends the answer back to the remote network management station that initiated the request. None of the remote network management stations have any knowledge that the SNMP agent calls on other processes to obtain an answer.

Communication between the SNMP agent and its clients (subagents) takes place over a stream connection. This is typically a TCP connection, but other stream-oriented transport mechanisms can be used (as an example, the VM SNMP agent allows DPI connections over IUCV).

The SNMP Agent DPI can:

- Create and delete subtrees in the MIB
- Create a register request packet for the subagent to inform the SNMP agent
- Create response packet for the subagent to answer the SNMP agent's request
- Create a TRAP request packet.

The following figure shows the flow between an SNMP agent and a subagent.

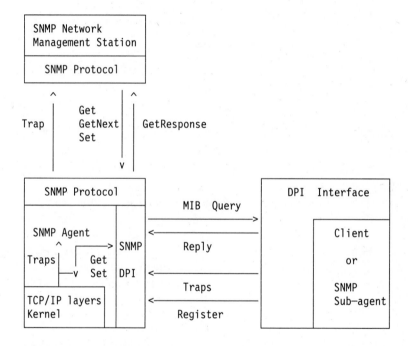

*Figure 4-64. SNMP DPI Overview*

- The SNMP agent communicates with the SNMP manager via the SNMP protocol.
- The SNMP agent communicates with the TCP/IP layers and kernel (OS) in an implementation-dependent manner. It potentially implements the standard MIB view in this way.

- An SNMP subagent, running as a separate process (potentially even on another machine), can register objects with the SNMP agent (`Register`).
- The SNMP agent will decode SNMP packets. If such a packet contains a Get/GetNext or Set request for an object registered by the subagent, it will send the request to the subagent via the corresponding query packet (`MIB query`).
- The SNMP sub-agent send responses back via a RESPONSE packet (`Reply`).
- The SNMP agent then encodes the reply into an SNMP packet and sends it back to the requesting SNMP manager.
- If the subagent wants to report an important state change, it sends a Trap packet to the SNMP agent, which will encode it into an SNMP trap and send it to the manager(s).

## 4.14.7  Simple Network Management Protocol Version 2 (SNMPv2)

The framework of version 2 of the Simple Network Management Protocol (SNMPv2) was published in April 1993 and consists of 12 RFCs including the first, RFC 1441, which is an introduction.  In August 1993 all 12 RFCs became a proposed standard with the status elective.

This framework consists of the following disciplines:

- Structure of Management Information (SMI)

  Definition of the OSI ASN.1 subset for creating MIB modules.  Description in RFC 1442.
- Textual conventions

  Definition of the initial set of textual conventions available to all MIB modules. Description in RFC 1443.
- Protocol operations

  Definition of protocol operations with respect to the sending and receiving of PDUs. Description in RFC 1448.
- Transport mappings

  Definition of mapping SNMPv2 onto an initial set of transport domains because it may be used over a variety of protocol suites.  The mapping onto UDP is the preferred mapping.  The RFC also defines OSI, AppleTalk, IPX etc.  Description in RFC 1449.
- Protocol instrumentation

  Definition of the MIB and Manager-to-Manager MIB for SNMPv2.  Description in RFCs 1450 and 1451.
- Administrative framework

  Definition of the SNMPv2 Party, Security Protocols and the Party MIB.  Description in RFCs 1445, 1446 and 1447.

- Conformance statements

  Definition of the notation *compliance* or *capability* of agents. Description in RFC 1444.

The following sections describe the major differences and improvements from SNMPv1 to SNMPv2.

### 4.14.7.1  SNMPv2 Entity

An SNMPv2 entity is an actual process which performs network management operations by generating and/or responding to SNMPv2 protocol messages by using the SNMPv2 protocol operations. All possible operations of an Entity can be restricted to a subset of all possible operations that belong to a particular administratively defined Party. Please refer to 4.14.7.2, "SNMPv2 Party" below. An SNMPv2 Entity could be member of multiple SNMPv2 Parties. The following local databases are maintained by an SNMPv2 Entity:

- One database for all Parties known by the SNMPv2 Entity which could be:
    - Operation realized locally
    - Operation realized by proxy interactions with remote Parties or devices
    - Operation realized by other SNMPv2 Entities
- Another database that represents all managed object resources which are known to that SNMPv2 entity.
- And at least a database that represents an access control policy that defines the access privileges accorded to known SNMPv2 parties

An SNMPv2 Entity can act as an SNMPv2 agent or manager.

### 4.14.7.2  SNMPv2 Party

An SNMPv2 party is a conceptual, virtual execution environment whose operation is restricted, for security or other purposes, to an administratively defined subset of all possible operations of a particular SNMPv2 entity. Please refer to 4.14.7.1, "SNMPv2 Entity" above. Architecturally, each SNMPv2 party comprises:

- A single, unique party identity
- A logical network location at which the party executes, characterized by a transport protocol domain and transport addressing information
- A single authentication protocol and associated parameters by which all protocol messages originated by the party are authenticated as to origin and integrity
- A single privacy protocol and associated parameters by which all protocol messages received by the party are protected from disclosure

## 4.14.7.3 GetBulkRequest

The GetBulkRequest is defined in RFC 1448 and is thus part of the protocol operations. A GetBulkRequest is generated and transmitted as a request of an SNMPv2 application. The purpose of the GetBulkRequest is to request the transfer of a potentially large amount of data, including, but not limited to, the efficient and rapid retrieval of large tables. The GetBulkRequest is more efficient than the GetNextRequest in case of retrieval of large MIB object tables. The syntax of the GetBulkRequest is:

```
GetBulkRequest [ non-repeaters = N, max-repetitions = M ]
                ( RequestedObjectName1,
                  RequestedObjectName2,
                  RequestedObjectName3 )
```

Where:

*RequestedObjectName1, 2, 3*

> MIB object identifier like sysUpTime etc. The objects are in a lexicographically ordered list. Each object identifier has a binding to at least one variable. For example, the object identifier *ipNetToMediaPhysAddress* has a variable binding for each IP address in the ARP table and the content is the associated MAC address.

*N*

> Specifies the non-repeaters value, which means that you request only the contents, of the variable next to the object specified in your request, of the first N objects named between the parentheses. This is the same function as provided by the GetNextRequest.

*M*

> Specifies the max-repetitions value, which means that you request from the remaining (number of requested objects - N) objects the contents of the M variables next to your object specified in the request. Similar to an iterated GetNextRequest but transmitted in only one request.

With the GetBulkRequest you can efficiently get the contents of only the next variable or the next M variables in only one request.

Assume the following ARP table in a host which runs an SNMPv2 agent:

| Interface-Number | Network-Address | Physical-Address | Type |
|---|---|---|---|
| 1 | 10.0.0.51 | 00:00:10:01:23:45 | static |
| 1 | 9.2.3.4 | 00:00:10:54:32:10 | dynamic |
| 2 | 10.0.0.15 | 00:00:10:98:76:54 | dynamic |

An SNMPv2 manager sends the following request to retrieve the sysUpTime and the complete ARP table:

```
GetBulkRequest [ non-repeaters = 1, max-repetitions = 2 ]
                ( sysUpTime,
                  ipNetToMediaPhysAddress,
                  ipNetToMediaType )
```

The SNMPv2 entity acting in an agent role responds with a Response-PDU:

```
Response (( sysUpTime.0 =  "123456" ),
          ( ipNetToMediaPhysAddress.1.9.2.3.4 =
                                     "000010543210" ),
          ( ipNetToMediaType.1.9.2.3.4 =  "dynamic" ),
          ( ipNetToMediaPhysAddress.1.10.0.0.51 =
                                     "000010012345" ),
          ( ipNetToMediaType.1.10.0.0.51 =  "static" ))
```

The SNMPv2 entity acting in a manager role continues with:

```
GetBulkRequest [ non-repeaters = 1, max-repetitions = 2 ]
                ( sysUpTime,
                  ipNetToMediaPhysAddress.1.10.0.0.51,
                  ipNetToMediaType.1.10.0.0.51 )
```

The SNMPv2 entity acting in an agent role responds with:

```
Response (( sysUpTime.0 =  "123466" ),
          ( ipNetToMediaPhysAddress.2.10.0.0.15 =
                                     ·"000010987654" ),
          ( ipNetToMediaType.2.10.0.0.15 =
                                        "dynamic" ),
          ( ipNetToMediaNetAddress.1.9.2.3.4 =
                                        "9.2.3.4" ),
          ( ipRoutingDiscards.0 =  "2" ))
```

This response signals the end of the table to the SNMPv2 entity acting in a manager role. With the GetNextRequest you would have needed four requests to retrieve the same information. If you had set the *max-repetition* value of the GetBulkRequest to three, in this example, you would have needed only one request.

### 4.14.7.4 InformRequest

An InformRequest is generated and transmitted as a request from an application in an SNMPv2 manager entity that wishes to notify another application, acting also in an SNMPv2 manager entity, of information in the MIB view[10] of a party local to the sending application. The packet is used as an indicative assertion to the manager of another party about information accessible to the originating party (manager-to-manager communication across party boundaries). The first two variables in the variable binding

---

[10] A MIB view is a subset of the set of all instances of all object types defined according to SMI.

list of an InformRequest are sysUpTime.0 and snmpEventID.i[11] respectively. Other
variables may follow.

## 4.14.8 MIB for SNMPv2

This MIB defines managed objects which describe the behavior of the SNMPv2 entity.

**Note:** This is not a replacement of the MIB-II.

Following are some object definitions to get an idea of the contents:

```
snmpORLastChange OBJECT-TYPE
    SYNTAX      TimeStamp
    MAX-ACCESS  read-only
    STATUS      current
    DESCRIPTION
            "The value of sysUpTime at the time of the most
            recent change in state or value of any instance of
            snmpORID."

warmStart NOTIFICATION-TYPE
    STATUS  current
    DESCRIPTION
            "A warmStart trap signifies that the SNMPv2
            entity, acting in an agent role, is reinitializing
            itself such that its configuration is unaltered."
```

## 4.14.9 Party MIB

The party MIB defines managed objects which correspond to the properties associated
with an SNMPv2 party. An example of some MIB objects:

```
partyIdentity OBJECT-TYPE
    SYNTAX      Party
    MAX-ACCESS  not-accessible
    STATUS      current
    DESCRIPTION
            "A party identifier uniquely identifying a
            particular SNMPv2 party."

partyAuthProtocol OBJECT-TYPE
    SYNTAX      OBJECT IDENTIFIER
    MAX-ACCESS  read-create
```

---

[11] snmpEventID.i is an SNMPv2 manager-to-manager MIB object which shows the authoritative identification
of an event.

```
STATUS       current
DESCRIPTION
        "The authentication protocol by which all messages
        generated by the party are authenticated as to
        origin and integrity.  The value noAuth signifies
        that messages generated by the party are not
        authenticated.

        Once an instance of this object is created, its
        value can not be changed."
```

### 4.14.9.1 Manager-to-Manager MIB

The purpose of this MIB is to provide the means for coordination between multiple management stations. That is, the means by which the controlling and monitoring functions of network management can be distributed amongst multiple management stations in a large network. Specifically, this MIB provides the means for one management station to request management services from another management station. Therefore, an SNMPv2 entity can act in a dual role; when providing management information to another manager the entity acts as an agent, and when requesting information, it acts as a manager. The manager-to-manager MIB consists of the following three tables:

- Alarms

- Events

- Notifications

Each alarm is a specific condition detected through the periodic, at a configured sampling interval, monitoring of the value of a specific management information variable. An example of an alarm condition is when the monitored variable falls outside a configured range. Each alarm condition triggers an event and each event can cause (one or more) notifications to be reported to other management stations using the InformRequest frame.

## 4.14.10  Single Authentication and Privacy Protocol

The authentication protocol provides a mechanism by which SNMPv2 management communications, transmitted by a party, may be reliably identified as having originated from that party.

The privacy protocol provides a mechanism by which SNMPv2 management communications, transmitted to a party, are protected from disclosure.

Principal threats against which the SNMPv2 security protocol provides protection are:

- Modification of information

- Masquerade

- Message stream modification

- Disclosure

The following security services provide protection against the above threats:

- Data integrity

  Provided by the MD5 message digest algorithm. A 128-bit digest is calculated over the designated portion of a SNMPv2 message and included as part of the message sent to the recipient.

- Data origin authentication

  Provided by prefixing each message with a secret value shared by the originator of that message and its intended recipient before digesting.

- Message delay or replay

  Provided by including a timestamp value in each message.

- Data confidentiality

  Provided by the symmetric privacy protocol which encrypts an appropriate portion of the message according to a secret key known only to the originator and recipient of the message. This protocol is used in conjunction with the symmetric encryption algorithm, in the cipher block chaining mode, which is part of the Data Encryption Standard (DES). The designated portion of an SNMPv2 message is encrypted and included as part of the message sent to the recipient.

## 4.14.11 The New Administrative Model

It is the purpose of the Administrative Model for SNMPv2, to define how the administrative framework is applied to realize effective network management in a variety of configurations and environments.

The model entails the use of distinct identities for peers that exchange SNMPv2 messages. Thus, it represents a departure from the community-based administrative model of the original SNMPv1. By unambiguously identifying the source and intended recipient of each SNMPv2 message, this new strategy improves upon the historical community scheme both by supporting a more convenient access control model and allowing for effective use of asymmetric (public key) security protocols in the future. Please refer to Figure 4-65 on page 4-188 for the new message format.

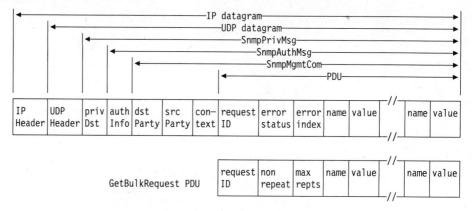

*Figure* **4-65.** *SNMP Version 2 Message Format*

PDU    Includes one of the following Protocol Data Units:

- GetRequest
- GetNextRequest
- Response
- SetRequest
- InformRequest
- SNMPv2-Trap

The GetBulkRequest has a different PDU format as shown above. Please also refer to 4.14.7.3, "GetBulkRequest" on page 4-183.

**Note:** The SNMP-Trap now has the same format as all the other requests.

*SnmpMgmtCom (SNMP Management Communication)*
    Adds the source party ID (srcParty), the destination party ID (dstParty) and the context to the PDU. The context specifies the SNMPv2 context containing the management information referenced by the communication.

*SnmpAuthMsg*
    This field is used as authentication information from the authentication protocol used by that party. The SnmpAuthMsg is serialized according to ASN.1 BER[12] and can then be encrypted.

*SnmpPrivMsg SNMP Private Message*
    An SNMPv2 Private Message is an SNMPv2 authenticated management communication that is (possibly) protected from disclosure. A private destination (privDst) is added to address the destination party.

---

[12] ASN.1 BER specifies the Basic Encoding Rules according to ISO 8825 which are used in OSI Abstract Syntax Notation one.

The message is then encapsulated in a normal UDP/IP datagram and sent to the destination across the network.

For further information please refer to the above mentioned RFCs.

# 4.14.12 Implementations

**Note:** The implementations described below only refer to the SNMP version 1.

## 4.14.12.1 VM and MVS

The TCP/IP for VM and MVS products provide both an SNMP client and an SNMP agent. They support the following MIB-II groups: system, interfaces, address translation, ip, icmp, tcp, udp and the IBM 3172 Enterprise Specific. Although no Exterior Gateway Protocol (EGP) is currently available under MVS or VM, you can query, from a VM or MVS manager, an agent that supports EGP. Of course a VM or an MVS agent will not be able to create EGP traps. The TCP/IP for VM and MVS products do not support the Set-Request PDU.

The traps generated by the SNMP agent (VM or MVS) are:

- COLD_START: signifies that the agent is reinitializing itself.
- AUTHENTICATION_FAILURE: signifies that an invalid community name has been provided from a manager within a GET PDU, for example.
- LINK_UP: signifies that the sending protocol entity recognizes that one of its communication links represented in the agent's configuration has come up.
- LINK_DOWN: signifies that the sending protocol entity recognizes a failure in one of its communication links represented in the agent's configuration.

The SNMP Agent DPI is also implemented under VM and MVS. This DPI allows external processes to generate SNMP traps.

The SNMP agent is provided within the SNMPD (*Simple Network Management Daemon*) Virtual Machine (VM) or Address Space (MVS).

The SNMP manager function requires that both NetView and the SNMPQE (*Simple Network Management Query Engine*) be up and running.

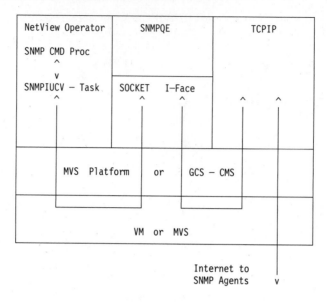

**Figure 4-66.** *Overview of NetView SNMP Support*

A description of the operation of the interface between TCP/IP and SNMP/NetView follows:

1. NetView operator or CLIST issues an SNMP command.

2. SNMP command is validated by SNMP Command Processor.

3. SNMP Command Processor passes the request to SNMPIUCV task.

4. SNMPIUCV task passes the request to SNMP Query Engine (SNMPQE).

5. SNMP Query Engine validates and encodes the request in ASN.1 and SNMP PDU (using the *tcpip*.MIB@DESC.DATA MVS data set or the MIB_DESC DATA VM file) and sends it to SNMP agent (variables must always be in ASN.1 notation when they are sent to an SNMP agent).

6. SNMP Query Engine receives a response from the SNMP agent.

7. SNMP Query Engine decodes the response and sends it to the NetView SNMPIUCV task.

8. SNMPIUCV task sends the response as a multi-line message to the requesting operator or authorized receiver.

To avoid unnecessary network traffic, each variable described in the customizable file, "MIB_DESC DATA" in VM or "*tcpip*.MIB@DESC.DATA" in MVS, has a *Time To Live (TTL)* value assigned. This specifies the number of seconds that the variable *lives* in the

Query Engine's internal cache. The value is obtained from the cache if multiple requests for the same variable are issued within the TTL period.

IBM 3172 support:

IBM TCP/IP supports *SNMP GET* and *SNMP GETNEXT* operations to request and retrieve the IBM 3172 enterprise-specific MIB variables. These requests will only be answered by those IBM 3172 devices connected to the MVS host's TCP/IP and whose *DEVICE* definition in the PROFILE.TCPIP data set includes the keyword NETMAN. Following is an example of such a definition:

```
DEVICE LCS1 LCS cuu NETMAN
LINK TR1 IBMTR 0 LCS1
LINK EN1 ETHERNET 1 LCS1
```

Please refer to *IBM TCP/IP Version 2 Release 3 for VM: Planning and Customization* and *IBM TCP/IP Version 3 Release 1 for MVS: Customization and Administration Guide* for details.

The SNMP starter set from TCP/IP for MVS provides NetView operators with the tool to manage the TCP/IP network. NetView commands can be entered from the SNMP main panel and standard PF key definitions used in the other NetView components are used within SNMP CLISTs.

Full documentation of the starter set is in member SNMPREXX in *tcpip.v3r1*.SEZAINST. The full screen panels require NetView Version 1 Release 3 (they are written in REXX).

The following screen output shows a sample MVS NetView session to another MVS host named **mvs20** using the community name **ITSC**:

```
snmp get mvs20 itsc sysdescr
SNM040I SNMP Request 1001 from LI Returned the following response:
SNM042I Variable name: 1.3.6.1.2.1.1.1.0
SNM043I Variable value type: 9
SNM044I Variable value: IBM , MVS TCP/IP V2R2
SNM049I SNMP Request 1001 End of response

snmpgrp mvs20 itsc sys
===================================================
    SYSTEM Group for MVS20
Descr:     IBM , MVS TCP/IP V2R2
ObjectId: 1.3.6.1.4.1.2.2.1.2.4
UpTime:    0 days/0 hours/34 minutes/6 seconds
Contact:   LADY LESIA OR SIR PHILIPPE
Name:      MVS20.ITSC.RALEIGH.IBM.COM
Location: COMPUTER ROOM BLDG 657
Services: 76
===================================================
```

The remote PING is implemented in TCP/IP for MVS. With this an SNMP monitor can send a remote PING via an SNMP GET request to the MVS TCP/IP SNMP agent. When the SNMP agent receives this SNMP GET request, it issues a PING command to the specified host and returns the round-trip time value as reply to the SNMP GET request.

### 4.14.12.2 AIX/ESA

AIX/ESA supports the SNMP agent functions and a limited set of client (manager) functions.

Its *SNMP* client (manager) provides the following functions:

- *snmpi* and *snmpt* support "primitive management station" functions.

Its SNMP agent provides the following functions:

- *snmpd* starts the SNMP agent. It does not currently support the SNMP set request. It supports an SNMP SMUX API based on RFC 1227. snmpd generates three types of Traps: *coldStart*, *linkDown* and *authenticationFailure*.

    The file */etc/snmpd.defs* stores the MIB-II variables.

For details, please refer to *AIX/ESA Network Application Programmer's Guide Version 2 Release 1, AIX/ESA System and Network Administrator's Reference Version 2 Release 1* and *AIX/ESA Network and Communications Administrator's Guide Version 2 Release 1.*

### 4.14.12.3 OS/400

The SNMP agent support provided in the OS/400 consists of three parts:

- SNMP agent

  The OS/400 SNMP agent provides configuration, performance, and problem management data concerning TCP/IP to an SNMP manager.

  Management Information Bases supported include:

  - MIB-II
  - Transmission Groups
  - APPN
  - Private

- SNMP framework

  The SNMP framework provides support for SNMP applications on the AS/400 system.

  The OS/400 SNMP framework supports:

  - Management applications that access SNMP management data throughout the network
  - SNMP sub-agent support, which provides the ability to dynamically add sub-agents that can supply additional management data

- TCP/IP protocol support

### 4.14.12.4 AIX/6000

AIX/6000 supports both the SNMP client and agent functions.

Its *SNMP* client (manager) provides the following functions:

- *snmpinfo* (same as *snmp_get*, *snmp_next* and *snmp_set*) supports the SNMP get, get-next and set requests. It obtains its objects descriptions of the MIB-II variables (described by RFC 1213) from the */etc/mib.defs* file.

- *IBM NetView for AIX V3*

  IBM NetView for AIX V3 provides a comprehensive network management solution for heterogeneous multivendor devices and open networks requiring SNMP. It facilitates network management in a multivendor TCP/IP network, provides management of TCP/IP devices that include Simple Network Management Protocol (SNMP) agents, and monitors IP-addressable devices.

  NetView for AIX features a graphical, object-oriented user interface built on background OSF/MOTIF, which allows the network to be displayed on top of meaningful pictures, such as maps, buildings, or devices. It also uses dynamic network discovery to maintain a current view of the network topography.

There is a variety of applications available based on NetView for AIX to provide a centralized management of a multivendor, heterogeneous network environment. Following is a brief description of these applications:

- IBM AIX LAN Management Utilities/6000

  There are LMU/6000 agents available for the following platforms: OS/2 LAN servers, Novell NetWare servers, OS/2, DOS Windows, DOS and Apple MacIntosh. Management access to all these clients is provided via the proxy agent LMU/2 because they are not directly SNMP accessible.

- IBM AIX Trouble Ticket/6000

  Trouble Ticket/6000 provides an integrated set of applications that includes functions such as trouble ticketing, systems inventory, and notifications. This unified set of applications enables pro-active management of the day-to-day problems encountered in the network environment.

- ATM Campus Manager for AIX

  ATMC Manager for AIX provides an automatic topology which is fully integrated in the NetView for AIX topology database. Therefore it is possible to navigate from the NetView for AIX IP map to the ATM topology map using the protocol switching function.

- Intelligent Hub Manager for AIX

  Hub Manager for AIX is a program which facilitates management of local area networks (LANs) built with IBM intelligent hubs. It offers MOTIF-based realistic resizable hub views with easy-to-identify and color-coded icons. Hub Manager for AIX provides an autotopology function which is integrated in the NetView for AIX topology database. Therefore it is possible to navigate from the NetView for AIX IP map to the hubs topology map using the protocol switching function.

- AIX Router and Bridge Manager/6000

  The IBM AIX Router and Bridge Manager/6000 (RandB Manager/6000) is an SNMP management application for managing router bridges. RandB Manager/6000's includes support for the IBM 6611 Network Processor, the IBM 2210 Nways Multiprotocol Router, the router blade in the IBM 8250 and 8260 Intelligent Switching Hub and selected models of other vendors' routers. Support also includes bridges which have SNMP agents such as the IBM 8229 LAN Bridge and IBM RouteXpander/2.                    In addition, there are unique features for management of Advanced Peer-to-Peer Networking topologies and Data Link Switching (DLSw) topologies provided.

- AIX Systems Network Architecture Manager/6000

  IBM AIX Systems Network Architecture Manager/6000 provides visibility and management of Systems Network Architecture (SNA) subarea resources. NetView Version 2 Release 3 or later on an MVS or VM platform is required.

- LAN Network Manager for AIX

  The LNM for AIX program in conjunction with agents provides views of a logical topology of the LAN, which allows you to correlate different protocol views with the underlying physical topology.

- AIX NetView Service Point

  AIX NetView Service Point provides the NetView/370 interface for NetView for AIX in order to exchange network management information.

- Systems Monitor for AIX

  Systems Monitor for AIX provides user-configurable systems management of LAN nodes and segments. Also provided is a fault and performance management, including automation capabilities from managed nodes rather than from a central NetView for AIX. It is designed to complement NetView for AIX by offloading polling tasks from the network management platform to the managed systems, while maintaining the centralized management control for both network and systems management at the management platform.

For more details on these please refer to *NetView for AIX Version 3 Release 1 Concepts* or to the related product publications.

The SNMP agent of AIX/6000 provides the following functions:

- *snmpd* starts the SNMP agent. It supports the following groups of MIBs: system, interface, address translation, ip, icmp, tcp, udp, egp, transmission and snmp. It also supports an SNMP API, which allows external processes to display/save traps, build SNMP request packets and SNMP get, next and save commands. For details, please refer to *AIX Version 3.2 for RISC System/6000 General Programming Concepts*. snmpd generates four types of Traps: *coldStart*, *linkUp*, *linkDown* and *authenticationFailure*. The *gated* daemon generates an *egpNeighborLoss* TRAP whenever it puts an Exterior Gateway Protocol (EGP) neighbor into the down state.

  The files /etc/mib.defs and /etc/mib_desc store the MIB-II variables used by various programs. New MIB objects can be added by using the mosy command. Please refer to the *AIX Version 3.2 for RISC System/6000 General Programming Concepts* for more details.

The following screen output shows a sample session from an AIX/6000 host named rs60002 to another AIX/6000 host and an MVS host, using the community name ITSC:

```
<rs60002>:# snmp_get rs60003 ITSC sysDescr
1.3.6.1.2.1.1.1.0 = IBM RISC System/6000
Machine Type: 0x0010 Processor id: 000105681000
The Base Operating System AIX version: 03.02.0000.0000
TCPIP Applications version: 03.02.0000.0000

<rs60002:/># snmpinfo -m get -h mvs20 -c ITSC -v sysContact
sysContact.0 = "LADY LESIA OR SIR PHILIPPE"
```

### 4.14.12.5 OS/2

TCP/IP for OS/2 provides both an SNMP client and an SNMP agent.

Its SNMP client (manager) provides the following functions:

- *SNMPGRP* can retrieve values from the following groups of MIBs: system, interfaces, address translation, ip, icmp, tcp and udp.

- *SNMP* can retrieve values from a single MIB. It does not support the SetRequest PDU.

- *SNMPTRAP* is an OS/2 PM application which receives and displays unsolicited notification of traps from SNMP agents. If the window is minimized, the icon shown is black. It turns red when a trap is received.

- *SNMPREQD* verifies incoming responses with outstanding requests. It must be started before any SNMP client commands.

Its SNMP agent provides the following functions:

- *SNMPD* starts the SNMP agent. It supports the following groups of MIBs: system, interface, address translation, ip, icmp, tcp and udp. It also supports the SNMP agent DPI, which allows external processes to generate SNMP Traps. For details, please refer to &os2pr.. SNMPD generates three types of Traps: *coldStart*, *authenticationFailure* and *enterpriseSpecific*.

  The file *MIB2.TBL* in your ETC subdirectory stores the MIB-II variables. It can be customized for your network environment. New MIB objects can be added as needed. Please refer to *IBM TCP/IP Version 2.0 for OS/2: User's Guide* for more details.

The following screen output shows a sample session from an OS/2 host to another OS/2 host named ps2fred using the community name ITSC:

```
[C:\]snmpgrp ps2fred ITSC sys
SYSTEM group
Descr  OS/2 SNMP AGENT version 1.2
ObjectId  1.3.6.1.4.1.2.2.1.2.2
UpTime  788974
Contact  Sir Fred
Name  ps2fred
Location  room BB117, Green Road, Raleigh
Services  76

[C:\]snmp get ps2fred ITSC sysdescr
Value of sysdescr is OS/2 SNMP AGENT version 1.2
[C:\]snmp next ps2fred ITSC sysdescr
Value of sysObjectID is 1.3.6.1.4.1.2.2.1.2.2
```

NetView for OS/2 delivers a comprehensive SNMP platform for management of systems and heterogeneous multivendor networks. This support allows NetView for OS/2 to manage any device having an SNMP agent.

NetView for OS/2 includes agents for management of OS/2, OS/2 LAN Server and OS/2 LAN Requester.

NetView for OS/2 V2.1 will include agents for OS/2 Communications Manager V1.1, and IBM DB2/2 V1.1.

### 4.14.12.6 DOS

TCP/IP for DOS Version 2.1.1 supports the SNMP agent function. It supports MIB-II data collection as well as provides unsolicited notifications of significant events to a SNMP monitor.

NetView for Windows is a new low-end SNMP management platform. This product provides fault, configuration and performance management capabilities for hubs, bridges, routers and switches. It also includes trouble ticketing, Telnet capabilities, TCP/IP communications, an integrated object-oriented database, and can operate in both the Ethernet and token-ring environments.

## 4.15  NetBIOS Services Protocol

NetBIOS Services Protocol is a *standard protocol*. Its status is *elective*.

A relevant application protocol is described in RFCs 1001 and 1002. They describe the standard to implement the IBM NetBIOS services (as described in *IBM Technical*

*Reference PC Network*) on top of the TCP and UDP protocol layers. Remember that many of today's IBM token-ring applications use the NetBIOS services to communicate over the IBM Token-Ring Network. Examples are the OS/2 LAN Server and the DOS LAN Requester. Among the OEM applications which use NetBIOS services is Lotus Notes.

All of today's NetBIOS applications run on PCs and PS/2s. Implementation of NetBIOS on TCP/IP would bring the power of mini and large computers to the PC user. A typical application would be to use large systems as file servers.

## 4.15.1 Implementations

### 4.15.1.1 OS/2

This section gives an overview of the functions of the NetBIOS Kit of TCP/IP V2.0 for OS/2, also known as TCP/NetBIOS.

TCP/NetBIOS enables NetBIOS applications running on OS/2 workstations with IBM TCP/IP to communicate, over a TCP/IP network, with other OS/2 workstations with TCP/IP and TCP/NetBIOS, or other vendor platforms running equivalent RFC 1001 and RFC 1002 compliant TCP/IP support. TCP/NetBIOS does not communicate with native NetBIOS nodes, but users who presently have native NetBIOS networks can operate TCP/NetBIOS networks concurrently on the same local area network. The two NetBIOS networks will be independent and will not communicate with each other.

TCP/NetBIOS is compatible with both IBM's NetBIOS and Microsoft's NetBIOS specifications.

TCP/NetBIOS can be used with any adapter supported by TCP/IP V2.0 for OS/2. It replaces the NetBIOS support provided with the OS/2 Communications Manager. NetBIOS application programs remain unchanged, but will now communicate over TCP/IP instead of directly over a LAN. TCP/NetBIOS is a TCP/IP application but application programs that interface with TCP/NetBIOS for communications are not TCP/IP applications because they do not interface directly with TCP/IP.

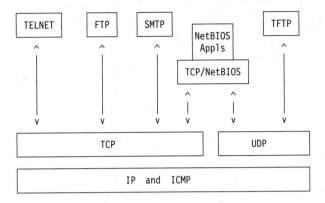

*Figure*   *4-67.* *TCP/IP and NetBIOS*

Two levels of OS/2 interfaces exist for the NetBIOS. An application program can use a Dynamic Link Routine interface, or a Device Driver interface. An application program may use either type of OS/2 interface, but cannot use both interfaces at the same time if it wishes to be considered as a single application. Resources provided to and resources obtained from one of the OS/2 interfaces cannot be used at the other OS/2 interfaces. In order for an application program to use a Device Driver interface, the application program itself must be a device driver or have a device driver as one of its components. The application program device driver must be set up to support communication between device drivers. In doing this, the application program device driver can be called by the NetBIOS for the posting of events.

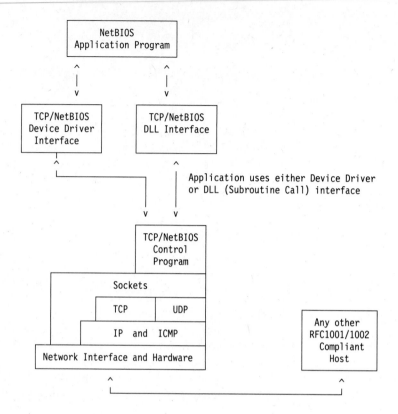

*Figure* *4-68.* *NetBIOS Kit of TCP/IP V2.0 for OS/2*

NetBIOS provides four kinds of services:

1. Name management services.

   It provides support for:

   - Name registration:

     Verifies that a NetBIOS name is not already being used on the network. The registration process starts with a broadcast, asking the network whether anyone is using the name. A node using the name will answer the broadcast. If no answer is received from the broadcast, NetBIOS can register the name.
   - Name defense:

     Makes sure that once a name is registered, no other node uses the name. The NetBIOS program will respond to a broadcast from another node to prevent the name from being used by the other node.
   - Name search:

     Finds the network address of a node known by a NetBIOS name only. The network address is usually obtained via a broadcast procedure.

2. Session services.

   A session is a connection-oriented service used for reliable data transfer. It has three phases:

   - Session establishment:

     It is during this phase that the IP address and TCP port of the called name are determined, and a TCP connection is established with the remote party.
   - Steady state:

     Once the connection (session) is established, simple "Send" and "Receive" verbs are provided for data transfer.
   - Session close:

     The session is closed whenever either a party (in the session) closes the session or it is determined that one of the parties has gone down.

3. Datagram services.

   Connectionless services are available through the use of monocast, multicast and broadcast messages. They are used to support low-overhead communications with minimal error checking. NetBIOS datagrams are carried within UDP packets.

4. Miscellaneous services.

   They are used to handle unusual situations such as errors.

Both session and datagram services use the logical network names to address recipients.

The RFCs define three modes of operations:

1. *Broadcast* or *B-node*:

   This mode uses broadcast to identify the target node and then establish point-to-point communications between B-nodes. This is the most commonly implemented mode. This covers TCP/IP implemented in environments which support broadcast, particularly Ethernet.

2. *Point-to-Point* or *P-node*:

   This mode requires the use of a *NetBIOS Name Server* and a *NetBIOS Datagram Distribution Server*. These servers are complex and difficult to implement. P-nodes operate in an environment where there are no broadcasts, only point-to-point connections.

3. *Mixed mode* or *M-node*:

   M-nodes are the same as P-nodes but with the ability to perform broadcasts.

TCP/NetBIOS supports the B-node class of implementation with some P-node extensions.

The RFCs cover naming conventions:

- Conversion algorithms for mapping names are required because NetBIOS addresses are 16-alphanumeric-character names, but TCP/IP addresses are 32 bits long. The NetBIOS names are also not directly compatible with the TCP/IP domain names because they can contain blanks.

- The RFCs define an additional name field: the *scope*.

  The scope limits the range of a NetBIOS name in order to avoid conflicts in a large network. The NetBIOS name *SCOPE* is hidden from the casual user. For example a name JOE in a headquarter network could be internally *JOE.HEQ* and another JOE in the laboratory could be *JOE.LAB*, where *HEQ* and *LAB* are scope names. The users only need to use the name JOE. The two JOEs cannot communicate because they are in different scopes.

TCP/NetBIOS provides the basic NetBIOS services required for B-nodes and provides some P-node extensions. This allows TCP/NetBIOS to operate through routers and to use TCP/IP domain name servers. The extensions do not alter the protocol as seen by a B-node. The extensions are implemented by two additional files (the *BROADCAST* file and the *NAME* file) and the use of the *Domain Scope String*.

- *BROADCAST* file:

  This file is loaded at startup. It contains a list of remote TCP/IP addresses, which the user wants to have included in a broadcast. The addresses are in other networks or subnetworks and can only be reached via routers. This file is needed to extend broadcasts across the router boundaries into other networks because normal broadcasts are limited to a single network. The TCP/IP address can be in dotted decimal format (9.3.124.5) or in domain name format (joe.raleigh.ibm.com). In the latter, a TCP/IP domain name server or a host table will be used to find the 32-bit TCP/IP address.

- *NAME* file:

  This file is accessed at each search. New users can be added without restarting TCP/NetBIOS. This file contains a cross reference of NetBIOS names to TCP/IP addresses. The TCP/IP address can be in dotted decimal format (9.3.124.5) or in domain name format (joe.raleigh.ibm.com). In the latter, a TCP/IP domain name server or a host table will be used to find the 32-bit TCP/IP address. The nodes in this file will be contacted in point-to-point mode and will *not* be included in broadcasts. Typically, this file can be used to access a server whose TCP/IP address is known.

- *Domain Scope String*:

  Because of the possibility of operating NetBIOS over a very large and dispersed TCP/IP network, and because NetBIOS names are to be unique, the RFCs specify an expanded form of NetBIOS name. This addition is called the NetBIOS name scope, because it has the effect of limiting the scope of a NetBIOS name. This surname is hidden from the casual user. The idea is that two RFC-compliant NetBIOS nodes can communicate only if they have the same NetBIOS name scope. For example, a NetBIOS name ERNIE may have a scope HQ. The name transmitted on the network will contain both parts of the name, as ERNIE.HQ.

When an application requests NetBIOS to locate a host, that is, to find the TCP/IP address of the NetBIOS name, it uses three algorithms:

1. The first is a NetBIOS broadcast. It will look for the node using both the TCP/IP broadcast address, which will result in a broadcast to the local nodes, and the addresses found in the *BROADCAST* file. The node that has the requested name will send a positive response to the originating host. When a positive response is received, communication can begin. If the broadcast is unsuccessful, then the next algorithm will be invoked.
2. The second is the use of the *NAME*. The NetBIOS name is matched against the name file. If a match is found, TCP/NetBIOS will use the corresponding TCP/IP address to communicate directly with the remote host. If the name is not found, then the next algorithm will be invoked.
3. The third is the use of the *Domain Scope String*. TCP/IP NetBIOS will encode the NetBIOS name into the domain name format and query the TCP/IP name server or the host table.

Finally, if a match is still not found, the program generates an error message.

**OS/2 LAN Server V4.0:**  An alternative implementation of RFCs 1001 and 1002 is provided in the TCPBEUI component of OS/2 LAN Server V4.0.  TCP/IP communications is basically provided in the MPTS support included in LAN Server. This, together with TCPBEUI, provides an implementation of RFC 1001/1002 which is similar to that described earlier for TCP/IP V2.0 for OS/2.  Both LAN Server and LAN Requester are able to use this support.  Performance is generally better using TCPBEUI than it is using the TCP/NetBIOS support described earlier.

### 4.15.1.2 DOS

TCP/IP V2.1.1 for DOS offers, as a separately orderable kit, an implementation of TCP/NetBIOS which is similar in terms of function to the OS/2 implementation described in the previous section.

### 4.15.1.3 AIX/6000

NetBIOS and IPX support for AIX is provided by the product AIX NetBIOS and IPX Support/6000.  The product includes industry standard communications protocol support for NetBIOS (NetBEUI), IPX/SPX and RFC 1001/1002. With this you have additional network application programming interfaces to allow you seamless access to existing systems.

# 4.16  Line Printer Daemon

The Line Printer Daemon protocol is an *informational protocol*. Its status is *limited use*. The current specification is in RFC 1179.  Note that this RFC does not specify an Internet standard.  However, the function has been part of UNIX systems for a long time (in *uucp*).

## 4.16.1  Implementations

### 4.16.1.1  VM

The LPR client and server functions are supported by VM TCP/IP.

The server runs in the *LPSERVE* virtual machine and allows you to print on local (VM printer or punch), remote (for example, a printer attached to an OS/2 workstation and managed by an LPR server) or RSCS printers. The RSCS printers can be connected to the RSCS subsystem in the same system as the *LPSERVE* virtual machine or to a remote RSCS. In the latter, the remote host does not need to have TCP/IP installed, but the two VM systems must be connected via RSCS.

Using the LPR server function on a VM system, it is possible to submit a job on an MVS system, if the VM and MVS system are connected. Once again, the MVS system does not need TCP/IP. MVS will send the job output back to the *LPSERVE* VM user ID (this can be overridden with the /*ROUTE PUNCH VM.USER and /*ROUTE PRINT VM.USER parameters where VM is the node ID of the VM system and USER is the user ID that will receive the output). It is not possible to route the output back to the originating workstation.

### 4.16.1.2  MVS

Both the LPR (client) and LPD (server) functions are supported by MVS TCP/IP.

The LPD (server) runs in a separate address space in your MVS system.  It listens on TCP port 515. The printers supported can be locally attached, NJE network-attached or remotely attached to another TCP/IP LPD server.

The following LPR (client) user commands are available:

- LPRSET: to set your default TCP/IP printer

- LPR: to print a file on a remote printer

- LPQ: to list the printer queue on a printer

- LPRM: to remove a job from the printer queue on a host

Please refer to *IBM TCP/IP Version 3 Release 1 for MVS: User's Guide* for more details.

**Network Print Facility (NPF):** The Network Print Facility allows users to send print output to LPD print servers on the TCP/IP network. JES2 and JES3 output and VTAM SNA character stream (SCS or LU type 1) and 3270 data stream output (LU types 0 and 3) may be printed on the TCP/IP network printers.

**Note:** The NPF feature has to be ordered separately. There is no extra charge.

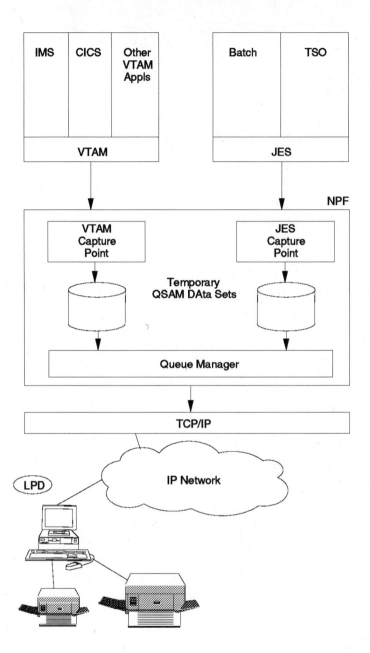

*Figure* *4-69.* *NPF Overview*

Please refer to *IBM TCP/IP Version 3 Release 1 for MVS: Network Print Facility* for more details.

### 4.16.1.3 OS/400

The LPR client and LPD server functions are supported by OS/400.

### 4.16.1.4 AIX/6000

The print server application consists of:

- A client back-end program called *LPRBE* which sends the file to be printed to a specified print-server host and to a specified print queue.

- The server application *lpd* (also called the *lpd daemon* in UNIX terminology). The server will accept print requests only from foreign hosts listed in its control file */etc/hosts.lpd*. This is further limited to the foreign hosts listed in the /etc/hosts.equiv. It also implements spooling/queuing for the jobs to be printed, provides for separator and banner pages, etc.

The print server function uses TCP/IP port number 515. Each print request consists of three parts:

- Control file: contains name(s) of data file(s) to be printed, together with information about the print job, such as the information that should go on the title page.
- Data file(s) to be printed.
- Temporary file used to create the print job.

The print client opens the printer port 515 on the remote host, and then sends lines of text to the server, first the control file, followed by the data file(s).

**AIX Print Services Facility/6000:**   This product implements the IBM Advanced Function Printing (AFP) capabilities to the RISC System/6000.

You can move data, manage resources, and provide connectivity to AIX, UNIX, MVS, VM, OS/2, OS/400 and DOS environments by using TCP/IP and Network File System (NFS) protocols. With the lpr command you can submit print jobs from the afore-mentioned environments. The use of networked resources allows you to maintain print resources on the system where they were created and attach them with NFS to the PSF/6000 server with the NFS mount command. For example, overlays created with Overlay Generation Language/370 (OGL/370) and existing in MVS system libraries or on a Conversational Monitoring System (CMS) minidisk can be remotely mounted for use with PSF/6000 by means of NFS.

For more detail please refer to *IBM Print Services Facility/6000: Print Services Facility for AIX Users*.

## 4.16.1.5 OS/2

The LPR client and LPD server functions are supported by TCP/IP for OS/2.

The following commands are available:

- LPD starts the LPD server on your local host.

- LPQ allows you to query a remote printer attached to a network host that provides print spooling services.

- LPRM allows you to remove a job that is printing on a remote printer attached to a network host that provides print spooling services.

- LPR allows you to transfer the contents of a file from your PC to a network host that provides print spooling services.

- LPRMON allows you to redirect the output of a parallel port from your PC to a network host that provides print spooling services. This allows you to print to an LPR server without an application using the Line Printer protocol directly. Please refer to *IBM TCP/IP Version 2.0 for OS/2: User's Guide* for more details.

- LPRPORTD: a Workplace Shell application that allows you to redirect, using the "drag and drop" technique, the output of a parallel port on your PC to a network host that provides print spooling services.

## 4.16.1.6 DOS

TCP/IP for DOS provides both the client (LPR) and server (LPD) functions.

The *LPR*, *LPQ*, *LPRM* and *LPRMON* commands are supported. Please refer to *IBM TCP/IP Version 2.1.1 for DOS: User's Guide* for more details.

# 4.17 BOOTstrap Protocol — BOOTP

BOOTP is a *draft standard protocol*. Its status is *recommended*. The BOOTP specifications can be found in *RFC 951 — Bootstrap Protocol* and *RFC 1497 — BOOTP Vendor Information Extensions*.

There are also updates to BOOTP that allow it to interoperate with DHCP (see 4.18, "Dynamic Host Configuration Protocol (DHCP)" on page 4-214). These are described in *RFC 1542 — Clarifications and Extensions for the Bootstrap Protocol* which updates RFC 951 and *RFC 1533 — DHCP Options and BOOTP Vendor Extensions*, which obsoletes RFC 1497. These updates to BOOTP are *proposed standards* with a status of *elective*.

LANs make it possible to use diskless hosts as workstations, routers, terminal concentrators and so on. Diskless hosts require a mechanism to boot remotely over a network. The BOOTP protocol is used for remote booting over IP networks. It allows a minimum IP protocol stack with no configuration information, typically stored in ROM, to obtain enough information to begin the process of downloading the necessary boot code. BOOTP does not define how the downloading is done, but this process typically uses TFTP (see also 4.3, "Trivial File Transfer Protocol (TFTP)" on page 4-21) as described in *RFC 906 — Bootstrap loading using TFTP*.

The BOOTP process involves the following steps:

1. The client determines its own hardware address; this is normally in a ROM on the hardware.

2. A BOOTP client sends its hardware address in a UDP datagram to the server. The full contents of this datagram are shown in Figure 4-70. If the client knows its IP address and/or the address of the server, it should use them, but in general BOOTP clients have no IP configuration data at all. If the client does not know its own IP address, it uses 0.0.0.0. If the client does not know the server's IP address, it uses the limited broadcast address (255.255.255.255). The UDP port number is 67.

3. The server receives the datagram and looks up the hardware address of the client in its configuration file, which contains the client's IP address. The server fills in the remaining fields in the UDP datagram and returns it to the client using UDP port 68. One of three methods may be used to do this:

   - If the client knew its own IP address (it was included in the BOOTP request), then the server returns the datagram directly to this address. It is likely that the ARP cache in the server's protocol stack will not know the hardware address matching the IP address. ARP will be used to determine it as normal.

   - If the client did not know its own IP address (it 0.0.0.0 in the BOOTP request), then the server must concern itself with its own ARP cache. ARP on the server cannot be used to find the hardware address of the client because the client does not know its IP address and so cannot reply to an ARP request. This is called the "chicken and egg" problem. There are two possible solutions:

- If the server has a mechanism for directly updating its own ARP cache without using ARP itself, it does so and then sends the datagram directly.

- If the server cannot update its own ARP cache, it must send a broadcast reply.

4. When it receives the reply, the BOOTP client will record its own IP address (allowing it to respond to ARP requests) and begin the bootstrap process.

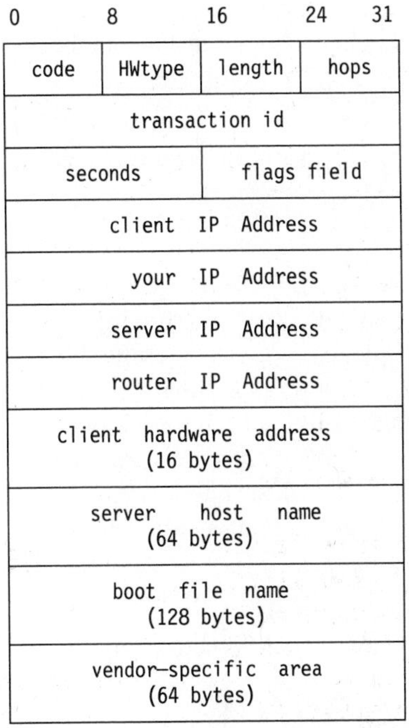

```
 0        8       16      24    31

 ┌────────┬────────┬────────┬────────┐
 │  code  │ HWtype │ length │  hops  │
 ├────────┴────────┴────────┴────────┤
 │          transaction id           │
 ├─────────────────┬─────────────────┤
 │     seconds     │   flags field   │
 ├─────────────────┴─────────────────┤
 │        client  IP  Address        │
 ├───────────────────────────────────┤
 │         your  IP  Address         │
 ├───────────────────────────────────┤
 │        server  IP  Address        │
 ├───────────────────────────────────┤
 │        router  IP  Address        │
 ├───────────────────────────────────┤
 │     client  hardware  address     │
 │            (16 bytes)             │
 ├───────────────────────────────────┤
 │      server    host    name       │
 │            (64 bytes)             │
 ├───────────────────────────────────┤
 │       boot   file   name          │
 │            (128 bytes)            │
 ├───────────────────────────────────┤
 │     vendor—specific   area        │
 │            (64 bytes)             │
 └───────────────────────────────────┘
```

*Figure*   *4-70.  BOOTP Message Format*

*code*

Indicates a request or a reply

*1* Request
*2* Reply

*HWtype*

The type of hardware, for example:

*1* Ethernet

6 IEEE 802 Networks

Refer to *STD 2 — Assigned Internet Numbers* for a complete list.

*length*

Hardware address length in bytes. Ethernet and token-ring both use 6, for example.

*hops*

The client sets this to 0. It is incremented by a router which relays the request to another server and is used to identify loops. RFC 951 suggests that a value of 3 indicates a loop.

*Transaction ID*

A random number used to match this boot request with the response it generates.

*Seconds*

Set by the client. It is the elapsed time in seconds since the client started its boot process.

*Flags Field*

The most significant bit of the flags field is used as broadcast flag. All other bits must be set to zero; they are reserved for future use. Normally, BOOTP servers attempt to deliver BOOTREPLY messages directly to a client using unicast delivery. The destination address in the IP header is set to the BOOTP *your IP address* and the MAC address is set to the BOOTP *client hardware address*. If a host is unable to receive a unicast IP datagram until it knows its IP address, then this broadcast bit must be set to indicate the server that the BOOTREPLY must be sent as an IP and MAC broadcast. Otherwise this bit must be set to zero.

*Client IP address*

Set by the client. Either its known IP address, or 0.0.0.0.

*Your IP Address*

Set by the server if the Client IP address field was 0.0.0.0.

*Server IP address*

Set by the server.

*Router IP address*

Set by the forwarding router if BOOTP forwarding is being used.

*Client hardware address*

Set by the client and used by the server to identify which registered client is booting.

*Server host name*

Optional server host name terminated by X′ 00′ .

*Boot file name*

The client either leaves this null or specifies a generic name, such as "router" indicating the type of boot file to be used. The server returns the fully qualified filename of a boot file suitable for the client. The value is terminated by terminated by X′ 00′ .

*Vendor-specific area*

Optional vendor-specific area. It is recommended that clients always fill the first four bytes with a "magic cookie." If a vendor-specific "magic cookie" is not used the client should use 99.130.83.99 followed by an end tag (255) and set the remaining bytes to zero. Please see RFC 1533 for details.

One restriction with this scheme is the use of the limited broadcast address for BOOTP requests; it requires that the server is on the same subnet as the recipient. BOOTP forwarding is a mechanism for routers to forward BOOTP requests. It is a configuration option available on some routers, including the IBM 6611 and 2210 Network Processors. See RFC 951 for more information about BOOTP forwarding.

Once the BOOTP client has processed the reply, it may proceed with the transfer of the boot file and execute the full boot process. See RFC 906 for the specification of how this is done with TFTP. The full boot process will replace the minimum IP protocol stack used by BOOTP and TFTP by a normal IP protocol stack transferred as part of the boot file and containing the correct customization for the client.

# 4.17.1 Implementations

## 4.17.1.1 AIX/6000

The BOOTP server function is implemented in the *bootpd* daemon. This daemon is a subserver controlled by the inetd superdaemon. Bootpd searches the */etc/bootptab* file for hardware addresses. For details on the file format, please refer to the online InfoExplorer.

The BOOTP client function is used in conjunction with TFTP to load executable modules (X stations, diskless workstations) or configuration files (intelligent hubs, routers) automatically at system startup.

**Note:** BOOTP requests from a BOOTP client are not able to pass an IP router if not explicitly customized.

## 4.17.1.2 OS/2

Both client and server functions are provided.

- Server function: The BOOTPD command starts the server. When the BOOTP server receives the hardware address it looks for a match in the /ETC/BOOTPTAB file. Upon finding a matching hardware address, the server sends back (in the UDP packet) an internet address, a subnet mask, and other information to the client. Please refer to *IBM TCP/IP Version 2.0 for OS/2: User's Guide* for more details about the /ETC/BOOTTAB file. BOOTP broadcast packets are used for transfer and reside only on the local network. They do not pass through a router to another network.

- Client function: the BOOTP command starts the client. The client will execute and print out the response from the server as soon as the connection is made.

### 4.17.1.3 DOS
TCP/IP for DOS provides the BOOTP client function. The BOOTP command initiates this client function which can be very useful in establishing SLIP connections (since BOOTP can be used to assign your IP address, you do not need to know the IP address before the connection is made).

# 4.18  Dynamic Host Configuration Protocol (DHCP)

DHCP is a *proposed standard protocol*. Its status is *elective*. The current DHCP specifications can be found in *RFC 1541 — Dynamic Host Configuration Protocol* and *RFC 1533 — DHCP Options and BOOTP Vendor Extensions*.

The Dynamic Host Configuration Protocol (DHCP) provides a framework for passing configuration information to hosts on a TCP/IP network. DHCP is based on the BOOTP protocol, adding the capability of automatic allocation of reusable network addresses and additional configuration options. For information according to BOOTP please refer to 4.17, "BOOTstrap Protocol — BOOTP" on page 4-210. DHCP participants can interoperate with BOOTP participants (RFC 1534).

DHCP consists of two components:

1. A protocol that delivers host-specific configuration parameters from a DHCP server to a host.
2. A mechanism for the allocation of network addresses to hosts.

IP requires the setting of many parameters within the protocol implementation software. Because IP can be used on many dissimilar kinds of network hardware, values for those parameters cannot be guessed at or assumed to have correct defaults. The use of a distributed address allocation scheme based on a polling/defense mechanism, for discovery of network addresses already in use, cannot guarantee unique network addresses because hosts may not always be able to defend their network addresses.

DHCP supports three mechanisms for IP address allocation:

1. Automatic allocation

   DHCP assigns a permanent IP address to the host.

2. Dynamic allocation

   DHCP assigns an IP address for a limited period of time. Such a network address is called a *lease*. This is the only mechanism that allows automatic reuse of addresses that are no longer needed by the host to which it was assigned.

3. Manual allocation

   The host's address is assigned by a network administrator.

The format of a DHCP message:

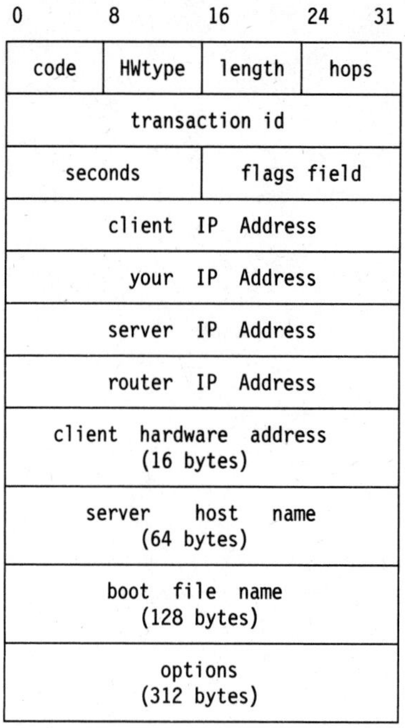

```
 0        8        16       24     31
┌────────┬────────┬────────┬────────┐
│  code  │ HWtype │ length │  hops  │
├────────┴────────┴────────┴────────┤
│          transaction id           │
├────────────────┬──────────────────┤
│    seconds     │   flags field    │
├────────────────┴──────────────────┤
│       client  IP  Address         │
├───────────────────────────────────┤
│         your  IP  Address         │
├───────────────────────────────────┤
│       server  IP  Address         │
├───────────────────────────────────┤
│       router  IP  Address         │
├───────────────────────────────────┤
│    client  hardware  address      │
│           (16 bytes)              │
├───────────────────────────────────┤
│     server    host    name        │
│           (64 bytes)              │
├───────────────────────────────────┤
│      boot  file  name             │
│          (128 bytes)              │
├───────────────────────────────────┤
│           options                 │
│          (312 bytes)              │
└───────────────────────────────────┘
```

*Figure 4-71. DHCP Message Format*

*code*

Indicates a request or a reply

*1* Request
*2* Reply

*HWtype*

The type of hardware, for example:

*1* Ethernet
*6* IEEE 802 Networks

Refer to *STD 2 — Assigned Internet Numbers* for a complete list.

*length*

Hardware address length in bytes. Ethernet and token-ring both use 6, for example.

*hops*

> The client sets this to 0. It is incremented by a router which relays the request to another server and is used to identify loops. RFC 951 suggests that a value of 3 indicates a loop.

*Transaction ID*

> A random number used to match this boot request with the response it generates.

*Seconds*

> Set by the client. It is the elapsed time in seconds since the client started its boot process.

*Flags Field*

> The most significant bit of the flags field is used as a broadcast flag. All other bits must be set to zero, and are reserved for future use. Normally, DHCP servers attempt to deliver DHCP messages directly to a client using unicast delivery. The destination address in the IP header is set to the DHCP *your IP address* and the MAC address is set to the DHCP *client hardware address*. If a host is unable to receive a unicast IP datagram until it knows its IP address, then this broadcast bit must be set to indicate to the server that the DHCP reply must be sent as an IP and MAC broadcast. Otherwise this bit must be set to zero.

*Client IP address*

> Set by the client. Either its known IP address, or 0.0.0.0.

*Your IP Address*

> Set by the server if the Client IP address field was 0.0.0.0.

*Server IP address*

> Set by the server.

*Router IP address*

> Set by the forwarding router if BOOTP forwarding is being used.

*Client hardware address*

> Set by the client. DHCP defines a "client identifier" option which is used for client identification. If this option is not used the client is identified by its MAC address.

*Server host name*

> Optional server host name terminated by X′ 00′ .

*Boot file name*

> The client either leaves this null or specifies a generic name, like "router" indicating the type of boot file to be used. In a DHCPDISCOVER request this is set to null. The server returns a fully-qualified directory-path name in a DHCPOFFER request. The value is terminated by X′ 00′ .

*Options*

The first four bytes of the options field of the DHCP message contain the "magic cookie" (99.130.83.99). The remainder of the *options* field consists of tagged parameters that are called *options*. Please see RFC 1533 for details.

### 4.18.1.1 Configuration Parameters Repository

DHCP provides persistent storage of network parameters for network clients. The model of DHCP persistent storage is that the DHCP service stores a key-value entry for each client, where the key is some unique identifier, for example an IP subnet number and a unique identifier within the subnet, and the value contains the configuration parameters for this particular client.

### 4.18.1.2 Allocating a New Network Address

This section describes the client/server interaction if the client does not know its network address. Assume that the DHCP server has a block of network addresses from which it can satisfy requests for new addresses. Each server also maintains a database of allocated addresses and leases in permanent local storage.

1. The client broadcasts a DHCPDISCOVER message on its local physical subnet. The DHCPDISCOVER message may include some options like network address suggestion or lease duration etc.

2. Each server may respond with a DHCPOFFER message that includes an available network address and other configuration options.

3. The client receives one or more DHCPOFFER messages from one or more servers. The client chooses one based on the configuration parameters offered and broadcasts a DHCPREQUEST message which includes the "server identifier" option to indicate which message it has selected.

4. The servers receive the DHCPREQUEST broadcast from the client. Those servers not selected by the DHCPREQUEST message use the message as notification that the client has declined that server's offer. The server selected in the DHCPREQUEST message commits the binding for the client to persistent storage and responds with a DHCPACK message containing the configuration parameters for the requesting client. The combination of client hardware and assigned network address constitute a unique identifier for the client's lease and are used by both the client and server to identify a lease referred to in any DHCP messages. The "your IP address" field in the DHCPACK messages is filled in with the selected network address.

5. The client receives the DHCPACK message with configuration parameters. The client performs a final check on the parameters, for example with ARP for allocated network address, and notes the duration of the lease and the lease identification cookie specified in the DHCPACK message. At this point, the client is configured.

If the client detects a problem with the parameters in the DHCPACK message, the client sends a DHCPDECLINE message to the server and restarts the configuration process. The client should wait a minimum of ten seconds before restarting the configuration process to avoid excessive network traffic in case of looping.

If the client receives a DHCPNAK message, the client restarts the configuration process.

6. The client may choose to relinquish its lease on a network address by sending a DHCPRELEASE message to the server. The client identifies the lease to be released by including its network address and its hardware address.

## 4.18.1.3 Reusing a Previously Allocated Network Address

If the client remembers and wishes to reuse a previously allocated network address then the following steps are processed:

1. The client broadcasts a DHCPREQUEST message on its local subnet. The DHCPREQUEST message includes the client's network address.

2. Servers with knowledge of the client's configuration parameters respond with a DHCPACK message to the client.

3. The client receives the DHCPACK message with configuration parameters. The client performs a final check on the parameters and notes the duration of the lease and the lease identification cookie specified in the DHCPACK     message. At this point, the client is configured.

   If the client detects a problem with the parameters in the DHCPACK message, the client sends a DHCPDECLINE message to the server and restarts the configuration process by requesting a new network address. If the client receives a DHCPNAK message, it cannot reuse its remembered network address. It must instead request a new address by restarting the configuration process as described in 4.18.1.2, "Allocating a New Network Address" on page 4-218. The client may choose to relinquish its lease on a network address by sending a DHCPRELEASE message to the server. The client identifies the lease to be released with the lease identification cookie.

**Note:**  A host should use DHCP to reacquire or verify its IP address and network parameters whenever the local network parameters have changed, for example at system boot time or after a disconnection from the local network, as the local network configuration may change without the host's or user's knowledge.

For further information please refer to the above mentioned RFCs.

# 4.19 NETSTAT

The NETSTAT command is used to query TCP/IP about the network status of the local host. The exact syntax of this command is very implementation-dependent. See the *User's Guide* or the *Command Reference Manual* of your implementation for full details. It is a useful tool for debugging purposes.

In general, NETSTAT will provide information on:

- Active TCP connections at this local host.
- State of all TCP/IP servers on this local host and the sockets used by them.
- Devices and links used by TCP/IP.
- The IP routing tables (gateway tables) in use at this local host.

The NETSTAT command is implemented in TCP/IP for VM, MVS, OS/400, OS/2, DOS and all AIX systems.

# 4.20 Finger Protocol

Finger is a *draft standard protocol*. Its status is *elective*. The current finger specification can be found in *RFC 1288 — The Finger User Information Protocol*.

The finger command displays information about users of a remote host. Finger is a UNIX command. Its format is:

```
finger user@host
or
finger @host
```

The information provided by the finger command about a user depends on the implementation of the finger server. If a user is not specified, the information will typically be a list of all users currently logged on to this host.

Connections are established through TCP port 79 (decimal). The client sends an ASCII command string, ending with <CRLF>. The server responds with one or more ASCII strings, until the server closes the connection.

## 4.20.1.1 Implementations

AIX systems have both the client finger command and the server fingerd daemon. TCP/IP for DOS and TCP/IP for OS/2 implementations provide the client finger function.

# 4.21  Whois Protocol

Whois is a *draft standard protocol*. Its status is *elective*. The current Whois specification can be found in *RFC 954 — NICNAME/WHOIS*.

The Whois program is commonly used in the UNIX environment to connect to a Whois server. The purpose of the server is to provide directory type services. The original Whois server was set up so that the Network Information Center could maintain a contact list for networks connected to the Internet. However, many sites now use Whois to provide local directory services.

The Whois server is based upon TCP and uses well-known port 43. Requests and replies exchanged between the client and server use NVT ASCII.

The most widely used Whois server is maintained by the InterNIC and can be reached at rs.internic.net.

### 4.21.1.1  Implementations
AIX systems implement both the Whois client and server. Warp Internet Connection provides the Whois client.

# 4.22  Time and Daytime Protocols

Time is a *standard protocol*. Its status is *elective*. The current TIME specification can be found in *RFC 868 - Time Server Protocol*.

Daytime is a *standard protocol*. Its status is *elective*. The current daytime specification can be found in *RFC 867 - Daytime Protocol*.

### 4.22.1.1  Concept
The time protocol provides a machine-readable date and time. It uses TCP or UDP as the transport vehicle. Port 37 (decimal) is used.

1. Used via TCP:

    S: listen on port 37
    C: connect to port 37
    S: send the time as a 32-bit binary number
    C: receive the number
    C: close the connection

2. Used via UDP:

    S: listen on port 37
    C: send empty datagram to port 37

S: receive empty datagram
S: send datagram containing the time as a 32-bit number
C: receive the datagram

The 32-bit number represents the number of elapsed seconds since midnight on January 1st 1900 (GMT). It is suitable for a machine to set its own clock to this, but it is not very human-readable.

The daytime protocol is similar in concept, but the server will now send a readable ASCII character string back to the client. The format of this ASCII string is not formalized. Port 13 (decimal) is used for this protocol.

### 4.22.1.2 Implementations

AIX/6000 provides both the client and server functions. The server function is included in the base *inetd* process; the client part is provided through the *setclock* command.

TCP/IP for DOS provides the client function with the *setclock* command.

# 4.23 Other Application Protocols

There are a number of other application protocols which are not documented in the RFCs, but are implemented by various products. The following sections describe some of these protocols.

## 4.23.1 Network Database (NDB)

The Network Database (NDB) protocol is not an Internet standard.

NDB defines a protocol for use with relational database systems in a TCP/IP environment. It has the following objectives:

- To allow any workstation/mainframe users and applications to issue SQL statements interactively or imbedded within the application programs, to access any database on any operating system.

- To distribute the applications of a database host to a requester machine.

NDB is built on the Remote Procedure Call (any arbitrary implementation of RPC) using the client/server model. Please see Figure 4-72 on page 4-223 for an overview of the various NDB components.

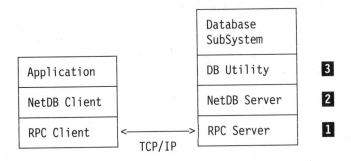

*Figure* *4-72.* *Components in the Network Database (NDB) Protocol*

**1** The **RPC client/server** layer is concerned with the transport of data across the TCP/IP network: creating sockets, interfacing with PORTMAP, sending and receiving data.

**2** The **NetDB client/server** layer manages Units of Work(UOWs), multi-threading, and also data conversion to/from the ASN.1 (Abstract Syntax Notation 1, ISO standard 8824) format.

**3** The **DB Utility** layer serves as the interface to the actual database.

### 4.23.1.1 Implementations

The TCP/IP for MVS and TCP/IP for VM both implement a NDB server and provide sample NDB client source code for AIX/6000 and SUN workstations. The supported database products are DB2 in MVS and SQL/DS in VM.

The current VM server implementation only supports the SQL SELECT DML function.

The current MVS server implementation supports all SQL statements that can be dynamically prepared in an MVS DB2 environment.

For details on the NDB implementations, please refer to *IBM TCP/IP Version 3 Release 1 for MVS: Customization and Administration Guide* and *IBM TCP/IP Version 2 Release 3 for VM: Planning and Customization.*

## 4.23.2 Network Information Systems (NIS)

The Network Information Systems (NIS) is not an Internet standard. It was developed by Sun Microsystems, Inc. It was originally known as the Yellow Pages.

NIS is a distributed database system which allows the sharing of system information in an AIX- or UNIX-based environment. Examples of system information that can be shared include the /etc/passwd, /etc/group and /etc/hosts files. NIS has the following advantages:

- Provides a consistent user ID and group ID name space across a large number of systems.

- Reduces the time and effort by users in managing their user IDs, group IDs and NFS file system ownerships.

- Reduces the time and effort by system administrators in managing user IDs, group IDs and NFS file system ownerships.

NIS is built on the SUN-RPC. It employs the client/server model. An NIS domain is a collection of systems consisting of:

**NIS master server**         maintains *maps*, or databases, containing the system information such as passwords and host names.

**NIS slave server(s)**        can be defined to offload the processing from the master NIS server or when the NIS master server is unavailable.

**NIS client(s)**             are the remaining systems which are served by the NIS servers.

The NIS clients do not maintain NIS maps; they query NIS servers for system information. Any changes to an NIS map is done only to the NIS master server (via RPC). The master server then propagates the changes to the NIS slave servers.

Note that the speed of a network determines the performance and availability of the NIS maps. When using NIS, the number of slave servers should be tuned in order to achieve these goals.

### 4.23.2.1 Implementations
AIX/6000 and AIX/ESA Version 2 all support NIS.

Note that the AIX/ESA implementation is provided by the licensed program *Network File System For AIX/ESA Version 2*. In all implementations, NFS must be configured before using NIS.

## 4.23.3 CICS Socket Interface
Customer Information Control System (CICS) is a high-performance transaction-processing system. It is developed by IBM and has product implementations in MVS/ESA, MVS, VSE, OS/400, OS/2, AIX/6000.

CICS is the most widely used OLTP (Online Transaction Processing) system in the marketplace today. It provides a rich set of CICS *command level* APIs to the application transaction programs for data communications (using SNA) and database (using VSAM, IMS or DB2).

Given the need for interoperability among heterogeneous network protocols, there is a requirement to enhance the CICS data communications interface to include support for TCP/IP in addition to SNA. The *IBM Sockets Interface for CICS* is a first step towards addressing this requirement.

### 4.23.3.1 Implementations

TCP/IP for MVS implements the *IBM Socket Interface for CICS*. Both CICS/MVS Version 2 and CICS/ESA Version 3 are supported.

The support provides a sockets environment to any C, COBOL, PL/I or Assembler language programs running under CICS, for communications with any sockets application programs running in any (local or foreign) systems. The interface is implemented, in CICS terms, using a CICS *Task Related User Exit (TRUE)*. (This is similar to the TRUE implementation of the CICS-DB2 SQL interface.)

For details on the IBM Socket Interface for CICS, please refer to *IBM Sockets Interface for CICS-Using TCP/IP Version 3 Release 1 for MVS: User's Guide.*

## 4.23.4 IMS Socket Interface

The IMS Socket Interface is implemented in TCP/IP for MVS Version 3.1 only.

The IMS to TCP/IP sockets interface allows you to develop IMS message processing programs which can conduct a conversation with peer programs in other TCP/IP hosts. The applications may be either client or server applications. The IMS to TCP/IP sockets interface includes socket interfaces for IBM C/370, assembler language, COBOL, and PL/I languages to use stream (connection oriented) sockets. It also provides ASCII-EBCDIC conversion routines, an ASSIST module which permits the use of conventional IMS calls for TCP/IP communications, and a Listener function to listen for and accept connection requests and start the appropriate IMS transaction to service those requests.

For details on the IBM Socket Interface for IMS, please refer to *IBM Sockets Interface for CICS-Using TCP/IP Version 3 Release 1 for MVS: User's Guide.*

## 4.23.5 Sockets Extended

The Sockets Extended information described here is related to the implementation in MVS only.

Sockets Extended provides programmers writing in assembler language, COBOL, or PL/I with an application program interface that may be used to conduct peer-to-peer conversations with other hosts in the TCP/IP networks. You can develop applications for TSO, batch, CICS, or IMS using this API. The applications may be designed to be reentrant and multithreaded depending upon the application requirements. Typically server applications will be multithreaded while client applications may not be.

For details on the IBM Sockets Extended for MVS TCP/IP, please refer to *IBM Sockets Interface for CICS-Using TCP/IP Version 3 Release 1 for MVS: User's Guide*.

## 4.23.6  REXX Sockets

REXX sockets allow you to develop REXX applications that communicate over a TCP/IP network. Calls are provided to initialize sockets, exchange data via sockets, perform management activities, and close the sockets.

The REXX Socket APIs are implemented in TCP/IP for MVS and OS/2.

## 4.23.7  RFC 1006

Programs that were originally written to the X/Open Transport Interface (XTI) may be used with the TCP/IP stack. RFC 1006 defines a protocol mapping component to enable these programs to be used in a TCP/IP network.

The RFC 1006 is implemented in the following IBM products:

- IBM TCP/IP Version 3 Release 1 for MVS
- AIX OSI Services/6000
- IBM AIX Distributed Computing Environment Global Directory Services Version 1.1 for AIX/6000
- VERITAS for IBM AIX/ESA
- IBM AIX Distributed Computing Environment/ESA

# 4.24  Summaries

## 4.24.1  Client/Server Relationships

The following figure shows which TCP/IP application is implemented under which operating system.

| | S/370 | | | PS/2 | | RISC/6000 | AS/400 |
|---|---|---|---|---|---|---|---|
| | MVS | VM | AIX | DOS | OS/2 | AIX | OS/400 |
| FTP | c/s | c/s | c/s | c/s | c/s | c/s | c/s |
| TELNET | c/s | c/s | c/s | c/ | c/s | c/s | c/s |
| TN3270 | c/s | c/s | c/ | c/ | c/ | c/ | c/s |
| SMTP | c/s | c/s | c/s | c/s | c/s | c/s | c/s |
| SUN RPC | c/s | c/s | c/s | c/ | c/s | c/s | c/s |
| NFS V2 | /s | /s | c/s4 | c/ | c/s | c/s 4 | c/s |
| NCS | c/s | c/s | | | c/s | c/s | |
| X Window | c/ | c/ | c/ | | c/s | c/s | |
| REXEC | c/s | c/s | c/s | c/ | c/s | c/s | |
| TFTP | | c/ | c/s | c/s | c/s | c/s | |
| LPR/LPD | c/s | c/s | c/s | c/s | c/s | c/s | c/s |
| SNMP | m/a | m/a | | m/a | m*/a | m/a | /a |
| Sockets | c/s | c/s | c/s | c/s | c/s | c/s | c/s |
| Kerberos | c/s | c/s | | | c/s | | |
| DNS | r/s | r/s | r/s | r/ | r/s | r/s | r/ |
| TALK | | | c/s | | c/s | c/s | |
| Finger | | | c/s | c/ | c/ | c/s | |
| PING | x | x | x | x | x | x | x |
| NETSTAT | x | x | x | x | x | x | x |
| RIP | x | x | x | x | x | x | |

```
4    = support SUN PC-NFS 4.0
c/s  = client/server support
m/a  = monitor/agent support, monitor for DOS: NetView for Windows
r/s  = resolver/server support
*    = with NetView for OS/2
SOD  = Statement of Direction for client/server
cSOD = Statement of Direction for client support
sSOD = Statement of Direction for server support
aSOD = Statement of Direction for agent support
x    = noted function exists for the product
```

*Figure   4-73.  Client/Server Relationships*

## 4.24.2 APIs by Operating System

The following figure shows which TCP/IP API is implemented under which operating system.

| | S/370 | | | PS/2 | | RISC/6000 | AS/400 |
|---|---|---|---|---|---|---|---|
| | MVS | VM | AIX | DOS | OS/2 | AIX | OS/400 |
| TCP,UDP | C&P | C&P | x | | | x | x |
| IP | C&P | C&P | x | | | x | |
| FTP | | | | C | C | | |
| SNMP DPI | | C | | | C | | |
| Sockets | M | C | x | C | C | x | x |
| RPC | C | C | x | C | C | x | x |
| NCS | C | C | | | C | x | |
| X-Window | C | C | W | | W | x | |
| OSF/Motif | C | C | x | C/W | C | x | x |
| Kerberos | C | C | | | C | x | |
| Source avail. | x | x | | | x | | |

```
SOD  = Statement of Direction
C    = C Language
C/W  = C Language with Windows
P    = Pascal Language
x    = noted function exists for the product
W    = Athena Widget library
M    = CICS, IMS, REXX, RFC 1006 Sockets
```

*Figure   4-74.  APIs for TCP/IP*

# 4.25  APIs by Protocol

The following chart shows the layered model of the TCP/IP protocol suite and also indicates the application programming interfaces (API) available to the user.

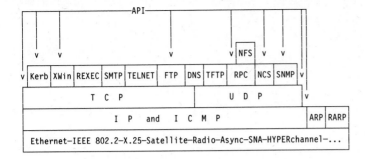

*Figure* *4-75. TCP/IP Layered Model*

Remote Procedure Call uses both TCP and UDP. It has been placed upon UDP here since NFS only uses RPC over UDP.

ARP and RARP are only used on local area networks.

The IP/TCP/UDP socket API has been mentioned in 2.10, "Ports and Sockets" on page 2-81. The other APIs were explained earlier in this chapter:

- Kerberos (see 4.13, "Kerberos Authentication and Authorization System" on page 4-155)
- X Window (see 4.9, "X Window System" on page 4-118)
- FTP (see 4.4, "File Transfer Protocol (FTP)" on page 4-25)
- RPC (see 4.10, "Remote Procedure Call (RPC)" on page 4-129)
- NCS (see 4.11, "Network Computing System (NCS)" on page 4-136)
- SNMP DPI (see 4.14, "Network Management" on page 4-166)
- CICS Socket Interface (see 4.23.3, "CICS Socket Interface" on page 4-224)

# Chapter 5.  Connections

This chapter describes the connectivity options available to the various IBM TCP/IP products. Each section presents a different connectivity option and its support for the TCP/IP products.  The last section contains a summary.

## 5.1  IBM 3172 Interconnect Controller

The IBM 3172 Interconnect Controller can be configured as a LAN gateway, an offload gateway or a remote channel-to-channel controller, to provide high-performance interconnection from the S/370 and S/390 hosts to the LAN environments.

The following tables show the various connections supported by the three models of the 3172.

| Host Software | Type of LAN | | | | |
| --- | --- | --- | --- | --- | --- |
| | Ethernet V2 | IEEE 802.3 | Token— Ring | PCNET | FDDI |
| TCP/IP VM   V2.3 | all | all | all | 1 | 2+3 |
| TCP/IP MVS V3.1 | all | all | all | 1 | 2+3 |
| AIX/ESA     V2.2 | all | all | all | | 2+3 |

all = 3172 Model 1, 2 & 3

*Figure*  *5-1.*  *LAN Types Supported on the 3172 with Interconnect Control Program (ICP)*

| Host Software | Type of LAN | | | | |
|---|---|---|---|---|---|
| | Ethernet V2 | IEEE 802.3 | Token–Ring | PCNET | FDDI |
| TCP/IP VM   V2.3<br>TCP/IP MVS V3.1<br>AIX/ESA    V2.2 | X | X | X | | X |

*Figure  5-2. LAN Types Supported on the 3172-3 with the Offload Feature*

**Notes:**

1. ICP stands for the 3172 Interconnect Control Program Version 3.3 which runs in the 3172 hardware.

2. Offload stands for OS/2 V2.11, TCP/IP Version 2.0 for OS/2, and the 3172-3 Offload hardware feature.

3. The 3172-1 and -3 connect to the host via either a parallel channel adapter or an ESCON channel adapter.

4. The 3172-2 connects to the host via a parallel channel adapter.

5. The 3172 with ICP supports other host software, such as SNA VTAM, OSI/CS and DECnet (please refer to the *IBM 3172 Planning Guide* for details).

Both the MVS and VM TCP/IP provide the SNMP subagent functions for the 3172 running ICP. They also provide 3172-specific MIB support.

## 5.1.1  3172 TCP/IP Offload

The 3172 Model 3 can be configured to provide an Offload function to the TCP/IP for MVS Version 3.1. This function offloads some of the TCP/IP processing from the MVS host to the 3172. The current estimates show that this function can achieve 30% reduction in the host CPU cycles.

This configuration of the 3172-3 requires OS/2 V2.11 (OS/2 SE V1.3.2 is also supported, but OS/2 V2.11 is recommended), TCP/IP Version 2.0 for OS/2, the TCP/IP MVS Offload feature, the 3172-3 Offload hardware feature and the appropriate hardware adapters.

The 3172-3 is channel-attached to the MVS host, using one subchannel pair. The TCP/IP MVS offload processing uses the CLAW (Common Link Access for Workstation) protocol for communicating between the TCP/IP MVS host and the 3172-3 Offload host. Two logical links are used over the subchannel pair (please see Figure 5-3 on page 5-4):

1. An **API link**

   All TCP, UDP and IP header processing for the data transferred to and from the MVS host is performed in the 3172-3. The data is passed, via the API link, directly to the API interface on the TCP/IP MVS host, bypassing the IP, TCP and UDP layers on the TCP/IP MVS host.

2. An **IP link**

   Other datagrams not destined for the MVS host are routed by the IP layer of the TCP/IP MVS host over the IP link.

CLAW is designed to achieve two goals:

1. All 370 subchannels driven by CLAW should remain 100% busy for as long as there is data transfer between the MVS host and the Offload host.

2. No 370 I/O interrupts should occur as long as the TCP/IP address space is not in an idle state.

This implies that the MIH (Missing Interrupt Handler) must be disabled for the subchannel pair used by the offload processing; otherwise, a channel interrupt will cause the CLAW algorithm to fail.

TCP/IP MVS creates and updates the routing table on the offload 3172-3 based on its own routing table.

**Note:** Since the 3172-3 offload function handles all ICMP packets, it responds to ICMP echo requests (from ping, for example) even if TCP/IP MVS is not running.

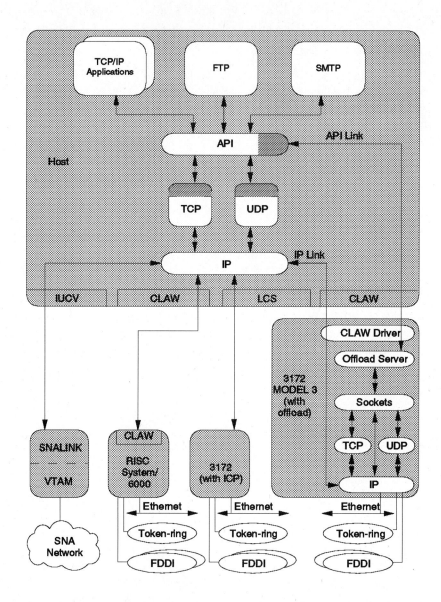

*Figure*  *5-3.*  *IBM 3172-3 Interconnect Controller.*  TCP/IP Offload Processing.

For more details on TCP/IP Offload processing, please refer to the *IBM TCP/IP Version 3 Release 1 for MVS: Offload of TCP/IP Processing.*

# 5.2 HYPERchannel Adapter

HYPERchannel A is a 50 Mbps, baseband, CSMA with collision avoidance network using a coaxial bus cable. Each network adapter can control up to four trunks (coaxial cable). It is used to interconnect large mainframe computers and high-speed peripherals. This adapter has to be connected to a BLKMPXR channel. It appears as a 64-address control unit to the operating system.

Both TCP/IP for VM and TCP/IP for MVS support HYPERchannel Series A devices. In addition, TCP/IP for VM and MVS supports the HYPERchannel Series DX devices, provided they function as Series A devices.

AIX/ESA supports the HYPERchannel Series DX devices.

TCP/IP for VM and TCP/IP for MVS support the HYPERchannel adapter A220, using the 16-bit address mode.

## 5.2.1 Addressing Particularities

Unlike most datagram delivery systems, the HYPERchannel network message consists of two parts. The first part is a message header, containing information required for the delivery. The second part is the associated data. Its length is literally unlimited. The header consists of several fields, each of them giving a value for TO and FROM trunks, adapters, and ports. The corresponding protocol does not support link-level broadcast, and therefore neither the Address Resolution Protocol (ARP) nor the IP broadcast can be used.

Connected to IBM channels, the entire logical TO field is interpreted as the subchannel on which the incoming data is to be presented.

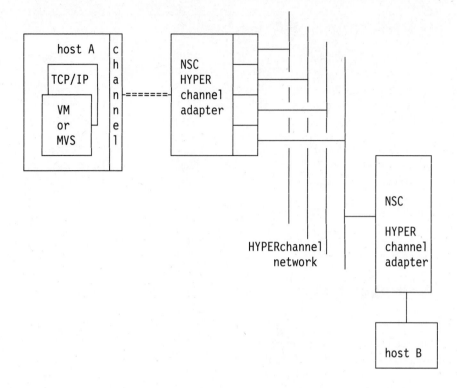

*Figure* **5-4.** *HYPERchannel Network*

For more information on HYPERchannel contact your Network Systems Corporation representative.

## 5.3 The IBM High-Performance Parallel Interface (HIPPI)

The IBM High-Performance Parallel Interface (HIPPI) is an 800 Mbps data transfer device that operates in a variety of high-speed computer environments. It is an implementation of the ANSI X3.183-1991 High-Performance Parallel Interface (HIPPI-PH) standard.

The IBM HIPPI can attach devices that comply with the ANSI standard to selected members of the IBM Enterprise System/3090 (ES/3090) and IBM Enterprise System/9000 (ES/9000) family of computers. Some examples of these devices are high-resolution real-time visualization devices, file servers, workstations or supercomputers.

## 5.3.1 Implementations

### 5.3.1.1 MVS

One of the following hardware RPQs is required for the HIPPI-supported ES/3090 or ES/9000 family of computers: 8P1347, 8P1348, 8P1353 or 8P1354.

The HIPPI software (RPQ P88039, program number 5799-DKW) makes the function of the HIPPI available to the HIPPI application programs. MVS TCP/IP V3R1 is one such program.

The IBM HIPPI software actually provides both a high-level, multiplexing interface and a low-level, exclusive-use interface. Basically, the high-level multiplexed interface gives several applications the ability to use HIPPI at the same time. This interface complies with the ANSI HIPPI-FP framing protocol. The low-level, exclusive-use interface allows only a single application to establish an association with it.

**Note:** MVS TCP/IP V3R1 was implemented to use the low-level interface. This means that other software may not use HIPPI while MVS TCP/IP is using it.

Please see Figure 5-5 for an overview of the relationship of the various components.

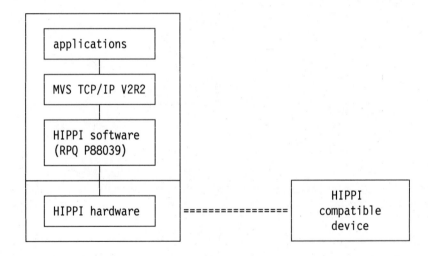

*Figure*   *5-5.  IBM HIPPI and MVS TCP/IP*

## 5.3.2 HIPPI Draft Standards and Internet-Draft

The ANSI X3T9.3 HIPPI working group drafted four standards covering:

- (HIPPI-PH) the physical and electrical specification

- (HIPPI-FP) the framing protocol of a point-to-point interface

- (HIPPI-LE) the encapsulation of IEEE 802.2 LLC data packets

- (HIPPI-SC) the control of HIPPI physical layer switches

Please see Figure 5-6 for an overview of the relationship of the various ANSI draft standards.

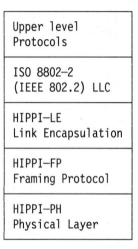

*Figure* **5-6.** *Relationship of ANSI HIPPI Draft Standards*

The Internet-Draft "IP and ARP on HIPPI" by A. Nicholson, June 1992, describes the HIPPI interface between a host and a crosspoint switch that complies with the HIPPI-SC draft standard. This is a *working draft* which is intended to become an Internet standard in the future.

**Note:** The HIPPI-SC switches are devices which allow a single HIPPI device to switch between multiple HIPPI devices without involving protocols above the HIPPI-PH layer.

## 5.3.3 Relationship of IBM HIPPI and the ANSI Draft Standards

The current IBM HIPPI does not support two items in the ANSI draft standard X3.183-1991 (HIPPI-PH):

- The IBM HIPPI does not support microbursts. Data is exchanged in packet sizes that are integral multiples of 4096 bytes.

- The IBM HIPPI does not have a means for software to deactivate the REQUEST signal of the IBM outbound channel once a program activates REQUEST by setting the clear bit in the outbound control word.

Please refer to *IBM HIPPI User's Guide and Programmer's Reference* for details.

## 5.4 CTC (Channel To Channel)

Both TCP/IP for MVS and TCP/IP for VM support the CTC (Channel-to-Channel, 3088) for S/370 host interconnection. The CTC device driver uses the CTC-to-transport IP packets without using VTAM and has a substantial performance benefit over SNALINK (see 5.6, "SNALINK" on page 5-11).

## 5.5 Continuously Executing Transfer Interface (CETI)

The CETI interface allows communication from S/370 and ESA/390 hosts to all other IEEE 802.3, Ethernet Version 2, and IEEE 802.5 LAN-attached hosts, controllers, workstations and devices where matching line protocols are available. This includes the attachment of non-IBM network controllers.

The CETI interface minimizes the use of SIO instructions and I/O interruptions in the S/370 and ESA/390 host processors.

For more details about the CETI and its relationship to the S/370 and ESA/390 software on the S/370 and ESA/390 *channel command* base, please refer to *ES/9000 Token-Ring and IEEE 802.3 LAN Programming Information*. Figure 5-7 on page 5-10 shows an overview of the CETI environments.

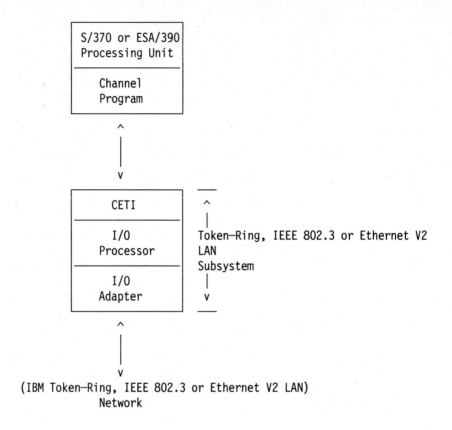

*Figure   5-7.  CETI Connection*

## 5.5.1 Implementations

TCP/IP for MVS supports the CETI.

For information about CETI support in TCP/IP for MVS, please refer to *IBM TCP/IP Version 3 Release 1 for MVS: Customization and Administration Guide.*

# 5.6 SNALINK

Both TCP/IP for VM and TCP/IP for MVS are implemented with the SNAlink function. This function allows the use of an SNA backbone to transfer TCP/IP protocols. A system equipped with TCP/IP and VTAM can be an originator, destination, or router of data originating from such a system.

In order to use this function of TCP/IP, you must have VTAM and TCP/IP installed on each host to be connected via SNAlink. There are two types of SNAlink implementations:

1. SNALINK, a VTAM application using the VTAM LU 0 protocol

2. SNALNK62, a VTAM application using the VTAM LU 6.2 protocol

Both SNALINK and SNALNK62 run in a separate address space (in MVS) or virtual machine (in VM) and are used to communicate between TCP/IP and VTAM. (Please see Figure 5-8 on page 5-12.) Both communicate with TCP/IP using IUCV.

SNALINK communicates via VTAM to its SNALINK partner on the remote host using the LU 0 protocol.

SNALNK62 communicates via VTAM to its SNALNK62 partner on the remote host using the LU 6.2 protocol.

For more details, please refer to the *IBM TCP/IP Version 3 Release 1 for MVS: Customization and Administration Guide* and *IBM TCP/IP Version 2 Release 3 for VM: Planning and Customization*.

TCP/IP for OS/2 provides support for an SNAlink LU 6.2 connection in its Extended Networking Kit. For more information refer to *TCP/IP V2.0 for OS/2 Extended Networking Guide, SC31-7071*.

Note that there is an Internet-Draft describing a method for the transmission of IP over SNA LU6.2. For details, please see [Stevenson, Schwell and Siddall] listed in Appendix A, "Bibliography" on page A-1.

## 5.6.1 Example

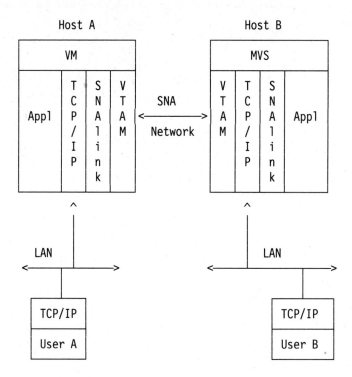

**Figure 5-8.** *Principle of SNAlink Function*

From a workstation connected to a LAN using basic TCP/IP functions, User A can access applications on Host A. In addition, User A can *TELNET* or *FTP*, via the Host A (transparently using the SNAlink function through a SNA backbone) to Host B.

# 5.7 Fiber Distributed Data Interface (FDDI)

The FDDI specifications define a family of standards for 100 Mbps fiber optic LANs that provides the physical layer and media access control sublayer of the data link layer as defined by the ISO/OSI Model.

IP-FDDI is a *draft standard protocol*. Its status is *elective*. It defines the encapsulating of IP datagrams and ARP requests and replies in FDDI frames. Figure 5-9 on page 5-13 shows the related protocol layers.

It is defined in *RFC 1188 - A Proposed Standard for the Transmission of IP Datagrams over FDDI Networks* for single MAC stations. Operation on dual MAC stations will be described in a forthcoming RFC.

RFC 1188 states that all frames are transmitted in standard IEEE 802.2 LLC Type 1 Unnumbered Information format, with the DSAP and SSAP fields of the 802.2 header set to the assigned global SAP value for SNAP (decimal 170). The 24-bit Organization Code in the SNAP header is set to zero, and the remaining 16 bits are the EtherType from Assigned Numbers (see RFC 1340), that is:

- 2048 for IP
- 2054 for ARP

The mapping of 32-bit Internet addresses to 48-bit FDDI addresses is done via the ARP dynamic discovery procedure. The broadcast Internet addresses (whose <host address> is set to all ones) are mapped to the broadcast FDDI address (all ones).

IP datagrams are transmitted as series of 8-bit bytes using the usual TCP/IP transmission order called "big-endian" or "network byte order".

The FDDI MAC specification (*ISO 9314-2 - ISO, Fiber Distributed Data Interface - Media Access Control*) defines a maximum frame size of 4500 bytes for all frame fields. After taking the LLC/SNAP header into account, and to allow future extensions to the MAC header and frame status fields, the MTU of FDDI networks is set to 4532 bytes.

Please refer to *LAN Concepts and Products,* GG24-3178 for more details on the FDDI architecture.

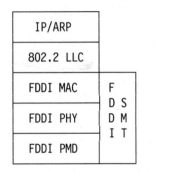

Figure  *5-9.  IP and ARP over FDDI*

## 5.7.1.1 Implementations
TCP/IP for MVS, TCP/IP for VM, and TCP/IP for AIX/ESA all support the FDDI Controller.

AIX/6000 supports FDDI connectivity through the RISC System/6000 Fiber Distributed Data Interface (FDDI) and the RISC System/6000 Serial Optical Channel Converter (SOCC) adapters.

# 5.8 Serial Line IP (SLIP)

The TCP/IP protocol family runs over a variety of network media: IEEE 802.3 and 802.5 LANs, X.25 lines, satellite links, and serial lines. Standards for the encapsulation of IP packets have been defined for many of these networks, but there is no standard for serial lines. SLIP is currently a *de facto* standard, commonly used for point-to-point serial connections running TCP/IP. It is not an Internet standard.

SLIP is just a very simple protocol designed quite a long time ago and is merely a packet framing protocol. It defines a sequence of characters that frame IP packets on a serial line, and nothing more. It does not provide any:

- Addressing: both computers on a SLIP link need to know each other's IP address for routing purposes.

- Packet type identification: thus, only one protocol can be run over a SLIP connection.

- Error detection/correction: error detection is not absolutely necessary at the SLIP level because any IP application should detect corrupted packets (IP header and UDP/TCP checksums should be sufficient). Because it takes so long to retransmit a packet that was altered, it would be efficient if SLIP could provide some sort of simple error correction mechanism of its own.

- Compression.

The SLIP protocol is expected to be replaced by the Point-to-Point Protocol (PPP). Please see 5.9, "Point-to-Point Protocol (PPP)" on page 5-15.

## 5.8.1 Implementations

SLIP is implemented in TCP/IP for OS/2, TCP/IP for DOS, and in AIX/6000.

## 5.8.2 Example

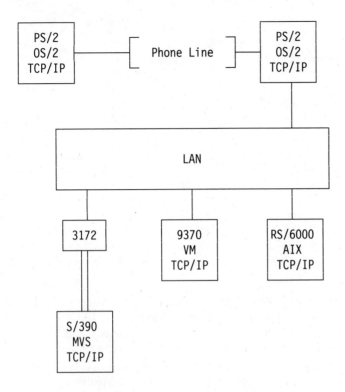

*Figure* **5-10.** *SLIP Example*

In Figure 5-10, the OS/2 workstation, connected to the LAN using a SLIP connection, can access all the other workstations, assuming that the necessary routing information has been set up. Conversely, all the workstations and hosts connected to the LAN can access the OS/2.

# 5.9 Point-to-Point Protocol (PPP)

PPP is a *network-specific standard protocol* with STD number 51. Its status is *elective*. It is described in RFC 1661 and RFC 1662.

There are a large number of *proposed standard protocols* which specify the operation of PPP over different kinds of point-to-point link. Each has a status of *elective*. The reader is advised to consult *STD 1 — Internet Official Protocol Standards* for a list of PPP-related RFCs which are on the Standards Track.

Point-to-Point circuits in the form of asynchronous and synchronous lines have long been the mainstay for data communications. In the TCP/IP world, the de facto standard SLIP protocol has served admirably in this area, and is still in widespread use for dial-up TCP/IP connections. However, SLIP has a number of drawbacks:

- SLIP defines only the encapsulation protocol, not any form of handshaking or link control. Links are manually connected and configured, including the specification of the IP address.

- SLIP is only defined for asynchronous links.

- SLIP cannot support multiple protocols across a single link; all packets must be IP datagrams.

- SLIP does no form of frame error detection which forces re-transmission by higher level protocols in the case of errors on noisy lines.

- SLIP provides no mechanism for compressing frequently used IP header fields. Many applications over slow serial links tend to be single-user interactive TCP traffic such as TELNET. This frequently involves small packet sizes and therefore a relatively large overhead in TCP and IP headers which do not change much between datagrams, but which can have a noticeably detrimental effect on interactive response times.

  However, many SLIP implementations now use *Van Jacobsen Header Compression*. This is used to reduce the size of the combined IP and TCP headers from 40 bytes to 8 bytes by recording the states of a set of TCP connections at each end of the link and replacing the full headers with encoded updates for the normal case where many of the fields are unchanged or are incremented by small amounts between successive IP datagrams for a session. This compression is described in RFC 1144.

The Point-to-Point protocol addresses these problems.

PPP has three main components:

1. A method for encapsulating datagrams over serial links.

2. A *Link Control Protocol (LCP)* for establishing, configuring, and testing the data-link connection.

3. A family of *Network Control Protocols (NCPs)* for establishing and configuring different network-layer protocols. PPP is designed to allow the simultaneous use of multiple network-layer protocols.

Before a link is considered to be ready for use by network-layer protocols, a specific sequence of events must happen. The LCP provides a method of establishing, configuring, maintaining and terminating the connection. LCP goes through the following phases:

1. Link establishment and configuration negotiation:

In this phase, link control packets are exchanged and link configuration options are negotiated. Once options are agreed upon, the link is *open*, but not necessarily *ready* for network-layer protocols to be started.

2. Link quality determination:

   This phase is optional. PPP does not specify the policy for determining quality, but does provide low-level tools, such as echo request and reply.

3. Authentication:

   This phase is optional. Each end of the link authenticates itself with the remote end using authentication methods agreed to during phase 1.

4. Network-layer protocol configuration negotiation:

   Once LCP has finished the previous phase, network-layer protocols may be separately configured by the appropriate NCP.

5. Link termination:

   LCP may terminate the link at any time. This will usually be done at the request of a human user, but may happen because of a physical event.

The *IP Control Protocol (IPCP)* is the NCP for IP and is responsible for configuring, enabling and disabling the IP protocol on both ends of the point-to-point link. The IPCP options negotiation sequence is the same as for LCP, thus allowing the possibility of reusing the code.

One important option used with IPCP is *Van Jacobsen Header Compression* which is used to reduce the size of the combined IP and TCP headers from 40 bytes to approximately 4 by recording the states of a set of TCP connections at each end of the link and replacing the full headers with encoded updates for the normal case where many of the fields are unchanged or are incremented by small amounts between successive IP datagrams for a session. This compression is described in RFC 1144.

# 5.10  TCP/IP and X.25

IP-X25 is a *standard protocol*. Its status is *elective*.

For detail on the Internet Protocol on X.25 networks, please refer to RFC 877 and RFC 1356.

## 5.10.1  Implementations
MVS, VM, OS/2, OS/400 and AIX/6000 all support TCP/IP over X.25 networks.

### 5.10.1.1 MVS

The TCPIPX25 address space runs a VTAM application program called XNX25IPI, which is the interface between the TCPIP address space's IUCV driver and your X.25 network. XNX25IPI communicates with the NPSI (X.25 NCP Packet Switching Interface) in a front-end IBM 37XX Communications Controller.

For more details, please refer to the *IBM TCP/IP Version 3 Release 1 for MVS: Customization and Administration Guide* and *X.25 Network Control Program Packet Switching Interface Planning and Installation.*

### 5.10.1.2 VM

The X25IPI virtual machine runs a GCS (Group Control System) application program called X25IPI, which is the interface between the TCPIP virtual machine's IUCV driver and your X.25 network. X25IPI communicates with the NPSI (X.25 NCP Packet Switching Interface) in a front-end IBM 37XX Communications Controller.

For more details, please refer to the *IBM TCP/IP Version 2 Release 3 for VM: Planning and Customization* and *X.25 Network Control Program Packet Switching Interface Planning and Installation.*

The IBM 9370 X.25 Communication Subsystem Controller provides support for non-SNA users. It is designed to support communications between hosts running TCP/IP over an X.25 network. For more details, please refer to *IBM 9370 Information System X.25 Communications Subsystem Description.*

### 5.10.1.3 X.25 Scenario using the IBM 9370

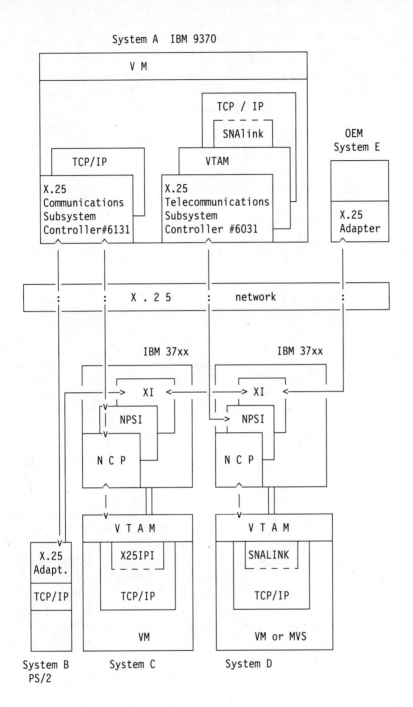

*Figure* **5-11.** *X.25 Example Scenario*

Using the two 9370 adapters, XI, NPSI, and standard functions of TCP/IP, we may build a network allowing the following possibilities:

- From System A, a user can access System B using the IBM 9370 X.25 Communication Subsystem Controller supported by TCP/IP. This is transparent for the user doing a TELNET or FTP, which are standard functions of TCP/IP.
- From System A to System C, the user enters the SNA world by an access to NPSI. Then we are in the VTAM area. The link between VTAM and TCP/IP is realized by X25IPI, which is a virtual machine owned by TCP/IP.
- From System A to System D, the TCP/IP connection is an SNA link over an X.25 network. Viewed from TCP/IP, the physical network can be any one supported by SNA.
- System B and System E may be linked through XI capabilities.

**Note:** The X.25 Telecommunication Subsystem Controller integrated into the IBM 9370 is only supported by the Virtual Telecommunication Access Method (VTAM). It is designed as a part of System Network Achitecture (SNA). On the other hand, the IBM 9370 X.25 Communication Subsystem Controller is supported only by TCP/IP.

## 5.11 3745 and Ethernet Adapter

The 3745 when installed with an ESS (3745 Ethernet SubSystem), and running the NCP (Network Control Program) Version 6, support the routing of IP and ARP Ethernet traffic. Both Ethernet V2 and IEEE 802.3 frames are supported by the 3745 ESS. It supports communication from:

- Ethernet IP workstation/host to Ethernet IP workstation/host

- Ethernet IP workstation/host to VM/MVS TCP/IP host.

### 5.11.1 Principle of Operation

NCP IP routing uses SNA sessions to transport IP datagrams across an SNA backbone network. SNA sessions are established from NCP IP nodes to other NCP IP nodes and SNALINK TCP/IP hosts. IP datagrams are enveloped at an IP node into an SNA RU and sent across an SNA session to a destination NCP IP node or SNALINK TCP/IP host. The routing mechanism is based on static NCP routing tables. The destination NCP IP node or SNALINK TCP/IP host de-envelopes the IP datagrams and sends the frames to an Ethernet/802.3 LAN or a TCP/IP host subsystem respectively. NCP also supports the TCP/IP Address Resolution Protocol (ARP). IP traffic will benefit from NCP routing of IP within the SNA backbone network (error recovery, flow control, etc.).

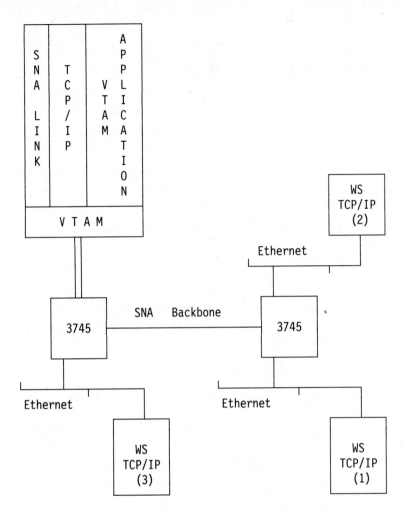

*Figure* **5-12.** *3745 and Ethernet Adapter*

## 5.11.2 Example

All the workstations can access a VTAM application in the host using TELNET.

All the workstations can access a TCP/IP application in the host (for example FTP).

Workstation 1 can communicate with workstation 2 (Ethernet-to-Ethernet in the same 3745).

Workstation 1 can communicate with workstation 3 (Ethernet-to-Ethernet in different 3745s using the SNA backbone).

# 5.12  3174 Establishment Controller

The IBM 3174 Establishment Controller Configuration Support-C Release 6 provides TCP/IP TELNET client support, to communicate with TCP/IP TELNET servers via its token-ring interface, for the following attached devices:

- 3270 CUT-mode terminals and ASCII display stations

- intelligent workstations coaxially attached (installed with either OS/2 with TCP/IP for OS/2, or DOS with TCP/IP for DOS and the IBM Workstation Peer Communication Support Program)

The TELNET hosts (servers) may be attached directly to the same token-ring which the 3174 is connected to, or they may exist anywhere in the network reachable via that token-ring and any bridges or routers. These TELNET hosts can also be non-IBM hosts that provide TELNET server support.

### 5.12.1.1  3174 Supported TELNET Terminal Types

For the coaxially attached display terminals, the 3174 supports the following 24x80 full-screen terminal types:  IBM3101, DEC VT100, DEC VT220 and Data General D210.

For the ASCII-Emulation Adapter-attached ASCII display terminals, the 3174 passes the terminal data stream transparently to the TELNET server.  This means that the TELNET server manages the display terminal as if it were a locally attached ASCII terminal.

The TELNET line mode is also supported for all displays.

In addition, TN3270 protocol support and Ethernet connectivity support are provided. TN3270 support allows the 3174 to support 3270 data stream traffic across TCP/IP links.

LPD and LPR printing functions are also supported.

# 5.13 PC and PS/2 Connections

## 5.13.1 Connections Supported by TCP/IP for OS/2

TCP/IP for OS/2 conforms to the Networks Device Interface Specification (NDIS) and has been tested with the following network adapters:

For Micro Channel workstations:

- IBM Token-Ring Network Adapter/A
- IBM Token-Ring Network 16/4 Adapter/A
- IBM Token-Ring Network Bus Master 16/4 Adapter
- IBM PC Network Adapter
- IBM 3174 Peer Communications Network Adapter
- IBM PS/2 Adapter/A for Ethernet Networks
- 3Com Etherlink/MC Network Adapter
- Western Digital Ethercard PLUS/A Adapter
- Ungerman-Bass NIUpc Network Adapter
- IBM X.25 Interface Coprocessor/2

For AT workstations:

- IBM Token-Ring Network Adapter
- IBM Token-Ring Network Adapter II
- IBM Token-Ring Network 16/4 Adapter
- IBM PC Network Adapter
- IBM 3174 Peer Communications Network Adapter
- 3Com Etherlink II Network Adapter
- Western Digital Ethercard PLUS Network Adapter
- Ungerman-Bass NIUpc Network Adapter
- Other adapters with NDIS Device Drivers

## 5.13.2 Connections Supported by TCP/IP for DOS

TCP/IP for DOS conforms to the Networks Device Interface Specification. The following connections and adapters are supported:

For PC AT, PS/2 Model 25 or 30 (EISA):

- IBM Token-Ring Network using:
  - IBM Token-Ring Network PC Adapter
  - IBM Token-Ring Network PC Adapter II
  - IBM Token-Ring Network 16/4 Adapter
  - IBM Token-Ring Network 16/4 Adapter II
- IBM PC Network using:

- IBM PC Network Adapter II
- IBM PC Network Baseband Adapter
- IBM PC Network Adapter II Frequency 2
- IBM PC Network Adapter II Frequency 3
- Ethernet Network using:
  - IBM LAN Adapter for Ethernet
  - 3Com Etherlink Adapter (Model 3C501)
  - 3Com Etherlink II Adapter (Model 3C503)
  - Western Digital Ethercard PLUS Adapter
  - Ungerman-Bass PC-NIC Adapter
  - Other Ethernet Network Adapters using Packet Device Drivers
- SLIP using:
  - Standard RS-232 compatible serial interface and a modem or a serial connection modem cable
- Coax using:
  - IBM 3270 Connection Card, or IBM 3278/3279 Emulation Adapter using IBM 3174 Peer Communications Support Program with NDIS

For PS/2 models with Micro Channel architecture:

- IBM Token-Ring Network using:
  - IBM Token-Ring Network Adapter/A
  - IBM Token-Ring Network 16/4 Adapter/A
- IBM PC Network using:
  - IBM PC Network Baseband Adapter/A
  - IBM PC Network Adapter II/A
  - IBM PC Network Adapter II/A Frequency 2
  - IBM PC Network Adapter II/A Frequency 3
- Ethernet Network using:
  - IBM LAN Adapter/A for Ethernet
  - IBM PS/2 Adapter/A for Ethernet Networks
  - IBM PS/2 Adapter/A for Ethernet Twisted Pair Networks
  - 3Com Etherlink/MC Adapter (Model 3C523)
  - Western Digital Ethercard PLUS/A Adapter
  - Ungerman-Bass NICps/2 Adapter
  - Other Ethernet Network adapters using NDIS Device Drivers or Packet Device Drivers
- SLIP using:
  - Standard RS-232 compatible serial interface and a modem or a serial connection modem cable
- Coax using:
  - IBM 3270 Connection Card, or IBM 3278/3279 Emulation Adapter using IBM 3174 Peer Communications Support Program with NDIS

# 5.14  AIX/ESA Connections

AIX/ESA provides support for the following connections:

- Channel-to-channel (CTC) using:
  - ESCON channels
  - 3088 Channel-to-Channel Adapter
  - S/370 CTC Adapter
- LAN connections using:
  - 8232 LAN Channel Station (token-ring, IEEE 802.3 and Ethernet V2)
  - 3172 Interconnect Controller Model 1 or 3 (token-ring, IEEE 802.3 and Ethernet V2, FDDI)
  - 3172 Interconnect Controller Model 2 (FDDI)
- HYPERchannel connection:
  - NSC HYPERchannel-DX devices (for example FDDI, Ethernet, T1, T3, and RISC System/6000 via the IBM Serial Optical Channel Converter)
- RISC System/6000 connections using:
  - Block multiplexer channel adapter (CLAW)
  - ESCON Control Unit Adapter (CLAW)

# 5.15  RISC System/6000 Connections

The RISC System/6000 provides support for the following connections:

- LAN connections (token-ring, Ethernet and FDDI) using:
  - Token-Ring High-Performance Network Adapter
  - Ethernet High-Performance LAN Adapter
  - Fiber Distributed Data Interface (FDDI) (single and dual ring)
- WAN connections:
  - 4-Port Multiprotocol Communications Controller
  - X.25 Interface Co-Processor/2
- Host connections (also see 5.15.1, "RISC System/6000 Parallel Channel Attachment" on page  5-26):
  - Block Multiplexor Channel Adapter
  - Serial Optical Channel Converter
  - RISC System/6000 ESCON Control Unit Adapter
    It enables the connection to one or more System/390 host systems via ESCON channel using 3088 or CLAW.
- Asynchronous connections:
  - 8 and 16 Port Asynchronous Adapters (RS232 and RS422)
  - 64 Port Asynchronous Adapter (RS232)
  - 4 Port Multiprotocol Communications Controller (RS232, RS422, V.35, X.21)

## 5.15.1 RISC System/6000 Parallel Channel Attachment

The RISC System/6000 supports the RISC System/6000 Block Multiplexer Channel Adapter. This provides high-speed parallel attachment between the RISC System/6000 and ES/9000, 3090, 308X and 4381 systems. A programming interface is provided at the device driver level to AIX.

The adapter device driver communicates to the same CLAW (Common Link Access to Workstation) device driver in MVS and VM as the 3172-3 mentioned in 5.1.1, "3172 TCP/IP Offload" on page 5-2.

TCP/IP for MVS V3R1, TCP/IP for VM V2R3 and AIX/ESA all support this RISC System/6000 PCA.

For more details, please refer to *AIX Block Multiplexer Channel Adapter User's Guide and Programming Reference*.

## 5.15.2 RISC System/6000 ESCON Control Unit Adapter

The implementation of the ESCON Control Unit Adapter is very similar to the Block Multiplexer.

For more details, please refer to *Enterprise Systems Connection Adapter Guide and Service Information*.

# 5.16 The IBM Nways Router Family

IBM offers two different multiprotocol routers:

- IBM 6611 Nways Network Processor

  Full function, multiprotocol, multiport router and bridge, based on IBM RISC technology.

- IBM 2210 Nways Multiprotocol Router

  Full function, low cost, entry node for small workgroups or remote offices based on the MC68360 processor.

Following is a brief description of both routers and their major functions.

## 5.16.1 IBM 6611 Network Processor

This router is offered in four different models, 120, 125, 145 and 175. The second digit of the model number represents the number of available slots for network adapter cards. The model 120 is offered in 10 fixed configurations while all others can hold any of the following adapters:

- 2-Port Multi-Interface Serial Adapter
- 4-Port Multi-Interface Serial Adapter
- 2-Port Token-Ring Network 16/4 Adapter
- Multi-Interface Serial/Token-Ring Adapter
- 2-Port Ethernet Adapter
- Multi-Interface Serial/Ethernet Adapter
- 4-Port SDLC Adapter

For more details, please refer to *IBM 6611 Network Processor Introduction and Planning Guide*.

The software support of the 6611 is provided by the preloaded *IBM Multiprotocol Network Program 1.3 (MPNP 5648-016)*. It provides the following major protocol functions:

- TCP/IP

  RIP, RIP V2 with variable subnet masking, OSPF, EGP, BGP, BOOTP request/reply forwarding for centrally located BOOTP server

- IPX
- DECnet (Phase IV and Phase IV-Prime)
- AppleTalk (Phase 2)
- Banyan VINES
- XNS
- Source-route bridging
- Transparent bridging
- Translational bridging
- Frame Relay

  RFC 1490: Multiprotocol Interconnect over Frame Relay supported for all protocols

  RFC 1293: InARP support for all protocols

- PPP

RFCs: 1171, 1331, 1332, 1333, 1548, 1549 and others for specific protocols.

All protocols are supported on PPP

Link quality monitoring is supported

- X.25

- SNA (over DLSw) and APPN

  Integration of SNA and APPN in the multiprotocol network

- NetBIOS (over DLSw)

### 5.16.1.1 Configuration, Management and Maintenance

The *Configuration Program* enables you to create a 6611 configuration which defines the interfaces and protocols you want to run. This program runs on the AIX/6000, OS/2 and DOS Windows platform and provides a graphical user interface for easy configuration. After you have finished the configuration the program creates a diskette with the binary files for the 6611.

The *System Manager* provides menu-driven and command line interfaces to view statistics, perform problem determination, install and update software, access other nodes in the network or make configuration changes.

The SNMP agent includes the following major functions:

- All standard MIB II objects

- Enterprise-specific 6611 MIBs

- RFC 1493 - Definitions of Managed Objects for Bridges

- RFC 1525 - Definitions of Managed Objects for Source Routing Bridges

- TRAP generation and GET/SET support, for example, SNMP SET Activate/Deactivate APPN Ports

The IBM 6611 is fully interoperable with the IBM 2210 and routers from other vendors if they comply with the open standards.

The newest 6611 MIB is available from the anonymous FTP server: ftp://venera.isi.edu/mib on the Internet.

For more details, please refer to *IBM Multiprotocol Network Program: User's Guide*.

## 5.16.2 IBM 2210 Nways Multiprotocol Router

This is a low-cost router with very rich functionality for branch office environments which need to be connected to the multiprotocol backbone of an enterprise. All configurations offer at least one LAN and two serial ports. Optionally, there is an ISDN-BRI interface which became available in April 1995 in selected European countries and Japan. The planar board includes processor, memory and interfaces for LAN, WAN and ISDN. The hardware is preconfigured and reconfiguration is not possible. Table 5-1 gives you an overview of the different models and included interfaces. The models with larger memory should be considered for larger networks.

*Table 5-1. IBM 2210 Model and Connectivity Offerings*

| Model | Dual Serial | Token Ring | Ethernet | 2/4 MB flash/ DRAM | 4/8 MB flash/ DRAM | ISDN |
|-------|-------------|------------|----------|--------------------|--------------------|------|
| 121 | x | x | | x | | |
| 122 | x | | x | x | | |
| 123 | x | x | | | x | |
| 124 | x | | x | | x | |
| 125 | x | x | | x | | x |
| 126 | x | | x | x | | x |
| 127 | x | x | | | x | x |
| 128 | x | | x | | x | x |

The IBM 2210 offers a variety of interfaces and connectivity options:

- Ethernet at 10 Mbps

- Token-ring at either 4 or 16 Mbps

- Serial ports for V.35/V.36 (9.6 kbps to 2.048 Mbps), EIA232-D/V.24 (4.8 Kbps to 19.2 Kbps and X.21 at speeds from 2.4 Kbps to 2.048 Mbps supporting PPP, Frame Relay, X.25 and SDLC

- ISDN Basic Rate Interface (BRI, 2B+D) supporting the commonly used S/T interface in Europe and Asia

For more information refer to the *IBM Nways 2210 Multiprotocol Router Planning and Setup Guide*.

All models are shipped preloaded with IBM's Nways Multiprotocol Routing Network Services program (5765-368). The current version is 1.1.0 which provides the following protocol support:

- TCP/IP
  - Routing with RIP or OSPF

- TCP/IP filtering based on TCP/UDP well-known ports to allow or deny a particular application for security reasons

- BOOTP request/reply forwarding

- Variable subnet masking

- Optional routing of IPX over PPP, Frame Relay, X.25, and LANs

- Optional routing of AppleTalk over PPP and LANs

- Bridging:

  - Source-Route Bridging (SRB) over token-ring

  - Transparent Bridging (TB) over Ethernet

  - Source-Route Transparent (SRT) bridging over token-ring

  - Translational bridging (transparent bridging and IBM 8209/8229 emulation) between remote token-rings and Ethernets

- Wide Area Network (WAN) protocols:

  - Point-to-Point Protocol (PPP)

  - Bandwidth reservation over PPP

  - Frame Relay

  - X.25, complies with CCITT 1980 and 1984 specifications

  - Synchronous Data Link Control (SDLC)

  - PU 2.0 or PU 2.1

- Data Link Switching (DLSw), RFC 1434

- SNA

## 5.16.2.1 Configuration, Management and Maintenance

The IBM 2210 comes with a configuration program similar to the IBM 6611. It runs on DOS/Windows, OS/2 and AIX platforms. This program aids you in configuring ports and software functions and allows you to make remote configuration changes while the 2210 is operational. All the configuration is done with an easy-to-use graphical user interface.

The SNMP agent includes the following:

- All standard MIB II objects

- Enterprise-specific 2210 MIBs for features like DLSw as well as Vital Product Data information

- RFC MIBs for protocols like PPP and Frame Relay

- TRAP generation and GET support

The IBM 2210 is fully interoperable with the IBM 6611.

The newest 2210 MIB is available from the anonymous FTP server: ftp://venera.isi.edu/mib on the Internet.

For more details, please refer to *IBM Nways Multiprotocol Routing Network Services: Software User's Guide*.

The product *AIX Router and Bridge Manager/6000* based on *NetView for AIX* provides a graphical user interface in order to manage both the 6611s and the 2210s in your network.

# 5.17 IBM 8229 Local Area Network Bridge

The IBM 8229 Bridge replaces the withdrawn IBM 8209 LAN Bridge.

There are three models available:

- Model 1: Providing a connection between two local token-ring segments
- Model 2: Providing a connection between a local token-ring segment and a local Ethernet segment
- Model 3: Providing a connection between a local token-ring segment and a remote token-ring segment via a WAN at speeds up to T1/E1

The IBM 8229 Local Area Network Bridge allows devices on an IBM token-ring LAN to communicate with devices on an Ethernet V2 or IEEE 802.3 LAN. The 8229 converts the data exchange between the two LANs. To a device on the token-ring LAN, the 8229 appears as a bridge to another token-ring LAN. The 8229 is functionally transparent to any device on the Ethernet V2 or IEEE 802.3 LANs.

In addition, the 8229:

- Supports Ethernet V2 and IEEE 802.3 traffic at the same time
- Supports either a 4 or a 16 Mbps token-ring LAN and does not affect communications between token-ring stations
- Supports the IBM LAN Network Manager and NetView/390 for network management (LLC Type 2)
- Provides an SNMP agent to support an SNMP manager like NetView for AIX with the following MIBs:
  - MIB II (RFC 1213)

– Standard Bridge MIB (RFC 1286)

– IBM Enterprise MIB

- Provides flash memory for code download

- Provides RS-232 port for out-of-band code download (XMODEM)

- Can be configured as the secondary bridge of the following IBM split bridges:

  – IBM Token Ring Bridge Program Version 2.2

  – IBM Remote Token-Ring Bridge/DOS Version 1.0

- Is rack mountable

- Provides isolation between the LANs so unnecessary Ethernet LAN activity does not intrude into the token-ring LAN environment and vice versa

Figure 5-13 shows a simple 8229 connection diagram.

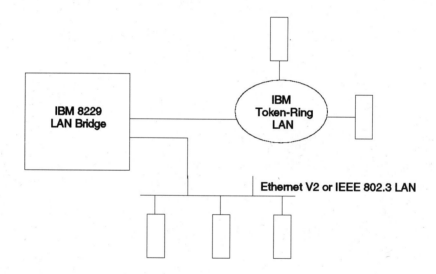

*Figure 5-13. 8229 Connection Diagram*

The 8229 is configured to operate in one of two modes:

- Mode 1 - When the 8229 is configured to operate in mode 1, performing subnetwork access protocol (SNAP) header processing, the TCP/IP or IPX protocol is supported. Logical Link Control (LLC) based protocols, such as SNA or NetBIOS, are also supported in this mode through token-ring to Ethernet conversion for LLC-based protocols.

- Mode 2 - When the 8229 is configured in mode 2, as a transparent MAC bridge, the 8229 transparently supports the transfer of LLC data. Protocols that are LLC-based and that may use the 8229 in this mode are the SNA and NetBIOS protocols.

Mode 1 is described in more detail as it supports the TCP/IP protocol. In mode 1 two different conversions are supported: token-ring to Ethernet and Ethernet to token-ring. Figure 5-14 shows a layered diagram of 8229 TCP/IP support.

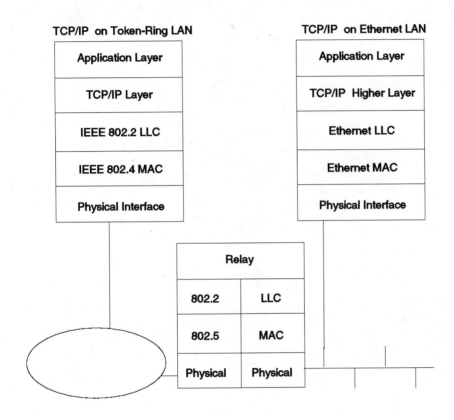

*Figure* *5-14.* *8229 TCP/IP Support.* Layered diagram.

Figure 5-15 on page 5-34 shows the conversion process.

Token–Ring to Ethernet Conversion

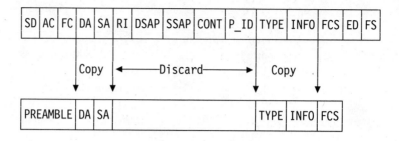

Ethernet to Token–Ring Conversion

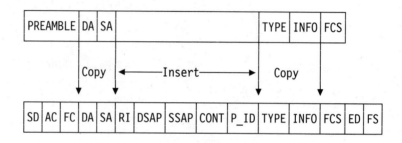

*Figure* **5-15.** *8229 TCP/IP Support.* Conversion process.

In the Ethernet to token-ring conversion the 8229 retrieves the source routing information associated with the token-ring destination address and inserts these fields and the fixed hex values AA AA 03 00 00 00 (SNAP header) representing the DSAP, SSAP, control and protocol ID fields into the frame.

The 8229 provides the following connections:

- Token-ring (all models)
  - DB-9 connector for STP cable (150 Ohms)
  - RJ-45 connector for UTP cable (100 Ohms)
- Ethernet/802.3 (Model 2)
  - AUI connector for 10Base-5 or 10Base-2 attachment
  - RJ-45 connector for 10Base-T attachment
- WAN (Model 3 only)
  - RS-232

- V.35
- X.21

# 5.18 IBM 8271 EtherStreamer Switch

LAN switches are a new family of network building blocks designed to increase the performance of departmental LANs and distributed workgroups and to do so in a cost effective manner. LAN segmentation, the separation of a population of LAN users into separate but interconnected LAN segments, is a popular technique for improving LAN performance by reducing contention. LAN switches offer a high performance, low cost alternative method for interconnecting LAN segments. The IBM 8271 creates multiple, high-speed, parallel paths among the connected Ethernet LAN segments and devices. Since each of these parallel paths supports the full 10 Mbps Ethernet bandwidth, total bandwidth of Ethernet networks segmented using the IBM 8271 can be expanded to up to 400% of previous levels.

The IBM 8271 supports full-duplex (bidirectional) communication with LAN stations equipped with Full-Duplex Ethernet adapters, such as the IBM EtherStreamer MC 32 Adapter. Full-duplex Ethernet connections can provide up to twice the bandwidth of standard half-duplex connections, that is, up to 20 Mbps on each of the switch ports (max. 8). A typical network would benefit from using the IBM 8271 by placing each server on a dedicated full-duplex segment and placing client workstations on shared segments using standard Ethernet concentrators, such as the IBM 8222 6-Port 10BaseT Workgroup Hub.

The IBM 8271 works like a normal Ethernet transparent multiport bridge and supports the spanning tree algorithm.

The SNMP agent has the following functionality:

- MIB II
- 8271 specific MIB
- SNMP GET/SET support
- Possible TRAPs:
  - Cold Start
  - Warm Start
  - Authentication Failure
  - New Root (related to spanning tree)
  - Topology Change (related to spanning tree)

TFTP/BOOTP is provided for microcode or configuration download.

For graphical management there is a Product Specific Module (PSM) available for use with the application *NetView for Windows* which greatly simplifies the management.

For further information please refer to *IBM 8271 Etherstreamer Switch Planning Guide*.

# 5.19  The IBM Hubs Family

Basically a hub is a wiring concentrator which connects the participating LAN workstations in a star-wired cabling system. Therefore a hub is mostly located in the wiring closet or near the workgroups. Today the term hub is used to describe multiprotocol devices offering sophisticated network management features and great flexibility for configuration.

One of the trends in networking is the move to centralize network functions in the wiring closet. This goes along with the trend toward collapsed backbones. A collapsed backbone uses the intelligent hub as the network backbone rather than using a segment of cable. Thus the backbone of the network is collapsed into the intelligent hub. This allows the network administrator to consolidate many network functions into a fault tolerant intelligent hub.

Hubs have been used in networks for wiring concentration for many years. Early hubs were passive devices that only provided for network connection such as the 8228. New hubs are becoming more sophisticated and they can do much more than act as wiring concentrators.

The following network functions can be consolidated in the intelligent hub:

- Port concentration
- Software bank and port switching - you can switch a user or a group of users from one network to another through software which saves time when making changes in the network
- Network management
- Terminal attachment - there are modules for attaching asynchronous terminals and 3270 terminals
- Bridging (SRB, TB, SRT, Translational Bridging)
- Switching - similar to bridging but faster

IBM offers a large variety of hub products to build a secure, reliable and manageable LAN. Hubs can be divided into two major groups: the first group, which supports only one specific LAN protocol token-ring or FDDI (workgroup hubs) for example, and the second which supports multiple LAN protocols in a single box (intelligent hubs). In this section you get a brief description of the different available hubs and the major information from a TCP/IP point of view.

## 5.19.1 IBM 8230 Token-Ring Controlled Access Unit

The IBM 8230 is an intelligent token-ring network wiring concentrator, providing enhanced levels of control and reliability over passive token-ring network wiring concentrators, such as the IBM 8228.

The 8230 is a rack mountable device that:

- Supports ring operation at 4 and 16 Mbps
- Is able to function as a repeater in both ring directions (on main and backup path)
- Has pluggable ring-in and ring-out modules to support copper and fiber cable
- Has token-ring MAC appearances on both the main and backup ring path
- May have its microcode loaded from the IBM LAN Network Manager, or from a diagnostic utility, which is provided
- The IBM 8230 supports  the IBM LAN Network Manager over CMOL by:
  - Maintaining the IBM LAN Network Manager's configuration table
  - Providing access control by reporting station insertions
  - Asset control in conjunction with IBM LAN Network Manager
- With the new Models 003 and 013 you have the ability to select either the CMOL or the SNMP management option with a switch on the front panel. There is a Product Specific Module (PSM) provided in order to manage this device graphically from NetView for Windows.
- The SNMP agent supports the following functions:
  - MIB II
  - Enterprise-specific MIB
  - Trap sending
  - GET/SET ability to enable/disable ports etc.

  All SNMP setup is done via the out-of-band management port (RS-232).

  The microcode update is done over TFTP.

  The CMOL management provides the same functionality.

For further information please refer to *IBM 8230 Model 3 Planning Guide*.

## 5.19.2  IBM 8222 Workgroup Hub

The IBM 8222 offers low-cost attachment for six 10Base-T nodes and has no in- or out-of-band network management.  One of the six ports can be used to cascade to another 10BaseT concentrator when expansion is needed.  Its suitable environment could be in small offices, using either permanently installed UTP or short lengths of UTP between devices that are in close proximity to one another. However, the modular expandability of Ethernet and relatively easy connection to the earlier bus topologies allow the IBM 8222 to be used as part of larger, even establishment-wide, LANs.

For further information please refer to *IBM 6-Port 10Base-T Workgroup Hub Installation & Planning Guide*.

## 5.19.3  IBM 8224 Ethernet Stackable Hub

The 8224 is IBM's newest Ethernet/802.3 hub. It provides low cost connectivity for 10Base-T networks.  It can be managed through SNMP and it can connect to existing 10Base-5, 10Base-2, 10Base-T, and fiber networks.

The 8224 is a stackable, SNMP manageable Ethernet hub for 10Base-T networks. The following is a list of 8224 features:

- 16 10Base-T ports

- Up to 10 8224s in a stack

- Model 2 is SNMP manageable

  Supported are RFC 1213 MIB II, RFC 1516 Hub Repeater MIB for 802.3 and Novell Repeater MIB. The SNMP agent uses either IP or IPX as a networking protocol. Therefore the 8224 can be managed with an SNMP manager or Novell's NetWare Management Station. There is a Product Specific Module (PSM) available to manage this hub graphically from the IBM NetView for Windows application.

- Up to 9 8224 Model 1s can be managed by a Model 2

- Optional media expansion port to attach to 10Base-2, 10Base-5, fiber

- A stack of 8224s can be segmented into separate Ethernet segments

For further information please refer to *IBM 8224 Ethernet Stackable Hub Installation and User' Guide*.

## 5.19.4  IBM 8244 FDDI Workgroup Concentrator

The IBM 8244 Fiber Distributed Data Interface (FDDI) Workgroup Concentrator is the primary attachment to the FDDI dual ring for attaching workstations to the backbone. The 8244 FDDI concentrator allows attaching up to 12 devices to a 100 Mbps network. These devices may be connected via:

- Multimode optical fiber, or

- IBM Cabling System's shielded twisted pair (STP) copper cable, or

- Unshielded twisted pair (UTP-5) copper cable

The 8244 can provide connection for FDDI devices that are based on the ANSI and ISO standards. The 8244 will operate with management entities that support the ANSI Station Management (SMT) 7.3 frame-based protocols.

Concentrator management is made possible via the imbedded FDDI SNMP agent. This agent will maintain the concentrator's FDDI MIB for SMT 7.3 (RFC 1512) and MIB II (RFC 1213) parameters for use by NetView for AIX or any original equipment manufacturer (OEM) SNMP-based network management system.

Network management is further enhanced by use of the complementary FDDI SNMP Proxy Agent on the OS/2 platform. This agent will convert SMT to SNMP protocols for use by NetView for AIX or any OEM SNMP-based network management system.

For further information please refer to *IBM 8244 FDDI Workgroup Concentrator: User' Guide*.

## 5.19.5  IBM 8250 Multiprotocol Intelligent Hub

The IBM 8250 Multiprotocol Intelligent Hub is a family of products designed to provide the platform to build LANs meeting the requirements of customers using various types of cabling systems (such as STP, UTP, fiber and coax) and different types of LANs (such as token-ring, Ethernet, and FDDI).

The 8250 family consists of four models of rack-mountable chassis, each offering an advanced backplane architecture, which allows the concurrent operation of several LANs using various LAN protocols. A range of media and management modules are also provided to allow the design of networks addressing the individual needs of each organization.

8250 modules can be added, removed or reconfigured while the 8250 is in operation. This allows changes to the configuration of the network without affecting the operation of the other users on the network.

For management purposes you need at least one management module per hub. This module can be one of the available management modules, a basic token-ring management module for example. Each of these modules includes a media access adapter, depending on the type of module, for in-band management and a RS-232 interface for out-of-band management. The module also includes the SNMP agent function with MIB II and a specific 8250 MIB and a TELNET server for remote configuration. The management module has access to all other modules residing in the same hub via the management bus on the backplane. This gives you the ability to change the port assignments for example of a token-ring media module from an Ethernet management module without the need to buy a protocol specific management module for each supported protocol in the hub. Of course you won't get any media specific statistics or failures from another segment or LAN type.

The microcode update can be done by TFTP.

Management can be simplified by using the graphical application *IBM Intelligent Hub Manager for AIX*.

The newest 8250 MIB is available from the anonymous FTP server: ftp://venera.isi.edu/mib on the Internet.

For further information please refer to *IBM 8250 Multiprotocol Intelligent Hub and IBM 8260 Multiprotocol Intelligent Switching Hub Planning and Site Preparation Guide*.

## 5.19.6  IBM 8260 Multiprotocol Intelligent Hub

The 8260 is IBM's newest intelligent hub. It is a hub platform for enterprise networking with an option of ATM for future growth. It can use existing 8250 modules so customers who have invested in 8250s can move to the 8260 without discarding their modules.

It can be used as a data center hub for consolidation of enterprise network functions. It also can be used as a wiring closet hub for port concentration and management.

It has all the features of the 8250 and the following new features:

- Increased LAN capacity
- Power supply load sharing for increased fault tolerance
- Distributed management architecture
- ATM upgrade option
- ATM media modules

The management of the 8260 hub is similar to the 8250 but more flexible. You can manage multiple LAN segments concurrently with only one management module because of the distributed architecture. The SNMP agent with the MIB II, the 8260 specific MIB, the TELNET server and all the IP functionality resides in the Distributed Management Module (DMM). The media access is provided by Media Access Cards (MAC) which can reside either as daughter cards directly on the media module or on the DMM carrier module. With this architecture you can "watch" up to 6 segments with only one DMM card. This saves space for other media modules and increases the maximum port density.

Management can be simplified by using the graphical application *IBM Intelligent Hub Manager for AIX*.

ATM management

The 8260 Switch/Control Point Module implements an SNMP ATM agent that includes objects defined by the standards bodies, as well as IBM specific extensions for superior manageability of ATM networks from the network management station

This SNMP agent features the following functions:

- Full SNMP support (get, getnext, set and traps) allowing complete control and monitoring through SNMP commands
- Support of IP over ATM (RFC 1577) for node management and services. Network management stations can therefore contact the switch/control point module agent either through direct connection to the ATM network using IP over ATM, or connected to a traditional LAN that is routed to the ATM subnetwork
- MIB 2 support
- Full ILMI[1] (ATM Forum V3.0) support (at UNI[2] and from network management station)
- IETF AToMIB, allowing the network administrator to display the status and configuration of 8260 ATM interfaces, including active VPCs and VCCs. Statistics on ATM interfaces are also collected via this MIB
- MIB support for topology and route computation management, allowing the display from the central management station of the topology of the 8260 network and the set of attached ATM stations
- IBM-specific extensions

With the graphical application *IBM ATM Campus Manager for AIX* the management is greatly simplified.

The newest 8260 MIB is available from the anonymous FTP server: *ftp://venera.isi.edu/mib* on the Internet.

For further information please refer to *IBM 8250 Multiprotocol Intelligent Hub and IBM 8260 Multiprotocol Intelligent Switching Hub Planning and Site Preparation Guide.*

---

1 ILMI (Interim Local Management Interface) defined by ATM Forum to provide standardized management information and formats until the official ITU-T (former CCITT) standard is produced.

2 UNI(User Network Interface)

## 5.20 Connectivity Summary

The following table shows operating system support for selected connectivity options.

| | S/370 | | | PS/2 | | RISC/6000 | AS/400 |
|---|---|---|---|---|---|---|---|
| | MVS | VM | AIX | DOS | OS/2 | AIX | OS/400 |
| Token–Ring | x | x | x | x | x | x | x |
| Ethernet V2 | x | x | x | x | x | x | x |
| 802.3 | x | x | x | x | x | x | x |
| FDDI | x | x | x | x | x | x | x |
| PC Network | x | x | | x | x | | |
| X.25 | x | x | PS/2 | | x | x | x |
| SLIP | | | | x | x | x | |
| SNALINK LU0 | x | x | | | | | |
| LU6.2 | x | x | | | x | | |
| HYPERchannel | x | x | x | | | | |
| HIPPI | x | | x | | | | |
| CTC | x | x | | | | | |
| CETI | x | | | | | | |
| RS/6000 PCA | x | x | x | | | x | |
| RS/6000 ECUA | x | x | x | | | x | |
| 3172 Offload | x | x | | | | | |
| 3745 ESS | x | x | | | | | |
| 3174 Telnetd | x | x | x | | x | x | x |

```
SOD          = Statement of Direction
PCA          = Parallel Channel Attachment
ECUA         = ESCON Control Unit Adapter
3745 ESS     = 3745 Ethernet SubSystem support for IP and ARP routing
3174 Telnetd = Telnet Server support for the 3174 Telnet Client function
```

*Figure   5-16.  Connectivity Summary*

# Chapter 6.  Internet Access

In the past the Internet was reserved for researchers, scientists and academics to exchange or provide world-wide information. The major tools for communication across the network were E-Mail, FTP, and TELNET. Internet access for private individuals was very difficult and its use for commercial purposes was strictly forbidden because the Internet was largely funded by the government. The capability of the hardware (non-programmable terminals), the modem speeds and the bandwidth of the network made graphical presentation of information impossible.

The Internet gradually became more open to the wider world, as the Internet access provider companies offered Internet access that was affordable to private individuals. This process was driven by a fall in technology costs, including telecommunications services, hence making it more economical to access the Internet. Associated with this change has been the need to find effective navigation tools for exploring the Internet. The goals for an Internet front end system are:

- Ease of installation and use

- Navigation support

- Provide access to complex Internet technologies like TELNET, Gopher, USENET, FTP, mail, etc.

- Operating system independent

- Simple access to text, audio, video and graphics (one-button press only)

There is a variety of Internet navigators available. Each tool has particular strengths for certain types of applications. Here are the most popular tools with a brief description:

- WAIS Wide Area Information Services

  Well suited to index and search large databases. Widely used by librarians and researchers.

- Gopher

  Tool to provide menu access to existing information. Many organizations use this tool instead of an anonymous FTP site. See 6.1, "Gopher" on page  6-2.

- Veronica:

  Search tool for the Gopher environment. See 6.1.2, "Veronica" on page  6-5.

- Archie

  One of the first navigators, used to search files on FTP sites.

- WWW World Wide Web

Provides an index of existing information like Gopher but supports hypertext and hypermedia to create new documents containing text, audio, video and graphics. WWW has become very popular. See 6.2, "World Wide Web" on page 6-6.

But on the other hand what about security? All these new possibilities to retrieve or provide information on the Internet imply that your network has access to the world-wide Internet and all others have access to your network. What you want is to connect to the Internet so that you can use all these new services to find and retrieve all the wonderful new information out there, but you don't want network "hackers" to be able to access your files.

IBM offers the product *IBM NetSP Secured Network Gateway* to build a secured network access for your network. The *firewall* concepts are described later in this chapter.

## 6.1 Gopher

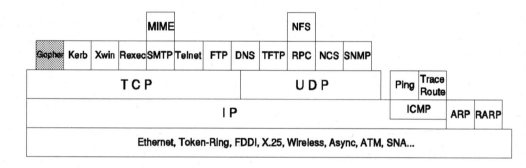

*Figure 6-1. Gopher*

In short, the Internet Gopher is a distributed document search and retrieval system. It combines the best features of browsing through collections of information and fully indexed databases. The protocol and software follow a client/server model and permit users on a heterogeneous mix of desktop systems to browse, search, and retrieve documents residing on multiple distributed server machines.

The Gopher protocol was developed at the University of Minnesota and is available under RFC 1436. Its state is *informational*.

The reason for developing Gopher was the need for a campus-wide information system which enables anybody to be able to publish documents or information even with a small desktop computer. Gopher client software presents users with a hierarchy of items and directories much like a file system. In fact, the Gopher interface is designed to resemble a file system since a file system is a good model for locating documents and services. So if you are connected to a Gopher server you get a list of different items, similar to the display of a root directory from a PC. After selecting a menu item for example you get all the items included, similar to a subdirectory and so forth. If you select a file item for example the file is automatically transmitted and displayed at the client. It is not necessary for the file to reside on the same Gopher server where you got the information. A Gopher menu can include items from different Gopher servers and the user gets automatically connected to the server where the selected item points to and so on. The user does not know or care that the items up for selection may reside on many different machines anywhere on the Internet.

A simple example:

You would like to have a look at the menu of your canteen.

1. Start your Gopher client and connect to the main Gopher server

2. Find an item which could include the menu and select it. For example: Facilities

3. The sub-items of Facilities are displayed

4. One of the items may be "Today's Menu" which is a file residing on the canteen's Gopher server

5. If you select it your Gopher client automatically establishes a connection to the server pointed to in the item, retrieves and displays the file

The path to the file could be very complex and Gopher servers around the world could be involved.

To implement the above mentioned hierarchy the Gopher client needs some information of the object type in order to display a file or a directory icon for example. The Gopher type is coded as a single digit at the beginning of each line. Following is a list of known Gopher types included in the RFC:

- 0 - Item is a file
- 1 - Item is a directory
- 2 - Item is a CSO (qi) phone-book server
- 3 - Error
- 4 - Item is a BinHexed Macintosh file
- 5 - Item is a DOS binary archive of some sort
- 6 - Item is a UNIX uuencoded file
- 7 - Item is an Index-Search server
- 8 - Item points to a text-based telnet session

- 9 - Item is a binary file
- T - TN3270 connection
- s - Sound type. Data stream is a mulaw sound
- g - GIF type
- M - Item contains MIME data
- h - html type
- I - Image type
- i - "inline" text type

The following paragraphs describe the basic functionality of the Gopher protocol.

In essence, the Gopher protocol consists of a client connecting to a server and sending the server a selector (a line of text, which may be empty) via a TCP connection. The server responds with a block of text terminated with a period on a line by itself, and closes the connection. No state is retained by the server between transactions with a client. Let's assume a Gopher server listens to port 70. The only configuration information the client software retains is this server's name and port number (in this example that machine is rawBits.micro.umn.edu and the port 70). In the example below the F character denotes the TAB character.

```
Client: {Opens connection to rawBits.micro.umn.edu at port 70}
Server: {Accepts connection but says nothing}

Client: <CR><LF> {Sends an empty line: Meaning "list what you have"}
Server: {Sends a series of lines, each ending with CR LF}
0About internet GopherFStuff:About usFrawBits.micro.umn.eduF70
1Around University of MinnesotaFZ,5692,AUMFunderdog.micro.umn.eduF70
1Microcomputer News & PricesFPrices/Fpserver.bookstore.umn.eduF70
1Courses, Schedules, CalendarsFFevents.ais.umn.eduF9120
1Student-Staff DirectoriesFFuinfo.ais.umn.eduF70
1Departmental PublicationsFStuff:DP:FrawBits.micro.umn.eduF70
                        {.....etc.....}
       .                {Period on a line by itself}
                        {Server closes connection}
```

The first character on each line describes the Gopher type as shown above. The succeeding characters up to the tab build the display string to be shown to the user for making a selection. The characters following the tab, up to the next tab form a selector string that the client software must send to the server to retrieve the document (or directory listing). In practice, the selector string is often a path name or other file selector used by the server to locate the item desired. The next two tab delimited fields denote the domain-name of the host that has this document (or directory), and the port at which to connect. A CR/LF denotes the end of the item. The client may present the above data stream as follows:

```
About Internet Gopher
Around the University of Minnesota...
Microcomputer News & Prices...
Courses, Schedules, Calendars...
Student-Staff Directories...
Departmental Publications...
```

In this case, directories are displayed with an ellipsis and files are displayed without any. However, depending on the platform the client is written for and the author's taste, item types could be denoted by other text tags or by icons.

In the example, line 1 describes a document the user will see as "*About Internet Gopher*". To retrieve this document, the client software must send the retrieval string: "*Stuff:About us" to rawBits.micro.umn.edu at port 70*. If the client does this, the server will respond with the contents of the document, terminated by a period on a line by itself. As you can see in this example the user does not know or care that the items up for selection may reside on many different machines anywhere on the Internet. The connection between server and client only exists while the information is transferred. After this the client may connect to a different server in order to get the contents of a displayed directory.

For further information about the Gopher protocol please refer to the *RFC 1436*. For a list of frequently asked questions including the anonymous FTP sites for retrieving the Gopher client and server code please get the following file from anonymous FTP: URL:ftp://rtfm.mit.edu/pub/usenet/news.answers/gopher-faq.

## 6.1.1 Implementations
A Gopher client is implemented in OS/2 Warp V3.0 and Internet Connection V3.0 for Windows.

## 6.1.2 Veronica
As interesting as it can be to explore "Gopherspace", one day you might want to retrieve some information or a file from a Gopher server. The problem is how to get the right servers providing the information needed without calling up endless Gopher menus. Fortunately there is a way to make even Gophers easier to use.

This tool is called Veronica (Very Easy Rodent-Oriented Net-wide Index to Computerized Archives) and does for Gopherspace what *Archie* does for FTP sites.

Veronica is a resource-discovery system providing access to information resources held on most ( 99% + ) of the world's Gopher servers. In addition to native Gopher data, Veronica includes references to many resources provided by other types of information servers, such as WWW servers, usenet archives, and telnet-accessible information services.

Veronica queries are keyword-in-title searches. A simple query can be quite powerful because a large number of information servers are included in the index.

Veronica is accessed through Gopher client software. A Veronica user submits a query (via a Gopher client) which may contain boolean keyword expressions as well as special Veronica directives. The result of a Veronica search is a Gopher menu comprising information items whose titles contain the specified keywords. The results menu may be browsed like any other Gopher menu.

In January 1995, 5057 Gopher servers were indexed. The index also includes items from approximately 5000 other servers, in cases where those servers are referenced on Gopher menus. These other servers include 3905 WWW servers and about 1000 TELNET-type services.

On most Gopher servers you will find Veronica by selecting Other Gopher and Information Services at the main menu and then Searching through Gopherspace using Veronica. If your Gopher server does not provide the above items connect directly to Veronica via gopher://veronica.scs.unr.edu.:70/11/veronica. There you will also find additional information about Veronica.

## 6.2 World Wide Web

The World Wide Web is a global hypertext system which was initially developed in 1989 by Tim Berners Lee at the European Laboratory for Particle Physics, CERN in Swizerland. In 1993 the Web started to grow rapidly which was mainly due to the NCSA (National Center for Supercomputing Applications) developing a Web browser program called Mosaic, an X Windows-based application. This application provided the first graphical user interface to the Web and made browsing more convenient.

Today there are Web browsers and servers available for nearly all platforms. You can get them either from an FTP site for free or buy a licensed copy. The rapid growth in popularity of the Web is due to the flexible way people can navigate through world-wide resources in the Internet and retrieve them. To get an idea of the growth of the Web, here are some statistics:

- June 1993 - only 130 Web sites available
- December 1994 - over 11500 Web sites available

The number of Web servers is growing very rapidly (between 50 and 100 daily) and the traffic over port 80, which is the *well known* Web port, on the NSF backbone has a phenomenal rate of growth too.

There are already some companies doing business on the Web. You can look at prospectuses and product offerings and of course order products over the Web. Most of the multinational companies have a Web server in place to distribute product specific information, their portfolio or simply to get in contact with customers. IBM of course has a Web home page with a large number of interesting items. A *page* is just the Web term for a document and the *home page* is a starting point to a collection of documents. It is, if you will, the table of contents of a Web site. From there you can easily explore and search the whole Web. Please see http://www.ibm.com which is the IBM home page.

Presenting a document in hypertext has certain advantages for the user. For example, if you want more information about a particular subject mentioned, you can usually "just click on it" to read further details. Subjects with a link to another document can be easily identified through highlighting. In fact, documents can be and often are linked to other documents by completely different authors, much like footnoting, but you can get the referenced document or graphic instantly displayed. A document on the Web could include links to other documents residing on different Web sites. If you activate the link, mostly done by a mouse click, the other document is automatically retrieved from the corresponding server and displayed. This document could include links to other resources as well and so on.

The standard communication protocol between Web servers and clients is the Hypertext Transfer Protocol (HTTP) which is a draft Internet standard. The HTTP is a generic stateless object-oriented protocol. The IETF has set up a working group to improve the performance of HTTP. Web browsers can also use many other Internet protocols like FTP, Gopher, WAIS and NNTP (Network News Transfer Protocol) for example. So you don't need a particular client product to get access to all these other resources also available on the Net. How the Web browser can differentiate between all these different protocols and which protocols are supported is explained later in this section.

An HTTP transaction consists basically of:

*Connection*
> The establishment of a connection by the client to the server. TCP/IP port 80 is the well-known port, but other non-reserved ports may be specified in the URL.

*Request*  The sending, by the client, of a request message to the server.

*Response*  The sending, by the server, of a response to the client.

*Close*  The closing of the connection by either or both parties.

For a more detailed description of HTTP please refer to the draft documents of the corresponding IETF working group.

The standard markup language for Web documents is HTML (Hypertext Markup Language) which is a draft Internet standard and is presently under construction by several IETF working groups. HTML is an SGML (Standard Generalized Markup

Language) application. IBM's GML is very similar as you can see in the example below. If you want to create a Web document you have to use the HTML tags to build the logical structure of the document, for example headers, lists and paragraphs. There are some tags available to define links to other documents or to imbed a picture in your text.

```
<HTML>  <!-- Begin of document -->
 <HEAD>  <!-- A sample document -->
  <TITLE>This is a Sample</TITLE>
 </HEAD>  <!-- End of the heading section -->
 <BODY>  <!-- Begin of text body -->
  <H1>First Header</H1>
   <P>The first paragraph.
   <UL>  <!-- unordered list -->
    <LI>Item one
   </UL> <!-- End of list -->
 </BODY> <!-- End of text body -->
</HTML> <!-- End of document -->
```

If you who would like an introduction to HTML please refer to the following document: http://info.cern.ch/hypertext/WWW/MarkUp/MarkUp.html.

All documents, images, audio or video clips on the Web are called resources. To address and identify the access method for these resources the Web uses URLs (Uniform Resource Locators). URL is an Internet standards track protocol and can be found under RFC 1738. The global framework for building new addressing schemes to encode names and addresses of objects on the Internet is described in the informational RFC 1630. This RFC introduces the term URI (Universal Resource Identifiers) as a more theoretical model for building these schemes. URIs which refer to an object address (IP address and path information) mapped to an access method using an existing network protocol like HTTP or FTP for example are known as URLs. Therefore an URL is a specific form of a URI. In general, URLs are written as follows:

```
<scheme>:<scheme-specific-part>
```

An URL contains the name of the scheme being used (<scheme>) followed by a colon and then a string (the <scheme-specific-part>) whose interpretation depends on the scheme. The following schemes are covered by the RFC, and other schemes may follow in the future:

- ftp - File Transfer protocol
- http - HyperText Transfer Protocol
- gopher - The Gopher protocol
- mailto - Electronic mail address
- news - USENET news
- nntp - USENET news using NNTP access
- telnet - Interactive sessions

- wais - Wide Area Information Servers
- file - Host-specific file names
- prospero - Prospero Directory Service

While the syntax for the rest of the URL may vary depending on the particular scheme selected, URL schemes that involve the direct use of an IP-based protocol to a specified host on the Internet use a common syntax for the scheme-specific data:

```
//<user>:<password>@<host>:<port>/<url-path>
```

Some or all of the parts "<user>:<password>@", ":<password>", ":<port>", and "/<url-path>" may be excluded. The scheme specific data starts with a double slash "//" to indicate that it complies with the common Internet scheme syntax.

The "url-path" at the end of the scheme supplies the details of how the specified resource can be accessed. Note that the "/" between the host (or port) and the url-path is not part of the url-path.

According to the definition above the HTTP URL looks like this:

```
http://<host>:<port>/<path>?<searchpart>
```

Where:

host        The fully qualified domain name of a network host or a dotted decimal IP address (for example, www.ibm.com).

port        The port number to connect to. If this parameter is omitted in an HTTP URL, it defaults to 80.

path        The path specifies the HTTP selector, a route to an HTML document for example.

? searchpart
            The searchpart is a query string which is indicated with a preceding question mark.

The URL of the RFC 1630 for example looks like this:

```
http://info.cern.ch/hypertext/WWW/Addressing/URL/URI_Overview.html
```

The syntax of all the other defined schemes like FTP and Gopher for example are explained in the RFC 1738.

There are three ways to access the Web:

- Use a Web browser on your own machine

  This is the best option but your corporate LAN must have access to the Internet. In most cases these networks have no direct Internet access, but are connected via a firewall to the Internet. In this case you have to specify either a SOCKS server or a proxy gateway where you are registered to get Internet access. Another way to get connected is the use of the SLIP protocol. With this you set up your own modem connection to an Internet access provider. See 6.3.1, "IBM NetSP Secured Network Gateway" on page 6-11.

- Use a browser on a machine to which you have TELNET access (not as good but also possible).

- Access the Web by E-mail (not very attractive but still possible).

Web browsers are available for most platforms. To get a list of FTP sites providing Web browsers and other useful information please look at ftp://rtfm.mit.edu/pub/usenet/news.answers/www/faq and get the two files located in this subdirectory by anonymous FTP.

These files include the frequently asked questions for Web users. Also included are the host names for TELNET or E-mail access to the Web. Look for the host closest to you.

## 6.2.1 Implementations

The OS/2 Internet Connection shipped with the Bonus Pack of OS/2 Warp includes the IBM WebExplorer.

Internet Connection V3.0 for Windows contains WebExplorer Mosaic.

# 6.3 Firewalls

In essence, a firewall is a barrier between a secure, internal private network and another (non-secure) network or the Internet. The purpose of a firewall is to prevent unwanted or unauthorized communication into or out of the secure network. The firewall has two jobs:

- To keep users in your own network from freely exchanging information with users outside your network

- To keep users who are outside your network from coming in to compromise or attack your network

Normally, hosts in a secure network cannot access the outside network. This reduces the risk of being intruded upon by unauthorized users from the Internet but denies Internet accessibility to users within the secure network. Without Internet accessibility, users in the secure network cannot access important tools, such as TELNET, FTP, Gopher, and World Wide Web, to access the resources available in the Internet.

There are several ways a firewall can protect your network. A firewall can provide screening services that deny or grant access based on such things as user name, host name, and TCP/IP protocol. A firewall can also provide a variety of services that let authorized users through while keeping unauthorized users out. At the same time, it ensures that all communications between your network and the Internet appear to end at the firewall, allowing the outside world no glimpse of the structure of your network.

# 6.3.1 IBM NetSP Secured Network Gateway

The IBM NetSP Secured Network Gateway (NetSP) is a network security firewall program for AIX/6000. NetSP offers a secure internal network and is very selective about who it lets in. In order to control access between your network and the Internet and facilitate authorized transactions, the NetSP Secured Network Gateway provides these services and barriers:

*Proxy Servers*

A proxy server is, in essence, an application gateway. A gateway from one network to another for a specific network application like TELNET or FTP for example. To get to a TELNET or FTP server outside the secured network the user has to go through a two step process:

1. The workstation user starts his TELNET or FTP client to connect to the proxy server at the firewall. The proxy server then asks the user for the name of the remote host to be accessed.

2. The proxy server relays an authorized TELNET or FTP request to the intended remote host.

For example a user inside a secure network would use TELNET to log into the firewall's proxy TELNET server, *telnetd*. Once *telnetd* checks the user's credentials, and the user's permission to cross the firewall with TELNET, *telnetd*, in turn, logs into the remote host specified by the user. It appears that data and commands then flow through the proxy TELNET server as if it were not there. The disadvantage of this concept is that the real TCP/IP function is performed in the firewall and not in the client workstation. This causes more processing load in the firewall than using SOCKS Services.

*SOCKS Servers*

SOCKS servers (SOCKets Secure) intercept and redirect all TCP/IP requests at the firewall. It handles data to and from many types of applications such as TELNET, FTP, Mosaic, WebExplorer and Gopher. The *sockd* daemon is a secure Internet socket server that provides users in a secure network access to resources outside that network by directing data through the firewall. To cross the firewall users must use client programs that are designed especially to work with the *sockd* server. These "SOCKS-ified" clients replace their normal TCP/IP counterparts. The Secured Network Gateway provides the following AIX servers:

• rtelnet in place of telnet

- rftp in place of ftp
- rfinger in place of finger
- rwhois in place of whois

The only difference between a normal and a "SOCKS-ified" client are the socket calls used by the client application. The normal C library socket calls are replaced by SOCKS library calls. The SOCKS routine names are the C sockets names preceded by an "R", for example connect() becomes Rconnect(). The parameters accepted are the same. The client application uses remote sockets residing on the firewall.

A TELNET connection for example works like this:

1. You start the *rtelnet* application to log into a remote host outside the secure network.
2. The *rtelnet* sends that TELNET request to the SOCKS server (*sockd*) in the firewall host.
3. *sockd* checks the user's identity and, if correct, connects the user to the requested remote host.
4. After establishing the connection, the SOCKS server acts as a secure pipeline to the remote host. The TELNET user is unaware of its existence.

To the user, this is only a one-step process.

The advantage of this concept is that the real TCP/IP application (TELNET for example) runs on the client workstation, not in the firewall. This saves processing in the firewall.

In summary, you need only the SOCKS version of the client at the workstations in your network. You can remove, or save and rename, standard versions and rename the SOCKS versions to replace them. For example save the standard *telnet* and rename *rtelnet* to *telnet*. The users will not see the difference.

The IBM WebExplorer shipped with OS/2 Warp supports SOCKS. You only have to name your SOCKS server at the Configure - Servers menu.

*Filters*     Provide ways to limit user access into or out of a secure network based on:

- Source IP address
- Destination IP address
- IP protocol (UDP, ICMP, TCP and TCP-with-acknowledgment)
- Port
- Network adapter (secure or non-secure)
- Direction

By default the firewall denies all access between the secure and non-secure network.

*Domain Name Service*

If you want to isolate the domain name services that are accessible from the secure network from those outside your network so that your internal network structure is not visible outside, you need two domain name servers:

- One domain name server, on the firewall host, responds to requests from outside your network, and resolves outside host names in response to requests from inside the secure network. The response to external requests includes the IP address only to hide the internal network structure.

- Another domain server, inside the secure network, resolves secure addresses in response to requests from inside the secure network. The internal nameserver knows all the internal hosts and consults the domain name server on the firewall if it cannot satisfy a request.

*Mail Handler*

NetSP provides mail handling at the firewall host. You provide a secure mail handler in the secure network. When mail arrives at the firewall, the firewall domain name server and the firewall mail handler forward the incoming mail to your internal mail server which, in turn, forwards it to the target host. For mail going out to the non-secure network, your secure hosts send their mail to the secure mail server which, in turn, sends it via the mail handler in the firewall to the non-secure network. Users outside see only the host name and the address of the firewall and not any secure host.

For further information please refer to *IBM NetSP Secured Network Gateway Installation, Configuration, and Administration Guide, SC31-8113-00.*

# Appendix A. Bibliography

## A.1 International Technical Support Center Publications

- *TCP/IP V3R1 for MVS Implementation Guide*, GG24-3687.
- *TCP/IP V2R2 for VM Installation and Interoperability*, GG24-3624.
- *TCP/IP V2.0 for OS/2 Installation and Interoperability*, GG24-3531.
- *TCP/IP for DOS/Windows Interoperability and Coexistence*, GG24-4374.
- *TCP/IP and National Language Support*, GG24-3840.
- *TCP/IP for MVS, VM, OS/2 and DOS: Troubleshooting Guide*, GG24-3852.
- *TCP/IP for MVS, VM, OS/2 and DOS: X Window System Guide*, GG24-3911.
- *Using NFS in a Multivendor Environment*, GG24-4087.
- *Overview and Examples of Using AIX NetView/6000*, GG24-3804.
- *IBM AIXwindows Programming Guide*, GG24-3382.
- *AIX Distributed Environments: NFS, NCS, RPC, DS Migration, LAN Maintenance and Everything*, GG24-3489.
- *AS/400 TCP/IP Configuration and Operation*, GG24-3442.
- *The AS/400 as a TCP/IP Network File Server*, GG24-4092.
- *AS/400 Communication Definition Examples III*, GG24-4386.
- *Local Area Network Concepts and Products*, GG24-3178.
- *MVS/ESA OpenEdition DCE: RACF and DCE Security Interoperation*, GG24-2526.
- *Developing DCE Applications for AIX, OS/2 and Windows*, GG24-4090.
- *OSF DCE for AIX, OS/2 and DOS*, GG24-4144.
- *MVS/ESA OpenEdition DCE Presentation Guide*, GG24-4240.
- *Using and Administering AIX DCE*, GG24-4348.
- *MVS/ESA OpenEdition DCE: Installation and Configuration Guide*, GG24-4480.
- *MVS/ESA OpenEdition DCE: Application Development Cookbook*, GG24-4481.
- *MVS/ESA OpenEdition DCE: Application Support Servers CICS and IMS*, GG24-4482.

- *LAN HOST Gateways Function and Selection Guide*, ZZ81-0299.

- *NCP V6 Planning and Implementation Guide*, GG24-3785.

A complete list of International Technical Support Center publications, with a brief description of each, may be found in:

*International Technical Support Organization Bibliography of Redbooks*, GG24-3070.

## A.2 VM Publications

- *IBM TCP/IP Version 2 Release 3 for VM: Planning and Customization*, SC31-6082.

- *IBM TCP/IP Version 2 Release 3 for VM: User's Guide*, SC31-6081.

- *IBM TCP/IP Version 2 Release 3 for VM: Programmer's Reference*, SC31-6084.

- *PROFS Extended Mail, User's Guide and Installation Manual*, SH21-0044.

## A.3 MVS Publications

- *IBM TCP/IP Version 3 Release 1 for MVS: User's Guide*, SC31-7136

- *IBM TCP/IP Version 3 Release 1 for MVS: Planning and Migration Guide*, SC31-7189

- *IBM TCP/IP Version 3 Release 1 for MVS: Offload of TCP/IP Processing*, SC31-7133

- *IBM TCP/IP Version 3 Release 1 for MVS: Programmer's Reference*, SC31-7135

- *IBM MVS/DFP Version 3 Release 3: Customizing and Operating the Network File System Server*, SC26-4832.

- *IBM MVS/DFP Version 3 Release 3: Using the Network File System Server*, SC26-4732.

## A.4 DOS Publications

- *IBM TCP/IP Version 2.1.1 for DOS: User's Guide*, SC31-7045.

- *IBM TCP/IP Version 2.1.1 for DOS: Installation and Administration Guide*, SC31-7047.

- *IBM TCP/IP Version 2.1.1 for DOS: Programmer's Reference*, SC31-7046.

- *IBM TCP/IP Version 2.1.1 for DOS: Command Reference*, SX75-0083.

## A.5 OS/2 Publications

- *IBM TCP/IP Version 2.0 for OS/2: User's Guide*, SC31-6076.
- *IBM TCP/IP Version 2.0 for OS/2: Installation and Administration*, SC31-6075.
- *&os2pr.*, SC31-6077.
- *IBM TCP/IP Version 2.0 for OS/2: Network File System Guide*, SC31-7069.
- *IBM TCP/IP Version 2.0 for OS/2: Extended Networking Guide*, SC31-7071.
- *&os2xc.*, SC31-7087.
- *IBM TCP/IP Version 2.0 for OS/2: X Window System Server Guide*, SC31-7070.
- *IBM TCP/IP Version 2.0 for OS/2: Domain Name Server Guide*, SC31-7174.
- *IBM TCP/IP Version 2.0 for OS/2: NetBIOS Guide*, SC31-6122.
- *IBM TCP/IP Version 2.0 for OS/2: Ultimail Guide*, SC31-7120.

## A.6 AIX for RISC/6000 Publications

- *IBM AIX for RISC System/6000, Communications Programming Concepts*, SC23-2206.
- *IBM AIXwindows Environment/6000 AIXwindows and AIXwindows Desktop User's Guide*, GC23-2432.
- *IBM AIXwindows Desktop to CDE Migration Guide*, SC23-2531..
- *AIX Graphics Programming Concepts for IBM RISC System/6000*, SC23-2208.
- *AIX User Interface Programming Concepts for IBM RISC System/6000*, SC23-2209.
- *IBM AIX for RISC System/6000 Technical Reference*, SBOF-1539.
- *AIX NetView/6000 Administration Reference*, SC31-6196.
- *AIX NetView/6000 at a Glance*, GC31-6175.
- *AIX Block Multiplexer Channel Adapter User's Guide and Programming Reference*, SC23-2427.

## A.7 AIX/ESA

- *AIX/ESA Network Application Programmer's Guide Version 2 Release 1*, SC23-3073.
- *AIX/ESA System and Network Administrator's Reference Version 2 Release 1*, SC23-3069.

- *AIX/ESA Network and Communications Administrator's Guide Version 2 Release 1,* SC23-3068.

- *IBM AIXwindows Environment/ESA Application Programmer's Reference, Volume 1,2,3* SC23-3097, SC23-3098, SC23-3099.

- *IBM AIXwindows Environment/ESA Application Programmer's Guide, Volume 2 ,* SC23-3112.

- *IBM AIXwindows Environment/ESA and AIXwindows Desktop User's Guide,* SC23-3114.

- *Network Computing System for AIX/ESA Planning and Administration,* SC23-3105.

- *AIX/ESA Security Features User's Guide,* SC23-3081.

## A.8  AIX General

- *IBM Enterprise Solutions for the 1990s,* G320-9929.

## A.9  AS/400 Publications

- *AS/400 Communications: TCP/IP Guide,* SC41-9875.

- *AS/400 TCP/IP Programmer and Operator Guide,* SC21-9875.

- *TCP/IP File Server Support/400,* SC41-0125.

- *OS/400 TCP/IP Configuration and Reference,* SC41-3420.

## A.10  CETI Publications

- *ES/9000 Token-Ring and IEEE 802.3 LAN Programming Information,* SA33-1600.

## A.11  HIPPI Publications

- *IBM HIPPI User's Guide and Programmer's Reference,* SA23-0369.

## A.12  X.25 NPSI Publications

- *X.25 Network Control Program Packet Switching Interface Planning and Installation,* SC30-3470.

- *X.25 Network Control Program Packet Switching Interface Host Programming,* SC30-3502.

## A.13 3172 Interconnect Controller Publications

- *IBM 3172 Interconnect Controller Planning Guide*, GA27-3867.
- *IBM 3172 Interconnect Controller Technical Overview and Installation Guide*, GG66-3210.

## A.14 6611 Network Processor Publications

- *IBM 6611 Network Processor Introduction and Planning Guide*, GK2T-0334.
- *IBM Multiprotocol Network Program: User's Guide*, SC30-3559.
- *The IBM 6611 Network Processor*, GG24-3870.

## A.15 8229 LAN Bridge Publications

- *IBM 8229 LAN Bridge Manual*, GA27-4025.
- *IBM 8250 8229 Hub Module Installation and Operation Guide*, SA33-0341.

## A.16 Other IBM Systems Publications

- *Introducing IBM's TCP/IP Products for OS/2, VM, and MVS*, GC31-6080.
- *Project Athena: Supporting Distributed Computing at MIT*, IBM Systems Journal, Volume 31, No. 3, 1992.
- *IBM TMC Raleigh, TCP/IP Bulletin*, Alan Reinhold, GG22-9125.
- *Technical Computing Systems Solutions in Networking*, G360-1034-04.

## A.17 DDN Network Information Center Publications

- *DDN Protocol Handbook, Volume 1*, NIC 50004.
- *DDN Protocol Handbook, Volume 2*, NIC 50005.
- *DDN Protocol Handbook, Volume 3*, NIC 50006.
- *DDN Protocol Implementations and Vendor's Guide*, NIC 50002.

## A.18  OSF Publications

- *Introduction to OSF DCE,* Prentice Hall, Inc., 1992, ISBN 0-13-490624-1.

- *Understanding DCE,* O'Reilly and Associates, Inc., 1994, ISBN 1-56592-005-8.

- *OSF DCE Version 1.0 - DCE Administration Guide,* December 1991.

- *OSF DCE Version 1.0 - DCE Application Development Guide,* December 1991.

- *OSF DCE Version 1.0 - DCE User's Guide and Reference,* December 1991.

## A.19  ANSI Publications

- *ANSI X3.183-1991 HIGH-PERFORMANCE PARALLEL INTERFACE - Mechanical, Electrical, and Signalling Protocol Specification (HIPPI-PH)*

- *ANSI X3.210-199x HIGH-PERFORMANCE PARALLEL INTERFACE - Framing Protocol (HIPPI-FP)*

- *ANSI X3.218-199x HIGH-PERFORMANCE PARALLEL INTERFACE - Encapsulation of ISO 8802.2 (IEEE Std 802.2) Logical Link Control Protocol Data Units (802.2 Link Encapsulation) (HIPPI-LE)*

- *ANSI X3.222-199x HIGH-PERFORMANCE PARALLEL INTERFACE - Physical Switch Control (HIPPI-SC)*

## A.20  Other Publications

- APOLLO Computer Inc., *Network Computing System (NCS) Reference,* APOLLO Computer Inc.

- Ben-Artzi, A., *The CMOT Network Management Architecture,* ConneXions, Volume 3, No.3., March 1989.

- Bertsekas, D., Gallager, R., *Data Networks,* second edition, Prentice Hall, Inc., 1992, ISBN 0-13-200916-1.

- Bowers, K.L., LaQuey, T.L., Reynolds, J.K., Roubicek, K., Stahl, M.K. and Yuan, A., *FYI on where to start: A bibliography of internetworking information,* RFC 1175, 1991.

- Case, L.D., Davin, J.R., Fedor, M.S. and Schoffstall, M.L., *Network Management and the Design of SNMP,* ConneXions, Volume 3, No.3., March 1989.

- Champine, G., *MIT Project Athena, A Model for Distributed Campus Computing,* Digital Press, 1991, DP ISBN 1-55558-072-6, PH ISBN 0-13-585324-9.

- Coltun, R., *The OSPF Routing Protocol,* ConneXions, Volume 3, No.8., August 1989.

- Comer, D., *Internetworking with TCP/IP, Volume I, Principles, Protocols and Architecture,* second edition, Prentice Hall, Inc., 1991, ISBN 0-13-468505-9, IBM order number SC31-6144.

- Comer, D. and Stevens, D., *Internetworking with TCP/IP, Volume II, Design, Implementation and Internals,* Prentice Hall, Inc., 1991, ISBN 0-13-472242-6, IBM order number SC31-6145.

- Comer, D., Stevens, D., *Internetworking with TCP/IP, Volume III, Client-Server Programming and Applications, BSD Socket Version,* Prentice Hall, Inc., 1993, ISBN 0-13-474222-2.

- Conklin, D., *OS/2 Notebook,* Microsoft Press, 1990, ISBN 1-55615-316-3, IBM order number G362-0003.

- Cypser, R., *Communications for Cooperating Systems, OSI, SNA, and TCP/IP,* Addison-Wesley, Inc., 1991, ISBN 0-201-50775-7, IBM order number ZE19-6006.

- Dern, D.P., *The ARPANET is Twenty - What We Have Learned and The Fun We Had,* ConneXions, Volume 3, No.10., October 1989.

- Dunphy, E., *The UNIX Industry - Evolution, Concepts, Architecture, Applications and Standards,* QED Information Sciences, Inc., 1991, ISBN 0-89435-390-X.

- Dyksen, W.R. and Korb, J.T., *A Programmer's Overview of X,* ConneXions, Volume 4, No.10., October 1990.

- Ford, A., *Spinning the Web: How to Provide Information on the Internet,* Van Nostrand Reinhold, 1995, ISBN 0-442-01996-3.

- Gray, P., *Open Systems, A Business Strategy for the 1990s,* McGraw-Hill, 1991, ISBN 0-07-707244-8.

- Hagens, R., *Components of OSI: ES-IS Routing,* ConneXions, Volume 3, No.8., August 1989.

- Hancock, B., *Designing and Implementing Ethernet Networks,* second edition, QED Information Sciences, Inc., ISBN 0-89435-366-7.

- Hunt, C., *TCP/IP Network Administration,* O'Reilly & Associates, Inc., August 1992, ISBN 0-937175-82-X.

- IBM Corp., *NSFNET - The National Science Foundation Computer Network for Research and Education,* IBM order number GK21-0104.

- Jolitz, W., *The X Window System,* ConneXions, Volume 4, No.5., May 1990.

- Jones, O., *Introduction to the X Window System, updated for XV11R4,* Prentice Hall, Inc., 1989, ISBN 0-13-499997-5.

- Kehoe, B., *Zen and the Art of the Internet, A Beginner's Guide,* Prentice Hall, Inc., 1993, ISBN 0-13-010778-6.

- Kelleher, L., *Merit/NSFNET Information Services,* ConneXions, Volume 3, No.6., June 1989.

- Kohl, J.T., Neuman, B.C. and Ts'o, T.Y., *The Evolution of the Kerberos Authentication Service.* Retrieve file */pub/kerberos/doc/krb_evol.ps* via anonymous FTP to *athena-dist.mit.edu* (18.71.0.38).

- Krol, E., *The Whole Internet - User's Guide & Catalog,* O'Reilly & Associates, Inc., September 1992, ISBN 1-56592-025-2.

- LaQuey, T., *The User's Directory of Computer Networks,* Digital Press, 1990, DP ISBN 1-55558-047-5, PH ISBN 0-13-950262-9.

- Lyons, T., *Network Computing System Tutorial,* Prentice Hall, Inc., 1991, ISBN 0-13-617242-3.

- Madron, T., *Local Area Networks,* John Wiley & Sons, Inc., 1988, ISBN 0-471-52250-3.

- Malamud, C., *Exploring the Internet, a Technical Travelogue,* Prentice Hall, Inc., 1992, ISBN 0-13-296898-3.

- Malamud, C., *Stacks - Interoperability in Today's Computer Networks,* Prentice Hall, Inc., 1992, ISBN 0-13-484080-1.

- Merit Corp., *NSFNET, The National Science Foundation Network,* Merit Corp.

- McCloghrie, K. and Rose, M.T., *Network Management of TCP/IP-based Internets,* ConneXions, Volume 3, No.3., March 1989.

- Miller, M., *Troubleshooting Internetworks, Tools, Techniques, and Protocols,* M&T Books, 1991, ISBN 1-55851-236-5.

- Miller, S.P., Neuman, B.C., Schiller, J.I. and Saltzer, J.H., *Section E.2.1: Kerberos Authentication and Authorization System,* M.I.T. Project Athena, Cambridge, Massachusetts, December 1987.

- Mogul, J., *Booting Diskless Hosts: The BOOTP Protocol,* ConneXions, Volume 2, No.10., October 1988.

- Orfali, R., Harkey, D., *Client/Server Programming with OS/2 2.0,* second edition, Van Nostrand Reinhold, 1992, ISBN 0-442-01219-5, IBM order number G325-0650-01.

- Perlman, R., *Interconnections, Bridges and Routers,* Addison-Wesley, Inc., 1992, ISBN 0-201-56332-0.

- Quarterman, J., *The Matrix, Computer Networks and Conferencing Systems Worlwide,* Digital Press, 1990, PH ISBN 0-13-565607-9, DP ISBN 1-55558-033-5.

- Réseaux Associés pour la Recherche Européenne (RARE), *Réseaux Associés pour la Recherche Européenne (RARE), Networking for Researchers in Europe,* ConneXions, Volume 6, No.1, January 1992.

- Rose, M., *The Internet Message, Closing the Book with Electronic Mail,* Prentice Hall, Inc., 1992, ISBN 0-13-092941-7.

- Rose, M., *The Open Book, a Practical Perspective on OSI,* Prentice Hall, Inc., 1991, ISBN 0-13-643016-3.

- Rose, M., *The Simple Book, an Introduction to Management of TCP/IP-based internets,* second edition, Prentice Hall, Inc., 1994, ISBN 0-13-177254-6.

- Schiller, J.I., *Kerberos: Network Authentication for Today's Open Networks,* ConneXions, Volume 4, No.1., January 1990.

- Slone, J., Drinan, A., *Handbook of Local Area Networks,* Auerbach Publishers, 1991, ISBN 0-7913-0868-5.

- Socolofsky, T.J. and Kale, C.J., *TCP/IP Tutorial,* RFC 1180, 1991.

- Stevens, W.R., *UNIX Network Programming,* Prentice Hall, Inc., 1990, ISBN 0-13-949876-1.

- Stevens, W.R., *TCP/IP Illustrated, Volume 1,* Addison Wesley, 1994, ISBN 0-201-63346-9.

- Stevens, W.R., *TCP/IP Illustrated, Volume 2,* Addison Wesley, 1995, ISBN 0-201-63354-X.

- Stockman, B., *Current Status on Networking in Europe,* ConneXions, Volume 5, No.7, July 1991.

- Stoll C., *The Cuckoo's Egg - Tracking a Spy Through the Maze of Computer Espionage,* Pocket Books, 1990, ISBN 0-671-72688-9.

- SUN Microsystems, Inc., *Network File System (NFS) Protocol Specification.*

- Tsuchiya, P., *Components of OSI: IS-IS Intra Domain Routing,* ConneXions, Volume 3, No.8., August 1989.

- *TCP/IP Network Management with an Eye Towards OSI,* Data Communications, August 1989.

- *The Internet Unleashed,* Sams Publishing, 1994, ISBN 0-672-30466-X.

- *The World Wide Web Unleashed,* Sams Publishing, 1994, ISBN 0-672-30617-4.

# Appendix B. Distributed Computing Environment (DCE)

DCE is becoming a very important technology in building distributed applications in an open and heterogeneous environment. It is analogous to the role TCP/IP plays in a distributed networking environment. In this chapter, we summarize the history of DCE, its main components and its implementations.

## B.1 History

Open Software Foundation (OSF) is a not-for-profit research and development organization that supplies software essential for creating open systems computing environment. Originally founded by IBM, DEC, Apollo, HP, Groupe Bull, Nixdorf and Siemens, OSF now has over 350 members worldwide.

OSF has defined a Distributed Computing Environment (DCE) to simplify building computer systems applications in a heterogeneous environment.

Founded in 1984, X/Open is a worldwide, independent open systems organization dedicated to developing an open, multivendor Common Applications Environment (CAE) based on de facto and international standards.

In August of 1992, X/Open and OSF announced a joint effort to integrate OSF's DCE into X/Open's Common Applications Environment (CAE).

## B.2 Overview of DCE Technology Components

DCE consists of the following components:

- **DCE Threads**: supports multithreading within a single process.

- **DCE RPC**: consists of both a development tool and a runtime library. When using its compatibility features, DCE RPC is compatible with the NCS Version 1.5.1. However, future enhancements to DCE RPC will cause their incompatibility.

- **DCE Directory Service**: provides a central repository for information about resources in the distributed environment.

- **DCE Distributed Time Service (DTS)**: makes sure the clocks in the distributed systems are synchronized.

- **DCE Security Service**: provides the security functions based on the M.I.T. Kerberos Version 5.

- **DCE Distributed File Service (DFS)**: provides an advanced file system based on the Andrew File System (AFS, a distributed file system originally developed by IBM and Carnegie-Mellon University, now marketed by Transarc Corporation).

- **DCE Diskless Support Service**: allows a diskless system to operate in a DCE environment.

The current DCE is at Version 1.1 which was released to developers in November 1994. Among the new features provided are:

- Enhanced administrator functions: These include a common user interface across all DCE components allowing remote startup, administration and shutdown of DCE services. Also included are enhanced diagnostic messages that will assist the troubleshooter in the heterogeneous networks in which DCE is implemented.

- Improved security: Systems that are not based on RPC are now able to use DCE security. In addition, auditing procedures, password and pre-authentication functions have been improved.

- National language support: DCE messages can be presented in the local language and RPC applications can be set up to convert data to the local language.

- Performance improvements: The Interface Definition Language (IDL) now produces more efficient and streamlined code. RPC has also been enhanced and optimized.

- NFS/DFS gateway: Allows NFS access through the gateway to DFS.

Version 1.2 is scheduled to start testing in the summer of 1995. It is expected to include new administrative and interoperability features as well as the addition of scalability and network management functions.

For more details, please refer to the OSF publications listed in Appendix A, "Bibliography" on page A-1.

## B.3 Implementations

All major IBM platforms implement DCE. The various implementations are detailed below.

The Open Software Foundation (OSF) on April 7th 1995 named IBM's AIX Distributed Computing Environment (AIX/DCE) as the industry's first certified implementation. The certification process assures customers that any implementation of DCE, a base for open, distributed, client/server computing, fully interoperates with other certified DCE solutions. IBM intends to submit all of its DCE implementations for certification with OS/2 DCE the next in line.

## B.3.1 MVS
DCE support is provided in the following features of MVS/ESA SP V5 OpenEdition:

- MVS/ESA OpenEdition DCE Base Services Feature

- MVS/ESA OpenEdition DCE User Data Privacy Feature

- MVS/ESA OpenEdition DCE Application Support (orderable as a separate product)

IBM intends to upgrade MVS/ESA OpenEdition DCE to OSF DCE Version 1.1. OSF DCE Version 1.1 will provide a foundation for RACF-DCE interoperation and for support of single sign-on between MVS/ESA and DCE environments.

MVS/ESA OpenEdition DCE will provide support for DCE RPC over SNA networks in addition to the TCP/IP networks supported today.

IBM also intends to enhance and extend the set of MVS/ESA OpenEdition DCE servers. The MVS/ESA OpenEdition DCE Application Support Program Product will be enhanced to exploit the security extensions provided in the MVS/ESA OpenEdition DCE Base Services and additional IMS transaction types will be supported.

New MVS/ESA OpenEdition DCE servers will include DCE Security Server and DFS Program Products.

## B.3.2 VM
DCE support is provided in VM/ESA V2 with OpenEdition VM/ESA. VM/ESA V2 OpenEdition is based on OSF's DCE V1.02 and provides DCE RPC, DCE Threads, DCE Cell Directory Service (CDS) client support and DCE Security Service client support.

## B.3.3 OS/400
DCE support is provided in DCE Base Services/400 V3. The following services are provided:

- Remote Procedure Call (RPC)

- Cell Directory Client function

- Security Client function

- Time Services

In order to develop DCE applications in the OS/400 environment the following is required:

- Integrated Language Environment C/400

## B.3.4 AIX/6000

The IBM DCE for AIX family of products for AIX/6000 V3.2.5 was extended in October 1994 with the addition of two new members:

- IBM DCE Manager for AIX V1.3

- IBM DCE NFS to DFS Authenticating Gateway for AIX V1.3

In addition the family includes the following members:

- IBM DCE Base for AIX V1.3

- IBM DCE Security Server for AIX V1.3

- IBM DCE Cell Directory Server for AIX V1.3

- IBM DCE Global Directory Server for AIX V1.3

- IBM DCE Enhanced Distributed File System for AIX V1.3

- IBM DCE Threads for AIX V1.3

- IBM DCE Global Directory Client for AIX V1.3

IBM DCE for AIX V1.3 is not compatible with AIX V4. However, IBM plans to provide these functions on an AIX V4 base in 1995.

## B.3.5 OS/2 and Windows

DCE support is provided in:

- DCE Software Developer's Kit (SDK) for OS/2 and Windows V1.0

- DCE Client for OS/2 V1.0

- DCE Client for Windows V1.0

DCE for OS2 and DCE for Windows consist of:

- Security Services

- Directory Services

- Time Services

- RPC

- Threads

# Glossary

## A

**abstract syntax**. A description of a data structure that is independent of machine-oriented structures and encodings.

**ACSE: Association Control Service Element**. The method used in OSI for establishing a call between two applications. Checks the identities and contexts of the application entities, and could apply an authentication security check.

**active gateway**. A gateway that is treated like a network interface, in that it is expected to exchange routing information, and if it does not do so for a period of time, the route associated with the gateway will be deleted.

**address mask**. A bit mask used to select bits from an Internet address for subnet addressing. The mask is 32 bits long and selects the network portion of the Internet address and one or more bits of the local portion. Sometimes called subnet mask.

**address resolution**. A means for mapping Network Layer addresses onto media-specific address. See ARP.

**ADMD**. Administration Management Domain. An X.400 Message Handling System public service carrier. Examples: MCImail and ATTmail in the U.S., British Telecom Gold400mail in the U.K. The ADMDs in all countries worldwide together provide the X.400 backbone. See PRMD.

**agent**. In the client-server model, the part of the system that performs information preparation and exchange on behalf of a client or server application. See NMS, DUA, MTA.

**ANSI**. American National Standards Institute. The U.S. standardization body. ANSI is a member of the International Organization for Standardization (ISO).

**API**. Application Program Interface. A set of calling conventions defining how a service is invoked through a software package.

**application layer**. The top-most layer in the OSI Reference Model providing such communication services as electronic mail and file transfer.

**Archie**. One of the first Internet navigators, used to search for files at FTP sites.

**ARP**. Address Resolution Protocol. The Internet protocol used to dynamically map Internet addresses to physical (hardware) addresses on local area networks. Limited to networks that support hardware broadcast.

**ARPA**. Advanced Research Projects Agency. Now called DARPA, the U.S. government agency that funded the ARPANET.

**ARPANET**. A packet switched network developed in the early 1970s. The "grandfather" of today's Internet. ARPANET was decommissioned in June 1990.

**ASN.1**. Abstract Syntax Notation One. The OSI language for describing abstract syntax. See BER.

**attribute**. The form of information items provided by the X.500 Directory Service. The directory information base consists of entries, each containing one or more attributes. Each attribute consists of a type identifier together with one or more values. Each directory Read operation can retrieve some or all attributes from a designated entry.

**X-1**

**Autonomous System**. Internet (TCP/IP) terminology for a collection of gateways (routers) that fall under one administrative entity and cooperate using a common Interior Gateway Protocol (IGP). See subnetwork.

# B

**background process**. (1) A process that does not require operator intervention that can be run by the computer while the workstation is used to do another work. (2) A mode of program execution in which the shell does not wait for program completion before prompting the user for another command.

**backbone**. The primary connectivity mechanism of a hierarchical distributed system. All systems which have connectivity to an intermediate system on the backbone are assured of connectivity to each other. This does not prevent systems from setting up private arrangements with each other to bypass the backbone for reasons of cost, performance, or security.

**baseband**. Characteristic of any network technology that uses a single carrier frequency and requires all stations attached to the network to participate in every transmission. See broadband.

**BER**. Basic Encoding Rules. Standard rules for encoding data units described in ASN.1. Sometimes incorrectly lumped under the term ASN.1, which properly refers only to the abstract syntax description language, not the encoding technique.

**BGP**. Border Gateway Protocol. A connection-oriented routing protocol (using TCP) that was developed based upon experience using EGP. See EGP.

**big-endian**. A format for storage or transmission of binary data in which the most

significant bit (or byte) comes first. The reverse convention is called little-endian.

**BITNET**. Because It's Time NETwork. An academic computer network based originally on IBM mainframe systems interconnected via leased 9600 bps lines. BITNET was eventually merged with CSNET, The Computer+Science Network (another academic computer network) to form CREN: The Corporation for Research and Educational Networking. See CSNET.

**bridge**. (1) A device that connects two or more physical networks and forwards packets between them. Bridges can usually be made to filter packets, that is, to forward only certain traffic. Related devices are: repeaters which simply forward electrical signals from one cable to another, and full-fledged routers which make routing decisions based on several criteria. (2) A functional unit that connects two local area networks (LANs) that use the same logical link control (LLC) procedure but may use different medium access control (MAC) procedures.

**broadband**. Characteristic of any network that multiplexes multiple, independent network carriers onto a single cable. This is usually done using frequency division multiplexing. Broadband technology allows several networks to coexist on one single cable; traffic from one network does not interfere with traffic from another since the "conversations" happen on different frequencies in the "ether," rather like the commercial radio system.

**broadcast**. A packet delivery system where a copy of a given packet is given to all hosts attached to the network. Example: Ethernet.

**BSD**. Berkeley Software Distribution. Term used when describing different versions of the Berkeley UNIX software, as in "4.3BSD UNIX."

# C

**catenet**. A network in which hosts are connected to networks with varying characteristics, and the networks are interconnected by gateways (routers). The Internet is an example of a catenet. See IONL.

**CCR**. Commitment, Concurrency, and Recovery. An OSI application service element used to create atomic operations across distributed systems. Used primarily to implement two-phase commit for transactions and nonstop operations.

**child process**. a child is a process spawned by a parent process that shares resources of parent process.

**client/server model**. A common way to describe network services and the model user processes (programs) of those services. Examples include the name-server/name-resolver paradigm of the DNS and file- server/file-client relationships such as NFS and diskless hosts.

**CLNP**. Connectionless Network Protocol. The OSI protocol for providing the OSI Connectionless Network Service (datagram service). CLNP is the OSI equivalent to Internet IP, and is sometimes called ISO IP.

**CLTP**. Connectionless Transport Protocol. Provides for end-to-end Transport data addressing (via Transport selector) and error control (via checksum), but cannot guarantee delivery or provide flow control. The OSI equivalent of UDP.

**CMIP**. Common Management Information Protocol. The OSI network management protocol.

**CMOT**. CMIP Over TCP. An effort to use the OSI network management protocol to manage TCP/IP networks.

**connectionless**. The model of interconnection in which communication takes place without first establishing a connection. Sometimes (imprecisely) called datagram. Examples: LANs, Internet IP and OSI CLNP, UDP, ordinary postcards.

**connection-oriented**. The model of interconnection in which communication proceeds through three well-defined phases: connection establishment, data transfer, connection release. Examples: X.25, Internet TCP and OSI TP4, ordinary telephone calls.

**core gateway**. Historically, one of a set of gateways (routers) operated by the Internet Network Operations Center at BBN. The core gateway system forms a central part of Internet routing in that all groups must advertise paths to their networks from a core gateway, using the Exterior Gateway Protocol (EGP). See EGP, backbone.

**COS**. Corporation for Open Systems. A vendor and user group for conformance testing, certification, and promotion of OSI products.

**COSINE**. Cooperation for Open Systems Interconnection Networking in Europe. A program sponsored by the European Commission, aimed at using OSI to tie together European research networks.

**CREN**. See BITNET and CSNET.

**CSMA/CD**. Carrier Sense Multiple Access with Collision Detection. The access method used by local area networking technologies such as Ethernet.

**CSNET**. Computer+Science Network. A large computer network, mostly in the U.S. but with international connections. CSNET sites include universities, research labs, and some commercial companies. Now merged with BITNET to form CREN. See BITNET.

# D

**DARPA**.  Defense Advanced Research Projects Agency.  The U.S.  government agency that funded the ARPANET.

**data link layer**.  The OSI layer that is responsible for data transfer across a single physical connection, or series of bridged connections, between two network entities.

**DCA**.  Defense Communications Agency.  The government agency responsible for the Defense Data Network (DDN).

**DCE**.  Distributed Computing Environment.  An architecture of standard programming interfaces, conventions, and server functionalities (for example naming, distributed file system, remote procedure call) for distributing applications transparently across networks of heterogeneous computers.  Promoted and controlled by the Open Software Foundation (OSF), a consortium led by HP, DEC, and IBM.  See ONC.

**DDN**.  Defense Data Network.  Comprises the MILNET and several other DoD networks.

**DECnet**.  Digital Equipment Corporation's proprietary network architecture.

**DNS**.  Domain Name System.  The distributed name/address mechanism used in the Internet.

**domain**.  In the Internet, a part of a naming hierarchy.  Syntactically, an Internet domain name consists of a sequence of names (labels) separated by periods (dots), for example, "tundra.mpk.ca.us."  In OSI, "domain" is generally used as an administrative partition of a complex distributed system, as in MHS Private Management Domain (PRMD), and Directory Management Domain (DMD).

**dotted decimal notation**.  The syntactic representation for a 32-bit integer that consists of four 8-bit numbers written in base 10 with periods (dots) separating them.  Used to represent IP addresses in the Internet as in: 192.67.67.20.

**DSA**.  Directory System Agent.  The software that provides the X.500 Directory Service for a portion of the directory information base.  Generally, each DSA is responsible for the directory information for a single organization or organizational unit.

**DUA**.  Directory User Agent.  The software that accesses the X.500 Directory Service on behalf of the directory user.  The directory user may be a person or another software element.

# E

**EARN**.  European Academic Research Network.  A network using BITNET technology connecting universities and research labs in Europe.

**EGP**.  Exterior Gateway Protocol.  A reachability routing protocol used by gateways in a two-level internet.  EGP is used in the Internet core system.  See core gateway.

**encapsulation**.  The technique used by layered protocols in which a layer adds header information to the protocol data unit (PDU) from the layer above.  As an example, in Internet terminology, a packet would contain a header from the physical layer, followed by a header from the network layer (IP), followed by a header from the transport layer (TCP), followed by the application protocol data.

**end system**.  An OSI system which contains application processes capable of communicating through all seven layers of OSI protocols.  Equivalent to Internet host.

**entity**.  OSI terminology for a layer protocol machine.  An entity within a layer performs the functions of the layer within a single computer system, accessing the layer entity below and providing services to the layer entity above at local service access points.

**ES-IS**.  End system to Intermediate system protocol.  The OSI protocol by which end systems announce themselves to intermediate systems.

**Ethernet**.  A 10 Mbps baseband local area network using CSMA/CD (Carrier Sense Multiple Acess with Collision Detection). The network allows multiple stations to access the medium at will without prior coordination; avoid contention by using carrier sense and deference; and resolve contention by using collision detection and retransmission.

**EUnet**.  European UNIX Network.

**EUUG**.  European UNIX Users Group.

**extended character**.  A character other than a 7-bit ASCII character. An extended character can be a 1-byte code point with the 8th bit set (ordinal 128-255) or a 2-byte code point (ordinal 256 and greater).

**EWOS**.  European Workshop for Open Systems.  The OSI Implementors Workshop for Europe.  See OIW.

# F

**FARNET**.  Federation of American Research Networks.

**FDDI**.  Fiber Distributed Data Interface.  An emerging high-speed networking standard. The underlying medium is fiber optics, and the topology is a dual-attached, counter-rotating token-ring.  FDDI networks can often be spotted by the orange fiber "cable."

**fragmentation**.  The process in which an IP datagram is broken into smaller pieces to fit the requirements of a given physical network. The reverse process is termed reassembly. See MTU.

**FNC**.  Federal Networking Council. The group of representatives from those federal agencies involved in the development and use of federal networking, especially those networks using TCP/IP, and the connected Internet. The FNC coordinates research and engineering. Current members include representatives from DOD, DOE, DARPA, NSF, NASA and HHS.

**FRICC**.  Federal Research Internet Coordinating Committee. Now replaced by the FNC.

**FTAM**.  File Transfer, Access, and Management.  The OSI remote file service and protocol.

**FTP**.  File Transfer Protocol.  The Internet protocol (and program) used to transfer files between hosts.  See FTAM.

# G

**gateway**.  The original Internet term for what is now called router or more precisely, IP router.  In modern usage, the terms "gateway" and "application gateway" refer to systems which do translation from some native format to another.  Examples include X.400 to/from RFC 822 electronic mail gateways.  See router.

**gopher**.  Internet navigation tool that provides menu access to information.  Many organizations use this tool instead of an anonymous FTP site.  See Veronica.

**GOSIP**.  Government OSI Profile.  A U.S. Government procurement specification for OSI protocols.

# I

**IAB**.  Internet Activities Board.  The technical body that oversees the development of the Internet suite of protocols (commonly referred to as "TCP/IP").  It has two task forces (the IRTF and the IETF) each charged with investigating a particular area.

**IANA**.  Internet Assigned Numbers Authority. The technical body inside the IAB that manages the Internet protocol standards. It coordinates the assignment of values to the parameters of protocols.

**ICMP**.  Internet Control Message Protocol. The protocol used to handle errors and control messages at the IP layer.  ICMP is actually part of the IP protocol.

**IESG**.  Internet Engineering Steering Group. The executive committee of the IETF.

**IETF**.  Internet Engineering Task Force. One of the task forces of the IAB.  The IETF is responsible for solving short-term engineering needs of the Internet.  It has over 40 Working Groups.

**IGP**.  Interior Gateway Protocol.  The protocol used to exchange routing information between collaborating routers in the Internet. RIP and OSPF are examples of IGPs.

**IGRP**.  Internet Gateway Routing Protocol. A proprietary IGP used by Cisco System's routers.

**intermediate system**.  An OSI system which is not an end system, but which serves instead to relay communications between end systems.  See repeater, bridge, and router.

**internet**.  A collection of networks interconnected by a set of routers which allow them to function as a single, large virtual network.

**Internet**.  (note the capital "I") The largest internet in the world consisting of large national backbone nets (such as MILNET, NSFNET, and CREN) and a myriad of regional and local campus networks all over the world.  The Internet uses the Internet protocol suite.  To be on the Internet you must have IP connectivity, i.e., be able to TELNET to--or ping--other systems.  Networks with only E-mail connectivity are not actually classified as being on the Internet.

**internet address**.  A 32-bit address assigned to hosts using TCP/IP.  See dotted decimal notation.

**IONL**.  Internal Organization of the Network Layer.  The OSI standard for the detailed architecture of the network layer.  Basically, it partitions the network layer into subnetworks interconnected by convergence protocols (equivalent to internetworking protocols), creating what Internet calls a catenet or internet.

**IP**.  Internet Protocol.  The network layer protocol for the Internet protocol suite.

**IP datagram**.  The fundamental unit of information passed across the Internet. Contains source and destination addresses along with data and a number of fields which define such things as the length of the datagram, the header checksum, and flags to say whether the datagram can be (or has been) fragmented.

**IRTF**.  Internet Research Task Force.  One of the task forces of the IAB.  The group responsible for research and development of the Internet protocol suite.

**ISDN**.  Integrated Services Digital Network. An emerging technology which is beginning to be offered by the telephone carriers of the world.  ISDN combines voice and digital network services in a single medium making it possible to offer customers digital data services as well as voice connections through a single "wire." The standards that define ISDN are specified by CCITT.

**IS-IS**. Intermediate system to Intermediate system protocol. The OSI protocol by which intermediate systems exchange routing information.

**ISO**. International Organization for Standardization. Best known for the seven-layer OSI Reference Model. See OSI.

**ISODE**. ISO Development Environment. A popular implementation of the upper layers of OSI. Pronounced eye-so-dee-eee.

# J

**JANET**. Joint Academic Network. A university network in the U.K.

**JUNET**. Japan UNIX Network.

# K

**KA9Q**. A popular implementation of TCP/IP and associated protocols for amateur packet radio systems.

**Kermit**. A popular file transfer and terminal emulation program.

# L

**little-endian**. A format for storage or transmission of binary data in which the least significant byte (bit) comes first. See big-endian.

# M

**mail exploder**. Part of an electronic mail delivery system which allows a message to be delivered to a list of addressees. Mail exploders are used to implement mailing lists. Users send messages to a single address (for example hacks@somehost.edu) and the mail exploder takes care of delivery to the individual mailboxes in the list.

**mail gateway**. A machine that connects two or more electronic mail systems (especially dissimilar mail systems on two different networks) and transfers messages between them. Sometimes the mapping and translation can be quite complex, and generally it requires a store-and-forward scheme whereby the message is received from one system completely before it is transmitted to the next system after suitable translations.

**Martian**. Humorous term applied to packets that turn up unexpectedly on the wrong network because of bogus routing entries. Also used as a name for a packet which has an altogether bogus (non-registered or ill-formed) Internet address.

**MHS**. Message Handling System. The system of message user agents, message transfer agents, message stores, and access units which together provide OSI electronic mail. MHS is specified in the CCITT X.400 Series of Recommendations.

**MIB**. Management Information Base. A collection of objects that can be accessed via a network management protocol. See SMI.

**MILNET**. Military Network. Originally part of the ARPANET, MILNET was partitioned in 1984 to make it possible for military installations to have reliable network service, while the ARPANET continued to be used for research. See DDN.

**MIME**. Multipurpose Internet Mail Extensions. A mail protocol that provides support for multimedia (graphics, audio, video) as well as basic compatibility with SMTP. MIME is described in RFCs 1521 and 1522. See SMTP.

**MTA**. Message Transfer Agent. An OSI application process used to store and forward messages in the X.400 Message Handling System. Equivalent to Internet mail agent.

**MTU**. Maximum Transmission Unit. The largest possible unit of data that can be sent on a given physical medium. Example: the MTU of Ethernet is 1500 bytes. See fragmentation.

**multicast**. A special form of broadcast where copies of the packet are delivered to only a subset of all possible destinations. See broadcast.

**multi-homed host**. A computer connected to more than one physical data link. The data links may or may not be attached to the same network.

# N

**name resolution**. The process of mapping a name into the corresponding address. See DNS.

**NetBIOS**. Network Basic Input Output System. The standard interface to networks on IBM PC and compatible systems.

**Network Address**. See Internet address or OSI Network Address.

**network layer**. The OSI layer that is responsible for routing, switching, and subnetwork access across the entire OSI environment.

**NFS**. Network File System. A distributed file system developed by SUN Microsystems which allows a set of computers to cooperatively access each other's files in a transparent manner.

**NIC**. Network Information Center. Originally there was only one, located at SRI International which had the task of serving the ARPANET (and later DDN) community. Today, there are many NICs, operated by local, regional, and national networks all over the world. Such centers provide user assistance, document service, training, and much more.

**NIST**. National Institute of Standards and Technology. (Formerly NBS.) See OIW.

**NMS**. Network Management Station. The system responsible for managing a (portion of a) network. The NMS talks to network management agents, which reside in the managed nodes, via a network management protocol. See agent.

**NOC**. Network Operations Center. Any center given the task of managing the operational aspects of a production network. These tasks include monitoring and control, trouble-shooting, user assistance, and so on.

**NSAP**. Network Service Access Point. The point at which the OSI Network Service is made available to a transport entity. The NSAPs are identified by OSI Network Addresses.

**NSF**. National Science Foundation. Sponsors of the NSFNET (National Science Foundation Network). A collection of local, regional, and mid-level networks in the U.S. tied together by a high-speed backbone. NSFNET provides scientists access to a number of supercomputers across the country.

# O

**OIW**. Workshop for Implementors of OSI. Frequently called NIST OIW or the NIST Workshop, this is the North American regional forum at which OSI implementation agreements are decided. It is equivalent to EWOS in Europe and AOW in the Pacific.

**ONC**. Open Network Computing. A distributed applications architecture promoted and controlled by a consortium led by Sun Microsystems.

**OSI**. Open Systems Interconnection. An international standardization program to facilitate communications among computers from different manufacturers. See ISO.

**OSI Network Address**. The address, consisting of up to 20 octets, used to locate an OSI Transport entity. The address is formatted into an Initial Domain Part which is standardized for each of several addressing domains, and a Domain Specific Part which is the responsibility of the addressing authority for that domain.

**OSI Presentation Address**. The address used to locate an OSI Application entity. It consists of an OSI Network Address and up to three selectors, one each for use by the Transport, Session, and Presentation entities.

**OSPF**. Open Shortest Path First. A "Proposed Standard" IGP for the Internet. See IGP.

# P

**PCI**. Protocol Control Information. The protocol information added by an OSI entity to the service data unit passed down from the layer above, all together forming a Protocol Data Unit (PDU).

**PDU**. Protocol Data Unit. This is OSI terminology for "packet." A PDU is a data object exchanged by protocol machines (entities) within a given layer. PDUs consist of both Protocol Control Information (PCI) and user data.

**physical layer**. The OSI layer that provides the means to activate and use physical connections for bit transmission. In plain terms, the physical layer provides the procedures for transferring a single bit across a physical media.

**physical media**. Any means in the physical world for transferring signals between OSI systems. Considered to be outside the OSI Model, and therefore sometimes referred to as "Layer 0." The physical connector to the media can be considered as defining the bottom interface of the physical layer, i.e., the bottom of the OSI Reference Model.

**ping**. Packet internet groper. A program used to test reachability of destinations by sending them an ICMP echo request and waiting for a reply. The term is used as a verb: "Ping host X to see if it is up!"

**port**. The abstraction used by Internet transport protocols to distinguish among multiple simultaneous connections to a single destination host. See selector.

**POSI**. Promoting Conference for OSI. The OSI "800-pound gorilla" in Japan. Consists of executives from the six major Japanese computer manufacturers and Nippon Telephone and Telegraph. They set policies and commit resources to promote OSI.

**PPP**. Point-to-Point Protocol. The successor to SLIP, PPP provides router-to-router and host-to-network connections over both synchronous and asynchronous circuits. See SLIP.

**Presentation Address**. See OSI Presentation Address.

**presentation layer**. The OSI layer that determines how Application information is represented (i.e., encoded) while in transit between two end systems.

**PRMD**. Private Management Domain. An X.400 Message Handling System private organization mail system. Example: NASAmail. See ADMD.

**protocol**. A formal description of messages to be exchanged and rules to be followed for two or more systems to exchange information.

**proxy**. The mechanism whereby one system "fronts for" another system in responding to protocol requests. Proxy systems are used in network management to avoid having to implement full protocol stacks in simple devices, such as modems.

**proxy ARP**. The technique in which one machine, usually a router, answers ARP requests intended for another machine. By "faking" its identity, the router accepts responsibility for routing packets to the "real" destination. Proxy ARP allows a site to use a single IP address with two physical networks. Subnetting would normally be a better solution.

**PSN**. Packet-Switched Node. The modern term used for nodes in the ARPANET and MILNET. These used to be called IMPs (Interface Message Processors). PSNs are currently implemented with BBN C30 or C300 minicomputers.

# R

**RARE**. Reseaux Associes pour la Recherche Europeenne. European association of research networks.

**RARP**. Reverse Address Resolution Protocol. The Internet protocol a diskless host uses to find its Internet address at startup.

RARP maps a physical (hardware) address to an Internet address. See ARP.

**repeater**. A device which propagates electrical signals from one cable to another without making routing decisions or providing packet filtering. In OSI terminology, a repeater is a physical layer intermediate system. See bridge and router.

**RFC**. Request For Comments. The document series, begun in 1969, which describes the Internet suite of protocols and related experiments. Not all (in fact very few) RFCs describe Internet standards, but all Internet standards are written up as RFCs.

**RFS**. Remote File System. A distributed file system, similar to NFS, developed by AT&T and distributed with their UNIX System V operating system. See NFS.

**RIP**. Routing Information Protocol. An Interior Gateway Protocol (IGP) supplied with Berkeley UNIX.

**RIPE**. Reseaux IP Europeens. European continental TCP/IP network operated by EUnet. See EUnet.

**rlogin**. A service offered by Berkeley UNIX which allows users of one machine to log into other UNIX systems (for which they are authorized) and interact as if their terminals were connected directly. Similar to TELNET.

**ROSE**. Remote Operations Service Element. A lightweight RPC protocol, used in OSI Message Handling, Directory, and Network Management application protocols.

**router**. A system responsible for making decisions about which of several paths network (or Internet) traffic will follow. To do this it uses a routing protocol to gain information about the network, and algorithms to choose the best route based on several criteria known as "routing metrics." In OSI terminology, a router is a network layer intermediate system. See gateway, bridge and repeater.

**RPC**. Remote Procedure Call. An easy and popular paradigm for implementing the client/server model of distributed computing. A request is sent to a remote system to execute a designated procedure, using arguments supplied, and the result returned to the caller. There are many variations and subtleties, resulting in a variety of different RPC protocols.

**RTSE**. Reliable Transfer Service Element. A lightweight OSI application service used above X.25 networks to handshake application PDUs across the Session Service and TP0. Not needed with TP4, and not recommended for use in the U.S. except when talking to X.400 ADMDs.

# S

**SAP**. Service Access Point. The point at which the services of an OSI layer are made available to the next higher layer. The SAP is named according to the layer providing the services: for example, transport services are provided at a Transport SAP (TSAP) at the top of the transport layer.

**selector**. The identifier used by an OSI entity to distinguish among multiple SAPs at which it provides services to the layer above. See port.

**session layer**. The OSI layer that provides means for dialogue control between end systems.

**SGMP**. Simple Gateway Management Protocol. The predecessor to SNMP. See SNMP.

**SLIP**. Serial Line IP. An Internet protocol used to run IP over serial lines such as telephone circuits or RS-232 cables interconnecting two systems. SLIP is now being replaced by PPP. See PPP.

**SMDS**. Switched Multimegabit Data Service. An emerging high-speed networking technology to be offered by the telephone companies in the U.S.

**SMI**. Structure of Management Information. The rules used to define the objects that can be accessed via a network management protocol. See MIB.

**SMTP**. Simple Mail Transfer Protocol. The Internet electronic mail protocol. Defined in RFC 821, with associated message format descriptions in RFC 822.

**SNA**. Systems Network Architecture. IBM's proprietary network architecture.

**SNMP**. Simple Network Management Protocol. The network management protocol of choice for TCP/IP-based internets.

**SPAG**. Standards Promotion and Application Group. A group of European OSI manufacturers which chooses option subsets and publishes these in a "Guide to the Use of Standards" (GUS).

**SQL**. Structured Query Language. The international standard language for defining and accessing relational databases.

**subnet mask**. See address mask.

**subnetwork**. A collection of OSI end systems and intermediate systems under the control of a single administrative domain and utilizing a single network access protocol. Examples: private X.25 networks, collection of bridged LANs.

## T

**TCP**.  Transmission Control Protocol.  The major transport protocol in the Internet suite of protocols providing reliable, connection-oriented, full-duplex streams. Uses IP for delivery.  See TP4.

**Telnet**.  The virtual terminal protocol in the Internet suite of protocols.  Allows users of one host to log into a remote host and interact as normal terminal users of that host.

**three-way-handshake**.  The process whereby two protocol entities synchronize during connection establishment.

**TP0**.  OSI Transport Protocol Class 0 (Simple Class).  This is the simplest OSI Transport Protocol, useful only on top of an X.25 network (or other network that does not lose or damage data).

**TP4**.  OSI Transport Protocol Class 4 (Error Detection and Recovery Class).  This is the most powerful OSI Transport protocol, useful on top of any type of network.  TP4 is the OSI equivalent to TCP.

**transceiver**.  Transmitter-receiver.  The physical device that connects a host interface to a local area network, such as Ethernet. Ethernet transceivers contain electronics that apply signals to the cable and sense collisions.

**transport layer**.  The OSI layer that is responsible for reliable end-to-end data transfer between end systems.

## U

**UA**.  User Agent. An OSI application process that represents a human user or organization in the X.400 Message Handling System. Creates, submits, and takes delivery of messages on the user's behalf.

**UDP**.  User Datagram Protocol.  A transport protocol in the Internet suite of protocols. UDP, like TCP, uses IP for delivery; however, unlike TCP, UDP provides for exchange of datagrams without acknowledgements or guaranteed delivery. See CLTP.

**UUCP**.  UNIX to UNIX Copy Program.  A protocol used for communication between consenting UNIX systems.

## V

**Veronica**.  Search tool for the gopher environment.  See gopher.

## W

**WWW**.  World Wide Web. A global hypertext system that supports multimedia communications on the Internet.

## X

**XDR**.  eXternal Data Representation.  A standard for machine-independent data structures developed by SUN Microsystems. Similar to ASN.1.

**X/Open**.  A group of computer manufacturers that promotes the development of portable applications based on UNIX. They publish a document called the *X/Open Portability Guide*.

**X Recommendations**.  The CCITT documents that describe data communication network standards.  Well-known ones include: X.25 Packet Switching standard, X.400 Message Handling System, and X.500 Directory Services.

**The X Window System**.  A popular window system developed by MIT and implemented on a number of workstations.

# Index

dotted decimal form   2-8
  subnet address   2-10
  subnetID   2-10
DRI
  *See* Defense Research Internet (DRI)
DRM
  *See* Data Replication Manager (DRM)
DSAP
  *See* Destination Service Access Point
    (DSAP)
Dynamic Host Configuration Protocol
  (DHCP)   4-210, 4-214
  message format   4-216

# E
E-mail   4-64
EARN
  *See* European Academic Research
    Network (EARN)
EBONE   1-6
EGP
  *See* Exterior Gateway Protocol (EGP)
  *See* exterior routing protocol
Electronic Mail   4-64
Entity
  *See* SNMPv2 Entity
Ethernet
  *See also* IBM 8222 Workgroup Hub
  *See also* IBM 8224 Ethernet Stackable
    Hub
  *See also* IBM 8250 Multiprotocol
    Intelligent Hub
  *See also* IBM 8260 Multiprotocol
    Intelligent Hub
  *See also* IBM 8271 EtherStreamer Switch
  3745 adapter   5-20
  8229 conversion process   5-34
  frame format   2-69
ETSI
  *See* European Telecommunications
    Standards Institute (ETSI)
European Academic Research Network
  (EARN)   1-7

European Telecommunications Standards
  Institute (ETSI)   1-8
European Workshop for Open Systems
  (EWOS)   1-8
EWOS
  *See* European Workshop for Open Systems
    (EWOS)
exterior   3-49
Exterior Gateway Protocol (EGP)   3-5, 3-6,
  3-49
  *See also* exterior routing protocol
  definition   3-5
  description   3-49—3-52
  features   3-50
  gated daemon   3-70
  IBM 2210 Nways Network
    Processor   3-70
  IBM 6611 Network Processor   3-70
  message types   3-50
  routing update message   3-51
exterior routing protocol   3-49
  *See also* Border Gateway Protocol (BGP)
  *See also* Exterior Gateway Protocol (EGP)
  protocol descriptions   3-49—3-69
External Data Representation (XDR)   4-129

# F
FDDI   5-12
  *See also* IBM 8244 FDDI Workgroup
    Concentrator
  *See also* IBM 8250 Multiprotocol
    Intelligent Hub
  *See also* IBM 8260 Multiprotocol
    Intelligent Hub
File Transfer Protocol (FTP)   4-25
  Anonymous FTP   4-31
  end the transfer session   4-28
  implementations   4-31
  job submission   4-33
  login   4-27
  operations   4-26
  PIOAM support   4-32
  reply codes   4-28

multicast
  *See also* Internet Group Management
    Protocol (IGMP)
  All hosts group   2-67
  Class D address   2-9
  description   2-19
  expanding ring search   2-68
  host group   2-19
  multicast group address   2-19
  single hop groups   2-68
  TTL   2-20
  TTL value   2-67
Multiprotocol Encapsulation   2-110
Multiprotocol Transport Networking (MPTN)
  *See* IBM Open Blueprint

# N
N-1net   1-8
NACSIS
  *See* National Center for Science and
    Information Systems (NACSIS)
NASA   1-20
National Center for Science and Information
  Systems (NACSIS)   1-8
National Science Founfation Network
  (NFSNET)   1-4, 3-53
  BGP-3   3-53
  routing architecture   3-8
NCS
  *See* Network Computing System (NCS)
NDB   4-222
  *See also* Network Database Protocol
    (NDB)
NE
  *See* Simple Network Management Protocol
    (SNMP), Network Element (NE)
NetBIOS
  *See* Data Link Switching:
    Switch-to-Switch Protocol
NetBIOS Services Protocol
  broadcast (B-node)   4-202
  BROADCAST file   4-202
  datagram services   4-201

NetBIOS Services Protocol *(continued)*
  Domain Scope String   4-203
  mixed (M-node)   4-202
  NAME file   4-203
  name management services   4-201
  naming conventions   4-202
  point-to-point (P-node)   4-202
  session services   4-201
NetSP
  *See* IBM NetSP Secured Network
    Gateway
NETSTAT   4-220
Network Access Point (NAP)   1-20
Network Computing System (NCS)   4-136
  binding   4-138
  calls   4-138
  implementations   4-141
  location broker   4-140
    GLB   4-140
    global location broker (GLB)   4-140
    LLB   4-140
    local location broker (LLB)   4-140
    locateion broker database   4-140
    location broker client agent   4-140
  Network Computing Architecture   4-136
  Network Computing Kernel   4-137
  Network Interface Definition Language
    (NIDL)   4-139
  Remote Procedure Call   4-137
  stubs   4-138
Network Database Protocol (NDB)   4-222
Network Element (NE)
Network File System (NFS)
  concept   4-144
  file system   4-148
  implementations   4-149
  MOUNT command   4-145
    options   4-145
  Mount protocol   4-144
  NFS protocol   4-147
  Remote Procedure Call   4-144
Network Information Systems (NIS)   4-223
Network Interface Definition Language
  (NIDL)

SNMP Distributed Programming Interface
  (SNMP DPI) *(continued)*
    *See* network management
SNMP DPI
    *See* SNMP Distributed Programming
      Interface (SNMP DPI)
SNMPv2
    *See* Version 2 of the Simple Network
      Management Protocol (SNMPv2)
SNMPv2 Entity  4-182
SNMPv2 Party  4-182
socket
    address  2-81
    association  2-81
    conversation  2-81
    datagram type  2-86
    definition  2-81
    half-association  2-82
    interface  2-82
    IUCV domain  2-86
    raw type  2-86
    stream type  2-86
    system call  2-84
    transport address  2-82
SOCKS Servers  6-11
Source Service Access Point (SSAP)  2-71
SPF
    *See* algorithm, shortest path first (SPF)
Split Bridge  5-31
split horizon
    *See* Routing Information Protocol (RIP)
SSAP
    *See* Source Service Access Point (SSAP)
Standard Protocol Numbers (STD)  1-24
    *See also* Request for Comments (RFC)
    referenced in this book
        STD 1  1-25, 3-19, 5-15
        STD 2  1-25, 2-19, 2-40, 2-133, 4-10,
          4-93
        STD 3  1-25, 4-53
        STD 4  1-25
        STD 5  2-36, 2-52, 2-66
        STD 6  2-88
        STD 7  2-92
        STD 8  4-3

Standard Protocol Numbers (STD)
  *(continued)*
    referenced in this book *(continued)*
        STD 9  4-25
        STD 10  4-64, 4-90
        STD 11  4-64, 4-91
        STD 13  2-31, 4-39
        STD 14  4-65
        STD 27  4-7
        STD 28  4-7
        STD 29  4-7
        STD 30  4-7
        STD 31  4-7
        STD 32  4-7
        STD 33  4-21
        STD 34  3-17
        STD 51  5-15
state machine  3-25
STD
    *See* Standard Protocol Numbers (STD)
Structure and Identification of Management
  Information (SMI)
    *See* network management
Sub-Network Access Protocol
  (SNAP)  2-71, 5-13
subagent  4-179
subnet
    introduction  2-10
    IP routing  2-14
    obtaining a subnet mask  2-16
    sample configuration  2-13
    static subnetting  2-11
    subnet mask  2-10
    subnet number  2-10
    variable length subnetting  2-11
subnet mask
    *See* subnet
subnet-directed broadcast address  2-18
supernetting  2-27
    *See also* classless inter-domain routing
      (CIDR)
SVC  2-105
System Management Application Process
  (SMAP)

System Management Application Process
(SMAP) *(continued)*
   *See* network management

# T

TCP
   *See* Transmission Control Protocol (TCP)
TCP and UDP using Bigger Addresses
(TUBA)
   *See* IP: the Next Generation (IPng)
TCP/IP protocol suite   2-1
TCP/IP versus OSI
   application-layer gateways   2-120
   coexistence considerations   2-120
   differences   2-117
   dual stacks   2-120
   functional positioning   2-116
   network tunnels   2-124
   the Internet world and OSI   2-118
   transport-layer gateways   2-122
   transport-service bridges   2-123
TCP/NetBIOS
   *See* NetBIOS Services Protocol
TELNET   4-3
   3270 full-screen cross table   4-19
   basic commands   4-10
   client/server cross table   4-19
   command structure   4-8
   full-screen capability   4-8
   implementations   4-10
   Network Virtual Terminal   4-5
   Network Virtual Terminal (NVT)   4-4
   NVT   4-4
   NVT printer   4-6
   option negotiation   4-9
   principle of operation   4-4
   scenario   4-20
TFTP
   *See* Trivial File Transfer Protocol (TFTP)
TGS
   *See* Ticket-Granting Server (TGS)
Ticket-Granting Server (TGS)   4-159

Time protocol   4-221
time-to-live
   *See* Domain Name System (DNS)
   *See* IP datagram
   *See* multicast
TISN   1-8
Token Ring
   *See* IBM 8250 Multiprotocol Intelligent
      Hub
   *See* IBM 8260 Multiprotocol Intelligent
      Hub
Token-Ring
   *See* IBM 8230 Token-Ring Controlled
      Access Unit
traceroute   2-65
transit routing domain (TRD)   2-28
transit traffic   2-28, 3-55
Transmission Control Protocol (TCP)
   acknowledgment   2-100
   application programming interface   2-103
   characteristics   2-93
   checksum   2-99
   connection establishment   2-102
   definition   2-92
   flow control   2-94
   full duplex   2-94
   half-association   2-92
   logical connection   2-94
   multiplexing   2-94
   push   2-93
   reliability   2-94
   retransmission   2-100
   segment   2-93, 2-98
      format   2-98
      mapped on IP datagrams   2-103
      options   2-100
   socket   2-92
   stream data transfer   2-93
   three-way handshake   2-102
   variable timeout interval   2-101
   window   2-97
transparent subnetting
   *See* proxy-ARP